GUIDE TO RURAL ENGLAND

THE SOUTH EAST OF ENGLAND

By Hugh Taylor and
Moira McCrossan

© Travel Publishing Ltd.

Published by:
Travel Publishing Ltd
7a Apollo House, Calleva Park
Aldermaston, Berks, RG7 8TN
ISBN 1-902-00778-6
© Travel Publishing Ltd

Country Living is a registered trademark of The National Magazine
Company Limited.

First Published: *2002*

COUNTRY LIVING GUIDES TO RURAL ENGLAND:

East Anglia
The South East
The South
The West Country

PLEASE NOTE:

All advertisements in this publication have been accepted in good faith
by Travel Publishing and they have not necessarily been endorsed by
Country Living Magazine.

All information is included by the publishers in good faith and is believed
to be correct at the time of going to press. No responsibility can be
accepted for errors.

Editor: Hugh Taylor and Moira McCrossan

Printing by: Scotprint, Haddington

Location Maps: © Maps in Minutes ™ (2000)   © Crown Copyright, Ordnance Survey 2001

Walk Maps: Reproduced from the 2001 Pathfinder 1:25,000 Ordnance Survey Maps by
                 permission of Ordnance Survey on behalf of the Controller of Her Majesty's
                 Stationery Office, © Crown Copyright MC 100035812

Cover Design: Lines & Words, Aldermaston

Cover Photo: Countryside around Shere, Surrey © www.britainonview.com

Text Photos: Text photos have been kindly supplied by the Britain on View photo library
                 and the South East Regional Tourist Board © www.britainonview.com
                 © South East Regional Tourist Board

Foreword

From a bracing walk across the hills and tarns of The Lake District to a relaxing weekend spent discovering the unspoilt hamlets of East Anglia, nothing quite matches getting off the beaten track and exploring Britain's areas of outstanding beauty.

Each month, *Country Living Magazine* celebrates the richness and diversity of our countryside with features on rural Britain and the traditions that have their roots there. So it is with great pleasure that I introduce you to the *Country Living Magazine Guide to Rural England* series. Packed with information about unusual and unique aspects of our countryside, the guides will point both fair-weather and intrepid travellers in the right direction.

Each chapter provides a fascinating tour of the South East of England, with insights into local heritage and history and easy-to-read facts on a wealth of places to visit, stay, eat, drink and shop.

I hope that this guide will help make your visit a rewarding and stimulating experience and that you will return inspired, refreshed and ready to head off on your next countryside adventure.

Susy Smith

Susy Smith, Editor of Country Living *Magazine*

P.S. To subscribe to Country Living *Magazine every month, call 01858 438844.*

Introduction

Moira McCrossan and Hugh Taylor are professional travel writers who have written for national newspapers such as *The Glasgow Herald* and magazines such as *Classic Travel* and *Woman's Realm* as well as for several travel guides published by the AA, Thomas Cook and Insight. Hugh has also produced radio series for the BBC and has contributed to a number of its travel programmes. Their vast experience of travel writing has been used to good effect in the South East edition of **The Country Living Magazine Guide to England** which is packed with vivid descriptions, historical stories, amusing anecdotes and interesting facts on hundreds of places in Surrey, Sussex and Kent.

The coloured advertising panels within each chapter provide further information on places to see, stay, eat, drink, shop and even exercise! We have also selected a number of walks from Jarrold's Pathfinder Guides which we highly recommend if you wish to appreciate fully the beauty and charm of the varied rural landscapes of the South East of England.

The guide however is not simply an "armchair tour". Its prime aim is to encourage the reader to visit the places described and discover much more about the wonderful towns, villages and countryside of Surrey, Sussex and Kent. Whether you decide to explore this region by wheeled transport or by foot we are sure you will find it a very uplifting experience.

We are always interested in receiving comments on places covered (or not covered) in our guides so please do not hesitate to use the reader reaction form provided at the rear of this guide to give us your considered comments. This will help us refine and improve the content of the next edition. We also welcome any general comments which will help improve the overall presentation of the guides themselves.

Finally, for more information on the full range of travel guides published by Travel Publishing please refer to the details and order form at the rear of this guide or log on to our website at www.travelpublishing.co.uk

Travel Publishing

Locator Map

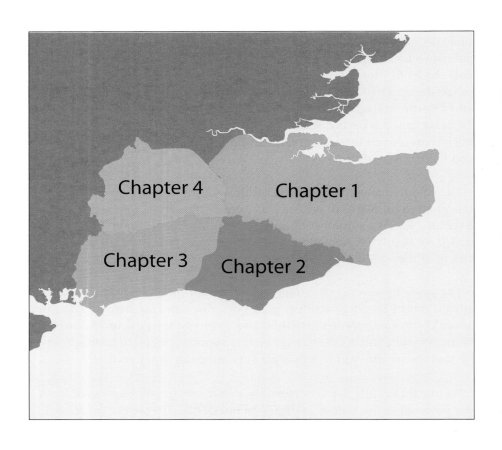

Chapter 4

Chapter 1

Chapter 3

Chapter 2

Contents

1 KENT

Water dominates the history of Kent. A land of gardens and orchards, of historic castles and churches, of pretty villages and fine market towns, but above all it is a land, inescapably linked to the sea. Its proximity to Europe across the narrow channel means that invaders through the centuries have chosen the Kent coast as a gateway to Britain. The Romans landed here over 2,000 years ago, the Vikings followed almost a 1,000 years later and the land was widely settled by the Normans following the defeat of Harold in 1066. All these peoples and the prehistoric tribes that preceded them have left their mark on the landscape and the language. Many place names, such as Rochester and Whitstable, are derived from Roman, Saxon or Norman origins. Norman churches and castles in various states of ruin or preservation still stand in the tranquil rural countryside that belies the bloodshed of centuries of successive invasions.

Orchards around Ashford

On the south coast the Cinque Ports were set up in the 11th century as a commercial alliance of significant ports, although silting up of channels over the centuries has left many of them several miles from the sea. Henry VIII established a dockyard at Chatham, which was the beginning of the Royal Navy and was a major factor in Britain's dominance of the seas in the centuries that followed. The whole length of the Kent coast has been the historic haven of smugglers, and every rocky cove and sheltered bay has seen daring and ruthless smugglers pursued by brave and determined

Oast Houses, Lenham

but generally ineffective excise men. In villages across Kent, ancient smugglers' tales are told and houses, churches and caves are pointed out, where the smugglers' booty was hidden away. However Kent's maritime tradition did not depend entirely on lawlessness and many villages plied a legitimate trade in fishing. Ancient fishing villages like Deal retain the quaint alleyways and traditional fishermen's cottages around the harbour areas. Whitstable has been famed for centuries for oyster fishing and Whitstable oysters are still regarded as gourmet fare. In the 19th century as the fashion grew for taking holidays by the sea, seaside towns and resorts grew up in former fishing ports like Herne Bay. Margate with its glorious sands was one of the first resorts to attract visitors. Even before the railways, pleasure boats brought Londoners to Margate in search of sun, sea and sands.

Churchill, Darwin and Charles Dickens have all had homes in Kent. Geoffrey Chaucer and the Elizabethan playwright and spy Christopher Marlowe as well as Somerset Maugham and Mary Tourtel, the creator of Rupert Bear lived at Canterbury. The abbey and cathedral here, along with St Martin's Church, form a fascinating World Heritage Site, where St Augustine brought Christianity to England in the 6th century.

Although Kent lies very close to the spreading suburban sprawl of Greater London, it has managed to retain a tranquil rural feel, despite commuter developments. Rolling wooded countryside is dotted with windmills and attractive villages, surrounded by orchards, market gardens, hop fields and countless gardens.

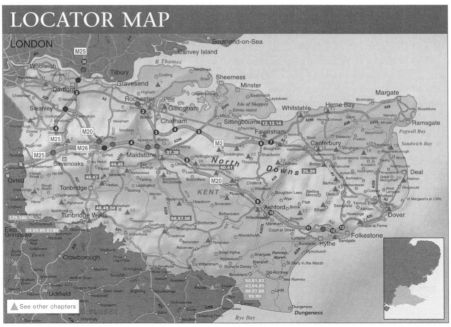

LOCATOR MAP

ADVERTISERS AND PLACES OF INTEREST

WEST KENT

Although this western region of Kent lies so close to the spreading suburban areas of Greater London, it has still managed to maintain an identity that is all its own particularly with the offbeat pronunciations of its towns and villages that defeat outsiders. Water dominates much of the history of Kent, reflected in the strong maritime heritage along the banks of the River Thames. The glorious countryside attracts many visitors yet it still manages to retain a tranquil rural feel. The short crossing to Europe via Dover and the Thames Estuary have always made this one of the first targets for invaders.

Prehistoric remains can be found here along with evidence of Roman occupation at Lullingstone near Eynsford and Croft Roman Villa at Orpington. Danes and Vikings also invaded and the now picturesque village of Aylesford has, over the centuries, been witness to more than its fair share of bloodshed.

More peaceful times saw the creation of grand manor houses and the conversion of castles into more comfortable homes and this area abounds with interesting and historic

places such as Cobham Hall, Knole House, Old Soar Manor, Ightham Mote, Penshurst Place and magnificent Hever Castle.

However, whilst these houses have much to offer visitors, both outside and within, two places stand out as being of particular interest. Chartwell, the home of Sir Winston and Lady Churchill from the 1920s until the great statesman's death in the 1960s, has been left just as it was when the couple were still alive and it remains a lasting tribute to this extraordinary man. At Downe just south of Farnborough, lies Down House, the home of Charles Darwin and the place where he formulated his theories of evolution and wrote his most famous work *The Origin of Species by Means of Natural Selection*.

GRAVESEND

The Thames is half a mile wide at Gravesend. This is where ships take on board a river pilot for the journey upstream. It is a busy maritime community, with cutters and tugs helping to maintain a steady flow of river traffic. Gravesend is where the bodies of those who had died on board were unloaded before the ships entered London. However the name Gravesend is not a reference to its being the last resting place of these poor unfortunates but is derived from 'Grove's End' from the Old English 'graf' meaning grove and 'ende' meaning end or boundary.

Much of the town was destroyed by fire in 1727. One of the many buildings that did not survive the fire was the parish **Church of St**

Penshurst Place

George, and the building seen today was rebuilt after the disaster in Georgian style. However the graveyard is more interesting than the church as this is thought to be the final resting place of the famous Red Indian princess, Pocahontas. Pocahontas was the daughter of a native American chieftain, who reputedly saved the life of the English settler, John Smith, in Virginia. She died on board ship (either from small pox, fever or tuberculosis) in 1617 whilst she was on her way back to America with her husband, John Rolfe. A life-sized statue marks Pocahontas' supposed burial place in the churchyard.

Cobham Village

A building of interest in the town, that did survive the 18th century fire, is 14th century **Milton Chantry**. A chantry is a place set aside for saying prayers for the dead. This small building was the chantry of the de Valence and Monechais families. It later became an inn and, in 1780, part of a fort. Milton Chantry is now a heritage centre with fascinating displays detailing the history and varied uses of the building.

AROUND GRAVESEND

COBHAM

4 miles SE of Gravesend off the A2

This picturesque village is home to one of the largest and finest houses in Kent - **Cobham Hall** - an outstanding red brick mansion that dates from 1584. Set in 150 acres of parkland and demonstrating architectural styles from Elizabethan, Jacobean and Carolean eras and the 18th century, the house has much to offer those interested in art, history and architecture. The Elizabethan wings date from the late 16th century. The central section of the house is later and here can be found the magnificent Gilt Hall that was decorated by Inigo Jones's famous pupil, John Webb, in 1654. Elsewhere in the house there are several superb marble fireplaces. The beautiful **Gardens** were landscaped by Humphry Repton for the 4th Earl of Darnley. Over the centuries many notable people have stayed here, including English monarchs from Elizabeth I to Edward VIII, and Charles Dickens used to walk through the grounds from his home at Higham to Cobham's village pub. However, perhaps Cobham Hall's most famous claim to fame dates back to 1883 when Ivo Blight, who later became the 8th Earl of Darnley, led the English cricket team to victory against Australia and brought the Ashes home to Cobham. Today, the hall is a private girls' boarding school and is occasionally open to visitors.

Back in the village more evidence can be found of past members of the Cobham family and, in the 13th century parish church of **St Mary Magdalene**, a series of superb commemorative floor brasses can be seen that date back to the late Middle Ages. Behind the church are some **Almshouses** that incorporate a 14th century kitchen and hall that were once part of the Old College that was founded by the 3rd Lord Cobham. The lord endowed them as living quarters for five priests who were to pray for the repose of his soul and after 1537, when the college was suppressed, the buildings became almshouses.

Leather Bottle Inn

Finally, in the heart of the village lies the half-timbered **Leather Bottle Inn** that was made famous by Charles Dickens when he featured his favourite inn in the novel *The Pickwick Papers*. It was at the Leather Bottle Inn that Tracey Tupman was discovered by Mr Pickwick after having been jilted by Rachel Wardle.

Close by, just to the north of the village, lies **Owletts** a lovely red brick house that was built, in the late 17th century, by a Cobham farmer. Still retaining a charming sense of rural comfort the house has an imposing staircase and a notable 17th century plaster ceiling but Owletts main appeal is its modest proportions and beautiful garden.

HEXTABLE

8½ miles SW of Gravesend on the B258

Surrounded by market gardens and orchards, this village is home to **Hextable Gardens**. This heritage centre lies in the former Botany Laboratory of Swanley Horticultural College, believed to be the first horticultural college in the world. The Botany Lab is not listed but is an attractive 1930s white painted brick building with metal-framed windows, now sensitively restored. Also in the village is **Hextable Park**, a charming place that has been specifically designed to attract a wide variety of wildlife and butterflies. Pictorial information plaques aid visitors in identifying the many species found here.

CHISLEHURST

13 miles SW of Gravesend on the A208

Following the arrival of the railways, Chislehurst developed as one of London's more select and fashionable suburbs as businessmen took their homes here lured by the fresh air and the downland scenery that lies on the doorstep. The town has managed to remain relatively unspoilt by further development thanks, in large part, to **Chislehurst Common**, an oasis of greenery criss-crossed by a number of small roads.

The suburb is also home to **Chislehurst Caves**, one of Britain's most interesting networks of underground caverns. There are over 20 miles of caverns and passageways, dug over a period of 8000 years. The vast labyrinth of caves is a maze of ancient flint and chalk mines dug by hand over the centuries. It comprises three sections that each relate to a specific era and the oldest section, known as the Druids, dates back approximately 4,000 years. The largest section is Roman whilst the smallest, and youngest, was excavated some 1,400 years ago by the Saxons. Royalists took refuge here during the Civil War and the pit that was built to trap their Parliamentarian pursuers can still be seen. At the height of the Blitz during World War II, the caves became the world's

Chislehurst Pond

largest air raid shelter when some 15,000 people hid here from the German bombing raids. Visitors can take a lamp lit guided tour of the various sections including the air raid shelters, the Druid Altar and the Haunted Pool.

A quiet and pleasant residential area today, Chislehurst has two famous sons: William Willet Junior, the enthusiastic advocate of the Daylight Saving Scheme, who unfortunately died a year before British Summer Time (BST) was introduced in 1916, and Sir Malcolm Campbell, the racing driver and pioneering land and water speed record holder of the 1930s.

BEXLEYHEATH
10½ miles W of Gravesend on the A207

Despite being located between Dartford and Woolwich, Bexleyheath is somewhat surprising in that, although there was a great deal of development here in the 19th and early 20th centuries, expanses of parkland still remain. As the town's name might suggest, this area was once heathland and, following enclosure in 1814, some of this land has managed to escape the hands of the developers. In the heart of Bexleyheath lies one of these such areas, **Danson Park**, covering more

than 180 acres of land. Originally a private estate, the garden was landscaped by Capability Brown. The **Danson Mansion** within the park, a Grade 1 Listed Building, completed in 1762 and designed by Sir Robert Taylor, architect of the Bank of England, is sometimes open to the public. The Mansion has recently been restored by English Heritage. At the centre of the park, a great oak tree, which is over 200 years old, is now designated one of the "Great Trees of London".

To the southeast lies **Hall Place** (see panel on page 8) a charming country house that was built in 1540 for Sir John Champneis, a Lord Mayor of London and substantially added to around 100 years later. As well as the fine splendid great hall, the house is particularly noted for its beautiful award-winning formal gardens on the banks of the River Cray. Over the centuries, the house has served many purposes. It has been a school on three separate occasions and, during World War II, it was an American Army communications centre.

However, today, parts of Hall Place are open to the public and visitors here can see the magnificent Great Hall, the Tudor Parlour and the recently redecorated

Drawing Room and Long Gallery. Hall Place also contains Bexley Museum and some exhibitions galleries. The gardens, through which the River Cray flows, are impressive and perhaps most eye-catching of all is the outstanding topiary with its chess pieces and Queen's beasts. There are rose gardens laid out in the Tudor style, herb, rock and heather gardens and a nursery with a display of designs for the smaller garden. Guided tours can be booked of both the house and the gardens. Hall Place is open throughout the year whilst the summer opening Visitors Centre, that doubles as a Tourist Information Centre, hosts exhibitions on local history and arts and crafts.

One of Bexleyheath's most famous former residents lived at **The Red House**, in Red House Lane. Designed by Philip Webb, it was built in 1860 for William Morris. However Morris's own ideas on architecture and craftsmanship are in strong evidence in the design. The artist Dante Gabriel Rossetti, described the Red House as "...more a poem than a house - but an admirable place to live in too". The house is privately owned but is sometimes open to the public. The locality around it, including some old cottages, is now a conservation area.

The ruins of **Lesness Abbey** are in the area between Belvedere and Abbey Wood. The Augustinians occupied the abbey from 1178 until the 16th century when it

HALL PLACE

Bourne Road, Bexley, Kent DA5 1PQ
Tel: 01322 526574 Fax: 01322 52292
website: www.hallplaceandgardens.com

Surrounded by its award-winning gardens, **Hall Place** is an attractive mansion house that dates from the 16th century that was substantially added to around 100 years later.

Originally the home of Sir John Champneis, a Lord Mayor of London, the house, over the centuries, has served many purposes and it has been a school on three separate occasions and, during World War II, it was an American Army communications centre.

However, today, parts of the house are open to the public and visitors here can not only see the magnificent Great Hall, the Tudor Parlour and the recently redecorated Drawing Room and Long Gallery but Hall Place contains Bexley Museum and there are also exhibitions galleries. The gardens, through which the River Cray flows, are impressive and perhaps most eye-catching of all is the outstanding topiary with its chess pieces and Queen's beasts. Meanwhile, there are rose gardens laid out in the Tudor style, herb, rock and heather gardens and a nursery with a display of designs for the smaller garden. Guided tours can be booked of both the house and the gardens. Hall Place is open throughout the year whilst the summer opening Visitors Centre, that doubles as a Tourist Information Centre, hosts exhibitions on local history and arts and crafts.

was razed to the ground. The foundations excavated in the 20th century give a good idea of the layout of a monastic community.

CRAYFORD
8½ miles W of Gravesend on the A2018

Now more a district of the borough of Bexley, it is here that the Roman road, Watling Street, crosses the River Cray. The parish church St Paulinus dates back to the 12th century but additions have been made over the centuries. A settlement was discovered just to the west of St Paulinus where Iron Age pottery was unearthed.

On the banks of the River Cray, the **World of Silk** provides visitors with an insight into the historic and traditional craft of silk making and the origins of silk are explained. Believed to have been discovered in around 1640 BC by the Empress of China, Hsi-Ling-Shi, silk found its way to Europe along the arduous silk route and, from the humble silk worm through to the beautiful printed fabrics, the whole of the story of this luxury material is explained.

Dartford
8 miles W of Gravesend on the A206

This urban settlement is best known as the home of the **Dartford Tunnel**, that runs for roughly one mile beneath the River Thames, re-emerging on the Essex bank near West Thurrock. However, Dartford, though not seemingly apparent at first sight, has some historical significance. It stands on the old London to Dover road, at the crossing of the River Darent, and this is the reason for its name, which actually means 'Darent Ford'.

Local legend has it that Wat Tyler, leader of the Peasant's Revolt, was from Dartford. The revolt was supposedly sparked off when Tyler's daughter was indecently assaulted by a tax assessor. Deptford, Colchester and Maidstone also lay claims to Wat Tyler. However the historical sources are unreliable and the legend is perpetuated in Dartford, which even has a Wat Tyler Inn.

In the 20th century Dartford has changed from Victorian market town to sprawling commuter land with 80,000 residents. Most of the town's older buildings disappeared over the century, victims of war, modern transport systems or the dead hand of urban planning. Holy Trinity church, mainly 18th and 19th century with a Norman tower, a few cottages nearby and a couple of 18th century buildings on the High Street including the Bull and Victoria Hotel are

the only survivors of old Dartford. Ironically the town centre is now a conservation area when there is little left to conserve. Dartford is almost entirely 20th century.

Swanscombe
2½ miles W of Gravesend on the A226

This former agricultural village, which has long since been swamped by the growth of industry along the banks of the River Thames, was the site of an important archaeological find in 1935. Excavations in a gravel pit unearthed fragments of a human skull and analysis of the bones revealed that the skull (that of a woman) was around 200,000 years old, making them some of the oldest human remains found in Europe. This riverside settlement also has remnants from more recent historical periods and, while the parish church of Saints Peter and Paul dates mainly from the 12th century, its structure incorporates bricks from Roman times and parts of its tower predate the Norman invasion. Although the church was substantially restored in the Victorian era, making it difficult to detect the original features, it does provide tangible evidence of the many layers of human settlement here along the Thames.

SEVENOAKS

With its easy road and rail links with London and its leafy and relaxed atmosphere, Sevenoaks has come to epitomise the essence of the commuter belt. Whilst this perception is not far from the truth, the town retains a rural feel from the once wooded countryside that surrounded the ancient settlement that stood here some nine centuries ago.

Sevenoaks began as a market town in Saxon times, although an older settlement is believed to have been sited here previously, and it grew up around the meeting point of the roads from London and the Dartford river crossing as they headed south towards the coast.

The first recorded mention of the town came in 1114, when it was called 'Seovenaca' and local tradition has it that the name refers to the clump of seven oaks that once stood here and, though the trees are now long gone, they were ceremoniously replaced in 1955 with seven trees from Knole Park. These replacement trees made headline news in the autumn of 1987 when several were blown down in the Great Storm that hit the southeast of England in October.

Rural Sevenoaks changed little over the centuries until the arrival of the railway in 1864 and the town became a popular residential area for those working in London. Despite the development, that was again accelerated when the railway line was electrified in the 1930s, Sevenoaks has managed to maintain its individuality and there are still various traditional Kentish tile-hung cottages to be found here. Meanwhile, at the **Sevenoaks Library Gallery** an imaginative programme of contemporary exhibitions of modern art, by both local and international artists, shows that the town does not dwell in the past. Ranging from photography and textiles to fine art, among the various artists featured here over the years have been Andy Warhol and John Piper.

Not far from the centre of Sevenoaks is another reminder of the town's heritage in the form of the **Vine Cricket Ground** that lies on a rise to the south. It was given to the town in 1773 but the first recorded

match held here - between Kent and Sussex - was in 1782, when the Duke of Dorset (one of the Sackville family of Knole) and his estate workers defeated a team representing All England. This remarkable victory was particularly sweet as the Duke's team also won a bet of 1,000 guineas! The weatherboard pavilion at the club is 19th century. The Cricket Club pay Sevenoaks Town Council a peppercorn rent, literally 2 peppercorns per year - one for the ground and one for the pavilion. The council may be required to pay Lord Sackville one cricket ball each year, but only if he asks.

The pride of Sevenoaks and, for many, of Kent is **Knole House**, one of the largest private homes in England that lies to the southeast of the town and is surrounded by an extensive and majestic deer park. The huge manor house, with its 365 rooms, stands on the site of a much smaller house that was bought by the Archbishop of Canterbury in 1456 and used as an ecclesiastical palace until 1532 when it was taken over by Henry VIII. In 1603, Elizabeth I granted the house to the Sackville family and, although it is now in the ownership of the National Trust, the family still live here. A superb example of late medieval

Knole House

Bedroom, Knole House

architecture, with Jacobean embellishments that include superb carvings and plasterwork, visitors to Knole can also see the internationally renowned collection of Royal Stuart furnishings that are housed here. An important collection of paintings with works by Van Dyck, Gainsborough, Hoppner and Wootton can be seen too and there are works by Sir Joshua Reynolds, which were commissioned for the house by the 3rd Duke of Dorset. Little altered since the 18th century, it was here that Vita Sackville-West was born in 1892 and, as well as being the setting for Virgina Wolff's novel *Orlando*, it is

believed that Hitler intended to use Knole as his English headquarters. The house is open to the public on a limited basis.

AROUND SEVENOAKS

OTFORD

3 miles N of Sevenoaks off the A225

Found in a pleasant location beside the River Darent, this village has a history that stretches back to Roman times and beyond - as does much of the Darent Valley. Lying at an important crossroads for many centuries, it was here, in AD 775, that King Offa of Mercia won the battle which brought Kent into his kingdom and, several hundred years later, Henry VIII stopped at Otford on his way to the historic encounter with Francois I of France at the Field of the Cloth of Gold. The King is believed to have stayed the night at one of the many palaces belonging to the Archbishop of Canterbury. The palace at Otford, of which little of the original building now remains, stood adjacent to the Church of St Bartholomew and opposite the village's duck pond.

The **Pond**, which lies at the heart of Otford, is itself something of an historic curio as it was documented as early as

THE STUDIO

20 High Street, Otford, Sevenoaks, Kent TN14 5PQ
Tel: 01959 524784

Former art teacher, Wendy Peck, established **The Studio** 10 years ago, in what was originaly the Parish Workhouse. The cob walls, tiled floor and oak beams provide the ideal atmosphere for displaying Wendy's own watercolours and oils as well as the varied selection of works by UK based artists and craftsmen. As well as original paintings and contemporary art, Wendy also sells sculptures, jewellery, ceramics, scarfs, mirrors, collages and textile prints. She also offers a framing service and accepts portrait commissions.

the 11th century and it is thought to be
the only stretch of water in England to
be classified as a listed building. The
Otford Heritage Centre is just the place
to find out more about this interesting
village and here can be seen displays on
the village's natural history, geology and
archaeology, including artefacts from
nearby Roman sites and the medieval
Archbishop's Palace. However opening
times are very limited.

Connections with the Archbishops of
Canterbury continue at **Becket's Well**
that once supplied water to the palace
and that is thought to have miraculous
origins. Local folklore suggests that
when he was visiting Otford, Archbishop
Thomas à Becket was so displeased with
the quality of the local water that, to
remedy the situation, he struck the
ground with his crozier and two springs
of clear water bubbled up from the spot.

SHOREHAM
4 miles N of Sevenoaks off the A255

Shoreham is situated beside the River
Darent, which features prominently in
the village. As well as the footpaths that
run along its banks it is also crossed by a
handsome hump-backed bridge. Close to
this bridge lies the **Water House** that was
the home of Samuel Palmer, the great
Romantic painter, for some years. Here
Palmer entertained his friend the poet
and visionary William Blake.

On the hillside across the valley can be
seen a large cross, carved into the chalk
that commemorates those who died in
the two World Wars. **Shoreham Aircraft
Museum** is dedicated to the Battle of
Britain and the air war over southern
England. Among the numerous exhibits
are aviation relics and homefront
memorabilia from the 1940s. The
museum is open on a limited basis and
only in the summer.

EYNSFORD
6½ miles N of Sevenoaks off the A225

The centre of this pretty and picturesque
village manages to preserve a sense of
history and, crossing the River Darent,
there is a small hump-backed bridge and
an ancient ford along with a number of
old timbered cottages and a church with
a tall shingle spire. Though the ford,
which gives the village its name, is still
passable by cars there is a depth chart
beside it that shows that the depth of the
ford can reach six feet when the river is
swollen with floodwater.

Leslie Hore-Belisha made his home
here for a time and, if his name sounds
familiar, it was whilst Minister of
Transport in the 1930s that Leslie gave
his name to the Belisha beacon street
crossings and he also inaugurated the
driving test for motorists.

Just a short distance from the village
down a lane, is **Eagle Heights**, Kent's
bird of prey centre, established to further
the cause of British birds. Concentrating
on explaining the importance of
conservation and the birds'
environment, the centre hosts free flying
shows where visitors can see eagles
soaring high above the Darent Valley
and watch the Condor, the world's
largest bird of prey, fly. There are also
some indoor demonstrations, when
snakes can be handled.

Further down the lane lies
Lullingstone Roman Villa, only
uncovered in 1949 although its existence
had been known since the 18th century,
when farm labourers uncovered
fragments of mosaics that had been
pierced as the men drove fence posts into
the ground. Although not the largest
find in the country, Lullingstone is
recognised to be the most exciting of its
kind made in the 20th century. The villa,
which was first occupied in AD 80, has

splendid mosaic floors and one of the earliest private Christian chapels.

Close by, in a quiet spot beside the River Darent, lies **Lullingstone Castle**, a superb manor house whose 15th century gatehouse is one of the first ever to be built from bricks. The house remains in the hands of the descendants of **John Peche**, who built it. The house has some fine state rooms, as might be expected of a place that had associations with both Henry VIII and Queen Anne, as well as family portraits and armour on display. The castle is surrounded by beautiful grounds, that also house the tiny Norman church of St Botolph. A little further south again lies **Lullingstone Park and Visitor Centre** that incorporates both parkland, with ancient pollarded oaks, and chalk grassland. A full programme of guided walks, special events and children's activities take place from the visitor centre where there is a countryside interpretation exhibition.

Riverside, Farningham

FARNINGHAM

8 miles N of Sevenoaks off the A225

This attractive village, in the Darent valley, was once on the main London road and much of the Georgian architecture found in the village centre reflects the prosperity that Farningham once enjoyed. A handsome 18th century brick bridge stands by lawns that slope down to the river's edge, alongside which runs the **Darent Valley Path**, that follows the course of the river as far as Dartford. Despite its rural appeal, Farningham is close to the M25 and M20 motorway intersection, but **Farningham Woods Nature Reserve** provides a delightful area of natural countryside that supports a wide variety of rare plants and birdlife.

MEOPHAM

10 miles NE of Sevenoaks on the A227

This pretty village, whose name is pronounced 'Meppam', still acts as a trading centre for the surrounding smaller

Farningham Centre

villages and hamlets. In additioj to the well maintained cricket green, the village is home to **Meopham Windmill**, a fully restored black smock mill dating from 1821 that is unusual in that it has six sides. The village was the birthplace of the great 17th century naturalist and gardener John Tradescant, who introduced many non-native species of flowers and vegetables into England.

TROTTISCLIFFE

9½ miles NE of Sevenoaks off the A20

As its name, pronounced 'Trossley', implies, this village occupies a hillside position. A pretty, neat village with views over the North Downs, it was the beauty of this quiet place that lured the artist Graham Sutherland to make Trottiscliffe his home.

Just to the north of the village, on high ground that offers commanding views eastwards over the Medway Valley, stands **Coldrum Long Barrow**, some 24 columns of stone that once marked the perimeter of a circular long barrow that was originally 50 feet in diameter. Only four of the huge stones are still standing and, although the huge burial mound inside the circle has long since disappeared, this ancient site remains an evocative and mysterious place.

WROTHAM

6 miles NE of Sevenoaks off the A227

This ancient village was once a staging post on one of the important routes southeastwards from London. It was here, in 1536, that Henry VIII received news of the execution of his second wife, Anne Boleyn.

PLATT

6 miles E of Sevenoaks off the A25

This village lies close to **Great Comp Garden**, one of finest gardens in the country and one that has a truly unique atmosphere. Around the ruins of the house that once stood here, there are terraces and a sweeping lawn along with a breathtaking collection of trees, shrubs and perennials and tranquil woodland walks. The whole amazing garden was designed and created by Eric Cameron and his wife after they retired in 1957.

IGHTHAM

4½ miles E of Sevenoaks on the A227

This delightful village is a charming place of half-timbered houses and crooked lanes. Inside **Ightham Church** is a mural dedicated to Dame Dorothy Selby who, according to legend, was instrumental in uncovering the Gunpowder Plot. The story goes that James I showed Dame Dorothy an anonymous letter he had received that hinted at 'a terrible blow' that would soon befall Parliament and, whilst the king dismissed the letter as the work of a crank, Dame Dorothy, understanding the implications, urged him to take the warning with the utmost seriousness.

IVY HATCH

3½ miles E of Sevenoaks off the A227

Just to the south of this small village lies **Ightham Mote**, one of England's finest medieval manor houses, owned by the National Trust. Covering some 650 years of history, this beautiful moated house, set in a narrow, wooded valley, dates back to the 14th century. It is constructed around a central courtyard that retains the meeting place purpose that is referred to in its name - 'mote' probably comes from the Old English word meaning 'meeting place'. There is plenty to see here, from the medieval Great Hall and Tudor chapel to the Victorian housekeeper's room and the billiard room. The manor house had a crypt, where unlucky prisoners could be simply

Ightham Mote

manor house, dating from the late 13th century. Only the solar end of the old house survives on a tunnel vaulted undercroft as well as the chapel. An 18th century red brick house stands where the original hall would have been. Whilst the house itself is charming it is the idyllic setting of Old Soar Manor, with its surrounding orchards and copses, that makes this such a delightful place to visit. The woods grow more dense as they climb the ridge and rise up from the orchards and, at the top, is one of southern England's largest forests, **Mereworth Woods**. Wild boar once roamed through this forest of oak and beech trees and, though today the wildlife is of a tamer variety, the woods are still enchanting.

dispatched by the opening of a sluice gate from the moat. There was also a trap in the floor of a room in the tower from where unsuspecting victims could be dropped into a small dark hole.

There is also an exhibition that details the traditional skills that were used during the major conservation programme, which took place here in 1998. The delightful garden and grounds, with their lakes and woodland, provide numerous opportunities for pleasant country walks.

PLAXTOL

4½ miles E of Sevenoaks off the A227

This hilltop village, on a prominent ridge near Ightham Mote, has a charming row of traditional Kentish weatherboard cottages that surround the parish church. Just to the east of the village, and reached via a circuitous succession of narrow lanes, is **Old Soar Manor**, another fine National Trust owned

MEREWORTH

8 miles E of Sevenoaks on the A228

Found on the southern boundary of Mereworth Woods, the village is something of a curiosity. Early in the 18th century, John Fane, a local landowner, built himself a large Palladian mansion here. However, he soon became disappointed as the village obscured some of his views of the surrounding countryside and so he had the village demolished and moved to a site that could not be seen from his new home. The new village had houses for all the original inhabitants and Fane even built a new church. This being the 1740s, the church architecture owes a lot to the style of Sir Christopher Wren and the result is a faithful copy of St Martin in the Fields, London.

Biggin Hill

7½ miles NW of Sevenoaks on the A233

This village is best known for its association with the RAF and, in particular, with the role that the local station played in the Battle of Britain. A Spitfire and a Hurricane flank the entrance to **Biggin Hill RAF Station**. A chapel at the station commemorates the 453 pilots from Biggin Hill who lost their lives during the conflict.

The location of Biggin Hill - high on a plateau on the North Downs - made it an obvious choice for an airfield and the views from here, over the Darent Valley, are outstanding.

The village itself, which sprawls along this plateau, has a particularly interesting church. Saint Mark's was built between 1957 and 1959, using material from the derelict All Saints' Church at Peckham. The windows were engraved by the vicar - Rev V Symons.

Downe

7 miles NW of Sevenoaks off the A233

Found high up on the North Downs and commanding spectacular views, especially northwards towards London, Downe has managed to retain a real country atmosphere. Its central core of traditional flint cottages has not been engulfed by the growing tide of modern suburban housing spreading from the capital. Seemingly at a crossroads between Greater London and the countryside, Downe's natural setting, still

High Elms Country Park

Shire Lane, Farnborough, Kent BR6 7JH
Tel: 01689 862815 Fax: 01689 861347

Found on the rim of the River Thames basin, on a ridge of the North Downs, **High Elms Country Park** is a wonderful expanse of woodland, formal gardens and wildflower meadows yet it is only 15 miles from central London. Covering some 250 acres, the peaceful country park trails, that have been created to highlight various aspects of the park for visitors, tell little of the park's eventful history. Originally, along with adjacent golf course, this park formed the estate of High Elms that, in the early 19th century came into the hands of the Lubbock family. For the next 130 years or so the family farmed and expanded the estate and it was the 3rd Baronet, in the Victorian era, who commissioned the building of the grand mansion house along with the ornate Italian gardens. A race course too was built and the last race meeting held on the estate was attended by some 40,000 people.

From springtime, when the woodlands are carpeted with bluebells, to the summer meadows brimming with wildflowers such as oxeye daisies and bee orchids, to the glorious and rich colour of autumn, there is much to see here. The Nature Centre, an ideal place to begin a visit to High Elms, has exhibitions on wildlife that can be found here along with traditional country crafts and there are explanatory leaflets of the various country park trails. Dog walkers, picnickers, cyclists and riders are all catered for here and, whilst the park is certainly popular, there is ample space to find a quiet and peaceful corner. A Site of Special Scientific Interest and one that also hosts a number of annual events for all the family, the combination of managed conservation and informal leisure works harmoniously to provide a wonderful and interesting day out for everyone.

evident in the outskirts of the village, also marks something of a boundary as it is poised between the open uplands of the Downs themselves and the more wooded areas of Kent, such as the Weald, further south.

It was in this village, at **Down House**, that one of the world's greatest and best known scientists, Charles Darwin, lived for over 40 years until his death in 1882. Following his five year voyage on *HMS Beagle*, Darwin came back to this house where he worked on formalising his theory of evolution and it was here that he wrote his famous work *The Origin of Species by Means of Natural Selection* that was published in 1859. The house is now a museum dedicated to the life and work of this famous scientist and visitors can find out more about his revolutionary theory and gain an understanding of the man himself. The study, where he did much of his writing, still contains many personal belongings and the family rooms too have been painstakingly restored to provide a real insight into Charles Darwin, the scientist, husband and father. Down House is open to the public but pre-booking is required.

FARNBOROUGH
8 miles NW of Sevenoaks off the A223

Just to the south of the village lies **High Elms Country Park** (see panel opposite), a delightful park of woodlands, formal gardens and meadows, that was once part of the High Elms Estate

ORPINGTON
8 miles NW of Sevenoaks on the A232

Once a country village, between the two World Wars, Orpington changed dramatically into the commuter town that it is today. However, thanks to William Cook, a 19th century local poultry farmer, the town has not lost its rural connections as Cook introduced a breed of poultry - the Black Orpington - that was to become famous throughout the farming world in Britain, Europe and beyond. In the heart of the town, next to the library, stands **Bromley Museum**, which is an ideal starting point for an exploration of this area. Housed in a museum piece itself, an interesting medieval building dating from 1290, and surrounded by attractive gardens Bromley Museum has numerous exhibits and displays that cover the history of the area around Bromley. From prehistoric Stone Age tools, Roman lamps and Saxon jewellery to a recreated 1930s dining room and memorabilia from World War II there are many interesting items that will fire the imagination. The museum also houses an archaeological collection, put together by Sir John Lubbock of nearby Hall Place.

Close to the town centre, and protected from the elements by a modern cover building, is **Crofton Roman Villa**, built in around AD 140 and inhabited for over 250 years. Presumed to have been at the centre of a farming estate, the villa, which was altered several times

Bromley Museum

during its occupation, probably extended to some 20 rooms although the remains of only 10 have been uncovered. Evidence of the under-floor heating arrangements, or hypocaust, can still be seen as can some of the tiled floors and there is a display of the artefacts that were also uncovered during the excavations here.

TONBRIDGE

This pretty old town stands at the highest navigable point on the River Medway and, as well as having a Victorian cast iron bridge across the river, the substantial remains of Tonbridge's Norman **Castle** can be found on a rise in the town centre. The walls of the castle date from the 12th century while the shell of the keep, along with the massive gatehouse and drum towers, were built in the early 14th century. Within the castle walls is a mound that is believed to have been the site of an earlier Saxon fort that provides further evidence of the importance that the river crossing here once had. The castle was all but destroyed during the Civil War and, today, the ruins are surrounded by landscaped gardens.

Whilst the castle is certainly one of the town's oldest buildings, its most famous institution is **Tonbridge School**, founded in 1553 by Sir Andrew Judd, Master of the Skinners' Company and a former Lord Mayor of London. The school received a charter from Elizabeth I and, on Judd's death the administration was left in trust to the Skinners' Company which remain the

Governors to this day. The school is mainly housed in 19th century buildings on the High Street, where other attractive 18th and 19th century buildings can also be found.

AROUND TONBRIDGE

Penshurst
4½ miles SW of Tonbridge on the B2176

With its hilly, wooded setting and Tudor architecture, Penshurst is renowned as being one of Kent's prettiest villages. The houses at its core are all old, dating from 200 to 500 years ago, and each has its own sense of charm and identity. At the heart of the village, the Church of St John the Baptist appears completely 19th century from the outside but within the 13th century interior survives with architectural details from the intervening centuries. Particularly noteworthy is the carving on a mediaeval tomb of a supplicant woman. The entrance to the church is by an ancient lychgate. Close by is one of the village's equally ancient houses, a two storey Tudor dwelling that is particularly quaint with its bulging walls and crooked beams.

Just to the north of the village lies

Penshurst Village

Penshurst Place. Set in the peaceful landscape of the Weald of Kent, it is recognised as being one of the best examples of 14th century architecture in the country. The house was built of local sandstone in 1341 and, in 1552, Edward VI granted Penshurst Place to his steward and tutor, Sir William Sidney, grandfather of the famous Elizabethan poet, soldier and courtier, Sir Philip Sidney. Additions to the original house, over the centuries, have seen it become an imposing fortified manor house and it remains in the Sidney family today. Visitors to Penshurst Place have the opportunity not only to see the magnificent Barons Hall and the impressive staterooms but also a marvellous collection of paintings, furniture, tapestries, porcelain and armour.

The Gardens surrounding the house are equally impressive and are a rare example of Elizabethan design. The records here go back to 1346, making this one of the oldest gardens in private ownership, and over a mile of yew hedging separates the walled garden into a series of individually styled 'rooms'. Designed as a garden for all seasons, visitors here can enjoy a riot of colour from early springtime right through to the autumn.

Penshurst Place is also the home of a Toy Museum, where the world of the nursery is brought to life through an interesting collection of dolls, tin

PENSHURST VINEYARDS

Grove Road, Penshurst, Tonbridge, Kent TN11 8DU
Tel: 01892 870255 Fax: 01892 870255
website www.penshurst.co.uk

Penshurst Vineyards welcomes visitors to a vineyard with a difference. Not only are you offered an insight into the production of high quality wines, but you can also enjoy a unique collection of wildlife - a delightful combination that attracts thousands of visitors each year. The picturesque

location just outside the village of Penshurst, close to the Eden Valley, makes this an ideal family day out.

The wildlife collection includes a mob of wallabies which, with the black swans and flock of rare breed sheep, are a great attraction. The wallabies, which are bred here, feature strongly in the history of Penshurst Vineyard, with a picture of one being incorporated into the wine label! The estate has also become a breeding centre for more than 30 species of exotic wildfowl.

soldiers and many other toys that originally belonged to several generations of the Sidney family children. It is open to the public throughout the summer.

Also close by is one of the most modern vineyards in England, **Penshurst Vineyard** (see panel above), where adults can enjoy the lovely walks and the wine tastings, and children can watch the unusual range of animals, including wallabies, rare breeds of sheep and birds, that have their home here.

CHIDDINGSTONE
6 miles W of Tonbridge off the B2027

This pretty village, set in pleasant open woodland, is one of the most picturesque in Kent and it is owned by the National Trust. Along a footpath behind the main street, which is lined with houses from the 16th and 17th centuries that were built during the village's prosperous period, lies a block of sandstone known as the **Chiding Stone**. Legend has it that in the past miscreant, vagrants and assorted petty criminals were taken here for public humiliation

Also found in this village is one of Kent's best kept secrets, **Chiddingstone Castle**, a traditional country squire's house that has the appearance of a grand castle. In 1805 Henry Streatfield rebuilt his family home in grand Gothic style.

In 1955 the house was bought by connoisseur Denys Eyre Bower, a self-made man, whose particular passion was collecting. Today, the castle houses Bower's vast wide-ranging collection, covering such far-reaching themes as relics from ancient Egypt and artefacts from Japan to pictures and mementoes from the Royal Stuart dynasty.

Hever Castle

BOUGH BEECH

6½ miles W of Tonbridge on the B2027

To the north of this village lies **Bough Beech Reservoir** whose surrounding nature reserve provides excellent opportunities for bird watching. The reservoir's visitor centre has a series of exhibitions and displays on the local wildlife, the area's hop growing industry and the history of this reservoir.

HEVER

7½ miles W of Tonbridge off the B2027

This tiny village, set in a delightfully unspoilt countryside of orchards and woodlands, is home to one of Kent's star attractions - **Hever Castle**. The original castle, that consisted of the gatehouse, outer walls and inner moat, was built in the 1270s by Sir Stephen de Penchester, who received permission from Edward I to greatly fortify his home. Some two centuries later, the Bullen (or Boleyn) family purchased the property and they added the comfortable Tudor manor house that stands within the castle walls. Hever Castle was the childhood home of Anne Boleyn and the ill-fated mother of Elizabeth I was courted here by Henry VIII. Many of Anne's personal items, including two books of hours (prayer books) signed by Anne, along with other Tudor mementoes can be seen here.

In 1903, the castle was bought by the American millionaire, William Waldorf Astor and he used his great wealth to restore the original buildings and the grounds - work that included laying out and planting over 30 acres of formal gardens. Visitors are particularly drawn to these award-winning gardens but the castle also houses fine collections of paintings, furniture, tapestries and objects d'art.

EDENBRIDGE

9 miles W of Tonbridge on the B2026

This small town, found near the upper reaches of the River Eden, has been a settlement since Roman times and, although the present bridge spanning the river dates from the 1830s, there has been a bridge here since that early occupation. Its High Street is a straight line through the town and across the river. It was originally the Roman road and an important route through the forest of the Kentish Weald. Along its route can still be some found ancient coaching inns, some dating from as long ago as the 1370s, that catered to the needs of travellers.

The town's name seems to be simply explained since there is a bridge here and it passes over the River Eden. However, the bridge is actually named after a Saxon leader, Eadhelm, whose river crossing replaced the earlier Roman structure. The name of the town settled easily into Edenbridge and the river became known as the Eden.

IDE HILL

7½ miles NW of Tonbridge off the B2042

Situated in the upper Darent Valley, this remote little village is the highest spot in Kent at 800 feet above sea level. In by gone days the hill was used as a beacon to signal danger to Shooters Hill on the outskirts of London. From its elevated position, it has glorious, panoramic views stretching out over the Weald. During the 16th century its hunting grounds became a secret meeting place for Henry VIII and his future queen, Anne Boleyn of Hever.

Just outside the village, and set on a hillside of mature beech trees, is **Emmetts Garden** an informal National Trust maintained garden that boasts the highest tree top in Kent - a 100 foot Wellingtonia planted on Kent's highest

THE HAXTED MILL RIVERSIDE BRASSERIE AND BAR

Haxted road, Edenbridge, Kent TN8 6PU
Tel: 01732 862 914 Fax: 01732 865705
e-mail: david@haxtedmill.co.uk
website: www.haxtedmill.co.uk

Situated in the beautiful Eden Valley, **The Haxted Mill Riverside Brasserie and Bar** is well worth a visit. In winter, guests can dine on fresh fish and game in the cosy beamed dining room, while in summer the candlelit terrace, overlooking the mill race and pond, is a wonderful alfresco dining experience. Those with romance in mind can watch the sun go down over the fields while sipping a glass of well-chilled Chablis Premier Cru and enjoying the finest fruits de mer this side of the English Channel. The menu reflects the feel of summer and outdoor eating with light lunches, fruits de mer, lobsters, crabs, langoustines and prawns. Tourists can have a light lunch following a visit to the adjacent five hundred year old watermill with its working waterwheel

and exhibition of the history of milling. After lunch an afternoon of horse racing at Lingfield Park might conclude the perfect day out.

For those, who are cycling or walking in the area and just need some liquid refreshment, there is always a selection of chilled non-alcoholic drinks available to help them on their way on hot summer days or cups of tea to fend off chill winter winds. The Haxted Mill Brasserie is ideally situated for Hever Castle, and Chartwell, home of Sir Winston Churchill. At a mere 30 miles due south of London, it makes a lovely day out in the country for city dwellers.

point. Noted for its rare trees and shrubs, as well as its rose and rock gardens, Emmetts also offers wonderful views across the Kentish Weald.

French Street

8½ miles NW of Tonbridge off the B2042

A tiny hamlet, tucked away in the folds of narrow, wooded hills, French Street appears to be one of the most hidden away places in Kent. In fact, if it is was not for the famous house that lies close by, it is probable that few would find this charming spot. In 1924, Winston Churchill purchased **Chartwell** as a family home and, with its magnificent views looking out over the Kentish Weald, it is easy to see why the great statesman said of Chartwell "I love the place - a day away from Chartwell is a day wasted." From the 1920s until his death in the 1960s, Churchill lived here with his wife and the rooms have been left exactly as they were when the couple were alive: daily newspapers lie on the table, fresh flowers from the garden decorate the rooms and a box of his famous cigars lie ready. Meanwhile, the museum and exhibition rooms contain numerous mementoes from his life and political career whilst the garden studio contains many of his paintings along with his easel and paintbox.

The gardens too have been well maintained, just as they were during his lifetime, and here visitors can see not only the golden rose walk that the couple's children planted on the occasion of Sir Winston and Lady Churchill's 50th wedding anniversary but also the brick wall that Churchill built with his own hands. The house is now in the ownership of the National Trust.

Westerham

10 miles NW of Tonbridge on the A25

A pleasant, small town close to the Surrey border, the building of the M25 close by has eased the town's traffic congestion and it is now a quieter and calmer place that is more in keeping with its former days as a coaching station. Along the town's main street and around the tiny green are a number of old buildings, including two venerable coaching inns, whilst, in the town centre, by the green, are two statues of British heroes who had connections with Westerham. The first dates from 1969 and it is a tribute to Sir Winston Churchill, who made his home close by at Chartwell, and the other statue is that of General James Wolfe, who defeated the French at Quebec in 1759. Wolfe was born in Westerham and his childhood home, renamed **Quebec House**, can be found to the east of the town centre. Dating from the 17th century, this gabled red brick building, is now in the hands of the National Trust and here can be found portraits, prints and other memorabilia relating to the family, the general and his famous victory over the French.

There has been a house on the site that is now occupied by **Squerryes Court** since 1216 and, in 1658, when the diarist John Evelyn visited the medieval

Chartwell

here that, at the age of 14 James Wolfe received his first commission in 1741. One of the rooms has been set aside to display mementoes relating to the General. Outside lie superb gardens, now restored to their original formal state using a garden plan of 1719, following the Great Storm of 1987. Beyond lie the less formal landscaped grounds and parkland that was laid out in the mid 18th century.

NORTH KENT COAST

From Margate, on the northeastern tip of Kent, to Rochester, on the River Medway, the history of the north Kent coastal area has been dominated by the sea. It was invaded, over 2,000 years ago, by the Romans and, ever since, the land, villages and towns have endured occupation by successive invaders. Many of the place names, such as Rochester and Whitstable, are derived from Roman, Saxon or Norman origins.

The cathedral at Rochester was built on a Saxon site by William the Conqueror's architect Bishop Gundulph, and it was also he who designed the massive fortress of Rochester Castle. Whilst this ancient city, with numerous connections with Charles Dickens, is one of the best known places along the Medway, it is Chatham that really captures the imagination. Henry VIII, looking to increase his sea power, established a dockyard at this originally Saxon settlement. This was the beginning of the Royal Navy that was to be instrumental in the building and maintenance of the British Empire. The Naval Dockyards at Chatham, where Nelson's ship *HMS Victory* was built, and the Napoleonic fortress, Fort Amherst, are two of the best monuments to the great seafaring traditions of the whole country.

Squerryes Court

mansion he wrote the following description: "A pretty, finely wooded, well watered seate, the stables good, the house old but convenient." However, this building was not to last much longer as, in 1681, the then owner, Sir Nicholas Crisp, pulled it down and built in its place the glorious red brick house seen today. Bought by the Warde family in 1731, it remains in their hands today and Squerryes Court is perhaps best known for the important collection of 18th century English and 17th century Dutch paintings housed here - many of which were commissioned by the family. Meanwhile, there are also sumptuously decorated rooms that house some splendid furniture, porcelain and tapestries. Of interest to military historians is Squerryes Court's connections with General Wolfe. The families were friends and it was whilst

Meanwhile, in conjunction with the naval loyalties of Chatham, Gillingham is the home of the Royal Engineers and their museum highlights the valuable work that the Corps has done over the centuries in many areas, including civil engineering and surveying.

Further east lie the seaside towns and resorts of Whitstable, Herne Bay and Margate. Certainly the most popular is Margate, the natural destination for many people of southeast London looking for a day beside the sea. Whilst offering all the delights of the seaside, such as amusements, a fun fair, candyfloss and fish and chips, Margate is older than it seems. It is not surprising that the bathing machine was invented in the town. Whitstable, which remains famous for its oysters, presents a calmer and less brash appearance to those looking for a seaside break. With a history that goes back to Roman times,

this fishing village, that became the haunt of smugglers, has managed to retain an individuality that inspired writers such as Somerset Maughan and Charles Dickens.

ROCHESTER

First impressions of this riverside city are misleading as the pedestrianised main shopping area and steady flow of traffic hide a history that goes back over 2,000 years. Rochester was first settled by the Romans, whose Watling Street crossed the River Medway at this point. To protect this strategic crossing point, they fortified their camp here and, in so doing, created a walled city of some 23 acres. Some five centuries later the Saxons arrived. Still an important strategic town and port, it was at Rochester that King Alfred, determined

THE HUNT RANGE

8/10 Dickens Court, Enterprise Close, Medway City Estate, Rochester, Kent ME2 4LY
Tel: 01634 293308 Fax: 01634 724471
e-mail: Melanie@thehuntrange.freeserve.co.uk

This is a family run business established in 1977 by Ken Marsh, his wife Ade and daughter Melanie. Ken was originally a registered farrier. Melanie, who grew up with horses, is trained in stable management and business administration and Ade, who was Mayor of Rochester (1994-95), is the administrative head of the business. **The Hunt Range** premises at Dickens Court are divided into three sections, manufacturing, rug washing, saddlery and feed. Ken designs and manufactures a range of horse clothing on the premises at Dickens Court. Melanie organises the rug washing and repair service as well as supervising the saddlery and tack and running the supply of horse feed, supplements and wormers. Another important aspect of the business is the direct to the public mail order service.

The Hunt Range Rugs are made from a range of durable fabrics including heavy duty nylon with polyester and synthetic linings. Fleece under, travel or show rugs use Polar Fleece while the summer sheet is in cotton and quilted polycotton to aid the wicking process. Cooler rugs use a waffle material which allows wicking, achieves rapid drying and so preventing the horse from getting chilled. A vast range of horse feeds and supplements are stocked including Saracen, Baileys, Dengie, Horsage, Topscore, Dodson & Horrell and Spillers. Bedding is by Beddown and Saracen plus a selection of New Zealand Rugs, Stable Rugs and Summer rugs as well as yard equipment and horse care products. The Rug scrubbing service covers washing, proofing and repairs.

Rochester Castle

away and the tunnel collapsed that the barons surrendered. The collapsing of the tunnel also caused the massive tower above to collapse. This was later reconstructed in a round form rather than the original square shape, giving the castle its odd appearance. Rochester castle was again severely damaged during the Civil War and much of the building seen today is the result of restoration work undertaken in the 19th century.

As well as ordering the construction of the massive fortification, William the Conqueror also put his architect to the task of building **Rochester Cathedral** on the site of a Saxon church that was founded in AD 604. Today's building still contains the remains of the 12th century chapter house and priory, along with other Norman features, that, in particular, include the fine west doorway. Like the castle, the cathedral was badly damaged during the Civil War and restoration work was undertaken by the Victorians. The remains of former monastic buildings surround the cathedral and there are three ancient gates: Prior's Gate, Deanery Gate and Chertsey's Gate, that lead on to the High Street.

Found in the city's main street, not far from Rochester Bridge, is the **Guildhall Museum** that covers the history of this city from prehistoric times through to the mid 20th century. The Guildhall was built 1687 and features in Dickens's novel "Great Expectations" as the place where Pip goes as an apprentice. The reconstruction of a Medway prison hulk ship, from the turn of the 19th century covers three floors. It is undoubtedly the most haunting exhibit in the museum depicting the inhuman conditions on

to thwart Viking sea power, built a fleet of ships and thereby created the first English navy.

Following the Norman invasion in 1066, William the Conqueror, also aware of the importance of the town and its port, decreed that a castle be maintained here permanently and put his architect, Bishop Gundulph, to the task of designing a suitable fortification. Still dominating the city today, **Rochester Castle** is recognised to be one of the finest surviving examples of Norman architecture in England. Over 100 feet tall and with walls that are around 12 feet thick, this massive construction comprised four floors from which there were many look out points. Despite the solidity of the fortress, it has had a very chequered history and, over the centuries, was subjected to three sieges. In 1215 the rebellious barons were held here by King John for seven weeks. The barons withheld despite being bombarded by missiles thrown from huge siege engines and it was only when the props of a siege tunnel were burnt board. There are domestic reconstructions of Victorian and Edwardian vintage, and many exhibits relating to Rochester's maritime history. There are scale models of local sailing barges and a diorama of the Dutch raid of the Medway in 1667.

Although the castle, cathedral and river dominate Rochester, the city is perhaps most famous for its connections with the great Victorian novelist, Charles Dickens. The **Charles Dickens Centre**, housed in Eastgate House, an Elizabethan building that Dickens knew well, brings to life the characters and places of his novels through the use of the latest technology. Like many places in and around Rochester, Eastgate House featured in his novels. It was Westgate House in *The Pickwick Papers* and The Nun's House in *The Mystery of Edwin Drood*, Dickens last and unfinished work. The grim reality of life in Victorian times

is highlighted, and world events of that age all go to help visitors put the stories of the novels in context. In the garden is the fabricated chalet that Dickens had brought from Switzerland and placed in his own garden so that he could write in peace and quiet.

There are many other buildings in the city with a Dickens' connection that are well worth seeking out. **The Royal Victoria and Bull Hotel**, that remains a hotel and restaurant today, featured as The Bull in *The Pickwick Papers* and again in *Great Expectations* as The Blue Boar. The addition of the 'Royal Victoria' to the hotel's name came in the 1830s following a visit by the as yet uncrowned Queen Victoria, who was prevented from continuing to London by a violent storm in 1836. Much earlier, in 1573, Elizabeth I stayed in Rochester at the mansion house belonging to Richard Watts MP. Although now little remains of the

Homeleigh Nurseries

Ratcliffe Highway, Hoo, Near Rochester, Kent ME3 8QD
Tel/Fax: 01634 250235

This is a very friendly, family run business with a lot of firm, local support. It's a long established business dating back to before the Second World War and was taken over by Ron and Maureen Thorne in 1960. Their first day's takings amounted to the princely sum of £3.2.6d. They have come a long way since then, slowly building the business to the thriving venture it is today. Their son, Martin, is also now a partner. He has recently opened an equestrian area which specialises in horse accessories and feed, clothing, footwear, bridles, collars, rug cleaning and repairs.

The main core business still concentrates on supplying the top quality range of traditional garden plants, shrubs and bedding plants that **Homeleigh Nurseries** has built its reputation on. They also specialise in unusual plants, shrubs, conifers and patio plants. These include the Handkerchief Tree and Bamboos. The selection of unusual fruit trees is also incredible. Peaches, pineapple and figs sit

beside nectarines and apricots. Then there is a vast range of unusual climbers like Pandoria Jasminoides, Campsis, Solya and Fremontodendron and a wonderful collection of ornamental grasses.

Everyone here is jovial and friendly and will happily take the time to discuss customers' requirements or tell them in great detail about the various plants on show. There's also a small farm shop and a selection of pottery vases and pots, and some rather interesting carved wooden mushrooms and toadstools.

building, Elizabeth was said to be so satisfied with the hospitality extended to her that the house became known as Satis House - a name that Dickens used in *Great Expectations*.

Upnor Castle

The busy port here and the routes to and from London that pass through Rochester have always ensured that the city has a steady stream of visitors. After 11 years in exile, Charles II found himself staying overnight at Rochester whilst making his triumphal march from Dover to London in 1660. The mansion in which he found overnight hospitality was renamed Restoration House following the visit. On a less happy note, it was at Abdication House (now a bank on the High Street) that James II, fleeing from William of Orange in 1689, spent his last night in England.

AROUND ROCHESTER

UPNOR

2 miles NE of Rochester off the A228

With a river frontage along the Medway and a backdrop of wooded hills, Upnor became something of a resort for the people of the Medway towns. However, whilst this is indeed an ideal place to spend some leisure time, the village has not always been so peaceful. In the 16th century, Elizabeth I ordered the construction of several fortifications along the Medway estuary to protect her dockyard at Chatham from invasion and, in 1559, **Upnor Castle** was constructed. Fronted by a water bastion jutting out into the River Medway, this castle saw action in 1667 when the Dutch sailed up

the river with the intention of destroying the English naval fleet. The gun batteries at Upnor were the primary defence against this attack but they proved to be ineffective as the Dutch captured, and made off with, the British flag ship the *Royal Charles*.

After this failure, the castle became a magazine and, at one time, more gunpowder was stored here than at the Tower of London. One of the guns that failed to stop the Dutch has been salvaged from the river and now stands guard outside the entrance to the fort and visitors here can tour the gatehouse and main body of the castle.

Just up the river lies the **Royal Engineers' Upnor Base** where the testing and development of numerous devices and pieces of equipment relating to sea warfare took place.

COOLING

4½ miles N of Rochester off the A228

This isolated village lies on the Hoo peninsula an area of bleak marshland lying between the Medway and the Thames. In 1381, John de Cobham of Cooling applied to Richard II to be granted the right to fortify his manor house as, at that time, the sea came right up to his house and he feared a seaborne attack. His fear was very much justified as, a couple of years earlier, the French had sailed up the river and set alight several villages in the area. So the king was happy to allow the construction to go ahead. The result of de Cobham's work, which became known as **Cooling Castle**, can still be seen clearly from the road (although it is not open to the public) but the sea has receded over the years and no longer laps the castle's massive outer walls. In the 15th century, Cooling Castle became the home of Sir John Oldcastle, Lord of Cooling, who was executed in 1417 for the part he played in a plot against Henry V. Shakespeare is said to have modelled his character, Falstaff, on Sir John.

Close by the substantial castle remains stands **St James' Church** where, in the graveyard, there can be seen the 13 lozenge-shaped stones that mark the graves of various Comport children who all died of malaria in the 18th century. Not one of the children lived to be older than 17 months and these were, supposedly, the graves of Pip's brothers in Dickens's novel *Great Expectations*.

ALLHALLOWS
8 miles NE of Rochester off the A228

This remote village, that takes its name from its small 11th century church of All Saints, overlooks the River Thames estuary and, beyond, the busy Essex resort of Southend. Nearby, is an **Iron Beacon** that was erected in Elizabethan times and it is one of many such beacons that were set up along the coast to warn of imminent invasion. In the 1930s there were plans to develop the land to the north of the village, along the coast, as a holiday area and, although the resort never quite came to fruition, the Art Deco style railway station still remains and has been put to other uses.

GRAIN
10 miles NE of Rochester off the A228

This easternmost tip of the Hoo Peninsula is known as the **Isle of Grain** and from here there are sweeping views out across the Thames estuary but many are put off by the sight (and sometimes the smell) of the oil refineries and the power station that lie close by. It was from here that Sir Winston Churchill learned to fly from Grain's airfield.

CHATHAM
1 mile E of Rochester on the A2

Although there has been a settlement here since Saxon times, it was not until Henry VIII established a dockyard here that Chatham began to grow from being a sleepy, riverside backwater into a busy town. The dockyard flourished and was expanded by Elizabeth I during the time of the Armada. Sir Francis Drake, who took part in the defeat of the Spanish fleet in 1588, moved here with his family at the age of six and, whilst his father was chaplain to the fleet based here, the young Francis learned his sailing skills on the reaches around Chatham and Gillingham. Of the many famous ships that were built at the naval dockyard, perhaps the most famous is Nelson's *HMS Victory*, which was launched in 1765.

The naval connection continued to boost the growth of the town and its present commercial centre originally saw to the needs of navy personnel. Among these was John Dickens, who was employed by the Navy Pay Office. His son, Charles, spent some of his boyhood years at Chatham. The family moved to **2 Ordnance Terrace** (now number 11) when Charles was five and it was his father who was to provide the inspiration for the character Mr Micawber in *David Copperfield*.

Just to the north of the town centre on

the banks of the River Medway is **The Historic Dockyard**, Chatham's historic dockyard, founded by Henry VIII, which became the premier shipbuilding yard for the Royal Navy. With over 400 years of history, visitors can appreciate the scale of the 20th century submarine and battleship dry docked here and the architecture of the most complete Georgian dockyard in the world. Samuel Pepys, the famous diarist, first made reference to the dockyard in his diaries in 1661 and he was here to witness the audacious Dutch raid six years later when de Ruyter managed to capture the English flag ship, Royal Charles. The Ropery at Historic Dockyard is a building a quarter of a mile long. Rope can be seen being made in the traditional way here, using machines dating back to 1811. The 175 year history of the lifeboats is told at the National Collection of the RNLI. The dockyard has been the setting for a number of

films over the years, including *The Mummy* and *Tomorrow Never Dies*.

The Chatham dockyards were an obvious target for Hitler's bombers during World War II and, at **Fort Amherst Heritage Park and Caverns**, that lie close by, the secret underground telephone exchange, that co-ordinated the air raid warnings, can be seen. The country's premier Napoleonic fortress, Fort Amherst was built in 1756 to defend the naval dockyard from attack by land, and it continued to serve this purpose up until the end of World War II. Today, the fort offers visitors an insight into the daily lives of the soldiers who were stationed here, and their families, through a series of displays and through re-enactments in period costumes. The fort's most outstanding feature, and most interesting, is undoubtedly the underground maze of tunnels and caverns that were used as storage, magazines, barracks and guardrooms, and the guided tour around the underground workings highlights the skills of the military engineers.

The extensive outer fortification, that covers seven acres and includes battlements and earthworks, has been turned into a country park style area where visitors can enjoy a picnic or walk the various nature trails.

Like the dockyard, Fort Amherst has been used as a location by both film and television companies and it was here that Robert de Niro shot the prison cell scenes for *The Mission*, Val Kilmer worked on the remake of the 1960s series *The Saint* and the BBC filmed *The Phoenix and the Carpet*.

In a former church, opposite the fort, is the **Medway Heritage Centre** where every aspect of this working river is explored, including the lives of the men and women who worked on the banks and sailed on the water. Back in the

Covered Building Slip, 1838

main part of the town can be found the **Almshouses** that were built by one of the two charities that were established by the Elizabethan seafarer, Admiral Sir John Hawkins. As well as helping to defeat the Spanish Armada along with Sir Francis Drake, Hawkins was also an inventor and philanthropist and it was he who introduced 'copper bottoms' to help prevent the deterioration of ship's hulls below the waterline.

These almshouse at Chatham were originally designed as a hospital for retired seamen and their widows.

GILLINGHAM

2 miles E of Rochester on the A2

Although there is evidence of both prehistoric and Roman occupation of this area, a village did not really become established here until the 11th century. The oldest part of this, the largest of the Medway towns, is **The Green** and here

can be found the Norman parish church of St Mary that dates from the early 12th century. However, it was the establishment of the dockyard at neighbouring Chatham in the 16th century that saw Gillingham begin to expand as it became a centre for servicing the naval dockyard and depot. As with many towns along the Medway, Gillingham has many links with the sea and it was the story of the Gillingham sailor, Will Adams, that inspired the novel *Shogun* by James Clavell. In 1600, Adams sailed to Japan and there he befriended Ieyasu, the Shogun, learnt Japanese and was honoured as a Samurai warrior. Beside the A2 is the **Will Adams Monument**, a fitting tribute to the man who went on to become the Shogun's teacher and adviser.

All things maritime have influenced Gillingham greatly over the centuries, but the town is also the home of one of

FAIRHAVEN HOLIDAY COTTAGES

Derby House, 123 Watling Street, Gillingham, Kent ME7 2YY
Tel: 01634 300089 Fax: 01634 570157
e-mail: enquiry@fairhaven-holidays.co.uk
website: www. fairhaven-holidays.co.uk

Ann and John Campbell have been running one of the most experienced agencies in southeast England for over seventeen years. They provide holiday and long term letting accommodation throughout Kent and Sussex. **Fairhaven Holiday Cottages** are all of a superior nature and range from attractive oast houses and country houses to compact flats and seaside houses. Many of the properties are in out of the way places making them ideal for those looking to get away from it all or for someone looking for a quiet base to tour the area. There's a charming country property for two on the historic and scenic Pilgrims Way to Canterbury or a picturesque 270 year old cottage, complete with ancient beams, an open fireplace and sloping floors in the pretty village of Grafty Green. Near the historic town of Lewes is a delightful single storey barn conversion again in an exceptionally quiet area just outside the village of East

Hoathly. Tucked away in a rural farmyard close to the picturesque, historic church of Ryarsh is another 18th century converted cottage. The minimum standard for a Fairhaven Cottage is three star or three diamond and many are of a much higher standard.

Ann and John offer a very friendly service. Because they have a comprehensive local knowledge they are able to discuss clients' requirements in depth and find the perfect property for them. All of the cottages on Fairhaven's list have been personally visited by Ann and John to ensure that they meet their very high standards.

The Royal Engineers Museum

was attacked by thousands of Zulu warriors. More recently, the World War I General, Lord Kitchener, of the now infamous recruitment poster campaign, was also a Royal Engineer.

MILTON REGIS

10 miles E of Rochester off the A2

Once a royal borough, Milton Regis has been all but incorporated into the outskirts of Sittingbourne. However, in the still well defined village centre can be found the **Court Hall Museum** housed, as its name might suggest, in a 15th century timbered building that was originally Milton Regis's courthouse, school and town gaol. The museum has displays, photographs and documents that relate to the village and surrounding area.

Meanwhile, at **Milton Creek**, lies **Dolphin Yard Sailing Barge Museum** that lies in a traditional sailing barge yard where commercial work is still undertaken. Along with aiming to preserve the barges and other craft that have been used on the local estuaries for hundreds of years, the museum is also dedicated, in particular, to the sailing barge. While the creek provided a means of transport its waters were also used to power paper mills and paper manufacturing remains in evidence in this area today.

SITTINGBOURNE

10½ miles E of Rochester on the A2

Lying close to the Roman road, Watling Street, Sittingbourne was, during the Middle Ages, a stopping place for pilgrims on their way to Canterbury. As a result of this the town developed a thriving market that has continued to this day

The town was also a centre for barge making and for paper manufacturing.

the most fascinating military attractions - **The Royal Engineers Museum**. This museum reflects the diverse range of skills that the Corps has brought to bear both in peace-time and war. They were the creators of the Ordnance Survey, the designers of the Royal Albert Hall and the founders of the Royal Flying Corps in 1912. The Royal Engineers continue the dangerous work of bomb disposal and throughout the world they build roads and bridges, lay water pipes and assist in natural disasters. The new courtyard display illustrates the wide variety of activities the Corps has undertaken since the 1940s whilst, inside, there is a dignified medal gallery, a reconstruction of a World War I trench and numerous artefacts from around the world that have been acquired by members of the Corps. Both the nearby dockyards and Fort Amherst at Chatham, were built by the Royal Engineers and this superb museum tells of the diverse work of the Corps in both wartime and peacetime. Here visitors can see the original battlefield map prepared by the Corps and used by the Duke of Wellington to defeat Napoleon at the Battle of Waterloo in 1815. It was a Royal Engineer, Lieutenant John Chard VC, who played a key role in the defence of Rorkes Drift when the mission, with just 130 men,

DODDINGTON PLACE GARDENS

Doddington, Near Sittingbourne, Kent, ME9 0BB
Tel: 01795 886101 Fax: 01795 886155

Doddington Place was built in 1860 for Sir John Croft of the port and sherry family. It is now the home of the Oldfield family. Surrounded by wooded countryside, orchards and farmland, it is in an officially designated Area of Outstanding Natural Beauty. The lovely landscaped ten- acre gardens are recognised by English Heritage as being of special historical interest. The gardens include a notable woodland garden established in the 1960's which is spectacular in May and June. It includes many different kinds of rhododendron and azalea, camellias, acers and eucryphia. A large rock garden laid out c.1910 retains a strong Edwardian atmosphere, where the plants include sedum, sempervivens, Helianthemum, dianthus, naturalised cyclamen and irises. A formal sunk garden with borders - at their best in late summer and a spring garden with fruit trees under planted with bulbs.

There is also a fine avenue of Wellingtonia dating from the mid 19th century and a recently completed two storey brick and flint gothic folly. Extensive lawns are framed by impressive clipped yew hedges and many fine specimen trees. The avenues provide several fine walks including Woodland Garden, Pond and Folly Walks.

Another form of transport that was, at one time, much more common, is the steam train and from here the **Sittingbourne and Kemsley Light Railway** runs steam hauled passenger trains along two miles of preserved track. The railway was originally designed to transport paper and other bulk materials but now the journey is taken for pleasure by those fascinated by steam trains and those wishing to view this area of the Kentish countryside at close quarters.

BORSTAL

1½ miles S of Rochester off the B2097

Found on the eastern side of the elegant **Medway Bridge**, that carries the M2 over the River Medway, this is the village that is famous for giving its name to young offenders institutions when the first prison of this type was opened here in 1908. The original borstal buildings can still be seen.

STROOD

1 mile W of Rochester off the A228

Situated on the opposite bank of the River Medway from Rochester, it was here that, during the Roman invasion of Britain, masterminded by Claudius from Richborough, the Roman legions were halted by a force of Britons led by Caratacus. After two days, the Romans won the battle but only after Claudius had ordered some of his men to swim the river whilst others crossed higher up and surprised the Britons from behind.

However, it is as the home of **Temple Manor** that Strood is better known. Built in the 13th century by the Knights Templar, this was originally a hostel where the knights could find shelter, food and fresh horses whilst going to and from the Crusades. A building of simple design, this is all that survives from an earlier complex that would also have contained stables, kitchens and barns. Later, it became a nunnery that was dissolved under Henry VIII and eventually a farmhouse before falling into disrepair. Sympathetically restored after World War II, the original 13th century hall, with its vaulted undercroft, and the 17th century brick extensions have all survived. It is now open to the public throughout the summer.

A local legend tells that, during the bitter feuding between Henry II and Archbishop Thomas à Becket, the men of Strood, who were loyal to the king, cut off the tail of Becket's horse whilst he was riding through the town. Becket suggested that the descendants of those involved in the incident would be born with tails and so, apparently, they were!

As with other Medway towns, Strood has its connections with the sea and, moored at **Damhead Creek** is *The Medway Queen*, an old paddle steamer that was one of the many thousands of unlikely crafts that took part in the evacuation of Dunkirk in 1941.

HIGHAM

3 miles NW of Rochester off the A226

This scattered village, with its ancient and charming marshland church, is famous for being the home of Charles Dickens - the great novelist lived with his family at **Gad's Hill Place** from 1857 until his death in 1870. Originally dating from 1780, Dickens made various alterations to the house to accommodate his family and, in particular, he added a conservatory that, in 1995, was restored to its former glory. Whilst living at Gad's Hill, Dickens wrote several of his novels and he died before he could complete *The Mystery of*

Edwin Drood. Although the house is now a school, some of the rooms and the grounds that Dickens so loved are open to the public at various times throughout the year. Visitors can see the study where Dickens worked on his novels, the restored conservatory and stroll around the grounds.

MINSTER

This unprepossessing seaside town, situated on the northern coast of the Isle of Sheppey, is an unlikely place to find one of the oldest sites of Christianity in England. However, it was here, on the highest point of the island, that Sexburga, the widow of a Saxon king of Kent, founded a nunnery in the late 7th century. Sacked by the Danes in 855, **Minster Abbey** was rebuilt in around 1130 when it was also re-established as a priory for Benedictine nuns. Sometime later, in the 13th century, the parish church of Minster was built, adjoining the monastic church, and so, from the Middle Ages until the Dissolution of the Monasteries, the building served as a 'double church' with the nun's worshipping in the northern half of the building and the parishioners in the other. To the west of this unusual church

Minster Abbey Gatehouse

lies the 15th century abbey gatehouse that, today, is home to the **Minster Abbey Gatehouse Museum**. Here, there are displays on the history of Sheppey which is told through exhibits of fossils, tools and photographs. Opening times are limited.

In his *Ingoldsby Legends*, RH Barham retells the story of the fiery Sir Roger de Shurland, Lord of Sheppey who, in 1300, killed a monk who had disobeyed him. Dodging the county sheriff, Sir Roger swam out on horseback to Edward I's passing ship and received the king's pardon for his wicked act. On returning to shore, Sir Roger met a mysterious old hag who foretold that, having saved his life, Sir Roger's horse would also cause his death. On hearing this, the tempestuous knight drew his sword and beheaded his horse. Some time later, whilst walking on the beach, Sir Roger came across the head of his horse that had been washed ashore. In an angry rage, he kicked the head but one of the horse's teeth penetrated his boot and Sir Roger died later from the infection that developed in the wound. Sir Roger's tomb lies in the abbey church and close to the right foot of his stone effigy can be seen the head of a horse.

AROUND MINSTER

EASTCHURCH

2½ miles SE of Minster off the B2231

This village was once the home of the early pioneers of aviation and a young Sir Winston Churchill flew from the old Eastchurch aerodrome. Another early pilot, Lord Brabazon of Tara, was the holder of Pilot's Licence No 1. Close to the church is a stone memorial to the early pilots whilst, nearby, are the ruins of 16th century Shurland Hall, where

Henry VIII and Anne Boleyn stayed on their honeymoon.

A little outside the village lies **Norwood Manor** a charming old house that dates from the 17th century although the 'Northwoode' family have lived on this site since Norman times. On display in the house are numerous artefacts that relate to this long established Kentish family.

LEYSDOWN

5 miles SE of Minster on the B2231

A popular seaside place with visitors for many years - Henry VIII loved the Isle of Sheppey so much that he spent one of his honeymoons here - Leysdown is renowned for its sandy beaches while there are picnic areas and nature trails close by.

A little to the south, and found on the southeastern tip of the Isle of Sheppey, **The Swale National Nature Reserve** is home to numerous wildfowl and visitors here can combine watching the birds with coastal walking.

ELMLEY ISLAND

3 miles S of Minster off the A249

Situated on southern coastline of the Isle of Sheppey and overlooking The Swale and the north Kent coast, **Elmley Marshes Nature Reserve** is an area of salt marsh that is home to wetland birds, marsh frogs, numerous insects and many species of aquatic plants.

QUEENBOROUGH

3 miles W of Minster off the A249

An historic town that began as a Saxon settlement, Queenborough became an important wool port and a wealthy borough that was graced by a royal **Castle** built here by Edward III. The town's reliance on the sea for its prosperity also saw its courthouse captured by the Dutch during their invasion of the Medway in 1667. During the 18th century, the town's prosperity continued, based on the increased naval presence after the Dutch invasion. Many fine buildings were built, which still survive. However the first part of 19th century century saw Queenborough decline as enterprising neighbours like Sheerness grew. During World War II, Queenborough became the home of hundreds of mine-sweeping vessels. **The Guildhall Museum**, that is housed in the building that replaced the earlier courthouse, tells the fascinating story of this town, from Saxon times, through its rise at the hands of Victorian industrialists, to the important role Queenborough played during World War II. Queenborough is still a very busy boating centre with numerous boat builders and chandlers.

SHEERNESS

2½ miles NW of Minster on the A249

Overlooking the point where the River Medway meets the River Thames, Sheerness was once the site of a naval dockyard and it was the first to be surveyed, in the 17th century, by Samuel Pepys, the famous diarist, who held the position of Secretary of the Admiralty during the reign of Charles II. It was at Sheerness that, in 1805, *HMS Victory* docked when it brought Nelson's body back to England after the Battle of Trafalgar. In more recent times, Sheerness has developed into

a busy container and car ferry port and most of the Isle of Sheppey's wealth is centred on the town.

The Sheerness Heritage Centre is housed in a weatherboarded cottage that was built in the early 19th century as a dwelling for a dockyard worker. Despite being constructed of seemingly temporary building materials the house, as with its two neighbours, has lasted well. Over the years, it has been a baker's shop and a fish and chip shop. The rooms here have now been restored to reflect authentic 19th century rooms and are furnished with genuine pieces from that period. The heritage centre also has an exhibition describing the development of The Royal Dockyard here, which closed in the 1960s and a display of tools used by its workers.

WHITSTABLE

Anyone wandering around Whitstable will soon realise that this is no seaside resort but very much a working town that is centred around the busy commercial harbour that was originally the port for Canterbury. The old

Shell Fishing, Whitstable

fashioned streets of the town are lined with fisherman's cottages and the winding lanes are linked by narrow alleyways with eccentric names - such as **Squeeze Gut Alley** - that recall the town's rich maritime past. Sometimes referred to as the 'Pearl of Kent', Whitstable is as famous today for its oysters as it was in Roman times and it is probable that Caesar himself enjoyed Whitstable oysters. Wheelers Oyster bar in the town is one survivor of the numerous bars that were once here, where oysters can be enjoyed, along with other fish, fresh from the sea.

After the Roman occupation left Britain, the Saxons came to the area and they gave the town its name - then Witanstaple, meaning 'an assembly of wise men in the market'. This later became Whitstable. Later, the Normans built the parish church of All Saints, which provided medieval sailors with a

key navigation aid. The ownership of the manor of Whitstable in the Middle Ages proved to be something of a poisoned chalice. John de Stragboli was executed for murder, Bartholomew de Badlesmere was hanged for his part in the rebellion against Edward II and Robert de Vere was convicted for treason. Even in the 16th century, the owner of the manor fared no better and Sir John Gates was executed for his support of Lady Jane Grey over the Catholic Mary Tudor.

Along with oysters and a fishing industry that has lasted over 700 years, the discovery of iron pyrites deposits around Whitstable led to the development of the manufacture of copperas that was used for dyeing, making ink and some early medicines. However, it was the sea and the associated boat building and repair yards that were to continue to support many of those living in the town. Now many of

CRAB AND WINKLE SEAFOOD RETAURANT

South Quay, The Harbour, Whitstable, Kent CT5 1AB
Tel: 01227 779377 Fax: 01227 771249
e-mail: crab.winkle1@ukonline.co.uk
website: www.crab-winkle.co.uk

Peter and Eileen Bennet and their son Andrew run this growing family business on Whitstable harbour, where guests can enjoy some of the finest seafood in the area. Combining a fresh fish market with a seafood restaurant ensures that the fish could not be any fresher, coming direct from the

Dylan Woolf Photography

boats to the kitchen to your table. Situated right at the heart of this working harbour, every seat in the **Crab and Winkle Seafood Restaurant** has a view of the boats coming and going. Fish are landed daily and if visitors are there at the right time they can see the fish being landed which will shortly be on the slabs in the market and the plates of the restaurant.

Imaginative and tasty food is served from morning through to late evening, with breakfast and

bistro menus as well as the main menu. From a light lunch of seafood bake or steamed mussels eaten watching the busy harbour to a gourmet serving of whole local lobster or Cornish crab for a special occasion, the excellence of the food and the ambience of this traditional wooden fisherman's building make any meal an event to remember. There are meat and vegetarian choices although most people will be unable to resist the enormous selection of fresh fish dishes, particularly the chef's specials and the catch of the day. A children's menu is also available.

the yards have gone but, as recently as World War II, ships' lifeboats and other small craft were being built and launched at Whitstable. Going hand in hand with the town's maritime connections was the unofficial trade of smuggling and, during the 18th century, there were numerous battles between the gangs and the revenue men in and around the town.

Whilst the authorities clamped down hard on this illegal trading, there was one positive spin-off as the smugglers had such an intimate knowledge of the French coastline that Nelson consulted them whilst planning his naval campaigns.

On the harbour's East Quay is the **Oyster and Fishery Exhibition** telling the story of Whitstable's connections with seafood and fish. Visitors can also see the first commercial oyster hatchery in the world. Naturally, there are fresh Whitstable oysters and clams on the menu at the exhibition's café. Meanwhile, for a broader picture of the town, past and present, **Whitstable Museum and Gallery** explores the traditions and life of this ancient seafaring community. There are also references and information on the many 'firsts' to which the town lays claim: the first scheduled passenger train ran between Whitstable and Canterbury; the first steamship to sail to Australia from Britain left here in 1837; the diving helmet was invented in the town; and the country's first council houses were built at Whitstable.

However, not everyone is an inventor and visionary and, more recently, Whitstable has become fashionable with writers and those associated with the media industry. After his parents died, Somerset Maugham came to live with his uncle at Whitstable and the town features strongly in two of his novels, *Of Human Bondage* and *Cakes and Ale*. Charles Dickens visited here and wrote about the town whilst Robert Hitchens, the novelist and journalist, lived nearby at Tankerton. One of the town's less celebrated residents was William Joyce who worked in one of the town's radio shops before travelling to Germany to broadcast Nazi propaganda back to England as Lord Haw Haw.

AROUND WHITSTABLE

HERNE BAY
4½ miles NE of Whitstable on the B2205

Now one of the main resorts on the north Kent coast, Herne Bay was, originally, a fishing village that became notorious as a haunt for smugglers. Much of the town seen today was laid out in the mid 19th century as it was developed as a resort to attract Victorian middle classes looking for clean air and safe beaches. It still retains a quiet gentility that is reminiscent of that lost era and, at the **Herne Bay Museum Centre**, visitors can, through entertaining displays, discover the history of the town and the story of its famous pier. The museum also contains relics from prehistoric times such as fossils and stone tools. Also in the town is a superb landmark, the **Clock Tower**, that stands on the promenade and was given to Herne Bay by a wealthy London lady to commemorate Queen Victoria's coronation in 1836.

Just inland, at the ancient Saxon village of **Herne**, stands **Herne Mill**, a Kentish smock mill that has recently undergone extensive repair work. Dating from 1789, this particularly mill is the latest in a long line that have occupied this site.

VINCENT NURSERIES AND PLANT CENTRE

Eddington Lane, Herne Bay, Kent CT6 5TS
Tel: 01227 375806

Founded in 1947 by Philip Maunder, **Vincent Nurseries and Plant Centre** is still a family run business. Originally growing vegetables for the wholesale trade, the nursery moved into production of bedding plants and glasshouse crops in the 1960s and 70s. When the Maunder's daughter Christine graduated from Hadlow College in 1983, after a three year course in commercial horticulture, the family decided to give up wholesale production and concentrate on growing and retailing from their five acre site in Eddington Lane.

As its name explains, Vincent Nurseries is essentially a plant centre rather than a garden centre, although it does of course stock a good range of associated sundries, chemicals, fertilizers, compost, tools, aggregates etc. A large percentage of the plants on offer, particularly shrubs and seasonal bedding plants, are raised in the nurseries by an experienced team of staff which helps to ensure good quality plants. Those members of staff are always on hand to help with selecting plants as well as helping to solve pest and disease problems in the garden. Stock includes a wide

range of shrubs, trees, conifers, fruit trees, roses as well as climbing plants, perennials, alpines,seeds and bulbs, seasonal bedding and basket plants, and aquatic plants. For the indoor gardening enthusiast the plant centre offers houseplants, flowering plants and cut flowers from their extensive covered area. Indoors or out no garden is complete without some pots, and Vincent Nurseries stocks a wide range of terracotta and oriental pots as well as stoneware. Planted containers and baskets are available or can be planted to order. A local delivery service is also available.

RECULVER

7½ miles NE of Whitstable off the A299

Reculver is the site of the Roman Regulbium, one of the forts built in the 3rd century to defend the shores of Kent from Saxon invasion. Sometime later the site was taken over as a place of Christian worship and this early fort provided the building materials for the 7th century Saxon church that was later extended by the Normans. It was also around this time that the Normans built the two huge towers, within the remains of the Roman fort, that provided mariners with a landmark to guide them into the Thames estuary. Today, **Reculver Towers and Roman Fort** is under the management of English Heritage and has been preserved and, although there are only few remains of the fort, the towers

still stand overlooking the rocky beach and can be seen from several miles along the coast. Meanwhile, **Reculver Country Park** offers visitors a lovely walk to these remains, church and towers and the park's visitors' centre has some fascinating information on the history and natural history of this stretch of coastline.

Reculver Towers and Roman Fort

As a major historic site, Reculver has, of course, seen much archaeological activity over the years and, in the 1960s, an excavation unearthed several tiny skeletons that were buried not far from the towers. It is generally believed that these babies were buried alive as human sacrifices and, it is said, that on stormy nights the babies can be heard crying out. During World War II, the Barnes Wallace 'bouncing bomb' was tested off the coast of Reculver. Several of these were found on the shore in 1997. Fortunately they were found to contain no explosives.

Birchington

12 miles E of Whitstable on the A28

This quiet resort, with cliffs and bays, still retains its individuality despite the spread of the Margate conurbation from the east and it is a particular favourite for families with young children. At **All Saints' Church** there is a monument to one of the most famous British artists of the 19th century, Dante Gabriel Rossetti, the poet and artist who was instrumental in the formation of the Pre-Raphaelite Brotherhood. He lies buried in the doorway and a memorial stone, carved by his mentor, Ford Madox Brown, marks his grave.

About half a mile to the southeast of the village lies **Quex House**, a Regency gentleman's country house that was later expanded into the Victorian mansion seen today. It remains the home of the Powell-Cotton family and visitors looking around the rooms will find that the house still retains the atmosphere of a family home, complete with freshly cut flowers from the garden. A fine collection of period and oriental furniture, family portraits,

porcelain and silver can be seen by those wandering through the rooms. One particular member of the family, Major PHG Powell-Cotton, was a great explorer and whilst he was lured to exotic lands by big game, the Major was a true Victorian who also took an interest in the customs and beliefs of the people and tribes that he met on his travels. As a result he put together a vast collection, and the **Museum** here displays that collection in polished mahogany cases. From dioramas of animals and tribal art, costumes and weapons to European and Chinese porcelains and local archaeological finds, there is a vast range of exhibits from right around the world. As well as offering visitors a great deal to see inside the house, Quex is surrounded by some superb **Gardens**, parkland and woodlands that provide the perfect backdrop to this fascinating house. The gardens have wide lawns with mature trees and a walled kitchen garden. John Cotton-Powell's collection of cannon are also displayed in the grounds.

Margate

15 miles E of Whitstable on the A28

With its long stretch of golden sand, promenades, amusement arcades, candy floss and fun fairs, Margate is very much everyone's idea of a boisterous English

The Sands, Margate

seaside resort. This is a well deserved reputation that has grown up for over 200 years. Before the railway brought holidaymakers in droves from London from the 1840s onwards, those looking for a day by the sea came in sailing boats known as Margate hoys. Still often regarded as the first choice for a day out by those living in southeast London, many people return here time and time again to wander the pleasant streets of the old town and take the bracing sea air. With this background as a seaside resort, it is not surprising to find that the bathing machine was supposedly invented here, in 1752, by a Quaker glover and a Margate resident called Benjamin Beale.

However there is more to Margate than sun, sea, sand and fish and chips. In King Street, can be found the **Tudor House** that dates back to the early 16th century and the reign of Henry VIII. It is the oldest house in Margate and it holds a collection of seaside memorabilia.

Just inland, lies the medieval **Salmestone Grange** that originally belonged to St Augustine's Abbey at Canterbury. Arguably, one of the best preserved examples of a monastic grange in England, the chapel, crypt and kitchen can all still be seen.

Another building that has withstood the test of time is **Drapers Mill**, an old smock corn mill that was constructed in 1845 by John Holman. It continued to the powered by the wind until a gas engine was installed in 1916 and, after being made redundant in the 1930s, the mill was restored to working order in the 1970s.

SARRE

9 miles SE of Whitstable on the A28

This sunken village lies on the edge of marshland and it was, centuries ago, an important harbour and ferry point when

Sarre Mill

the Isle of Thanet was, indeed, an island. Today, it is home to one of the country's few remaining commercially working mills, **Sarre Mill**, a typical Kentish smock windmill built in 1820 by the Canterbury millwright John Holman. The addition of first steam and then gas power ensured that Sarre Mill remained in use well into the 20th century but in the 1940s milling ceased here. Fortunately, in the 1980s, the windmill was restored to working order. Today, Sarre Mill is producing high quality stoneground flour, and offering tours of the five floors of the mill. There are small farmyard animals that are sure to delight children and a rare portable steam engine dating from the 1860s that was used to crush apples for cider making. Numerous other items of rural interest, such as old agricultural machinery, farming implements and domestic pieces, are on display here in the exhibition of bygones.

HERNE COMMON
4 miles SE of Whitstable off the A291

Close to the village and found deep in a leafy forest is **Wildwood**, Kent's unique woodland discovery park that is also the home of the only breeding pack of endangered European wolves in Britain. Although wolves have not been living in the wild in this country for many years, tales of the savage packs that once roamed the countryside live on and, here, stories of the medieval hunters who killed them for bounty and of the fear of travellers alone on dark nights bring back those days. The Saxons called January 'Wulf monat' as this was when the hungry packs were at their most dangerous. However, Wildwood is not entirely devoted to wolves and here, in the forest, is a reconstruction of a Saxon village, Regia Anglorum, where living history is brought to life as village members, in authentic costume, go about their daily lives and practice the skills and crafts from centuries ago.

Other wildlife also abounds at Wildwood and, along with the badger colony here there are rabbits, polecats, shrews and hedgehogs all living in underground burrows. Living in a near natural environment is the park's herd of deer. Whilst this is an interesting, enjoyable and educational place to visit for all the family, much of the work of the park goes on behind the scenes, in the area of conservation, and two species in particular, water voles and hazel dormice, are bred here for re-introduction into the wild.

HERNHILL
5 miles SW of Whitstable off the A299

A secluded and tranquil village that is surrounded by orchards, Hernhill is also home to **Mount Ephraim Gardens**. This family estate also includes a house, woodland and fruit farm. There are magnificent views of both the Swale and Thames estuaries from the gardens. The gardens are essentially Edwardian offering a good balance between the formal and the informal through such delights as herbaceous borders, topiary, rose terraces, a Japanese garden, a rock garden, a vineyard and orchard trails.

FAVERSHAM
6 miles SW of Whitstable on the A2

As with many places in this area of Kent, Faversham was first settled by the Romans, who gave the town its name (it comes from 'faber' meaning blacksmith), and it was later inhabited by both the Jutes and the Saxons. Despite this period of turmoil, the town continued to grow, so much so in fact that, in 811, King Kenulf granted Faversham a charter and the market still plays an important part in the life of the town today. The Market Place, which is also the junction of three

BIRDS, BIRDS, BIRDS

4 Limes Place, Preston Street, Faversham, Kent ME13 8PQ
Tel: 01795 532370
e-mail: pauljcumberland@yahoo.co.uk

Paul and Susan Cumberland preside over a comprehensive and eclectic collection of ceramics, paintings, prints and glasswork all with one thing in common, birds. From the exquisite porcelain puffins made on the Isle of Arran, the Swedish glass birds of Matts Jonasson , hand painted figures from Florence to original paintings of birds, mainly by local artists, there is something to suit every taste and every pocket at **Birds, Birds, Birds**. And they sell bird feeders and birdfood.

MACKNADE FINE FOODS

Selling Road, Faversham, Kent ME13 8XF
Tel: 01795 534497
e-mail: macknade@aol.com

Patricia and Renato Cuomo started their business in 1979 as 'Fir Tree Farm' with 20 acres of land planted with 'Pick Your Own' crops and their shop was a tent attached to a caravan.   Twenty plus years later they have evolved into **Macknade Fine Foods** with an Aladdin's Cave of a shop jammed full of all manner of goodies. They supply a wide range of fresh produce as well as a vast selection of specialist and unusual foods. As far as possible they stock local produce whether it be fresh fruit and vegetables or ice cream, jam, wine, cider and beer. They also carry a comprehensive selection of foods ranging from the Mediterranean to the Far East.

By making frequent visits to London's Covent Garden market they have access to a huge variety of fruit and vegetables, and if a customer is looking for something they don't have in stock they will do their best to get it. The massive tables in the centre of the shop are piled with baskets and trays of every

type of fruit and vegetable imaginable. From the ceiling hang an unusual and varied choice of hand crafted wicker baskets and the walls are lined with shelves to delight a gourmet. Handmade Belgian chocolates sit alongside, fresh Italian Pestos, virgin olive oils and fresh apple juices. The selection of freshly ground coffees is without compare in the region as are the English jams, home made cakes and free-range eggs. They have a large car park in very attractive country surroundings where animals and colourful poultry can be seen roaming in their natural habitat. There's also a craft centre on the site with a coffee shop.

BROGDALE HOME OF FRUIT

Brogdale Road, Faversham, Nr Canterbury, Kent ME13 8XZ
Tel: 10795 535286 Fax: 01795 531710
e-mail: info@brogdale.org.uk website: www.brogdale.org.uk

Brogdale is home to the National Fruit Collections, the largest collection of fruit trees and plants in the world. Over 2,300 different varieties of apple, 550 of pear, 350 of plum, 220 of cherry and 320 varieties of bush fruits as well as smaller collections of nuts and vines are grown here in 150 acres of beautiful orchards. The varieties of fruit range from the sublime to the ridiculous. The ancient Romans would have munched on the Decio variety of apple, the Victorians loved their medlars and quinces, while other varieties of apple taste like pineapples or bananas.

Spectacular in bloom, the orchards are at their best in late summer and autumn when the fruit is ripe for picking. There are daily guided tours of the fruit collections which last about an hour or visitors can wander at will around the most attractive parts including the peaceful picnic area. Special

events throughout the year include Blossom Walks in the spring, a Summer Fruit Festival in July, the Great Apple celebration in October and a Christmas Craft Fair in December. There are also courses on all aspects of fruit cultivation from planting and pruning to grafting.

Brogdale Plant centre stocks hundreds of different varieties of apples, pears, plums, cherries, gages, and bush fruits. Bare rooted trees are available from November to March, while containerised trees are in stock the year round. Even if the centre does not have a particular variety in stock they will usually be able to 'bud' or 'graft' it on request.

of the town's oldest streets, is dominated by the **Guildhall**, which was built in the 16th century. Its open ground-floor pillared arcade provided cover for the market. Unusually it has a tower at one end. After the upper floor and tower were damaged by fire in the early 19th century, it was rebuilt and extended. However the rebuilding was wholly in keeping with the 16th century original. The clock in the tower was made in 1814 by a clock maker called Francis Crow, whose workshop was in the Market Place opposite the tower.

Globe House, Faversham

Although, over the centuries, Faversham market has dealt in a wide range of goods, the town was, for 400 years, the centre of the country's explosives industry and **Chart Gunpowder Mills** is a lasting monument to the industry that thrived here between 1560 and 1934. Dating from the 18th century, and now restored, these mills are the oldest of their kind in the world. The Mill can be fully working, if water is available. Chart Mills is an *incorporating* mill. Incorporating was the process by which the ingredients of gunpowder are *incorporated* together to become explosive. The Mills are open to the public on a limited basis in the summer.

Faversham has over 400 listed buildings and one that is well worth seeking out is the 15th century former inn that is now home to the **Fleur de Lis Heritage Centre**. Here, displays review the last 1,000 years and tell the story of the town's growth and prosperity. Of the numerous artefacts and exhibitions to be seen here one of the more impressive is Abbey Street, a 16th century thoroughfare that is complete and well preserved. Also featured are an Edwardian barber shop, a Victorian fireside, a typical village post office, working manual telephone exchange and costume displays. At the centre, too, visitors can walk through a doorway that was once used by James II and learn of the story behind the anonymous play *Arden of Feversham*.

Close by lies **Faversham Creek**, a tidal inlet of the River Swale, that is inextricably linked with the main town's prosperity as the Creek acted as Faversham's port. A limb of the Cinque Port

Queens Court, Faversham

THE TAPSTER BISTRO AND BAR AT SYNDALE VALLEY VINYARDS

Seed Lane, Newnham, Kent ME9 0NA
Tel: 01795 890711 Fax: 01795 890911

This magnificent establishment is situated in the old village of Newnham, nestling in a long, winding and tranquil downland valley which is easily accessible from the A20 or A2. The farmhouse called the Tapster was built on the site of an iron age burial place and an early first century Roman building. It still has its original oak beams and cosy inglenook fireplaces. The old glebe meadow adjoining the Tapster is called Wineycock, harking back to a time when it was farmed by the Knights Templar as a mediaeval vinyard of St John. Since 1980 wine has once again been made here with the Abbs family producing red, white and sparkling wines at the Tapster Vinyard. There's a field of lavender which is being cultivated for oil production. It is also sold in bunches for the dried flower market.

Jonathan Abbs, the proprietor and vintner, leaves the management of the **Tapster Bistro** to London trained chef, Mathew Levett and his wife Cheryl. Mathew has been part of the management team

since the start and his keen passion and commitment for fresh, quality food prepared from local produce is part of the great success of the bistro.

The Tapster provides classical English and Mediterranean dishes presented to an exceptionally high standard and at an affordable price. Some of the tastiest dishes on offer include a mouth-watering combination of black pudding fritters with tomato sauce and vegetable niçoise and that's just a starter. The main courses include a selection with a slightly Irish twist. Grilled cod with wild mushroom sauce and Colcannon potatoes or the succulent Irish stew, Mathew's way, served with Tuscan bread. The desserts are almost too wicked to mention. Don't count the calories but do try the orange and vanilla brûlée or the poached fruits in sweet stem ginger and crème fraîche.

Everything that comes out of Mathew's kitchen is freshly prepared and cooked to order so don't expect fast food. At peak times there can be a slight delay but the food will taste all the better for the wait. The staff are exceedingly friendly and if any visitors have special requirements or requests they will be accommodated if at all possible. The main restaurant in the Tapster offers a relaxed atmosphere and the large inglenook fireplace warms and cheers the room during the winter months. Downstairs in the bar is a fine a selection of real ales which do a lot to please the local branch of CAMRA. There's a fine selection of the most popular spirits and of course a comprehensive range of international wines as well as the Tapsters own famous brands.

Upstairs, adjacent to the restaurant, are a few wonderful bedrooms, all of which are en-suite. They make the Tapster an ideal base for a touring holiday of the area, for a short weekend or midweek break or just to retire to after a full and satisfying meal.

The Tapster is easy to find. Leave the A20 at the crossroads north of Lenham village. Follow the signs for Doddington and then on to Newnham. In the village centre turn sharp right at the vinyard sign and right again behind the church.

of Dover and with a shipbuilding tradition that is so rooted in history that the title of 'The King's Port' is retained as an acknowledgement of the royal gratitude for the provision of navy vessels, Faversham Creek is well worth a visit. Between here and Seasalter, to the east, lies the **South Swale Nature Reserve**, that concentrates on the legacy of natural history of this area. A wide range of wildfowl, including Brent geese, make their home along this stretch of coast. There is a pleasant coastal walk here between Seasalter and Faversham.

OSPRINGE

8 miles SW of Whitstable off the A2

This hamlet, just to the southwest of Faversham, was a thriving Roman settlement and around here numerous coins, medallions and household items have been unearthed that suggest that the community was quite sizeable. Various Roman artefacts that have been excavated here can be found, along with Saxon pottery, glass and jewellery and relics from medieval Ospringe, at **Maison Dieu**. The French Maison Dieu, meaning 'God's House' was in common usage in medieval times when a mix of French and English was spoken in England. It meant a house that provided hospitality of various kinds. Such houses would provide a haven for the sick as well as a resting place for travellers.

The exact name of this property was the Hospital of the Blessed Mary of Ospringe. Originally founded by Henry III in around 1230, the building served as a combination hospital and hostel for pilgrims on their way to and from Canterbury. As well as having some features still remaining from the 13th century, the house also displays beamed ceilings from the Tudor era. Along with the relics unearthed in the local area, the museum here also includes information on the fascinating history of Maison Dieu itself.

TEYNHAM

10 miles SW of Whitstable off the A2

In 1533, Henry VIII's fruiterer, Richard Harris, planted England's first cherry tree in the village, along with pippins and golden russet apple trees, and thus established Teynham as the birthplace of English orchards.

William Lamparde writing his *Perambulation of Kent* in the 16th century said that Teynham was "the cherry garden and apple orchard of Kent". This would appear still to be true as fruit trees can be seen in every direction.

CANTERBURY TO SANDWICH BAY

This ancient land, between the city of Canterbury and the east coast of Kent, has seen invaders come and go, religious houses founded and then dissolved under Henry VIII and the building of great fortresses. Certainly one of the best places to begin any tour of the area is Canterbury itself, the home of the Mother Church of the Anglican Communion, Canterbury Cathedral. The cathedral was founded by St Augustine in the late 6th century, along with an abbey, and both can still be seen today although the cathedral, that still dominates the city's skyline, is actually a Norman structure. The abbey and cathedral, along with St Martin's Church, the oldest parish church in England that is still in constant use, form a fascinating World Heritage Site.

However, it is not just ancient buildings that draw visitors to this very special city. There is much else to see here including the places that were known to the city's several famous literary connections: Geoffrey Chaucer, the Elizabethan playwright and spy Christopher Marlowe, Somerset Maugham and Mary Tourtel, the creator of Rupert Bear.

The land between Canterbury and the coast is characterised by pretty villages, whilst to the south around Barfreston, was the area of the East Kent coalfield. To the north, around Stourmouth, is an area of very fertile land, which is the home of market gardens and orchards. Centuries ago, the Wantsum Channel separated the Isle of Thanet from the rest of Kent. The channel silted up over the centuries becoming marshland. The land seen today is the result of the drainage of the marshland in the 16th and 17th centuries.

This eastern stretch of Kentish coastline supported numerous fishing villages but, with the constant threat of invasion, they became fortified, particularly in 16th century under Henry VIII. Deal Castle remains one of the best surviving examples of Tudor military architecture whilst its contemporary, Walmer Castle, has been turned into an elegant stately house that is the home of the Lord Warden of the Cinque Ports.

Set up in the 11th century, the Cinque Ports were a commercial alliance of south coast ports but today the title is chiefly ceremonial.

CANTERBURY

England's most famous cathedral city, and also one of the loveliest, Canterbury lies in one of the most attractive areas of rural Kent. It was here, in AD 597, that St Augustine founded an abbey, soon after his arrival from Rome, and it proved to be the roots of Christianity in England. Lying just outside the city walls, **St Augustine's Abbey** is now in ruins but there is an excellent museum and information centre here with

exhibits on display that have been excavated from the site. Founded in 598, it is one of the oldest monastic sites in Britain. Destroyed at the dissolution of the monasteries in the 16th century, visitors can see the ruins of the original Saxon and Norman churches as well as the remains of Tudor brickwork from a Royal Palace built by Henry VIII. Before St Augustine had finished the monastery, he worshipped at **St Martin's Church**, England's oldest parish church, which was named after the Bishop of Tours, France. The building is believed to date back to Roman times and it is still in constant use.

However, both these fine buildings are overshadowed by the Mother Church of the Anglican Communion, **Canterbury Cathedral**, that still dominates the city skyline today. Canterbury Cathedral has a tradition of welcoming visitors that

Canterbury Cathedral

goes back to the days of the medieval pilgrimage. It was founded in AD 597 by St Augustine who was sent to England by Pope Gregory the Great and, as the first archbishop, he made Canterbury his seat (or 'Cathedra'). The earliest part of the present building is the crypt that dates back to around 1100 and that is also the largest of its kind in the country. On top of this was built the quire that had to be replaced in the 12th century after the original construction was destroyed by fire. Gradually, the building was added too and extended over the centuries. There is the 14th century nave, with its tall columns rising up like trees to meet the delicate vaulted arches, and the late 15th century 'Bell Harry' tower.

The windows in the cathedral are magnificent. Fortunately they survived the ravages of Henry VIII's Dissolution of the Monasteries and Hitler's bombs that flattened much of the surrounding city.

However, the cathedral's library was not so lucky as this was damaged by a German air raid in 1942. The beautiful and historic stained glass at the cathedral had been removed earlier and only the plain, replacement windows were blown out with the force of the blast. Eight of the original twelve 12th century stained glass windows remain intact with amazing jewel bright colours.

Naturally, there is much to see here, from the medieval tombs of kings and numerous archbishops to splendid architecture, and the guided tours provide not only information about the building but also of those people who have been associated with it through the centuries. However, it is as the scene of the murder of Archbishop Thomas à Becket that the building is best known. Becket was killed on a December evening in the northwest transept by the knights of Henry II, who supposedly

Canterbury Cathedral

seems to have been more of a social event than an act of penance. As well as making the journey at least once himself, as the king's messenger, Chaucer also passed through Canterbury on numerous occasions on his way to the Continent. At the **Canterbury Tales Visitor Attraction** visitors are taken back to the 14th century and invited to embark on the same journey of pilgrimage that was undertaken by the characters in Chaucer's great poem. As they were making the journey, the Knight, the Miller, the Pardoner and the Wife of Bath, along with the other travellers, told tales to keep themselves amused. From the animated farmyard tale of a cock, a hen and a wily old fox to stories of love, rivalry and chivalry, the colourful tales are brought very much to life at this popular attraction. The medieval streets, houses and markets of the pilgrims are faithfully reconstructed as is Becket's shrine, their destination.

misunderstood the king's request to be rid of this troublesome priest. A penitent Henry, full of remorse for the death of his former friend, later came here on a pilgrimage. Unfortunately, Becket's tomb, said to have been covered in gold and jewels, was destroyed in 1538 by the agents of Henry VIII. However, from the time of his death, in 1170, Canterbury Cathedral has been one of the most famous places of pilgrimage in Europe and it continues to be so today. One of the best examples of ecclesiastical architecture in the country, the whole precincts of the cathedral, along with St Martin's Church and St Augustine's Abbey, form a World Heritage Site. The Archbishop of Canterbury is the Primate of All England, attends royal functions and sits in the House of Lords.

By the time that Geoffrey Chaucer was writing his *Canterbury Tales*, some two centuries after the death of Thomas à Becket in 1170, Canterbury had become one of the most popular places of pilgrimage after Rome and Jerusalem. Many of the pilgrims set out, on foot or by horse, from London, as did Chaucer himself, and, in many cases, the journey

Whilst Canterbury is certainly dominated by its great cathedral there is much more to the city than first appearances might suggest. The capital of the Iron Age kingdom, Cantii (a name that lives on in the city and in the county name of Kent), the Romans also settled here for a time and, at the **Roman Museum**, there is a fine display of unearthed remains from Dunrovernum Cantiacorum (the Roman name for Canterbury). This underground museum centres on the remains of a Roman town house and, along with the fine mosaic floors, there are also reconstructions of other Roman buildings, a gallery of household objects that were excavated in and around this ancient site and some reproduction artefacts that visitors can handle.

Another aspect of life in Kent can be discovered at **The Kent Masonic Library and Museum** where the history of freemasonry over the last 300 years is explored. The vast collections found here cover many aspects of masonic life, and visitors can see numerous pieces of Masonic regalia and a huge library of books covering all aspects of freemasonry. There are also fine paintings, glassware and porcelain and the Cornwallis collection of documents and presentation items. The museum has limited opening times.

Housed in the former Poor Priests' Hospital, which has some fine medieval

The Weavers House, Canterbury

interiors, is the **Canterbury Heritage Museum** that presents a full history of the city over the last 2,000 years. From the time of the Roman occupation through to Canterbury in World War II, this museum has a great wealth of treasures and award winning displays. Among the various displays here can be found memorabilia relating to Mary Tourtel, the creator of Rupert Bear, who was born in Canterbury in 1874.

In fact, Canterbury has had a surprisingly large number of connections with the literary world down the ages as, along with Mary Tourtel and, of course, Chaucer, Somerset Maugham went to King's School in the city in the 1890s as did the Elizabethan dramatist Christopher Marlowe centuries earlier. A contemporary of Shakespeare's and the author of *Dr Faustus* and *Edward II*, Marlowe, the son of a shoemaker, was born in 1564 in George Street, Canterbury and later went on to Benet (now Corpus Christi) College Cambridge. As a friend of Sir Francis Walsingham, Elizabeth I's Secretary of State, Marlowe supplemented his literary career by taking an active role as a spy. At only 29 years of age, he was stabbed to death in Deptford following what is officially referred to as a tavern brawl but may well have been a deliberately planned assassination. He is buried at the church of St Nicholas and the church records simply state: "Christopher Marlowe, slain by ffrancis Archer 1 June 1593." Canterbury's main theatrical venue, the **Marlowe Theatre**, is named after this famous son and, along with the **Gulbenkian Theatre** at the University of Kent, it plays host to the annual **Canterbury Festival** that presents a varied programme of performing arts.

AROUND CANTERBURY

Fordwich

2½ miles NE of Canterbury off the A28

This village was once a busy port, serving all of Canterbury's trade, on the River Stour that was tidal to this point. As the river silted up and commercial vessels became larger, Fordwich was robbed of its major economic activity and the once prosperous town became a quiet and peaceful backwater. However, remnants of the bustling trade that was carried out here remain and it is now the smallest town in Britain. Its town council meets in one of the smallest **Town Halls** in the county. Built in Tudor times and sited on the quay it is timber framed with the upper storey overhanging on all sides. On the upper floor was the courtroom and on the ground floor, the jail and the gaoler's quarters. There is a fascinating

collection of items here including the ancient chest with three locks in which all the town's important documents were kept. The building is open to the public on a limited basis.

Preston

7 miles NE of Canterbury off the A28

Listed in the Domesday Book as Prestetune, which means 'priest's farmstead or manor', the village church of St Mildred had, up until the early 18th century, suffered a period of decline and records show that animals were allowed to graze in the graveyard and that the church services were conducted improperly if they were conducted at all. However, some sort of order was returned to the parish when, in 1711, a house was left to the local church for use as a vicarage on condition that two services were held at the church each Sunday. The church itself is quaint in appearance,

---

KING WILLIAM IV

4 High Street, Littlebourne, Nr Canterbury, Kent CT3 1UN
Tel/Fax: 01227 721244
e-mail: KingwilliamIV@littlebourne.fslife.co.uk
website: www.littlebourne.fslife.co.uk

This charming 18th century village pub overlooking the village green and a Kentish oast house in the rural village of Littlebourne is a mere five minutes from historic Canterbury. Dave and Dawn Reed are the genial hosts of the **King William IV**, a three diamond graded, thriving country inn. It has a reputation for high standards of accommodation, good food and excellent service. Dave is from a fishing family, so naturally fresh fish, all caught locally, is a speciality of the restaurant menu. Sea bass, brill, Dover and lemon sole, turbot, lobster, crab and monkfish feature regularly in an imaginative and unusual menu. The steamed mussels in cider and thyme are exquisite as is the mouth-watering smoked oysters and bacon in lemon cream cheese baked in a filo basket.

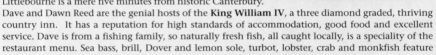

The traditionally furnished oak-beamed restaurant serves food from an early morning full English breakfast right through to dinner, which can be ordered from the constantly changing specials board and the monthly changing à la carte menu. All the food is home cooked, on the premises, by the two

full time chefs. Even the desserts and ice cream are prepared from scratch. The food is complemented by an excellent wine list featuring over fifty different wines.The bar is a delightful place to relax, over a pint of real ale or a glass from the collection of fine malt whiskies. The inn is a free house with a changing selection of ales and one or two regulars including Master Brew. On one wall of the bar is a display of original clippings from the Daily Telegraph of December 1863, which were discovered during a recent renovation.

14th century with a 19th century pyramidal cap on the tower and slightly odd triangular windows. There are also some beautiful 14th century stained glass windows.

STOURMOUTH
7½ miles NE of Canterbury off the A28

As the village is several miles from the sea, its name seems to make little sense but, centuries ago, this is where the River Stour fed into the **Wantsum Channel**, the stretch of water that separates the Isle of Thanet from the rest of Kent. In fact, such was the depth of the channel that, in AD 885, it was the site of a sea battle between King Alfred and Danish raiders who became trapped in the channel whilst attempting to attack and capture the City of Rochester.

The Wantsum Channel gradually silted up over the years and, in the 16th and 17th centuries, the resultant marshes were drained by Flemish refugees. Still criss-crossed by a network of drainage ditches today, this land remains very fertile and it is now home to market gardens, fruit farms and hops.

WINGHAM
6 miles E of Canterbury on the A257

On either side of the long tree-lined High Street, that runs through this large village, there are some fine and historic buildings, some of which date back to the reign of Henry VIII. There is an interesting story surrounding the wooden arcade of the **Norman parish church**. By the 16th century the building had fallen into a state of acute disrepair and George Ffoggarde, a local brewer, obtained a licence to raise funds for the church's repair. However, Ffoggarde embezzled all the £244 that he had collected and so the intended stone arcade, which was going to have been a feature of the repairs was replaced with a wooden one that was considerably cheaper. The village became renowned for rebellion as the villagers were not only active in the Peasants' Revolt of 1381 and other popular protests but they also took part in the Swing Riots of 1830 for which several inhabitants were transported to Australia.

Just to the northeast of the village lies **Wingham Bird Park** which aims to provide safe and secure habitats for many species of bird that are threatened in the wild. Among the many birds here visitors can see waterfowl, parrots, owls and emu whilst, in the Orchard Aviary, numerous smaller birds live alongside a range of furry mammals. Children, in particular, will enjoy the Pet Village where they can mingle with the animals and the Landscaped Lake where they can feed the ducks.

BEKESBOURNE
3 miles SE of Canterbury off the A2

Just to the north of the village and set within 70 acres of beautiful and ancient parkland, lies **Howletts Wild Animal Park** which was created by John Aspinall and is dedicated to the preservation of rare and endangered animals. Here, visitors can see the largest family groups of gorillas and breeding herds of Asian and African elephants. Other families of rare monkeys can be seen at the park along with both Indian and Siberian tigers, other large cats and many more endangered animals.

PATRIXBOURNE
3 miles SE of Canterbury off the A2

This handsome village, with a range of houses dating largely from the 17th and 18th centuries, also has newer dwellings, built in the 19th century. Carefully constructed in the Tudor style, they blend harmoniously with the existing buildings. The village church dates back to Norman times and has some wonderful carvings including the priest's door with a disfigured saint's head above. Bifrons, now demolished was, seat of the Marquess of Conyngham, the great favourite of George IV. Highland Court however remains. Built around 1904, this stone mansion was home to Count Louis Zborowski, the racing motorist who, built and raced the famous Chitty Chitty Bang Bang car.

AYLESHAM

6½ miles SE of Canterbury off the B2046

Following World War I, the eminent town planner, Professor Abercrombie, set out an ambitious scheme for a new town here that was to provide 2,000 houses. When development began in the 1920s, the plans were scaled down and the village provided 500 dwellings for miners and their families who worked in the East Kent coalfield and, in particular,

nearby Snowdown Colliery which closed in 1987.

GOODNESTONE

7 miles SE of Canterbury off the B2046

Close to the village lies Goodnestone Park, an estate that was originally owned by Brook Bridges, who held an important post in the Treasury during the reign of Charles II. In the 18th century, Jane Austen was a frequent visit to the house as her brother married Bridges' daughter and, during World War II, the house and park were requisitioned by the army and used as a tank repair depot. The estate is now in the ownership of Lord and Lady FitzWalter and **Goodnestone Park Gardens** are considered some of the best in the southeast of England. The formal gardens around the house contain several old specimen trees along with a walled garden that still has some of the original 17th century walls. New planting

---

SUMMERFIELD NURSERIES

Barnsole Road, Staple, Nr Canterbury, Kent CT3 1LD
Tel: 01304 812549 Fax: 01304 813417

This family run business was established 45 years ago and is still very much a family concern. Ron Sear is retired but still takes an active interest in everything, while his son Graham is responsible for growing the vast range of plants that the nursery produces. From 4½ acres of mainly glasshouses the nursery supplies the trade as well as retail. In spring and summer there is a profusion of bedding plants, as well as geraniums, fuchsias and pelargonium. Ron's daughter Karen is responsible for the gorgeous displays in the glasshouse as well as the wide range of prepared potted plants, patio tubs and hanging baskets. There is always a selection of terra cotta pots and other plant holders for those who want to produce their own displays and friendly and knowledgeable staff are on hand to advise on how to use them to best advantage.

Unlike many nurseries and despite its name, **Summerfield** blossoms in the winter. Anyone who

has ever despaired of the feeble examples of poinsettia available in supermarkets or even in most garden centres should visit Summerfield in November or December. A noted specialist in poinsettia, they produce over 12,000 plants in 30 different varieties. The displays are truly breathtaking. Inside the vast glasshouse, tables packed with fresh and healthy plants create a sea of vibrant colour stretching out as far as the eye can see. For the last five years the nursery has held poinsettia walks in November and December, with free tea and coffee and biscuits to allow people to enjoy the spectacle.

continues here all the time and beyond the formal garden areas lie mature woodlands with a 1920s rockery and pond.

NONINGTON

7 miles SE of Canterbury off the B2046

For many years there were several private estates, with grand and imposing houses, situated close to this village and one, **Fredville Park**, remains to the south of Nonington. Although the superb Georgian house that lay at the centre of this estate was burned to the ground in 1939, the park is still renowned for its collection of fine oak trees and, in particular, the **Fredville Oak** that is several hundred years old and has a circumference of 36 feet.

CHILLENDEN

8 miles SE of Canterbury off the B2046

Found in a prominent position, just outside this village, is **Chillenden Windmill**, one of the last 'open trestle' post windmills to be built in England and one of the last surviving such mills in Kent. It was built in 1868 for Brigadier Speed, who lived at Knowlton Court, although this exposed site has supported windmills for over 500 years. Restored recently and with a complete outward appearance, the mill contains some of the old machinery and it is open to the public on occasional days throughout the year.

KNOWLTON

8½ miles SE of Canterbury off the A256

The main street through this tiny hamlet leads to **Knowlton Court**, an Elizabethan house remodelled by Sir Reginald Blomfield in 1904. The Lodge was designed by Sir Edwin Lutyens in 1912. Down the years, Knowlton Court has been the home of several military and naval men. The Royalist

commander, Sir Thomas Peyton lived here around the time of the Civil War whilst, later, it was the home of Admiral Sir John Narborough. In 1707, Sir John's two sons were drowned off the Isles of Scilly following a naval disaster when navigational error caused the English fleet to be wrecked at night. A tomb in **Knowlton Church**, designed by Grinling Gibbons, illustrates the scene.

BARFRESTON

8½ miles SE of Canterbury off the A2

This pretty village lies in the heart of farming land, just to the north of Lyminge Forest, although, up until World War II much of the land in this immediate area was taken over by collieries. Barfreston's small **Norman church**, that dates from the 11th and 12th centuries, is remarkable for its detailed stone carvings the best examples of which can be seen around the east door. Representing an array of creatures, scenes from medieval life and religious symbols, an explanatory booklet on these delightful images can be obtained from the nearby public house. There is another curious feature to this church - the church bell can be found attached to a yew tree in the churchyard.

SHEPHERDSWELL

9 miles SE of Canterbury off the A2

This old village, which is sometimes referred to as Sibertswold, grew rapidly after 1861 when the London to Dover railway opened and, again, when housing was built here for the miners working at the nearby Tilmanstone Colliery. In 1911, a junction was established for the East Kent Light Railway, that served the colliery and, whilst the last passenger service ran in 1948, the railway continued its commercial operations until the colliery closed in 1987. Today, the **East Kent**

Railway is open once again and it carries passengers for pleasure from the village's charming station, to the nearby village of Eythorne, on restored trains including a steam train.

Those visiting the railway will find that there is also a museum of railway memorabilia, a buffet, a gift shop and a miniature railway to add to their enjoyment.

COLDRED

10 miles SE of Canterbury off the A2

The tidy little village of Coldred is one of the highest places in East Kent at nearly 400 feet above sea level. Its name may be from Ceoldred, King of Mercia, who supposedly helped the Kentish men against the Saxons or more likely from the Old English word for charcoal burning, which was a local industry. Next to the parish church of St Pancras lies a farm that was originally a manor house owned by Bishop Odo of Bayeux, half-brother to William the Conqueror. In fact, both the church and the farm stand on a site that was a fortified Saxon camp of the 8th century and a few remains can still be seen. Archaeological excavations in this ancient village have revealed not only finds from Saxon times but also evidence of earlier, Roman, occupation. More recently, the village pond was used for witch trials and, in the 1640s, it was recorded that Nell Garlige, an old woman of the parish, was tied up and thrown into the pond where, presumably, she drowned.

HARBLEDOWN

1 mile NW of Canterbury off the A2

This village was, for many pilgrims, their last stopping place before Canterbury and, so legend has it, the village well was called Black Prince's Well as the prince believed the waters to have healing properties. Despite drinking a flask of the water each day, the prince died in 1376, probably of syphilis that he contracted in Spain. The church of St Nicholas is still known locally as "The Leper Church". It was built by Archbishop Lanfranc around 1084 as the Chapel for the Leper Hospital, which he founded here. The chapel was extended in the 14th century, and there are four delightful 14th century stained glass windows in the chancel. The leper hospital was demolished as leprosy disappeared in England and the almshouses next to the church are Victorian.

Near Harbledon is **Bigbury Hill Fort**, where Caesar fought the local iron-age people in 54BC. The outline of the fort is still clearly visible on the skyline. The defensive ditches can still be seen. Excavations at the site have unearthed Belgic pottery and iron work, including an iron slave chain.

BLEAN

2½ miles NW of Canterbury on the A290

Close to the village lies **Druidstone Wildlife Park** where visitors can see a wide variety of animals and birds in a peaceful country setting. Along with the native species here, some of which are now rare, such as otters and owls, the park is also home to more exotic creatures including rhea, mara, wallabies and parrots. Younger children can make friends with the farmyard animals whilst there are walks through woodland where the park's herd of deer can be observed. Many of the animals and birds living here have been rescued whilst others play an important part in captive breeding programmes. The plant growth in the park provides interest, right throughout the year, from spring flowers to autumn fungi and winter buds.

RAMSGATE

For centuries, Ramsgate was a small fishing village until, in 1749, a harbour was built here and the town began to grow. After George IV landed here in 1822, (the **Obelisk** on the East Pier commemorates this historic event) the town adopted the title of 'Royal Harbour'. By the end of the 19th century, its fishing fleet had grown to make this the largest port on the south coast of England. However, at the beginning of World War I, the fishing industry began to decline and, with a seemingly uncertain future, Ramsgate enjoyed a brief moment of national glory when, in 1940, over 40,000 British troops, evacuated from the Dunkirk beaches by an armada of small boats and vessels, landed here.

The parish church of St George commemorates this important episode in Ramsgate's and England's history with a special stained glass window.

Still dominated by its harbour and shipping, the town is also home to the **Ramsgate Motor Museum** where visitors are offered a trip down memory lane and a journey back to the days of stylish motoring. Founded in 1982 and dedicated to the golden ages of motoring, the many cars, motorcycles and bicycles on display here are set out in scenes that depict the past, and cards record the world history of the year each vehicle was made.

Just to the south of Ramsgate lies **Pegwell Bay** that is, traditionally, said to have been the landing place of Hengist and Horsa who led the successful Jutish invasion

of Kent in AD 449. The badge of Kent today has on it a prancing white horse, the same image under which these Jutish warriors fought.

AROUND RAMSGATE

Broadstairs

2 miles N of Ramsgate on the A255

This family seaside resort, grew as an amalgamation of St Peter's inland and Broadstairs and Reading on the coast. It still retains its village atmosphere and is best known for its associations with Charles Dickens. Those coming in search of **Bleak House** will find it high up on the cliffs at the northern end of the town, overlooking the popular beach at Viking Bay. Charles Dickens spent his summers here for 20 years. He wrote David Copperfield here, at a desk at the window with a splendid view over the English Channel. The cellars of Bleak House have various displays on smuggling in Broadstairs. The town retains its links with the great Victorian novelist by holding an annual Charles

Broadstairs Beach

Dickens Festival.

Other famous people associated with the town include the politician Sir Edward Heath, who was born here in 1916, and another famous sailor, Sir Alec Rose, who lived in Broadstairs for many years. Writers too seem to have found inspiration along this stretch of coast as both Frank Richards, creator of Billy Bunter, and John Buchan, author of *The Thirty-Nine Steps* spy thriller, lived here. Buchan wrote the story at a house called St Cuby, on Cliff Promenade and the staircase that gave him the idea for the title stands opposite the house. Actually of 78 steps, this was halved by Buchan to provide a catchier title.

SANDWICH

5½ miles SW of Ramsgate off the A256

Though not a big town, Sandwich has its origins in Saxon times when a town was established here at the mouth of the River Stour. Since those days, the river has silted up and the town now stands a couple of miles from the coast but its maritime history still lives on here. It was one of the original Cinque ports, hard though it might be to believe today. Sandwich was one of the country's most important naval bases although, by the 15th century this period of its history was over as the harbour was no longer viable. The town turned to cloth manufacturing as its economic mainstay and, with the

help of Flemish refugees, the town once again prospered. Today, however, this industry has all but ceased and Sandwich has become simply a pleasant and peaceful place, renowned for its championship golf course, Royal St George's.

Sandwich does have plenty to offer the visitor and certainly one of the best places to begin exploration is the **Sandwich Guildhall Museum**. Telling the story of the town from early medieval times onwards, there are numerous artefacts here that date from as far back as the 13th century. Built in 1576, though it has been modified during the 20th century, the Guildhall itself can be toured and there are some fascinating historic items including the Moot Horn that was used as far back as the 12th century to summon the people of the town to hear important announcements. The Horn is still used today to announce the death of the monarch and the accession of their successor. Another fascinating item is the Hog Mace which, as the name implies, was used to round up straying animals after the Goose Bell had been rung and, all such animals, not repossessed by their owners on payment of a fine, were passed on to the Brothers and Sisters of St John's Hospital. Sandwich Town Council still meets in the Council Chamber here twice a month as

Church Street, Sandwich

strip, the waters have silted up. There are several buildings in Worth that have distinctive Dutch architectural features and these were constructed, in the 17th century, by Flemish and Huguenot refugees who fled from the Continent to escape persecution.

WOODNESBOROUGH

7 miles SW of Ramsgate off the A256

The hill at the centre of the village is Woden-hill derived from the Saxon God Woden, from which the village took its name. In the early 8th century the Battle of Wodnesbeorh took place here between the Saxons and the West Mercians. Legend has it, that Woden-hill is actually the burial heap of those who died in the battle. Death certainly seems to have been a feature of ancient Woodnesborough as this is also believed to be the burial place of Vortimer, King of the Saxons, who died in AD 457. Near the hill is the Parish Church of St Mary notable for the wooden tower which replaced its spire in 1745.

MANSTON

2 miles W of Ramsgate on the B2050

This quiet village, surrounded by rich farmland supports intensive market gardening, was, during World War II home to one of the country's major airfields. Featuring heavily in the Battle of Britain, RAF Manston was the closest airfield to the enemy coast and, as a consequence, it bore the brunt of the early Luftwaffe air attacks. The **Spitfire and Hurricane Memorial Building**, where the main attractions are the two aircraft themselves, provides visitors with an opportunity to gain an understanding

it has done for over 400 years. The Mayor's chair dates from 1561.

Elsewhere in Sandwich, visitors can see the **Barbican Gate**, a turreted 16th century gatehouse that guards the northern entrance into the town, and **St Bartholomew's Hospital**, which was founded in the 12th century and consists of a quadrangle of almshouses grouped around an old chapel.

Just over a mile northwest of the town is **Richborough Roman Fort**, believed to date from AD 43. These impressive ruins of a fort and supporting township include the massive foundations of a triumphal arch that stood some 80 feet high. The extensive fortifications, which still dominate the surrounding flat land, were designed to repel Saxon invaders in the 3rd to 5th centuries and, at one time, this was the most important Roman military base in Britain. The museum here gives a real insight into life during the heyday of this busy Roman town.

WORTH

6 miles SW of Ramsgate off the A258

The pond in the centre of this pretty village was once part of a navigable creek that lead out to the sea but, over the centuries, as with much of this coastal of just what life was like for the pilots and other staff stationed at the airfield in the 1940s. Photographs and other memorabilia are on sale here whilst there is a cafeteria with fine views out across the airfield.

MINSTER

4½ miles W of Ramsgate off the A299

It is likely that there were settlements in the area around this village, overlooking Minster Marshes, well before the invasion of the Romans and it is generally accepted that, later, the Isle of Thanet was the first landing place for invading Saxons. Among the many old buildings in the village, some of which date back to the Middle Ages, of particular note are the **Old House**, built in 1350 and the **Oak House** that is almost as old. One of the country's first nunneries was established at Minster in the 7th century, on land granted to Princess Ermenburga, who is usually better known by her religious name - Domneva. King Egbert, her uncle, gave the land to Ermenburga as compensation when her two brothers were murdered by one of his men, the thane, Thunor. Legend has it that Thunor secured the throne of Kent for Egbert by murdering the two princes, Ethelbert and Ethelred, and he buried their bodies, secretly, in the grounds of the royal palace. The graves were soon found, revealed, so it is said, by mysterious columns of light, and a penitent King Egbert let loose a deer to run free, declaring that all the land that it encompassed by its route would be given to Ermenburga. As Thunor watched he became alarmed at the distance that the deer was covering and set out to try halt it but he fell, with his horse, into a ditch and was drowned.

In the end, Ermenburga received over 1,000 acres and the story of the manner in which it was acquired is illustrated in the windows of the parish church of St Mary. Ermenburga founded **Minster Abbey** in 670 and, although the nunnery was later sacked by the Danes, it became part of the estate of St Augustine's Abbey, Canterbury. The monks set about rebuilding the abbey, adding a grange, and much of the Norman work can still be seen in the cloisters and other parts of the ruins. In the grounds of Minster Abbey is **Minster's Agricultural and Rural Life Museum** centred on the Old Tithe Barn, parts of which date back to 8th Century A.D. Agricultural machinery and implements depict farming methods and daily life in a rural community from the early 19th century.

DEAL

This delightful fishing town has changed little in character since the 18th century thanks, in part, to its shingle rather than sandy beach, which meant that Deal escaped Victorian development into a full-blown seaside resort. The fishing industry has always played a major role along this stretch of coastline and the roots of that trade are still very much in evidence in the town today. Deal's seafront is one of the most picturesque along the southeast coast and, with its quaint alleyways, traditional fishermen's cottages and old houses, the town is well worth exploring. Not surprisingly, given its history, Deal was also the haunt of smugglers and these illegal activities were centred around Middle Street. It was in a house along this street that, in 1801, Nelson's great friend, Captain Edward Parker, died from wounds that he received following a raid on Boulogne. Nelson was a frequent visitor to the town and, in the early 19th century, he outraged local society by staying at the Royal Hotel with his mistress, Lady Emma Hamilton.

Deal Castle

The **Maritime and Local History Museum** is an excellent place to begin as the displays here cover many aspects of the life of the town and its people. Housed in stables that were once used to shelter army mules, the museum has a large collection of real and model boats, figureheads, compasses and other navigational aids, pilot's relics and memorabilia that relate to Deal's seafaring and fishing past. On the site of the old Naval yard stands the distinctive **Timeball Tower** that was built in 1795 and that was used to give time signals to ships in the English Channel. The four storey building had a curious device whereby a black copper ball was dropped down its central shaft at exactly one o'clock to warn ships just off the coast to be ready to set their chronometers. Although this original system has long since been replaced by a modern radio time signal, a replica ball still drops down the shaft each day. The tower is also home to a museum devoted to time and telegraphy.

Not far from the Timeball Tower stands the menacing fortress of **Deal Castle** which was built by Henry VIII in the early 1540s as one of a number of forts designed to protect the south coast from invasion by the French and Spanish,

angered over Henry's divorce of his Catholic wife, Catherine of Aragon. The castle was designed to resemble a Tudor rose and the distinctive 'lily-pad' shape can only really be appreciated from the air or by looking at plans of the site. A huge bastion, Deal Castle had 119 guns trained out across the sea and it must have been a very formidable sight to anyone thinking of making an attack. Despite all these precautions, Deal Castle never came under attack from foreign invaders and it was not until the Civil War that the fortress saw action. In 1648, the castle, that was held on behalf of Charles I, came under fire from the Parliamentarians and, although it was extensively damaged, the castle was not attacked again until it was hit by a bomb during World War II. A superb place to explore as there are long dark passages, battlements and a huge basement. The castle also has an exhibition on its history and the various defensive castles that were constructed under Henry VIII. At the northern end of the town lies another of Henry VIII's great fortresses, **Sandown Castle**, but unfortunately time has not been so kind to Sandown and all that remains are some ruined buttresses.

The quiet waters just off the coast of Deal are known as **The Downs** and they create a safe anchorage for ships that might otherwise run aground on the treacherous **Goodwin Sands**. In fact, the sands, for centuries, have proved to be a graveyard for unwary vessels and the sad sight of shipwrecks, with their masts poking above the water, can still be seen at low tide. These sands were mentioned by Shakespeare, in the *Merchant of Venice*, as a place where the merchant lost one of his ships. As many as 50,000 men may have perished on these sands and there are numerous tales of 'ghost ships' that have been sighted here.

AROUND DEAL

WALMER
1½ miles S of Deal on the A258

This residential seaside town merges, almost imperceptibly with its neighbour, Deal, to the north but Walmer does have its very own, distinct, history. It is firmly believed

Walmer Castle and Gardens

that it was here, in 55 BC, that Julius Caesar and his legions landed in England. However, the town is now best known for its sister castle to Deal, **Walmer Castle** that, whilst being built as one of Henry VIII's line of coastal defences in the 1540s, has become, over the years, an elegant stately home. Today it is the official residence of the Lord Warden of the Cinque Ports, a title that has been held by William Pitt the Younger, the Duke of Wellington and Sir Winston Churchill as well as HM Queen Elizabeth, The Queen Mother. A charming and delightful place, visitors to the castle can see the Duke of Wellington's rooms, and even his famous boots, as well as stroll around the **Gardens**. In honour of the late Queen Mother's 95th birthday (in

August 1995), a special garden was planted and, along with the rest of the beautiful, well kept grounds, there is a charming tearoom. One time owners of the castle, the Beauchamp family, were the inspiration for the Flyte family that featured in Evelyn Waugh's novel *Brideshead Revisited*.

RINGWOULD
3 miles S of Deal on the A258

Centuries ago, this village stood on the edge of a vast forest that extended westwards almost to the city of Canterbury. The oldest building in the village is undoubtedly the 12th century **Church of St Nicholas** whose curious onion dome was added to the 17th century tower to act as a navigation aid for ships out in the English Channel.

The village's old forge too had maritime connections and this is where iron carriage wheels and chains were made to be used at the naval dockyard in the nearby town of Deal.

St Margaret's at Cliffe
5½ miles S of Deal off the A258

This small town stands on cliffs overlooking **St Margaret's Bay**. It was, before World War II, a secluded seaside resort with a number of hotels along the beach. It was the home of playwright Noel Coward. Another famous resident, Ian Fleming, the author of the James Bond spy thrillers, later bought Coward's house. As this is the nearest point to the French coast, which lies some 21 miles away, St Margaret's has always been the traditional starting place for cross channel swimmers and, also because of its position, a gun emplacement was built here during World War II to protect the Channel and ward off any German invasion. Despite seeming to be a relatively new settlement, St Margaret's possesses an ancient parish church, the 12th century **Church of St Margaret of Antioch**, that features some interesting rounded arches and an intricately carved doorway.

Just to the south of the town lies **The Pines**, a six acre park, created in 1970, that is renowned for its trees, plants, shrubs and ornamental lake. The brainchild of a wealthy local builder and philanthropist Fred Cleary, the gardens' imaginative layout includes a Romany caravan, a statue of Sir Winston Churchill and a waterfall. It is a perfect tranquil setting to enjoy the glorious views over the White Cliffs. Opposite The Pines, and opened in 1989, is **St Margaret's Museum** containing collections of artefacts put together by Fred Cleary relating to local or maritime themes and others of world-wide interest.

A little further south again lies **South Foreland Lighthouse**, the highlight of the White Cliffs and a distinctive landmark overlooking the Straits of Dover. Erected in 1843, the lighthouse was used by radio pioneer, Marconi, for his early experiments and it was from here that he made the world's first ship to shore radio transmission. A guided tour takes visitors around the lighthouse where its history can be learned and from where there are magnificent long-ranging views.

Great Mongeham
2 miles SW of Deal off the A258

High on the wall of the chancel of the local parish church of St Martin hanging from an iron pole, is a helmet said to have been worn at the Battle of Hastings in 1066. More credible, is a brass plaque on a pillar that bears a Greek verse written by the poet, Robert Bridges, in memory of his nurse who lies buried in the church.

West Langdon
5 miles SW of Deal off the A256

Close to this small village can be seen the scant remains of **Langdon Abbey**, founded in 1189 by Premonstratensian Canons. Dissolved by Henry VIII, an inspection made here on behalf of the king in 1535 reported that the canons' behaviour was immoral and that the abbot kept a mistress. After the dissolution, much of the masonry of the abbey was carted to the coast and used in the construction of Henry VIII's coastal defences and, later, a farmhouse was built on the abbey site.

Northbourne
3 miles W of Deal off the A256

In the church of this small country village can be found a monument to Sir

Edwin Sandys who was responsible for the drawing up of the constitution of Virginia, in America, and who was born in the village at Northbourne Court. Edwin's son also made a name for himself as he became a prominent commander in the Civil War on the Parliamentarian side, renowned for his cruelty. Colonel Edwin Sandys died in the village in 1642 as a result of the injuries he sustained during the battle of Worcester. Although the house that these two gentlemen knew was demolished in the 18th century, the **Ornamental Gardens** survive and they are occasionally open to the public.

TILMANSTONE
4½ miles W of Deal off the A256

At one time the largest mine of the East Kent coalfield, Tilmanstone Colliery, could be found just to the south of the village. When the mine closed, in 1987, this ended mining in east Kent and the site of the colliery has been turned into an industrial estate.

EASTRY
4½ miles E of Deal off the A256

Situated along the Roman road that linked Richborough with Dover, this ancient village has a couple of interesting historic connections. It was here, in 1164, that Thomas à Becket hid whilst waiting to travel to Flanders after his quarrel with Henry II. Lord Nelson also visited the village and one of his officers, Captain John Harvey, lies buried in the local churchyard.

NORTH DOWNS TO DOVER

Following the North Downs eastwards to the coast, this area ends, or begins, at Dover, the traditional 'Gateway to England'. As Britain's major cross

Channel port, this is where many start their holiday in England (or leave to go abroad) but the town is well used to 'invaders' and, during the Roman occupation, it was at Dover that they stationed their navy. Still dominated by its castle, set high above the famous White Cliffs, this originally Norman fortress has, over the centuries, been an impressive repellent to unfriendly foes thinking of mounting an attack.

Whilst the huge structure of the castle makes this is wonderful place to wander around, it is the Secret Wartime Tunnels that attract much of the attention. This is a labyrinthine maze of tunnels cut into the cliffs, where during World War II, the evacuation of Dunkirk was masterminded by Winston Churchill and Admiral Ramsey.

Although defence of the country from sea attack is a key aspect of this stretch of coast, it was overhead that one of the great battles of World War II took place and close to the coast are both the Battle of Britain Memorial and the Kent Battle of Britain Museum. They each play tribute, in separate ways, to the courage of the young pilots who fought to win air supremacy over the skies of England and so prevent a German invasion.

It may seem that this area is given over to war but the idyllic nature of many of the rural villages of this region portray a picture that is both peaceful and tranquil. Very much part of the 'Garden of England', further inland lies the National Fruit Collection, where literally hundred of apples, pears, plums and numerous other fruit trees are grown, and the famous Wye College, the agricultural institution that is now part of the University of London. There are also ancient country houses that open their glorious, gardens to the public such as Beech Court Gardens and Belmont.

At the heart of the rural idyll lies Ashford which, like many places in Kent has a history that goes back to Roman times. The central location of the town has led it, over the centuries, to become a meeting place for people, farmers and travellers and, today, with the opening of the Channel Tunnel and its International Station it is beginning to rival Dover for the title 'Gateway to Britain'.

ASHFORD

In the heart of the Garden of England, Ashford boasts some fine Georgian houses and is surrounded by countryside, which has inspired such famous writers as HE Bates, Jane Austen and HG Wells. The town itself is dominated by the great central tower of St Mary's, its splendid 15th century parish church rising high above the other town buildings, each of its four pinnacles crowned by a golden arrow-shaped weathervane.

Ashford's central location makes it an ideal base from which to visit many of the county's attractions but it is well worth spending time here and, at the **Ashford Borough Museum**, where visitors can find out more about this interesting and historic place. Housed in Dr Wilks' Hall, which was formerly the Old Grammar School, the museum has a varied collection that ranges from Victorian patchwork to equipment used by the town's fire brigade.

Ashford is proud that it is the home of the first volunteer Fire Service in the country, formed in 1826 and which purchased its first manual fire engine some 10 years later. In 1925, the first Leyland motor fire engine went into service at Ashford and the funds required to buy the appliance were raised by public subscription. Unfortunately, the

THE CHILLI BITE

63 High Street, Ashford, Kent TN24 8SG
Tel: 01233 650051 Fax: 01233 650051

Robert and Tania Lewin, the proprietors, bring over 25 years of experience in the food industry to the running of **The Chilli Bite**. She is responsible for all the daily preparation and cooking and he was a former senior food buyer for Selfridges in London. The attractive, bow windowed frontage is situated

in the pedestrian area of the High Street in a building dating from 1450, which was formerly the Turk's Head, an original English ale house. Inside, the display counter holds a mouth-watering selection of cheeses and salads. The two small dining areas are light and airy with a relaxed atmosphere created by a combination of linen tablecloths and old, beamed ceilings, contrasted with magnificent chilli pepper wallpaper. Tania's authentic recipes are enhanced by the addition of secret ingredients and naturally she won't reveal what they are but it is fun trying to identify them.

There is an excellent range of deep filled sandwiches and baguettes with specials including The Manhattan, with pastrami, cheese, salad, salsa and chutney and, reflecting their South African origins,

the Boerewors Special. This spicy, sensation contains sausage, chutney, onions and tomatoes. Other dishes available include curries, meats and salad platters. Breakfast is another speciality of the house either the full English or the South African variety which includes sausage, eggs, bacon, hot potato salad with chilli, fried onions and tomatoes. The couple aim to provide top quality food at reasonable prices. They also run an outside catering service supplying everything from authentic curries to luxury items including caviar, foie gras and smoked salmon.

original fire station has since been demolished and replaced with shops.

The town's central location, as well as being at a major crossing point of two important routes, saw a Roman settlement established here in around the 1st century and, for several centuries before the Norman Conquest, records show that a town, called Esseteford, could be found here. Growing into a flourishing market town that served the surrounding area, Ashford developed further with the building of, first, turnpike roads and then the arrival of the railway in 1842.

Today, the railway still influences the town and, with the completion of the Channel Tunnel, a range of Continental European destinations can be reached in just a few of hours from Ashford's **International Station**.

AROUND ASHFORD

BOUGHTON LEES
2½ miles N of Ashford on the A251

This delightful village, along with its neighbour Boughton Aluph, lies on the southern fringes of the North Downs, where the wooded hills give way to hedgerows, meadows, field and a network of narrow, twisting lanes. The long distance footpath, the **North Downs Way**, makes the descent from the higher ground at this point and it passes right alongside the parish church of Boughton Aluph. A similar network of footpaths and narrow lanes leads southwards to Boughton Lees.

CHALLOCK
4½ miles N of Ashford off the A251

This pretty village, centred around its wide and spacious green, is set in the dense woodlands known as **Challock Forest**. Like so many villages with its roots in the Middle Ages, Challock was built around its church in a forest clearing. However, when the Black Plague struck, the villagers moved to a new site, a mile or so from the church. Dedicated to Saints Cosmus and Damian, the church was the victim of a direct bomb hit during World War II and, now restored, it is worth visiting, not just for its location but also because some fine wall paintings were added in the 1950s as part of the restoration.

Set around a medieval farmhouse, **Beech Court Gardens** provides something of interest for everyone right throughout the seasons. A riot of colour in the spring when the azaleas, vibernums and rhododendrons are in flower, the garden has brilliant summer borders and roses whilst, in the autumn, there are the rich tones of the acers. Well known for its relaxing atmosphere, the garden has more than 90 named trees, woody areas and extensive lawns.

Just to the south of the village lies **Eastwell Park**,

Eastwell Park

which has a public footpath through its 3000 acres of parkland. On the northern edge of the vast Eastwell Lake is a ruined church that reputedly houses the bones of Richard Plantagenet, son of Richard III. According to local legend, in the mid 15th century, when Sir Thomas Moyle was building his new mansion on the estate, he was surprised to find that his foreman bricklayer was reading a book in Latin. Thomas asked the bricklayer where he received his education and was told that in 1485, when he was a young man, the bricklayer had been summoned to Bosworth Field, where he was told that he had received such an education as he was the illegitimate son of Richard III and the king was ready to acknowledge him as his rightful heir. The next day, at the Battle of Bosworth, Richard III was killed and the king's son fled the battlefield. Disguising himself as a humble bricklayer to avoid being recognised, the king's son continued at this trade from then onwards. Moved by the story, Thomas gave the man a house on the estate and, after his death, had this entry made in the burial register: "December 22, 1550: Richard Plantagenet."

THROWLEY

7½ miles N of Ashford off the A251

Tucked away amid the orchards of Kent and close to the village lies **Belmont** (see panel) a beautiful Georgian mansion house and estate.

SHELDWICH

8½ miles N of Ashford on the A251

Standing at the point where the landscape blends gently from scattered woodlands to open meadows and then farms and orchards, Sheldwich has, at its centre, a Norman parish church with a distinctive squat steeple that is visible from miles around. Just to the north, at **Brogdale**, can be found the **National Fruit Collection**. Home to the largest collection of fruit trees and plants in the world, visitors here can see over 2,300 varieties of apples, 550 pears, and numerous plums, cherries and bush fruits along with smaller collections of

---

BELMONT

Belmont Park, Throwley,
Faversham, Kent ME13 0HH
Tel: 01795 890202

Commanding stunning views across the rolling Kent countryside, **Belmont** is a marvellous example of Georgian architecture that has remained completely unspoilt. Until Edward Wilks, the store-keeper of the Royal Powder Mills at Faversham bought this land in 1769 there was no house or estate of Belmont. The house that he had built still survives as a wing of the present building and that in turn was constructed to the designs of Samuel Wyatt between 1789 and 1793 for the new owner, Colonel John Montresor of the Royal Engineers. It was the Colonel who is responsible for creating much of the estate seen today but, unfortunately, his career ended prematurely when he was accused of embezzlement and, in 1801, the estate was purchased, at auction, by General George Harris, with money earned during his successful military career in India.

Created a lord in 1815 following his victory at Seringapatam, he and successive Lords Harris have continued to live at Belmont and also play a distinguished role in the expansion of the British Empire. It is the magnificent clock collection put together by the 5th Lord Harris that takes pride of place and it is the most extensive to be found in private hands.

Meanwhile, the surrounding gardens are equally impressive and here there is not only a walled garden and a pinetum, with a Victorian Shell Grotto, but also an Orangery, designed as an extension to the house, that is planted with orange trees, palms and other tropical trees.

WELLBROOK FARMHOUSE

South Street, Boughton, Kent, ME13 9NA
Tel: 01227 750941 e-mail: info@wellbrookfarmhouse.co.uk
website: www.wellbrookfarmhouse.co.uk

Situated in a quiet rural location, convenient for Faversham, Whitstable and Canterbury, **Wellbrook Farmhouse** is a listed period property dating from the 16th century, with an 18th century facade. It stands in two acres of pasture and natural gardens with mature trees. The elegant accommodation, with its well equipped private facilities, is in keeping with the classic simplicity of the house. Visitors are provided with their own keys and have full use of the panelled drawing room in the exclusive guest area of the house.

CHILHAM SHOP

Canterbury Road, Chilham, Nr Canterbury, Kent CT4 8DX
Tel: 01227 730348 Fax: 01227 752657

The modest frontage of the family run **Chilham Shop** belies the depths within and the richness of the produce on offer. Thought to be the one first 'farm shops' in the county, it was taken over by George and Peter Higgs in 1983 and is popular with the local farming community for both buying and selling. There is a wide range of fresh fruit and vegetables, much of it locally grown as well as a range of other local produce including eggs, jams and baking. Fresh locally baked bread is available every day as well as biscuits, cakes and shortbread. For a picnic or lunch on the run, it is a convenient stopping place to pick up fresh sandwiches, home-made pies or pasties. Situated on the A28, the main road between Ashford and Canterbury, with ample parking on the large forecourt, many people find it a handy stopping place to collect general groceries as well as fresh local produce. Many others go out of their way to shop here for the quality.

In summer there is a variety of perennials, shrubs and bedding plants, mostly grown in the family's own nursery at Selling, while all year round they stock a range of garden requisites and ceramic and terracotta pots. For that last minute gift customers will always find cut flowers, pot plants, hand-made items or exotic sweets. In short, this is the convenience store with everything. It is family run with friendly service, easy parking and a wide range of high quality produce supplied by local farmers and artisans.

HODE POTTERY

Staddlecombe, Pett Bottom, Bridge, Canterbury, Kent CT4 5PE
Tel: 01227 830225
e-mail: hodepots@dircon.co.uk

Mary and Nigel Chapman work from the idyllic setting of their 17th century cottage, in the middle of the peaceful Kent countryside. The elegant designs produced in stoneware clay at **Hode Pottery**, inspired by the Mediterranean, are strong and impervious to frost. There are pots for every shape and size of plant from ornamental trees to pot plants. The warm toasted finish ensures that they look good in any setting. They will also take special orders.

nuts and vines that are all grown in the beautiful orchards. Particularly spectacular when the blossom is out, there are guided tours around the fruit collections and visitors can see new varieties of fruit such as apples that taste like pineapples.

BOUGHTON

10½ miles N of Ashford off the A2

Although close to the main road and other major routes to Kent's coast, it is well worth pausing a while here and exploring **Farming World at Nash Court**. Almost every aspect of farming is mentioned here, one way or another, and, with beautiful surrounding countryside and marked trails for walking, there is plenty here to keep the whole family amused for hours. Farming World's extensive breeding programme ensures that there are usually lots of young animals here, such as lambs, kids, calves and chicks, but it is also home to a variety of rarer breeds like miniature Shetland ponies, llamas and Britain's smallest breed of cattle.

Along with the animals, the birds of prey and the heavy horses, Farming World has a **Museum** where a fascinating collection of agricultural implements are on display. Throughout the year there are demonstrations on the ancient and traditional skills of farming and other crafts whilst specialist talks on a wide range of subjects, including bee keeping, animal husbandry and falconry, are also held here.

CHILHAM

7½ miles NE of Ashford on the A252

This well preserved village is one of Kent's show piece places and, particularly the area around the village square, is often used as a location for filming. The houses here are primarily Tudor and

Chilham in the Snow

Jacobean and they are a delightfully haphazard mix of gabled, half-timbered houses, shops and ancient inns that date from the Middle Ages. A stopping place for pilgrims on their way to the shrine of Thomas à Becket in Canterbury Cathedral, Chilham today plays host to other visitors who, now, walk the nearby **North Downs Way**.

The village is also the home of **Chilham Castle**, a Jacobean Mansion built on to a Norman Keep built on Roman foundations. The Jacobean house was built for Sir Dudley Digges, an official of James I and the spacious grounds around the castle were first laid out by Charles I's gardener, John Tradescan. Tthey were reworked in the 18th century by Capability Brown. The lodge gates in the village square, were added in the 20th century. It was close to Chilham that the Romans fought their last great battle in Britain and the site is known as Julieberrie Downs in honour of Julius Laberius who was killed there in 54 BC.

BRIDGE

12½ miles NE of Ashford off the A2

The village stands at a river crossing, where the old Dover Road from London

HIGHAM PARK HOUSE AND GARDENS

Higham Park, Bridge, Canterbury, Kent CT4 5BE
Tel: 01227 830830 Fax: 01227 830830
e-mail: highampark@aol.com
website: www.higham-park.co.uk

When Amanda Harris Deans and Patricia Gibb first visited the almost derelict **Higham House** in 1994, they had no idea that this house would become for them a labour of love consuming all their waking hours. One of England's most beautiful country houses, fronted by a magnificent four columned neo-classical façade in Portland stone, its past can be traced back to the 14ᵗʰ century. Although it captured their hearts, it was in a parlous state when they first saw it, with crumbling masonry, collapsed ceilings, dry rot in the roof and 25 acres of neglected undergrowth which had once been a beautiful garden. Amanda and Patricia pooled their resources and to their surprise their modest offer was accepted. The house was theirs and the concept of leisure disappeared from their lives.

Gradually the pair, whose gardening knowledge was minimal, have laid out and restored acres of formal gardens, embellishing them with rare plants in complex patterns. Among the delights of the garden is the replacement of garden follies, such as the attractive Classical Temple in the Peto designed Yew hedged Italian Water garden and a beautiful stag on a most appropriate base. Colour and delightful scents now abound from the huge drifts of golden daffodils in early spring, followed by the pink hues of 2,500 tulips and alliums, through the richness of summer until the leaves fall in the splendour of autumn.

Inside, the task of restoration was equally challenging. Patricia and Amanda have turned their hands to most trades as they have painstakingly scratched out the thick paint deposits masking the fine detail of the plaster mouldings, ground off the cement covering the Portland stone floor of the hallway and replaced the tiles blown off the roof in a gale. They've now opened the house to the public and, as with the garden, part of the pleasure of a visit to Higham House is seeing this wonderful historic house rise phoenix-like from the ashes of dereliction.

Amanda on a house tour, explains the trials and tribulations of Higham; history comes to life from 1320 with Edward II, Thomas Culpepper, Countess Margaret Zborowski (nee Aster) and her son Louis, creator of the legendary Chitty Chitty Bang Bang racing cars that inspired Ian Fleming, who stayed at Higham, to write about Chitty and 007 James Bond. If your schedule is too hectic you can just visit for coffee, succulent light lunches or scrumptious afternoon teas with home-made scones, cakes and jams.

Higham is just off the A2 at Bridge between Canterbury and the Channel ports. Open April to September, Sundays to Thursdays 11.00am - 5.00pm. Admission prices at time of press: House tour £2.00, Gardens £3.00. Group rates also available.

crosses a tributary of the River Stour, and this is, obviously, the source of the village's name. Now by-passed by the main A2 dual carriageway, this village was, for many years, subjected to a constant stream of heavy traffic and the villagers, in the 1970s, caused such a bottleneck whilst protesting to have the road through the village re-routed that the government relented and the by-pass was opened in 1976.

Close to the bridge lies **Higham Park** (see panel opposite) a mansion that was altered for Count Zabrowski of *Chitty Chitty Bang Bang* fame.

STELLING MINNIS
8 miles NE of Ashford off the B2068

Minnis means 'common' and on the edge of what remains of the once great Lyminge Forest, this village has an attractive rural atmosphere. On the outskirts of Stelling Minnis stands **Davison's Mill**, a smock mill built in 1866 that continued to grind corn commercially until 1970. The mill wheels were rotated by either wind or the mill's 1912 Ruston and Hornsby oil engine and the museum here has displays of some of the original mill maintenance tools along with other milling implements. It is unlikely that it will ever be able to run wind-powered again but it is still in working order. It is open on a limited basis to the public.

WYE
3 miles NE of Ashford off the A28

This attractive old market town, on the North Downs, has some fine Georgian houses as well as some half-timbered buildings in the area surrounding its 15th century collegiate church. However, it is not these buildings that have made the town famous but its agricultural college - **Wye College**, now affiliated to the University of London. Occupying the buildings of a priests' college, built in 1447 by John Kempe, then Archbishop of Canterbury, the college combines teaching and internationally respected research into all areas of agriculture including plants and pests, soils, animals and agricultural economics.

BROOK
3 miles E of Ashford off the A28

A scattered village in the wooded farmland that lies beneath the North Downs, Brook is home to an **Agricultural Museum** that occupies old farm buildings that stand on a site that dates back to Saxon times. Originally beginning as a small collection of farm implements and tools that were in the hands of nearby Wye College, the collection has grown and it now includes such items as ploughs, man traps, shepherd's crooks and domestic artefacts like butter pats and flat irons. However, it is not just the collection that is of interest here as two of the buildings in which the displays can be seen are worthy of special note. The barn was constructed in the 1370s and its oak framework is particularly interesting, revealing the skills of the craftsmen involved in its construction. It is about 120 feet long by about 30 feet wide with a Kent peg tile roof. The oast house, dating from 1815, is an early example of one with a round kiln - thought to give the hops more even drying - and it is possibly unique in having four fireplaces rather that just a single one.

SMEETH
4½ miles SE of Ashford on the A20

A charming and traditional Kentish village, where authentic games are still played. Smeeth's name means 'a smooth clearing in the woods' and though, today, most of the woods have long since

BULLTOWN FARMHOUSE

Bulltown, W. Brabourne, Ashford, Kent TN25 5NB
Tel: 01223 813505 Fax: 01223 813505
e-mail: wilton@bulltown.fsnet.co.uk

Lilly and Julian Wilton bought **Bulltown Farmhouse** in 1995 and totally renovated it before opening for bed and breakfast in 1997. This 15th century timber-framed Kentish farmhouse is a haven of peace and tranquillity from which to go out exploring the area. Every room overlooks delightful views of the countryside while inside the lounge and dining room have beamed ceilings, antique furniture and wood-burning stoves. The bedrooms too are decorated in keeping with the historic house, so that visitors may feel that they have slipped into a delightful time warp. However all the rooms are comfortable with en-suite facilities, ensuring that guests enjoy the ambience without suffering the privations of a by-gone age. The no smoking rule of the house is

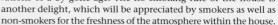

another delight, which will be appreciated by smokers as well as non-smokers for the freshness of the atmosphere within the house.

Conveniently situated 4 miles from Wye, 12 miles from Canterbury, 7 miles from Ashford and 10 miles from Dover, this is an ideal location from which to sample the delights of Kent and the southeast coast. For those who enjoy walking its situation on the edge of the North Downs and Pilgrim's way gives easy access to superb walks and glorious countryside. Its proximity to the Channel Ports makes it the perfect stop for travellers from the north heading for the continent.

CHURCH HILL COTTAGE GARDENS

Church Hill, Charing Heath, Ashford, Kent TN27 0BU
Tel/Fax: 01233 712522

Michael, Margaret and Jeremy Metianu are pleased to welcome visitors to their spell-binding cottage garden. This is a small slice of heaven in the Kentish countryside and just the place to come and relax. Visitors can wander through **Church Hill Cottage Gardens**, viewing the plants, or just sit and absorb the atmosphere in one of the many seats placed in a secluded corner. Set in one and a half acres surrounding their charming 16th century Kentish cottage, the garden is arranged in several separate connecting areas like the rooms of a house, with each one presenting a different vista. Round the cottage groups of plants grow in sinks and pots.

This is a gardener's garden, crammed full with an extensive collection of plants, many of them rare and unusual. No matter what the time of year, there are always plants in flower. There is also a well-stocked nursery containing many of the plants which can be seen growing in the garden. The masses of old-fashioned roses evoke images of yesteryear with their sweet aromas. There is an abundance of hostas, ferns, dianthus, violas and a wide variety of other perennial plants. One of the family is always on hand to help and advise visitors on selections for their own gardens. Church Hill Cottage is located eight miles northwest of Ashford. Leave the A20 after Charing, following the signs for Charing Heath and Egerton. After one mile bear right at the Red Lion, then immediately right again. The gardens are 250 yards on the right. Dogs are not allowed in the garden.

gone remains of ancient forests, such as Lyminge to the north, can still be found.

WILLESBOROUGH

1½ miles SE of Ashford off the A20

Now almost swallowed up by the expansion of Ashford, this once rural village is home to **Willesborough Windmill**, a smock mill that dates back to 1869 and which was restored in 1991. Visitors here can take a guided tour around the mill and see just what life was like for a miller at the beginning of the 20th century whilst the mill is also home to a collection of artefacts that relate to Ashford's industrial heritage.

WESTWELL

2½ miles NW of Ashford off the A20

Now a quiet village, Westwell was originally a Saxon settlement that was further developed by the Normans who built the lovely parish church.

CHARING

5 miles NW of Ashford on the A20

There has been a settlement here for centuries. There is a line of springs close to the village and the earliest archaeological evidence is of an Iron Age flint workings. Archaeologists suggest that there could well have been a Roman villa close by and the village's name is said to be derived from that of a local Jutish chief. In the late 8th century, Charing was given to Canterbury Cathedral by Egbert II, King of Kent. The manor here remained the property of the archbishops until 1545 when Henry VIII confiscated it from Archbishop Cranmer. The little that remains of this archbishop's palace today dates from the early 14th century and many of the buildings have been incorporated into a private farm. However, when visiting the parish church of St Peter and St Paul in

Charing Countryside

the village, the archbishop still robes in this ancient palace.

The village lies one day's journey from Canterbury and Charing became one of the many stopping places, in the Middle Ages, where pilgrims would seek rest, shelter and food on their pilgrimage. Just outside the gates of the manor house was a flourishing market, which, due to its antiquity, never required a charter. At the top of the street there are some fine red brick houses dating mainly to the 17th and 18th century although Pierce House is 16th century with an even older building beside it, believed to be 13th century.

PLUCKLEY

5½ miles NW of Ashford off the A20

This charming little village clusters around a tidy little square and the surrounding cottages all have a curious feature - 'Dering' windows. Sir Edward Cholmeley Dering, a 19th century landowner, added these distinctive arched windows to all the houses of his estate because he thought them lucky. One of his ancestors had supposedly escaped from the Roundheads through such a window during the Civil War. He

THE DERING ARMS

Station Road, Pluckley, Kent TN27 0RR
Tel: 01233 840371 Fax: 01233 840498

The Dering Arms was built in the 1840s originally as a Hunting Lodge serving the Dering Estate, one of the largest estates in the area at that time. It was built as a replica of the main manor house but to a smaller scale. The building with its grand façade and impressive Dutch gables has been an inn for over a century. James Buss, the owner/chef took over the inn in 1984. He has created an award-winning restaurant, where all meals are prepared to order using only the best quality produce, much of it local. Everything is home made on the premises right down to the marmalade on the breakfast table.   James loves fresh fish and seafood and the menu reflects this. He is particularly proud of having won The Egon Ronay Seafood Pub of the Year for the South East of England in 1997 and the A.A. Pub Guide Seafood Authority Seafood Pub of the Year for the South of England 2002. Just two of many awards the Dering Arms has picked up over the years. The restaurant seats 25 people and throughout the winter, it is the popular venue for a series of black tie gourmet evenings, where diners feast on a seven course banquet from a set menu. The dishes featured are some of the more unusual creations that James produces. Because of the high demand, booking is essential for gourmet evenings.

The inn has three comfortable bedrooms, offering accommodation at a reasonable price and two traditional bars, where guests can relax after a hard day's touring. Both have antique furniture and open fires and there are no noisy distractions like piped music, electronic machines or juke box to detract from the wonderful old world ambience of this excellent establishment.

also put them into his own mansion but this appears to be where his luck ended as the great house burnt down. Pluckley featured in the successful television series *The Darling Buds of May* and according to The Guinness Book of Records, it is the most haunted village in England.

DODDINGTON

10 miles NW of Ashford off the A2

The landscaped gardens of **Doddington Place**, in this traditional little rural village, are truly magnificent and comprise lawns, avenues and clipped yew hedges. The 10 acre garden was created by the renowned 19th century gardener William Nesfield. The display of rhododendrons and azaleas in the spring is brilliant whilst there are also large rock gardens and a formal sunken garden to view.

HARRIETSHAM

11 miles NW of Ashford on the A20

Harrietsham is a pleasant village with views stretching southwards over the Weald of Kent and with the North Downs as a backdrop. However, before the completion of the M20 motorway, life in the village was much less peaceful

Doddington Gardens

as the A20, that cuts it into two, was the major route between Maidstone and Folkestone.

HOLLINGBOURNE
13 miles NW of Ashford off the A20

Along with the adjoining hamlet, **Eythorne Street**, Hollingbourne forms a linear village stretching out below the rising North Downs. Of the two, Eythorne Street is the older and here a number of timber-framed and traditional, weatherboarded houses can be found. The 14th century All Saints Church lies by the village pond. In Upper Hollingbourne is the Grade 1 listed Elizabethan manor house, Hollingbourne Manor, once home to a prominent Kentish family, the Culpeppers. This tall Tudor manor house was acquired by Francis Culpeper, in 1590.

DETLING
16 miles NW of Ashford off the A249

Sheltered by the North Downs and by-passed by the main road, this village has remained relatively unspoilt and, today, it is visited by many walking the nearby **Pilgrims Way** footpath. In earlier times, this was an important coaching stop on several major routes that linked Maidstone with Sittingbourne, Faversham and other towns to the north. The High Street, that had been the main thoroughfare for the stagecoaches, is now more tranquil and along here, and elsewhere in the village, there are quaint old cottages to be found. On top of nearby Delting Hill lies the **Kent County Agricultural Show Ground**, the venue for the county's major annual agricultural, and social events, and where also some World War II buildings still remain from the days when this site was used as an airfield.

BOXLEY
18 miles NW of Ashford off the A249

Very much a hidden village, lying tucked away below the North Downs surrounded by major roads and motorways, Boxley is a small and traditional village of weatherboarded and red brick cottages. Just outside the village, to the west, lie the remains of **Boxley Abbey**, now part of a private house and not open to the public although the abbey's late 13th century ragstone barn can be seen from the road.

Back in the village stands the 13th century **All Saints' Church**, that still retains some features from the original Norman building and, inside, visitors can see a monument that recalls the gratitude of one of the village's residents had for a cat. In 1483, Sir Henry Wyatt was imprisoned in the Tower of London for denying Richard III's claim to the throne of England. Sir Henry was left to starve to death in one of the tower's cold, damp cells but a cat, by sleeping on his chest at night and bringing him pigeons to eat during the day, saved his life.

DOVER

This ancient town, which is often referred to as the 'Gateway to England', is Britain's major cross Channel port and, as well as the freight traffic, it is from Dover that many holidaymakers set out for France and beyond whilst others arrive looking to explore England. Many pass through but few stay in and around Dover. However its long history going back to Roman times, is a good reason for visitors to tarry here awhile. It was the Romans who first developed Dover, basing their navy here, and right up to the present day, the town has relied on shipping and seafaring for its prosperity.

DOVER MUSEUM & THE DOVER BRONZE AGE GALLERY

Market Square, Dover, Kent CT16 1PB
Tel: 01304 201066 Fax: 01304 241186
e-mail: museum@dover.gov.uk
website: www.dovermusuem.co.uk

Dover Museum and the Dover Bronze Age Boat Gallery tell the story of the town and port since prehistoric times, a town that for centuries has been the gateway to England. The Archaeology gallery on the ground floor shows Dover's history as a Roman port and fortress and also includes finds from nearby Buckland Anglo-Saxon cemetery, one of the largest and most important found in Britain.

The first floor is devoted to a programme of special exhibitions on a variety of themes of both local and national interest. Floor two covers Dover's history from 1066 to the present day and includes six large scale models of the town through the centuries, Cinque Port history, Victorian objects and displays on the First and Second World Wars. There are cannons from a bye-gone age complete with life size models of soldiers showing how they

would be fired. For the less war-like there's some interesting pieces of social history like a fine William and Mary dish from the late 17th century. The world's oldest known sea-going boat is on display here in the Bronze Age Boat Gallery. The boat, found in Dover in 1992 is a remarkable survivor from the Bronze Age. It is 3,550 years old, older than Tutankhamun and as old as Stonehenge. This unique archaeological treasure was saved for posterity by the Dover Bronze Age Boat Trust and its sponsors, and with money from the Heritage Lottery Fund. It took about seven years of conservation work, fundraising and research before the boat could be put on display in its new state-of-the-art gallery. But the hard work paid off with the gallery winning both the ICI British Archaeology Award and an Interpret Britain Award in the Millennium year.

As well as the boat there is a large collection of other treasures from the Bronze Age and the gallery also contains a full-scale reproduction of a home from that period. The film show and interactive section are very popular, particularly with children. Children can become scientists in the Bronze Age Gallery Lab with its puzzles, games, video microscopes and a bank of multimedia computers with touch screens, which can answer just about any question they could ask about Bronze Age Britain and of course the boat. They can even try building their own boat and then see if it will cross the Channel or sink. Family activity days are held regularly and are designed for adults and children to enjoy. Experts and specialists lead the fun activities and all materials are provided free with participants taking home anything they make. The Museum's Education Officer gives guided tours of the special exhibition and visitors get a chance to handle real objects from the collection. The Museum is open every day except Christmas Day, Boxing Day and New years Day and is fully accessible for wheelchair users.

Dover Castle

A founder member of the Confederation of Cinque Ports, founded by Edward I, as the old harbour silted up a new harbour was constructed, out into the English Channel, in the 19th century. Much of the older part of Dover was destroyed by enemy bombs during both World Wars but, amongst the jumble of modern streets, some of the surviving ancient buildings can still be found.

Situated high on a hill above the cliff tops, and dominating the town from almost every angle, stands **Dover Castle**, dating back to 1180. Although the castle was begun by William the Conqueror it was under Henry II that the great keep was constructed and the fortress was completed by another surrounding wall which was studded with square towers and two barbicans. Throughout its long life the castle has had an interesting history and one event, in particular, occurred towards the end of the reign of King John. By 1216, the barons had become increasingly frustrated with their king and they invited the heir to the French throne, Prince Louis, to invade and take over. He landed with his army at Dover and laid siege to the castle, which was, at that time, held by Hubert de Burgh, a baron loyal to King John. Powerful though the castle's walls were, the French managed to gain access to the

outer barbican and began to undermine the gate to the inner enclosure. At this point, King John died and the barons declared their allegiance to his successor, Henry III, and Prince Louis went home empty handed.

Today, the castle has much to offer the visitor. It is home to the **Princess of Wales' Royal Regiment Museum**, and there are also the remains of a Roman lighthouse and a small Saxon church within the grounds. However, one of the most spectacular sights and, one of World War II's best kept secrets, are the **Secret Wartime Tunnels** that were cut into Dover's famous white cliffs. Now open to the public and reconstructed to provide the most realistic wartime experience possible, it was from this labyrinth of tunnels that Winston Churchill and Admiral Ramsey masterminded the evacuation of nearly 350,000 troops from the beaches of Dunkirk. Also in this maze of caves was an operating theatre and underground hospital and, as the lights dim and bombs drop overhead, the atmosphere of wartime Britain is brought back to life.

Back in the heart of Dover, in New Street, can be found another of Dover's popular attractions - the **Roman Painted**

Roman Painted House

House, often dubbed Britain's buried Pompeii. An exceptionally well preserved town house, thought to date from around AD 200, the building was used as a hotel for official travellers and the excavated remains have revealed extensive wall paintings and an elaborate under-floor heating system. Only discovered in 1970, the house, which has a Roman fort wall built through it, is covered by a modern structure that also houses a major display on Roman Dover.

The Victorian Town Hall incorporates the magnificent **Maison Dieu**, a hostel for Canterbury pilgrims that was founded in the early 13th century as well as typically grand Victorian Council Chambers and function rooms. Beneath the building lies the gruesome **Dover Old Town Gaol** where the horrors of Victorian prison life can be experienced. Now fully restored, the tour of the old gaol begins in the Court Room, where Thomas Wells can be seen being convicted of shooting dead a stationmaster, a crime for which he was later hanged.

Visitors then have the chance to meet other inmates (using the latest 'talking head' technology), such as the young rabbit thieves and the cunning trickster, before trying out a cell that measures just six feet by four feet for themselves!

In the Market Square can be found the area's largest and newest museum, **Dover Museum** (see panel on page 74), which has an amazing range of items that illustrate the history of the town from prehistoric times onwards. There are artefacts from the time that Dover was a Roman port and fortress, along with finds from one of the most important archaeological sites in Britain, the nearby Buckland Saxon cemetery. The story of Dover as a Cinque Port, the town through both World Wars and numerous Victorian objects all add to the interesting picture of the town that the

White Cliffs, Dover

museum portrays. However, one of the newest exhibits is one of the museum's oldest. After seven years conservation, a 3,500 year old Bronze Age Boat, is now on display. Opposite the museum is the **White Cliffs Experience** where visitors can step back to the time of the Roman invasion or relive the dark days of Dover during World War II. Overlooking the Straits of Dover and one of world's busiest shipping lanes, this internationally famous attraction is an excellent way to get to know the 'Gateway to Britain'.

Just away from the town centre, lies **The Western Heights**, a vast area that stands on what was one of the largest and strongest fortresses in the country. There are some five miles of dry ditches and numerous gun batteries and defences. Some parts date from the late 18th and early 19th centuries, a time when England was expecting to have to defend its shores from French invasion. Other parts date only to World War II. The huge complex has been preserved to include, along with many of the defensive structures, much of the wildlife and the plants that have since colonised the site. The first buildings were erected here in the summer of 1779 and, when Napoleon posed a threat from France, further work was undertaken, in 1804, to strengthen and fortify the area further. There is the Drop Redoubt, a sunken fortress of the early 19th century that could fire guns in all directions, the 19th century three-gun emplacement and St Martin's Battery, which was upgraded and saw service during World War II. The Grand Shaft is a triple spiral staircase built to allow the soldiers to descend quickly from the Heights to the harbour. It is open at certain times.

One final place of interest, particularly to those who remember World War II, is the **Women's Land Army Museum**, housed on a farm, that pays tribute to the women who served their country by working on the land. Among the numerous exhibits on display are personal letters, uniforms and a wealth of factual information.

AROUND DOVER

CAPEL LE FERNE
5 miles SW of Dover off the B2011

This village, close to the cliffs between Folkestone and Dover, is home to the **Battle of Britain Memorial** (see panel below) that commemorates the fierce 1940 air battle that took place in the skies overhead.

HAWKINGE
6 miles SW of Dover on the A260

Close to the village, at Hawkinge Airfield, can be found the **Kent Battle of Britain Museum** that is the home of the country's largest collection of 1940 related artefacts on display to the public. Along with the full size replicas of the planes that played such a part in the battle - a Hurricane, Spitfire and Messerschmitt have been painstakingly rebuilt from as many original parts as possible - the museum houses an important collection of both British and
(Continued Page 80)

THE BATTLE OF BRITAIN MEMORIAL

Capel le Ferne, Folkestone, Kent

On a spectacular clifftop position can be found the Battle of Britain Memorial that was built to commemorate those who fought and lost their lives in the summer of 1940. Taking the form of an immense three bladed propeller cut into the chalk hillside with, at its centre, the statue of a lone seated airman, this is a fitting tribute to those young men who so bravely and unselfishly served their country. The memorial was unveiled by HM Queen Elizabeth the Queen Mother in 1993 and an annual memorial day is held here on the Sunday that lies closest to 10th July, the start of the air battle.

The siting of the memorial here is particularly poignant as it was in the skies above, in the summer of 1940, that the RAF struggled to gain air supremacy over the Luftwaffe and so prevent the otherwise inevitable German invasion. The battle, that cost so many their lives, lasted until the end of October and, as well as being the last major conflict over British soil, the victory marked the turning point of World War II. Close to the memorial, by the flagpole that originally stood at RAF Biggin Hill, is a memorial wall on which Winston Churchill's immortal words, "Never in the field of human conflict was so much owed by so many to so few", are carved. At the adjacent visitors' centre visitors can purchase a range of souvenirs and it should be remembered that this memorial and the site on which it stands relies on public donation for its maintenance.

WALK 1

Elham and Acrise

Start	Elham
Distance	4 miles (6.5km)
Approximate time	2 hours
Parking	The Square, Elham
Refreshments	Pubs at Elham
Ordnance Survey maps	Landrangers 179 (Canterbury & East Kent) and 189 (Ashford & Romney Marsh), Explorer 138 (Dover, Folkestone &Hythe)

Ancient Elham lies snug in its valley, clustered about the medieval church, and its attractive situation is well seen at the beginning of this walk from the path which climbs up the steep side of the valley. Field paths lead to Acrise, a forgotten village with a tiny, hidden church. The return is also mainly on field paths which are usually kept clear by farmers where they cross cultivated land.

Walk down Duck Lane on the north side of Elham church, ignoring the footpath which crosses the lane on the edge of the village. Climb up the narrow lane and when it bends sharply to the left Ⓐ turn on to the footpath on the right and climb to the field gate and stile. Cross the meadow beyond diagonally up to a stile at the top corner. There are fine views of Elham and its valley from here. After the stile walk across the neck of another meadow to a fence and then follow this to a stile at the top of the field. The path continues along the field edge on a generous headland and soon reaches a road.

Cross the road on to another pleasant field-edge path which drops down to Standardhill Plantation, where there is a pond with a pylon standing in it. The plantation itself has sadly been much depleted but it has been replanted. Climb up by the side of a line of oaks and Scots

pines to a large field at the top Ⓑ. Continue straight across this, heading for an electric post bearing a transformer which stands beyond a lone pine tree. There is also a fence ahead which ends with a distinctive tall post. At the post it is easy to find the way into the meadow to the south of Garden Wood, where the pine noted earlier stands close to a stile. Climb up to the stile by the electric post and turn left on to the road.

The second driveway on the right goes to the tiny Acrise church, but the route continues along the road opposite, which goes to Swingfield and Lydden. Turn left off this road at a right-hand bend Ⓒ and walk down the drive to the Old Rectory (do not take the bridleway to the left of the drive). Opposite the house climb over a stile on the right, continue to the gate at the corner of the paddock and then walk across the field to a gate on the far side by Parsonage Wood. After another gate on the other side of this copse turn left and head along the edge of the field towards Standardhill Farm.

The path descends to the bottom of a valley, on the other side of which there is a concrete track. Climb up this until it swings to the left. Cross a stile here and walk across the field to a gate into the farmyard and thus reach the road.

Turn left and then right down the lane which is opposite the farmhouse. When this bends to the left after a copse 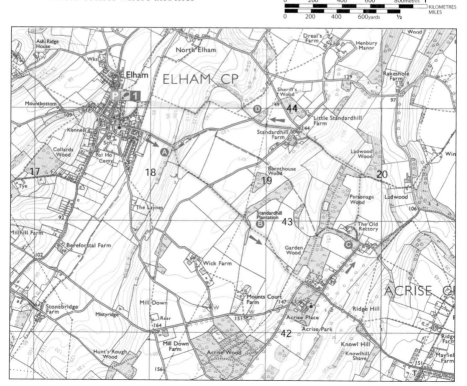D take the footpath on the right. The farmer has left a broad headland on the left side of the fence so walk along this to a field corner where another

footpath joins from the right. From this point the course of the footpath is obviously straight across the field to its lowest point. Elham again comes into view. Climb over a stile and follow the fence down in a south-westerly direction until you reach another stile. After this the path goes straight across a field to a gate and a bridge over the Nail Bourne.

Cross the bridge and then walk diagonally across a meadow to Cock Lane which leads directly into The Square, the starting point.

German flying equipment of that era. Many of the items on display have been recovered from aircraft, which were shot down, on both sides, and there are also weapons, vehicles and exhibits relating to the home front to see here.

ALKHAM

4 miles W of Dover off the A20

Fortunately, plans to turn this charming village, in the steep Alkham Valley, into a large residential area for miners working in the expanding East Kent coalfield never came to fruition, and the village remains much as it has done for centuries. A good place from which to begin a walk in the pleasant countryside around this coastal chalk downland, Alkham is also a pleasant place to stroll around as it has retained its Norman church, 18th century mellow red brick rectory, ancient houses and, perhaps most importantly, its old coaching inn.

SWINGFIELD

6½ miles W of Dover on the A260

At **MacFarlanes Butterfly and Garden Centre** visitors can walk around the tropical green houses, which not only contain exotic plants but also many varieties of colourful butterflies from all over the world that are allowed to fly freely. The life cycle of the butterfly, from the courtship displays, through the egg and caterpillar stages, to the chrysalis and finally the butterfly, are explained and can be observed at close quarters. Exotic plants on which the butterflies live - such as bougainvillaea, banana and oleander - can also be studied.

ELHAM

9 miles W of Dover off the A260

This relatively unspoilt village, whose name is pronounced 'Eelham', is the starting point for a number of footpaths that lead through the Elham Valley.

ELHAM ANTIQUES

High Street, Elham, Nr Canterbury, Kent CT4 6TB
Tel: 01303 840085

Elham Antiques was established in Elham in 1995 by local husband and wife team Julian and Lin Chambers. In the centre of this delightful conservation village, the shop is in a converted bakery with five large rooms displaying a varied and eclectic range of antiques.

This is the place to find solid country furniture, where the constantly changing choice may include a ten foot pine dresser, a Georgian oak table, a 17th century oak coffer or a Georgian mahogany chair

Now refurbished to include the architectural antiques from The Warehouse in Dover, there is a selection of genuine Georgian, Victorian and Edwardian fireplaces, restored to their original beauty in marble, slate, cast iron or wood with tiled inserts, as well as fenders, fire baskets and coal buckets. Original Georgian doors, garden statuary and pots jostle for position with such unusual finds as a font or a 17th century cannon. An unexpected specialism here is in '0' gauge trains including Hornby, Marklin and Bing as well as tin plate toys and perhaps an old pedal car.

Part of the old Bakery has been converted into two comfortable flats with polished oak floors, wood burning stoves and a modern fitted kitchen, retaining the atmosphere of the building with antique furnishings. Situated in the centre of the village of Elham, close to Canterbury and the south coast, the flats provide an ideal base to explore this lovely area. They sleep two to four and are available all year round.

During World War II, the now disused railway line through the village carried an 18-inch 'Boche Buster' gun, actually of World War I vintage, that fired shells seven feet long.

In the heart of the Elham Valley lies Parsonage Farm, a designated Area of Outstanding Natural Beauty, and its **Rural Heritage Centre**. The farm here has a long history that dates back to medieval times and it also has connections with the University of Oxford. The heritage centre explores over 600 years of history, associated with the farm and many of the traditional farm animals seen here are old and rare breeds. After, watching the sheep, cattle, pigs, horses and other animals, there is the peace and quiet of the old **Elham Valley railway trail** that provides the opportunity to observe the amazing number of wild mammals, birds, insects and plant life that have made their home along this long since disused track. Other attractions include Grandfather George Palmer's old office in the medieval undercroft, the photographs and implements that explain past and present cereal production on the farm and the barns of old farming equipment.

River

1 mile NW of Dover on the A2

Now more a suburb of Dover, this village stands on the banks of a river that has, over the centuries, powered several mills as its meanders its way out to sea. Of those long ago mills **Crabble Corn Mill** survives and this beautiful Georgian mill (dating from 1812) is still set to work on a regular basis. Visitors here can join the guided tour of the windmill and see the unique set of automatic 19th century flour mills. Just to the southwest of the village of River lie the ruins of the 12th century **St Radigunds Abbey** founded by French monks.

Whitfield

2 miles NW of Dover on the A2

For centuries this village has stood at an important crossroads where the routes to Canterbury, Dover and Sandwich met and it was also the site of several manor houses. One of the ancient lords of the manor had a particularly unusual service in that it was his duty to hold the king's head whenever he made a Channel crossing and support him through any seasickness to which he might succumb. This village, which is now more a suburb of Dover, is home to the **Dover Transport Museum** where a whole range of vehicles, from bicycles to buses, can be seen along with model railways and tramways. Offering a history of the local transport, the museum also includes exhibits on the East Kent coalfield and the area's maritime heritage.

Temple Ewell

2½ miles NW of Dover off the A2

This ancient village, in the valley of the River Dour, was mentioned in a charter as long ago as 772 and for centuries it came under the control of successive religious orders: first the Knights Templar and then the Knights of the Order of St John of Jerusalem. As with the village of River, further down the River Dour, there were two mills in the valley here that were driven by the Dour's waters.

Wootton

6½ miles NW of Dover off the A260

This village was the home of Thomas Digges, the inventor of the early telescope, who, during the reign of Elizabeth I, was the builder of the original harbour complex at Dover, which is now incorporated into the Western Docks. Unfortunately, nothing remains of the manor house, demolished in 1952, which was Digges's home.

THE JACKDAW

The Street, Denton, Nr. Canterbury, Kent CT4 6QZ
Tel: 01303 844663 Fax: 01303 844216

Bob and Caroline Hopkins took over the **Jackdaw** in 1998 and own and run it together. The specials on the menu change daily and there is an excellent selection of fish and vegetarian dishes but the speciality of the house is meat, particularly steaks. The Jackdaw 20oz Mixed Grill is a meal to satisfy the famished meat lover for a week. An 8oz steak, a gammon steak, a lamb chop, pork sausage and lambs kidneys with chips, mushrooms and all the usual accompaniments are piled high on the plate. However, for the intrepid trencherman who could eat more, the challenge is the legendary Jackdaw 32oz Meat Feast, comprising 12oz Aberdeen Angus steak, gammon steak, pork loin chop, lamb chop, pork sausage and lambs kidney and of course the usual chips and vegetables.

Another speciality of the house is the vast selection of guest ales. Five are changed every week and the inn is listed in CAMRA. It is a great place to pop in for a pint or to linger to chat in one of the bars or secluded corners. The main bar has comfortable seating on wing back leather chairs and sofas and two open brick fires with a friendly invitation to throw a log on the fire when you feel like it. The

conservatory with its wooden beamed ceiling and piano overlooks the secluded garden, where meals are served in summer. The dining areas have low, beamed ceilings and assorted stout wooden tables and chairs. The ambience of this Grade II listed building with its cosy nooks and crannies is part of its charm.

Originally a farmhouse belonging to Thomas Leythorpe of Eltham, the house dates back to 1645, the nineteenth year of the reign of Charles I. At Leythorpe's death in 1672 it passed to his nephew by marriage Francis Wyatt and thereafter to various others, all of whom leased it out. It was in 1756, that the tenant, Andrew Snell, was first granted a licence to sell ales and ciders from premises in Denton, which he called the 'Red Lion'. One of his regular customers was Thomas Gray, the celebrated poet. He ran the business until his death in 1792, when his widow took over until she died in 1801. Since then, passing through various hands, it has continued as a hostelry to the present day. In 1962 it was extensively refurbished and

renamed the 'Jackdaw' in honour of one its regulars of the 19th century, Richard Harris Barham, who wrote a famous poem 'The Jackdaw of Rheims'. Over the intervening years its reputation has grown as a country pub and restaurant providing good food and excellent ales in the warm and welcoming atmosphere of this ancient inn.

A more recent claim to fame is being featured in the epic film 'Battle of Britain' and an area beside the bar is dedicated to Battle of Britain pilots with memorabilia and photos adorning the walls. The Battle of Britain Museum is nearby at Hawkinge, a famous Battle of Britain airfield.

DENTON

7 miles NW of Dover on the A260

This charming village has a green surrounded by pretty half-timbered cottages. Next to the small 13th century church of St Mary Magdalene, nestling among ancient trees, can be found **Denton Court**, where the poet, Thomas Gray, was a frequent visitor. Close by are two other interesting, historic houses, **Broome Park**, dating from 1635 and designed by Inigo Jones, was, at one time, the home of Field Marshall Lord Kitchener, the World War I military leader. The other house, **Tappington Hall** was built by Thomas Marsh in about 1628. Richard Barham wrote many of his *Ingoldsby Legends* here, featuring the Ingoldsby family of Tappington-Everard. The hall is associated with several ghost stories. One suggests that it is haunted by a Royalist killed during the Civil War by his brother, who was fighting for the Parliamentarian cause.

BARHAM

8½ miles NW of Dover off the A2

The village is set in a delightful river valley near the point where the woodlands of the North Downs give way to the flatter agricultural lands. This area was first mentioned in the Arthurian legends as being the site of a great battle and the land around the village was used as a military camp in the early 19th century when an invasion by Napoleon was anticipated.

WOODLANDS AND MARSHES

This southernmost area of Kent is characterised by two diverse landscapes, the woodland, or once wooded, area around Tenterden and the marshlands of

STABLEGATE ANTIQUES

Derrington Hill Farm, Barham, Nr. Canterbury, Kent CT4 6QD
Tel: 01227 831639 Fax: 01227 831639

Stablegate Antiques was established in the early 80s in Canterbury but Michael and Christian Giuntini are of a family with an interest in fine art and antiques. Michael's grandfather was a sculptor and artist with a studio in Cheyne Walk, Chelsea. Michael himself has been involved in the business since 1963. Gaye, Michael's wife also has had a long-standing interest in antiques. Stablegate exhibits at most of the leading antique fairs including Claridges at the National Exhibition Centre in London.

The main showroom is in a delightful 17th century farmhouse at Barham. Inside, in the beamed rooms of the historic farmhouse there are two floors of exquisite Georgian and Victorian furniture.

Visitors can browse through seven rooms hung with varied prints, pictures and mirrors, furnished with dining tables and chairs and sideboards laden with a delightful selection of china, glass and silver plate. Blue china hangs on the red brick wall, copper kettles glow against white walls while the rich gleam of walnut and mahogany reflect delicate china or polished silver. The essence of Stablegate is quality, and all the items, so beautifully displayed here, are worthy of their place, personally selected by the Giuntinis with their specialist knowledge and wide experience of the Georgian and Victorian period.

Romney and Welland. Often dubbed the 'Jewel in the Weald', Tenterden lies on the eastern border of the Weald and this place, like other villages and towns close by, has the suffix '-den' that indicates a former setting in a woodland clearing. Developed on the wealth of the woollen trade in the Middle Ages and then becoming a key market place for the area, Tenterden has a pleasing mix of old buildings and it is an excellent place to begin a tour of southern Kent. Around it are numerous charming villages including the delightful Biddenden, where lived and died the Biddenden Maids, 12th century Siamese twins. Bethersden has become best known for its marble - a fossil encrusted stone - that has been used in the building work of Kent's two cathedrals and numerous parish churches.

Situated at the northern edge of the marshland lies Folkestone, once a small and ancient fishing village that, after the arrival of the railway in 1842, developed into a fashionable seaside resort. From here, in the 19th century, ships ferried passengers across the Channel. Today, the trains take holidaymakers to France through the Channel Tunnel. To the south are the delightful former ports of Hythe, Dymchurch and New Romney that were linked in the 1920s by the charming and much loved Romney Hythe and Dymchurch Railway. Built for

an eccentric millionaire racing driver to one third scale, this railway is still a much loved attraction carrying passengers down the coast to Dungeness.

Finally there are the remote and isolated marshes that are protected from the sea by the Dymchurch Wall and by the Royal Military Canal and an old cliff line. Once a bay of the sea, draining and reclamation of the land began as long ago as Roman times, and today it is an area of rich farmland and the home of the hardy Romney sheep. This was also the preserve of smugglers who hid their ill-gotten gains in drainage ditches, isolated farm buildings and even in churches.

TENTERDEN

Often referred to as the 'Jewel of the Weald', despite being situated right on the border between the dense woodlands of the Weald and the flatter farmland that leads eastwards to Romney Marsh, Tenterden is a charming town of considerable age. Today's well-earned nickname is, however, a far cry from its earliest days when it was known as 'Tenet-ware-den' or 'pig pasture of Thanet'. Although pigs certainly did flourish here and in the surrounding area, sheep became more profitable. The town developed quickly as the wool trade

---

Tenterden

newspaper, Franklin came to England to work in a British printing office for 18 months before returning home to set up his own newspaper. Later, and then acting as an agent for several American provinces, he moved back to England for 18 years when also, as a result of his experiments with electricity and his invention of the lightning conductor, he was elected a Fellow of the Royal Society.

grew. In 1331, the far-sighted Edward III prohibited the export of unwashed wool and encouraged weavers from Flanders to settle here and bring their dyeing and weaving techniques to England. The town prospered and became one of the most important centres for the manufacture of broadcloth during the Middle Ages. However, in the 16th century, the fortunes of the clothiers were altered by an act of Parliament and the wool trade began to decline. There are still buildings in the town built with the profits of the wool trade, along with elegant 18th century houses constructed during Tenterden's days as an agricultural market place serving the surrounding towns and villages.

The **Church of St Mildred**, in the heart of Tenterden, dates from 1180 and its most interesting feature is its unusual twin doors at the western end. From the top of its 15th century tower - some 125 feet above the town - there are panoramic views out across the Weald and to the Channel coast. Another place of prayer, a Unitarian chapel, built in 1695, is particularly interesting as this is where, in 1783, Dr Benjamin Franklin, the American statesman, philosopher and scientist, worshipped. As an apprentice typesetter in his brother's

For a real insight into the history of the town and the local area a visit to the **Tenterden and District Museum** is well worth while. The displays here cover over 1,000 years of history and they relate to hop-picking, farming, the area of the Weald, the Cinque Ports and Victorian domestic life. Lying close to the town's steam railway, the museum is housed in an interesting 19th century weatherboarded building that was originally a coach house and stables. Comprising six rooms, on two floors, the museum's collections are extensive and diverse, including exhibits ranging from a 1500 BC flint axe head to a recreation of a typical Victorian kitchen.

Tenterden is also the home of the **Kent and East Sussex Railway** that runs between the town and Northiam just over the county border in East Sussex. When the railway opened in 1900 it was the first full size light railway in the world. Passengers today can journey in beautifully restored carriages dating from Victorian times up until the 1960s, pulled by one of the railway's dozen steam locomotives, travelling through glorious, unspoilt countryside, that will be familiar to anyone who saw the television series *The Darling Buds of May*. Adjacent to the station at Tenterden is

Kent and East Sussex Railway

the **Colonel Stephens' Railway Museum** where the fascinating story of the Colonel, who built and ran this railway along with several other independent lines, is told.

AROUND TENTERDEN

SMARDEN
5½ miles N of Tenterden off the A262

This ancient Wealden market town's name comes from a Saxon word meaning 'butter valley and pasture' and this charming place has managed to keep its original character along with some beautiful old half-timbered cottages and houses set along the single main street. A centre for the cloth industry in the Middle Ages, the village's 14th century church has become known as the 'Barn of Kent' because of its huge roof.

BETHERSDEN
5 miles NE of Tenterden on the A28

This small village has long been associated with its 'marble' that was quarried in medieval times and used in many of Kent's churches and its two cathedrals. Calling the stone 'marble' is a little misleading as it is actually a type

of fossil encrusted stone. Although the village is situated on the main Tenterden to Ashford road and had an abundance of local building materials, Bethersden was considered, in the 18th century, to have some of the worst roads in the County.

WOODCHURCH
4 miles E of Tenterden off the B2067

In the heart of this large village lies the green around which are grouped several charming typically Kentish houses - including one dating back to Tudor times and others from the Georgian period. It was on this green, in 1826, that a battle took place between a smuggling gang and the Dragoons. The gang members were caught, tried, sentenced and then transported to Australia.

One of the fine buildings to be found here is **Woodchurch Windmill**, an impressive white smock mill that was constructed in 1820. Fully renovated and with its original machinery restored to full working order, the mill also houses a display of photographs that tell of its history and illustrate the restoration work. From the mill there are spectacular views over the marshes to the Channel coast. It is open to the public on a limited basis.

Also found at Woodchurch is the **South of England Rare Breeds Centre** that, as its name might suggest, is home to a large collection of rare British farm breeds, such as the Lincoln Longwool sheep that date back to Roman times and the Bagot goat that was brought to Britain by the Crusaders. Young visitors can meet many of the centre's animals in the Children's Barn and there are trailer rides and woodland walks to enjoy.

SMALL HYTHE

2 miles S of Tenterden on the B2082

Hard though it might be to imagine today, this little hamlet was once a flourishing port and shipbuilding centre. In the Middle Ages, the River Rother flowed past Small Hythe and it was wide enough and deep enough to accommodate the ships of those days. One of Henry VIII's warships was built here. Today, there is little trace of this village's past life or, indeed, of the river as, even in the wettest weather, it is little more than a tiny stream. One clue, however, to those long ago days lies in the name of the Small Hythe bus stop, called The Ferry.

Close to the village lies **Smallhythe Place** a charming 16ᵗʰ century half-timbered house, best known for being the home of the famous Shakespearean actress Ellen Terry, between 1899 and 1928. The house, now in the ownership of the National Trust, contains many of her personal items, including some of her stage costumes and numerous artefacts relating to other great thespians. The house retains many of its original features and, outside, there is a delightful cottage garden and an

Elizabethan barn that was adapted into a theatre in the late 1920s.

Small Hythe is also the home of **Tenterden Vineyard** where visitors can walk around the growing vines, tour the herb garden and take in the rural museum.

WITTERSHAM

4 miles S of Tenterden on the B2082

Situated high above the Rother Levels, some 200 feet above sea level, and right in the middle of the Isle of Oxney, Wittersham has been given the affectionate title of the 'Capital of the Isle' despite being not significantly larger, or more important, than many of the area's other villages. The skeleton of a prehistoric iguanadon was uncovered here and, more recently, Wittersham was a mooring site for airships during World War I. Nearby, lies **Stocks Mill**, the tallest post mill in Kent, erected on this site in 1781 and restored by the County Council in 1980 and open to the public on a limited basis.

BIDDENDEN

4 miles NW of Tenterden on the A262

Well recognised as one of the finest villages in the Weald of Kent, Biddenden has an attractive main street, lined with charming half-timbered houses. Ranging from medieval times through to the 17ᵗʰ century, there are many fine examples of period architecture and also some interesting old weaver's houses - situated on the south side of the street to make the most of the available light - that date back to the time when this was a centre of the cloth

Half Timbered House, Small Hythe

trade. Now converted into shops, above the door of one of these old houses is a carved wooden head that is said to have come from a Spanish ship, wrecked during the Armada.

At the western end of the main street stands **All Saints' Church**, founded by the Saxons but the oldest parts remaining, such as the nave, chancel and south aisle, date from the 13th century. The tower, which was funded by the thriving cloth trade, was erected in 1400 and it is made from Bethersden marble.

Although this is undoubtedly a delightful place to visit with some fine buildings to see it is the **Biddenden Maids** that arouse most visitors' curiosity. Said to have been born in Biddenden in 1100, Eliza and Mary Chulkhurst were Siamese twins who, despite being joined at both the hip and shoulders, lived to be 34 years old. A rare occurrence today, the birth of these special twins would have been an occasion of unheralded novelty in a medieval community. Local legend has it that, when one of the sisters died the other refused to be separated from her twin, saying, "As we came together we will also go together", and she died some six hours later. Although the twins, obviously, had problems of their own they bequeathed some land for the poor and needy of Biddenden that is still generating money today. Although there is no real historical evidence of their existence, the women are remembered through various traditions. Cakes bearing the womens' images are given to strangers in the village each Easter and a quantity of loaves and cheese, known as **Biddenden Dole** are distributed to the poor of the parish.

HEADCORN

7½ miles NW of Tenterden on the A274

This is another of the charming and ancient Wealden villages, scattered over this area of the county and, as with many of its neighbours, Headcorn was a thriving centre of cloth manufacturing. Evidence of this wealth remains in the many fine buildings to be seen here, including **Shakespeare House** and **The Chequers**, both excellent examples of Elizabethan timbered buildings. Beyond the large 14th century church, constructed of local Bethersden marble, lies **Headcorn Manor**, a magnificent Wealden house that has changed little since it was erected some 500 years ago. Despite all this antiquity, Headcorn is also a modern village and it provides shopping facilities for the

Biddenden

Oast Houses, Headcorn

ferry people across the English Channel to Boulogne and, even then, the journey time from London to Paris was just 12 hours. Much of the town dates from the Victorian age whilst the wide avenues and formal gardens remain a legacy of the elegant Edwardian era. What is most unusual about this particular seaside resort, however, is that it does not have a recognisable seafront but, instead, it has **The Leas**, a wide and sweeping promenade with a series of delightful cliff top lawns and flower gardens, with a distinctly Mediterranean feel. The name comes from a Kent dialect word meaning an open space. The **Leas Cliff Lift**, the oldest water-balanced lift in the country, carries people from the clifftops to the beach below. Not far from the lower lift entrance lies **The Rotunda Fun Park**, with its traditional seaside amusements.

Throughout all this development in the late 19th and early 20th century Folkestone has managed to retain its

smaller surrounding communities.

Just to the south of the village, at **Lashenden**, is the **Lashenden Air Warfare Museum** that commemorates the role played by this area of Kent during World War II and the Battle of Britain in particular. On display are numerous wartime exhibits, from both Britain and Germany, including a piloted V1 flying bomb, ration books and many photographs.

FOLKESTONE

A port and small fishing village since Saxon times, it was the arrival of the South Eastern railway in 1842 that transformed Folkestone into the major port and elegant resort that it is today. Within a year of the first passenger train service running, passenger ships had started to

Folkestone Harbour

original ancient fishing village and this is concentrated in an area known as **The Lanterns**. One of the oldest buildings in the town is its parish **Church of St Mary and St Eanswythe** that dates back to the 13th century. St Eanswythe was a Kent princess who founded a nunnery in what is now Folkestone in the 7th century and her bones are buried here. The church also remembers the town's most famous son, William Harvey, in its west window. Born in Church Street, a part of the town that was home to traders of cloth and silk, in 1578, Harvey was a physician to both James I and Charles I but he is best remembered for his discovery of the circulation of blood in the human body. Unfortunately, it would seem that all of Harvey's medical skills counted for nothing when it came to his own fate for he is reputed to have committed suicide in 1657 after discovering that he was going blind.

The story of the town, from its Saxon roots right through to the present day, is told at the **Folkestone Museum** and the numerous displays and exhibits here range from the early traders, the growth of the medieval port and the town as a smugglers' haven to its development into a fashionable resort. The geology of this corner of Kent is also explored and, hundreds of millions of years ago, this area was deep under a tropical sea. At **Martello Tower No 3**, one of numerous such towers that were built as a defence against the possible invasion of the country by Napoleon, there is an exhibition that illustrates the measures taken to defend the south coast.

As long ago as the early 19th century, when a French engineer presented Napoleon with plans for a tunnel linking France and England, the idea of such a thoroughfare, then designed for horse-drawn carriages, has captured the imagination. So much so, in fact, that,

in 1877, a tunnel was started, from both sides, but work on this ceased, almost before it had begun, because of the public outcry in England. However, in 1986, work on the present Channel Tunnel began. Now complete, the **Channel Tunnel Terminal** in England is at Folkestone, where both passenger cars and freight lorries join the trains that take them under the Channel to continental Europe.

A far cry from the bustle associated with the tunnel terminal, **The Folkestone Warren** is a peaceful country park that provides a habitat for numerous birds, insects and small mammals. The clifftop grasslands that were once grazed by sheep and cattle have now been colonised by, in some cases, rare wild flowers while there are also beautiful plants, such as Wild Cabbage and Rock Samphire, growing on the chalk cliffs.

AROUND FOLKESTONE

SANDGATE

1 mile SW of Folkestone on the A259

Now more a suburb of Folkestone that a village in its own right, Sandgate is a haven for collectors as its main street is littered with interesting antique shops. This is a peaceful place now but, during the threat of an invasion by Napoleon, no less that six Martello Towers were built in the area and these impressive granite structures overlook the village.

In 1898 and aged 32, the by then famous author HG Wells moved to Sandgate. In 1900, on the proceeds of his successful novels, he moved into **Spade House**, specially designed for him by CF Voysey. Situated at the foot of Sandgate Hill, it was here that he entertained his literary friends and continued to write

David M Lancefield

53 Sandgate High Street, Sandgate, Folkstone, Kent CT20 3AH
Tel/Fax: 01303 850149
e-mail: david@antiquedirect.freeserve.co.uk
website: www.davidmlancefield.co.uk

David Lancefield specialises in genuine antiques and interior design. With a constantly changing stock there is every reason to become a regular visitor. David has been supplying the American and continental European trade for a quarter century and more. His dedicated team of suppliers and decorators are based in this Kentish seaside town renowned for its choice selection of antique and fine art establishments. The shop's traditional, bow windowed frontage looks small from the outside, but it opens into a series of interconnected rooms spreading over two floors. The place is full of furniture, silver and metalware, ceramics, bronzes, ivory, clocks, watches, jewellery, paintings, prints and all manner of objets d'art.

On any visit you might discover a handsome rosewood table, perhaps with a set of balloon back chairs, a mahogany Georgian chest of drawers or a Victorian desk and display cabinet. The tables are set with an exquisite collection of dinner services, cutlery, glasses and decanters - to re-create an historic dining room. There is also a fine selection of skilfully made classic reproductions. Regency inspired

sabre leg chairs are available in a range of colour combinations in either carver style or as side chairs. They can be covered with a choice of fabrics or with that supplied by the client. The warmth and luxury of the Roman Baths of ancient Pompeii can be recaptured with a series of hand painted wall panels. Available in portrait or landscape they can be designed to individual requirements. To accompany them there are Roman inspired, hand carved and decorated seats complete with imitation animal skin fabrics.

articles and papers advocating social and political change as well as many of his successful novels. Spade House is not open to the public.

Hythe

4 miles W of Folkestone on the A259

The recorded history of Hythe goes back to AD 732 when Elthelred, King of the Saxons, first granted it a charter and its name, which means 'landing place', refers to the time when there was a busy harbour here and Hythe played an important role as one of the Cinque Ports.

However, decline set in as the harbour began to silt up and today this historic town lies half a mile from the sea and no sign of its harbour remains.

Hythe is a delightful and ancient town to visit with plenty to offer visitors, particularly those interested in beautiful old buildings. The skyline is dominated by the Norman tower of **St Leonard's Church**, built in 1080 but much extended in the 13th century. It has a **Crypt** where over 2,000 skulls and

Hythe Beach

various other assorted human bones, dating back to before the Norman invasion, are on display. For more information on the history of Hythe, the **Hythe Local History Room** is the ideal place to visit. This fascinating museum has numerous artefacts on display and a model of the town dated 1907.

Today, this charming place is best known as one of the terminals for the **Romney Hythe and Dymchurch Railway**, offering passengers a 14 mile journey, by steam train, across the edge of Romney Marsh to Dungeness.

A mile to the north of Hythe lies **Saltwood Castle**. It is not open to the public but can be seen from a nearby bridleway. It was once the residence of the Archbishop of Canterbury and it was here that Becket's murderers stayed whilst journeying from France to commit their evil act. More recently, Lord Clark, the famous art historian and presenter of the pioneering television series *Civilisation* made this his home when he purchased the estate from Bill Deedes, the veteran journalist. After his death his son, Alan Clark, a Conservative member of Parliament, lived here undertaking considerable restoration work. He died in 1999.

LYMPNE

2½ miles W of Folkestone off the B2067

Pronounced 'Limm', Lympne was established by the Romans as a port, known as Portus Lemanis, and, in the 3rd century, they built a fort here. Now standing on the site of this ancient fort is **Lympne Castle**, a fortified manor house with Norman towers that has been extensively remodelled since it was first built in the 12th century. In 1905 Sir Robert Lorimer restored the now almost derelict castle, managing to preserve many original features in the rebuilding.

The castle now operates as a hotel for business functions and weddings. From here, there are glorious panoramic views out across Romney Marsh, along the line of the Royal Military Canal and down the coast to Dungeness.

Just beyond the castle lies **Port Lympne Wild Animal Park** that was created by John Aspinall and shares the same aim, of the preserving of rare and endangered species, as its sister park Howletts. The large wild animal wilderness is home to many animals, including Indian elephants, tigers, lions, gorillas and monkeys, and also the largest captive group of black rhino in the world. After taking a safari trailer ride around the park, visitors have the opportunity to discover the delights of the park's historic mansion house, built by Sir Philip Sassoon MP, in 1915. In particular, the house is home to the Spencer Roberts Animal Mural Room, where the walls are covered with colourful paintings of the exotic animals, whilst, outside, there are beautiful landscaped gardens.

COURT-AT-STREET

4 miles W of Folkestone on the B2067

The ruined chapel here is connected with the tragic tale of the Holy Maid of Kent, Elizabeth Arton who, in 1525, claimed that she had direct communication with the Mother of God. Her pronouncements made her famous and she was persuaded to enter a convent at Canterbury by clergy seeking to capitalise financially on the increasing public interest in her powers. However, in 1533 Elizabeth made the mistake of suggesting that Henry VIII would die if he divorced his first wife, Queen Catherine, and married Anne Boleyn and she (along with those clerics who had faith in her) was hanged at Tyburn in 1534.

MERSHAM

10 miles NW of Folkestone off the A20

To the southwest of this village lies **Swanton Mill**, a charming old rural watermill powered by the River East Stour that is surrounded by a beautiful garden. The restoration work undertaken on the mill has won awards and, today, the mill is still working and produces wholemeal flour.

NEW ROMNEY

Known as the 'Capital of the Marsh', New Romney is an attractive old town with some fine Georgian houses, that was, at one time, the most important of the Cinque Ports. However, in 1287 a great storm choked the River Rother, on which the town stood, with shingle and caused the river's course to be diverted to Rye. The town lost its harbour and its status. Although the Cinque Port documents are still housed at the guildhall, New Romney now lies a mile from the sea. The sole survivor of the four churches in the town that were recorded in the Domesday Book, **St Nicholas' Church** still dominates the town's skyline with its 100 foot high west tower. However, of more interest to most visitors are the floodmarks that can be seen on the pillars inside the church indicating just how high the floodwaters rose in late 13th century.

The town is best known as being home to the main station of the **Romney Hythe and Dymchurch Railway**, a charming one third scale railway that was built in the 1920s for the millionaire racing driver, Captain Howey. Opened in 1927 as the 'World's Smallest Public Railway', and running between Hythe and Dungeness, it was not uncommon for train loads of holidaymakers to find that their carriages were being pulled by a locomotive driven by a famous friend of the Captain. During World War II, the railway was run by the army who used it move both troops and supplies along this stretch of the south coast. Although revived in the post war boom years, the railway struggled to attract visitors in the 1960s but it was, fortunately, saved by a group of enthusiastic businessmen. Whilst not necessarily as popular today as it has been, the railway is still a delightful way to explore this coastline and makes a fascinating day out for all the family. At the New Romney station can be found the **Romney Toy and Model Museum** housing a wonderful collection of old and not so old toys, dolls, models, posters and photographs. There are also two magnificent working model railways that are sure to captivate children of all ages.

AROUND NEW ROMNEY

ST MARY IN THE MARSH

2 miles N of New Romney off the A259

Set on the lonely and remote flats of Romney Marsh, this village's church steeple is crowned by an interesting ball and weather vane. The ball was obviously used by the villagers for target practice as, during restoration work, honey, from the bees, who had made their hive in the ball, was oozing from the bullet holes. In the churchyard lies the simple grave of E. Nesbit, the author of many children's books whose most famous novel is *The Railway Children*.

DYMCHURCH

3½ miles NE of New Romney on the A259

This small town's name is derived from 'Deme' the medieval English word meaning judge or arbiter and the town was the home of the governors of

St Mary's Bay

Visitors can go from one formidable defence to another at Dymchurch as the **Martello Tower** here is, arguably, the best example of its kind in the country. Now fully restored and with its original 24 pounder gun, complete with traversing carriage, still on the roof, this is one of the 74 such towers that were built along the coast as protection against invasion by Napoleon. Their name is derived from their 'pepper-pot' shape as they are similar in style to a tower that stood at Cape Mortella in Corsica. This was an ironic choice of model as Napoleon himself was born on that Mediterranean island.

From the 1890s onwards the children's author, Edith Nesbit (but always E. Nesbit on her novels), came to Dymchurch and other places around Romney Marsh to work on her novels. As well as writing she would explore the marshland churches, riding first on a bicycle and later in a dog cart.

Romney Marsh. Known as the Lords of the Level, it was these men who saw that swift justice was carried out on anyone endangering the well being of marshes and they still meet today. Visitors can find out more about the history of Romney Marsh at the **Lords of the Level**, a small museum housed in the town's old courtroom.

At one time a quiet and secluded village, Dymchurch has become a busy seaside resort with a five mile stretch of sandy beach and all the usual amusements arcades, giftshops and cafés. However, what does make it rather different from other such resorts is the **Dymchurch Wall**, that prevents water from flooding both the town and marsh as Dymchurch lies about seven-and-a-half feet below the level of the high tide. A barrier of some kind has existed here since Roman times.

BURMARSH

5 miles NE of New Romney off the A259

At the northern end of Romney Marsh, this village is home to one of the area's marshland churches, All Saints' Church, which boasts an impressive Norman doorway that is crowned by a grotesque man's face. Two of the original late 14th century bells are still rung today whilst another, dedicated to Magdalene, has been preserved. At nearby **Lathe Barn**, children get the opportunity to meet and befriend a whole range of farm animals including ducks, chicks, barn owls, rabbits, donkeys' calves and sheep.

DUNGENESS

5 miles S of New Romney off the B2075

This southern most corner of Kent, with its shingle beach, has been a treacherous headland, feared by sailors for centuries. Originally simple fires were lit on the beach to warn shipping of the dangers around this headland and, in 1615, the first proper lighthouse was erected. As the sea has retreated a succession of lighthouses has been built and today there are now two at Dungeness. The **Old Lighthouse** dates from 1901 and its modern and current successor, Lighthouse number five was opened in 1961. The Old lighthouse is open to the public and at the top of its 169 steps, there are glorious views out to sea and, inland, over the marshes. As well as the makeshift fishermen's shacks, and the lighthouses, the other key building on the headland is **Dungeness Power Station** where, at the **Visitor Centre**, there is an exhibition on electricity and the generation of nuclear energy. Guided tours of the power station can also be taken. The headland is also home to the **Dungeness Nature Reserve** whose unique shingle flat lands have been described as "the last natural undisturbed area in the South East and larger than any similar stretch of land in Europe". This RSPB reserve is noted for the many rare and migrating birds that come here to rest and feed in spring and autumn and a breeding colony of gulls and terns which nest in summer.

LYDD

3 miles SE of New Romney on the B2076

Like Old Romney, Lydd was once a busy port, linked to the Cinque Port of New Romney, but the changing of the course of the River Rother and the steady build up of land along the marsh put paid to this. Despite the loss of the port trade and now lying some three miles from the sea, Lydd is an attractive place that has retained many mementoes of its more prosperous past. Along with some fine merchants' houses and the handsome guildhall, the town is home to one of the tallest and longest parish churches in Kent, the 13th century **All Saints' Church**, often referred to as the 'Cathedral of the Marsh'. Whilst the church was being restored following bomb damage it sustained in 1940, a stone altar that had been thrown out by Reformers was rediscovered and it now stands in the north chancel. Before his meteoric rise to fame, Cardinal Wolsey was the rector of Lydd in 1503.

Housed in the old fire station, **Lydd Town Museum** has a fascinating collection of memorabilia on the history of the town and local area along with a Merryweather fire engine and an early 20th century horsebus. At Lydd Library, the **Romney Marsh Craft Gallery** has a permanent display of crafts from both Romney Marsh and further afield that can be purchased.

OLD ROMNEY

2 miles W of New Romney on the A259

With its setting in the remote Romney Marsh, this tiny village has a forlorn feel and it is hard to imagine that this place was once a prosperous port. However, the Domesday Book records that Old Romney had three fisheries, a mill and a wharf, thereby indicating that it had a waterfront. As the marsh gained more land from the sea, Romney's position - which had been as a busy island - became landlocked and trading became seriously hampered. So Old Romney lost out to New Romney, which ironically also found itself victim of the gradually accretion of land in the marsh.

Just its name, **Romney Marsh**, is enough to conjure up images of smugglers lugging their contraband across the misty marshland and, for centuries, this whole area profited from the illegal trade that was known locally as 'owling' because of the coded calls the smugglers used in order to avoid the excise men. Whilst Rudyard Kipling has painted a charming and romantic picture of the marsh in his poetry, another writer, Russell Thorndyke, told of a rougher side in his children's novel, *Dr Syn*, published in 1915. As well as being the vicar of Dymchurch, Dr Syn was the leader of a gang of smugglers in the 18th century who killed excise men, fought battles with the militia and stored their contraband in the marshland churches.

BROOKLAND
4½ miles W of New Romney on the A259

Brookland certainly has a name that describes its setting - on the southern fringes of Romney Marsh where the landscape is one of flooded meadows, small ditches and dykes. Despite its location, the village is home to an impressive church, that of St Augustine, said to be built from the timber of local shipwrecks. Whilst, inside, the church has some fine features - such as the medieval wall painting of the murder of Thomas à Becket and a cylindrical lead Norman font that is unique in Britain - it is the church's belfry that is most interesting. Built in three vertical wooden stages, it stands quite apart from the rest of the church in much the same way that the campanile of an Italian church or cathedral is separate. Dating from the 13th century, architectural historians suspect that the medieval builders feared that the church, built on such damp foundations, would not support the extra weight of a belfry if it was added to the original building.

BRENZETT
4 miles NW of New Romney off the A259

This small settlement, lying on the probably Roman **Rhee Wall** sea embankment, is home to one of the smallest of the marshland churches, St Eanswith's Church. Thought to have been founded in the 7th century,

although no traces of this building survive, there is an interesting tomb to local landowner John Fagge and his son to be seen here. The **Brenzett Aeronautical Museum** houses a unique collection of wartime aircraft memorabilia including equipment and articles recovered from crash sites.

APPLEDORE
7 miles NW of New Romney on the A2080

Appledore was originally a port on the estuary of the River Rother. A violent storm in the 13th century, changed the course of the river and the resultant silting up has left Appledore some eight miles from the sea. However, this did not prevent French raiders, in 1380, arriving here and setting fire to the village's 13th century church. The **Royal Military Canal**, built in 1806 as a defence against Napoleon, passes through the village. Encircling Romney Marsh, the canal's sweeping bends meant that the whole length of the waterway could be protected by cannon fire and it was designed as a means of quickly flooding the marshland in the event of the expected invasion. However, by the time that the canal had been completed, in 1807, the threat of invasion had ended but, during World War II, when it seemed likely that Hitler would try to land his forces on English soil, pillboxes were built along the length of the canal. Now there is a public footpath along the full length of the canal with interpretation panels detailing its history. The canal also provides a wonderful habitat for a variety of wildlife including dragonflies and Marsh Frogs.

SNARGATE
5 miles NW of New Romney off the B2080

In the heart of the Romney Marsh, this village's remote location conjures up the days when smugglers plied their illicit trade under the cover of darkness and hid their ill-gotten gains in reed lined streams or in disused and isolated farm buildings. The 600 year old parish **Church of St Dunstan**, built in an exposed position, seems, on first impressions, to be disproportionately large for the size of this village. However, this extra space was a boon for smugglers as they used it to store their contraband. An excise raid in 1743 uncovered a cask of gin in the vestry and tobacco in the belfry. In the early 19th century the vicar here was the Rev Richard Barham and during his time at Snargate he wrote his humorous tales, the *Ingoldsby Legends*, some of which relate to the people of the marsh. As he lived at some distance from the village Barham was unaware of the night time activity in and around his church.

STONE-IN-OXNEY
8 miles NW of New Romney off the B2080

Strikingly situated on the eastern flank of the inland island known as the Isle of Oxney, the stone that gives the village its name is Roman and can be found, preserved, in the parish Church of St Mary. Other archaeological remains within the church suggest that this site once served as a temple to Mithras, a Persian deity beloved of Roman soldiers.

THE WEALD OF KENT

The Weald of Kent is a name to be reckoned with and one that conjures up, quite rightly, images of rolling wooded countryside, orchards and hop fields. Cranbrook, often dubbed the 'Capital of the Kentish Weald', is typical of many of the towns and villages of this area. It is a charming place that prospered in the Middle Ages with the growth of the woollen trade and that, when this industry declined, reverted to being a market town serving the surrounding communities.

Further north lies Maidstone, on the River Medway that forms the border between the Kentish Men and the Men of Kent. In bygone days Kent was divided into two parts, East (Men of Kent), administered from Canterbury, and West (Kentish Men), from Maidstone. In 1814 the two came together and Maidstone became the county town. Of the places to visit here, some of the most interesting, such as Allington Castle and the Museum of Kent Life, can be found beside this main waterway just north of the town. However, Maidstone is home to a 14th century Archbishop's Palace that was a resting place for the clergy travelling between London

Orchards, Paddock Wood

CORNFIELD MINIATURES

Unit 11B, The Corn Exchange, Market Buildings, Maidstone,
Kent ME14 1HP   Tel: 01622 755116
e-mail: Cornmin@barclays.net website: www.cornfieldminiatures.co.uk

Situated in the centre of Kent's county town and within walking distance of
the museum **Cornfield Miniatures** grew from a hobby. Josie Turner, who
owns and runs the shop with her husband Graham, originally collected full
size tea pots. Lack of space at home led to her collecting miniature tea pots
instead. The Doll's House shop opened in 1996 and a year later Josie and
Graham had acquired it. The collection of doll's houses is incredible. All shapes
and sizes, colours and prices. There's single storey cottages and bungalows
right through to three storey Georgian mansions, half timbered Tudor houses,
even the odd château as well as garden sheds,
summer houses and greenhouses. Much of the stock is by British manufacturers
with houses, shops and room boxes by Anglesey, Sid Cooke, Toy Workshop,
Dolls House Emporium and Jim Cutler's exclusive Georgian Houses.

Naturally when someone purchases a miniature house they will require
some tiny furniture to fill it with. Josie and Graham stock a complete range-
electric lighting that works, carpets, wallpaper and furniture. Everything in
fact right down to the silverware, china, glass and DIY items. It's not just
doll's houses that are sold here. There is also a wide selection of goods made
by local crafts people. Speciality items include Valerie Casson's miniature
teapots and ceramics, Silver by Royal Tunbridge Wells, Simply Silver and
Stokesay Ware China. Finally they also sell knitting needles, patterns, 1 ply
wool and flower thread.

MAIDSTONE MUSEUM AND BENTLIF ART GALLERY

St Faiths Street, Maidstone, Kent ME14 1LH
Tel: 01622 754497 Fax: 01622 685022
website: www.museum.maidstone.gov.uk

This exceptional museum is based in a charming Elizabethan manor house
in the centre of the county town of Kent. It contains a series of galleries
covering history from over 4.5 billion years ago right up to the present
time. It's a place visitors will want to return to again and again and given
the free admission policy there is no reason why they should not. The
comprehensive archaeology collection includes objects recovered from
Stone Age tombs, Maidstone's Roman villa and Anglo Saxon graves. The
Ceramics gallery has a wide ranging collection of English, European,
Chinese and Japanese pottery and porcelain dating from 1120 to the late 20th century and the medieval
gallery holds the only copy in the world of the Lambeth Bible, a 12th century illuminated manuscript.

Other galleries cover ancient Egypt, Japan during the Edo
Period (1660 – 1868), Victoriana, fine art from Dutch and Italian
Old Masters to Victorian and contemporary British paintings
and some work by local water colourist, Albert Goodwin (1845
–1932). The Queens Own Royal West Kent   Regimental
museum occupies a gallery with its display of uniforms, medals,
weapons, pictures and a hip flask that saved a life. There is also
an internationally recognised carriage collection, called the
Tyrwhitt - Drake Museum. Add to that some recent additions
one of which tells the history of the town which grew up around
the Archbishops Palace and 200 years of women's fashion.

and Canterbury and that stands on the site of a building mentioned in the Domesday Book.

Close to the county border with East Sussex lies Royal Tunbridge Wells, a particularly charming town that, unlike many places in the Kent, was no more than a forest clearing until the early 17th century when health-restoring waters were discovered here. Developed to provide accommodation and entertainment, with the help of Beau Nash, to those coming here to take the waters, the town also received royal patronage that led to the addition of the prefix granted by Edward VII.

In between these key towns, the countryside is dotted with attractive villages and small towns, surrounded by the orchards and hop fields that typify the Weald. This area is also home to two of the most popular attractions in the county, if not England. Situated on two islands and surrounded by glorious gardens, the former royal palace of Leeds Castle, that was so beloved by Henry VIII, is a wonderful example of Norman defensive architecture that was thankfully restored by Lady Braillie from 1926 onwards. The other is Sissinghurst Castle, the ruin bought by Vita Sackville-West and her husband, Harold Nicholson in 1930, where they lovingly restored the gardens in the Elizabethan style. There are also other, less famous gardens that are sure to enchant visitors such as Scotney Castle, Groombridge Place and Owl House.

MAIDSTONE

Maidstone grew up on the site of an important meeting place and this is reflected in the town's name that means 'the people's stone'. The River Medway, on which it stands, is the ancient boundary that separated East and West Kent with the Kentish Men living in the west and, to the east of the river, the Men of Kent. This important distinction is still used proudly by many of the county's inhabitants today. Despite being extensively developed in the 20th century, Maidstone has retained many handsome Elizabethan and Georgian buildings. **Chillington Manor** is a beautiful Elizabethan residence, now home to the **Maidstone Museum and Art Gallery** (see panel opposite), founded by generous Maidstone Victorian gentlemen and holding one of the finest collections in the south east. The many exhibits here cover a wide range of interests including oriental art, ethnography, archaeology and social history. The museum also has The Lambeth Bible Volume Two, a particularly outstanding example of 12th century illumination, and a real Egyptian mummy. The equally impressive art gallery includes works by both English and continental old masters among its permanent displays.

Another part of the museum's collection can be found at **The Tyrwhitt-Drake Museum of Carriage** where visitors can see a marvellous range of horse drawn carriages that were enthusiastically collected by Sir Garrard Tyrwhitt-Drake, a former mayor of the town, who wanted to preserve this method of transport as it was being replaced by motorcars. The first collection of its kind in Britain, the museum opened in 1946 and it is housed, appropriately enough, in some stables that once belonged to the archbishops of Canterbury. Opposite these stables is the **Archbishop's Palace** that dates from the 14th century. An older building stood here at the time of the Domesday Book and it was used as a resting place by the archbishops as they

Archbishops Palace

travelled between London and Canterbury. Restored and recently refurbished, the palace still retains many of its original features, including the historic meeting room. Meanwhile, close by are the **Dungeons**, a 14th century building from which, it is alleged, Wat Tyler, leader of the Peasants' Revolt in 1381, released John Ball, the 'mad priest of Kent'.

Other interesting buildings in the town that are worth seeking out include the **College of Priests**, that was founded in 1395 and is now used by the Kent Music School, and the early 15th century **Corpus Christi Fraternity Hall**, where business was carried out in medieval times and which housed the Grammar School for over 300 years until the Education Act of 1870.

Just north of the town centre, at **Sandling**, on the banks of the River Medway, stands **Allington Castle**, the earliest parts of which are 13th century. However a fire around 1600 destroyed a

large part of it and it was not until the early 20th century that it was restored. It was once the home of Sir Thomas Wyatt, one of the 'silver poets' of the 16th century and author of *They flee from me that sometime did me seek*. He shares, with the Earl of Surrey, the credit for introducing into English poetry the sonnet form, popularised by the Italian poet, Petrarch, and that Shakespeare later went on to perfect. It was also at this castle that Henry VIII is said to have first met Anne Boleyn and, now housed in Maidstone Museum, is a chair from the castle that bears the following inscription: "... of this (chay)re iss entytled too one salute from everie ladie thott settes downe in itt - Castell Alynton 1530 - Hen. 8 Rex". The castle now belongs to a closed order of nuns and is not open to the public.

Lying on the opposite bank of the Medway from the castle is **Tyland Barn** a beautifully restored 17th century building that houses the **Museum of Kent Life**. Reflecting the unique character of this area of Britain and set in some 50 acres of land at the foot of the North Downs, the museum covers many aspects of the county from some of its historic buildings, hops and a working farm to riverside and country walks.

AROUND MAIDSTONE

OTHAM

3 miles SE of Maidstone off the A274

Despite being only a short distance from Maidstone, this elevated village is a haven of tranquillity with its restored

14th century church, solid yeomen's houses and surrounding orchards. William Stevens, the eccentric writer who called himself 'Nobody' and founded the society of 'Nobody's Friends' lies buried in the churchyard. **Stoneacre**, a National Trust property, is a small and charming 15th century half-timbered yeoman's house, complete with a great hall with a crownpost roof. It was sensitively restored from a state of near dereliction in the early 20th century using windows, fireplaces and wood from other ruined period buildings. The delightful gardens here have been restored to their original cottage style.

Thorpe Hall Drawing Room

LEEDS

4½ miles SE of Maidstone on the B2163

Whilst most people come to the village on their way to see the 'most beautiful castle in the World', it would be a mistake not to spend some time looking around Leeds itself. The village stands on the grounds of a former abbey, that flourished until the Dissolution in the 16th century, and many of the older buildings in Leeds, such as its oast houses, Norman Church of St Nicholas, and surrounding farms, were part of the abbey complex.

Covering almost 1,200 years of history, **Leeds Castle** stands on two islands in the middle of the River Len and, while the peaceful moat is the home of swans and ducks, the castle itself is surrounded by beautifully landscaped **Gardens**. Built on the site of a manor house that was owned by Saxon kings, the present castle was built just after the Norman Conquest and, when Edward I came to the throne, it became a royal palace. Beloved by Henry VIII, Leeds Castle was relinquished by the crown in the mid 16th century and, from then onwards, it has been in private hands. The last owner, an American heiress, Olive, Lady Baillie, bought the estate in 1926 and it is thanks to her vision, determination and hard work that Leeds Castle is so impressive today. One of the most popular visitor attractions in the country, there is plenty to delight and interest the public both inside and in the gardens. There is a collection of furnishings, tapestries and

Leeds Castle

RINGLESTONE INN AND FARMHOUSE HOTEL

Ringlestone Hamlet, Nr Harrietsham, Maidstone, Kent ME17 1NX
Tel: 01622 859900 Fax: 01622 859966
e-mail: bookings@ringlestone.com website: www.ringlestone.com

Deep in the heart of the North Downs yet only five minutes from Leeds Castle and the M20, **Ringlestone Inn** is an unspoilt, medieval lamp-lit tavern and farmhouse inn. Built in 1533 as a hospice for monks, by 1615 it had become an early ale house. Little seems changed from those bygone days. The original brick and flint walls remain, along with the floors, inglenooks and centuries old English furniture, which by rights should be on display in a museum. Even the furniture in the dining room, which was a later addition, was made from an 18th century Thames barge. The impressive English oak sideboard greets guests with a message, carved into the wood in 1632. 'A Ryghte joyouse and welcome greetynge to ye all'.

It's not just the atmosphere that makes the Ringlestone special. It has been consistently listed in distinguished food guides since 1983 and offers a superb help yourself buffet lunch and extensive evening menus with waitress service. Most of the food is home created using local Kentish produce where possible. Try the chicken casserole in cider with leeks and herbs or the lamb, coconut and banana curry or local delicacies like Kentish sausages and the tantalising little lamb and stilton pies -and that's just the buffet lunch. In the evening the feast might include game pie with redcurrant wine, a spectacular home-cooked dish containing venison, wild duck, rabbit and pheasant. Above all this is a place to relax and soak up the atmosphere. It's a great place to stay and you will be sure of a relaxing sleep in one of the three comfortable guest rooms.

GOLDSMITHS' FINE ART

9, High Street, Lenham, Nr. Maidstone, Kent ME17 2QD
Tel: 01622 850011 Fax: 01622 850011
e-mail: goldfineart@FSBDial.co.uk

Goldsmiths' Fine Art has been at its present address for two years but in Lenham for 16 years. Established by Christine Goldsmith, current proprietor Simon Bate joined in 1995, becoming a partner in 2000. For him it was a natural progression from his former career in interior design. Situated in the Lenham High Street, adjoining the village square, the gallery is a 16th century Grade II listed building with a Georgian façade. The interior of the building echoes the elegance of the exterior. Two well-lit rooms display a constantly changing selection of etchings, original water colours and limited edition prints, all by both well-known and local artists. There is also a range of sculptures and ceramics as well as an enticing array of greetings cards.

The gallery always features the work of notable artists such as the enchanting animal studies of Nigel Hemming.Also well-represented is the work of Rowland Hilder, for whose estate Goldsmiths' is the official agent, distributing his remaining limited edition work to galleries worldwide, as well as selling to local customers. Hilder, who died in 1993 at the age of 88, was one of the best known English artists of the 20th century. He lived at Blackheath for most of his life and has been described as 'the Turner of his generation' for the way he captured the essence of the Kent countryside he loved. Goldsmiths' also provides a professional picture framing and restoration service.

paintings and an idiosyncratic museum of dog collars. Many of the gardens have been restored including the maze and grotto and the informal and typically English Culpepper Garden. One new garden is particularly interesting - the Lady Baillie Garden, honouring the woman who put so much back into the castle before her death in 1974. Here are planted numerous sub-tropical species like bananas and tree palms that flourish in this south facing site.

BROOMFIELD

5 miles SE of Maidstone off the A20

This picturesque village in the Len Valley was mentioned in the Domesday Book and, in the churchyard of its 12th century church, lie buried several members of both the Wykeham-Martins and Fairfax families of Leeds Castle along with Frederick Hollands, a 19th century county cricketer from Broomfield. It is also the home of a spectacular 1,000 year old yew tree.

LOOSE

2½ miles S of Maidstone off the A229

Pronounced 'Looze', the older part of this delightful village lies in a narrow little valley and the cottages rise in terraces above the stream. The power of the stream, along with its purity and the availability of Fullers Earth, helped to established a flourishing woollen

industry here in the 16th century but, as the trade declined, some of the mills were converted to paper making. This change of direction brought about more contact with Maidstone, just to the north, and the village is slowly being absorbed by its larger neighbour. The viaduct that carries the main road from Maidstone across the Loose valley was built by Thomas Telford in 1829 and, along this stretch of road, can be seen large stones that were used, with the help of ropes, to pull heavy wagons up the steep hill.

BOUGHTON MONCHELSEA

3½ miles S of Maidstone on the B2163

On a ridge overlooking the Weald of Kent, this pleasant village was at the centre of Kentish ragstone quarrying and, not surprisingly, this local building material features heavily here. The quarries, on the edge of the village, have been worked almost continuously for seven centuries but archaeologists suggest that they were used longer ago than that as both the Romans and the Saxon used the stone in their buildings. Some of these stones were used in the construction of Westminster Abbey and Henry III ordered a number of cannonballs to be made from Kentish ragstone. Naturally, the village's 13th century parish Church of St Peter was built with this readily available material.

LENHAM ANTIQUE CENTRE

Lenham Square, Lenham, Kent ME17 2PQ
Tel: 01622 858050

The privately owned **Lenham Antique Centre** is within the 14th century former Hall House on the Village Square in Lenham. The interior has been sensitively restored and original features include exposed beams and the crown post. The two floors house an extensive collection of antiques, jewellery, pictures, bric-a-brac and some modern items. On the ground floor a dress agency sells nearly new designer and chain store clothes, while the gift shop has a good selection of modern gifts, pot pourri and soft toys.

It is also home to one of the oldest lychgates in England - erected in 1470 the gate was built entirely without nails.

To the north of the church lies **Boughton Monchelsea Place**, a beautiful fortified ragstone manor house, originally built in 1567. Inside, the house visitors can see a wealth of antique furniture, pictures and tapestries ranging in style from Tudor to Victorian. The house itself is little altered since the late 18th century, retaining 16th century stained glass windows, Elizabethan wall panellings, a galleried Jacobean staircase and original oak floors and marble fireplaces. To the front, it has breathtaking views of the private deer park and unspoilt countryside. To the rear is courtyard featuring a Georgian clock tower and ornamental pond and beyond that delightful walled gardens. One of these includes the kitchen garden

RALPH'S FARMSHOP AND NURSERY

Marlpit Farm, Wierton Road, Boughton Monchelsea,
Maidstone, Kent ME17 4JW
Tel: 01622 743851

Ralph's Farmshop and Nursery is an absolute gem, bursting with colour in season and one of the friendliest places in the area. Bernard and Anne Ralph have been running this family business since 1979. Originally founded by Bernard's parents in 1955 it has been substantially developed by the couple since they took over.

They specialise in bedding plants, hardy ferns, shrubs, alpines, starter plants and perennials. Plants are raised in a series of huge heated glasshouses and carefully nurtured from seed by Bernard and Anne. They also run a farm shop selling their own grown and locally produced fruit and vegetables as well as a selection of garden and pet accessories, local apple juice and honey. Each year they grow their own runner beans and celery as well as strawberries and cherries in season. Also

on sale are other local grown award-winning cherries. Ralph's is very popular with people looking for hanging baskets and a grand selection is usually available. They are also happy to refill customers own hanging baskets for them.

Some rather delightful little characters can been seen about the Nursery. Reminiscent of 'Bill and Ben' these tiny 'Flowerpot men' are made from terracotta flower pots joined together and fitted with a set of lead overalls. They come in three sizes ranging upwards from 18 inches and are made by Bernard and Anne and only available from them.

CHARITY CORNER NURSERIES

Charity, Headcorn Road, Hawkenbury, Staplehurst, Kent TN12 0DU
Tel: 01580 891628 Fax: 01580 891628

Christopher Wenman has a National Certificate in Horticulture and a National Diploma from Cannington Agricultural and Horticultural College in Somerset. He established **Charity Corner Nurseries** nine years ago on very fertile land last farmed during WWII. He's also developing a shelter belt, with wildlife, and an arboretum. And the river at the end is a Site of Special Scientific Interest. Situated in the beautiful Kent countryside it's a mere three miles from Sissinghurst Gardens (NT). It's a plant only nursery specialising in Salvias and unusual perennials and doesn't stock the usual garden centre items of peat, compost or furniture and accessories.

among gravel walks, box hedged beds and climbing roses. The other is the orchard and still contains old fruit trees as well as roses and shrubs.

MARDEN

7 miles S of Maidstone on the B2079

Surrounded by orchards and hop fields, the old part of the village is centred around a main street lined with attractive tile hung and weather-boarded houses. This village was, centuries ago, part of a Royal Hundred and, as it was exempt from the jurisdiction of the County Sheriff, it had its own court. This ancient court house still stands in the old square but the village stocks have been moved and can now be found on display in the porch of Marden's 13th century church.

STAPLEHURST

8 miles S of Maidstone on the A229

There was once a stronghold in the village but, today, all that can be seen is a tree covered mound and little is known of the fortification's history. In 1865, the novelist Charles Dickens was involved in a serious train accident at the point where the track crosses the River Beult, that lies to the east of Staplehurst, and he makes a reference to this in a postscript to his novel *Our Mutual Friend*.

A garden with a difference, **Iden Croft Herbs** has wonderful displays of herbs, aromatic wild flowers and plants that particularly attract butterflies, in both open and walled gardens. It is also home to the national oreganum and mentha collections. Another place in the village that is well worth a visit, is the charming and interesting museum, **Brattle**

Farm Museum, where a wide-ranging collection of vintage cars, tractors, veterinary equipment, horses and harnesses, weights and measures and Victorian and Edwardian household items are displayed along with other exhibits that relate to rural life.

EAST FARLEIGH

2 miles SW of Maidstone on the B2010

Standing on steeply rising ground on the side of the River Medway, East Farleigh is surrounded by orchards and overlooks a graceful 14th century bridge. It was over this superb five-arched river crossing that Parliamentary soldiers marched, in 1648, on their way to capture Maidstone from the Royalists during the Civil War. One of the most important engagements in the war, the battle left 300 of the King's supporters dead and more than 1,000 were taken prisoner. In the churchyard of the village's ancient church, a cross marks the final resting place of 43 hop pickers who died of cholera whilst working here in 1849. Also in the churchyard can be found the graves of the artist Donald Maxwell and Barbara Spooner, the wife of the reformer William Wilberforce, two of whose sons were vicars here.

Cottage and Old English Garden, Benover

THE GRANARY BED AND BREAKFAST

Rock farm, Gibbs, Hill, Nettlestead, Maidstone,Kent, ME18 5HT
Tel: 01622 814547 Fax: 01622 813905
e-mail: robcorfe@thegranary-bnb.co.uk
website: www.thegranary-bnb.co.uk

Gail Corfe's outstanding guesthouse is a beautiful Georgian granary recently converted into a large family farmhouse. This is a perfect spot to enjoy walks round the farmland, along the nearby River Medway and to Nettlestead Place. Guests enjoy large luxurious well-appointed bedrooms and have a large sitting room with log fire. Full facilities and plentiful breakfasts. Non smoking.

ROCK FARM HOUSE BED AND BREAKFAST

Rock farm, Gibbs Hill, Nettlestead, Maidstone,
Kent, ME18 5HT
Tel/Fax: 01622 812244
website: www.rockfarmhousebandb.co.uk

Sue Corfe's delightful 18th century Kentish farmhouse occupies an idyllic location in an area of outstanding beauty. It is surrounded by two acres of magnificent gardens, which are open to the public through the 'Yellow Book' of the National Gardens Scheme. The gardens are the habitat of a wide selection of birds and wildlife. The rooms are spacious and very comfortable with full facilities and the splendid breakfast includes homemade and local produce. Non smoking

NETTLESTEAD

5 miles SW of Maidstone on the B2015

A quiet village set on a bank above a particularly pleasant stretch of the River Medway, Nettlestead is home to two buildings that are thought to have been founded by Bishop Odo, the half-brother of William the Conqueror. The present parish **Church of St Mary** was rebuilt in 1420 and it contains some lovely stained glass windows that were greatly damaged in 1763 when a thunderstorm unleashed 10 inch hailstones on the village. Beside the church stands **Nettlestead Place**. Restored in the early 20th century, this ancient private house still retains its old stone gatehouse and medieval undercroft.

YALDING

5 miles SW of Maidstone on the B2010

This lovely village's position, at the confluence of the Rivers Medway, Beult and Teise, provides ample irrigation for the fertile soil so it is not surprising that Yalding lies in one of the largest hop-growing parishes in England. Each of the three rivers here is crossed by its own medieval bridge whilst the delightful high street is lined with charming weather-boarded houses that date back to the 17th century. At **Yalding Organic Gardens** visitors can see 14 individual gardens, including a Tudor garden, a Victorian garden and a wildlife garden, that illustrate the history of gardening from medieval times through to the present day. Changing ideas and themes down the ages are also highlighted such as stewardship of resource, the importance of genetic engineering and organic horticulture.

LADDINGFORD

6½ miles SW of Maidstone off the A228

This ancient village is really little more

than a hamlet around a ford on a tributary of the River Medway. In nearly every direction there are orchards but looking south from the village, there is a wooded ridge with the village of Goudhurst at its crest.

BELTRING
7½ miles SW of Maidstone on the A228

This neat little village is home to one of the county's major attractions - the **Whitbread Hop Farm**. Situated on a 1,000 acre working hop farm, this agricultural complex was originally a hop-drying centre supplying this major brewery but it has grown to house a museum, a rural crafts centre and a natural trail. Visitors can learn about the history and purpose of hops in the brewing process (until the 14th century cloves were more commonly used as flavouring) and also about the brewing industry itself. Visitors, particularly

children, will also enjoy meeting the famous Whitbread shire horses and the smaller animals at the pets' corner. A collection of agricultural machinery is on display along with an interesting exhibition of rural crafts.

HADLOW
9 miles SW of Maidstone on the A26

Lying in the Medway Valley, this attractive village has a wide main street where a number of its older houses can be found. These, and the rest of the village, are, however, completely overshadowed by the curiosity known as **May's Folly**. A tower some 170 feet high, this is all that remains of Hadlow Castle that was built by the eccentric industrialist Walter Barton May over a number of years and was finally finished in the early 19th century. A landmark for miles around, May built the tower so that he would have a view that extended as

(Continued page 110)

DOWNDERRY NURSERY

Pillar Box Lane, Hadlow, Tonbridge, Kent TN11 9SW
Tel: 01732 810081 Fax: 01732 811398
e-mail: info@downderry-nursery.co.uk
website: www.downderry-nursery.co.uk

Set in the peaceful beauty of an old walled garden, **Downderry** is home to the National Plant collection of Lavender and Rosemary. A visit here is very much a tranquil and sensual experience. Simon Charlesworth, the owner, and his team have perfected their craft over many years and the evidence is there to see and to smell. It is backed up by the awards that they have received from top international flower shows, including for the last three years, gold medals from Hampton Court Palace Flower show.

RIVERSIDE NURSERIES

Hamptons Road, Hamptons, Near Hadlow, Kent TN11 9RG
Tel: 01732 811449

This, friendly, family-run business is operated by Paul Hollobon and his mother Michelle. Paul, a trained horticulturist, founded the nursery with his father and has been running it for 13 years. The shrub selection at **Riverside Nurseries** is constantly changing according to season. The perennials are field grown but potted up for selling. In addition they sell, bedding plants, hanging baskets, trees, roses, grasses, geraniums and alpines. All their plants are grown cold so that they last longer and perform better in the garden.

WALK 2

Mereworth Woods and West Peckham

Start	Mereworth church
Distance	6 miles (9.5km)
Approximate time	3 hours
Parking	On road in Mereworth
Refreshments	Pub at West Peckham
Ordnance Survey maps	Landranger 188 (Maidstone & The Weald of Kent), Explorer 148 (Maidstone & the Medway Towns)

This invigorating walk uses an attractive part of the Wealdway, climbing through Hurst Wood and returning by West Peckham, where church and pub beside the village green make a perfect picture if cricket is being played. After this there is a climb to the top of the Wealden ridge before the return to Mereworth.

From the church walk down the street to the pub, the Torrington Arms, where a short lane on its far side leads to a narrow enclosed path which has an orchard to the right. Very soon another narrow path leaves to the right **A**. Take this and climb up to join a driveway from a large white house which reaches a lane on a sharp bend. Keep straight on here and bear left at the next road junction, with Horns Lane. There are good views back to Mereworth as you approach the following junction, with New Pound Lane. Keep ahead here to reach the main road and go directly across to the footpath opposite. This follows a farm track, with poplars to the left sheltering a field of fruit bushes.

Turn left when the track reaches a lane and then right after a pond to walk up another track past a cottage and through a meadow. When the track reaches Hurst Wood **B**, at a 'Private' notice, turn right by the edge of the trees and follow the wood round to find a further track to the left which climbs up into the wood from the meadow.

The right of way is a humble, often muddy, track which climbs steadily up a valley to reach a vast coppice of beech and ash trees. Keep straight on when another path crosses, continuing the steady climb.

Turn left at the next track **C**, just below the summit. There are two great beech trees here, one with exposed, convoluted roots. The path, now level, soon reaches a further crossways. Go straight over here but turn left at the next crossing **D** on to a broader track heading south – there is a metal gate to the right. Cross straight over a lane, following the Wealdway logo, to a path above another lane. This is Gover Hill, the small sector of Mereworth Woods owned by the National Trust. Soon the path descends to reach the road **E**.

Cross straight over this complex junction to a track to the left of a white cottage. Just before the track reaches the trees at the bottom look for a Wealdway sign pointing to the left **F** and follow this to cross a stile on to a path which follows the edge of a long field with a spinney to the right. At the end of the field the path swings to the right to join a farm track.

The track meets the road at East Lodge. Turn left and then look for the white railings to the right where the footpath runs above the lane, and parallel to it for a short distance. A little further on the path leaves the lane, bearing to the south-east with a row of poplars to the left and an orchard beyond as it heads down towards a white bungalow. An unusual feature here are the ancient buses parked about the fields close to West Peckham. They are hired by film and TV companies.

Turn left at the bungalow **G** to head towards the tower of West Peckham church, emerging on to the beautiful village green with the pub at one corner and the church at another. The church is a place of great beauty and peace. Continue eastwards from the church and turn left into Forge Lane towards Plaxtol. Fork right into Stan Lane when the lane divides and climb to the top of this quiet byway, passing to the left of Beech Farm.

The lane begins to level at the modern house named Hurst Folly on the left. Opposite this house **H** turn into a bridleway on the right and a wonderful view opens up almost immediately but is soon masked by conifers planted as shelter for the fruit bushes on the left. The path continues to descend after the row of trees ends and Mereworth Castle can be seen in the distance ahead – a rare glimpse of this private house. The path swings around a bungalow and the unusual spire of Mereworth church comes into view. It then skirts the rear of Yotes Court, swinging to the right to approach the farmyard. Just beyond a cottage with pointed windows on the left, turn left on to a muddy track which passes cattlesheds on the other side of a hedge to the right.

This track narrows and then skirts a spinney before reaching the road by a renovated gate-lodge. Cross over the main road into Mereworth and continue along the street back to the church. ●

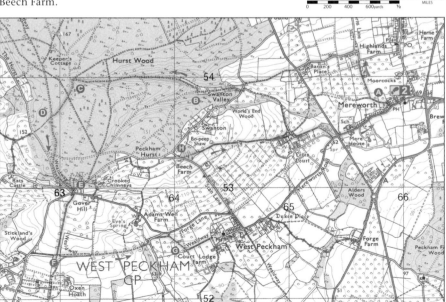

far as the south coast but, unfortunately, the South Downs made this particular dream of his impossible.

Anyone looking for gardening ideas in the heart of the Garden of England should pay a visit to **Broadview Gardens** where the belief of the success of a garden lying in its design is firmly held. There are a wide range of gardens to see here - from subtropical, stone and water, oriental and Italian to mixed borders, cottage, bog and wildlife. Beside the more traditional gardens there are experimental areas and this is an ideal place to come to for anyone looking for gardening inspiration.

Aylesford

13 miles NE of Sevenoaks off the A20

This charming village, on the banks of the River Medway, is not only one of Kent's oldest villages but it has, over the centuries, seen more than its fair share of fighting. Having travelled many miles from Pegwell Bay, the Jutish leaders Hengist and Horsa defeated the ancient Britons here in a great battle in AD 455. Though Horsa died in the battle, Hengist along with his son Aesc established a kingdom here (Cantware - or 'Men of Kent') and, for the next 300 years, the land was ruled by the descendants of Aesc, the dynasty of the Eskings. Later, in 893, the Danes were seen off by King Alfred whilst, soon afterwards, in 918, Edmund Ironside defeated Canute and the Vikings at Aylesford.

Aylesford has been an important river crossing for centuries and records recall that there was a bridge spanning the river here as long ago as 1287. However, the beautiful five-arched **Bridge** seen today dates from the 14th century and from it there is an excellent view of Aylesford's delightful half-timbered, steeply gabled cottages.

In 1242, when the first Carmelites arrived here from the Holy Land, they founded **Aylesford Priory**. After the Dissolution in the 16th century, the priory became a private house and was rebuilt in 1675 only to be destroyed by a fire in the 1930s. After World War II, in 1949, the Carmelites took over the house and, having restored it to its former glory, they have re-established the priory - now calling it **The Friars** to use its traditional name. Today, it is a peaceful and tranquil retreat set in acres of well tended grounds in which visitors are invited to picnic. The restored 17th century barn acts as a tea rooms, as well as a gift and bookshop, whilst the chapels contain some outstanding modern works of religious art. Still a popular place for pilgrimage, there is also a guesthouse here that offers peace and quiet to individuals, groups and families and extensive conference facilities.

Just north of the village lies further evidence of the long history of settlement in and around Aylesford in the form of **Kits Coty House**. Situated on Blue Bell Hill, this is a Neolithic burial chamber (with a capstone lying across three huge upright stones) that is reputed to be the tomb of a British chieftain who was killed by the Jutish leader Horsa. Whether this is true or just local legend matters little as the views from the monument, out across the valley to the Medway Gap, make a walk to this site very worth while.

ROYAL TUNBRIDGE WELLS

Surrounded by the unspoilt beauty of the Weald, some of the most scenic areas of countryside in England, Royal Tunbridge Wells is a pretty and attractive town that has been a popular place to visit for several hundred years. However, unlike many of the major towns and cities of Kent, Royal Tunbridge Wells has no Roman or ecclesiastical heritage and, during the Middle Ages, when many towns were establishing their trading reputations, it was little more than a forest. The secret of how this charming place gained such prominence lies in the 'Royal' and 'Wells' of its name. In 1606, the courtier, Dudley, Lord North, found chalybeate springs here and he rushed back to court to break the news of his discovery of what he declared to be health-giving waters. Soon the fashionable from London were taking the water and spreading the word of their health-restoring qualities but, for three decades, there were still no buildings beside the springs.

In 1630, Tunbridge Wells received its first royal visitor when Queen Henrietta Maria, the wife of Charles I, came here to recuperate after giving birth to the future Charles II. She and her entourage, like other visitors, camped on the grounds by the springs. However, soon afterwards, enterprising local people began to build here but the real development of the town into one of the most popular spas of the 18th and 19th centuries was due to the Earl of Abergavenny. In order to increase the popularity of the spa, Beau Nash, the famous dandy who played an important role in the development of another spa town, Bath, came here as Master of Ceremonies in 1735. With Nash at the helm, guiding and even dictating fashion, Tunbridge Wells went from strength to strength and, whilst royalty had always found the town to their liking, it was granted its 'Royal' prefix in 1909 by Edward VII.

The chalybeate spring that was accidentally discovered by Lord North whilst out riding in what was then Waterdown Forest still flows in front of the **Bath House**, which was built in 1804 on top of the original Cold Bath. Meanwhile, close to the original springs was a grassy promenade known as The Walks where those coming to take the waters could take some exercise. In 1699 Princess Anne visited Tunbridge Wells with her son, the Duke of Gloucester, who slipped and hurt himself along The Walks. The irate Princess complained and the town authorities tiled over the grass and so created **The Pantiles** that remains, today, a lovely shaded walk, lined with elegant shops. The Pantiles were the central focal point for the hectic social life arranged by Beau Nash and there were concerts and balls throughout the season along with gambling houses. Also in this area of the town is the **Church of King Charles the Martyr**, often dubbed the 'jewel of the Pantiles'. Originally established as a chapel in 1678 for those coming to take the waters, the church has been extended and one of its

THACKERAY'S

85 London Road, Tunbridge Wells, Kent TN1 1EA
Tel: 01892 511921 Fax: 01892 527561
e-mail: reservations@thakeryrestaurant.co.uk
website: www. thakeryrestaurant.co.uk

Thackeray's is a new restaurant serving the highest standards of modern French cuisine within an elegant and contemporary interior located in one of the oldest and finest buildings in town. Partners Paul Smith, Richard Phillips and Mark Pullinger have brought London dining standards to the country. Richard is also head chef. During his career he has worked with some of the most famous names in the business including the Roux Brothers and Marco Pierre White. More recently he was executive chef at London's St Martin's Lane Hotel.

A series of intimate dining spaces has been created by interior designer Mark Pimlitt. These range from classic to spectacular. One room is decorated in gold leaf while another, called the Goldfish room has goldfish, in bowls, on all the tables - and all this in a magnificent old building with low ceilings and ancient floorboards. The result is a wonderful ambience, which provides something for everyone whether it's an intimate supper for two or a family party. But above all else it's the food that attracts

the clientele. Mouth-watering starters, innovative main courses and deliciously decadent desserts are all offered in abundance. Try the Irish rock oysters with lime crème fraîche or the roasted sea scallops and pan fried black pudding with caramelised apples and grain mustard sauce. Follow with the pan-fried 'mille feuille of Dutch calves liver, roasted shallots, chestnuts and Madeira wine sauce. Then top that with the assiette of chocolate with butterscotch sauce. The beauty of it all is the very reasonable prices. The lunch menu is a particularly fine bargain.

TREVOR MOTTRAM LTD

33-37 The Pantiles, Tunbridge Wells, Kent, TN2 5TE
Tel: 01892 538915 Fax: 01892 523712

Trevor Mottram's is a specialist cookshop with a formidable range of products covering every conceivable tool for the kitchen of every size. It's one of only five cookshops recommended on the Delia Online website and the friendly and superbly efficient service matches the extensive stock. Tableware and glassware sits beside a growing range of electrical goods including Dualit, Kitchen Aid and Gaggia. Trevor Mottram's first shop, opened in 1976 and was one of the earliest cookshops. Developing and expanding over the years as it gained momentum and reputation, it was taken over in March 2000 by Sarah and Alan Wood, the current owners. Both are enthusiastic cooks and relate easily to the business.

Sarah is a chef's daughter and grew up in hotels and restaurants while Alan is a Chartered Accountant who has held Finance Director and management roles in large organisations with turnovers ranging from £5 to £150 million. The shop now occupies one of the oldest buildings in Tunbridge Wells, a

Georgian, five storey building in the historic Pantiles . Previously a seed merchants it retains many original features including a sack loading door on the first floor balcony and an ancient dumb waiter. The large glass frontage is crammed full of stock enticing the browser through the doors to find 8000 product lines from 150 different suppliers on display. Recent acquisition of the adjacent property will provide a ground floor display area of 2400 sq ft, allowing the product range to be increased, mainly in dining and tableware with porcelain from Richard Ginori and Laure Japy and glassware from Nason and Moretti. The new demonstration area will allow in-shop cooking experiences.

The Wells Exhibit

Once part of the extensive network of railway lines in Kent and neighbouring East Sussex, **Spa Valley Railway** is a restored and preserved section of this system that was re-opened in 1996. Now running between Royal Tunbridge Wells and High Rocks, the trains leave Tunbridge Wells West station and take passengers on a pleasant journey through the Wealden countryside.

most interesting features is the charming clock that was donated to the church in 1760 by Lavinia Fenton, the actress and mistress of the Duke of Bolton. Inside, there is a superb ceiling that was created by Henry Doogood, the chief plasterer to Sir Christopher Wren.

For a greater insight into the history and development of the town, a visit to the **Royal Tunbridge Wells Museum and Art Galley**, opened in 1952 is a must. Amongst the displays and exhibits on natural history and art, there is an exhibition of local history and a collection of Tunbridge ware - the decorative woodwork that is unique to the area.

AROUND ROYAL TUNBRIDGE WELLS

MATFIELD
5 miles NE of Royal Tunbridge Wells on the B2160

The village name is derived from the Anglo Saxon name 'Matta' and 'feld' meaning large clearing and appropriately at the centre of this village is one of the largest village greens in Kent. Around it old and new houses blend harmoniously including several fine tile hung, typically Kentish houses and an impressive Georgian dwelling built in 1728.

RIGHT ON THE GREEN

15, Church Road, Southborough, Tunbridge Wells, Kent TN4 0RX
Tel: 01892 513161

Dine by candlelight in this award winning restaurant with its delicious, innovative cuisine accompanied by a fine selection of wines. Husband and wife team Peter and Paula, became the proud new owners in August 2000 and have not looked back. Peter's excellent culinary history started with his Roux apprenticeship, followed by patisserie perfection at le Notre and seasons in Switzerland, France and Paris and is now evolving and creating superb cuisine within his own restaurant. Private Dining and Canapé parties are also hosted in the Georgian Room.

HORSMONDEN

7½ miles E of Tunbridge Wells on the B2162

Pronounced 'Horzm'den', it is hard to imagine that this delightful village, tucked amongst orchards and fields, was once a thriving industrial centre. Although little evidence of this remains today the key to the village's prosperity lies in the pond found just to the west of Horsmonden. Known as a furnace pond, it supplied water to the ironworks that flourished throughout the Weald of Kent. Now, nature is reclaiming the pond and it will soon be indistinguishable from other expanses of water in and around the village.

From the village green, known as The Heath, a footpath leads to the village church, some two miles to the west. This is a walk worth making as the countryside is pleasant and, on reaching the church, visitors can see a memorial to John Read, who died in 1847, and is best known for having invented the stomach pump.

GOUDHURST

9 miles E of Tunbridge Wells on the A262

Standing on a hill and with sweeping views across the surrounding orchards and hop fields, and especially over the Weald, Goudhurst (that is pronounced 'Gowdhurst') is a picturesque place that draws many visitors, not least because of its main street, lined with traditional tile hung, weather-boarded cottages. The solidity of the village reflects the prosperity it enjoyed when the woollen industry was introduced here in the Middle Ages. The village church, which stands on the hilltop, begun as a chapel in 1119, dates chiefly from the 15th century and, inside, there are many memorials to the leading local family, the Culpeppers. From the church tower it

MARLE PLACE GARDENS AND GALLERY

Marle Place Road, Brenchley, Near Tonbridge, Kent TN12 7HS
Tel: 01892 722304 Fax: 01892 722099

Marle Place is a peaceful, privately owned garden, with ten acres of formal planting and many more acres of woodland and orchard. It is a plantsman and artist's garden, featuring a Victorian gazebo, Edwardian rockery, a walled fragrant garden, a restored 19th century greenhouse and orchid collection, a mosaic terrace and ornamental ponds. The house with a massive chimney is 17th century is of great architectural interest but not open to the public. The gardens have been designed as a combination of hedged rooms and tree lined avenues set on a south-east slope ending in woodland planted with specimen trees and bordered by a stream. Scent and colour are a major feature throughout the year. Spring bulbs are followed by masses of old fashioned roses and herbaceous borders, annual plants and unusual shrubs.

A gentle walk meanders through the woodland, following the stream through new tree planting and old woods, skirting two ponds, one dating to a bygone age. Many varieties of wild plants and

creatures live in this magical habitat and the path returns, via a red bridge over a bog garden. The woodland and areas of long grass are the perfect place to enjoy a picnic. Teas, herbals teas, coffee and cake are always on sale in the cart bay. Exhibitions are held throughout the season in the Gallery, by a variety of contemporary painters, sculptors, potters and most work is for sale. On occasion the studios of the resident artists are open and artwork is often on view in the grounds. Open 28th March until 6th October, 10.00 a.m. to 5.30 p.m.

was said that 51 other churches could be seen on a clear day. This may have been possible when the tower was higher, but whatever the truth of the 51 churches it is certainly possible today to see Canary Wharf Tower in London, which is 40 miles away.

Just to the southwest of the village lies **Finchcocks** a charming Georgian manor house, with a dramatic frontage, that is named after the family who lived on this land in the 13th century. Built for the barrister, Edward Bathurst in 1725, the house has managed to retain many of its original features despite having changed hands several times over the years. In 1970, Finchcocks was bought by Richard Burnett, a leading exponent of the early piano and, today, it is home to his magnificent collection of historic keyboard instruments. The high ceilings and oak panelled rooms are the ideal setting for this collection of beautiful instruments, which includes chamber organs, harpsichords, spinets and early pianos and, whenever the house is open to the public those instruments restored to concert standard are played. Along with these instruments Finchcocks also houses some fine pictures and prints and an exhibition on 18th century pleasure gardens. Tucked away behind the elegant house are four acres of beautiful gardens, which provide a dramatic setting for outside events. The gardens are mainly of Victorian design, except the walled garden, which was designed in 1992, as an 18th century Pleasure Garden.

Further south again and adjoining the county border with East Sussex lies **Bedgebury National Pinetum and Forest Gardens**, founded jointly by the Forestry Commission and the Royal Botanic Gardens at Kew in the 1920s. Today, Bedgebury is home to the National Conifer Collection, the finest collection of conifers in the world, where some of the most famous conifers, including large Californian redwoods are to be found.

LAMBERHURST
6 miles E of Royal Tunbridge Wells on the A21

As this village lies on the main road between Royal Tunbridge Wells and Hastings, it once played an important role as a coaching stop but much of the village's prosperity is due to the iron industry of the Weald. The high street here is lined with attractive old houses and other buildings dating from those days. Lamberhurst produced iron railings, which are also in evidence at St Paul's Cathedral, can be seen along this road. Lamberhurst's 14th century church, set some way from the village centre in the valley of the River Teise, has been remodelled to accommodate a smaller congregation than those it attracted

Oast Houses, Lamberhurst

during the years of Lamberhurst's heyday. Today, the village is associated with viticulture and the first vineyard was established here in 1972.

To the northwest of the village lies **The Owl House** a particularly pretty little cottage whose tenants, according to records dating from 1522, paid the monks at Bayham Abbey an annual rental of one white cockerel. Later the house became associated with night smugglers or 'owlers' (hence its name) who traded English wool for French brandy and avoided the tax inspectors by giving out coded hoot calls. In 1952, the house was bought by Lady Dufferin and, while this

Scotney Castle

is not open to the public, the beautiful **Gardens** that she planted are. There are extensive lawns and walks through woodland of birch, beech and English oak as well as spring bulbs, roses, flowering shrubs and ornamental fruit trees. As this was once the site of the

BEWL WATER

The Estate Office, Bewlwater, Lamberhurst, Kent TN3 8JH
Tel: 01892 890661 Fax: 01892 890232
e-mail: bewl@southerwater.co.uk   website: www.bewl.co.uk

Set in an area of outstanding natural beauty in the heart of the High Weald, **Bewl Water** is the largest body of inland water in the south east. It supports a great variety of wildlife as well as a wide range of sporting and leisure activities. However Bewl Water is not a natural feature, but a reservoir constructed to provide efficient and sustainable water supplies for Kent. Before the reservoir was built this was a picturesque agricultural valley, but it had long been recognised that the water supplies were inadequate to meet the needs of the area. The construction of Bewl Water reservoir started in 1973. Woodland was cleared, roads were rerouted and historic houses were dismantled and rebuilt elsewhere. The water supply was secured for the future, and visitors to Bewl can find out about its sources and conservation at Southern Water's interactive exhibition.

However over the years Bewl water has developed as one of the most popular leisure attractions in the area. Visitors can appreciate the wildlife on a picturesque 13 mile walk around the water. A route map is available in the Visitor Centre. The route is also open for horse riding or cycling and during the summer months cycles are offered for hire at the car park. Other sports on offer include fly-fishing, sailing, wind-surfing and canoeing. Beginners courses are available for these and other activities. Less energetic visitors can take to the water with a trip on the passenger boat Swallow from Easter to September or simply enjoy the scenery from the Look Out restaurant.

CREATIVE IRONWORK CO. LTD

Unit 5 B.Y.G. Business Units, Bayham Road, Bells Yew Green
Tunbridge Wells, Kent TN3 9BJ
Tel/Fax: 01892 750324
e-mail: mxforge@lineone.net website: www.thecreativeironworkco.co.uk

Established in August 2000 by Giles Blakely, **Creative Ironwork Co Ltd.** produces
distinctive works of art for practical application, visual impact and eccentricity.
Giles Blakely is a skilled and creative artist blacksmith with over twenty years
experience of creating beautiful objects from wrought iron, copper and mild
steel. He blends the ideas of his customers with his own artistic flair to produce
a complete custom-made work of art.

iron works that made some of the
fitments for St Paul's Cathedral, there are
also hammer ponds and these have been
creatively converted into informal water
gardens surrounded by willows, camellias
and rhododendrons.

To the east of the Lamberhurst lies
Scotney Castle, a massive, rust-stained
tower that was built by Roger de
Ashburnham in 1378 and that now
incorporates the ruins of a Tudor house.
However, what especially draws people to
Scotney are the romantic **Gardens** that
are renowned for their autumn colours
but are beautiful through out the
seasons. The water lily filled moat
around the ruins provides the perfect
center piece to the wealth of plants
found in the gardens and there are
also delightful countryside walks around
the estate.

GROOMBRIDGE

4 miles SW of Royal Tunbridge Wells on the B2110

Straddling the county border between
Kent and Sussex, it is generally
recognised that the Kent side of this
village is the prettier and more
interesting as this is where the triangular
village green lies, overlooked by the tile
hung cottages of the Groombridge estate.
This charming village centre piece is also
overlooked by **Groombridge Place**, a
classical 17th century manor house that
stands on the site of a medieval castle.
The house is surrounded by superb
parkland and **Gardens**, designed by the
famous Jacobean diarist John Evelyn in a
formal manner. Likened to a series of
rooms, the walled gardens are
complemented by extensive herbaceous
borders whilst, high above these, there is

GROOMBRIDGE PLACE GARDENS AND ENCHANTED FOREST

Groombridge Place, Groombridge,
Near Royal Tunbridge Wells, Kent TN3 9QG
Tel: 01892 863999 e-mail: office@groombridge.co.uk
Fax: 01892 863996 website: www.groombridge.co.uk

These award winning gardens, set against the romantic
backdrop of a 17th century moated manor, feature
magnificent walled gardens with herbaceous borders, rose
garden, secret garden, drunken topiary and much more. In
the ancient woodland of the 'Enchanted Forest' there's
mystery, innovation and excitement for all ages. It's a great
place to take children for a day out and it has a restaurant,
picnic area and gift shop.

HARVEYS OF CRANBROOK

11 - 13 Stone Street, Cranbrook, Kent TN17 3HF
Tel: 01580 712345 Fax: 01580 720352
e-mail: markharvey1@talk21.com

Harveys of Cranbrook is a veritable gastronomic Aladdin's cave, situated in a listed building, part of a conservation area, just off the High Street. Inside the double windowed shop Mark and Debbie Harvey preside over a mouth-watering selection of delicatessen items specialising in a wide range of produce from Italy.

Just inside the front door is a large deli counter, jam packed with exotic delights including a range of over 70 cheeses, salads, pasta dishes, olives and seasonal Italian goodies. Hanging from hooks on the shelves behind are sausages, salamis and hams. On top of the deli counter is a collection of jars, bottles and tins containing preserved fruits, roasted onions and artichokes, while the shelves behind the counter contain various exotic olive oils, vinegars, jams, preserves and mustards. Sweet tasting, seasonal, titbits make an appearance too with an excellent

choice, which includes Amaretto biscuits and the delicious Panetone.There is also a large selection of local produce with some particularly fine preserves and honey. The friendly staff always seem to have the time to discuss the produce with customers while still managing to keep the sales ticking over.

Wine is another speciality of Harveys. Fine wines from around the world fill the shelves. Riojas from Spain, Chianti and Frascati from Italy and an eclectic mix of bottles from the New World. Customers can choose from their established USA favourites from Southern California or from some of the newly fashionable wine producing countries such as Chile.

No deli could survive without a decent range of coffees and Harvey's is no exception. They sell it ground or as roasted beans and also have their own label blend.

To the rear of the shop is a wonderful new coffee bar that the Harvey's opened in December 2001. It has a wonderful light and airy ambience created by a combination of bright lemon walls, the polished wooden floor and the plain, light pine, tables. The prints on the wall enhance the decor but are constantly changing as customers buy their favourites. This is the place to come for morning coffee or an afternoon tea break in the midst of a busy day's touring or shopping. It's an even better idea to stop for a light lunch, relax in the pleasant surroundings and sample the produce of the deli before making a purchase. Of course the menu has a predominance of Mediterranean dishes, pastas, salads, meats, olives and tapas. As it is also licensed the wines can be sampled as well beers and ciders.

Harveys is open 7 days a week from 8.45am to 5pm Monday to Friday and 10am to 2pm on Sundays. It is best to ring as opening times may vary according to the season.

The Enchanted Forest a magical and imaginative series of mysterious gardens that are a delight to explore.

RUSTHALL

1½ miles W of Royal Tunbridge Wells off the A264

Although Rusthall lies on the outskirts of Royal Tunbridge Wells it has managed to retain some of its original rural character and not become completely engulfed by its much larger neighbour. A lovely common marks the heart of the village and some of the unusual rock structures that can be found in Royal Tunbridge Wells can also be seen here, in particular, there is **Toad Rock**, a natural rock formation, so called because of its remarkable resemblance to a giant toad balanced atop a rock.

SPELDHURST

2½ miles NW of Royal Tunbridge Wells off the A26

This attractive chiefly residential village was mentioned as early as the 8th century and, though close to Royal Tunbridge Wells, still manages to preserve a cohesive sense of village identity and a rural atmosphere. At its heart lies the village church, built on the foundations of a much older Norman church that was struck by lightning in 1791. Great care was taken by the Victorians when the church was rebuilt and it is worth visiting to view the colourful stained glass windows, designed by Burne-Jones.

CRANBROOK

Originally a little hamlet lying in the hills close to the source of the River Crane, Cranbrook began to grow in the 11th century and, by the end of the 13th century, it was sufficiently well established to be granted a market charter by Edward I. However, it was the introduction of the wool weaving from Flanders, in the 14th century that really changed the town's fortunes and, for the next few centuries, Cranbrook prospered. Several old buildings date back to this period of wealth including the church and the Cloth Halls and winding streets lined with weather boarded houses and shops. However, the industry began to decline and, by the 17th century, agriculture had taken over and, like other Wealden places, Cranbrook was transformed into a market town serving the needs of the surrounding area.

Often dubbed the 'Capital of the Kentish Weald', one of the best places to start any exploration of the town is at the **Cranbrook Museum** that is housed in a museum piece itself. Dating back to 1480, the museum is a fine example of a timber-framed building that is held together by elaborate joints. Opened in 1974, the displays and exhibitions here cover many aspects of Wealden life, from agriculture and local crafts to Victorian and wartime memorabilia. Naturally the

---

THE CRAFT SHOP

High Street, Cranbrook, Kent TN17 3DP
Tel: 01580 712668

Eleven years ago Madeline gave up her job as an art teacher in Sheffield to start her own craft business. Her tiny shop front in a building dating back to the 17th century disguises the fact that inside is a veritable Aladdin's Cave of Crafts. As a teacher she specialised in textiles so it is no surprise that she has a wide range in the **Craft Shop**. She also stocks an eclectic range of English and Scottish glassware, craft jewellery, lino prints, wood engravings and amazing stainless steel sculptures from a local artist.

Cranbrook Windmill

now rare.

The parish church, **St Dunstan's**, is believed to have been built on the site of first a Saxon and then a Norman church. Locally known as the 'Cathedral of the Weald' and built between the 14th and the 16th centuries, the size of this church reflects the prosperity of the town at the time. Above the porch, reached by a stone staircase, is a room known as 'Baker's Jail' where, in the reign of Mary Tudor, Sir John Baker, sometimes known as 'Bloody Baker' imprisoned the numerous Protestants he had convicted to await their execution. Originally, the room was intended to hold church valuables.

town's reliance on the weaving industry is highlighted and, along with the collection of prints by the 19th century Cranbrook colony of artists, there is a display of local birds, many of which are

Although St Dunstan's church tower is tall, the town is dominated by the tallest smock mill in England, **Union Mill**, which is around 70 feet high. Built in 1814, the windmill was fully restored in the 1960s and, wind permitting, it still

grinds corn into the flour that is sold here. It is open to the public on a limited basis.

AROUND CRANBROOK

SISSINGHURST

1½ miles NW of Cranbrook on the A262

The main street of this village is lined with old weather boarded houses that have been built over a period of several centuries. Many of the larger houses were erected by prosperous weavers who worked in the thriving industry that was introduced to Sissinghurst during the reign of Edward III.

Sissinghurst is, of course, famous for the lovely gardens that were the creation of the writer Vita Sackville-West and her husband Harold Nicholson. When, in 1930, the couple bought **Sissinghurst Castle** it was all but a ruin. The castle was originally built in Tudor times by Sir John Baker, who, during the reign of Mary Tudor, sent so many Protestants to their deaths that he became known as 'Bloody' Baker. Such was Sir John's reputation that local legend tells that when two women working at the castle heard him approaching, they hid under the main staircase. From their hiding place they saw that their master was being followed by a servant carrying the body of a murdered woman. As the men climbed

Sissinghurst Gardens

the staircase, one of the dead woman's hands became caught in the banisters. Impatient to continue whatever gruesome tasks he was about to perform, Sir John quickly hacked the hand from the body and he and his servant continued up the stairs. Meanwhile, the severed hand fell into the lap of one of the women hiding below. Later, during the Seven Years War in the 18th century, the castle was used as a prison for 3,000 French troops and, by the time they had left, only a few parts of the original building were left standing. Decades of neglect and a short time as a workhouse finally saw the castle descend to the wrecked state of the 1930s.

Restoring what they could of the castle, the couple concentrated on creating the famous **Gardens** that, today, bring so much pleasure to visitors. Laid out in the Elizabethan style, there are a series of formal gardens, or 'rooms', that each have a different theme such as the White Garden where only silver leafed, white flowering plants are grown. Away from this formality there are also woodland and lakeside walks and the estate's oast house is home to an interesting exhibition.

BENENDEN

3 miles SE of Cranbrook on the B2086

This attractive village is strung out along a ridge. It is famous for its girls' public school, also called **Benenden**, that is housed in a mock Elizabethan house dating from 1859 to the west of the village centre. However, Benenden village itself is also famous - for cricket - that is played on most summer evenings on the village's large green.

ROLVENDEN

5 miles SE of Cranbrook on the A28

Surrounded by orchards and hop fields, this large village stands on the eastern fringe of the Weald and on the edge of the Isle of Oxney. A place of white weather-boarded and tile hung houses, the village is home to the **CM Booth Collection of Historic Vehicles**, that is chiefly centred on a unique collection of Morgan three-wheeled cars that date from 1913 to 1935. However, there is much more to discover at this fascinating museum, such as a 1904 Humber Tricar, numerous bicycles and motorcycles, toy and model cars and a whole host of other motorcar related memorabilia.

Close to the village lies **Great Maytham Hall** a charming country house, renovated by Sir Edwin Lutyens, which stands in glorious grounds. At the turn of the 20th century, the novelist Frances Hodgson Burnett, who spent most of her life in America, leased the house. While staying here, she fell in love with the particularly beautiful walled kitchen garden that was to inspire her to write the classic children's book *The Secret Garden*. The garden is open to the public on a limited basis.

SANDHURST

5 miles S of Cranbrook on the A268

Visitors coming here expecting to find the Royal Military Academy will be disappointed as this is located at Sandhurst, Berkshire. However, Sandhurst, Kent, is an attractive place that deserves a visit in its own right. Set in reasonably hilly terrain this feature of the countryside gave rise to the name of the local inn, The Missing Link, which refers to the practice of linking extra horses to the wagons in order to pull heavy loads up the hill.

INGRID NILSON

By appointment only
Newenden, Kent TN18 5PL
Tel: 01797 252030 e-mail: ingrid@ingridnilson.com
Fax: 01797 252030 website: www.ingridnilson.com

Ingrid Nilson specialises in decorative antique prints from the 17th and 18th centuries. She has over 17 years of experience in the British antiques trade and a BA degree in history of art from Uppsala University in Sweden. She is a member of LAPADA, which is open only to those who meet the Association's stringent requirements as to experience, quality of stock and knowledge of their subject. This enables

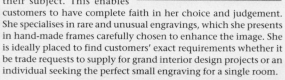

customers to have complete faith in her choice and judgement. She specialises in rare and unusual engravings, which she presents in hand-made frames carefully chosen to enhance the image. She is ideally placed to find customers' exact requirements whether it be trade requests to supply for grand interior design projects or an individual seeking the perfect small engraving for a single room.

Framed antique prints are an ideal complement to any décor, hung individually or in groups. Maps make excellent gifts since they can be related to people's backgrounds or interests. Other subjects include flowers and animals, originally used as illustrations for scientific works, household goods which figured in catalogues or houses, castles and exotic geographic locations. Ingrid will search out a particular subject for customers if she doesn't have it in stock.

2 EAST SUSSEX

East Sussex was the location of some of the most famous events in the history of England. The coastal village of Pevensey was the landing place of William, Duke of Normandy and his army in 1066 and as every school child knows, William proceeded to defeat Harold near Hastings and claim the crown of England. Hastings and Battle, the town that grew up around the site of the battlefield, have museums and exhibitions on these momentous historical events. The victorious Normans soon set about building castles and fortifications from which to defend their new territory, along with religious buildings and the area is still rich in Norman architecture.

South Downs, East Sussex

The south coast was always susceptible to invasion and, in the days before the Royal Navy, the confederation of Cinque Ports was established to provide a fleet of ships to defend the coast. Many Sussex towns, now some distance from the sea, were part of the confederation. The silting up of the harbours has changed the landscape of the East Sussex coast considerably in the last 1,000 years.

Nowadays the coast is the preserve of holiday makers, taking advantage of the moderate climate and sea air. The thriving resorts of Brighton and

Hastings Town

Eastbourne began life as quiet fishing villages but developed rapidly at the beginning of the 19th century. Brighton is best known for its exotic Royal Pavilion, designed by John Nash for the Prince Regent, in magnificent Indian style, with minarets and domes. Eastbourne, by contrast, was carefully planned and laid out in genteel style, by William Cavendish, the 7th Duke of Devonshire, close to the chalk cliffs of Beachy Head. St Leonards and Bexhill are quieter resorts and perhaps the most picturesque is Rye, with its many medieval buildings.

Away from the coast, on the high ridges of the Weald, is the largest area in southeast England that has never been ploughed and put to agricultural use. Ashdown Forest was a royal hunting ground and its thriving population of deer made it a favourite sporting place. The network of tracks across the forest goes back to prehistoric times, the Romans built a road straight across it and the rights of commoners to gather wood for fuel, cut peat and graze cattle, were well established by Norman times. Although much of the woodland has been lost as fuel and for shipbuilding over the centuries, the remaining forest is protected as an Area of Outstanding Natural Beauty and Site of Special

Eastbourne

Scientific Interest. The surrounding area is characterised by small towns and villages of weather boarded cottages, traditional hall houses and unspoilt farmsteads.

Many artists and writers of the 19th and 20th centuries chose to live here. A.A. Milne set the *Winnie the Pooh* stories in Ashdown Forest and surrounding area. Virginia Woolf and her husband Leonard lived at Monk's House, Rodmell, whilst her sister, Vanessa Bell, was at nearby Charleston Farmhouse, in Selmeston. The Elms at Rottingdean was the home of Rudyard Kipling until 1902, when he moved to Burwash, and the village of Ditchling was home to several artists and crafts people at the centre of the Arts and Crafts Movement.

LOCATOR MAP

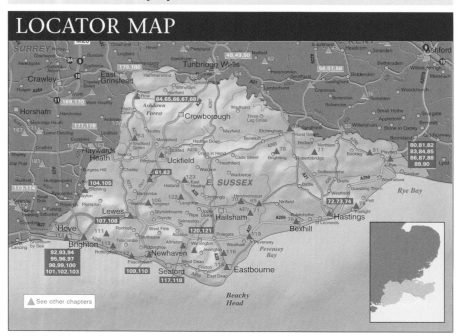

Advertisers and Places of Interest

ASHDOWN FOREST AND THE SUSSEX WEALD

This region of East Sussex is centred around the ancient Ashdown Forest, a royal hunting ground that also provided the fuel for the area's iron industry. Much of the actual woodland has been lost both as fuel and for shipbuilding and the area is characterised by small towns and villages of weather-boarded cottages, traditional hall houses and unspoilt farms. There is evidence in ancient tracks that the area has been inhabited since prehistoric times, but the exciting discovery of a supposedly 150,000 year old skull in 1912 at the village of Piltdown, was proved some 40 years later to be a clever hoax.

Over the centuries there have been many fine houses and castles in the area and, in particular, there is the still impressive Herstmonceux Castle. Home of the Royal Observatory from 1948 until the 1980s, this magnificent medieval brick fortress, which also provided comfortable living accommodation for its inhabitants, is set in the most glorious gardens and parkland.

Other houses here have a more personal appeal and one, Bateman's at Burwash, was the home of Rudyard Kipling from 1902 until his death in 1936. A quiet place in a secluded position, the house has been left as it was when Kipling died and is full of his personal possessions. Ashdown Forest and Hartfield are linked with another 20th century novelist - A.A. Milne. He lived close by and wrote the *Winnie the Pooh* stories, set in the forest and surrounding area, for his son Christopher Robin.

CROWBOROUGH

This Wealden town, on the eastern edge of Ashdown Forest, is, at over 750 feet above sea level, one of the highest towns in Sussex. Before the arrival of the railways, in the 1860s, this was a small community of iron smelters and brigands centred around the parish church and vicarage which dates from the 18th century. At the heart of the town is a triangular green, where can be found the grey stone classical church dating from 1744, although it was unfortunately extended and remodelled in the late 18th century.

However, the railways put Crowborough within easy reach of London and it was gradually transformed into the flourishing residential town it is today. Though a relatively uneventful place, its convenient location meant that the town attracted a number of well-known late 19th century writers including Sir Arthur Conan Doyle, creator of the famous Sherlock Holmes.

South Downs, East Sussex

On the highest place in Crowborough stands **Beacon House**, one of the town's oldest buildings, built in 1838.

AROUND CROWBOROUGH

GROOMBRIDGE
4 miles N of Crowborough on the B2110

This unspoilt village straddles the county border with Kent and, whilst the Sussex part of the village, which grew up around the railway station has little to offer, the Kent side is particularly charming. The name is said to be derived from the Saxon 'Gromen', meaning man as in bridegroom. Centred around a triangular green, there are attractive 15th and 16th century estate cottages and a superb manor house **Groombridge Place**, dating from the 17th century. However, the site on which the foundations were laid is much older and there is some evidence that there was first a Saxon then a Norman castle here. Built by Charles Packer, the Clerk of the Privy Seal, who accompanied Charles I on his unsuccessful journey to Spain to ask for the Infanta's hand in marriage, Groombridge Place is a splendid red brick house surrounded by a moat. Set within beautiful terraced gardens, there is a small museum dedicated to Conan Doyle who was a frequent visitor to the house and the surrounding woodland, dubbed the Enchanted Forest. This is indeed a magical place with a wild wood area, a Celtic Forest, a North American Wood and a Jurassic Valley. The gardens and woodlands are open throughout the summer months.

HADLOW DOWN
4 miles SE of Crowborough on the A272

This handsome hamlet is surrounded by winding lanes that weave their way through some of the most glorious Wealden countryside. Just outside Hadlow Down the **Wilderness Wood**, is a living museum of woodland management that does much to maintain the crafts and techniques of woodland management. Visitors can see the woodland being tended in the traditional chestnut coppices and plantations of pine, beech and fir. The wood is then harvested and the timber fashioned, using traditional techniques, into all manner of implements in the centre's workshops. There are also woodland trails, a bluebell walk and an adventure playground for children.

WALDRON
7 miles S of Crowborough off the B2192

The 13th century village **Church of All Saints** has a lovely kingpost roof and, unusually for its age, a very wide aisle and nave the reason for which has never quite been explained.

BUXTED
5 miles SW of Crowborough on the A272

This village has long been dominated by the great house of **Buxted Park**. This Grade II listed building was built along classical lines in 1725. Almost destroyed by fire in 1940, it was restored by architect Basil Ionides. Although altered from its original design, it was sensitively rebuilt using numerous period pieces from other locations. There are doors and chimney pieces by Robert Adam, cabinets and pillars from grand London houses and country mansions and a particularly fine staircase from a house in Old Burlington Street in London. It is now a hotel and the 312 acres of gardens and parkland are open to visitors taking afternoon teas.

In the 19TH century the house was the home of Lord Liverpool and, wishing to give himself more privacy, the noble earl

BLACKBOYS NURSERY

Blackboys, Uckfield, East Sussex TN22 5LS
Tel: 01825 890858 Fax: 01825 890878
e-mail: enquiries@plants4us.co.uk website: www.plants4us.co.uk

Phil and Sue Flagg bought this established nursery in 1997. They have invested in **Blackboys** to increase the range of plants and improve quality and choice. As a horticulture business, their overheads are lower than Garden Centres and so are their prices. Most of the plants are grown by them and they can offer advice with every plant they sell. They stock over 1,000 varieties including alpines, shrubs, fuchsias, pelargoniums, herbs, bedding and basket plants.

THE FAULKNERS

Isfield, East Sussex, TN22 5XG
Tel: 01825 750344 Fax: 01825 750577

Celia Rigby is the owner of this 15th century, grade II listed, former Wealden Hall House set in six acres of gardens with two large ponds a walled garden and herb garden. The superb service matches the surroundings in this 4 diamond, gold award, establishment. The dining room has a refectory table and a large inglenook of wood and stone while the lounge has a wood burning stove and a television. Breakfast at the **Faulkners** includes fresh local produce, free range eggs and home made preserves.

THE LAUGHING FISH

Station Road, Isfield, East Sussex, TN22 5XB
Tel: 01825 750349
e-mail: laughingfish1@aol.com
website: www.laughingfish.org.uk

This excellent hostelry was built as the Station Hotel in the 1870s. Sometime in the 1960s the landlord purchased a glass etching of a Laughing Fish that is still in the front porch window and it is thought the name was changed because of that. The railway station closed in 1969 and lay derelict for years. It was restored in the 1980s and now operates as the Lavender Line, a flourishing steam railway. Andy Brooks and his wife Linda are the warm and friendly owners. **The Laughing Fish** is a real ale pub specialising in some of the great English beers like Greene King IPA, Old Speckled Hen and Ruddles County. These are augmented by a changing list of guest ales. An annual Beer Race has been held here for over 40 years. Every Easter Monday the contestants line up outside the pub with a half pint jug of beer and have to run to the mill and back a round trip of a mile and a half. The winner is the contestant with the most beer still in their glass. They receive a cup and a bottle of champagne.

Food is another important part of the service with Linda doing all the cooking and producing superb English cuisine. Everything is freshly cooked using local produce from the Sunday roast to the special farm sausages and freshly baked local bread. Entertainment is a regular feature with monthly folk and jazz nights, quizzes, darts and bar billiards. It is the headquarters of the local angling society and visitors can purchase permits to fish locally.

decided to move the village further away. The villagers were incensed and refused to move so, reaching a stalemate, Lord Liverpool declined to repair their estate cottages. Eventually the villagers gave way and moved to the rather ordinary village that is now Buxted. However, several buildings have remained in the old location including, at the entrance to the park gates, the half timbered **Hogge House**. Dating back to the 16th century, the house was once the home of Ralph Hogge, who is said to have been the first man to cast guns in England in 1543. The much-restored 13th century parish church also remains in the park's grounds and the Jacobean pulpit was once used by William Wordsworth's brother who was vicar here for a time.

MARESFIELD
5½ miles SW of Crowborough off the A22

Before the turnpikes between London and the south coast were laid through the Weald, this was a remote place. However in the 18th century, its position at a crossroads on the turnpike ensured its development. The tall Georgian Chequers Inn is arguably the village's oldest building and a fine example of a coaching inn. Close by is a white painted iron milestone with 41 and four bells and bows in outline. One of a whole chain of such milestones that stood on the old turnpike road, this is a particularly witty one as it refers to the distance, in miles, from Maresfield to Bow Bells, London.

PILTDOWN
7½ miles SW of Crowborough off the A272

Though the village itself is not well known, its name is famous, particularly in academic circles. In 1912, an ancient skull was discovered by the Lewes solicitor and amateur archaeologist, Charles Dawson, in the grounds of

Barcombe Manor. At the time, archaeologists the world over were looking for a 'missing link' between man and the ape and the skull seemed to fit the bill. It had a human braincase and an ape like jaw. Believed to be about 150,000 years old it was not until the 1950s, and with much-improved scientific dating techniques, that the skull was shown to be a fake. It was, in fact, the braincase of a medieval man who had suffered a bone thickening disease and the jaw of an orang-utan. The perpetrator of the hoax was never discovered. It certainly could have been Dawson himself but various other theories have been put forward including one which points to Sir Arthur Conan Doyle, the author of the Sherlock Holmes stories and a well-known Christian fundamentalist.

Though the skull has been proved a hoax, the village inn, which changed its name to the **Piltdown Man** in 1912, still carries the name and an inn sign with the famous skull on one side and a stone-carrying humanoid on the other.

UCKFIELD
7 miles SW of Crowborough on the B2102

Situated in the woodland of the Weald, on the River Uck, this was once a small village at the intersection of the London to Brighton turnpike road with an ancient pilgrims' way between Canterbury and Winchester. When the stage-coaches arrived a number of coaching inns sprang up. Before this, the village had been a centre of the iron industry thanks to its plentiful supplies of wood and water. However, despite these advantages, Uckfield remained small until the 19th century, when a period of rapid expansion followed the arrival of the railway.

Several of the old coaching inns survived the move from horse-drawn to

THE NATIONAL TRUST SHEFFIELD PARK GARDEN

The National Trust

Sheffield Park, East Sussex, TN22 3QX
Tel: 01825 790231 e-mail: sheffieldpark@nltrust.org.uk
Fax: 01825 791264 website: www.nationaltrust.org.uk

This is a magnificent landscaped garden, laid out in the 18th century by 'Capability' Brown and further developed in the early years of the 20th century by its owner, Arthur G. Soames. The centre piece is the original series of four lakes. There are dramatic shows of daffodils and bluebells in spring, and the rhododendrons, azaleas and stream garden are spectacular in early summer. Autumn brings stunning colours from the many rare trees and shrubs. The short walk towards the neo-Gothic Sheffield Park House is bordered by several autumn foliage trees and shrubs including maples, photinias, nyssas and fothergillas.

Even in winter there are spectacular views and many splendid walks, the most spectacular of which, is the Big Tree Walk with its fine specimens of North American Sequoia. The walk goes past oak and beech under planted with hardy hybrid rhododendrons and towards the end of the first lake is a

superb specimen of the rare, Mexican Pinus Montezumae planted in 1910.

At the head of the first and second lakes is a fine specimen of Blue Cedar. The banks of those lakes are broken by rounded clumps of pink, white and crimson rhododendrons. Just past the first bridge the main path goes through groups of deciduous and evergreen azaleas and some fine old lime trees. Beyond the lower bridge is a fine view of a magnificent waterfall and in summer the lake is covered with deep pink and white flowered water lilies. The path continues to a large Copper Beech and a Cedrus Atlantica, where superb views across the first lake take in a landscape full of silver birch, oaks and conifers.

An extended tour of the gardens should include the Aucklandii Walk with its Hydrangea ' Blue Wave', a small specimen of Eucalyptus Gunnii, some wonderful Rhododendron 'Angelo' and several large groups of pink Japanese azaleas. The Conifer Walk although devastated by the storm of 1987 contains many young specimens propagated from the original trees as well as a fine Acer saccharinum. The Gentian Walk, with its two long beds of blue Chinese gentian, leads into the Stream Garden and the Seven Sisters Glade. The former is at its best in the late spring and early summer when its plantings of hostas, astilbes, ferns, Siberian iris, lilies and Asiatic primulas are at their peak. The Giant Lily of the Himalayas is undoubtedly the top attraction here with

its large scented white flowers on stems at least eight feet high. Beyond the Glade, replanted after the storm, is a grove of, superb, autumn-coloured, Tupelo trees that have already reached sixty feet in height.

On the bank of the fourth lake two fine specimens of Dawn Redwood and Swamp Cypress stand in front of clumps of the huge Brazilian Gunnera with its six-foot wide leaves. The Cascade Bridge, which crosses the cascade between the third and four lakes is haunted, according to legend, by a headless woman, who vanishes when approached.

steam-powered travel and, amongst the Victorian buildings, lies **Bridge Cottage**, a very fine example of a 15th century hall house.

SHEFFIELD GREEN

8 miles SW of Crowborough on the A275

The village takes its name from the manor house, a Tudor building that was remodelled in the 1770s by James Wyatt for John Baker Holroyd, MP, the 1st Earl of Sheffield. At the same time as creating his mansion, **Sheffield Park**, the earl had Capability Brown and Humphrey Repton landscape the gardens (see panel opposite). During his time here, the earl's great friend, Edward Gibbon, came to stay during the last months of his life, and it was while here that he wrote much of his epic *Decline and Fall of the Roman Empire* in the library.

A later inhabitant, the 3rd Earl of Sheffield, was a keen cricketer and was the first to organise the test tours between England and Australia. At the same time he began a tradition that the visiting team came to Sheffield Park to play their first match against the Earl of Sheffield's XI. Though the house remains in private hands, the splendid gardens belong to the National Trust and are open to the public. From the mass of

daffodils and bluebells in spring to the blaze of colour from the rare trees and shrubs in autumn there is always plenty to look at and enjoy.

Not far from the house, in the village, lies the **Sheffield Arms**, a coaching inn, built by the 1st Earl in the 18th century. Local stories told of a cave behind the inn with an underground passageway to a nearby farmhouse that was used by smugglers and, in order to test out the truth of the tales, three ducks were shut into the cave. After ten days, one of the ducks reappeared - in the cellars of the farmhouse.

The village is also the terminus of the **Bluebell Railway** and the cricketing earl would surely have been pleased with the railway's success today as he was on the board of the Lewes and East Grinstead Railway that originally built the line. The other terminus can be found near East Grinstead.

CHAILEY

9 miles SW of Crowborough on the A275

This large and scattered parish comprises three villages: North Chailey, Chailey and South Common. Though small, Chailey has some impressive old buildings including the 13th century parish church and a moated rectory. To the north, lies **Chailey Common**, a nature reserve covering some 450 acres of wet and dry heathland where also can be found **Chailey Windmill**. Unlike many Sussex windmills, Chailey's splendid smock mill was saved from ruin just in time.

Overlooking the common is **Chailey Heritage**, which was founded in 1903 as a home for boys with tuberculosis from the East

Sheffield Park Gardens

ASHDOWN FOREST LLAMA PARK

Wych Cross, Forest Row, East Sussex, RH18 5JN
Tel: 01825 712040 Fax: 01825 713698
e-mail: info@llamapark.co.uk website: www.llamapark.co.uk

This is one of the leading llama breeding centres in the country and offers visitors the opportunity to discover for themselves all about these fascinating animals. The centre was created round three 18th century Sussex barns and a brand new visitor centre. Running now for over five years, **Ashdown Forest Llama Park** is one of the top visitor attractions in Sussex. A leisurely stroll around the farm walk offers visitors stunning views over Ashdown Forest and the chance to encounter a whole host of llama and alpacas, all of them captivating and engaging characters.

One of the barns in the complex has been converted to a museum where the story is told of how llamas and alpacas were first domesticated in South America over 5,000 years ago. There is also a shop containing a wonderful array of South American craft goods, alpaca knitwear and rugs. Look out for the designer alpaca knitwear from Spirit of the Andes and the Alpaca Collection as well as ethnic South American designs in natural colours. There is a superb range of toys and novelties and of course most of the items in the shop make lovely gifts. The adventure playground is a huge hit with children of all ages and they are happy to play there while their parents enjoy a pot of tea or coffee and a snack at one of the outdoor tables or lunch inside in the fully licensed coffee shop and patio. Even if the weather is bad this is a great place to come as many of the animals are housed in buildings close to the entrance.

TABLEHURST FARM

Forest Row, East Sussex, RH18 5DP Tel: 01342 823173
Fax: 01342 824873 e-mail: Tablehurst_Farm@talk21.com

The land here has been farmed organically for over thirty years. No artificial fertilisers are used and crop rotation, compost manure and homeopathic preparations are what sustain the venture year after year from its own resources. It's run as a co-operative owned by the village and they positively welcome people to come and see how they operate. Produce is sold from the on-site farm shop where Barry the Butcher dispenses beef from the closed herd of Sussex cattle. He also sells pork, lamb and chicken and makes renowned sausages and burgers. As well as meat produce there is a large range of organic eggs, vegetables, flour milled on the farm and honey.

PLAW HATCH FARM LTD

Sharpthorne, West Sussex, RH19 4JL Tel: 01342 810652

Now part of the Tablehurst and Plaw Hatch Community Farm this was previously part of a charitable trust set up in 1981 to foster ecologically and economically sound agriculture. It's a mixed bio-dynamic farm of 210 acres supporting a herd of horned dairy cattle, some pigs, a flock of chickens, cereal and vegetable enterprise. Like Tablehurst no artificial fertilisers or chemical are applied here. Dairy produce is the mainstay, with much of the milk being processed to yoghurt and cheese, the remainder being sold in the shop or delivered locally. The co-op produces an excellent selection of cheeses ranging from soft to hard and the organic farm shop also sells cream, ice cream, eggs, vegetables, poultry and honey and stocks organic fruit, locally produced organic bread and organic lamb.

End of London. As treatments for the now less prevalent disease have progressed, the home has become a learning centre for children with disabilities and has a world-wide reputation.

NEWICK

9 miles SW of Crowborough on the A272

The village is centred around its large green on which stands an unusual long-handled pump, erected to mark Queen Victoria's Diamond Jubilee in 1897. The actor, Dirk Bogarde, was brought up in the area and was given his first big acting part in an amateur production here in the 1930s.

NUTLEY

5 miles SW of Crowborough on the A22

The village is home to **Nutley Windmill**, Sussex's oldest working windmill. It was restored in 1968 by a group of enthusiasts after it had stood unused and neglected from the turn of the century.

ASHDOWN FOREST

3 miles W of Crowborough on the B2026

This ancient tract of sandy heathland and woodland on the high ridges of the Weald is the largest area in southeast England that has never been ploughed and put to agricultural use. The original meaning of 'forest' was as a royal hunting ground and this is exactly what Ashdown Forest was. The earliest record dates from 1268 and its thriving population of deer made it a favourite sporting place. However, the area was used long before this and, in prehistoric times, there was a network of tracks across the forest. Later, the Romans built a road straight across it and, by the time of the Norman invasion, the rights of the commoners living on its fringes, to gather wood for fuel, cut peat and graze cattle, were well established.

During medieval times it was a great place for sport and a 'pale', or ditch, was dug around it to maintain the deer within its confines. A famous sporting owner was John of Gaunt, the Duke of Lancaster and during his ownership the forest became known as Lancaster Great Park. Henry VIII and James I were also frequent visitors. By the end of the 15th century much of the woodland had gone as fuel for the area's iron industry, during the Civil War the forest was neglected and by 1657 no deer remained.

Today, the forest is designated an Area of Outstanding Natural Beauty, a Site of Special Scientific Interest and a Special Protection Area for birds. It is a place of recreation with many picnic areas and scenic viewpoints and open access for walking throughout. The deer have returned and the clumps of Scotch pines that make prominent landmarks on the higher points of the forest were planted in the 19th century.

WYCH CROSS

6 miles W of Crowborough on the A275

Marking the western limit of Ashdown Forest, local folklore has it that the village's name is derived from a cross that was erected on the spot where the body of Richard de Wyche, Bishop of Chichester, rested overnight on the journey from Kent to its burial place in Chichester during the 13th century.

FOREST ROW

6 miles NW of Crowborough on the A22

This hillside village in Ashdown Forest is a popular place with walkers and also a good starting point for wonderful forest drives. The village was founded in the late Middle Ages when the forest was still extremely dense in places and provided a thick swathe of vegetation between the Thames valley and the south coast.

Unusually many of the village's

SEASONS

10/11 Hartfield Road, Forest Row,
East Sussex RH18 5DN
Tel: 01342 824673 Fax: 01342 826119

John Walden who has managed this shop for over
20 years is a committed green vegetarian. Established
in 1971 the business consists of two shops and is run
as a community business working closely with Old
Plaw Hatch and Tablehurst, two local organic farms.
Both shops carry a full range of wholefoods including dairy produce, fresh fruit and vegetables, a
range of natural cosmetics, wooden toys and books.

FALCON ANTIQUES

Lower Square, Lewes Road, Forest Row, East Sussex, RH18 5ES
Tel: 01342 826224 Fax: 01342 826224
e-mail: fallont@tinyworld.co.uk

Terence Fallon OBE, the friendly, knowledgeable, owner has dealt
in antiques over a number of years. He moved from his previous
shop in Brasted to open this gallery in 1999 with the object of
providing furniture and objets d'art from the 17th - 19th centuries.
Although Falcon Antiques specialises in these fields, it also stocks
original paintings in watercolour and oil, fine English and continental porcelain, silverware and
Victorian jewellery. Visitors are welcome to browse his three, well stocked, showrooms.

buildings are older than the parish
church, which only dates from 1836. The
village is also the proud owner of a stone
wall which commemorates a visit made
by President John F. Kennedy.

HAMMERWOOD

7 miles NW of Crowborough off the A264

Here lies, down a potholed lane,
Hammerwood Park, a splendid mansion
that was built in 1792 by Benjamin
Latrobe, the architect of the Capitol and
the White House in Washington DC.
The house has had a chequered history.
Divided into flats in the 1960s, it was
bought by the rock group Led Zeppelin
in the 1970s and was rescued from ruin
in the 1980s. Extensive and meticulous
restoration work has been undertaken by
the present owner David Pinnegar and
his family, with help from volunteers and
some support from English Heritage. The
dining room remains derelict and there is

still a massive amount of work to be
done inside and out. The house is open
on a limited basis during the summer.

HARTFIELD

4 miles NW of Crowborough on the B2026

An old hunting settlement on the edge of
the Ashdown Forest, which takes its
name from the adult male red deer, or
hart, the village is very closely associated
with A.A.Milne and *Winnie the Pooh*.
Milne lived at Cotchford Farm, just
outside Hartfield and he set his famous
books, which he wrote in the 1920s, in
the forest. Designed to entertain his son,
Christopher Robin, the books have been
delighting children ever since and, with
the help of illustrations by E.H.Shepard,
the landscape around Hartfield has been
brought to millions around the world.

   In the village lies the 300 year-old
sweet shop to which Christopher Robin
was taken each week by his nanny. Now

called **Pooh Corner**, this is a special place to visit for both children and those who remember the stories from their own childhood. Full of Winnie the Pooh memorabilia, the shop caters for all tastes as long as it involves Winnie. All of the famous Enchanted Places lie within the parish of Hartfield. **Poohsticks Bridge**, a timber bridge spanning a small tributary of the River Medway, was fully restored in 1979.

WITHYHAM

3½ miles NW of Crowborough on the B2110

This small village, with its church and pub, was the home of the Sackville family from around 1200. The original village church was struck by lightning in 1663. The lightning was said to have come in through the steeple, melted the bells and left through the chancel, tearing apart monuments on its route. Completely rebuilt following the destruction, the church incorporates some original 14th century features including the west tower. The Sackville Chapel was commissioned in 1677 to house a memorial to Thomas Sackville, who had died aged 13. The marble memorial incorporates life size figures of the boy

and his parents sensitively rendered. There is also a memorial to Vita Sackville-West, the poet and owner of Sissinghurst Castle in Kent who died in 1962.

BURWASH

Standing on a hill, which is surrounded by land that is marsh for part of the year, Burwash is an exceptionally pretty village, whose High Street is lined with delightful 17th and 18th century timber framed and weather-boarded cottages. Among the buildings found here is **Rampyndene**, a handsome timber framed house with a sweeping roof that was built in 1699 by a wealthy local timber merchant. Burwash was, between the 15th and 17th centuries, a major centre of the Wealden iron industry and this brought much prosperity to the village.

However, it is not the village that brings most people to Burwash, though it certainly deserves attention, but a house just outside. In 1902, Rudyard Kipling moved from Rottingdean to **Bateman's** to combat the growing problem of over-enthusiastic sightseers. Located down a steep and narrow lane, the Jacobean

Bateman's, Burwash

house was originally built in 1634 for a prosperous local ironmaster. With its surrounding 33 acres of beautiful grounds, landscaped by Kipling and his wife, it proved the perfect retreat.

Kipling and his wife lived here until their deaths - he in 1936 and she just three years later - and during his time here the author wrote many of the famous works including *Puck of Pook's Corner*, the poem *If* and

(Continued page 138)

WALK 3

Burwash and Bateman's

Start	Burwash
Distance	5 miles (8km)
Approximate time	2½ hours
Parking	Burwash – car park next to Bear Inn
Refreshments	Pubs and cafés at Burwash, National Trust tearoom at Bateman's
Ordnance Survey maps	Landranger 199 (Eastbourne & Hastings), Explorer 136 (The Weald)

This walk features views over unspoilt countryside, and much of the return half is over National Trust land surrounding Rudyard Kipling's former home, Bateman's. A bridleway may be muddy.

Burwash is a most attractive village with some handsome houses and a church that retains its Norman tower. Turn right out of the car park onto the village street and then left just after the post office down the lane leading to the Rose and Crown pub and the fire station. Take the track (Ham Lane) between the fire station and a playing-field. After ½ mile (800m), just before an iron gate, turn left to an adjacent stile. Climb this and a second stile and follow an arrow across the meadow, descending to a stile at the back of barns into woodland. The clearly defined path winds through trees to another meadow. Bear right to a stile in the bottom left corner of this field, but do not climb this. Instead turn left to follow the stream and reach an iron gate in the corner of the field. Walk down the long, narrow meadow that follows and go through another iron gate at the end of this, on the right **Ⓐ**. Cross the stream and climb towards Mottynsden Farm, making for the iron gate to the right of the oast house. Go through this and pass between the farmhouse and the manor to find a driveway leading right towards a modern

house. Where the driveway curves right, continue ahead on a path that ascends the bank, passes the garage and enters an orchard. Turn right and shortly turn left at the end of the orchard. Climb by the hedgerow, turning left at the top of the orchard, to find an opening **Ⓑ**, which leads onto a farm track. Turn left, passing a plaque to Flight Lieutenant R.F. Rimmer, killed in action here during the Battle of Britain.

When the track meets a lane, turn left and pass Holton Farm before turning right onto a track at the side of the farm. Although muddy at times the bridleway is more often grassy and encroached by bracken and brambles. Glimpses of open countryside are the foretaste of a splendid panorama of pastoral landscape which will be enjoyed at the top of the hill. After this, the path descends gently through woodland to reach Woodlands Farm.

The bridleway passes to the right of the farm, and then on the left the bridleway joins a sunken track. This climbs and becomes narrow and overgrown. When the bridleway meets a farm track, bear left, but leave this before the top of the hill by turning left **C** to follow a further section of ancient enclosed trackway, to reach the A265 opposite Weald House and the Burwash Weald village sign.

Turn right and walk a short distance along the main road, turning left just beyond Weald House, past concrete posts, to join the drive to Burnt House Farm. Keep straight on at the end of the drive to pass between the houses (the one on the right incorporates oast houses), making for a metal gate leading into a paddock. Go through the gate and over a stile on the left to descend to another gateway. Pass through the gateway **D** and turn left, following the yellow arrow and an iron fence. Keep to the right of this fence to a gate, pass through and continue along the fence until it ends at a stile and gateway. Cross the next field to a stile, keeping close to the hedge on the right and then walk by a few trees (pond on the right) to cross another field. Half-way across, Bateman's comes into view ahead.

The path emerges onto an asphalted drive that becomes a farm track as its heads towards a barn. The track ends at a stile, where you bear right, and walk for a short distance, keeping the hedge on the right, to reach another stile. Turn right to cross the stream and then bear left to cross the

next, large field, making for the iron railings of a bridge in the fringe of trees on the far side. Cross the bridge, turn left and follow the path to a beautiful millpond, where it reaches a lane, and turn left.

The lane passes the north front of Bateman's, a fine 17th century building. Rudyard Kipling lived here until his death in 1936. At the front of the house, turn right **E** and after ¼ mile (400m) look for a stile on the left. Go over this and follow a line of old oaks to the right. Skirt the right side of a wood and from its corner go across the meadow to an old-fashioned curved stile on the far side. From here the path climbs towards Burwash. It follows the left-hand field edge, then directly crosses a field to a bridge by an oak tree. After this bear left and keep the hedge on the left until a stile is reached. Cross this to a short path back to the car park. ●

the Sussex poems. Now in the hands of the National Trust the rooms of the house have been left as they were when the Kiplings lived here, and among the personal items on display is a watercolour of Rudyard Lake in Staffordshire, the place where his parents met and which they nostalgically remembered at the time of their son's birth out in Bombay. Also here are a series of terracotta plaques that were designed by Kipling's father, Lockwood Kipling, and used to illustrate his novel *Kim*. Lockwood was an architectural sculptor and went to India as the principal of an art school; he later became the curator of Lahore Museum.

Whilst here the Kipling's only son, John, was killed on active duty during World War I at Loos, France in 1915. There is a tablet to the 18 year-old in the village church.

AROUND BURWASH

THREE LEG CROSS
4 miles N of Burwash off the B2099

In 1975, the Southern Water Authority dammed the River Bewl to create **Bewl Bridge Reservoir**, the largest area of inland water in the southeast of England (see panel on page 116). A great many buildings were lost under the water but one, the 15th century **Dunsters Mill**, was taken down, brick by brick, before the waters rose and placed above the high water level. Another couple of timber framed farm buildings in the valley were also uprooted and sent to the Weald and Downland Museum at Singleton.

More than just a reservoir, the land around Bewl Bridge is a Country Park and has much to offer including lakeside walks, trout fishing, pleasure boat trips and glorious countryside.

TICEHURST
3½ N of Burwash on the B2099

This ancient village is filled with attractive tile hung and white weather-boarded buildings that are so characteristic of the settlements along the Sussex and Kent border. Among the particularly noteworthy buildings here are **Furze House**, a former workhouse, and **Whatman's**, an old carpenter's cottage with strangely curving walls. The village is also home to **Pashley Manor Gardens**, which surround a Grade I listed timber frame house, which dates from 1550. With waterfalls, ponds and a moat, these romantic gardens are typically English with numerous varieties of shrub roses, hydrangea and peonies adding colour and lushness at every corner. Less formally there is a woodland area and a chain of ponds that are surrounded by rhododendrons, azaleas and climbing roses. The gardens and house are privately owned but the gardens are open to the public throughout the summer.

ETCHINGHAM
2 miles NE of Burwash on the A265

This scattered settlement, found in the broad lush valley of the River Rother, was home, in the Middle Ages, to the fortified manor of the de Echyngham family. Built to protect a crossing point on the River Rother, the house, which stood where the station now stands, has long gone. Just outside the village lies **Haremere Hall**, an impressive Jacobean manor house, which is now available as a holiday rental.

BRIGHTLING
2½ miles S of Burwash off the B2096

The character of this tiny hillside village is completely overshadowed by the character of one of its former residents.

It is certainly not unkind to say that the Georgian eccentric, 'Mad' Jack Fuller, was larger than life since he weighed some 22 stones and was affectionately referred to as the 'Hippopotamus'. A local ironmaster, squire and generous philanthropist, 'Mad' Jack, who sat as an MP for East Sussex between 1801 and 1812, was elected only after a campaign that had cost him and his supporters a massive £50,000. Fuller was one of the first people to recognise the talents of a young painter, J.M.W. Turner, and he was also responsible for saving Bodiam Castle from ruin.

However, it is for his series of imaginative follies that this colourful character is best remembered. He commissioned many of the buildings to provide work for his foundry employees during the decline of the iron industry and among those that remain today are Brightling Observatory, now a private house, a Rotunda Temple on his estate and the **Brightling Needle**. The 40 foot stone obelisk was built on a rise to the north of the village which is itself, 650 feet above sea level.

One of Fuller's more eccentric buildings was the result of a wager. Having bet with a friend on the number of spires that were visible from this home, Brightling Park, Fuller arrived back to find that, in fact, the steeple of Dallington church was not visible. In order to win the bet, Fuller quickly ordered his men to erect a 35 foot mock spire in a meadow on a direct line with Dallington and the monument is affectionately referred to as the **Sugar Loaf**. Perhaps, though Fuller's greatest structure is, in fact, his **Mausoleum**, a 25 foot pyramid, which he built in the parish churchyard some 24 years before his death. The story went around that Fuller was buried inside in a sitting position, wearing a top hat and holding a bottle of claret. However, despite the

The Chestnut Tree Restaurant

Boreham Street, East Sussex, BN27 4SF
Tel: 01323 833651
e-mail: thechestrest@aol.com

In the lovely village of Boreham Street on the A271 between Herstmonceux and Ninfield, this splendid restaurant is in the 15th century home of Tim and Julie Pain. The **Chestnut Tree** is a Wealden hall house, built in 1463 from local timber, mud and horsehair and hand made nails. For five centuries it was called 'Wilshams' but this was changed in 1948, when a horse chestnut towered over the house. The tree had to be felled in 1965 but its successor had been planted in the back garden. Over the centuries it has been home to a succession of yeomen farmers, a weaver, surgeon, mercer, collar maker, innkeeper, five butchers and since 1948, five restaurateurs.

All the food served here is prepared and cooked on the premises. Tim and Julie specialise in old fashioned, high quality, home cooked, seasonal English food. Many of their recipes are based on medieval cooking, adapted for modern tastes. All the ingredients will have been grown, caught, shot, fished, farmed, smoked or made in East Sussex. They use free range eggs from their own hens, cream from Northiam, cheese from Stonegate and Golden Cross. The fish comes fresh from Hastings, meat from Robertsbridge, fruit from Hooe and game from Brightling. A herd of wild boar has gradually re-established itself in the woods around Beckley and Peasmarsh. Meat from one of those, marinaded in cider is slowly stewed with sage, prunes, mushrooms and onion to produce one of the most original dishes on the menu. The restaurant has become a showcase for local artistic talent. High quality paintings adorn the walls and a selection of glassware is displayed on the windowsills. All of the art work is for sale.

appropriateness of this image of his life, the parish church quashed the idea by stating that he was buried in the normal, horizontal pose.

HERSTMONCEUX

8 miles S of Burwash on the A271

The village is famous as being the home of **Herstmonceux Castle**, which was built on the site of an early Norman manor house in 1440 by Sir Roger Fiennes. A remarkable building on two counts, it was one of the first large scale buildings in the country to be built of brick and it was also one of the first castles to combine the need for security with the comforts of the residents. As the castle was built on a lake there was added protection, and the impressive gatehouse, with its murder holes and arrow slits, presented an aggressive front to any would-be attackers.

Later, the castle passed into the hands of the Hare family, who presided over a

long period of decline for Herstmonceux, which culminated in most of the interior being stripped to provide building materials for another house in 1777. The castle sadly lay semi-derelict for 150 years before a major programme of restoration was undertaken in the 1930s under the supervision of a Lewes architect, W.H. Godfrey. His careful and inspired work saw the turrets and battlements restored to their former glory and, today, the castle is as pristine as it was when first built in its delicious romantic setting. There are guided tours of the castle on a limited basis. **Herstmonceux Castle Garden**, the 500 acres of grounds around the splendid moated castle are open for most the summer. Along with parkland and woodland there is an interesting Elizabethan garden.

In 1948, the Royal Observatory at Greenwich was looking for somewhere to move to away from the glow of the street lights of London. The Royal Observatory

The Truggery

Coopers Croft, Herstmonceux, Hailsham,
East Sussex, BN27 1QL
Tel: 01323 832314 Fax: 01323 832314
e-mail: sarah@truggery.fsnet.co.uk
website: www.truggery.co.uk

The traditional willow and chestnut baskets or trugs, crafted and sold at **The Truggery** are ideal for a wide variety of uses. Deriving from the Anglo-Saxon word 'trog', meaning a wooden vessel or boat shaped article, trugs are renowned for their strength, durability and beauty. After years of living away from her home area, Sarah Page returned to East Sussex and bought the house and business. Three generations of trug makers have worked here since it was established in 1899 and it is one of the few remaining trug makers in the country.

While Sarah runs the shop and business, maintains the website and deals with mail order customers, trug maker, Tim Franks is the sole craftsman in the workshop. He produces a vast range of Sussex trugs constructed for a wide variety of uses. From the smallish No 2 for use by amateur gardeners to the huge size No 8 used by celebrity gardener, Alan Titchmarsh and HRH Prince Charles, Tim has a size and design to suit everybody. Trugs can't be mass produced so each one is lovingly prepared by hand. The handle and rim are cut from sweet chestnut that is then steamed to make it easy to bend to shape. Then willow boards are shaped and nailed into place and finally feet are added. Many of the techniques are similar to those employed by coopers in the manufacture of barrels. A trug will last a lifetime and can easily be repaired, another service offered at the Truggery. The shop also sells English willow basket ware and a selection of local crafts. Visitors can also view the workshop in operation during the week.

WARTLING PLACE

Wartling, Herstmonceux, East Sussex, BN27 1RY
Tel: 01323 832590 Fax: 01323 831558
e-mail: accom@wartlingplace.prestel.co.uk
website: www.bestbandb.net

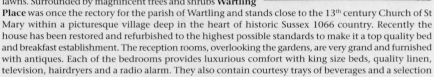

This Grade II listed Georgian country house is set in three acres of delightfully secluded mature gardens with formal lawns. Surrounded by magnificent trees and shrubs **Wartling Place** was once the rectory for the parish of Wartling and stands close to the 13th century Church of St Mary within a picturesque village deep in the heart of historic Sussex 1066 country. Recently the house has been restored and refurbished to the highest possible standards to make it a top quality bed and breakfast establishment. The reception rooms, overlooking the gardens, are very grand and furnished with antiques. Each of the bedrooms provides luxurious comfort with king size beds, quality linen, television, hairdryers and a radio alarm. They also contain courtesy trays of beverages and a selection of magazines. They are en suite with bath, shower and WC. Two of the rooms contain antique four

poster beds for that special occasion. Additionally there is a two bedroom self-contained lodge cottage in the grounds that can be rented on a weekly basis.

The house is non-smoking throughout and there is ample private parking. Rowena Gittoes, the owner provides her guests with a high standard of personal service in a relaxed and tranquil setting making Wartling Place ideal for those seeking a peaceful country retreat, a splendid base to tour the area and perfect for anyone wanting to experience old world English country living.

moved here and, after 20 careful years of planning and building, they opened the gigantic Isaac Newton telescope in the grounds. One of the five largest in the world it was officially opened in 1967. Although the Royal Observatory has moved on, the castle now has the **Herstmonceux Science Centre**, where, among the domes and telescopes that the astronomers used between the 1950s and the 1980s, visitors can experience the excitement of viewing the heavens. There are also hands on displays and an Astronomy Exhibition which traces the history and work of the world famous Royal Observatory.

WARBLETON

6 miles SW of Burwash off the B2203

Found amongst a series of crisscrossing lanes, the village is little more than its church and a handful of houses. Inside the church is a magnificent galleried pew

dating from the 18th century that has two compartments on a level with the first floor. Whether these were used for checking the church attendance or for dozing off in during a dreary sermon no one is quite sure.

CROSS IN HAND

8 miles W of Burwash on the A267

This intriguingly named settlement lies on a busy road junction that has a post mill standing in the triangle formed by the converging roads. Certainly worth a second glance, the windmill at one time stood five miles away at Uckfield.

CADE STREET

5 miles W of Burwash on the B2096

This hamlet, used as a street market until the early 20th century, is reputed to be the place where the notorious Jack Cade, leader of the Kentish rebellion, was killed in 1450 by the High Sheriff of Kent,

Alexander Iden. A stone memorial marks the spot where he fell and on it is inscribed the moral, 'This is the Success of all Rebels, and this Fortune chanceth ever to Traitors'.

HEATHFIELD
6 miles W of Burwash on the A265

To the east of the town centre lies the large expanse of **Heathfield Park**, once owned by General Sir George Augustus Elliot (later Lord Heathfield), the Governor of Gibraltar and commander of the British garrison that successfully withstood attacks from both France and Spain between 1779 and 1782. Despite the wall surrounding the grounds, **Gibraltar Tower**, a castellated folly erected on his estate in his honour, can be seen.

Heathfield remained a quiet and undistinguished town until the arrival of the Tunbridge Wells to Eastbourne railway in the 19th century and then it grew to become an important market town for the local area.

MAYFIELD
6 miles NW of Burwash off the A267

This ancient settlement possesses one of the finest main streets in East Sussex with a number of fine 15th to 17th century houses and it is certainly one of the most picturesque villages in the area. According to local legend, St Dunstan, a skilled blacksmith by trade, stopped here in the 10th century to preach Christianity to the pagan people of this remote Wealden community. Whilst working at his anvil, St Dunstan was confronted by the Devil disguised as a beautiful maiden. When she attempted to seduce the missionary, he spotted that her feet were cloven and grabbed her by the nose with a pair of red-hot tongs. The Devil gave out an almighty scream and beat a hasty retreat. But he soon returned, this time dressed as a traveller in need of new shoes for his horse. Dunstan again saw through the deception and, threatening Satan with his blacksmith's tools, forced him to promise never again to enter a house, which had a horseshoe above the door.

St Dunstan went on to become the Archbishop of Canterbury in 959 and, some time later, **Mayfield Palace**, one of the great residences of the medieval Archbishops of Canterbury was built here. Though little remains of the grand palace now, a Roman Catholic Convent School incorporates the surviving buildings. St Dunstan also founded here a simple timber church, replaced by a stone structure in the 13th century. It was rebuilt after a fire in the 14th century and again after a lightning strike in the 17th century. The present day **Church of St Dunstan** is a conglomeration of styles, incorporating a 13th century tower, a Jacobean pulpit, a font dated 1666 and some 17th and 18th century monuments to the Baker family.

WADHURST
5 miles NW of Burwash on the B2099

This was another great centre of the Wealden iron industry in the 17th and 18th centuries and it was also one of the last places in Sussex to hold out against the improved coal fired smelting techniques which had taken root in the north. Though the village **Church of St Peter and St Paul** is not quite built of iron the floor is almost entirely made up of iron tomb slabs, a unique collection which marks the graves of local ironmasters who died here between 1617 and 1772.

The village was dominated by iron and many of Wadhurst's fine buildings date from the industry's heyday, including the large Queen Anne vicarage, on the High Street, built by John Legas, the town's chief ironmaster. In the late 19th century, the village sought fame, when an important prize fight was held here with many of the spectators travelling down from London to this rather obscure venue by train.

THE CINQUE PORTS AND THE EAST SUSSEX COAST

The story of this area of the East Sussex Coast is, of course, that of the events leading up to October 14, 1066. William, Duke of Normandy came here to claim the throne of England and, after defeating Harold a few miles from the town of Hastings, this is exactly what he did. Hastings and Battle, the town that grew up around the abbey that was built on the site of the battlefield, have a concentration of museums and exhibitions on the events of the 11th century. The victorious Normans soon set about building castles and fortifications from which to defend their new territory along with religious buildings. Today this area is still rich in Norman architecture.

The South Coast was susceptible to invasion and, in the days before the Royal Navy, the confederation of Cinque Ports was established to provide a fleet of ships to defend the coast. Many of the towns that were part of the confederation seem unlikely sources of ships today but the silting up of many of the harbours has changed the landscape of the East Sussex coast considerably in the last 1,000 years.

More recently, the coast has been the preserve of

holiday makers taking advantage of a moderate climate and clean sea air. St Leonards was created in the 1820s and went on to become a fashionable resort whilst the small and more modest Bexhill-on-Sea is home to the impressive modern De La Warr Pavilion, constructed from steel in the 1930s.

Perhaps though the most picturesque of the coastal towns here is the ancient town of Rye. Situated on a hill and once a great haunt for smugglers, the changing fortunes of the town have left it with a great number of medieval buildings, which make it a charming place to visit.

HASTINGS

Long before William the Conqueror made his landing on the beaches of nearby Pevensey, Hastings was the principal town of a small Saxon province that straddled the county border between Sussex and Kent. Its name comes from 'Haestingas', a Saxon tribal name, and, during the reign of Edward the Confessor, the town was well known for its sailors and ships. In fact, the town became so important that it even had its

Hastings Town

Hastings Castle

by the movements of the townsfolk preparing to surprise their oppressors, alerted the occupying force to the uprising. As a vengeance on all cockerels, the people of Hastings instituted a game called 'cock in the pot', where sticks were thrown at an earthenware pot containing a bird. Whoever threw the stick that broke the pot was given the cockerel as his prize and the game continued to be played each Shrove Tuesday until the 19th century.

own mint. Earlier, during the 9th century, when the Danes were occupying the town, the crowing of a cockerel, awoken

Following the Battle of Hastings, which actually took place six miles away at Battle, the victorious William returned to

HASTINGS AND ST LEONARDS

Town Hall, Queens Road, Hastings, East Sussex TN34 1QR
Tel: 0800 181066 (ref: 1747)

Invaded by the Normans to establish a stronghold on the British throne; bombed by the Germans for being a suspected submarine base; attacked and inundated by the elements and the ocean; chosen by everyone from the Teletubbies to Lord Attenborough as a location for film and television productions; and enjoyed by thousands of foreign students as a place of study for the summer – Hastings and St Leonards have never had any trouble attracting attention and the same is true today. Three miles of coastal splendour offer wet sand at low tide and fine shingle for bathers and walkers alike. The nearby **Hastings Country Park** is one of the most remarkable expanses of unspoilt cliff top beauty in Britain and **Alexandra Park** is being restored to its original Victorian glory.

Hastings Castle houses the **1066 Story**, a stunning audio-visual account of the Norman invasion. The **West** and **East Hill Cliff Railways** provide spectacular views over the whole town – the former is also an enjoyable way of reaching both the castle and the **Smugglers Adventure**, a unique underground exhibition experience that captures the thrills and wonders of 18th century smuggling. Other key attractions include the impressive **Underwater World**, the **Shipwreck Heritage Centre** and Europe's largest beach-launched fishing fleet. **Hastings Museum and Art Gallery** contains a rich variety of displays including the Dinosaur Gallery and an Indian Palace while the **Carr Taylor Vineyards** provide a rare opportunity to tour their site and taste their wines.

The **White Rock**, **St Mary in the Castle** and the **Stables** are the town's three main theatres and offer a comprehensive programme of entertainment including everyone from Jack Dee and Jools Holland to the Divine Comedy and Mark Lamarr. A popular place with a wealth of visitor attractions, Hastings and St Leonards provide all the ingredients for an excellent British seaside holiday. Free accommodation brochures are available from the Tourism office.

TRINITY WHOLEFOODS

3 Trinity Street, Hastings, East Sussex, TN34 1HG
Tel: 01424 430473

Conveniently situated in the centre of Hastings this splendid workers' co-operative is owned and managed by local people. It was formed 16 years ago to promote the principles of eating wholefoods and to provide quality, fresh, organic produce in a fair and ethical trading environment. The shop is a large, glass-fronted unit with a warm and welcoming atmosphere. Inside the walls are lined with shelf units and chill cabinets, crammed full of all manner of good things. The range is wide and comprehensive and includes produce for those with special dietary requirements such as dairy-free and gluten-free. The non-dairy yoghurts and margarine are particularly popular. Healthcare is also covered by the range of natural remedies.

The co-operative's own bagged, dried fruits, nuts rice and breakfast cereals sit alongside an exceedingly large range of specialist teas and coffees. Organic wines are another speciality with a wide choice. Organic oriental meals are a breeze using ingredients from their selection of tofu, organic,

wholewheat, noodles, coconut milk, creamed coconut and coconut milk powder. **Trinity Wholefoods** is registered with the Soil Association and stocks a magnificent selection of fresh and delicious organic fruits and vegetables. A central display area is devoted in its entirety to a vast selection of environmentally friendly cleaning products and toiletries. Nearby is a selection of books, covering all aspects of healthy eating and living. Members of the highly knowledgeable staff are always on hand and will do their best to answer any questions on organics, wholefoods or alternative living.

Hastings where the Normans began to build their first stone castle in England. Choosing the high ground of West Hill as their site, the massive structure is now in ruins and all that can be seen on the cliff top are the original motte and parts of the curtain wall. However, there are commanding views from here and also the permanent display - **1066 Story at Hastings Castle**. Housed in a medieval siege tent, the exhibition transports visitors back to October 1066, through clever use of audio-visual techniques.

West Hill also contains a system of elaborate underground passages, known as **St Clement's Cave**, where the naturally formed tunnel network has been extended. The caves were leased to Joseph Golding, who spent a great deal of time fashioning the sandstone into sculptures, arcades and galleries and they became one of the town's first commercial sights. Used as air raid

shelters during World War II, the caves are now home to the **Smugglers Adventure**, where visitors are told stories of the town's illegal trade by a grizzly old smuggler known as Hairy Jack. After the Conquest, this already important port became a leading Cinque Port, a role it played until the harbour began to silt up in Elizabethan times. Nevertheless, the fishing industry has managed to survive here and today fishing vessels continue to be hoisted on to the shingle beach by a winch. One of the town's greatest features are the tall wooden huts that are used for drying nets and storing fishing tackle. Dating from the 17th century they are known as net shops or 'deezes'. The old fishermen's church of St Nicholas is now home to the **Fishermen's Museum**, which has, as its centrepiece, *The Enterprise*, one of the last of Hastings' sailing luggers. Also here, amongst the displays of fishing tackle, model boats and historic pictures and photographs, is *The Edward and Mary*, the first locally built boat to have an engine installed. Staying with a maritime theme, the **Shipwreck Heritage Centre** is an award winning museum that is devoted to the history of wrecked ships. Exhibits on display here include a medieval sailing barge sunk on the River Thames in London, the warship, *Anne*, that was beached near Hastings in 1690, and *Primrose*, the last Rye barge. Additional displays concern themselves with modern methods that help eliminate the possibility of a shipwreck, including radar and satellite navigation.

The old part of Hastings consists of a network of narrow streets and alleyways - or **'twittens'** - which lie between West and East Hill. There are two cliff railways, one running up each of the hills. West Hill railway runs underground taking passengers to

Hastings Castle and St Clement's Caves whilst the **East Hill Railway**, the steepest in England, takes passengers to the cliff top and the beginning of **Hastings Country Park.** This 500 acre park is unlike the cliff tops around Eastbourne as the drop here is not sheer but is split by a series of sloping glens over-hung with trees.

The best way to discover the town's many interesting old residential buildings, inns and churches is to take a walk up the High Street and All Saints Street. **St Clement's Church**, in the High Street, has two cannonballs embedded in its tower, one of which was fired from a French warship, while the **Stag Inn**, in All Saints Street, has a concealed entrance to a smugglers' secret passage and a pair of macabre 400 year-old mummified cats.

Occupying the old Town Hall, which was built in 1823, the **Museum of Local**

HASTINGS MARITIME STADE

c/o Stade Managers Office, Hastings Borough Council, 1st Floor, The Fishmarket, Rock-a-Nore Road, Hastings, Sussex, TN34 3DW
Tel: 01424 781377 Fax: 01424 781985
e-mail: tnewcomen@hastings.gov.uk
website: www.hastings.gov.uk

At the heart of the historic town of Hastings is the **Stade**, the shingle beach where the ancient Cinque Port meets the sea. Here is one of Britain's oldest and largest shore based fishing fleets, still using traditional wooden boats. Nearby wet fish shops sell fresh fish. The Net Shops are a series of black wooden huts standing in neat rows. Unique to Britain they were built to store fishing gear-with space at a premium they were built upwards like skyscrapers. A Fisherman's Museum in a former church contains a complete fishing boat. The 29 foot Enterprise is the last Hastings Lugger surviving in its original condition. Built on the Stade in 1912 it worked until 1955. The remains of a much older vessel can be found in the Shipwreck Heritage Centre. It's all that's left of a Roman ship. Also on display is the complete hull of a Victorian river barge and relics from a 1749 Dutch merchant ship whose wreck is visible at St Leonards at low tide. Both museums have free admission.

The sea creatures of the surrounding area can be seen at Underwater World where a dramatic glass tunnel under a huge tank allows visitors to walk under the ocean. Over 30 displays reveal all aspects of the lives of the local marine environment from shrimps to sharks. Built in 1902 the East Cliff Railway is one of the steepest in Britain and the journey to the top gives access to the Country Park and rewarding views of the Stade, Old Town and the coast.

History, is an excellent place to come to for more information on this historic town. Going right back to the Stone Age, and with a considerable section on the Norman Conquest, the museum also covers Hastings' more recent past by including displays on the rise of the Victorian resort, its life as a Napoleonic garrison and its role as a Cinque Port. By contrast, the **Hastings Museum and Art Gallery** covers a wider range of exhibits that also take in the county's ancient crafts. Hastings also contains a variety of attractions that are typical of a traditional seaside resort. The 600 foot long pier was completed in 1872 and had to be repaired after World War II when it was deliberately holed in two places to prevent it being used as a landing stage for Hitler's forces. According to local legend, the Conqueror's Stone at the head of the pier was used by William the Conqueror as a dining table for his first meal on English soil. The town also has its own version of the Bayeux Tapestry, made by the Royal School of Needlework, the **Hastings Embroidery** and completed in 1966, it was exhibited in the centenary year in the specially built Triodome on the pier. It comprises 27 panels covering all the major events of the last 1,000 years. Among the many scenes and events depicted is the gentleman John Logie Baird - the Scottish pioneer of television who carried out many of his early experiments in Hastings. The Triodome has gone but the Hastings Embroidery can still be seen, at least in part, at the **White Rock Theatre**.

AROUND HASTINGS

WESTFIELD
3½ miles N of Hastings on the A28

This modern red brick village, on the edge of Brede Level, has, at its old centre,

weather-boarded cottages and a Saxon church, with a beautiful Norman arch, that has suffered greatly at the hands of Victorians who added the various internal features.

Vineyards in this country are still something of a novelty, but the gentle rolling slopes of the South Downs and the high mineral content of the soil are ideal. At **Carr Taylor Vineyards**, visitors can follow the Vineyard Trail from the vines, to the massive presses which crush two tons of grapes in one load, right through to the bottling plant to see the fascinating process of turning grapes into wine.

BREDE
5 miles N of Hastings on the A28

Situated to the north of the River Brede, this compact village has a long history, shrouded in myth and tales of the supernatural. One particular legend is that of the Brede Giant, based around the 16th century owner of Brede Place, Sir Goddard Oxenbridge. At over seven feet tall he was certainly a giant and, by all accounts, he was a God fearing gentleman of the parish. However, some time after his death, stories spread that he was a child eating monster who was eventually killed by a band of Sussex children who, having got him drunk, sawed him in half - the children of East Sussex holding down one end of him with the children of West Sussex securing the other.

Tombs of the Oxenbridge family can be seen in the small Norman village church as can a wood carving of the Madonna created by Clare Sherida, a cousin of Sir Winston Churchill who died, aged 84, in 1970. A remarkable woman of her time, she travelled to America where she learnt to carve in wood whilst staying for six months on a Red Indian reservation. In the aftermath of the Russian revolution, she journeyed to Moscow and, staying for two months at the Kremlin, she carved busts of both Lenin and Trotsky.

NORTHIAM

9½ miles N of Hastings on the A28

In this large and picturesque village, characteristic white weather-boarded cottages and a number of fine 17th and 18th century buildings overlook the triangular green at its heart. Elizabeth I is known to have dined and rested on this green under a great oak tree on her journey through Kent and Sussex in 1573. Her green high heeled shoes must have been particularly uncomfortable as she took them off here and left them to the villagers, who saved them as a memento of her brief visit. Unfortunately, the vast oak tree, which was said to be over 1,000 years old and was held together by chains and clamps, has died recently and all that remains on the green is its giant stump.

Of the memorable buildings in the village, **Brickwall House** is one of the finest. This imposing 17th century gentleman's residence was the home of the Frewen family, an old local family, who had been living in Northiam since 1573 when the first Frewen came to the village as rector. Well known for its splendid plaster ceilings, there is also a comprehensive series of family portraits which begin in the 17th century. On display in the house are also Elizabeth I's famous green shoes and a sedan chair that belonged to Martha Frewen, who burnt to death in her bedroom in the 1750s. Several members of the family

were strict Puritans and one family named their two sons, Accepted and Thankful. Despite the handicap of these unusual names, Accepted went on to become first the president of Magdalen College, Oxford and then the Archbishop of York, while Thankful is remembered for having donated the communion rails to the church in 1683. The church is also home to an impressive 19th century family mausoleum. Brickwall House, which is so named as it and its grounds are surrounded by a high stone wall, also has some splendid topiary in the **Gardens**, as well as an arboretum and chess garden. Now a private school, the house and grounds are open by appointment only.

Just three miles northwest of Northiam lies **Great Dixter House and Gardens**, one of the finest examples of a late medieval hall house, surrounded by a very special garden. Built in the 1450s, the manor house was purchased, in 1910, by Nathaniel Lloyd, who then employed Edwin Lutyens to renovate and extend the property. He restored the house to its original medieval grandeur, as well as adding suitable domestic quarters for an Edwardian household. The Great Hall, constructed of Wealden oak and moved

Great Dixter House

here from nearby Benenden to be incorporated into the building, is one of the largest surviving timber framed rooms in the country. Open to the public, many of the original rooms have been filled with antique furniture and examples of 18th century needlework.

However, it is the gardens that make Great Dixter so special. The imaginative design was laid out by Lutyens and various new features were added such as the sunken garden, the topiary lawn and the meadow garden. Begun by Nathaniel Lloyd and his wife, Daisy, the gardens were added to by their son Christopher. A regular contributor on gardening to *Country Life*, Christopher's lively and inventive approach to horticulture obviously stems from working in the gardens. A mixture of formal and wild, there are many rare plant specimens on display here and the gardens are open to the public.

Northiam Station is also on the **Kent and East Sussex Railway**, which was restored in 1990 and has steam trains running on a track between Tenterden in Kent and Bodiam during the summer months. At one time too, the River Rother was navigable to this point and barges were brought upstream to be unloaded at the busy quay. This must have been an ancient port as, in the 1820s, the remains of a Viking long ship were found in the mud by the river where they must have lain hidden since the 9th century.

BODIAM

10½ miles N of Hastings off the B2244

Situated in the valley of the River Rother, this attractive village, whose name is pronounced 'Bodjem', is home to one of the most romantic castles in the country. In the 1380s, Richard II granted Sir Edward Dalyngrygge a licence to fortify his manor house in order to defend the

upper reaches of the then navigable River Rother. Thankfully, Dalyngrygge chose to interpret the licence liberally and one of the last great medieval fortresses in England was built. Construction on **Bodiam Castle** was begun in 1385 when the technology of castle building was at its peak and before the use of gunpowder. Completely surrounded by a wide moat, the arrow slits, cannon ports and aptly named murder holes (through which objects were thrown at attackers below) were never used in anger. However, there was a minor skirmish here in 1484 and, during the Civil War, the castle surrendered without a shot being fired.

A long period of decay followed, during the 17th and 18th centuries, until, in 1829, plans to dismantle the castle were thwarted by 'Mad' Jack Fuller of Brightling. A programme of restoration was begun, firstly by George Cubitt at the end of the 19th century, and completed by Lord Curzon in 1919. On his death in the 1920s, Lord Curzon left the castle to the National Trust and they have continued the restoration programme, including replacing the floors in the towers so that visitors can climb to the top of the battlements and gain a real feel of the security that Bodiam must have offered its inhabitants over the centuries. A popular film location, as the exterior is almost complete, the interior remains somewhat bare. Bodiam Station is now the terminal for the **Kent and East Sussex Railway**.

GUESTLING THORN

4½ miles NE of Hastings on the A259

With no real village centre and an isolated ancient church found down a small lane, it is hard now to believe that this was probably the meeting place for the important governing body of the Cinque Ports. However, as it lay on neutral territory and was not controlled by any of the ports, is would have been suitable to the parties concerned.

PETT

4 miles NE of Hastings off the A259

Situated on top of a hill the village overlooks, to the south, **Pett Level**, a vast expanse of drained marshland that now consists of watercourses and meadows. Dotted with small lakes the area provides a suitable sanctuary for wildfowl.

FAIRLIGHT

3 miles NE of Hastings off the A259

Separated from Hastings, to the west, by its country park, this village is a small settlement of, chiefly, old coastguard cottages. The 19th century grey stone church occupies a magnificent position overlooking the coast and its tower can be seen for miles out to sea. So much so, in fact, that when the weathervane blew down the villagers were inundated with requests from anxious sailors asking for it to be replaced. In the churchyard, among a number of elaborate tombstones, is the rather neglected final resting place of Richard D'Oyly Carte, the founder of the opera company that will be forever linked with Gilbert and Sullivan.

To the west of the village lies **Fairlight Glen**, an attractive place where a gentle stream approaches the sea through a steep side woodland valley. The Lovers'

Seat placed here is said to be in memory of a girl who waited on this spot for her lover to return to her from his ship. Unlike many similar tales, this one had a happy ending as, not only did the girl's lover return from overseas unharmed, but her parents also consented to their marriage. The beach here is now an unofficial naturist beach.

ST LEONARDS

1 mile W of Hastings on the A259

St Leonards was created in the 1820s as a fashionable seaside resort by the celebrated London architect, James Burton, who was responsible for designing much of Bloomsbury. The centrepiece of Burton's plans was the Royal Victoria Hotel, which, although still standing, is now rather over-shadowed by the vast **Marina Court**, built to resemble an ocean going liner in the 1930s. Assisted by his son, Decimus, a talented architect in his own right who later designed the Wellington Arch at Hyde Park Corner, London, James Burton went on to create a model seaside town that was designed to attract the wealthy and aristocratic.

In its heyday, St Leonard's formal social activities took place in the Assembly Rooms, behind the Royal Victoria Hotel, a classical building that had a tunnel running between the two so that the hotel could provide suitable

WHITE COTTAGE B & B

Battery Hill, Fairlight, Near Hastings, East Sussex, TN35 4AP
Tel: 01424 812528 Fax: 01424 812285
e-mail: johnamdjune@whitecottagebb.com

Set on the outskirts of a peaceful village **White Cottage** is a cheerful, clean and friendly bed and breakfast with beautiful gardens that are occasionally visited in the evening by foxes and badgers. The three rooms are en suite with colour television, tea and coffee making facilities. Two have views over the sea. There is a separate guest lounge, a breakfast room and a sun room.

refreshments for the wide variety of functions. The rooms are now the Masonic Hall. During the Victorian era, this well-organised town even had its own services area. Mercatoria was the tradesmen's quarters and Lavatoria the laundrywomen's.

The delightfully informal **St Leonards Gardens** stand a little way back from the seafront and they were originally private gardens maintained by subscriptions from the local residents. Acquired by the local council in 1880, they are a tranquil area of lakes, mature trees and gently sloping lawns that can now be enjoyed by everyone.

In the churchyard of the parish church, which was destroyed by a flying bomb in 1944 and rebuilt in a conservative modern style in the 1960s, lies James Burton's curious tomb - a pyramid vault where he and several other family members are buried.

BULVERHYTHE
3 miles W of Hastings on the A259

A port during the Middle Ages, in the 19th century the noise made by the shingle as it was washed by the tide was called the 'Bulverhythe Bells' and their sound was seen as an indicator of bad weather by local fishermen. Just off the coast, at very low tides, the remains of the wreck of the Dutch East Indiaman *Amsterdam* are clearly visible.

BEXHILL-ON-SEA
5 miles W of Hastings on the A259

This small seaside resort was founded in the 1880s by the influential De La Warr family, who lived at the original village of Bexhill, just a mile from the coast.

BEXHILL-ON-SEA

Bexhill Tourist Information Centre

For town guide contact:
Tel: 01424 732208
e-mail: bexhilltic@rother.gov.uk

Set in the midst of 1066 country **Bexhill-on-Sea** offers a quiet charm and elegance, missing from many larger, better-known coastal towns. It's a great place to unwind and relax, walking along the two miles of straight promenade, studying the marine life in the rock pools or stopping for lunch at one of the many pavement cafes and restaurants. This was a favourite resort for the Victorians and modern visitors can still sit in the classic shelters they used, enjoying the same stunning views of Eastbourne, Beachy Head, Hastings and across the Channel. Bexhill has some of the finest Victorian and Edwardian buildings in England but it is the splendid De La Warr Pavilion that is its gem. This Art Deco delight was opened in 1935 and is one of the world's most sublime examples of modernist architecture. It has appeared in countless period films and televisions series including Agatha Christie's Poirot.

British Motor racing was born here in 1902 when Bexhill's seafront cycling boulevard became an international motor racing track. Amongst the 200 or so competitors in the very first races were such notables as H.S Rolls, of Rolls Royce, Baron Rothschild and Herbert Austin. Although racing ceased here when Brooklands Circuit opened there is still an annual celebration over the May Bank Holiday weekend. The three-day, Bexhill 100 International Festival of Motoring, where the car is the star, attracts some 80,000 visitors. More subdued but no less popular are the twice-yearly Anglo Continental Markets where the town centre is filled with stalls offering a genuine taste of France, Spain, Germany and Italy.

The old Bexhill was an ancient place, with its roots well established in Saxon times, when the land around 'Bexlei' was granted to Bishop Oswald of Selsey by Offa, King of Mercia. Fortunately a good many of the older buildings have survived the late 19th century development including old weather-boarded cottages, a 14th century manor house and also the part Norman parish church.

Often referred to as Bexhill-on-Sea, the late 19th century new resort, though genteel, is rather modest and has never built a pier from the front though there is a promenade and some formal floral gardens. Among the many late Victorian buildings, the **De La Warr Pavilion** stands out. Built in the 1930s by Erich Mendelsohn and Serge Chermayeff, it is a fine and an early example of the functional style of architecture that was becoming fashionable at the time. Looking rather like an ocean going liner, with its welded steel frame, curves, abundance of glass and terraces, the Grade I listed building is now a renowned centre for arts and culture. With a 1,000 seater theatre, which attracts many international artists, a restaurant, bar and ball room it is very much a focal point of the town.

For what would appear today to be a relatively conservative resort, Bexhill was the first seaside town to allow mixed bathing on its beaches - in 1900! A very progressive move then, the gently sloping shingle beaches still offer safe and clean bathing as well as facilities for a range of watersports. The town has another first: in 1902, it played host to the birth of British motor racing when a race and other speed trials were held here. The huge Edwardian cars - nine litres were not uncommon - flew along the unmade roads around Galley Hill and stopping was a matter of applying the rear wheel brakes, brute force and luck.

The anniversary of this first race is celebrated each year in May with the **Bexhill Festival of Motoring**.

To discover more about the history of this seemingly modern but truly ancient settlement a visit to the **Bexhill Museum** is a must. As well as a range of exhibitions on local wildlife, history, geology and archaeology, there are also dinosaurs exhibits and even a Great Crab from Japan.

NINFIELD
7 miles NW of Hastings on the A269

To the north of this village, straggled along a ridge, lies Ashburnham Place, a red brick house that is much less impressive than it once was. The house was originally three storeys but there have been many alterations over the years, including the addition of a new block in the 1960s. However, the landscaped **Ashburnham Park**, has survived much as it was conceived by Capability Brown in the 18th century though a large number of trees were lost in the hurricane of 1987.

Close to the house lies the parish church where there are several monuments to the landowning Ashburnham family. One member of the family, John Ashburnham, was a supporter of the monarchy in the Civil War and he followed Charles I on his last journey to the scaffold in London. Imprisoned in the Tower by Cromwell, the late king's possessions that he was wearing on the day of his death - his shirt, underclothes, watch and the sheet in which his body was wrapped - came into the hands of the Ashburnham family. These relics were kept in the church following the restoration of Charles II to the throne and, for many years, they were believed to offer a cure for scrofula, a glandular disease called King's Evil.

BATTLE

6 miles NW of Hastings on the A2100

This historic settlement is, of course, renowned as being the site of the momentous battle, on 14th October 1066, between the armies of Harold, Saxon King of England, and William, Duke of Normandy. The Battle of Hastings actually took place on a hill, which the Normans called 'Senlac', meaning 'lake of blood', and even today some believe in the myth that blood seeps from the battlefield after heavy rain. However, any discolouration of the water is, in fact, due to iron oxide present in the subsoil. The battle was a particularly gruesome affair, even for those times, and it was not until late in the afternoon that Harold finally fell on the field. However, what happened to Harold's body remains a mystery. One story tells how it was buried by his mother at Waltham Abbey in Essex while another suggests that William the Conqueror wrapped it in purple cloth and buried it on the cliff top at Hastings.

Battle Abbey

After the battle and subsequent victory, William set about fulfilling his vow that, if he was victorious, he would build an abbey. Choosing the very spot where Harold fell, **Battle Abbey** was begun straight away and was consecrated in 1094. Throughout the Middle Ages the Benedictine abbey grew increasingly more wealthy and powerful as it extended its influence over wider and wider areas of East Sussex. This period of prosperity, however, came to an abrupt end in 1537 when Henry VIII dissolved the monasteries. The abbey buildings were granted to Sir Anthony Browne and, during a banquet to celebrate his good fortune, a monk is said to have appeared before Sir Anthony announcing that his family would be killed off by fire and water. The prophecy was forgotten as the family flourished until, some 200 years later, in 1793, the home of Sir Anthony's descendant, Cowdray Hall near Midhurst, burnt to the ground. A few days later another member of the family was drowned in the River Rhine in Germany.

Although little of the early Norman features remain, under the custodial care of English Heritage, Battle Abbey has much to offer the visitor. The most impressive part is the Great Gatehouse, a magnificent medieval abbey entrance, built around 1338. The **Prelude to Battle Exhibition** introduces visitors to the site and its history. This is followed by a 12-minute video on the Battle of Hastings. Other on-site attractions are a children's themed play and picnic area and an educational Discovery Centre.

There is more to Battle than the abbey and the battlefield, and any stroll around the streets will reveal some interesting buildings. The **Battle Museum of Local History** is an excellent place to discover more about the lives of those living in

ED'S NURSERY

Sunflower Garden, Cripps Corner Road, Staplecross,
Near Robertsbridge, East Sussex, TN32 5QA
Tel: 01580 830701 Fax: 01580 830701

Established 30 years ago, **Ed's Nursery** was taken over ten years
ago by Ed Rogers. Born locally, he has spent his life in
horticulture and agriculture and is very knowledgeable and
friendly. Most of the plants he sells are propagated on site in
the huge tunnels and glasshouses on the three-acre site. He
specialises in all year round items and has an excellent range of shrubs, roses, herbaceous plants,
climbers, bedding plants, fruit trees and hanging baskets.

East Sussex through the ages and there is
also a replica of the Bayeux Tapestry to
view. Opposite the abbey, and housed in
a 600 year-old Wealden hall house, is
Buckleys Yesterday's World, where more
than 50,000 objects are displayed in
authentic room settings, which cover the
period from 1850 to 1950. There are
even replicas of a Victorian kitchen, a
1930s country railway station and a
bicycle shop.

SEDLESCOMBE

6½ miles NW of Hastings on the B2244

This former flourishing iron founding
settlement, is a now a pleasant and pretty
village, stretched out along a long
sloping green, where the parish pump
still stands under a stone building of
1900. The interior of the village church,
on the northern edge of the village,
retains its seating plan of the mid 17th

SWALLOWFIELD FARM AND THE POTTING SHED

Brightling, East Sussex, TN32 5HB
Tel: 01424 838225 / 01424 838486 Fax: 01424 838885
websites/e-mail: www.swallowfieldfarm.freeserve.co.uk
    or: www.thepottin-shed.co.uk

This delightful cottage and the Elizabethan farmhouse are
set within thirty acres of outstanding natural beauty deep
within the 1066 Country and provides high quality bed
and breakfast accommodation in the three en-suite
bedrooms complete with tea and coffee making facilities
and colour televisions. A further six people can be
accommodated either self-catering or bed and breakfast in
Swallowfield Farm Cottage, completely detached from the farmhouse. An ideal base for touring the
historic villages or peaceful walks in the tranquil Sussex countryside.

    The Potting Shed within the grounds produces a
variety of hand-made items. Quelli and Gideon Coles
have built up a considerable reputation with their
sensational pots and ever-popular animal toast and
letter racks. Gideon, who worked for many years in
Portuguese potteries throws magnificent pots and
domestic tableware in the Majolica style. Quelli has
an outstanding range of toast and letter racks from
farm animals and cricket bats to authentically
reproduced breeds of dogs for which there is
overwhelming demand.

century, which lays out the hierarchy of this rural society in no uncertain terms. The front pew was retained for the Sackville family with the other villagers seated behind. Right at the back, the last few pews were kept for 'Youths and Strangers'.

To the southeast of the village, centred around an adapted 19th century country house, is the internationally renowned **Pestalozzi Children's Village**. Founded in 1959 to house children from Europe who had been displaced during World War II, the centre follows the theories of the Swiss educational reformer, Johann Heinrich Pestalozzi. The 19th century Swiss gentleman, who believed that young people of all nationalities should learn together and took into his care orphans from the Napoleonic Wars. The village now takes children from Third World countries, who live here in houses with others from their country under the care of a housemother of the same nationality. After studying for their first degree, the young adults return to their own countries where their newly learnt skills can be put to excellent use in the development of their homelands.

ROBERTSBRIDGE
10 miles NW of Hastings off the A21

Situated on a hillside overlooking the valley of the River Rother, the village's name is a corruption of "Rothersbridge". In the 12th century an annexe to a Cistercian Abbey was founded here, by the river, and today some of the buildings can be seen incorporated in a farm. The house's unusually high pitched roof protects the remains of the abbot's house and, in the garden, there are other ruins. Robertsbridge has long been associated with cricket and, in particular, the manufacture of cricket bats. The village establishment of Grey

HURST GREEN ANTIQUES
79 London Road, Hurst Green, East Sussex, TN19 7PN
Tel: 01580 860317 Mobile: 07966 256675

Stuart Atkinson and Kiel Shaw got involved in antiques some ten years ago. Both have travelled extensively through France in pursuit of their hobby and eventually gave up careers in social work and accounting to open their first shop. Both partners are friendly and knowledgeable and have a passionate interest in antiques that few other traders could match. They specialize in the country furniture of France, French linen, decorative white china, glass, period garden furniture and antique mirrors.

Weekly trips are made to France sourcing items to replace the stock they have sold. Anything requiring renovation or repair will be restored in their own workshop before being placed on sale. **Hurst Green Antiques** on the A21 in the middle of Hurst Green is a large double fronted unit with glass windows and is very well-stocked. Although the display is constantly changing, at any one time browsers might encounter farmhouse tables, chests and dressers, corner units, occasional tables, a variety of different styles of chair and huge ornate over-mantle mirrors. Most of the surfaces are covered with a selection of ceramics and glass. Complete dinner services sit beside a collection of antique medicine bottles or stoneware storage jars. Antique chandeliers, completely renovated for modern circuits, are joined by matched pairs of candlesticks and old oil lamps. In a quiet corner a superb wicker fishing basket hangs on a mahogany hall stand, while beside it on the wall an elegant sconce contains a modern church candle.

HOPE ANCHOR HOTEL

Watch Bell Street, Rye, East Sussex, TN31 7HA
Tel: 01797 222216 Fax: 01797 223796
e-mail: info@hotel-rye-freeserve.co.uk

Occupying a commanding position in one of Rye's most enchanting and interesting cobbled streets, the **Hope Anchor** has stunning views over the harbour, Romney marsh, Camber Castle and the rivers Brede and Rother. With Mermaid Street, Church Square, Lamb House and the 13th century Ypres Tower within a few minutes stroll it is an ideal base for exploring the area . Dating back to the mid 18th century the hotel has two bars, lounge, restaurant and 12 bedrooms each with individual character reflecting the nature of this beautiful old timbered house with its nooks, crannies and secret passages. Most of the rooms are en suite and all have tea and coffee making facilities. The Hope Anchor has an enviable reputation for the quality of its food. The resident chef uses local, seasonably available fresh produce to make mouth watering dishes, which compliment the excellent wine list.

WHITE VINE HOTEL

24 High Street, Rye, East Sussex, TN31 7JF
Tel: 01797 224748 Fax: 01797 223599
e-mail: Irene@whitevinehouse.freeserve.co.uk

Timber framed and built over one of the most outstanding medieval vaulted cellars in Rye, this gracious old house was once a private residence. The local historian, William Holloway, lived here and it was also home to one of the Mayors of Rye, Charles Pix Meryon, in the late 19th century. An earlier building on this site was the original Whyte Vyne Inn and the present cellar was part of it. Nowadays it has its own unique personality and relaxing atmosphere. Throughout the rooms are fresh flowers, pictures and an abundance of books. Guests can relax in the Elizabethan room, enjoy a magnificent country breakfast in the Sunflower room or retire to the privacy of Mistress Holloway's room with its antique four poster bed and timbered ceiling. The **White Vine Hotel** is becoming increasingly popular for family reunions, small conferences and weddings which are held in the oak panelled Elizabethan room. This small, personally run establishment offers a level of personal service seldom found in larger hotels.

FLETCHER'S HOUSE

Lion Street, Rye, East Sussex
Tel: 01797 222227

This popular and busy tea room sits at the top of Lion Street adjacent to the parish church of St Mary the Virgin. It is named after the Elizabethan dramatist, who was born here in 1579. The half-timbered and Sussex peg tile frontage reflect the antiquity of the building and inside is a classical old English tea room with wood strip floor and heavy oak beams. There are two open rooms, a large inglenook fireplace and crisp linen cloths on the tables. As might be expected **Fletcher's House** serves a large variety of teas and coffees. Food ranges from cakes and pastries through light lunches to the legendary Sussex cream teas. Much of the food is home made on the premises. Freshly cut sandwiches from locally baked bread, home made soup, jacket potatoes and ploughman's platters are amongst the favourite lunches while the mouth watering display of pastries and cakes in the window is more temptation than mere mortals can endure.

Nicholls has been making bats for many of the sport's famous names, including W.G. Grace, who once stayed at The George Inn in the village.

HURST GREEN
12 miles NW of Hastings of the A21

Set in four acres of gently sloping Weald farmland, close to the village, **Merriments Gardens**, is a place which never fails to delight its visitors. A naturalistic garden, where the deep borders are richly planted according to the prevailing conditions of the landscape, there is an abundance of rare plants here. By contrast, there are also borders that are planted in the traditional manner of an English garden and colour themed using a mix of trees, shrubs, perennials and grasses. Things change at the gardens all the time, with the seasons and as new ideas are put into operation.

Church Square, Rye

RYE

This old and very picturesque town was originally granted to the Abbey of Fecamp in Normandy, in 1027, and was only reclaimed by Henry III in 1247. It became a member of the confederacy of the Cinque Ports, joining Hastings, Romney, Hythe, Dover and Sandwich as the ports, which were a key part of the south coast's maritime defence and became a full Head Port in the 14th century. Over the years, this hill top town, which overlooks both the Rother estuary and the Romney Marshes, was subjected to many raids, including one by the French in 1377, which left no non-stone building still standing. Later, the harbour suffered the same fate as many ports along the south coast as it silted up and the harbour was moved to further down the estuary. **Rye Harbour Nature Reserve**, on the mouth of the River Rother, is a large area of sea, saltmarsh, sand and shingle which supports a wide range of both plant, animal and bird life.

Rye's prominent hill top position was a factor, which made it a strategically

ANN LINGARD

Rope Walk Antiques, Rope Walk, Rye, Sussex, TN31 7NA
Tel: 01797 223486 Fax: 01797 224700
e-mail: ann-lingard@ropewalkantiques.freeserve.co.uk

Ann Lingard has been selling antiques from this magnificent shop for over 25 years and won the BACA Award in June 2001. The spacious showrooms are crammed with British antique pine furniture ranging from dressers and wardrobes to tables, display cabinets and bookcases. There's an eclectic collection of antiques and bric-a-brac including, glassware, old model boats, wicker baskets, stoneware jars and bottles, kitchenware and even coal scuttles. It's a browsers' paradise and full of bargains.

CINQUE PORTS POTTERY

Conduit Hill, Rye, East Sussex, TN31 7LE
Tel: 01797 222033 Fax: 01797 222400
e-mail: cppottery@aol.com website: cinqueportspottery.com

Cinque Ports Pottery is housed in an Augustinian friary founded in 1379, commonly known as the Monastery. This magnificent building, with stone walls over two feet thick and Gothic arched windows, is situated in a steep cobbled way leading from the High Street. Stairs lead up the outside of the building into the ancient chapel, which now houses hand throwers of pottery. Next door is the casting section, where goods are sponged, fettled and dried. Downstairs are the glazing and painting departments. Every item is hand painted either for stock or individually commissioned. The viewing gallery enables visitors to follow the whole fascinating process of creating pottery from beginning to end, finishing of course in the showroom, where all the end products are available to buy.

There are commemorative pieces, house name plaques and many collectables designed by the imaginative in-house designer, James Elliott. The popular Country Gentlemen animal series includes Sir Freddy Fox in red or green hunting jacket and staid and solid Lord William Badger, who have recently been joined by their respective wives Felicity and Beatrice.

Visitors can also make a booking to paint their own pottery, creating a unique piece to keep or give as a present. Once the piece is chosen, help is on hand to plan the colours and design and paint the pot. After that it will be glazed and fired and one week later will be available to collect or can be sent out.

THE RYE BAKERY

89 High Street, Rye, East Sussex, TN31 7JN
Tel: 01797 222243/226522 Fax: 01797 227388
e-mail: hawthornsrye@hotmail.com

The Rye Bakery is a combination of tea shop, patisserie and bakery right in the middle of the High Street in Rye. Glenn and Donna Croucher have owned the business since 1985. Donna takes responsibility for administration while Glenn is a master baker, who trained at the National Bakery School in London and who has been involved with baking in Rye since 1975. He has won gold and silver medals in Bakery Championships and is a prominent member of the National Association of Master Bakers.

The shop is at least 120 years old and they keep up a long tradition of bread making with their speciality Wealden Loaf, made with local organic ingredients. It is brown and crusty and made in the old-fashioned way without the use of high speed mixers. As well as the popular Wealden Loaf they produce a range of fresh crusty bread fresh every day including wholemeal, granary and rye bread.

Their confectionery choice includes chocolate brownies, muffins, iced buns, doughnuts and carrot cake. The tea shop, opened in 1999, is light, airy and brightly decorated and has proved a popular meeting place for visitors and locals alike. They serve light lunches, soup, filled baguettes, an excellent range of filled rolls and sandwiches, obviously using the freshly baked bread of the bakery. This is an excellent place too, to pick up a picnic, buying ready filled rolls to take away or simply fresh bread to combine with cheese and fruit, which always tastes even better out in the open countryside.

Landgate, Rye

Found in the heart of this ancient town, **Durrant House Hotel** is a charming, spacious Georgian residence that also has a part to play in the history of Rye. Built for a local gentleman in the 17th century, the house was, like so much of the town, at the centre of the smuggling trade. However, in the 18th century the property was bought by Sir William Durrant, a friend of the Duke of Wellington, and gained respectability. During the Napoleonic Wars, it was an operations centre for the defence of the Channel port and a relay station for carrier pigeons bringing news of the victory at Waterloo.

(Continued page 162)

important town from early times. A substantial perimeter wall was built to defend the northern approaches and one of its four gateways, the **Landgate**, still survives today. This imposing structure is all that remains of the fortifications erected by Edward III in the 1340s.

MARTELLO BOOKSHOP

26 High Street, Rye, East Sussex, TN31 7JJ
Tel: 01797 222242 Fax: 01797 227335
e-mail: martbook@aol.com

This has been a booksellers since at least 1894 having a series of owners from A. Whiteman, publisher of Whiteman's Almanac, to Gouldens of Rye, founded by Fran Goulden in 1929. That family business continued as stationers and booksellers until taken over by the Reavells in 1975. They renovated the shop and named it **Martello Bookshop** after the Martello Towers that are such a feature of the coastal landscape in East Sussex. Terry and Wendy Harvey, the present owners, succeeded the Reavells in 1996 and have continued to develop the business.

This is a magnificent general bookshop, often having volumes signed by the author. There is a wide range of paperback fiction and sections on art, photography, crafts, cookery, gardening, sports, reference and childrens' books. This is also the best place to find books on local history, maps and wild life, as well as an outstanding section of cards and calendars.

Terry and Wendy formed the Martello Reading Circle in 1999. Each month, members read a chosen book and then discuss it in detail at the next meeting. Meetings are held monthly in the bookshop on a Monday evening.

The shop is also the venue throughout the year for occasional exhibitions of their photography and local crafts.

WALK 4

Rye and Winchelsea

Start	Rye
Distance	5½ miles (8.9km)
Approximate time	2½ hours
Parking	Rye
Refreshments	Pubs, cafés and restaurants at Rye, pubs and cafés at Winchelsea
Ordnance Survey maps	Landranger 189 (Ashford & Romney Marsh), Explorer 125 (Romney Marsh, Rye & Winchelsea)

Constant threat of invasion from the Continent is the dominant theme of this walk across the marshes that lie between Rye and Winchelsea, two of the medieval Cinque Ports. The towns themselves, together with Camber Castle, the Royal Military Canal and a martello tower, represent different reactions to invasion threats in the medieval, Tudor and Napoleonic eras. This is an easy walk across flat, fresh and open marshland, an extension of the larger Romney Marsh across the Kent border, but do keep a sharp look-out for half-hidden drainage channels on the first part of the walk; these are not always obvious and are potentially dangerous. Also, leave plenty of time to explore Rye and Winchelsea, two outstandingly attractive and fascinating towns.

As the title implies, the Cinque Ports were originally a confederation of five towns on the coast of Kent and Sussex. Their role was to provide ships and men for the defence of this highly vulnerable stretch of the English Channel in return for certain privileges. Rye and Winchelsea were later additions to the original five ports in the 14th century.

Rye occupies a hilltop site overlooking marshland, and the spire of its splendid, solid-looking church, despite being of the usual short and squat Sussex variety, dominates the surrounding countryside. Rye was an important and prosperous port in the Middle Ages, but its prosperity declined as the sea retreated, leaving behind one of the most delightful and unspoilt small towns in the country. Narrow cobbled streets of timber-fronted and tiled houses, shops and inns climb from the River Rother to the medieval church and Ypres Tower, and from many different points in the town there are extensive views across the reclaimed marshes to the sea, now 2 miles (3.2km) away. Mermaid Street is the most photogenic and best-known street but there are lots of other old streets, alleys and attractive little squares to explore.

Rye is not just a museum piece, however; there is plenty of bustle and there are still fishing vessels and boat-building yards down by the river.

The walk starts at Strand Quay by the bridge over the River Rother. Cross the bridge, walk along New Winchelsea Road and after a few yards turn right along a track, at a public footpath sign to Winchelsea. The track passes to the right of a farm, bends to the left and finishes in front of a metal gate. Go through the gate and keep straight ahead across a field to pass through two more metal gates in quick succession at the far end.

Follow the narrow but generally distinct and certainly well-waymarked path to Winchelsea, which is in sight on the wooded cliff ahead all the time, across flat fields and sheep pastures reclaimed from the sea. It is very important initially to keep to the left of a drainage channel, otherwise you will stray off the route and could easily fall into one of the numerous half-hidden channels. Indeed, for much of the way you keep along the left bank of a drainage channel, but look out for where yellow waymarks and footpath signs show deviations

WALK 4

from a generally straight line and direct you over a number of stiles and footbridges. All around are wide, open views: Winchelsea ahead, Rye on its hill behind, low hills to the right and flat marshes looking towards the coast on the left. Finally, the path bears right and heads across to a stile by a bridge .

Climb the stile, turn left to cross the bridge over the River Brede and walk along a lane to the main road where it bends sharply at the bottom of the hill on which Winchelsea stands. Turn left along the road for ¼ mile (400m) (there is a path) and look out for a flight of steps and a public footpath sign on the right **B**; the steps enable you to climb the steep, wooded cliff into Winchelsea. At the top of the steps turn right onto a narrow tarmac path and continue along a picturesque road of tile-hung cottages to a crossroads. The main part of the town is to the right.

Despite the obvious similarities between Rye and Winchelsea there are a number of differences. Winchelsea is smaller and quieter, more of a fossilised backwater, yet at the same time built on more spacious and symmetrical lines. This is because Winchelsea was built as a new town, commissioned by Edward I when Old Winchelsea was destroyed by storms in the 13th century, and it is laid out in a grid-iron pattern, a rare example of a planned medieval town. It was conceived on a large scale, intended to be the chief port for the flourishing French wine trade, but a combination of French raids and the receding of the sea meant that these grandiose ambitions were never realised. The main surviving monuments to its brief heyday are three of the four original gateways, the 14th century Court Hall and the large and imposing ruined church, the latter comprising just the east end as its nave and transepts were destroyed by the French.

At the crossroads, turn left and follow the road as it bends sharply left, passes through Strand Gate – one of Winchelsea's medieval gateways – and continues downhill. As you descend there are superb views across the marshes to Rye and the coast. At the bottom, turn right to rejoin the main road and, where it turns left, keep ahead in the direction of Winchelsea Beach to cross the Royal Military Canal, built in 1805 as a defence against a possible Napoleonic invasion. Continue along the road for ½ mile (800m) and, where it bends sharply to the right, keep ahead along a track **C**.

The track bends to the left; at a fork keep ahead along the left-hand concrete track. To the right Camber Castle can be seen in an isolated position on the marshes. This was an artillery fort built by Henry VIII at a time of an invasion scare in the 1530s. Where the concrete track turns right, go through a metal gate and continue along a grassy embankment raised above sheep pastures on both sides. This keeps close to the River Brede most of the time, but on two occasions bears right, away from it. On the first occasion you can make a short detour to the right, climbing a waymarked stile, if you want a closer look at Camber Castle. When the grassy track starts to bear right for the second time, keep ahead along a much narrower path by the river, go through a metal gate, then pass to the left of houses to rejoin the track and follow it to a road **D**.

Turn left over the river near its confluence with the Rother to a T-junction. Just ahead is a martello tower, one of over seventy built at the beginning of the 19th century as another defence against an anticipated French invasion, at the time of the Napoleonic Wars. Turn right to return to the start. ●

THE UNION INN

East Street, Rye, East Sussex, TN31 7YJ
Tel:01797 222334

This charming Sussex Inn is one of the oldest buildings in Rye. Dating from the 15th century it is a popular haunt with locals and visitors alike. It's so popular that some of the former clientele are apparently still lingering years after their deaths. The inn's three resident ghosts have been seen by locals and although an exorcism took place in the mid 1990s, they are still being seen today. They appear to be a benign lot of ghosts and have been the subject of a book and a television programme. Owner Steve Dartnall took over the **Union** in 1992 and enjoys his reputation as the 'Rudest Landlord in Rye' even though it's a myth. He welcomes guests to his historic pub with its whitewashed stone walls, casement windows and lanterns.

Show cases lining the walls contain a fine collection of militaria including etched line drawings of RAF Victoria Cross Holders. Steve has a wealth of knowledge about military history as well as being a font of interesting and amusing stories. The Union Inn is a free  house and maintains a splendid beer cellar. Guest ales are changed regularly but the standards, including, Bass, Harveys Best Bitter and the incredible Adnams Broadside are always on tap. The food is firmly based in the English tradition and the menu contains a lot of fish and game but there are also exotic items and visitors can dine on kangaroo, buffalo, springbok, emu, squirrel and even crocodile. Vegetarians are equally well catered for and all the food is freshly prepared from top quality ingredients.

JEAKE'S HOUSE

Mermaid Street, Rye, East Sussex, TN31 7FT
Tel: 01797 222828   Fax: 01797 222623
e-mail: jeakeshouse@btinternet.com   website: www.jeakeshouse.com

Jeake's House on an ancient cobbled street in the centre of Rye is ideal for the discerning visitor, who enjoys the feel of history all around yet does not wish to sacrifice modern comforts. It was originally built as a wool store in 1689 by the Jeakes family, who were strict Puritans. The adjoining building, known as the Quaker's House, was sold to the Baptists in 1753 and pulled down to make way for a chapel. In 1853 Jeake's became a school and in 1909 eventually a dwelling house, while the chapel became a men's club. They were both bought by the American writer Conrad Aiken in the 1920s and many of the famous literati of the day visited him in these premises.

He loved the house not only for its beautiful outlook over Romney Marsh and the channel but for its inner beauty 'Lighted by love, lighted by laughter, the kind of light that never goes out.'

The building is now owned by Jenny Hadfield and she has ensured that it is furnished in keeping with its rich history. The floors are not always level, the beams are very low and the doors may not quite fit but every room is warm and welcoming with traditional elegance combining with luxury and modern amenities in this unique setting. In the book-lined 'honesty' bar, furnished with old pews from the chapel, visitors can browse local restaurant menus over a pre-dinner drink. At breakfast, served in the elegant galleried hall of the chapel, there is always a wide choice including vegetarian, full traditional or continental options. Private car park nearby.

The town grew prosperous in the late medieval period due to the activities of its fishermen and the merchant fleets that traded with continental Europe. Though the loss of the harbour denied Rye the chief means of earning a living and the town fell into decline. Visitors today very much benefit from this turn of events as Rye still retains a large number of medieval buildings which would undoubtedly have made way for new structures if the town had been more prosperous.

Naturally, being a seafaring town, there is an abundance of old inns and the **Mermaid Inn**, an early timbered building down a cobbled street is one of the most famous. Rebuilt in 1420 after the devastating French raid over 40 years before, the inn was the headquarters of the notorious Hawkhurst Gang in the 18th century. The most infamous band of smugglers on the south coast, in their day, legend has it that they always sat with their pistols close to hand in case of a sudden raid by the excisemen.

Another interesting building is the handsome Georgian residence, **Lamb House**, built by a local wine merchant, James Lamb, in 1723 and now in the hands of the National Trust. The family was well known in the town and not without a certain amount of influence. Not long after the house was built, the family were involved in a famous murder when, in 1743, a local butcher named Breads killed James Lamb's brother-in-law by mistake. His intention had been to murder James, then the town's Lord Mayor, against whom he held a grudge. Tried and found guilty, Breads was hanged on a gibbet and his bones were stolen to be used as a cure for rheumatism. Only his skull remains and it can be seen, along with the gibbet, in Rye Town Hall.

CULPEPPERS

Love Lane, Rye, East Sussex, TN31 7NE
Tel: 01797 224411 Fax: 01797 224411
e-mail: peppersrye@aol.com
website: www.culpeppers-rye.com

Few things can be more satisfying at the end of a long hot day than to sit and relax in the large furnished summerhouse at **Culpeppers** and enjoy the fine views over the Mediterranean style terraced garden to the town of Rye and the surrounding countryside. Culpeppers is a name steeped in Sussex history but the house itself is modern and comfortable. Built in a former orchard it is adjacent to farmland and river paths yet within a few minutes walk of the centre of medieval town of Rye with its cobbled streets, ancient houses and 14th century inns.

South facing and situated at the end of a quiet cul-de-sac, Culpeppers is the home of Pat and John Ciccone, a friendly and welcoming couple, who go out of their way to ensure all their guests enjoy their stay, welcoming each with a cup of tea and some biscuits or cakes.   The guest bedrooms are comfortably furnished and have central heating, colour television, radio and a hospitality tray. The double/twin bedded room, has an en-suite bath and shower and has patio doors leading to a small balcony overlooking the pretty terraced garden. The other two are singles, overlooking the fields opposite the house. Pat and John go out of their way to ensure their guests' comfort and will provide hair dryers, dressing gowns, irons and ironing boards, hot water bottles, extra blankets and pillows as required. They are also happy to collect guests arriving by train from the station and return them there free of charge. This comfortable accommodation, with its friendly welcome, well deserves its 4 diamond rating and Silver Award from the English Tourist Board.

More recently, Lamb House, was the home of the novelist, Henry James, who lived here from 1898 to 1916 and many of his personal possessions are on show in the house. James was also responsible for laying out the gardens and he invited many of his friends to the house, including H.G. Wells, Rudyard Kipling, G.K. Chesterton and Joseph Conrad. The literary associations do not end there as, in the 1920s, the property was leased to E.F. Benson who is best remembered for his Mapp and Lucia novels, which include descriptions of the town, thinly disguised as 'Tilling'.

Ypres Tower, Rye

One of Rye's oldest surviving buildings is **Ypres Tower**, which forms part of the **Rye Castle Museum**, the other part being in East Street. The collection concentrates on the town's varied past and includes exhibitions on smuggling, law and order and the iron industry. On the second site, there is an old fire engine, pottery made in the town, nautical equipment and much more that tells the full history of Rye. Combining

RYE LODGE HOTEL

Hilders Cliff, Rye, East Sussex, TN31 7LD
Tel: 01797 223838 e-mail: info@ryelodge.co.uk
Fax: 01797 223585 website: www.ryelodge.co.uk

Standing in a unique and commanding position on the East Cliff, the Rye Lodge has stunning panoramas and views across the Romney Marshes and the Rother Estuary to the sea. Before it receded the sea once lapped the walls of this ancient Cinque Port town and access by land could only be gained through the Landgate, an ancient monument built in 1329 and now standing a few steps away from the hotel. This is an ideal base for exploring the town and is adjacent to the High Street with its many acclaimed restaurants, inns, tearooms, antique shops, art galleries, book shops, craft shops and potteries.

All of the rooms are luxurious and en suite, and the owners, the de Courcey family, pride themselves on the high level of personal service that they offer guests. One of the great features of the room service is breakfast in bed, available at any time of the day. The elegance of the marble floored Terrace

Room Restaurant ensures that each meal is a special occasion with superb food, served by candlelight and accompanied by wines from round the world, chosen from the extensive list. Specialities include the local Romney marsh lamb and a mouth-watering Rye Bay plaice.

The hotel's Venetian Leisure Centre has all the amenities for a relaxing stay. Beauty treatments, massage and reflexology are available and the indoor heated swimming pool, sauna and spa baths and an aromatherapy steam cabinet are perfect to sooth and relax the weary holidaymaker.

the traditional craft of model making with the latest electronic techniques, the **Rye Heritage Centre** presents a model of the town, complete with light and sound, that transports visitors back through the ages.

AROUND RYE

PLAYDEN
1 mile N of Rye off the A268

This smart hamlet has a rather battered old 12th century church, with a shingle broach spire. Inside there is an unusual memorial to a 16th century Flemish brewer, Cornelis Roetmans. A refugee from Spanish persecution in the Low Countries, he settled in the area along with a community of Huguenots and carried on his trade as brewer. After his death, he was remembered in the church by a memorial slab carved with beer barrels and mash forks - the tools of the brewing trade.

The country lanes to the northeast of Playden lead to the start of the **Royal Military Canal**, an unusual waterway, built in 1804 as part of the defences against a possible invasion by Napoleon. There is a 20 mile long towpath between Rye and Hythe, which now offers easy and attractive walking along the fringes of the now drained **Walland** and **Romney Marshes**.

CAMBER
3 miles SE of Rye off the A259

The village has seen a lot of development since World War II with the building of bungalows on the sand dunes. However, though the appearance is relatively modern, Camber is also home to **Camber Castle**, a fine example of a the coastal defences built by Henry VIII in the 16th century. The fortress seems rather far inland today but when it was built, it held a commanding position on a spit of land on one side of the Rother estuary. Now in the hands of English Heritage, the castle is open on a limited basis.

WINCHELSEA
2½ miles SW of Rye on the A259

Though Winchelsea lies only a short distance from Rye, there could be no greater contrast. While Rye is a place of tourist bustle, Winchelsea is a quiet place that time seems to have forgotten. An ancient Cinque Port and the smallest town in England, Winchelsea lay several miles to the south until the 13th century. This site was engulfed by the sea after a series of violent storms. The 'new' Winchelsea stands on a hill and it was built to a rigid grid pattern laid out by Edward I. The ambitious rectangular plan of 39 squares - a feature which can still be seen some 700 years later - became the home of some 6,000

FLACKLEY ASH HOTEL

Peasmarsh, Near Rye, East Sussex, TN31 6YH
Tel: 01797 230651 Fax: 01797 230510
e-mail: flackleyash@yahoo.co.uk   website: www.flackleyash.co.uk

The **Flackley Ash Hotel** in a quiet village four miles north west of Rye, is set in five acres of beautiful grounds. The accommodation includes four-poster beds, deluxe rooms and suites. The facilities include a swimming pool, steam room, sauna, whirlpool spa and gym. Meals in the candlelit restaurant are of the highest quality using fresh ingredients including local fish. This is an ideal base for exploring Rye and the historic countryside of Sussex and Kent.

inhabitants, nearly ten times the number of residents there today.

For a short time in the 14th century, Winchelsea prospered as the most important Channel port but again nature took its toll and the town lost its harbour. As a result of the Black Death and constant raids by the French, the town declined into almost complete obscurity. It was not until the mid 19th century that a successful recovery plan was put together to restore the town to something like its former grandeur and historic beauty. **Winchelsea Court Hall Museum** illustrates the events that led to the town's prosperity, culminating in it being made a Head Port of the confederation of Cinque Ports, and its gradual decline. The museum is housed in one of Winchelsea's oldest surviving buildings and, close by, can be seen the ruins of a 14th century **Franciscan Friary**.

BECKLEY

4½ miles NW of Rye on the B2088

When Alfred the Great died in 900, he referred to lands at 'Beccanleah' in his will and there was certainly a Saxon church here. A medieval building with a Norman tower, now stands on the site. Inside there are two grotesque stone heads with leaves protruding from the mouths that were known as 'jack in the greens'. On still nights, it is said that Sir Reginald Fitzurse can be heard riding furiously to the church for sanctuary after taking part in the murder of Thomas à Becket.

BRIGHTON AND THE EAST SUSSEX DOWNS

This coastal area of East Sussex centres around the thriving resorts of Brighton and Eastbourne. Both began life as a quiet fishing villages but, following

Royal visits, they developed rapidly at the beginning of the 19th century. Brighton, the favoured holiday resort of the Prince Regent, is best known for the lavish Royal Pavilion, a splendid monument to exotic architecture and design. However, its Lanes, the narrow streets and alleyways of the old village are a real treat for antique lovers.

Eastbourne has none of the grand architecture of its rival. Carefully planned and laid out by William Cavendish, the 7th Duke of Devonshire, this is a genteel resort close to the spectacular chalk cliffs of Beachy Head.

The county town of Lewes dates back to Saxon times and it benefited greatly just after the Norman Conquest, when both a great castle and the important St Pancras Priory were founded here by the Norman William de Warenne. Another coastal village, Pevensey, was the landing place of William, Duke of Normandy and his army.

Although many of the inland towns and villages have their roots in Saxon England they are also linked with artists and writers of the 19th and 20th centuries. Virginia Woolf and her husband Leonard lived at Monk's House, Rodmell, until Virginia's death in 1941 whilst her sister, Vanessa Bell, maintained her eccentric household at nearby Charleston Farmhouse, in Selmeston. The Elms at Rottingdean was the home of Rudyard Kipling until his success as a novelist forced him to move to a more secluded location in 1902, and the village of Ditchling was home to a group of artists and craftsmen at the centre of the Arts and Crafts Movement.

BRIGHTON

Before Dr Richard Russell of Lewes came here in the 1750s, this was an obscure little south coast fishing village called Brighthelmstone, dating back to medieval times. Dr Russell, a believer in the benefits of sea air and water, published a dissertation on *The Use of Sea Water in Diseases of the Glands*. Russell set about publicising the village as a place for taking sea air, bathing and even drinking sea water in order to gain relief from ailments and diseases. He also promoted the medicinal virtues of the mineral waters of St Ann's Well at Hove.

By the time of the Prince Regent's first visit to the village, at 21 years of age in 1783, it was already becoming a popular place but still remained concentrated around the old village of Brighthelmstone. The effect of royal patronage on the village was extraordinary and the growth here was rapid. By the time of the Prince Regent's last visit to Brighton, some 47 years after his first, the place had been completely transformed.

BOUDOIR

13 New Road, Brighton, East Sussex, BN1 1UF
Tel: 01273 710818 Fax: 01273 722549
e-mail: boudoir-brighton@hotmail.com

Located in a row of Georgian shops, opposite the Pavilion, amidst a busy and very spectacular area of Brighton, **Boudoir** is a cosy, classy shop containing everything for the bedroom. Antique French furniture blends with an eclectic mix of contemporary nightwear, accessories, soaps, scents and lighting. Kim Murphy realised a life-time ambition when she created Boudoir here two years ago and has gone on to build a loyal local following.

PASKINS TOWN HOUSE

18 – 19 Charlotte Street, Brighton, East Sussex, BN2 1AG
Tel: 01273 601203 Fax: 01273 621973
e-mail: welcome@paskins.co.uk
website: www.paskins.co.uk

All the staff pride themselves on the reputation they have established for this delightful small boutique hotel. There is a distinctive décor, a tranquil ambience, imaginative breakfasts, sourced from local and farm fresh produce including many vegetarian or vegan options. Above all you will get a warm welcome and informal hospitality. This 4 diamond, high-class, bed and breakfast with its Art Deco dining room evokes memories of a gracious past.

REDROASTER COFFEE HOUSE

1D St James's Street, Brighton BN2 1RE
Tel: 01273 686668 e-mail: redroaster.stj@virgin.net

Redroaster Coffee House is a homegrown gourmet café, established in St James's Street for three years. Redroaster's predecessor was set up in the Brighton Lanes in 1994. Redroaster roast their own beans behind the counter, so the coffee they serve is as fresh as possible. Freshly made savoury delicacies, croissants and cakes are also available throughout the day. Huge bags of coffee beans and large comfortable leather sofas line the walls, along with a customer donated piano. There is also a large collection of historical coffeemakers and the whole place has a light airy feel.

PAINT POTS

39, Trafalgar Street, Brighton, BN1 4ED
Tel: 01273 696682 Fax: 01273 696682

Paint Pots is centrally located just 100 yards from Brighton train station. Visitors to this lively studio can paint their own pottery and are guaranteed to have a unique piece. There is a choice from a wide selection of interesting shapes, including mugs, plates, bowls, teapots, picture frames, sushi plates, money pigs, planters and many more, all of which are ready to paint on. Customers pay for the pots plus a very reasonable studio fee, which includes paints, tuition, glazing and firing. Anyone can paint, even babies can make hand or footprints onto mugs or tiles or whatever, making brilliant

gifts for parents, grandparents or godparents. Toddlers love making blobs and smears on pots and all the paint is completely washable and non-toxic, so they can make as much mess as they like and still put their fingers in their mouths.

Painting pottery is very simple for all ages. Having chosen a pot, customers use a damp sponge to clean it, then draw on their own design in pencil and they are then ready to paint with expert help and advice on hand. The finished pot can be collected a couple of days later or it can be posted out to people who are not local. Paint Pots is perfect for parties for children or for adults and customers can bring their own food or buy it in from the excellent coffee shop and patisserie close by. For evening parties, although they don't supply the bottles of wine, they'll happily supply the glasses and corkscrews for visitors who bring their own bottles.

LANES DELI & PASTA SHOP

12 B Meeting House Lane, Brighton, East Sussex, BN1 1HB
Tel: 01273 723522
website: www.lanesdeli.co.uk

Right in the heart of Brighton the enchanting **Lanes Deli and Pasta Shop** is overflowing with some of the finest foods available in the south east of England. Previously owned by an elderly Italian lady, it had become very run down. However since it was taken over three years ago by Fiona Hayes, it has built up a well deserved reputation, for quality food, throughout Brighton. Situated within a historic part of The Lanes, it is very atmospheric and attracts a lot of passing trade. The brightly decorated frontage with a double window gives the first indication of the goodies that can be found within. Shelves, racks and display counters stuffed full of tins, jars and packets sit alongside a machine for making fresh pasta. Speciality foods from the continent include fresh anchovies, caper berries, marinated olives, sun blush tomatoes, stuffed vine leaves and home made pesto.

Amongst the cheese and meat selections can be found pecorino romano, parmigiano reggiano, manchego, provolone, taleggio, fontina, pancetta, san daniele parma ham, mortadella, milano and

napoli salami and of course chorizo. Added to this are delights such as aromatic coffees, olive oil, risotto rice, preserved truffles, dried fungi and pasta flour - everything in fact that is needed to make that special continental meal. For those who don't fancy the effort there's hot pasta and sauce to take away from a wide choice of 12 meat, veggie and fish sauces, freshly made on the premises. Try the vegetarian pizza slices or foccaccia and ciabatta rolls filled with any of the deli items on display or the delicious mushroom and mozzarella arancini rice balls.

The Prince Regent, later to become George IV, was so taken with the resort that he first took a house here and then built his famous **Royal Pavilion** in the resort. The small farmhouse on the site was transformed in 1787 by architect Henry Holland into a neoclassical building with a dome and rotunda. Finally between 1815 and 1822, the pavilion seen today was created in a magnificent Indian style, by John Nash. Based on a maharajah's palace, complete with minarets, onion shaped domes and pinnacles, the Royal Pavilion has been the most well-known Brighton landmark for almost 200 years.

The interior of the palace is one of the most lavish examples of Regency chinoiserie in the world. The detail in the decoration is astonishing, with imitation bamboo everywhere. Even the kitchens have flamboyant cast iron palm trees.

Brighton Pier

TERRE À TERRE

71 East Street, Brighton, Sussex BN1 1HQ
Tel: 01273 729051 e-mail: terreaterre.co.uk
Fax: 01273 327561 website: www.terreaterre.co.uk

This vegetarian restaurant, in Brighton's winding Lanes, has gained an outstanding reputation with veggies and carnivores alike. The food is simply brilliant. Paul Morgan, Lawrence Glass, Philip Taylor and Amanda Powley started seven years ago in smaller premises round the corner. Their amazing success enabled them to expand and they continue to go from strength to strength, gaining awards for their food and recommended by food critics in magazines and newspapers as well as by all who eat here.

The stripped pines floors, contemporary wooden tables and chairs and stylish interior create a relaxed yet sophisticated ambience for a leisurely lunch or dinner. But it is the food, which stars. The emphasis is on fresh and organic ingredients and practically all the food is prepared from scratch on the premises. There are choices for vegans as well as vegetarians and the unique menus combine flavours and ideas from all over the world. The food is hearty and satisfying rather than the vegetarian stereotype of slimming and good for you. Tasty oils, nuts and herbs flavour focaccio or onion and potato flat bread or any one of their range of fabulous breads. Salads may have deep fried potato with cheese, noodles and tofu soaked in an exotic plum sauce or kalamata, bread and feta. There is a plain leaf and herb salad, but of course it would never escape without a delicious oil and lemon dressing. Main courses have pasta with exotic cheeses, aubergine with garlic and Asian spices or comforting rosti with vegan bubble and squeak. The only problem at the end of the meal may be moving from the chair.

THE ALEXANDER GALLERY

7 East Street, Brighton, Sussex, BN1 1HP
Tel: 01273 321694 Fax: 01273 725959
e-mail: Karen@thealexandergallery.co.uk

The Alexander Gallery Exhibits individual designs produced by studio makers and has one of the largest selections of contemporary craft anywhere. They work very hard at maintaining an exceedingly high standard of excellence, style and individuality in the various items they display. Their exhibits include jewellery, glass, ceramics, wood, paintings and prints.

The gallery has been in Brighton for many years, originally trading as the Hugo Barclay after the founder. It was he who set the high standard of selection that, Karen Foster, the present proprietor aims to maintain while adding to the excellent range of makers and seeking new and original forms of decorative art.

A member of the Independent Craft and Galleries Association, The Alexander Gallery runs a series of shows and exhibitions each year where works of various talented makers are displayed. Work on display includes enigmatic pieces by Alasdair Neil MacDonell, ceramics by Peter Layton and delicate jewellery by Janet Perry. Despite the high quality of the pieces and the uniqueness of the designs the prices are reasonable, affordable and start at twenty pounds.

Ceramic Mask
Alasdair Neil MacDonell

BENVENUTI A PICCOLO

Ship Street, Brighton, BN1 1AF
Tel: 01273 203701 Fax: 01273 820820

This delightful Italian orientated restaurant is in a corner location in The Lanes, just 200 yards from the sea front. **Benvenuti a Piccolo** is ideal for a delicious lunch or snack in the centre of the main shopping area or for a leisurely gourmet meal in the evening. In attractive surroundings with bright modern frescoes, ornate ceilings and marble tables, guests can sit and watch the world go past through the large windows all round.

However the main attraction of this busy restaurant is the food. The chef is trained to international standards and the restaurant has a well deserved reputation for its innovative high quality menu. The à la carte menu has a wide range of Italian dishes including a wide choice of starters and salads as well as pizza and pasta. The specials board is the place to look for really mouth watering freshly made

creations like pasta with spicy Italian sausages, garlic, mustard and cream, or high quality fresh scallops, simply cooked in garlic and olive oil or rigatoni with avocado, pine kernels, mushrooms and basil in a cream sauce for vegetarians. For those looking for a romantic evening in with superb food cooked by someone else or for the intrepid tourist, who would just like to veg out for an evening in front of the television, the home delivery service from the delicatessen counter is perfect. Anything on the menu can be packed up and delivered to your home, ready to eat from 5.30pm onwards.

Royal Pavilion

out grounds. Beginning life as the Royal Pavilion's stables and once housing a riding school, **The Dome**, dated 1805, is now a superb concert hall. Another part of the complex has been converted into the **Brighton Museum and Art Gallery**. Opened in 1873, this outstanding museum houses collections of both national and international importance. Among the marvellous displays are art nouveau and art deco furniture, decorative art, non-western art and culture, archaeology from flint axes to silver coins and paintings by both British and European masters.

The gardens surrounding this seaside pleasure palace are also the work of John Nash though one ancient oak tree here is said to be the one in which Charles II hid after the Battle of Worcester. Although this is an unlikely claim, the tree certainly predates Nash's splendidly laid

The creation of the Royal Pavilion and the almost permanent residence of the Prince Regent in the resort certainly

ENGLISH'S OF BRIGHTON

East Street, Brighton, BN1 1HL
Tel: 01273 327980/328645 Fax: 01273 329754
e-mail: info@englishs.co.uk website: www.englishs.co.uk

Probably the most famous seafood restaurant on the south coast, **English's** has been owned by the Leigh-Jones family since 1945. The building, which houses the Oyster Bar began life as Braziers Fishmongers and the brasswork and marble display on the outside is original. In the early part of this century, Mr English married one of the Brazier daughters and established the Oyster Bar. When Clifford Leigh-Jones bought the restaurant, he acquired the two cottages on either side at the same time and was able to expand and extend the menu to include a comprehensive range of seafood dishes. The Red Room echoes back to Brighton's Edwardian heyday, with murals by local artist Marcus Stone combining with red velvet and intimate tables to evoke an atmosphere of days gone by. Three larger dining rooms upstairs and the Brazier Room mean that

English's can accommodate parties ranging from ten to 70 guests in charming surroundings. In 1996, two local art students, Catarina Perestrello and Mark Davies were commissioned to paint three series of murals for these rooms. The Spode Room has pictures depicting Edwardian dinner scenes, The Wedgwood Room, after dinner scenes and the Minton Room depicts the famous 'handbag' scene from *'The Importance of Being Ernest'*, watched over by Oscar Wilde himself.

English's prides itself in the fact that all soups and sauces are made on the premises from the freshest and most natural ingredients. The menu contains the chef's own interpretation of many classical dishes, many of which are available to take away. Specialities include the famous English Oysters which are available from September to April.

BLUE SHOP AND GALLERY

20 Church Street, Brighton, BN1 1RB
Tel: 01273 700370
e-mail: info@bluecrafts.co.uk
website: www.bluecrafts.co.uk

blue is a dynamic outlet for local and national designer makers, producing innovative, creative and exciting works. Situated in a corner property, it is unusually attractive and dates back to the 18th century. Mel Cartwright, the proprietor and a potter herself, started **blue** three years

ago and chose the name for its simplicity. Within the shops three showrooms is an incredible variety of arts and crafts from Brighton and beyond. There's even a ladies' clothes boutique to the rear, stocking Quiver clothing by designer Ione Harris - an effortlessly elegant but simple collection of women's wear in linens, silks and wools.

Elsewhere in this treasure trove, walls and shelves are adorned with crafts including jewellery by designers Annabet Wyndham and Penny Williams. There is a select collection of children's clothes and gifts, like beautiful cotton knit clothing by Lucinda Guy, and fabulous hats by Amanda Hawkins. There are ceramics, pictures, papier mache creatures, hats, bags, scarves and much more. All products are sourced by Mel, who scours the country looking for new designer-makers to feature. Everything stocked at **blue** is exclusive to the area, setting it apart from the other craft shops that all rely on buying from the same large trade shows.

CASALINGO RESTAURANT

29 Preston Street, Brighton, Sussex, BN1 2HP
Tel: 01273 328775 Fax: 01273 881010
e-mail: martinoli@btinternet.com

Angelo Martinoli, the owner of this superb Italian Restaurant was born near Lake Como, trained initially in Chiavenna and then worked at the Palace, Lucerne, Switzerland with the legendary Anton Mosiman of the Savoy, London. After a spell working on cruise liners he came to Brighton and worked at the Casalingo from 1979, finally taking it over with his wife, Gerry, in 1988. Situated in an area known as Restaurant Street, the **Casalingo** is close to the west pier and a mere 150 yards from the sea. Established in 1975, this fully air conditioned restaurant is exceedingly popular with locals as well as out of town

visitors and booking is advisable. The cosy interior has a smart modern décor and a wonderful ambience created by candle light and sympathetic background music. The waiting staff are very friendly and knowledgeable and go out of their way to help diners choose the best combination of dishes and wines for a superb evening out.

One of the secrets of the restaurant's success is the use of the best quality ingredients. Seasonal herbs and vegetables, locally caught fish and the finest of meats are freshly cooked to produce mouth watering dishes. Traditional dishes like pizza, pasta, chicken and veal are complemented by superb modern creations including spaghetti with lobster, king prawns, sea bass and pesce spada, grilled swordfish served in a sauce of fresh dill and mustard. The huge grilled steaks, cut from prime Angus beef, are absolutely awesome as is the filetto al dolcelatte, tender fillet in a creamy blue cheese and port sauce.

sealed Brighton's fate as a sought after seaside location and the town rapidly expanded - westwards until it met up with Hove and eastwards to **Kemp Town**, laid out by Thomas Reid Kemp, a local lord of the manor in the 1820s. Another notable feature of Brighton is **Royal Crescent**, an early example of town planning . Built in the late 1790s, this discreet row of little houses was built to face the sea rather than have their backs turned towards the coast as was the norm at the time.

For many visitors to Brighton a visit to **The Lanes**, the warren of narrow streets that represent what is left of the old village, is a must. Today, these tiny alleys are the preserve of smart boutiques, antique shops and restaurants. The old **Parish Church** standing outside the old part of Brighton is shown in ancient pictures as an isolated building. It has long since been engulfed. In the

churchyard is a curious gravestone to Phoebe Hessel. Born in 1713, she served in the army as a private and, after her retirement, she came to Brighton where she died, aged 108, in 1821.

Another church worth visiting is the Roman Catholic **Church of St John** in Kemp Town. However, it is not for any ancient feature that visitors make their way here but to see the last resting place of Mrs Fitzherbert, who died in 1837. Maria Anne Fitzherbert, twice a widow, was secretly married to the future George IV in London in 1785. They honeymooned in Brighton, where Mrs Fitzherbert took a house, said to be linked to the pavilion by an underground passage. Their marriage had to remain a secret as it was completely in breech of the Royal Marriages Act. Eventually, the Prince Regent, who could not acknowledge her publicly without renouncing the throne,

BRAMPTONS (BUTCHERS) LTD

114 St Georges Road, Kemp Town, Brighton, East Sussex, BN2 1EA
Tel: 01273 682611
e-mail: Bramptons_Butchers@hotmail.com

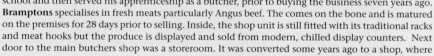

This traditional butcher's shop with its tiled double frontage has been operating here for over a century and received the Royal warrant from King Edward VII in 1902. The present proprietor, Paul Williams, trained as a chef after leaving school and then served his apprenticeship as a butcher, prior to buying the business seven years ago. **Bramptons** specialises in fresh meats particularly Angus beef. The comes on the bone and is matured on the premises for 28 days prior to selling. Inside, the shop unit is still fitted with its traditional racks and meat hooks but the produce is displayed and sold from modern, chilled display counters. Next door to the main butchers shop was a storeroom. It was converted some years ago to a shop, where

customers will find a magnificent variety of delicious cheeses. Paul Williams is noted for his 'naturally reared and produced' principles and products.

The shop is close to the town centre and a few minutes walk from the sea front making it an ideal choice for visitors looking for some quality cold meats for a picnic or for those in self catering accommodation to shop for fresh cheese, deliciously cured bacon, mouth watering sausages and tender, tasty, beef and steaks.

broke off their affair in 1811.

Just a short distance from the sea front lies **Preston Manor**, a delightful old house, now restored and refurbished in the style of an Edwardian gentleman's residence. Beginning life as a 13th century manor house, set within beautifully landscaped grounds, the manor was rebuilt in the 1730s and extended in 1905. Laid out on four floors, there are some 20 rooms to explore from the attics and nursery on the top floor to the servants' quarters at ground level. Within the pleasant grounds is a walled garden, a pets' cemetery and a croquet lawn.

Another lesser known place of interest in Brighton is **Stanmer Park and Rural Museum**. An excellent 200 acre country park centred around the fine early 18th century mansion that was once the home of the Earls of Chichester. The park now contains a large municipal nursery as well as glasshouses where flowers are grown. Behind Stanmer House is a unique collection of agricultural implements, including blacksmith's and wheelwright's tools. The late 17th century well house that was designed to supply water to the house and was, originally, powered by oxen can be seen here too.

For those wishing to take a step back into their childhood the **Sussex Toy and Model Museum**, under the arches of Brighton station, is the place. A fascinating display of trains, dolls, teddy bears, planes and much more will delight all members of the family - young and old. The world of natural history can also be discovered in Brighton, at the **Booth Museum of Natural History**, the creation of Edward Booth, a Victorian ornithologist. His original collection of some 500 species of bird, assembled between 1865 and 1890, has been extended by displays of butterflies, fossils and animal skeletons. **The Sea Life Centre** concentrates very much on live creatures and has the longest underwater viewing tunnel in Europe. The tunnel winds through a series of underwater habitats where both fresh and sea water creatures can be viewed. Although this is a an up to the minute centre, some of the original 19th century display cases are still in use in this Victorian building.

Brighton's **Palace Pier** is open every day of the year to amuse and entertain. For those looking for more refinement, the **Theatre Royal**, founded in 1774, remains one of the country's best and loveliest provincial theatres.

Naturally, Brighton also has a whole wealth of places to stay, from small bed and breakfast establishments to splendid five star hotels. Side by side on the front, are two superb hotels that symbolise Victorian holiday luxury, the white painted **Grand Hotel**, built in the 1860s and its neighbour the **Metropole Hotel**, completed in 1890. In 1984, during the Conservative Party Conference, an IRA bomb blew the Grand Hotel apart. Several people lost their lives in the tragedy and a great many more were injured. The hotel too suffered as the bomb had been strategically placed in its centre. However, just under two years later the hotel was once again fully open for business with no scars to show.

AROUND BRIGHTON

DITCHLING
6 miles N of Brighton on the B2116

This historic village, known as 'Diccelingas' in Saxon times, has records going back to 765. Once part of a royal estate belonging to Alfred the Great, it was passed on to Edward the Confessor and then to the Norman William de Warenne. The oldest building here, the parish **Church of St Margaret of Antioch**, dates from the 13th century though details from before the Norman Conquest can still be seen in the nave.

Close by the village green and opposite the church, stands **Wings Place**, an unusual Tudor house, also known as **Anne of Cleves' House**. There is no record that the fourth wife of Henry VIII ever stayed here but she is thought to have acquired the property as part of her divorce settlement.

At the beginning of the 20th century, this pretty village, at the foot of the South Downs, became the home of a lively group of artists and craftsmen including Eric Gill, Sir Frank Brangwyn and Edward Johnston. Today it remains a thriving artistic community with many studios and galleries.

To the north of the village lies **Ditchling Common Country Park**, a splendid nature reserve and beauty spot,

with a lake, stream and nature trails. Meanwhile, south of Ditchling lies the 813 foot summit of **Ditchling Beacon**, the third highest point on the South Downs. Once the site of an Iron Age hill fort and almost certainly occupied by the Romans, the beacon was used as a vantage point from which fires were lit to warn of the coming of the Spanish Armada. A magnificent place from which to view much of this area - southerly over the coast and northwards over the Weald - the beacon was given to the National Trust in memory of the owner's son who was killed during the Battle of Britain in 1940.

Visitors wanting to discover more about the locality's long and interesting history should make a point of calling in at the superb **Ditchling Museum**, which is located in the Victorian former village school. From the Iron Age, there has been evidence of settlement in this area

Spitfire Art

22/24 High Street, Ditchling, East Sussex, BN6 8TA
Tel: 01273 843749 Fax: 01273 842632
e-mail: art@spitfireart.com
website: www.spitfireart.com

A lifelong interest in aviation led Arthur Rayner to open his shop in September 1996. Since then he has concentrated on selling prints and originals, all of them with an aviation theme. His shop occupies the ground floor of an early 19th century building, which was until recently a butcher's shop in the High Street of the delightful village of Ditchling. **Spitfire Art** is small but extremely well stocked, containing over 500 prints from some twenty five artists including Taylor, Turner, Bailey, Champion and Postlethwaite.

Arthur is a WWI and WWII specialist and has probably the UK's most extensive selection of aviation art. His customers range from the mildly interested to the serious collector. Signed original paintings and limited editions make this shop a magnet for those looking for the rare and unusual. Now available is Nicolas Trudgian's new collection, Spitfire Country. This is a limited edition set of prints commemorating the Battle of Britain and the 'few' who successfully defended the country against overwhelming odds in the skies overhead. As well as Trudgian's signature each print will be signed by three Battle of Britain pilots, Flight Lieutenant Ludwik Martel, Wing Commander Peter Olver and Squadron Leader Basil Stapleton. Arthur produces a full colour catalogue at a reasonable price and also sells specialist books on aviation history and can arrange specialist commissions and a bespoke framing service. Non aviation items on sale include a selection of gift articles from the local area. His latest project involves plans to provide Bed and Breakfast accommodation of three bedrooms, all en suite.

CHESTERTON'S

1 High Street, Ditchling, East Sussex, BN6 8SY
Tel: 01273 846638 Fax: 01273 846582
website: www.chestertonsstores.co.uk

Robin, Ellen and Kenneth Fisher took over **Chesterton's** in the centre of this attractive village two years ago. It had always been a shop but at that time it was a rather sad and tired business. Robin, a former producer of animated commercials, and Ellen set about rejuvenating and expanding and have gradually built up a reputation for high quality, friendly service coupled with an amazing variety of produce. It's a typical old fashioned grocers shop reminiscent of a style, which was prevalent throughout England between the two world wars but which had all but disappeared by the 1970s. It is extremely well thought of and patronised, not just by the locals but by country people for many miles around. More of a food hall than a combined delicatessen, grocers and off licence, quality pervades every corner of the premises. The large, wood panelled, central display units hold everything from luxury potato crisps and boxes of chocolates to soft drinks and preserves. A large floor to ceiling wall display is devoted to over 120

varieties of international wines ranging from the inexpensive, suitable for everyday drinking, through to fine wines for that special occasion or celebration. Beer drinkers also have plenty of choice and can buy cans and bottles ready chilled or stored at room temperature.

Behind the great glass, chilled deli display counter are high wooden shelves jammed full of some of the finer things in life. Champagne and sparkling wine, racks of spirits and liqueurs and of course massive glass jars of coffee beans, which can be purchased whole or ground and in a wide variety of blends. There are large bags of speciality tea, chocolate eggs and some amazing extra virgin olive oils. Within the display cabinet is a mouth watering array of dishes and tubs filled to the brim with fresh and tasty food. Olives, black and green, from a variety of regions are available in oil or with herbs or perhaps garlic. Mixed salads and dips can be bought in small tubs or large dishes and with a little cheese, some fresh bread and a bottle of wine provide a splendid picnic for a sleepy summer afternoon in the countryside or by a riverbank. The selection of cheeses includes French and Italian alongside locally produced delicacies and regional and national favourites from the United Kingdom. Chesterton's also caters for visitors and tourists with a specially selected range of gifts.

Outside in the elegant courtyard garden customers can rest from the heat of the day under the shade of a parasol and enjoy a cup of tea or coffee along with their choice from the deliciously wicked selection of pastries and cakes. The courtyard has a typical mediterranean atmosphere with its plain brick walls and steps, beautifully scented garden borders and colourful hanging baskets.

and the museum's Attree Room shows archaeological finds from prehistoric sites nearby and remains of Roman pottery dug up to the east of the village. Here is also the history of the parish church and more recently of 17th century non-conformist worship in the village. As this remarkable village has an important place in the English Arts and Crafts movement, the museum features an important collection of work by 20th century artists and craftspeople, including stone carver and typographer Eric Gill, calligrapher Edward Johnston, painter and poet David Jones, weaver Ethel Mairet, silversmith Dunstan Pruden and artist Frank Brangwyn. The village school itself opened in 1838 and the schoolmaster's garden is stocked with fruits, flowers and vegetables as it would have been in the days of the first schoolmaster, George Verrall. Life in the village, at home and on the farm is shown in the schoolmaster's cottage.

PLUMPTON
6 miles NE of Brighton on the B2116

The village is divided in two: the modern Plumpton Green and the old village of Plumpton. **Plumpton Green**, to the north, grew up around the railway station and is the home of the famous **National Hunt Racecourse**. Spectators arriving by train should look out for the Victorian signal box, which has been designated a listed building following the persistent efforts of local railway enthusiasts to preserve it.

Old Plumpton is centred around its flint built church which dates from the 12th century. The elegant moated 16th century **Plumpton Place** was substantially remodelled by Lutyens in the 1920s. The then owner, Edward Hudson, was a wealthy magazine proprietor, who had already

commissioned Lutyens to renovate his other country property, Lindisfarne Castle, off the Northumberland coast. A previous Tudor owner, Leonard Mascall, was a great cultivator of apples, a tradition that is still maintained at the East Sussex Agricultural College here in Plumpton.

The site of an early Bronze Age settlement can be found up a footpath opposite the college and, nearby, is a sandstone block, which commemorates the Battle of Lewes, where Simon de Montfort defeated Henry III in 1264.

HAMSEY
8 miles NE of Brighton off the A275

This must have once been an important place for, in 925, King Athelstan held a meeting of his counsellors at Hamsey Manor. Today, though, all that remains of this hamlet is the old church that is reached through the yard of a 400 year-old farm.

BARCOMBE
9 miles NE of Brighton off the A275

On the banks of the River Ouse, which is tidal as far as this point, Barcombe is a tranquil place that was a favourite picnic place with the Edwardians. As well as fishing and picnicking, artists would come here to paint the dilapidated mill buildings in this splendid Ouse Valley setting. There is evidence that the Romans were here and the village was described as having a church and three and a half mills in the Domesday Book. The half mill was one that spanned the river and the other half was accredited to the village of Isfield.

The parish church of St Mary once lay at the heart of the village but, as the Black Death came to the area, the village was decimated and those who survived rebuilt their houses a mile away to the north. There are marvellous views of the South Downs from the churchyard.

RINGMER

9½ miles NE of Brighton on the B2192

This spacious village, familiar to anyone arriving at Glyndebourne by car, is one of the earliest recorded settlements in Sussex. Though nothing remains of the Saxon church that once stood close to the village's enormous green, there has been a place of worship here for over 1,000 years. The present church was built in 1884 by William Martin after fires in the 16th and 19th centuries had burnt down the previous buildings. Inside the church is a poignant memorial to the village's cricket team. During World War I they joined up en masse to fight at the front and, of the 34 club members who went to France, only six returned alive.

During the 17th century, this rural village, in a roundabout manner, played an important part in the history of America. Two young women of the parish married men who went on to become influential figures in the birth of the United States. Guglielma Springett, the daughter of Sir William who supported Parliament during the English Civil War, went on to marry William Penn, the founder of the state of Pennsylvania, while Ann Sadler married John Harvard, the founder of Harvard University.

Ringmer's most famous inhabitant was Timothy, a tortoise. He belonged to the aunt of the 18th century naturalist Gilbert White. During his visits to see his aunt, White became fascinated by Timothy's activities. After his aunt's death, White continued to study the tortoise and, in *The Natural History of Selbourne* he describes the tortoise's lethargic movements. Timothy's carapace can be seen in the Natural History Museum, London.

VIC STRINGER

Unit 5, Acorn House, The Broyle, Ringmer, Lewes BN8 5NN
Tel: 01273 814434 Fax: 01273 814434
e-mail: vsp47@hotmail.com

Vic Stringer has been in the antique trade in Lewes for over 30 years. Vic spent 15 years gaining experience and building up networks of contacts within the trade, working for an established repro-furniture company. Then he decided to use his skills and knowledge of antiques to set up his own company. He offers a painstaking restoration service of English antiques, including French polishing, re-upholstering, re-leathering and glazing. As well as restoration, Vic also makes repro-furniture pieces, including custom made antique reproduction pieces to order. Customers can also get expert help and advice on interior design, based on Vic's extensive knowledge of period furniture and classic interiors.

Vic was originally based in the centre of Lewes but traffic and parking problems in this busy county town made him decide to move out to a more accessible location. The short drive out from the attractions of medieval Lewes to Ringmer is well worth it to visit this busy and spacious workshop and view the range of repro-furniture, produced on the premises as well as the selection of antiques in the process of restoration. There is plenty of parking on this small industrial estate and easy access to Vic's workshop to browse or to collect furniture.

Vic's workshop is easily found by taking the Uckfield Road out of Lewes as far as the Ringmer turn off, sign-posted to the right.

LEWES

7 miles NE of Brighton on the A27

The county town of East Sussex, Lewes is an historic settlement that occupies a strategically important point where the River Ouse is crossed by an ancient east to west land route. Much of the town's street plan dates from Saxon times. It was one of the Saxon capitals visited by Alfred the Great and it was considered important enough to be allowed to mint currency. The Norman invasion in the 11th century

Lewes Castle

and William the Conqueror's success at Battle, however, really saw Lewes grow in stature.

Because of their closeness to the English Channel, William gave the Sussex estates to his most trusted barons, and the lands around Lewes were granted to his powerful friend, William de Warenne. De Warenne and his wife Gundrada began the construction of **Lewes Castle** and founded the great **Priory of St Pancras**. Today, a substantial part of the castle remains,

ANTIQUE INTERIORS LTD

7 Malling Street, Lewes, East Sussex, BN7 2RA
Tel: 01273 486822 fax: 01273 486769

Architectural antiques are the speciality of this fascinating Aladdin's Cave of a shop. Set in a splendid old listed building, opposite the Thomas à Becket church, there has been a shop here since it was built in the 18th century. Proprietors Liz Trunfull and Kevin Hillman have over 20 years of experience in the antique business. Prior to starting **Antique Interiors** ten years ago they specialised in brass and iron Victorian bedsteads. Now they supply architectural antiques for the home and garden.

Liz is responsible for buying all of the stock and for running the shop. Kevin is more often found in their huge workshop across the road carrying out restoration work, stripping, polishing and repairing or constructing the hand built kitchens, the business specialises in. He's also responsible for deliveries

and installations. The shop contains a wide variety of pieces collected from all over the world. Antique statues sit beside magnificent ornate beds and farmhouse dressers complete with dishes. In the corner may be found a hand-crafted sink unit complete with brass taps, a butlers sink and an overhead plate rack or a beautifully restored Victorian iron bath big enough to host a party. The prices are reasonable and the service is direct and friendly. Kevin and Liz are happy to advise on kitchen and bathroom fittings. Having restored several houses themselves they now have a wealth of experience that they can pass on to their clients.

including a section of the keep and two towers dating from the 13th century. During the early 19th century, the castle was owned by the Kemp family and they are responsible for the elegant Georgian façade to the **Barbican House**. Overshadowed by the Barbican Gate, the house is now home to the **Barbican House Museum** where relics found in the area, from prehistoric times through to the Middle Ages, are on display. Here, too, is the **Living History Museum**, with its superb scale model of Lewes set at the end of the 19th century. There are also splendid views over the town available to anyone climbing to the roof of the keep.

Anne of Cleves' House

Little remains of the Priory of St Pancras. Built on the foundations of a small Saxon church, the priory and a great deal of land were given to the abbey of Cluny in Burgundy. At its height, the priory had a church as large as Chichester Cathedral, with outbuildings to the same scale, but all were destroyed at the time of the Dissolution in the 16th century.

During the 14th century a feud developed between the 4th Earl de Warenne and Lord Pevensey. In order to settle their differences the two met, one May morning, under the walls of Lewes Castle. As they fought, Lord Pevensey cornered de Warenne and, as he was about to drive home his sword, Lady de Warenne began to pray to St Nicholas to save his life and she vowed that, should her husband be spared, her first born son would not marry until he had placed St Nicholas' belt on the tomb of the Blessed Virgin in Byzantium. At that moment, Lord Pevensey slipped and, as he fell, de Warenne drove home his sword. Years went by until the earl's eldest son, Lord Manfred, became engaged to Lady Edona and, halfway through a banquet to celebrate the 21st anniversary of de Warenne's victory, a vision of the combat appeared to all the guests. Understanding at once that the vow must be fulfilled before their son's

SAY CHEESE

Riverside, Cliffe High Street, Lewes, BN7 2AD
Tel:01273 487871 Fax: 01323 833871

Life long foodies, David and Eleanor Robins have been cheesemongers since 1989 and they love introducing people to different cheeses. They specialise in the farm cheeses of Sussex, Kent and Surrey, together with the best from the rest of the world. Riverside also has a butcher, a fishmonger, a chocolate shop and a wide range of hard to find ingredients. There is also a brasserie upstairs in this delightful 18th century converted warehouse alongside the River Ouse.

Southover Grange Gardens, Lewes

wedding, the earl and his wife sent Manfred to Byzantium. For over a year Lady Edona waited for him to return and, finally, his ship was sighted off Worthing. A welcoming party gathered and then, with every one watching, the ship struck a hidden rock and sank with all hands. Lady Edona, watching the ship go down, gave out a sigh and sank to the ground dead. A plinth stands in memory of Lady Edona who was buried where she fell.

Beside the priory ruins is a bronze memorial by the sculptor Enzo Plazzotti that was commissioned to commemorate the 700th anniversary of the **Battle of Lewes**. Fought on Offham Hill, the Battle of Lewes took place in May 1264, between the armies of Henry III and Simon de Montfort. The night before the battle, de Montfort and his troops were said to have kept vigil in a nearby church whilst Henry III and his men had a wild, and in some cases drunken, evening at the castle. Whether this was the reason for the king's defeat or whether it was down to bad military tactics is open to debate.

Another monument in the town is the **Martyrs' Memorial** erected in 1901 in memory of the 17 Protestant martyrs

who were burnt to death on Lewes High Street during the reign of Catholic Mary Tudor. The mainly Protestant inhabitants of Lewes found an outlet for their resentment at this treatment after the foiling of the Gunpowder Plot and the **Bonfire Celebrations**, which still take place here are elaborate affairs.

Like Ditchling, Lewes has an **Anne of Cleves' House**, in this case an early 16th century Wealden hall house which, again, formed part of Henry VIII's divorce settlement with his fourth wife. Also like the house in Ditchling, it is unlikely that the queen ever set foot in the building. Today, the house is open to the public and the rooms are furnished to give visitors an idea of life in the 17th and 18th centuries.

GLYNDEBOURNE
9½ miles NE of Brighton off the B9192

Glyndebourne, a part Tudor, part Victorian country house, just a mile north of Glynde village, is now the home of the world famous **Glyndebourne Opera House**. In the early 1930s, John Christie, a school master, music lover and inheritor of the house, married the accomplished opera singer Audrey Mildmay and, as regular visitors to European music festivals, they decided to bring opera to England and their friends. In the idyllic setting of their country estate, they built a modest theatre and, in 1934, Glyndebourne first opened with a performance of Mozart's *Marriage of Figaro*. However, their scheme was not an overnight success. On the second night only six people ventured here in evening dress. However, by the outbreak of World War II, they had extended the theatre to accommodate 600. Since the

Glyndebourne Audience

early 1950s, Glyndebourne has gone from strength to strength and, as well as extending the theatre further, the repertoire has also increased. Today, each summer season, from May to August, sees people venturing here dressed in evening gowns, laden with picnic hampers to enjoy a wide range of opera in a unique setting and to eat their picnics in the grounds during the long interval.

GLYNDE
9½ miles NE of Brighton off the A27

Situated at the foot of Mount Caburn, this small and attractive village is home to a splendid house and an ancient church. Overlooking the South Downs, **Glynde Place** was built in 1579 for William Morley from flint and Normandy stone that was brought across the Channel in barges. An undistinguished family, the only member of note was Colonel Herbert Morley, a Parliamentarian who was also one of the judges at the trial of Charles I. Fortunately for the family, Morley did not sign the king's death warrant and so, at the Restoration, the family was able to gain his pardon from Charles II. The

house passed by marriage into the Trevor family and, in 1743, it was inherited by the Bishop of Durham, Richard Trevor. He left the exterior of the house untouched whilst turning the interior into classical 18th century residence. The house is still in private hands and open to the public on a limited basis.

At the gates to the house stands the church built by the bishop in 1765 to the designs of Sir Thomas Robinson. Having recently visited Italy, Robinson was very enthusiastic about Renaissance architecture and, as a result, the church has a coved rococo ceiling, box pews and a gallery.

The village is also home of the black faced southdown sheep, first bred here by John Ellman who lived here between 1753 and 1832. A benevolent farmer, he built a school for his labourers' children and, when they married, he gave the couple a pig and a cow. He even allowed the single labourers to lodge under his own roof. However, Ellman would not allow a licensed house in the village although he did not mind if his men brewed their own beer at home.

The distinctive **Mount Caburn**, to the west of Glynde, can be reached along a footpath from the village. Many thousands of years ago, this steep sided chalk outcrop was separated from the rest of the Downs by the action of the River Glynde. This process created a mound about 500 feet in height whose natural defensive properties have not gone unnoticed over the centuries. The earthwork defences of an Iron Age hillfort can still be made out near the summit and there is evidence of an earlier Stone Age settlement.

WEST FIRLE
10 miles E of Brighton off the A27

Though the village is known as West Firle, there is no East Firle - or any other

Firle in the area. A feudal village of old flint cottages at the foot of the South Downs, it is dominated by **Firle Beacon** to the southeast, which rises to a height of 718 feet. As one of the highest points in the area, the importance of this vantage point has long been recognised. It was used by the Admiralty for a fire beacon to warn of the approaching Spanish Armada in the 16th century and remains of a Stone Age long barrow and a group of Bronze Age round barrows have been found on the summit. There was also a Roman observation point here. Today, the summit can be reached by taking a small detour off the South Downs Way and the breathtaking views make the climb well worth while.

Back in the village, and set in its own idyllic parkland, is **Firle Place**, the home of the Gage family for over 500 years. Built by Sir John Gage in the 15th century, this marvellous Tudor manor house was greatly altered some 300 years later and today it will be familiar to many who have seen it as a backdrop for major feature films or as a location for television series. Still very much a family home, today owned by the 7th Viscount, its rooms contain a wonderful collection of European and English Old Masters as well as some rare and notable examples of French and English furniture and Sèvres porcelain. The magnificent deer park, which surrounds the house, was landscaped by Capability Brown in the 18th century and it features a castellated tower and an ornamental lake. It is open to the public in the summer.

RODMELL

7 miles E of Brighton off the A26

This little village of thatched cottages is thought to have got its name from 'mill on the road' and, though no mill can be found here today, there is a Mill Road and, in the small 12th century church

there is a reference to the village's old name 'Rodmill'.

However, the village's main claim to fame is that it was the home of Virginia and Leonard Woolf from 1919 until her death in 1941. The couple, escaping the confining intellectual world of the Bloomsbury set in which they were influential figures, settled at **Monk's House**, a delightful early 18th century farmhouse that is now in the hands of the National Trust and open briefly in the summer. The garden, which is lush with hollyhocks, dahlias and hydrangeas, gives good views over the downs across the River Ouse.

During her time here, Virginia wrote many of her best remembered works, but throughout her life she suffered great bouts of depression and mental illness. Finally, in 1941, she took her own life by wading into the river with her pockets full of stones. Surprisingly for the disappearance of such a well-renowned figure, her body was not discovered for three weeks and then by some children playing on the riverbank. Her ashes, along with those of her husband who stayed here until his death in 1969, are scattered in the garden.

SOUTHEASE

7 miles E of Brighton off the A26

This tiny village, in a dip on the Lewes to Newhaven road, was first mentioned in a Saxon charter of 966, when King Edgar granted the church and manor here to Hyde Abbey in Winchester. Some 100 years later, at the time of the Domesday Survey, this was a flourishing village that was assessed as having 38,500 herrings as well as the usual farm produce. Inside the early 12th century church is a copy of King Edgar's charter. The original is in the British Museum, London. There is also an unusual organ built by Allen of Soho and installed in 1790. The only other organs of this kind known to be still in existence are in Buckingham Palace and York Minster.

TELSCOMBE
6 miles E of Brighton off the A26

Telscombe was once an important sheep rearing and a race horse training centre. In fact, the last man in England to be hanged for sheep stealing, in 1819, is believed to have come from the village. In 1902, the racing stables at Stud House trained the winner of the Grand National - Shannon Lass. The horse's owner, Ambrose Gorham, was so delighted with the win that he rebuilt the village church and each Christmas gave the children of the parish a book and a pair of Wellington boots.

PIDDINGHOE
7½ miles E of Brighton off the A26

Set on a wide curve of the River Ouse, this village - whose name is pronounced 'Piddnoo' by its older inhabitants - is a picturesque place, with a host of 17th century cottages and pleasant riverside walks. It was a great place for smugglers in days gone by. Today, however, the ships and boats that tie up at the quayside below the church belong to deep sea anglers and weekend sailors. The golden fish weather vane on top of the church tower was referred to by Kipling as a dolphin but it is, in fact, a sea trout.

NEWHAVEN
9 miles SE of Brighton on the A26

Newhaven itself is a relatively new settlement and it replaces the much older village of Meeching. Inhabited since the Iron Age, when a fort was built on Castle Hill, Meeching lay beside the River Ouse. However, in 1579 a great storm altered the course of the river and its outlet to the sea moved from Seaford to near

Meeching. Thus Newhaven was established at the new river mouth and it is now one of the county's two main harbours (the other is at Shoreham by Sea) with an important cross-Channel ferry/hovercraft service and also a cargo terminal.

Newhaven's rise began in the 19th century and it grew steadily busier once the rail link with London was established

NEWHAVEN FORT

Fort Road, Newhaven, East Sussex BN9 9DS
Tel: 01273 517622 Fax: 01273 51205
e-mail: enquiries@newhavenfort.org.uk
website: www.newhavenfort.org.uk

Built in the 1860s to deter invaders, **Newhaven Fort** is now home to a museum that offers an insight into the sights and sounds of wartime Britain. The life-size scenes, interactive exhibitions and audio-visual presentations vividly illustrate what conditions were like for those who remained at home during World War II. Here, visitors can take a look inside Anderson and Morrison air-raid shelters; walk through a blitzed house and experience an air-raid from inside an underground shelter.

In addition, a new World War I exhibition has been created within the fort's refurbished Officers' Quarters and, through interactive, audio-visual and film presentations, the origins of the war through to its aftermath are traced. The horrific conditions of the battlefront are also illustrated.

There is also plenty to discover outside, including underground tunnels, ramparts and cliff top guns, and children will enjoy the special Mission Trail, themed play area and souvenir shop. Special events are held throughout the year and the fort is open daily from the end of March to the beginning of November.

in 1847. Two of the earliest visitors to use the passenger steamer service to Dieppe were the fleeing King and Queen of France, Louis Phillippe and Marie Amelie who stayed at the Bridge Inn in 1848 after their sea journey before continuing to London by train where they were met by Queen Victoria's coach and taken to Buckingham Palace. In order to maintain their

Newhaven Harbour

anonymity, the couple registered themselves at the inn under the rather original names of Mr and Mrs Smith.

Also in the 19th century, during one of the periodic French invasion scares, **Newhaven Fort** (see panel opposite) was built. Consisting of a ring of casements

constructed around a large parade ground, the fort was equipped with modern guns during World War II and also received several direct hits from German bombs. Today, it is a **Museum** where visitors can explore the underground tunnels and galleries and

CATCHPENNY CRAFTS

40 High Street, Newhaven, East Sussex, BN9 9PD
Tel: 01273 611374 Fax: 01444 831582
e-mail: c.oakley@bushinternet.com

Carol and Steve Butler spent 15 years making and selling crafts at local craft fairs always working towards opening their own shop. They achieved their goal in March 2001 and have gained a loyal following amongst local people, who love the enormous range that **Catchpenny** carries. The shop is an Aladdin's cave full of gifts, cards and goodies. Shelves are crammed with quality hand-made crafts, whilst craft supplies bring a steady trade from other craft workers, who can shop here for their raw materials. Much of the stock is from the workshops of Carol and Steve, augmented by a wide range of crafts, gifts and cards from other craft workers and artists from throughout England, Scotland and Wales.

Handmade dolls sit next to flowerpot people on one shelf, while another contains pen sets for the desk of a busy executive. There are hand-painted mirrors, beautiful dried flower arrangements in baskets, glassware, scarves, clocks and barometers. Hanging from the ceiling is a wonderful collection of mobiles and exquisite wind chimes that fill the shop with their gentle music if the door is open. Greetings cards come in all shapes and sizes. Some hand-painted, others using dried and pressed flowers, shapes or materials. The stock of craft supplies is extensive and includes, papers and glues, parchments, dried flowers and even glass. As experienced craftspeople Carol and Steve are delighted to offer advice and help on any aspect of craftwork and assist their customers in choosing the right materials for the job.

COLOUR HEALING TAPESTRIES

82 Crescent Drive South, Woodingdean, Brighton, Sussex, BN 2 6RB
Tel:01273 303571 e-mail: teresa@colouhealingtapestries.co.uk
website: www.colourhealingtapestries.co.uk

Theresa Sundt was born in Thessaloniki, Greece and has been a professional weaver and artist for over 25 years. She has undertaken numerous public and private commissions during that time as well as teaching art to adults and children. At **Colour Healing Tapestries** visitors can enjoy Swedish massage and Indian Head massage, attend workshops and lectures. Weekend classes on weaving and colour healing last for a day and basic techniques are taught. The colours chosen are those most needed on the day to complement and balance personal well being. Other craft courses are available.

Theresa, Aimeé

AIMEÉ SAIC MOSART

Mosaic Studio and Art Gallery, 131A South Coast Road, Peacehaven, East Sussex, BN10 8PA
Tel:01273 589457 website: www.bamm.org.uk/ Aimeé Saic

Aimeé was runner up for the decorator of the year award in 1999 from *House Beautiful Magazine* for her craft of mosaic making. Successful completion of a restoration job on the mosaic floors in the lavatories of the Orient Express Pullman carriage led, in 2001, to a commission to design a new floor for the Minerva carriage. She opened **Mosart Gallery** in a small shop six miles from Brighton two years ago. It is busy but has a cosy relaxed atmosphere and the walls are lined with mosaic. Here Aimeé undertakes private and public commissions in mosaic art and also runs a series of weekend courses to teach this art to others. Theresa Sundt also teaches her Colour Healing Tapestry courses at this gallery and with the two disciplines complementing each other, people often cross over from one course to the other.

view the permanent Home Front exhibition. Meanwhile, the **Newhaven Local and Maritime Museum**, in Garden Paradise, contains a wealth of information relating to Newhaven's port, the town's history and its role in wartime. Here, also lies the **Planet Earth Exhibition**, which explores the world of natural history from millions of years ago to the present day.

PEACEHAVEN

9 miles SE of Brighton on the A259

If nearby Newhaven is a recent town, Peacehaven must be considered just a fledgling village. The brainchild of wealthy businessman, Charles Neville, it was planned and designed during World War I and the intention was to call the new town Anzac on Sea in honour of the Australian and New Zealand troops, who were stationed here before going off to fight in the trenches. However, after the

Armistice, it was renamed Peacehaven which very much caught the mood of the time. Laid out in the grid pattern and with no immediate connection with either the South Downs or the coast, it remains a quiet place off the usual South Coast tourist itinerary.

Along the cliff top promenade there is a 20 foot tall monument to King George V that also marks the line of the Greenwich Meridian.

ROTTINGDEAN

3½ miles SE of Brighton on the A259

Built in a gap in the cliffs between Newhaven and Brighton, Rottingdean was, naturally, a key place for smugglers at one time. However, more recently, it became the home of more artistic citizens. The artist Sir Edward Burne-Jones lived here for the last 20 years of his life in the rambling **North End House** by the green. During his time in

THE BEST OF BRIGHTON AND SUSSEX COTTAGES

Windmill Lodge, Vicarage lane, Rottingdean, Sussex, BN2 7HD
Tel: 01273 308779 e-mail: brightoncottages@pavilion.co.uk
Fax: 01273 300266 website: www.bestofbrighton.co.uk

This accommodation letting agency was started ten years ago by
Richard Harris who lives and works in the charming seaside village of
Rottingdean, three miles outside Brighton. They specialise in offering
fully furnished properties to the business, holiday and conference accommodation market in the
Brighton and Hove area, but can also offer longer term residential lets.

Accommodation is available throughout East and West Sussex. and includes seafront and town
centre properties in Brighton and Hove, unusual properties in the Sussex countryside, both inland
and along the coast between Eastbourne and Chichester, and a luxury apartment in the centre of
Paris. The properties on offer range from small studio flats, through standard two to three bedroom
properties, up to some magnificent five to eight bedroom properties, sleeping from 10 to 16 people.
Most of the properties are either owners' second homes or investment properties and great care and
pride is taken to ensure that they are presented in the best possible way. Every single property has been

visited by Richard, who takes a personal interest in the running of
the business. In addition some 95% of the properties have been
assessed by the English Tourism Council and display their star
grading. Most are four or five star and none have less than two
stars. Previous satisfied clients include stars and cast of major shows
and plays, members of parliament, sportspeople attending world
class events, ramblers, overseas language students and holidaymakers
of all kinds. All of the properties are regularly inspected, well-
managed and are let complete with all facilities.

Rottingdean, Burne-Jones designed seven
windows for the originally Saxon parish
church that were made up by William
Morris. After his death in 1898, his wife,
Lady Burne-Jones maintained her high
profile in Rottingdean and, in 1900,
caused uproar when she hung anti-war
banners from her windows following the
Relief of Mafeking.

Lady Burne-Jones was also Rudyard
Kipling's aunt, and he lived here, at **The
Elms**, for five years before moving to
Bateman's in 1902. Overlooking the
village pond, the gardens of The Elms are
open to the public. Surrounded by old
stone walls are formal rose gardens, wild
and scented gardens and a wealth of rare
plants. At the Museum of the
Rottingdean Preservation Society, at The
Grange in Rottingdean, there is a Kipling
Room, with a reconstruction of his study
in The Elms, and other exhibits devoted
to his work.

Another famous resident of
Rottingdean was J. Reuter, a German
bank clerk, who started a pigeon post to
bring back news from abroad that
expanded into the internationally
respected world wide news agency.

HOVE

2 miles W of Brighton on the A259

Nestling at the foot of the downs and
now joined to Brighton, Hove is a
genteel resort that is famous for its
Regency squares - such as Brunswick and
Palmeira - and broad tree lined avenues.
A former fishing village, major
development of Hove took place in the
early 19th century when the seafront was
built with its distinctive terraces. As well
as the usual spoils of the seaside town,
Hove is home to the Sussex County
Cricket Club and hosts teams from all
over the world at their ground.

The **Hove Museum and Art Gallery**,

AUDREY'S CHOCOLATES (HOVE) LTD

28 Holland Road, Hove, Sussex, BN3 1JJ
Tel: 01273 735561 Fax: 01273 735561
e-mail: info@audreyschocolates.co.uk
website: www.audreyschocolates.co.uk

Audrey's Chocolates has been in business making superb
hand- made chocolates and confectionery for more than 40
years. The chocolates and confectionery are made on the
premises at 28 Holland Road by a dedicated team of 23 people.
Behind this traditional frontage, with its old fashioned windows full of beautiful satin boxes decorated
with hand made paper and silk flowers, there are cabinets and shelves crammed with a wonderful
range of chocolates. Only the finest ingredients are used and the chocolatiers are trained to the very
highest standards. Specialities include traditional rose and violet creams, peppermints in bitter
chocolate, caramels, nougat and marzipan. For the connoisseur there are Morello cherries steeped in
the finest French brandy for two years before being dipped in plain chocolate.

Throughout the year there are seasonal specialities. At Christmas it will be chocolate Santas and
novelty boxes, while at Easter there are eggs of all sizes as well as
chocolate bunnies, chickens and fish and more decorated boxes.
Valentine's Day sees hearts popping up everywhere, chocolate
hearts and heart shaped boxes draped of course with masses of
satin, lace and ribbon. As well as the main premises at Hove there
is another shop in Brighton at 16 Regent Arcade. They also do
mail order to all parts of the world and customers can choose
from a range of decorative and special occasion boxes to fill with
confectionery of their choice.

outside which stands the splendid
wooden pavilion, **Jaipur Gateway**, an
elegantly carved structure that was
transported to England from Rajashtan
in 1886, contains a whole host of
exhibits on the history of the town.
There is also a superb collection of 20th
century paintings and drawings and 18th
century furniture. For history of a
different kind, the **British Engineerium**,
housed in a restored 19th century
pumping station, has all manner of
engines - from steam powered to electric.
Many of the model and life size displays
still work and the museum's working
beam engine is powered up on a regular
basis. Meanwhile, there is the Giant's
Toolbox, a hands on display of gears and
levers, cylinders and pistons that visitors
can discover for themselves.

For one of the most spectacular views
of the South Downs a visit to **Foredown
Tower** is a must. Housed in a beautifully

restored Edwardian water tower, there is
a viewing gallery with Sussex's only
operational camera obscura and a mass
of computers and countryside data that
tell the story of the local flora and fauna
as well as the geography of the night sky.

Also in Hove, and rather out of place
with the grand Regency squares and
avenues, is **West Blatchington
Windmill**. Built in the 1820s and still
with all its original machinery working
on all five floors, the mill has been
restored and continues to grind flour. As
well as watching the fascinating milling
process, visitors can view an exhibition
of agricultural equipment, which
includes an oat crusher and a threshing
machine.

EASTBOURNE

This stylish and genteel seaside resort,
which has managed to avoid both

becoming too brash or disappearing into shy gentility, takes its name from the stream, or bourne, which has its course in the old reservoir in the area of open land that is now known as Motcombe Gardens. When George III sent his children here in the summer of 1780, it was, in fact, two villages, the larger of which lay a mile inland from the coast. Slowly the villages were developed and merged but it was William Cavendish, later the 7th Duke of Devonshire, who really instigated Eastbourne's rapid growth as a seaside resort from the 1850s onwards.

As much of the land belonged to the Cavendish family, the expansion was well thought out and managed agreeably which leaves, today, an elegant town, well known for its delightful gardens. Among the first buildings that Cavendish had constructed are the handsome Regency style Burlington Hotel, St Saviour's Church, the town hall and the extremely elegant railway station. The classic pier was built in the 1880s and it remains one of the finest seaside piers in the country.

There are, however, several buildings, which pre-date the intervention of William Cavendish. The original parish church, inland from the coast, dates from the 12th century though it stands on the site of a previous Saxon place of worship. The excellent **Towner Art Gallery and Museum** is housed in a very sensible Georgian town house that was built by Dr Henry Lushington, a vicar of Eastbourne. It became home to the town's museum in the 1920s and it has a collection of 19th and 20th century British art, as well as displays on the history from the time of the Romans to the present day. The development of the old village into a seaside resort is told at the **Eastbourne Heritage Centre.** In the centre of Eastbourne is the **Museum of Shops** (see panel below) with its Victorian streets,

MUSEUM OF SHOPS

20 Cornfield Terrace, Eastbourne,
East Sussex BN21 4NS
Tel: 01323 737143

This famous **Museum of Shops** is in the centre of Eastbourne, just off the seafront between the War memorial roundabout and the main theatres. Visitors say this is one of the most comprehensive collections of its kind in the country as there are over 100,000 exhibits on four floors of old shops, room settings and displays depicting 100 years of Shopping and Social History. Certianly it's one of the oldest established having been amassed during the past 40 years by Jan and Graham Upton.

To the sounds of horses and carriages stroll through the Victorian styled streets, wonder at the chemist with his "cure all" preparations or remember "Five boys" chocolate. See the ironmonger, who sold everything from pot menders to mouse traps, the office or boot repairers, the draper's or tailor's and proud portraits in the photographer's. There's wind up gramaphones in the music shop whilst the toy shop is full of childhood memories.

Mr. Barton, the grocer, is selling biscuits from glass topped tins

and in the seafarer's inn the sailor is enjoying his pint. Re-live the Wartime and rationing - with the authentic kitchen/living room, complete with air raid shelter. See the Edwardian kitchen or village post office, "Christmas Past" or the jewellers and many other displays including eggcups and a huge collection of royal souvenirs. Opening Hours: 10.00 am to 5.30 pm every day (Summer). Details of winter hours, admission prices, party rates, worksheets, etc. upon application.

CHALK FARM HOTEL AND PLANT CENTRE

Coopers Hill, Willingdon, East Sussex, BN20 9JD
Tel: 01323 503800 Fax: 01323 520331
e-mail: chalkfarm@supa.com
website: www.chalkfarm.org

George Orwell's classic satire on the Russian Revolution, *Animal Farm*, centred on a takeover, by the animals, of Manor Farm in the village of Willingdon. Only one such village exists in all of England and although there is not a Manor Farm here there is considerable evidence pointing to Chalk Farm as Orwell's model. Nestling in the beautiful, tranquil South Downs, **Chalk Farm** is now a hotel, an ideal setting for holidays or business travellers. The house dates back to the 17th century and has retained many of the original features. It is surrounded by superb gardens and lawns maintained to the highest standard.

Eric Blair, who wrote as George Orwell, was born in 1903 and was educated from 1911 onwards at St Cyprian's School in Eastbourne, a two hour round walking trip from Chalk Farm. As a boy he

explored the South Downs and went on lengthy rambles and in a letter to his mother makes mention of the neighbouring village of Jevington. Blair never identified the site of Manor Farm but locals in Willingdon are convinced it is Chalk farm. And they have plenty of evidence from the book to back this up, Williingdon is mentioned eight times in the story. Manor Farm was described as having ' a good quarry of limestone' and old maps show the existence of a chalk pit and old limekilns close to the farm house. The farm is also described as being on a slope which 'led the way down to the five-barred gate that gave way onto the main road.' In Blair's time the main road was not, as it is known today, the A22 but the road known as Coopers Hill. Furthermore 'on Midsummer's Eve, which was a Saturday, Mr Jones went into Willingdon and got so drunk at the Red Lion that he did not come back until midday on Sunday.' And indeed the Red lion is still operating in the village today. There is a short walk round the village and farm which leads to the top of a grassy knoll, which corresponds with Orwell's description of '...the knoll where they (the animals) were lying gave them a wide prospect across the countryside. Most of Animal Farm was within their view; the hayfield, the spinney, the drinking pool, the ploughed fields, where the young wheat was thick and green and the red roofs of the farm building with the smoke curling from the chimneys'. The view remains, unchanged with the exception of some modern housing.

Guests in the hotel can of course wander round and see for themselves how Orwell's descriptions match reality. They can also enjoy the highest standard of accommodation and service, including the en suite bedrooms complete with tea and coffee making facilities and colour television. The traditional Old Barn Restaurant serves delicious English fare for lunch and dinner and there is morning coffee and mouth watering Sussex cream teas available in the comfortable lounges. The Plant Centre, which is part of the farm, was established in 1994 and stocks a wide range of hardy plants many of which are propagated and grown on site. The centre has for sale a large quantity of trees, shrubs, herbaceous plant, bedding plants and hanging baskets. They also provide a garden maintenance and a landscaping service.

room-settings and displays depicting shopping and social history over the last 100 years.

As a coastal town, during the scare of French invasions at the beginning of the 19th century, Eastbourne had its own defences. The **Martello Tower No 73**, one of 103 built along the south coast, is also referred to as the **Wish Tower**. Its rather odd name comes from the Saxon word 'wisc' which means marshy place and today the tower is home to a small **Puppet Museum**.

Eastbourne Town

Another Napoleonic defence, the **Redoubt Fortress**, was built between 1804 and 1810 on the seafront. Now the home of the **Military Museum of Sussex**, the exhibitions here cover some 300 years of conflict on land, sea and in the air. Highlights include, relics from the charge of the Light Brigade at Balaklava and Rommel's staff car from World War II.

The sea has always played an important part in the life of the town, from its early days as a fishing village and now as a resort offering a safe beach environment. Naturally, the lifeboats have played an important role through the years and, close to their lifeboat station, is the **RNLI Lifeboat Museum**. Here the history of the town's lifeboats, from 1853 onwards are charted through a series of interesting exhibits, including photographs of some of their most dramatic rescues.

Whilst the town is undoubtedly a charming and delightful place to explore and enjoy, most people wish to see **Beachy Head**. One of the most spectacular chalk precipices in England, with a sheer drop of over 500 feet in places, this very famous natural landmark lies just to the southwest of the town. The grand scale of the cliffs is brought home by the sight of the lighthouse, completely dwarfed at the cliff base. On the clifftop is the **Beachy Head Countryside Centre** which focuses on downland life, from the Bronze Age onwards, and includes numerous wildlife displays. This is also the end (or the beginning) of the **South Downs Way**, the long distance bridleway that was first established in 1972.

Beachy Head

LITLINGTON NURSERY

Litlington, Near Polegate, East Sussex, BN26 5RB
Tel: 01323 871211 Fax: 01323 871211

Litlington Nursery in this picturesque East Sussex village was once part of the famous Littleton Tea Gardens. Sara Webster and Nicholas Barratt took it over seven years ago in a very neglected state and since then have worked hard to reinvigorate it. They specialise in growing and propagating plants suited to the local chalk downs and the salt wind. They also sell a variety of garden objects made from natural wood and still run the tea room in the summer.

COTYLEDON COUNTRY CRAFTS

Litlington Tea Gardens, Litlington, Near Polgate, East Sussex, BN26 5RB
Tel:01323 871113
e-mail: cotyledon@litlington.fsnet.co.uk

Anthony Paine gave up being a fisherman to make pottery and stained glass. Working initially from home he soon needed more space and took over this shop seven years ago to start **Cotyledon Country Crafts**. He makes a wide variety of pottery and stained glass items, some with a seafaring theme. He also stocks aromatherapy oils, candles, angels and fairies, wooden carvings, fudge, honey and preserves and a range of pure health products.

AROUND EASTBOURNE

POLEGATE

4 miles N of Eastbourne on the A27

The village grew up in the 19th century around a railway junction and, today, it is almost a suburb of Eastbourne. Visitors generally make for the **Polegate Windmill and Museum**, a splendid red brick tower mill, built in 1817, that is one of the few tower mills open to the public (though on a limited basis). Restored as early as 1867, all its internal machinery is in working order and here, too, is a small but fascinating museum of milling.

HAILSHAM

7 miles N of Eastbourne on the A295

This market town, which first received its charter in 1252 from Henry III, is a pleasant town where the modern shopping facilities sit comfortably with the chiefly Georgian High Street. Once a thriving centre of the rope and string industry, Hailsham had the dubious honour of supplying all the rope for public executions. Now, its rope and string are put to less lethal uses. It maintains its rural roots and the three-acre cattle market is one of the largest in East Sussex.

PEVENSEY

4 miles NE of Eastbourne on the A259

On the coast, in the shelter of Pevensey Bay, Pevensey was the landing place for invading Roman legions and it was here they built a fortification to protect their anchorage. The fortress of Anderida, built around AD 280, was one of the first south coast defences. William the Conqueror landed here with his troops prior to the Battle of Hastings and left his half brother, Robert, here while he went off to defeat Harold. Robert built a Norman fortress here, which was joined, in the 13th century, by a stone curtain wall. **Pevensey Castle** seemed well able to withstand attack. Following the Battle of Lewes, Simon de Montfort laid siege here without success. However, the structure gradually fell into disrepair although it was brought back into service, briefly, during the advance of the Spanish Armada and again during World War II. Today, the castle is besieged only by visitors who can explore the ruins and follow its history, from the days of the Romans to the mid 20th century.

In the rest of the village there are several fine medieval buildings including the **Mint House**, a 14th century building that lies outside the castle gates. Coins have been minted on this site since 1076

and, though it is now an antiques showroom, visitors can see the priest's secret room and King Edward VI's bedroom. Any self respecting old building has a ghost and the Mint House is no exception. In the 1580s an Elizabethan woman, the mistress of the London merchant Thomas Dight, lived at the house. Coming back unexpectedly, Dight found her in bed with her lover. Incensed with jealousy, Dight ordered his servants to cut out her tongue and hold her whilst she was made to watch her lover being roasted to death over a fire. The lover's body was thrown into the harbour and the mistress lead to an upstairs room where she starved to death.

In the days prior to the founding of the Royal Navy, Pevensey served as one of the nation's Cinque Ports - that is to

HOREAU'S RESTAURANT

High Street, Westham, Pevensey, East Sussex, BN24 5LZ
Tel: 01323 741037
e-mail: info@horeaus.co.uk website: www.horeaus.co.uk

Seafood is the speciality of this superb little restaurant. Small but with a vibrant intimate atmosphere, **Horeau's** opened in June 2001 and has gone on to become a firm favourite with locals and visitors alike. Claude Horeau is from the Seychelles and it was his love of fish that prompted him to open this speciality restaurant with his wife Christine. Fresh fish and seafood predominates in an exciting and changing menu. Some of the fish is caught locally but the restaurant also receives daily deliveries of specialist and more exotic items. Scallops with vermouth and basil cream is a particularly tasty and unusual combination of flavours as a starter, followed by the delicate flavour of fillet of lemon sole with white wine and cream sauce. Vegetarians will just love the deep fried vegetable samosa, followed by a mouth watering aubergine lasagne

Meat is also available with game, rabbit, chicken, beef, lamb and guinea fowl appearing in various guises. The food is cooked by award winning chef David Bennet. He trained at the prestigious Gleneagles Hotel and was for five years head chef at Rules, Covent Garden, the oldest restaurant in England. To accompany his cooking there is an excellent selection of mainly French wines. The restaurant interior is light and airy, simple and tasteful with a plain wood floor and a small wooden bar. The tables are covered with fine linen cloths and decorated with freshly cut flowers. A new conservatory and lounge have been built at the rear to accommodate extra tables and a pre-meal reception area.

say, it was granted certain privileges by the Crown in return for providing ships and men in defence of the south coast.

Inland, lies the area of drained marshland known as the **Pevensey Levels**. At one time this was an area of tidal mudflats which were covered in shallow salt pans. Since then it has been reclaimed for agricultural use and is now covered in fertile arable fields.

WESTHAM
4 miles NE of Eastbourne on the B2191

This pretty village is home to one of the most ruggedly beautiful churches in Sussex, dating from the 14th century and much patched and braced over the years. Inside the parish church there is a memorial to John Thatcher who died in 1649 and left his estate to the 'Old Brethren' in the hope that Roman Catholicism would, once again, be the religion of England.

EAST DEAN
3 miles W of Eastbourne off the A259

This charming village at the foot of the South Downs is one of the county's most picturesque, with its village green surrounded by flint cottages, a pub and an ancient church.

During the 18th century, the local parson, Jonathan Darby, is said to have made a cave in the nearby cliffs from which he could display a huge lantern on stormy nights to warn sailors of the hidden rocks. However, some say that the reason for his retreat to the caves was actually to get away from Mrs Darby.

Just south of the village, right on the coast, is **Birling Gap**, a huge cleft in the

Seven Sisters

cliffs which offers the only access to the beach between Eastbourne and Cuckmere Haven. Naturally, this was a great place for smugglers who landed their contraband here before making their way up the steep steps to the cliff top. This stretch of the coast, during the 18th century, was controlled by a particularly notorious gang led by Stanton Collins. He had his headquarters in Alfriston and, on one particular night, the gang are said to have moved the lumps of chalk from the cliff path so that pursuing customs officers could not find their way. One unfortunate officer fell over the cliff edge but miraculously held on by his finger tips. Collins' gang came upon him and stamped on his finger-tips and he fell to his death.

To the east of the gap lie the **Seven Sisters**, huge great blocks of chalk, the highest is 260 feet, which guard the coast between Eastbourne and Seaford.

FRISTON
3½ miles W of Eastbourne on the A259

This is rather more a hamlet than a village, as only a part Norman church and a Tudor manor house can now be found around the village pond. The churchyard, however, is interesting as it contains the grave of the composer Frank Bridge, one of the pioneers of 20th century English music and also the teacher of Benjamin Britten. Born in Brighton, Bridge lived in Friston for much of his life though he died in Eastbourne in 1941 - the south door was placed here in his memory. The village pond, too, has a claim to fame as it was the first in the country to be designated an ancient monument.

To the north and west of the village lies **Friston Forest**, 1,600 acres of woodland, planted in 1927 by the Forestry Commission. Among the fast growing pine trees slower growing broad leaved trees have also been planted. There is a waymarked circular tour through the forest.

WEST DEAN
5 miles W of Eastbourne off the A259

Though the village is only a couple of miles from the south coast and close to Eastbourne, its position, hidden among trees in a downland combe, gives an impression that it is an isolated, timeless place. King Alfred is thought to have had a palace here and no more idyllic spot could be found for such a place. Known as Dene in Saxon times, Alfred the Great is also said to have kept a great fleet here on the River Cuckmere, which, then, formed a much deeper and wider estuary.

The village is now the home of **Charleston Manor**, an ancient house,

originally built in 1080 for William the Conqueror's cup bearer. Recorded in the Domesday Book as Cerlestone, the house has been added to over the years and it forms the centrepiece of a remarkable garden. Planted in the narrow valley, just north of Westdean's centre, the garden has more the feel of a Continental rather than an English garden with its parterres and terraces.

SEAFORD
8 miles W of Eastbourne on the A259

Once a thriving port on the River Ouse, Seaford was also a member of the confederation of Cinque Ports. Following the great storm in the 16th century which changed the course of the River Ouse, Seaford lost its harbour and also its livelihood to the newly established Newhaven. Traces of the old medieval seafaring town can still be seen around the old church but, overshadowed by Brighton and Eastbourne on either side, the town never gained the status of its neighbours. The building of the esplanade in the 1870s did bring some development as a modest resort but the constant pounding of the sea, particularly in winter, has kept the development small.

However, during the threat of a possible French invasion in the early 19th century, Seaford was considered important enough to be the site of the most westerly Martello Tower - this one number 74. Today it is the home of the **Seaford Museum of Local History** and amongst the exhibits in this friendly and lively museum are a World War II kitchen, radio sets, vintage lavatories and mementoes from shipwrecks. From the roof of the tower there are magnificent views over the town and beyond as well as the tower's original cannon.

To the west of the town lies **Seaford Head**, an excellent place from which to view the Seven Sisters. The nature reserve here is home to over 250 species of plants and the reserve supports a wealth of wildfowl on its 308 acres of mudflats, meadowland and downland.

JEVINGTON

3½ mile NW of Eastbourne off the A22

This old smugglers' village was established during the time of Alfred the Great by another Saxon called Jeva. Inside the parish church, which can be found up a tree lined lane, there is a primitive Saxon sculpture and the tower dates from the 10th century. During the 18th century, when smuggling was rife in the area, the local gang brought their illegal goods up here from Birling Gap and stored them in the cellars of the village rectory. The gang's headquarters were the local inn and, conveniently, their leader was the innkeeper who was also the ringleader of a group of

highwaymen until he was finally hanged in the 1760s.

ALFRISTON

6 miles NW of Eastbourne off the A27

Alfriston is one of the oldest and best preserved villages in Sussex. The settlement was founded in Saxon times and it grew to become an important port and market town on the River Cuckmere. The old market cross still stands in the square, one of two left in the county (the other is in Chichester). However, it has not escaped the ravages of time as it was smashed by a lorry and repaired by replacing the shaft.

One of the oldest buildings remaining in the town is the **Star Inn**, built in the early 15th century as a resting place for pilgrims on their way to and from the shrine of St Richard at Chichester. Inside can still be seen the original medieval carvings of animals on the ceiling beams.

MOONRAKERS RESTAURANT

High Street, Alfriston, East Sussex, BN26 5TD
Tel: 01323 870472 Fax: 01323 870472
e-mail: info@moonrakersrestaurant.co.uk
website: www.moonrakersrestaurnat.co.uk

This wonderful half-timbered 16th century building sits in the centre of a very attractive and typical South Downs village. Peter and Samantha Bronwich are the husband and wife team, who run this first class establishment. Between them they had years of experience in the catering industry before acquiring **Moonrakers** in June 2001. It is a long established business with a reputation that has been steadily built upon from its inception in 1953. Peter and Samantha are intent on further enhancing the quality and variety of the service and ensure that the menu changes at least once a month. The restaurant is in an attractive low beamed room part of which dates back to circa 1250.

The fresh, well laid out dining area with crisp linen table cloths looks out on the High Street through leaded glass windows. The food is modern European with an emphasis on Italian, Spanish, French and British. Peter and Samantha always use high quality fresh ingredients, as far as possible, produced locally. They have a very good source of fresh local fish available all year round and this is reflected in the menu with dishes like smoked haddock chowder, seared scallops and sauce vierge and roasted cod with sauce caponatta. Other tasty dishes include wild mushroom tart, parmesan soufflé and a mouth watering slow roasted duck with pomegranate sauce and celeriac mash. Fine wines to wash it all down can be selected from the extensive cellar, containing a selection of 65 wines from around the world.

RIVERDALE HOUSE

Seaford Avenue, Alfriston, East Sussex, BN26 5TR
Tel: 01323 871038 Fax: 01323 871038
e-mail: wells@riverdalebnb.freeserve.co.uk
website: www.cuckmere-valley.co.uk/riverdale

Alan and Melanie Wells have recently taken over this established bed and breakfast and are enthusiastically improving it. **Riverdale House** is a lovely and comfortable Victorian home, which combines the charm and informality of bed and breakfast with the comforts of a small hotel. Peacefully located at the edge of the famous and picturesque village of Alfriston, the house enjoys wonderful views of the South Downs. The bedrooms are comfortably furnished with all the usual facilities.

Another ancient inn, the **Market Cross**, had no less than six staircases and, during the 19th century was the headquarters of the notorious gang of smugglers led by Stanton Collins. Though he was never arrested for smuggling, Collins was eventually caught for sheep stealing and, as punishment, was transported to Australia. It was tales of Stanton Collins and other local gangs, which inspired Rudyard Kipling, living at nearby Rottingdean, to write his atmospheric poem, *A Smuggler's Song*.

The former prosperity of this town is reflected in its splendid 14th century parish church that is often referred to as **The Cathedral of the Downs**. As recently as the 1930s, local shepherds would be buried here with a scrap of raw wool in their hand - a custom, which served to inform the keeper of the gates of heaven that the deceased's poor church attendance was due to his obligation to his flock.

Beside the church is the thatched and timbered **Clergy House**, the first building to be acquired -for £10 - by the National Trust, in 1896. A marvellous example of a 14th century Wealden hall house, its splendid condition today is due to the skilful renovation of Alfred Powell who managed to save both its crown pot roof and the original timbers. Visitors to the house, which has limited opening, can see an interesting exhibition inside on medieval construction techniques. The house is surrounded by a magnificent and traditional cottage garden that includes rare flowers that have been grown since Roman times but are almost lost to cultivation.

By contrast, to the north of the village lies **Drusillas Park**, a child

Alfriston

friendly zoo that promises to be a hit with all the family. As well as housing over 90 species in imaginative and naturalistic enclosures there is also a creative play area, a train ride and attractive gardens.

WILMINGTON

5 miles NW of Eastbourne off the A27

This delightful village, with its mix of building styles, is home to the historic remains of **Wilmington Priory**. Founded in the 11th century by William the Conqueror's half brother, Robert de Mortain, as an outpost of the Benedictine Abbey of Grestain in Normandy, the priory was well into decline by the time of the Dissolution. Many of the buildings were incorporated into a farmhouse, but other parts remain on their own including the prior's chapel, which is now the parish church of St Mary and St Peter.

Cut into the chalk of Windover Hill is Wilmington's famous **Long Man**, which took its present form in 1874. There is much debate about the age of the Long Man and archaeologist and historians have been baffled for centuries. The earliest record of this giant is dated 1710 but this is inconclusive as it could be prehistoric or the work of an artistic monk from the local priory. However, what is known is that, at over 235 feet high, it is the largest such representation of a man in Europe. The giant, standing with a 250 foot long shaft in each hand, is remarkable as the design takes account of the slope of the hill and appears perfectly proportioned even when viewed from below. Covered up during World War II as the white chalk was thought to be a navigation aid to German bombers, the Long Man was outlined in concrete blocks in 1969.

ALCISTON

7½ miles NW of Eastbourne off the A27

This quiet hamlet, which once belonged to Battle Abbey, became known as the "forgotten village" after its inhabitants left following the ravages of the Black Death and settled close by. The villagers left, amongst other buildings, a 13th century church, which had been built on a hill on the foundations of a Saxon structure to avoid flooding, and 14th century Alciston Court, that was once used by the monks. During the Middle Ages, the tenant farmers paid a rent to the abbot of Battle in the form of one tenth of their annual farm output and, at harvest time each year, this was brought to the abbey's vast medieval tithe barn which still looms in front of the church. After the village was abandoned, Alciston Court became a farmhouse. The remains of a large **Medieval Dovecote** can also be seen close by. During the winter, large numbers of pigeons would be kept here to help supplement the villagers' dreary winter diet.

SELMESTON

8 miles NW of Eastbourne off the A27

This ancient hamlet, which is sometimes pronounced 'Simson', was the site where, during the 1930s, archaeologists discovered tools, weapons and pottery fragments in the churchyard, thought to date from the New Stone Age. However, though the finds are interesting in themselves, Selmeston is better remembered as being the home of Vanessa Bell, the artist. Vanessa moved here to **Charleston Farmhouse** in 1916, with her art critic husband, Clive, and her lover, fellow artist Duncan Grant.

Over the next 50 years, the intellectual and artist group that became known as the Bloomsbury set frequented the house. David Barnett, Maynard Keynes, E.M.

Forster, Roger Fry and Virginia and Leonard Woolf, who lived not far away at Rodmell, were all frequent visitors. During the 1930s, the interior of the house was completely transformed as the group used their artistic skills to cover almost every wall, floor, ceiling and even the furniture with

Charleston Farmhouse

their own murals, fabrics, carpets and wallpapers. They hung their own paintings on the walls, including a self portrait of Vanessa Bell and one of Grace Higgens, the valued housekeeper. The garden of the house too was not forgotten and a delightful walled cottage garden was created at the same time with carefully laid out mosaic pathways, tiled pools, sculptures and a scented rose garden. Following Duncan Grant's death in 1978, a trust was formed to save the house and garden, restoring them to their former glory. This unique task has been described as 'one of the most difficult and imaginative feats of restoration' to be carried out in Britain. The property is open to the public on a limited basis.

RIPE

9 miles NW of Eastbourne off the A27

Lying at the corner of a road grid laid out by the Romans, this quiet little village, obviously, has a long history. An attractive community, where there can be found a cottage faced with a remarkable set of wood carvings, Ripe lies on the fertile plain below the South Downs.

UPPER DICKER

8 miles NW of Eastbourne off the A22

This hamlet, which overlooks the River Cuckmere, is centred around a minor crossroads in an area that was once known as 'Dyker Waste'. In 1229, Augustinian canons chose this as the site for the beautiful **Michelham Priory**. Founded by Gilbert de Aquila, the Norman Lord of Pevensey, the six acre site is surrounded on three sides by the River Cuckmere and on the other by a slow flowing moat - England's longest water filled medieval moat. The slow moving water is still used to power an old mill where traditionally ground flour is produced in small batches. A splendid gatehouse to the priory was added in the 14th century and the priory continued to flourish until the Dissolution.

After the Dissolution the priory came into the hands of first the Pelham family and then the Sackville family who, in the 300 years of their ownership, incorporated some of the priory's buildings into a Tudor farmhouse which went on to become the focal point of a large agricultural estate. Today, the grand Tudor farmhouse rooms are furnished with a collection of Dutch paintings, Flemish tapestries and old English furniture and the gatehouse is home to a group of brass rubbings and a reconstructed forge.

Michelham Priory Gardens are equally interesting and they cover a range of styles. To the south of the house is a physic herb garden containing plants that were, and still are, grown for their medicinal and culinary benefits. There is also a recreated cloister garden, which illustrates the ability of the original monks to combine a pleasing garden with one that requires little maintenance. An Elizabethan barn can also be found in the grounds of the priory as can the working watermill, whilst, the river and moat attract a variety of waterfowl throughout the year.

LAUGHTON
11 miles NW of Eastbourne on the B2124

This scattered village, isolated on the Glynde Levels, was once home to flourishing marble mines, potteries and a brickworks. In fact, **Laughton Place**, built in 1534, was one of the first brick buildings constructed in Sussex. The interior of the village church, which lies some way from the village centre, is dominated by a stone war memorial which features a soldier and sailor, carved in minute detail.

HALLAND
13 miles NW of Eastbourne on the A22

Just to the south of Halland lies the interesting and fascinating **Bentley House and Motor Museum**. Covering

DAVID CARDOZA ANTIQUES

Milwards Farm, Lewes Road, Laughton, East Sussex, BN8 6BN   Tel:01323 811155
e-mail: dcardozaantiques@aol.com
website: www.davidcardozaantiques.co.uk

David and Christina Cardoza have been dealing in antiques for six years and have now converted the large barn at Milwards Farm into an elegant showroom. They provide a personal service by appointment for all types of customer including trade, interior designers or private individuals. The huge interior space is divided into two parts. One area is set out in booths of well-decorated carpeted rooms, giving customers an opportunity to see the antiques as part of a living room or bedroom or dining room. The other part has antique pieces awaiting restoration and display, which are also available for customers to buy.

The Cardozas specialise in importing 19th and 20th century French antiques and there is always an enormous range of furniture in this vast display area. The collection will include dining tables and chairs, chandeliers, mirrors, small decorative tables, armchairs and an excellent choice of antique beds

as well as dressing tables, bedside tables and much more. Whether customers are looking for ideas for a whole room, or house or just one special piece for a specific place, they are sure to find a selection here to choose from. Customers can buy un-restored pieces but the Cardozas offer a complete restoration and re-upholstery service if required.

Set just off the Lewes to Hailsham road a couple of miles from Lewes in beautiful countryside, they are open seven days a week but customers must telephone for an appointment.

some 100 acres of beautiful Sussex countryside, the estate cleverly combines a wildfowl reserve, a stately home and a museum in order to provide a fun day out for all the family. Originally a modest 17th century farmhouse, Bentley was transformed into the splendid Palladian mansion by the architect Raymond Erith who was also behind the restoration of 10, 11 and 12 Downing Street in the 1960s. Exquisitely furnished throughout, the house is particularly renowned for its Chinese Room and the Philip Rickman gallery, which contains a collection of over 150 wildfowl watercolours by the celebrated Sussex artist.

The formal gardens surrounding the house are laid out in a series of rooms, separated by yew hedges, and they often follow a colour theme. Beyond the house are the grounds and a woodland walk through the cool tranquillity of Glyndebourne Wood.

The Motor Museum comprises a superb collection of privately owned vintage cars and motorcycles, many of them roadworthy, which follow the history of motoring from its infancy in the Edwardian era to an elegant modern Lamborghini.

The waterfowl collection, which includes swans, geese, ducks and flamingos, was begun in the 1960s by the late Gerald Askew. Free to roam in the glorious parkland, the emphasis at the wildfowl centre is on conservation and breeding, particularly of the world's endangered birds. Here, the centre has at least 17 species breeding that are threatened with extinction in the wild.

EAST HOATHLY
12 miles NW of Eastbourne off the A22

Situated some 20 miles from West Hoathly, this compact village was immortalised by Thomas Turner in his *Diary of East Hoathly*. Although the village church was almost completely rebuilt in the mid 19th century, the 15th century squat tower remains from the original building. Known as a Pelham Tower, because it was built by the local Pelham family, the structure has a belt buckle carved on it on either side of the door. This distinctive emblem was awarded to Sir John Pelham for his part in capturing King John of France at Poitiers in 1356.

One of the door emblems has a deep slit in it that was supposedly caused by a bullet fired at Sir Nicholas Pelham in the 17th century. The failed murderer is said to have been a Cavalier, Thomas Lunsford, who joined the French army after being exiled for the attempted murder. He returned to Britain to fight with the king during the Civil War, then

CLARA'S

9 High Street, East Hoathly, Near Lewes, East Sussex, BN8 6DR
Tel: 01825 840339 Fax: 01825 841179
e-mail: claras@netway.co.uk
website: www.netway.co.uk/users/claras

This teashop in a pretty 18th century building opposite the former home of diarist Thomas Turner, complete with Victorian shop front and traditional oak beams is also a 21st century cyber-cafe. Jane Seabrook has been running **Clara's** for ten years and the wide range of crafts and goods available reflects her wide interests. Visitors can enjoy teas and light lunches, purchase gifts and keep in touch by email, surf the net or send faxes.

emigrated to America and died in Virginia in the 1650s.

CHIDDINGLY

10½ miles NW of Eastbourne off the A22

This small village is dominated by the tall 15th century spire of its church, which, at 130 feet is a useful local landmark. Inside the church is a impressive monument to Sir John Jefferary, Baron of the Exchequer under Queen Elizabeth, who lived at nearby Chiddingly Place - a once splendid Tudor mansion that is now in ruins. However, his memorial is overshadowed by that of his daughter and son-in-law, who both appear to be standing on drums. Tradition has it that the Jefferay family once laid a line of cheeses from their manor house to the church door so that they would not get their feet wet. So the large discs of Sussex marble could, in fact, be a reference to those cheeses!

Curiously, the monuments have lost hands and fingers over the years as enraged locals knocked them off, thinking that the family were related to Judge Jefferies who presided at the Bloody Assizes.

Despite being home to an international airport at Gatwick, which is a transport hub for road and rail as well as air travel, West Sussex remains an essentially rural landscape dominated by the South Downs, a magnificent range of chalk hills. The South Downs Way, a 100 mile bridleway along the crest of the hills from Winchester to Beachy Head, has panoramic views across the Weald to the north and south to the sea. It traces the long history of this area along ancient trails, passing Bronze Age barrows and Iron Age hill forts. On the coast, Chichester, the county town, once a busy haunt of smugglers, is now a thriving sailing centre, while the small fishing villages of the past are quiet holiday resorts like Littlehampton, Bognor Regis and Worthing. The ancient woodland of the West Sussex Weald is now a landscape of pastures and hedgerows and small country villages. The trees were felled for fuel to drive the furnaces of the iron industry, which

Bosham

flourished here for centuries. The legacy of this prosperous industry can be seen in the wealth of elaborate buildings, particularly churches, built on the profits.

   Evidence of human habitation and culture abound in this area. The Romans settled in Chichester in the 1st century, and it later became a great medieval religious centre with a fine Norman cathedral. At Fishbourne, the Roman remains of a splendid palace built for the Celtic King Cogidubnus, were discovered in 1960. At Arundel, the original Norman motte and double bailey design of its magnificent castle is still visible as well as the alterations and additions of subsequent generations. Norman churches are everywhere, often little altered over the centuries. In the tiny village of Sompting, there is a Saxon church with a pyramid capped tower, unique in England. Near Ardingly, Wakehurst Place is the striking Elizabethan mansion of the Culpeper family, with a magnificent collection of trees and shrubs. Wakehurst Place is also home to the **Millennium Seed Bank**, a project, which aims to ensure the continued survival of over 24,000 plant species worldwide. Petworth House is an elegant late 17th century building, reminiscent of a French château with a garden landscaped by Capability Brown. Close to East Grinstead, the remarkable Victorian country house, Standen ,has been sensitively restored to its original Arts and Crafts Movement style.

Many great artists and literary figures have found this region inspirational. Turner loved to paint its landscapes and harbours. H.G. Wells, Anthony Trollope and Tennyson all lived here. The composer Edward Elgar wrote his famous cello concerto at Fittleworth in 1917. And at Hurstpierpoint, at the Elizabeth mansion, Danny, Lloyd George and his war

Steyning Village

cabinet drew up the terms of the armistice, which ended World War I.

Within easy reach of London by rail or road but not so near as to suffer too much from commuter belt blight, served by an international airport and close to channel ports for travel to the continent, it is no surprise that many notable people continue to make their homes here. Few places so elegantly combine 21st century convenience with the unspoiled charm of a rich historic heritage.

LOCATOR MAP

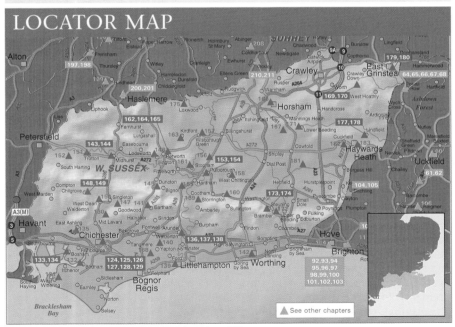

© MAPS IN MINUTES ™ 2001　© Crown Copyright, Ordnance Survey 2001

ADVERTISERS AND PLACES OF INTEREST

CHICHESTER CATHEDRAL

West Street, Chichester, West Sussex, PO19 1PX
Tel: 01243 782595 Fax: 01243 536190
e-mail: vo@chicath.freeserve.co.uk
website: www.chichester-cathedral.org.uk

Chichester's Cathedral, rich in history, architecture, music and art, provides the focus for any visit to the city. Guided tours are available whilst, the splendid Cathedral Precinct and the delightful Bishop's Garden are also open to the public and a joy to explore. The children's education centre offers special childrens tours and activities linked to the school National Curriculum. Situated next to the main shopping area and within walking distance of other notable attractions, it is possible to combine a visit to the Cathedral with other venues such as Pallant House Art Gallery or Chichester Festival Theatre. For shoppers it's an easy matter to take a break, pop into the Cathedral Bell Rooms restaurant for morning coffee, afternoon tea or a full meal, then resume shopping. In the summer visitors can sit in the tranquil walled garden and admire the splendour of the Cathedral and surrounding buildings. In the detached 15th century Bell Tower is the Cathedral gift shop where guide books, postcards, souvenirs and gifts may be purchased.

Visitors are very welcome to join with the congregation in acts of worship. Evensong at 5.30pm each evening (3.30 pm on Sundays) is when the renowned Cathedral Choir, with its ley vicars and boy choiristers can be heard on most days. Visitors are also welcome to the Sung Eucharist at 11am on Sunday and to join the community for a cup of coffee afterwards.

One of the great features of Chichester Cathedral is the use of modern works of art to invigorate and beautify the Cathedral. Paintings, stained glass, tapestries and embroideries have all been employed. Look out in particular for the painting of 'The Baptism of Christ' by Hans Feibusch (1951), Graham Sutherland's ' Noli me Tangere' from 1960 and Patrick Procktor's stunning ' Baptism' from 1984. Marc Chagall's 1978 stained glass window should not be missed. Based on the theme of Psalm 150 '...let everything that hath breath praise the Lord', it is one of the finest examples of its type from the late 20th century. There's a tapestry by John Piper, completed in 1966, as a reredos to the high altar and another, from 1985, by Ursula Benker-Schirmer in the retro-choir. Behind the Bishop's throne is a magnificent embroidered panel designed by Joan Freeman in 1993. Also worth a close look are the sculptures, Virgin and Child from 1988, by John Skelton and Christ in Judgement executed by Philip Jackson ten years later. Don't miss Skelton's polished polyphant stone and beaten copper font from 1983. Outside, by the bell tower, is an impressive statue in bronze of St. Richard by Philip Jackson.

All these are set in an ancient building that has stood here from Norman times. It was destroyed by fire in 1114 and the present building and additions date from then. The Cathedral suffered from years of neglect but since the mid 19th century a continuing programme of restoration has been taking place.

A great deal has been achieved in recent years to ensure that the structure of the Cathedral is in good order. The interior stonework has been thoroughly cleaned, the ceilings restored and their beauty enhanced by the installation of up-lighting. Among the many early features worth looking at are the 12th century Chichester Reliefs, two carved stone panels depicting part of the story of the raising of Lazarus, and a collection of 16th century paintings by Lambert Barnard of past bishops and the Kings and Queens of England.

Guided Tours: am and pm Easter to end of October. For special arrangements and group bookings, contact the booking officer. For children's and educational visits, contact the education officer.

CHICHESTER AND THE WEST SUSSEX COAST

This western, coastal region of West Sussex is centred around Chichester, the county town, Arundel, with its magnificent castle, and the resorts of Littlehampton, Bognor Regis and Worthing. Founded by the Romans in the 1st century, Chichester was an ecclesiastical centre for over 900 years. Its fine, natural harbour, once a busy place for trade and smugglers, is now a lively yachting centre with delightful old fishing villages along its inlets. Nearby, at Fishbourne, the grateful Roman conquerors built a splendid palace for the Celtic King Cogidubnus who collaborated with the invaders. The largest estate north of the Alps, the Roman remains were only uncovered this century while a new water mains was being installed.

The inland town of Arundel is home to a marvellous castle beside the River Arun and to the area's second cathedral. Built by the Roman Catholic family living at the castle, Arundel Cathedral is famous for its Corpus Christi Festival.

On the coast the stylish resorts of Littlehampton, Bognor Regis and Worthing, which were once small fishing villages, have much to offer visitors in an unbrash and timeless manner. Finally, the small town of Selsey and Selsey Bill, the most southwesterly tip of West Sussex, is a charming place with as much history as there are pleasant walks along the coastline.

CHICHESTER

Set on the low-lying plain between the south coast and the South Downs, Chichester, the county town of West Sussex, was founded by the Romans in the 1st century. The invading Roman legions used the town as a base camp, christening it *Noviomagus*, "the new city of the plain", and both the city walls and the four major thoroughfares - North, South, East and West Streets - follow the original Roman town plan. They cross at the point where a fine 16th century **Butter Cross** now stands; an ornate structure built in 1500 by Bishop Edward Story to provide shelter for the many traders who came to sell their wares at the busy market.

The city walls, originally consisting of raised earthwork embankments built in an irregular 11-sided shape, were constructed around AD 200. Over the subsequent centuries alterations and improvements were made and, today, the remaining walls largely date from medieval times and large sections still form the boundary between the old and new city. After the Romans left, the

Chichester Butter Cross

ROYAL MILITARY POLICE MUSEUM

The Keep, Roussillon Barracks, Chichester, West Sussex, PO19 6BL
Tel: 01243 534225 Fax: 01243 534288
e-mail: museum@rhqrmp.freeserve.co.uk
website: www.rmpmuseum.org.uk

This is an essential visit for anyone interested in military history and a fascinating insight into the history and workings of the **Royal Military Police** for anyone else. Established in 1979, the present museum was formally opened in 1985 and has full registration with the Museums and Galleries Commission. Military Police, also known as redcaps because of their distinctive headgear, have been around for a long time. Walking through the various fascinating exhibits, it is possible to trace their entire history from Tudor times to the recent conflicts in the former Yugoslavia. Display cases contain life size models of military policemen dressed in the varieties of uniforms they have used at different times and at different points of the globe.

Everything is there from full camouflage combat gear to the dress uniform worn by a mounted officer at a ceremonial occasion. Also included are maps, weapons and communications equipment the corps have used in their various theatres of operations.

Visitors can try on some of the uniforms, have their fingerprints taken and learn about the diverse role of the military police. A .22 palm pistol is part of a haul of weapons confiscated during the RMP operations, aimed at reducing weapon holding, in Republica Serbska during 1996-97. This murderous little device is lethal at close quarters and easily concealed. From the period at the end of WWII is a complicated looking illicit still recovered from a displaced persons camp in Hamburg, 1946. From the same period is the Walther P38 pistol used in the murder of Sergeant Southcott. He and two others arrested Teofil Walasek on charges of murder, rape and robbery. When they apprehended him at the railway station he was searched but they neglected to check his overcoat. Back at HQ Walasek produced the pistol, killed Southcott, wounded two others and escaped but was later recaptured and sentenced to death.

Amongst the exhibits is a ferret armoured car of the type used extensively by the Redcaps in anti-terrorist operations in Cyprus and Malaya during the 1950s. This one, which sits outside the museum, is in the livery of 17 Ghurkha Division Provost Company and was crewed entirely by RMP NCOs providing close escort to the general officer commanding the division during road moves.   A BSA motorcycle was in use from 1939-1964. Many modern exhibits are on display from theatres of operations ranging from Northern Ireland to Bosnia and Kosovo. The Northern Ireland exhibits include captured terrorist weapons, commercially and home-made, uniform items and accounts of incidents in which the RMP were involved. Outside the building are two imposing statues of Military Policemen, one standing at ease upon a large block the other on horseback. In the purpose built Broakes Room is a comprehensive collection of medals awarded to members of the RMP over the years of its existence.

Chichester Cathedral

Chichester in the 13th century. A venerated bishop who was canonised in 1262, Richard of Chichester was subsequently adopted as the city's patron saint.

Lying in the heart of the city, **Chichester Cathedral** (see panel on page 206), a centre for Christian worship for over 900 years, is unique on two counts. Firstly, it is the only medieval English cathedral that can be seen from the sea rather than being secluded by its own close and, secondly, it has a detached belfry. The existing tower was thought not to have been sturdy enough to take the cathedral bells and another separate building was needed. In 1861, the cathedral spire blew down in a storm and demolished a large section of the nave. The present 277 foot spire was designed by Sir Gilbert Scott, in keeping with the building's original style, and it can also be seen for miles around from all directions.

Among the treasures within the cathedral is the Shrine of St Richard of Chichester along with some fine Norman arches, a set of 14th century choir stalls and some excellent modern works of art. There is an altar tapestry by John Piper, a stained glass window by Marc Chagall and a painting by Graham Sutherland of

Saxons came in AD 500, and Chichester's modern name is derived from *Cissa's ceaster* after the Saxon King Cissa.

Chichester also has a long and colourful ecclesiastical history and, although St Wilfrid chose nearby Selsey as the site of the area's first cathedral, the conquering Normans, who moved all country bishoprics to towns, built a new cathedral on the present site in the late 11th century. Resting on Roman foundations, the construction work began in 1091 and the finished building was finally consecrated in 1184. A fire, just three years later, all but destroyed the cathedral and a rebuilding programme was started by Richard of

Chichester Cathedral

In House

Unit 1, The Old theatre, 43 South
Street, Chichester, PO19 1DX
Tel/Fax: 01243 775495

One of the latest additions to the shopping experience in the historic town of Chichester is In House, an Aladdin's cave of an establishment that has become a Mecca for bargain hunters. Jerry Fettroll, the proprietor is an experienced retailer who has traded throughout the UK. He has set up his linen and furniture showrooms within the red brick frontage of a former theatre building in the main street.

Inside the triple glass fronted shop is a massive open plan shopping area with shelves and display areas jammed full with one of the most eclectic selections of goods in the area. The selection of house ware products is comprehensive and includes bales of linen and towels, sets of fine china, household crockery, and kitchenware and kitchen

equipment. In this browsers' paradise the visitor could spend hours marvelling at the range and diversity of the stock. Hundreds of bargains can be unearthed from throw overs to coffee cups, electric toasters to cutlery. Then there's the candle collection. In House is the biggest retailer of candles outside of London, specialising in the famous American Yankee Candles, probably the finest available in the world. There's also the most amazing collection of Indian teak furniture. Sourced from the Far East and available at unbelievable prices, the range includes everything from coffee tables to bookcases, display units to a splendid Thakat dining table and set of eight chairs. Displayed on top and around the furniture is a mind-boggling collection of goods. Candlesticks, mug trees, wine racks, table lamps, CD racks, vases and even an ornamental birdcage. In House may not stock everything from a pin to an anchor but they get very close.

The people of Chichester are always on the lookout for new and innovative products and In House keeps pace with this demand by introducing small quantities of new items on a regular basis and Jerry Fettroll is proud of his ability to offer all his customers the widest and best possible choices.

One thing that is guaranteed during a shopping experience at In House is friendly and personal service. There is no pressure on browsers to buy but should advice be needed it is readily available and the attentive staff are delighted to assist with

colour selection, advice and even design ideas. In House also operates an interior design and porcelain service.

Christ appearing to Mary Magdalene. However, the most important treasures to be seen are the Norman sculptures: *The Raising of Lazarus* and *Christ Arriving in Bethany*, which can be found on the south wall. The **Prebendal School**, the cathedral choir school, is the oldest school in Sussex and it stands alongside the main building.

From the Middle Ages until the 18th century, Chichester was a major trading and exporting centre for the Sussex woollen trade and some handsome merchants' houses were built using these profits. The city's oldest building, **St Mary's Hospital**, dating from the 13th century, was established to house the deserving elderly of Chichester.

The almshouses that were built into the hospital walls are still inhabited and the chapel has some unique misericords. The city's **Guildhall**, built in the 1270s as the church of the Franciscans, is also well worth seeing. Later becoming Chichester's town hall and law courts it was here, in 1804, that the poet William Blake was tried for treason and acquitted. Today, it is home to a display telling the story of the building and the surrounding Priory Park in which it stands.

There are also some fine Georgian buildings to be found here and, in the area known as The Pallants, lies **Pallant House**. A fine example of a red brick town house, it was built in 1713 by the local wine merchant Henry 'Lisbon' Peckham and the building is guarded by a wonderful pair of carved stone dodos, which have given rise to its local nickname - the Dodo House. Another curious feature is the observation tower on the house from which Peckham would look out for his merchant ships returning laden with goods from the Iberian Peninsula. Today, the house is the **Pallant House Gallery**, one of the

BOND-A-FRAME

15A St Pancras, Chichester, West Sussex, PO19 7SJ
Tel: 01243 789343 Fax: 01243 786345
e-mail: sales@bondaframe.co.uk
website: www.bondaframe.co.uk

In 1983 Mike and Bettine Bond opened their framing shop in Chichester. Today **bond-a-frame** is a retail picture framing business unlike its competitors; the customers make their own frames on the premises. Mike has fitted his shop with the latest, state of the art framing technology and it's that which enables ordinary mortals to make professional frames with no training. Of course people can still have frames made to order if they wish by the three trained staff. That usually takes about a week. The staff spend a considerable time with the customers, helping them to choose the right mount and frame for their pictures. Mike, a former boatbuilder, likes 'out of the ordinary challenges' which are thrown at him from time to time.

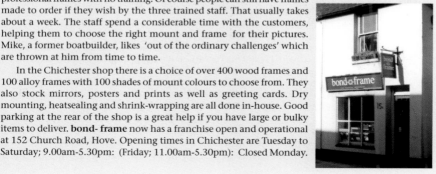

In the Chichester shop there is a choice of over 400 wood frames and 100 alloy frames with 100 shades of mount colours to choose from. They also stock mirrors, posters and prints as well as greeting cards. Dry mounting, heatsealing and shrink-wrapping are all done in-house. Good parking at the rear of the shop is a great help if you have large or bulky items to deliver. **bond- frame** now has a franchise open and operational at 152 Church Road, Hove. Opening times in Chichester are Tuesday to Saturday; 9.00am-5.30pm: (Friday; 11.00am-5.30pm): Closed Monday.

finest galleries outside London, and home to a modern art collection that includes fine works by Moore, Sutherland, Piper, Klée and Cèzanne.

One of the city's most distinctive modern buildings can be found at Oaklands Park, close by the city walls. The **Chichester Festival Theatre** was opened in 1962 and the splendid hexagonal building has since gained a reputation for staging the finest classical and contemporary drama, opera and ballet. The theatre and the cathedral are the focal points of the annual Chichester Festival for two weeks during July, the city is alive with a myriad of cultural events. For those with quieter interests, the **Mechanical Music and Doll Collection** (see panel opposite) represents a fascinating walk through the last 100 years of mechanical music. Playing the tunes of late 19th century public houses through to genteel

Victorian parlour songs, the beautifully restored instruments are put through their paces on a regular basis. Also to be seen with the collection are Edison phonographs, early horned gramophones, stereoscopic viewers and over 100 dolls spanning the years from 1830 to 1930.

The **Royal Military Police Museum** is housed in the Keep at Roussillon Barracks and is a must for anyone interested in military history (see panel on page 208)

Once a busy port, the city is now a haven for boat lovers and yachtsmen with 12,000 resident boats in one of Europe's largest marinas. From the bustling harbour visitors can take a boat trip around this stretch of sheltered water with its sand dunes, mudflats, shingle and woodlands providing habitats for varied sea birds. A particularly pleasant waterside walk can be taken from the city's impressive canal

MECHANICAL MUSIC AND DOLL COLLECTION

Church Road, Portfield, Chichester, West Sussex PO19 4HN
Tel: 01243 372646 Fax: 01243 370299

In a former Victorian church, a mile to the east of Chichester city centre, can be found this magical collection of mechanical musical instruments. There are musical boxes, barrel pianos, organs etc. and on Wednesday afternoons in the summer

visitors have the chance to hear them. Listen to the lively music of the Victorian parlours, streets and pubs, and the glorious sounds of orchestrions that filled the dance halls in the twenties. You can even take groups there by appointment for a tour any time throughout the year. Children adore these music machines, and adults sometimes remember the tunes!

basin, along the **Chichester Canal** to Chichester Harbour. The canal opened in 1822, taking vessels up to 150 tons from Arundel to Portsmouth. The last commercial cargo travelled the route in 1928 but now, after restoration work, this shorter stretch provides a delightful walk with a cruise boat at the other end on which to make the return journey.

Housed in an 18th century corn store, **Chichester District Museum** explores local history through displays and hands-on activities. Visitors can find out about local geology and prehistory, including Boxgrove Man, believed to have lived around 500,000 years ago. The remains, consisting of part of a human shinbone and two human teet, are the earliest remains of human-like species found in Britain. They were found during excavations in the 1990s along with bones of butchered animals and tools. Life in Roman, Saxon and medieval Chichester can also be discovered. There are displays on Chichester during the Civil War and visitors can see how the city changed during Georgian and

Victorian times. The story is brought right up to date with displays on Chichester since 1900.

AROUND CHICHESTER

MID LAVANT

2 miles N of Chichester on the A286

This attractive village, along with its neighbour East Lavant, is named after the small river, which flows from Singleton into Chichester Harbour. There are spectacular views from here northwards over the South Downs and it is said that these were the inspiration for the words 'England's green and pleasant land' which appear in William Blake's famous poem, *Jerusalem*.

GOODWOOD

3 miles NE of Chichester off the A285

This is not a village but the spectacular country home of the Dukes of Richmond, **Goodwood House**. It was first acquired by the 1st Duke of Richmond (the natural son of Charles II and his beautiful French mistress, Louise de Keroualle) in 1697 so that he could ride with the local hunt. The original, modest hunting lodge still remains in the grounds, but has been superseded by the present mansion, built on a grand scale in the late 18th century for the 3rd Duke by the architect James Wyatt. At the same time the splendid stables were added. Now refurbished by the Earl and Countess of March, several rooms in this impressive house, including the state apartments, are open to visitors. The state apartments are magnificent examples of the luxury of the period with an Egyptian state dining room, grand yellow drawing room and an elegant ballroom. Among the items on display, are paintings by Canaletto and Stubbs, fine Sèvres procelain collected by the 3rd Duke whilst he was Ambassador to Paris, gruesome relics from the Napoleonic Wars and French and English furniture.

Viewers of the BBC television drama *Aristocrats* will recognise the house as it was used as the location for the series. Not only was the drama filmed here but the story was that of the independent minded and glamorous daughters of the 2nd Duke of Richmond. The girls grew up both at Goodwood House and at the Duke's London residence, Richmond House, and the whole family were enthusiastic leaders of early Georgian society. Goodwood House was the setting for Sarah's banishment from society and it was also here that Kildare

Goodwood House

wooed Emily. On display in the house is a painting by Stubbs which features Caroline's husband, Lord Holland, and the Meissen snuff box the couple gave to the duchess four years after their elopement.

The house is the focal point of the Goodwood Estate, some 12,000 acres of downland which also incorporate the world famous **Goodwood Racecourse**. A

THE FLINT HOUSE

Pook Lane, East Lavant, Chichester, West Sussex
Tel: 01243 773482 e-mail: theflinthouse@ukonline.co.uk

Situated in a peaceful rural setting on the edge of the South Downs between East Lavant and Goodwood, **The Flint House** is one of the hidden gems of Sussex. Built by Napoleonic prisoners of war in the early 19th century it has a large garden, a tennis court, which guests may use and ample parking. Originally built as two farm cottages, it was later converted to one house. The exterior is of flint stone with a tiled roof. The guests have their own entrance to the house. All of the large, sunny bedrooms are on the ground floor. Tastefully decorated to reflect the ambience of the house they have television, radio, hairdryers, tea and coffee making facilities and freshly cut flowers. Vivien Read, the owner, enjoys entertaining her guests and nothing is too much trouble for her. Full English breakfast is served, freshly cooked using local produce, organic where possible and home-made preserves.

The high standard of service has been recognised by an award of the English Tourist Council 5 Diamonds and a Silver Award. Flint House is very quiet and secluded making it ideal for that 'get away from it all' break or a pleasant place to return to after a day's touring to relax in a hot bath or stroll through the gardens. As an alternative, guests can enjoy a game of pool in the library room. Some excellent walks are situated nearby as are some exceedingly fine English country pubs. Chichester, Arundel, Midhurst, Petworth and the coast are all within easy reach of the Flint House.

favourite venue with the rich, racing has taken place here for nearly 200 years and, in particular, there is the Glorious Goodwood meeting. First introduced by the 4th Duke of Richmond in 1814, just 12 years after racing began here, this prestigious five-day meeting is one of the major events in the calendar and has long been a much anticipated part of the summer season. Further, the estate contains a golf course, motor racing circuit and children's adventure play area.

HALNAKER

3½ miles NE of Chichester on the A285

Pronounced Hannacker, this village was the seat of the influential and powerful De La Warr family. The present **Halnaker House**, designed by Edwin Lutyens in 1938, is a splendid modern country house. However, just to the north lies the original Halnaker House, which was allowed to fall into decay around 1800. Built in medieval times, the old house was originally the home of the De Haye family who were also the founders of Boxgrove Priory.

Above the village, on Halnaker Hill, stands an early 18th century tower windmill, **Halnaker Windmill**, which was painted by Turner. It remained in use until 1905 when it, too, was allowed to fall into ruin. In 1912, Hilaire Belloc mentioned the windmill in a poem where he compares the decay of agriculture in Britain with the neglected mill. The exterior, however, was restored in 1934 and the windmill was used as an observation tower during World War II. It was restored once again in 1955 by the county council.

BOXGROVE

2 miles NE of Chichester off the A27

This attractive village is home to the remains of **Boxgrove Priory**, a cell of the Benedictine Lessay Abbey in France,

which was founded in around 1115. Initially a community of just three monks, over the centuries the priory expanded and grew into one of the most influential in Sussex. However, all that remains today are the Guest House, Chapter House and the Church, which is now the parish Church of St Mary and St Blaise. Its sumptuous interior reflects the priory's former importance and, before the Dissolution of the Monasteries, the De La Warr Chantry Chapel was built like a 'church within a church' to be the final resting place of the family.

Unfortunately, Henry VIII forced De La Warr to dispose of the priory and the family was eventually buried at Broadwater near Worthing. Though it is still empty, the extravagant marble chapel has survived.

A fascinating discovery was made, in 1993, by local archaeologists who unearthed prehistoric remains in a local sand and gravel pit. Amongst the finds was an early hominid thigh bone and, although there is still some debate over the precise age of the bone, the find has been named **Boxgrove Man**.

TANGMERE

2 miles E of Chichester off the A27

The village is still very much associated with the nearby former Battle of Britain base, RAF Tangmere and, although the runways have now been turned back into farmland or housing estates, the efforts of the pilots are remembered at the local pub, The Bader Arms (named after pilot Douglas Bader) and the **Tangmere Military Aviation Museum**. The museum, based at the airfield, tells the story, through replica aircraft, photographs, pictures, models and memorabilia, of military flying from the earliest days during World War I to the present time. The Battle of Britain Hall tells its own story with aircraft remains, personal effects and true accounts from both British and German pilots of those desperate days in 1940. On display are two historic aircraft, each of which beat the World Air Speed record in their day. Finally, it was whilst at RAF Tangmere during World War II that E.H. Bates completed his novel *Fair Stood the Wind for France*.

SIDLESHAM
4 miles S of Chichester on the B2145

A pleasant village, which is home to the information and interpretation centre for **Pagham Harbour Nature Reserve.** The harbour was formed when the sea breached reclaimed land in 1910 and it is now a well known breeding ground for many rare birds. The tidal mud flats attract an abundance of wildfowl and also many species of animals and marine life. Sidlesham Ferry is the starting point for guided walks around this important conservation area.

NORTON
6 miles S of Chichester on the B2145

One of the original communities that made up Selsey, Norton's first church was probably built on, or close to, the site of the cathedral that St Wilfrid erected when he became Bishop of the South Saxons in AD 681. Following the Norman Conquest, the country bishoprics were moved into the towns and Selsey's bishop transferred to Chichester. In the 1860s, the decision to move the medieval parish Church of St Peter from its isolated site to Selsey was taken. But, according to ecclesiastical law, a church chancel cannot be moved, so it remains here as **St Wilfrid's Chapel.**

SELSEY
7 miles S of Chichester on the B2145

Once an important Saxon town, fishing has been the main stay of life here for many centuries. However, according to accounts by the Venerable Bede, St Wilfrid, whilst Bishop of the South Saxons, discovered that the Selsey fishermen were unsuccessful and such was their shortage of food that they were prepared to throw themselves off nearby cliffs. St Wilfrid taught them to fish and the town has thrived ever since and, until recently, only Selsey crabs were served on the QE2.

Now a more modest town yet still a popular resort, the main street looks much as it did in the 18th century. The **Sessions House**, where the Lord of Selsey Manor held court, was probably built in the early 17th century though it contains the exposed beams and wooden panelling of an earlier age. There are also several thatched cottages to be seen, including the 18th century cottage and the 16th century farmhouse known as The Homestead. Perhaps, though, the most impressive building here is **Selsey Windmill**. Today's mill was built in 1820 as the previous late 17th century timber construction had suffered greatly from weather damage. A tower mill built from local red bricks, though it ceased milling flour in 1910, the mill continued to grind pepper into the 1920s. Now rescued and restored, it is a pleasant local landmark.

With so many of the townsfolk dependant upon the sea for their living, the Lifeboat Station was established here in 1860. The present building was erected 100 years later and there is also an interesting little **Lifeboat Museum**.

For many years the town's **East Beach** was a well-known site for smuggling, which, was a full time occupation for many local inhabitants in the 18th century. In fact, whilst the French were in the throes of their revolution the villagers of Selsey were busy smuggling ashore over 12,000 gallons of spirits. Much later, during World War II, East

Beach was used as a gathering point for sections of the famous Mulberry Harbour that was transported across the Channel as part of the D-Day landings. Just inland from the beach, now on a roundabout, is a small building called the **Listening Post**. During World War I it was used as a naval observation post, with personnel listening out for the sound of invading German airships, and as such it acted as an early warning system long before radar was established.

Just outside the town is **Northcommon Farm Centre**. Offering an interesting day out for all the family, the centre has a wide selection of farm animals, including cows and calves, sheep and lambs, donkeys, goats and pigs as well as miniature ponies, horses and llamas. There are tractor and trailer rides to take visitors around this old farm.

Geographically, **Selsey Bill**, the extreme southwest of Sussex, is an island with the English Channel on two sides, Pagham Harbour to the northeast and a brook running from the harbour to Bracklesham Bay which cuts the land off from the remainder of the Manhood Peninsular. However, Ferry Banks, built in 1809, links the bill with the mainland. Over the centuries this part of the coastline has been gradually eroded and many of the area's historic remains have now been lost beneath the encroaching tides.

EARNLEY
6 miles SW of Chichester off the B2198

This charming small village is home to **Earnley Gardens**, a delightful five acres of themed gardens, exotic birds and butterflies. It also has a fascinating small museum of ephemera. **Rejectamenta**,

the Museum of 20th Century Memorabilia, displays thousands of everyday items, reflecting the changes in lifestyle over the past 100 years. There is everything here from old washing powder packets and winklepickers to stylophones and space hoppers.

WEST WITTERING
7 miles SW of Chichester on the B2179

West Wittering and its larger neighbour, **East Wittering**, both lie close to the beautiful inlet that is Chichester's natural harbour. A charming seaside village, West Wittering overlooks the narrow entrance to the harbour and this former fishing village has developed into a much sought after residential area and select holiday resort. Here, too, lies **Cakeham Manor House**, with its distinctive early 16th century brick tower that was once the summer palace of the bishops of Chichester. A splendid part medieval, part Tudor and part Georgian house, it was in the manor's studio that Sir Henry Royce, of Rolls Royce, designed many of his inventions.

Both villages have easy access to excellent sandy beaches and the headland that forms the eastern approach to Chichester Harbour, **East Head**, which is

West Wittering

HOME FARM HOUSE

Elms Lane, West Wittering, West Sussex, PO20 8LW
Tel: 01243 514252 Fax: 01243 512804
e-mail: peter-paddymorton@talk21.com

This is a very spacious modern house situated in a peaceful country lane and surrounded by half an acre of exceedingly pretty garden. **Home Farm House** is less than a mile from the National Trust coastline, bird sanctuary and safe sandy beach where swimming, sail boarding and surfing are popular. Locally there are many excellent country walks and the sleepy, winding country lanes and by-ways are excellent for cycle touring. Bicycles are available for hire. This pleasant and friendly bed and breakfast is run by Paddy Morton who, with her husband Peter, owns the house. Paddy is addicted to gardens and gardening and this certainly shows in her large private garden.

The accommodation is splendid and spacious. One double bedroom is en suite with bath and shower. The other has its own private bathroom and there is a single bedroom, suitable for a relative or child. All are equipped with colour television, hostess trays, hair driers and toiletries. Full English

breakfast is served each day in the dining room. Within West Wittering is a good selection of places for eating out. Two miles away is East Wittering, which has a good range of shops, banks, cafes and restaurants. Home Farm House can be reached from the A27 to Chichester by turning onto the A286 signposted Witterings and continuing for seven miles. Once in the village of West Wittering, pass the four village shops and turn left at the memorial hall into Elms Lane. The house is three hundred metres on the right.

FUCHSIAS GALORE

Tawny Nurseries, Bell lane, Birdham, Nr Chichester, West Sussex, PO20 7HY
Tel:01243 512168 Fax: 01243 514908
website: www.fuchsias-galore.co.uk

Over 20 years ago Derek Howell and his wife were looking for a new way of life. Leaning on the five bar gate of a field that would eventually become their

nursery they saw a tawny owl flying low across the ground. That gave them the name. Many years later, and a lot of very hard work by this likeable family and the business is well-established with a countrywide reputation for top quality. Derek has now been joined in the business by his son Adrian and daughter Gloria. As the name suggests fuchsias are the game and at Tawny Nurseries they have over 1,000 varieties. They're geranium specialists as well with over 250 varieties. The family have won many professional awards over the years particularly for their hanging baskets that can be purchased from the small retail area on site or made to order. The gardening and display areas are a delight to stroll through in season with magnificent splashes of colours and wonderful scents hanging in the air everywhere. The nursery has an open parking space and also operates a Caravan Club site.

now a nature reserve. A sand and shingle spit which supports a variety of bird, plant and marine life, marram grass has been introduced to the sand dunes to help reduce the ravages of the sea and wind.

ITCHENOR
5 miles SW of Chichester off the B2179

Originally a Saxon settlement called Icenore, in the 13th century the villagers of Itchenor built a church, which they chose to dedicate to St Nicholas, the guardian of seafarers. As the village overlooks the sheltered waters of Chichester Harbour, shipbuilding was an obvious industry to become established here and, as early as the 1600s, there was a shipyard at Itchenor. The last ships built here were minesweepers during World War II but the village today is a busy sailing and yachting centre as well as being the customs clearance port for Chichester Harbour.

BIRDHAM
4 miles SW of Chichester on the A286

The setting for Turner's famous painting of Chichester Harbour (which can be seen at Petworth House), this delightful place is as charming today as it was when the views captured the great artist's imagination. Here, too, can be found the **Sussex Falconry Centre**, which was originally set up as a breeding and rescue centre for indigenous birds of prey. In 1991, the centre started to exhibit the birds to the public and, as well as viewing and watching the birds fly, visitors can also take advantage of the centre's falconry and hawking courses.

FISHBOURNE
2 miles W of Chichester on A286

This unremarkable village would not appear on anyone's list of places to visit in West Sussex if it was not for the splendid Roman remains discovered in 1960 when a new water main was cut. **Fishbourne Roman Palace** was built around AD 75 for the Celtic King Cogidubnus, who collaborated with the Roman conquerors. As well as taking on the role of Viceroy, Cogidubnus was rewarded with this magnificent palace with underfloor heating, hot baths, a colonnade, an ornamental courtyard garden and lavish decorations. This was the largest residential building north of the Alps and among the superb remains are a garden and numerous mosaic floors, including the famous **Cupid on a Dolphin** mosaic.

As well as walking through the excavated remains of the north wing, visitors can see the formal garden, which has been replanted to the original Roman plan. When the palace was first constructed the sea came right up to its outer walls and the building remained in use until around AD 320 when a fire largely destroyed the site. The history of the palace, along with many of the artefacts rescued during the excavations, can be discovered in the site museum,

Fishbourne Roman Palace

(Continued page 222)

WALK 5

Bosham and Fishbourne

Start	Bosham
Distance	8½ miles (13.7km). Shorter version 5 miles (8km)
Approximate time	4½ hours (2½ hours for shorter version)
Parking	Bosham
Refreshments	Pubs and tearoom at Bosham, pubs at Fishbourne and Dell Quay
Ordnance Survey maps	Landranger 197 (Chichester & The Downs), Explorer 120 (Chichester, South Harting & Selsey)

The picturesque creek to the south of Bosham provides the opening section of this walk. It then strikes across country to the highest reach of Chichester harbour – an area of reedy wilderness and a sanctuary for waders and other waterbirds. The eastern shore of the estuary is equally attractive; the waterside path ends at Dell Quay. The return, which repeats a short stretch of the walk by the estuary, gives the opportunity of seeing a secluded medieval church and its neighbouring tower-house. There can be few walks which will be more enjoyable to an ornithologist. The shorter version omits the eastern shore. It should be warned that there is often high tide between Points D and E.

Bosham, a key port in Saxon and medieval times and now a popular sailing centre, is a most attractive village with a number of historic associations. The ancient church contains the coffin of one of Canute's daughters, and it was from here that Harold, Earl of Wessex, sailed on his ill-fated trip to Normandy to his future conqueror and successor; the Bayeux Tapestry shows Harold praying in Bosham church before departure.

Turn left from the car park to reach Bosham waterfront and then left again to continue along the shore of the creek. If there is a high tide you may be forced to walk on the flood wall. At the head of the creek, by a grassy triangle **A**, look for a footpath sign on the other side of The Drive, to the left of a white chalet-bungalow. This is an enclosed path at the back of gardens which emerges at a road. Go straight over this onto a field path which after 1 mile (1.6km) reaches Park

Lane. Turn right onto this quiet road which runs through a flat, hedgeless landscape that is reminiscent of East Anglia. At Church Farm **B** bear left onto a private tarmac road, passing through a metal gate. There is a lovely distant view of Chichester Cathedral on the left. The tarmac road ends at Hook Creek **C**, where the right of way is to the left, on a farm track which turns away from the estuary following a footpath sign with a curlew emblem. The track becomes a little-used footpath, and Chichester Cathedral now has a foreground of river. At a footpath junction **D** turn right and walk to the river, with a hedge on the right, turning left at the tideline.

Birdlife abounds here: look out for curlews, oyster-catchers, shelducks, redshanks, red-breasted mergansers, herons, Sandwich and little terns, Brent geese, kingfishers and various migrants. The path skirts the shoreline, often on the flood wall, which is an excellent vantage-point for bird-watching. Eventually the path reaches the upper end of the estuary at Fishbourne, near a thatched cottage picturesquely situated by the millpond **E**.

For the shorter version of the walk, turn left onto Mill Lane here and follow route directions after **E** below.

Cross over the road here (a bridleway to the 'harbour') and go through a kissing-gate, following the direction of the sign for Dell Quay. Keep bearing right through the meadows, keeping as close as possible to the shoreline (though there is a short-cut across a meadow at one point on the landward side), before reaching the Crown and Anchor on Dell Quay **F**.

Take the road from the pub, walking eastwards for about ½ mile (800m) before taking the left turn to Apuldram. Keep on past the drive to the Aviation Museum and Rosefield. Before the second part of a Z-bend **G** turn left to pass by Rymans, an early 15th-century tower-house built by William Ryman and substantially enlarged in later centuries. The stone for the medieval house was brought from a quarry at Ventnor on the Isle of Wight, which was also the source for the bell-tower of Chichester Cathedral. The path leads into Apuldram churchyard, where the church itself is one of the county's lesser-known gems. Its interior was comprehensively restored by a wealthy 19th-century parson who kept his steam yacht on the river nearby.

The footpath continues from the west end of the churchyard and soon reaches the waterside footpath trodden

earlier. Turn right onto this and retrace your footsteps to the millpond at Fishbourne **E**. Turn right onto Mill Lane and left at the end when it reaches the main road by the Bull's Head pub.

Walk down the road towards Bosham, passing a road on the right leading to Fishbourne Roman Palace. The remains contain fine mosaics and exhibits, and a reconstruction of a Roman garden. The palace is thought to have belonged to a native British chief who co-operated with the Romans and was well rewarded for his loyalty. It was discovered by accident in 1960 by a water-board workman.

Keep on the main road to the Black Boys pub, where you fork left down Old Park Lane. Carry straight on down a private road when the lane bends left **H**. There is a footpath sign at this point. After the infilled Bullrush Pond the path continues by the side of a fine line of poplars, with a tree nursery to the right, and eventually ends when it meets a road at an acute bend. Keep straight on here and at a subsequent junction to return to Bosham.

●

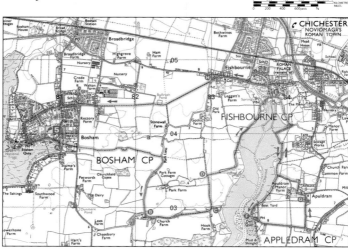

where there is also an exhibition area on Roman gardening.

BOSHAM

3½ miles W of Chichester off the A286

Pronounced Bozzum, this pleasant village is well known for both its history and its charm. Though it was the Irish monk Dicul who built a small religious house here, Bishop Wilfrid is credited with bringing Christianity to the area in AD 681 and Bosham is probably the first place in Sussex where he preached. Later, in the 10th century, Danish raiders landed here and, amongst the items that they stole, was the church's tenor bell. As the Danes left and took to their boats, the remaining bells were rung to sound the all clear and to indicate to the villagers that they could leave the nearby woods and return to their homes. As the last peal of bells rang out, the tenor bell, in one of the Danish boats, is said to

have joined in and, in doing so, capsized the boat. Both the bell and the sailors sank to the bottom of the creek and the place is now known as Bell Hole. Whether the story is true or not, Bosham certainly has its fair share of local legends as the village has strong associations with King Canute. It was here, on the shore, that the king, in the early 11th century, is said to have ordered back the waves in an attempt to demonstrate his kingly powers. King Canute's daughter is also buried in the once important Saxon parish church.

Later in the 11th century, King Harold sailed from Bosham, in 1064, on his ill-fated trip to Normandy to appease his rival, William of Normandy, for the English throne. However, Harold's plans went awry when he was taken captive and made to swear to William to aid his claim to the crown - a promise which, famously, Harold did not keep. It was

---

BOSHAM WALK CRAFT CENTRE

Bosham Walk, Bosham, Near Chichester, West Sussex, PO18 8HX
Tel: 01243 572475 Fax: 01243 576058

This spacious gallery is located in one of the oldest, most picturesque villages in Sussex. The **Bosham Walk Craft Centre** is marked by the sign of the fisherman. Inside is a fascinating collection of little shops and showcases in an old world setting. Here are antiques and crafts not to mention many of the artists and craftspeople happy to be watched at work. Periodically there are special exhibitions and demonstrations by visiting artists.

MILLSTREAM HOTEL AND RESTAURANT

Bosham, Chichester, West Sussex, PO18 8HL
Tel: 01243 573234 e-mail: info@millstream-hotel.co.uk
Fax: 01243 573459 website: www.millstream-hotel.co.uk

In the heart of the historic village of Old Bosham on the shores of Chichester harbour, the **Millstream Hotel** combines the elegance of a small English country house with the character and charm of an 18th century malthouse cottage. The fine restaurant overlooks charming gardens and the millstream. The menu is English and European, with dishes made from fresh local produce. This hotel is one of only two in the county to have the English Tourist Council Gold Award.

Bosham Village

variety of distinguished guests, including royalty, over the centuries. The house was built on its present site in 1668 for Richard Lumley - probably by the architect William Talman. Heavily altered in the following two centuries, it was burnt to the ground in 1900 but, in 1903, the house was rebuilt to the exact plans of Richard Lumley's grand mansion.

Now open to visitors, on a limited basis, the house is home to the late Lord Bessborough's collection of paintings and furnishings, including some fine 18th century tapestries. The **Below Stairs Experience** transports visitors to the old kitchen, pantry, servants' hall, living quarters and wine cellars. The surrounding grounds are renowned for their peace and tranquillity and the **Stansted Park Garden Centre** in the original walled garden has restored Victorian glasshouses, including a palm house, camellia house, fernery and vine house.

EAST ASHLING

3 miles NW of Chichester on B2178

A couple of miles to the north of East Ashling lies **Kingley Vale National Nature Reserve**, which contains the largest forest of yews in Britain. The trees were protected until the mid 16th century as they were used for making long bows, England's successful weapon against crossbows. Yews are a long lived species - 100 years is nothing in the life of a yew tree. Here at Kingley Vale, there are several 500 year-old trees, although most of the forest is made up of trees approaching their 100th birthday. Towards the summit of **Bow Hill**, the trees give way to heather and open

the breaking of the promise that caused William to set forth with his army a couple of years later. As a result, Harold's lands in Sussex were some of the first to be taken by the conquering Norman army and Bosham church's spire can be seen alongside Harold's ship in the Bayeux Tapestry.

An important port in the Middle Ages and particularly, between the 1800s and the 20th century, when it was alive with oyster smacks, today's Bosham is a place for keen yachtsmen as well as a charming place to explore. The narrow streets that lead down to the harbour are filled with elegant 17th and 18th century flint and brick buildings amongst which is the **Bosham Walk Craft Centre**. This fascinating collection of little shops selling all manner of arts, crafts, fashions and antiques within a old courtyard setting, also holds craft demonstrations and exhibitions throughout the season.

WALDERTON

6 miles NW of Chichester off the B2146

Just to the west of the village lies **Stansted House**, a splendid example of late 17th century architecture, built on the site of Henry II's 11th century hunting lodge. Stansted has played host to a

HORSE AND GROOM

East Ashling, Chichester, West Sussex, PO18 9AX
Tel: 01243 575339 e-mail: horseandgroomea@aol.com
Fax: 01243 575560 website: www.horseandgroom.sageweb.co.uk

This delightful 17th century inn, situated in a pretty West Sussex village in the South Downs, is a superb starting point for walking, cycling and riding breaks. The welcoming frontage is festooned with hanging baskets and pots overflowing with a riot of colour. Inside, the bar area retains the charm of a country pub and features a Victorian cast iron range in the old open fireplace. On top of the range is a traditional black cast iron pot of the type, which used to be suspended over the fire on a chain and several other cooking utensils from a bygone age. Nearby an old baker's oven is set into the wall.

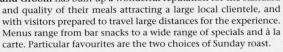

The separate restaurant can seat 60 people and is light and airy with brick and half-panelled walls and old timber beams. **The Horse and Groom** has built up a wonderful reputation for the standard

and quality of their meals attracting a large local clientele, and with visitors prepared to travel large distances for the experience. Menus range from bar snacks to a wide range of specials and à la carte. Particular favourites are the two choices of Sunday roast.

To the rear of the pub is a fully enclosed beer garden offering a sheltered haven to enjoy a quiet drink on a hot summer day or alfresco dining on a balmy evening. If you are thinking of staying over, there are also 11 en suite rooms available on a bed and breakfast basis all with television, tea and coffee making facilities.

---

heathland and it is here a group of four Bronze Age burial mounds, known as the King's Graves or Devil's Humps, can be found.

ARUNDEL

A settlement since before the Romans invaded, this quiet and peaceful town, which lies beneath the battlements of one of the most impressive castles in the country, is a strategically important site where the major east-west route through Sussex crosses the River Arun. It was one of William the Conqueror's most favoured knights, Roger de Montgomery, who first built a castle here, on the high ground overlooking the river, in the late 11th century. With a similar plan to that of Windsor castle, **Arundel Castle**

consisted of a motte with a double bailey, a design which, despite several alterations and rebuildings, remains clearly visible today. The second largest castle in England, it has been the seat of the Dukes of Norfolk and the Earls of Arun for over 700 years.

It was damaged in 1643 when, during the Civil War, Parliamentarian forces bombarded it with canons fired from the

Arundel Castle

Arundel Village

profits from the family's ownership of the newly prosperous steel town of Sheffield. Unfortunately, all that remains today of the original construction are the 12th century shell keep and parts of the 13th century barbican and curtain wall.

However the castle is still an atmospheric place to visit. The state apartments and main rooms contain some fine furniture dating from the 16th century and there are some excellent tapestries and paintings by Reynolds, Van Dyck, Gainsborough, Holbein and Constable on show. Also on display are some possessions of Mary, Queen of Scots and a selection of heraldic artefacts from the Duke of Norfolk's collection. The title, the Duke of Norfolk, was first

church tower. A programme of restoration took place during the late 18th century to make it habitable once more. A second programme of rebuilding was undertaken 100 years later by the 15th Duke of Norfolk, using

(Continued page 228)

ANTIQUITIES

5-7 Tarrant Street, Arundel, West Sussex, BN18 9DG
Tel: 01903 884355 Fax: 01903 884355
e-mail: antiquities@btconnect.com

Ian and Christina Fenwick are the friendly and professional proprietors of this shop dedicated to supplying high quality decorative antiques, country and formal furniture. Both have years of experience in the trade and are happy to deal with enquiries. They have been trading for 12 years in a traditional double-fronted

shop. Inside the open plan showrooms are crammed full of a superb selection of items that are constantly changing. This may include a large Victorian glass-fronted bookcase complete with a splendid set of tooled leather books. An antique model yacht, its sails displaying the patina of age sits on top of a

mahogany sideboard. Nearby is a wall mounted rack containing a delightful collection of Victorian kitchenware - huge burnished copper pots and containers, jelly pans and measuring jugs. Elsewhere are 19th century mirrors, cupboards, chests of drawers, tables, chairs, light fittings and paintings as well as a large and varied collection of ceramics, Staffordshire, majolica and glassware.

Ian and Christina also have three other bulging warehouses so it pays to ask what else they have in stock. A large part of their trade is to the American market and they can arrange shipping.

WALK 6

Arundel Park & South Stoke

Start	Arundel
Distance	7 miles (11.3km)
Approximate time	3½ hours
Parking	Mill Road car park
Refreshments	Pubs and cafés at Arundel, pub at Offham
Ordnance Survey maps	Landranger 197 (Chichester & The Downs), Explorer 121 (Arundel & Pulborough)

This lovely walk begins under the walls of Arundel Castle and then passes through the impressive park which surrounds the castle, the home of the dukes of Norfolk for 500 years. The return part of the route follows the course of the River Arun eastwards and southwards, at first through rich woodland high on a cliff overlooking the valley and then on the banks of the river itself. Note that dogs are restricted to public rights-of-way in Arundel Park.

Castle, church and Catholic cathedral perched above a bend in the river give Arundel a continental air. The juxtaposition of the buildings reflects the uneasy relationship that existed from the Reformation to the present century between the mainly Protestant townspeople and the Catholic dukes of Norfolk, owners of the castle and premier peers of the realm.

The extensive walls and towers of Arundel Castle make a splendid sight. It is mainly a 19th century reconstruction of the original Norman castle but some earlier work remains, including the 11th century shell keep. Close by is the medieval church, unique in that the nave is Anglican and the east end Catholic. For a long time the two parts were walled off from each other but now they are separated by a glass screen that can be opened on ecumenical occasions. The cathedral, an imposing building in the French Gothic style, was erected by a duke of Norfolk in the late 19th century only after the Catholic Church in England was allowed to organise itself into dioceses.

From the car park, turn left and then right when you reach the High Street. The

tourist information centre is on the left side of the High Street, which climbs steeply past the medieval parish church on the right and the Catholic cathedral on the left. Opposite a primary school on the left, bear right to enter Arundel Park **Ⓐ**.

Follow the driveway into the park through a kissing-gate by a road gate. Bear right at a notice 'No unauthorised vehicles beyond this point' onto a track and continue, with the Hiorne Tower – built by Francis Hiorne in 1790 – to your left. Cross the end of the gallop (look out for racehorses here), then turn left **Ⓑ**. On your left can be seen some of the extensive re-afforestaton that has been carried out following the devastation of the 1987 storm. Continue along the track skirting a wood on the right to a field gate and stile. The track then begins a descent into a steep-sided dry valley. This part of the walk is a delight with a wide view of the park to the right and woods to the left.

At the bottom of the valley, at a three-way footpath sign, cross over to a track that climbs, via a gate in a fence, steeply heading towards Duke's Plantation, not immediately visible on the skyline. After ¼

WALK 6

mile (400m) on this track, swing left **C** up the slope of the valley, heading north to climb to the crest of the ridge. Head for the left-hand edge of Dry Lodge Plantation.

Walk along the track here, enjoying the fine view on the left towards Duchess Lodge; behind is another splendid panorama – on a clear day you can see the Isle of Wight beyond Chichester harbour. The view ahead opens up at the top of the plantation, where a finger-post points the direction of the footpath as it leaves the track, turning half-right to head for a distant chalky cliff. You soon come to a stile by a gate, which is another excellent vantage-point for vistas over the Arun valley. Follow the track down and turn right when this meets another track at the bottom.

Turn left immediately before the next gateway to leave the track and follow a faint path down by a fence, which leads into dense woodland. This becomes steep and dark and there is an old flint wall on the right. Go through a gap in this at the bottom to reach the bridleway **D** which follows the south bank of the River Arun. Take a few steps to the left to view the river or turn sharp right to begin the return leg of the walk.

The bridleway twists its way through woodland which screens views of the river, and eventually it leaves the wood through a gateway to reach the top of a cliff. Another climb follows, and the track becomes a field-edge path leading into South Stoke. Turn right to pass behind a cart shed, which used to have accommodation for labourers on its upper floor, and reach the lane **E** into the hamlet. Turn left here to visit the unpretentious and utterly peaceful little St Lawrence Church, its interior dominated by an enormous cast-iron stove. It is usually open. Continue

down the lane to the bridge and turn right along the path on the west bank of the river.

The walking now is undemanding, the tranquillity disturbed only by the passing of a train or, rarely, a boat. You may see herons here and some less common waterbirds. Burpham church can be seen nestling among trees as a navigational cut truncates the eastern meander of the river. The dramatic silhouette of Arundel Castle appears as the footpath approaches a cattle bridge across the river at Offham Farm, but the apparent distance to Arundel is deceptive since the river makes another meander eastwards before reaching the town. Before this final section the riverside path passes a pub. The path ends back at Mill Road car park. ●

conferred on Sir John Howard in 1483, by his friend Richard III. Carrying the hereditary office of Earl Marshal of England, the Duke of Norfolk is the premier duke of England.

Perhaps the most gruesome item to be seen at the castle can be found, not surprisingly, in the armoury. The **Morglay Sword**, which measures five feet nine inches long, is believed to have belonged to Bevis, a castle warden who was so tall that it was said he could walk from Southampton to Cowes without getting his head wet. In order to

determine his final resting place, Bevis, so the story goes, threw his sword off the castle's battlements and, half a mile away, where the sword landed, is a mound that is still known as Bevis's Grave.

The period of stability that the castle brought to the town in the late medieval times turned Arundel into an important port and market town. In fact, the port of Arundel was mentioned in the Domesday Book and it continued to operate until the 20th century when it finally closed in 1927 - the last Harbour Master was moved to Shoreham and the

ARUNDEL WILDFOWL AND WETLANDS CENTRE

Mill Road, Arundel, West Sussex, BN18 9PB
Tel: 01903 883355 Fax: 01903 884834
e-mail: info.arundel@wwt.org.uk website: www.wwt.org.uk

Have a fantastic day out seeing, feeding, and learning about wetland birds and wildlife, and at the same time help the Wildfowl & Wetlands Trust to conserve wetland habitats and their biodiversity.

WWT was founded in 1946 by the artist and naturalist Sir Peter Scott and is the largest international wetland conservation charity in the UK. WWT Arundel is one of 9 centres and it consists of more than 60 beautiful acres of ponds, lakes and reed beds. WWT Arundel is home to over 1000 of the world's most spectacular ducks, geese and swans, many of which are rare or endangered. This includes the world's rarest goose, the Nene, which was saved from extinction by WWT. Also see the New Zealand Blue Ducks - WWT Arundel is also the only site in the world outside of New Zealand where Blue Ducks have successfully bred. You can enjoy an atmospheric stroll through the reed beds on the new boardwalk, or watch wild birds from one of the many hides. Kids can follow the themed Discovery trail through the grounds. WWT Arundel also features the award winning recreation of the volcanic Lake Myvatin, complete with lava formations, waterfalls, and it's native duck the common Scoter which is part of a specialist breeding programme. There is also plenty to do inside the centre - the new Eye of the Wind wildlife art gallery shows a continuous programme of local and national wildlife artists, many of whom host art workshops at the centre. You can enjoy superb homemade food in the Waters Edge Restaurant situated in the main viewing gallery overlooking swan lake, or browse through the gift shop or *In Focus* (telescope and binocular specialists) shop.

Special events run throughout the year, and there are children's crafts every school holiday. Open every day except Christmas day. Less than 1 mile from Arundel town centre (follow the brown duck signs). Free parking. 20 minute walk from Arundel train station.

WWT Arundel – the most complete year round wildlife experience in Sussex!

THE ARUNDEL BOOKSHOP

10 The High Street, Arundel, Sussex, BN18 9AB
Tel: 01903 882680

The Arundel Bookshop has been here since 1977 and it is the ideal place for a good old-fashioned browse through the shelves. The books are crammed into every inch of the three floors of the shop and cover every subject in print and range from antique to the latest publications. All interests and age groups are catered for. Open seven days a week this is a book-lovers' paradise.

port transferred to Littlehampton.

It was also during this peaceful period that the 14th century parish Church of St Nicholas was built, a unique church in that it is divided into separate Catholic and Anglican areas by a Sussex iron screen. Despite religious persecution, particularly during the 16th century, the Fitzalan family and the successive Dukes of Norfolk remained staunch Catholics. So much so that the 15th Duke, who was responsible for the 19th century rebuilding of the castle, also commissioned the substantial Catholic Church of St Philip Heri which was designed by J.A. Hansom and Son, the inventors of the Hansom cab, in 1870. In 1965, this impressive building became the seat of the Catholic bishopric of Brighton and Arundel and was renamed the **Cathedral of Our Lady and St Philip Howard**. (Sir Philip was the 13th Earl of Arundel who died in prison after being sentenced to death by Elizabeth I for his beliefs.) Each June, the cathedral hosts the two-day Corpus Christi Festival during which the entire length of the aisle is laid out with a carpet of flowers.

Other historic sites in the town include the **Maison Dieu**, a medieval hospital outside one of the castle's lodges, founded by Richard Fitzalan in 1345. Dissolved by Henry VIII 200 years later, this semi-monastic institution combined the roles of clinic, hotel and almshouse.

For a greater insight into the history of the town and its various inhabitants down the ages, the **Arundel Museum and Heritage Centre** is well worth a visit. With imaginative use of models, old photographs and historic artefacts, the story of Arundel, from Roman times to the present day, is told.

Just to the north of the town, is the **Wildlife and Wetland Trust** (see panel opposite), a wonderful place that plays host to a wide variety of ducks, geese, swans and other migratory birds from all over the world. There is a trail around the various lakes and ponds and an award-winning visitor centre.

AROUND ARUNDEL

BURPHAM
2 miles NE of Arundel off the A27

This charming and attractive downland village of flint and brick built thatched cottages overlooks the River Arun and provides excellent views of Arundel Castle. The peace and quiet found here seems far removed from the days when the Saxons built defensive earthworks in an attempt to keep the invading Danes at bay. Later, during the Middle Ages, one of the farms on nearby Wepham Down was a leper colony and the track leading down into the village is still known as Lepers' Way.

LYMINSTER

1½ miles S of Arundel on the A284

Lyminster is an ancient settlement of flint cottages and protective walls, which appears, as *Lullyngminster*, in Alfred the Great's will of AD 901. From the village there is a marvellous view of Arundel Castle across the water meadows of the lower River Arun. Local legend has it that the deep pool, known as the **Knuckler Hole**, which lies northwest of Lyminster church, was once inhabited by a savage sea dragon, whose only food was fair maidens. This monster was said to have terrorised the local population to such an extent that the King of Wessex offered half his kingdom and his daughter's hand in marriage to the man who killed the beast. The dragon was finally slain after a terrible fight though there is some confusion regarding the identity of the brave dragon slayer. This was either a gallant young farm boy known as Jim Pulk or a handsome knight. The early Norman coffin slab in the north transept of the church is where the conquering hero was finally laid to rest and it is still known as the **Slayer's Stone**.

LITTLEHAMPTON

3 miles S of Arundel on the A284

This is a charming maritime town, at the mouth of the River Arun. Signs of Roman occupation have been discovered here

and the local manor is mentioned in the Domesday Book. Following the Norman invasion, Littlehampton became an important Channel port (declining considerably in the 1500s), exporting timber from the Sussex Weald and importing stone from Caen, France. It was here, too, that Queen Matilda arrived from France, in 1139, to stake her unsuccessful claim to the English throne from Stephen.

Now a quiet and pleasant coastal town and a popular holiday resort, though not as fashionable as many of its larger neighbours, Littlehampton has all the ingredients for a traditional seaside break. There is a large amusement complex, a boating marina, a promenade and a harbour. **Littlehampton Fort** was built in 1854 to protect the entrance to the River Arun . Although the site is fenced off and heavily overgrown, it is visible from the path and there is a plaque with historical details. However, the town's most charming feature is, undoubtedly, the large green, which lies between the seafront and the first row of houses.

In the old manor house in Church Street, **Littlehampton Museum** tells the history of the town, including its maritime past, through a series of informative displays. Also worthy of a visit is the **Body Shop Tour**, which takes place each Friday throughout the

BAILIFFSCOURT HOTEL

Climping, Near Littlehampton, West Sussex, BN17 5RW
Tel: 01903 723511 e-mail: bailiffscourt@hshotels.co.uk
Fax: 01903 723107 website: www.hshotels.co.uk

Bailiffscourt has the tranquil and timeless quality of an ancient country house but is in fact comparatively modern. Built in 1933 for Lord Moyne of the Guiness brewing family, it was created in the style of earlier medieval buildings. Many salvaged architectural features like the 15th century oak door and the entrance archway provide an authentic medieval atmosphere. It's been a hotel since 1948 allowing guests to sample the luxury enjoyed by the aristocracy between the wars.

summer. The Body Shop Headquarters lie just outside the town, which is the birthplace of both the company and its founder Anita Roddick, and the tour shows visitors just how some of the company's environmentally and animal friendly products are made.

FORD

2½ miles S of Arundel off the A259

Situated on an ancient ford crossing of the River Arun, this village is dwarfed by the prison on the site of an old RAF station. However, this does little to spoil the splendid and isolated setting of the old **Saxon parish church** that stands alone by the river.

FELPHAM

5 miles SW of Arundel off the A259

This is the village to which the poet and artist, William Blake, moved, along with his wife and sister, in 1800 to undertake some engraving work for William Hayley, a gentleman of the period. The cottage where the Blakes lived can still be seen down Blake's Road and it was here that he wrote '*Away to sweet Felpham for Heaven is there*', which recalls the view of the sea from his window. He left the village a few years later after being acquitted of a charge of sedition.

BOGNOR REGIS

6 miles SW of Arundel on the A259

Towards the end of the 18th century Sir Richard Hotham, a wealthy London milliner, sought to transform Bognor from a quiet fishing village into a fashionable resort to rival Brighton. He set about constructing some imposing residences, including The Dome in Upper Bognor Road, and even planned to have the town renamed Hothampton. Unfortunately, the fashionable set of the day stayed away and Hotham's dream was never realised - at least not in his

THE FLOWER BARN

37 Hill Lane, Barnham, West Sussex, PO22 0BL
Tel: 01243 553490 Fax: 01243 554995
website: www.Flowerbarn.co.uk

Down a quiet country lane, deep in the heart of the Sussex countryside is this well-established, specialist, family business. Lyn and Andrew Tulett are growers of dried flowers and in the **Flower Barn** probably offer the largest and choicest selection of dried flowers to be found anywhere in England. But dried flowers are just part of the picture. Now the Barn specialises in interior design accessories - the finishing touches to any room. The stock changes with every season, their range of Christmas products being especially spectacular. Although well off the beaten track, this remarkable enterprise stocks the very latest continental designed products from Europe's leading suppliers. This keeps the Flower Barn in the forefront, making it a magnet for interior designers in the South of England.

As well as dried flowers the Barn stocks hops, fruit and berries, candles, ribbons, baskets, terra cotta, china, glass, metalware and the finest silk flowers. Arrangements are ready made or to order. Thousands of bunches hang from the ceiling, thousands more cascade from baskets lining the walls and the floor. Everywhere is the delightful scent of roses, the sweet perfume of lavender, and the most evocative smell of a country childhood, a summer hay meadow. The Flower Barn is both wholesale and retail.

lifetime. However, in 1929, George V came to the resort to convalesce following a serious illness and, on the strength of his stay, the town was granted the title Regis (meaning of the King). Today, the town is a pleasant coastal resort with some elegant Georgian features, traditional public gardens, a promenade and safe, sandy beaches. The large central **Hotham Park** is another feature of this charming town where visitors can enjoy concerts given at the bandstand, clock golf and tennis. The naturally planted gardens are perfect to stroll in, picnic or just watch the squirrels. The **Bognor Regis Museum**, housed in a lodge of Hotham Park, plays tribute to Sir Richard Hotham as well as telling the story of the famous bathing machine lady, Mary Wheatland. Mary Wheatland was a well known Bognor Regis character. Born in 1835 in the nearby village of Aldinbourne, she hired

out bathing machines as well as teaching children to swim. She also saved many souls from drowning for which she received medals and recognition from the Royal Humane Society. The sea air and exercise must have done the eccentric lady a great deal of good as she lived to be 89 years old.

Perhaps, more than anything else, the resort is known for its "Birdmen" and the annual international **Birdman Rally** held in August. The competitors, in a variety of classes, take it in turns to hurl themselves off the pier in an attempt to make the longest un-powered flight and so win the coveted competition.

YAPTON

3½ miles SW of Arundel on the B2233

Set amid the wheatfields of the coastal plain, this village has a charming 12th century church, the tower of which leans at an alarming angle.

THE GEORGE INN

Eartham, Nr Chichester, West Sussex, PO18 0LT
Tel: 01243 814340 Fax: 01243 814725

This family run country freehouse is off the beaten track but only 6 miles from Chichester, within ten miles of Arundel, Petworth and Midhurst, and within 3 miles of both Goodwood and Fontwell racecourses. Your hosts are John and Val Ednie. John was formerly an officer with the Metropolitan Police, while wife Val was a pottery tutor. Their head chef is their son Russell, who trained at Brooklands College Weybridge, then worked as a head chef in London before coming to the **George**. They offer a warm welcome and delicious, freshly prepared meals and snacks from an imaginative and varied menu. The specials board has a frequently changed selection of traditional meals, while the à la carte menu has a wide choice of cosmopolitan cuisine.
Visitors can eat in the non-smoking restaurant, which seats 40 or in the inviting lounge bar with its

open fire or in the village bar with flagstone floors and dartboard. There is a wide selection of real ales including some from small local breweries. The guest ales are changed frequently and Greene King, Old Speckled Hen and Arundel Classic are among the great ales regularly available here.

There is plenty of convenient parking and a large garden to enjoy, where customers can dine alfresco in the summer. Just ½ mile from Stane Street, the George is an ideal stopping place for walkers. Children are welcome, making it perfect for family lunch on an outing and dog lovers can bring their canine companions into the garden and the village bar.

WALBERTON

3 miles W of Arundel off the B2132

Down a narrow country lane, this pleasant village has obviously been settled for centuries as the local parish church is built on Saxon foundations and it still contains an ancient Saxon tub shaped font.

FONTWELL

3½ miles W of Arundel off the A27

The village is well known to followers of horse racing as it is home to the pleasantly situated **Fontwell Park National Hunt Racecourse**. First opened in 1921, the unusual 'figure of eight' track holds 15 meetings between August and May and remains a firm favourite with jumping enthusiasts. Fontwell is also home of **Denman's Garden**, a beautifully sheltered, semi-wild, 20th century garden where the emphasis in planting has been on colour, shape and texture which can be seen all year round.

EARTHAM

5 miles NW of Arundel off the A285

The village was the home of the 19th century Member of Parliament, William Huskisson, the gentleman who was famously knocked down by Stevenson's *Rocket* during its inaugural run in 1830. Thus, Huskisson was able to claim the dubious honour of being the world's first recorded victim of a railway accident.

SLINDON

3 miles NW of Arundel off the A29

With a dramatic setting on the side of a slope of the South Downs, the name Slindon is derived from the Saxon word for sloping hill. This picturesque village has splendid views over the coastal plain to the English Channel and numerous lovely old cottages. As an excellent observation point, it has been occupied

from Neolithic times and many fine examples of early flint tools have been found in the area.

The village was the estate village for Slindon House. Today, the **Slindon Estate** is owned by the National Trust and most of the village, the woodlands and Slindon House (now let to Slindon College) come under its care. The largest Trust-owned estate in Sussex, there is plenty to see here as well as excellent opportunities for walking and birdwatching. Slindon House was originally founded as a residence for the Archbishops of Canterbury. (Archbishop Stephen Langton, a negotiator and signatory of the Magna Carta, spent the last weeks of his life here in 1228.) Rebuilt in the 1560s and extensively re-modelled during the 1920s, the house is now a private boys' school. The estate's wonderful post office is an amalgamation of two 400 year-old cottages and it is the village's only remaining thatched building. The focal point of the village is the crossroads where a tree stands in a small open area close to the village church. Dating from the 12th century, this charming flint built church contains an unusual reclining effigy of a Tudor knight, Sir Anthony St Leger, the only wooden carving of its kind in Sussex. Finally, just to the north lies the cricket field where Sir Richard Newland is said to have refined the modern game over 200 years ago.

From the village there is a splendid walk around the estate that takes in the ancient deer park of Slindon House as well as other remains such as the summerhouse. The magnificent beech trees in the woodland were once highly prized and their seeds were sold worldwide. Unfortunately, the severe storm of October 1987 flattened many of these splendid trees, some of which had stood for 250 years. Though most of the fallen trees were cleared, some were left and the dead wood has provided new habitats for a whole range of insects and fungi. Birds and other wild-life also abound in the Slindon woodlands and, in May, the woodland floor is a carpet of bluebells.

Also at the Slindon Estate is **Gumber Bothy Camping Barn**, a stone tent now fully restored by the National Trust, which provides simple overnight accommodation just off the South Downs Way. Originally an outbuilding of Gumber Farm, a secluded working farm in the folds of the South Downs, the bothy is available to anyone over the age of five who enjoys the outdoor life. Sleeping up to 27 in three dormitory style rooms, the other facilities include showers, a drying room, a well-equipped kitchen and a common room. There is also a field for campers and, though no dogs are allowed, sociable horses can be accommodated overnight in a shared horse paddock.

WORTHING

Despite having been inhabited since the Stone Age, Worthing remained a small and isolated fishing community until the end of the 18th century when the popularity of sea bathing among the rich and fashionable set led to a period of rapid development. The climax to this period of development occurred in 1798, when George III sent his 16 year-old daughter, Princess Amelia, to Worthing to recuperate from an ill-fated affair with one of his royal equerries. By 1830, however, Worthing's Golden Age was at an end but fortunately many of the Georgian town houses, villas and streets can still be seen today, just as they were nearly 200 years ago. Further development work was hampered by the cholera and typhoid outbreaks of the 1850s and 1890s although, between the two World Wars, some more modest expansion was undertaken.

Throughout much of the 19th century, Worthing remained a popular resort with both royalty and the famous. It was here, in the summer of 1894, that Oscar Wilde wrote *The Importance of Being Ernest* and immortalised its name in the central character, Jack Worthing. **Worthing's Pier**, one of the country's oldest, was built in the 1860s as a pier was a must for any successful Victorian seaside resort. An elegant construction with a 1930s pavilion at the end, it has, during its lifetime, been blown down, burnt down and blown up. Of the more recent buildings to be found here, the **English Martyrs Catholic Church**, just west of the town centre, is a recommended stopping point as, painted on the ceiling, is a replica of

Michelangelo's Sistine Chapel fresco that was completed by a local artist in 1993.

It also plays host to the **National Bowls Championships** that take place in Beach House Park.

For a real insight into the history of this town a visit to the **Worthing Museum and Art Gallery** is essential. Through a series of fascinating displays, tales of smuggling, the town riots of the 19th century, top secret activities during World War II and the early life of this fishing village are told. The museum is also home to a nationally important costume and toy collection and, in the surrounding museum grounds, there is a sculpture garden.

As Worthing expanded it also swallowed up a number of ancient nearby settlements including Broadwater with its fine cottages and Norman church and West Tarring where the remains of a 13th century palace belonging to the Archbishops of Canterbury now double as the village hall and primary school annexe.

AROUND WORTHING

HIGH SALVINGTON

1½ miles N of Worthing on the A24

This village, now almost entirely engulfed by Worthing, is home to the last survivor of several windmills that once stood in the area. **High Salvington Windmill**, a black post mill, was built between 1700 and 1720 and its design is one that had been used since the Middle Ages - a heavy cross shaped base with a strong central upright (or post) around which the sails and timber superstructure could pivot. The mill stopped working in 1897 but, following extensive restoration in the 1970s, it has now been restored to full working order. It is now

open on a limited basis with afternoon tea available.

FINDON

3 miles N of Worthing off the A24

An attractive village, Findon's main square is surrounded by some elegant 18th century houses. Situated within the South Downs Area of Outstanding Natural Beauty, Findon is famous for being the venue of one of the two great Sussex sheep fairs - the other is at Lewes. Markets have been held on Nepcote Green since the 13th century and the Findon **Sheep Fair** has been an annual event each September since the 18th century. The village has a festival atmosphere and thousands of sheep change hands here during the fair. Despite a gap year in 2001 due to foot and mouth disease, the fair returns to business as usual in 2002.

From Findon there is also easy access to **Cissbury Ring**, the largest Iron Age hillfort on the South Downs. Overshadowed only by Dorset's Maiden Castle, this impressive hilltop site covers an area of 65 acres and is surrounded by a double rampart almost a mile in circumference. Archaeologists have estimated that over 50,000 tons of chalk, soil and boulders would have had to be moved in the fort's construction, which would indicate that this was once a sizeable community in the 3rd century BC. However, the site is much older than this as Neolithic flint mines dating back 6,000 years have also been discovered here, which makes Cissbury one of the oldest industrial sites in the country. Today, the site is owned by the National Trust and is open to the public.

COOMBES

4 miles NE of Worthing off the A27

This tiny settlement of just a few houses and a farm is worthy of a visit if just to see the village church, which stands in the farmyard. An unassuming Norman church, it contains some exceptional 12th century murals that were only uncovered in 1949 and are believed to have been painted by monks from St Pancras Priory, Lewes. Just to the north of the hamlet lies **Annington Hill** from where there are glorious views over the Adur valley and also there is access to a section of the South Downs Way footpath.

SHOREHAM-BY-SEA
4½ miles E of Worthing on the A259

There has been a harbour here, on the River Adur estuary, since Roman times and, though evidence of both Roman and Saxon occupations have been found, it was not until the Norman period that the town developed into an important port. At that time the River Adur was navigable as far as Bramber and the main port was situated a mile or so upstream, where the Norman church of St Nicholas still stands today.

However, towards the end of the 11th century, the river estuary began to silt up and the old port and toll bridge were abandoned in favour of New Shoreham, which was built at the river mouth. Again, the Normans built a church close to the harbour and both churches remain key features of the town. The old town lapsed into the life of a quiet village while, during the 12th and 13th centuries, New Shoreham was one of the most important Channel ports. It was here, in 1199, that King John landed with an army to succeed to the throne of England following the death of Richard the Lionheart and, in 1346, Shoreham was asked to raise 26 ships, more than both Dover and Bristol, to fight the French. Perhaps, though, the town's most historic moment came in 1651 when Charles II fled from here to France, following defeat at the Battle of

Worcester, on board the ship of Captain Nicholas Tettersell.

The new port flourished until the 16th century when, once again, silting, in the form of a shingle spit, which diverted the river's course, had disastrous economic consequences. The next 200 years or so saw a period of decline in Shoreham, which was only relieved by the rise in popularity of nearby Brighton and the excavation of a new river course in 1818. To reflect its new importance, **Shoreham Fort** was constructed at the eastern end of the beach as part of Palmerston's coastal defence system. A half-moon shape, the fort was capable of accommodating six guns, which could each fire 80 pounds of shot. The fort has been restored and is now open to visitors who will also have a superb view of the still busy harbour.

The history of Shoreham-by-Sea and, in particular, its maritime past, are explored at **Marlipins Museum**. The museum is, itself, interesting, as it is housed in one of the oldest surviving non-religious buildings in the country. A Norman customs warehouse, an unusual knapped flint and Caen stone patterned façade was added in the 14th century and it has a single 42 foot beam supporting the first floor.

Though the town's past is, undoubtedly, built upon its port, **Shoreham Airport**, opened in 1934, is the country's oldest commercial airport. Still a major base for recreational flying, the lovely art deco terminal acts as a departure and arrivals hall for many business passengers travelling to and from the Channel Islands and Western Europe. Also here, housed in a World War II blister hangar, is the **Museum of D-Day Aviation**. With a unique collection of early aircraft, artefacts, uniforms and medals from the desperate days of 1940, this is an interesting and unusual place to visit. Tours of the airport can also be booked.

North Lancing

3 miles E of Worthing off the A27

This attractive downland village, with its curved streets, has one of the most ancient Saxon names in Sussex. It is derived from Wlencing, one of the sons of Aella, who led the first Saxon invasion to the area in AD 477. Apart from the old flint cottages on the High Street, the old 13th century church adds to the timeless atmosphere of the village. However, North Lancing is dominated by a more recent addition to its skyline - **Lancing College**. Set high up on a beautiful site overlooking the River Adur, the college was founded in 1848 by Nathaniel Woodward, whose aim was to establish a group of classless schools. By the time of his death in 1891, there were 15 schools in the Woodward Federation and, today, Lancing College is an independent secondary school. Of the college buildings, the splendid 19th century Gothic style chapel is the most striking and it is considered to be one of the finest examples of its kind.

Sompting

2 miles E of Worthing off the A27

This village, the name of which means marshy ground, has, as its pride and joy, a church that is unique in Britain. Built on foundations, which can be traced back to AD 960, the **Church of St Mary** has a distinctive spire that consists of four diamond shaped faces which taper to a point. Known as a Rhenish helm, the design was popular in German Rhineland but is not found elsewhere in this country. In 1154, the church was given to the Knights Templar who completely rebuilt it except for the spire, which they left untouched. Just over 150 years later the building came into the hands of their rivals, the Knights Hospitallers, who were responsible for the present design of the church as they returned it to its original Saxon style.

Goring-By-Sea

1½ miles W of Worthing on the A259

Until the arrival of the railway in the mid 19th century, this was a small fishing village. However, the Victorians love of a day by the seaside saw the rapid growth of Goring and today it is a genteel place with a pleasant suburban air.

To the northwest stands the cone-shaped **Highdown Hill**, which, although only 266 feet high, stands out above the surrounding coastal plain. Its prominent nature has made a much sought after vantage point over the centuries. It has been an Iron Age hillfort, a Roman bath house and a Saxon graveyard.

Close by **Highdown Gardens** are the creation of Sir Frederick and Lady Stern, who spent over 50 years turning what was originally a chalk pit into this splendid garden. One of the least known gardens in the area, Highdown has a unique collection of rare plants and trees which the couple brought back from their expeditions to the Himalayas and China in the mid 20th century. The garden was left to the local borough council on the death of Sir Frederick in 1967 and it has been now declared a national collection.

On the south side of the main A27 is **Castle Goring**, built for the grandfather of the poet Percy Bysshe Shelley. It is not exactly a castle although the castellated frontage and the arched windows with their elaborate tracery are believed to be based on Arundel Castle. The south frontage is quite different with pillars and pediments resembling a Roman villa. The building is currently a private English language school.

THE WEST SUSSEX DOWNS

The southern boundary to this part of West Sussex is the South Downs, a magnificent range of chalk hills extending for over 100 miles. The South Downs Way, a long distance bridleway follows the crest of the hills from Winchester to Beachy Head at Eastbourne and, whether taken as a whole or enjoyed in sections, it provides splendid views of this Area of Outstanding Natural Beauty as well as a wealth of delightful rural hamlets and villages to discover.

To the north of the Downs lies Midhurst, the home of the area's most famous ruin - Cowdray Park. Though the once splendid Tudor mansion has been reduced to a burnt out shell following a fire in the late 18th century, the ruins provide a haunting backdrop to the parkland's famous polo matches. In better condition are Uppark, where H.G. Wells spent many hours in the great library as a boy and Petworth House, an elegant late 17th century building that is very reminiscent of a French château.

Other great names from the world of the arts have also found this region inspirational. The novelist Anthony Trollope spent his last years at South Harting, the poet Tennyson lived under the wooded slopes of Black Down and the composer Edward Elgar visited Fittleworth several times and wrote his famous cello concerto while staying there in 1917.

MIDHURST

Though this quiet and prosperous market town has its origins in the early Middle Ages, its name is Saxon and suggests that once it was surrounded by forest. It was the Norman lord, Savaric Fitzcane, who first built a fortified house here, on the summit of St Ann's Hill, and, though only a few stones remain today, the views from this natural vantage point over the River Rother are worth the walk.

The town of Midhurst grew up at the castle gates. By 1300, when the de Bohuns (the then lords of the manor) moved from their hilltop position the town was well established. Choosing a new site by the river in a coudrier, or hazel grove, gave the family the name for their new estate - **Cowdray**. In the 1490s, the estate passed, by marriage, to Sir David Owen, who built the splendid Tudor courtyard mansion. However, due to rising debts he was forced to sell the house to Sir William Fitzwilliam, a leading figure in the court of Henry VIII and the 1st Earl of Southampton. He and his family added the finishing touches and, when complete, the

The Angel Hotel

North Street, Midhurst, West Sussex, GU29 9D
Tel:01730 812421 Fax: 01730 815928
e-mail: Angel@hshotels.co.uk website: www.hshotels.co.uk

The elegant Georgian façade of **The Angel** hides a much older building full of warmth and character. This former 16th century coaching inn is situated in the centre of a delightful Sussex market town surrounded by the beauty of the South Downs. The cosy lounge with its open log fire is just the place to relax after a day at Goodwood races or polo at Cowdray Park, before dining in the informal brasserie or the splendid Court Room.

magnificent house was a rival to Hampton Court. Indeed, the house played host to many notable visitors including both Henry VIII and Elizabeth I who were frequently entertained here. Even though the house is in ruins following a devastating fire in 1793, it is still a splendid monument to courtly Tudor architecture. Today, visitors can view the roofless remains of the east side of the quadrangle court, along with parts of the west side where the turreted three-storey gatehouse still remains largely intact. However, most visitors come to **Cowdray Park** to watch the polo matches that take place every weekend and sometimes during the week from April until July.

Back in the town, on the opposite side of the River Rother from Cowdray Park, there are some impressive buildings. The 16th century timber framed **Market Hall** stands in front of the even older **Spread Eagle Inn**, an old coaching inn, dating from the 1400s, where Elizabeth I is reputed to have stayed. Nearby is the famous **Midhurst Grammar School**, founded in 1672 by Gilbert Hanniman and now a successful comprehensive school. Though the centre of the town has migrated away from its old heart around the

market square and the church, the custom of ringing the curfew each night at eight o'clock from the heavily restored church continues and is said to be in memory of a legendary commercial traveller. Whilst endeavouring to reach Midhurst, the traveller got lost in the local woods at dusk and, on hearing the sound of the church bells, was able to find his way safely to the town.

For most people visiting Midhurst, it is through the books of H.G. Wells that they feel that they already know the town. Wells' maternal grandmother came from Midhurst and his mother worked at nearby Uppark where, as a young boy, Wells spent many hours in the library. At the age of 15, Herbert George was apprenticed to a chemist in the town and also enrolled at the Grammar School for evening classes.

Cowdray House

Though he left Midhurst for some years, Wells later returned to the Grammar School as a teacher. As well as providing the inspiration for his most famous book *The Invisible Man*, Midhurst has been the setting for many of his short stories including *The Man Who Could Work Miracles*. The great novelist and science fiction writer obviously had fond recollections of his time in the town for he wrote in his autobiography: "Midhurst has always been a happy place for me. I suppose it rained there at times, but all my memories of Midhurst are in sunshine."

AROUND MIDHURST

EASEBOURNE

1 mile N of Midhurst on the A272

This delightful estate village, which has some superb half-timbered houses, was the home of an Augustinian convent of the Blessed Virgin Mary. Founded in the 13th century, the convent prospered until 1478, when the prioress and some of her nuns were accused of gross immorality and squandering the convent's funds on hunting and extravagant entertaining. All that remains today of the priory is the church now the parish church. Another interesting building here is **Budgenor Lodge**, built in 1793, it was a model workhouse and now occupied by the Christ for the Nation Training Centre.

FERNHURST

4½ miles N of Midhurst on the A286

Just to the east of this pretty village, with its assorted tile hung cottages surrounding the village green, lies **Black Down**, rising abruptly from the Sussex Weald. A sandstone hill covered in heather, gorse and silver birch, that is an ideal environment for a variety of upland birdlife, the summit is the highest point

in Sussex and from here there are views over the Weald and South Downs to the English Channel.

A particularly fine viewpoint lies on the southern crest and one of the footpaths up the hill has been named locally as **Tennyson's Lane**, after the famous poet who lived for 20 years in the area. At one time a Royal navy signal tower stood on Tally Knob, a prominent outcrop to the southeast of the Temple of the Winds. A development of the tried and tested system of fire beacons, in 1796 the Admiralty introduced the Shutter Telegraph here as a more sophisticated means of passing messages between Portsmouth and London. Though ingenious, the system was found to be impractical and was soon abandoned.

To the west of Fernhurst, in the late 12th century, an Augustinian priory, on smaller scale then the magnificent Michelham Priory near Upper Dicker, was founded. At the time of the Dissolution the priory became a farmhouse. One of the first floor rooms, which was originally the prior's chamber, is decorated with Tudor murals and although it is a private house, **Shulbrede Priory** is occasionally open to the public.

LURGASHALL

4½ miles NE of Midhurst off the A283

This delightful rural village has, as a backdrop, the wooded slopes of Black Down, where Tennyson lived at **Aldworth House**. The village's largely Saxon church has an unusual loggia, or porch, outside where those who had travelled from afar could eat and rest before or after the service.

LODSWORTH

2½ miles E of Midhurst off the A272

Situated on the River Lod, a small tributary of the River Rother, this old community has some fine buildings including a 13ᵗʰ century manor house and an early 18ᵗʰ century Dower House. The whitewashed village Church of St Peter lies on the outskirts of Lodsworth and, just to the north, is **St Peter's Well**, the water of which is supposed to have healing qualities.

TILLINGTON

5 miles E of Midhurst on the A272

Dating back to the days before the Norman Conquest, the village appeared in the Domesday Book as Tolinstone . Tillington lies beside the western walls of Petworth House. The local landmark here, however, is **All Hallows' Church** and, in particular, its tower. Built in 1810, the tower is topped by stone pinnacles and a crown that is very reminiscent of the lower stage of the Eiffel Tower. Known as a Scots Crown, the church and its tower have featured in paintings by both Turner and Constable.

DUNCTON

5 miles SE of Midhurst on the A285

Sheltered beneath Duncton Hill, beside Burton Park, the main building of St Michael's Girls' School, stands a small church on the wall of which can be seen the Royal Arms of Charles I dated 1636.

SINGLETON

5½ miles S of Midhurst on the A286

Lying in the folds of the South Downs, in the valley of the River Lavant, Singleton, owned by Earl Godwin of Wessex, father of King Harold, was one of the largest and wealthiest manors in England. Little remains here from Saxon times, except an ancient barn on the village green, though the 13ᵗʰ century church was built on the foundations of its Saxon predecessor. Inside the church, in the south aisle, is a memorial to Thomas Johnson, a huntsman of the nearby Charlton Hunt who died in 1744. There

THE WHITE HORSE INN

The Street, Sutton, West Sussex, RH20 1PS
Tel: 01798 869221 Fax: 01798 869291

Situated in the lovely flint and stone village of Sutton, the **White Horse** has a mellow exterior, hidden for much of the year by Virginia creeper. For two and a half centuries this has been the village ale house. Tastefully restored, it now has the comforts of the 21ˢᵗ century, whilst maintaining the charm and character of a by-gone age. With a blazing log fire and half-clad walls this is one of the most comfortable hostelries in the county.

HORSE GUARDS INN

Tillington, West Sussex, GU28 9AE
Tel: 01798 342332

Paul and Susannah Brett delight in welcoming guests to their 18ᵗʰ century inn on a hillside on the edge of Petworth Park. The **Horse Guards Inn** is renowned for the standard of its haute cuisine and its extensive and high quality wine list. Originally named the New Star it was renamed in 1840 in honour of the Horse Guards who used it as a regular watering hole whilst

transporting gold from London to Portsmouth or dealing with local smugglers and highwaymen.

Weald and Downland Open Air Museum

a Victorian tollhouse from Bramber, a schoolroom from West Wittering, a working blacksmith's forge and the watermill from Lurgashall which produces flour everyday for sale in the shop and use in the lakeside café. Several interiors have been furnished as they may have been during the building's heyday and visitors can take a look at the Tudor farmstead, with its fireplace in the middle of the hall, traditional farmyard animals and gardens, and the Victorian schoolroom is complete with blackboard, benches and school bell. To complement the buildings, five historic gardens have been carefully researched and planted, using traditional methods, to demonstrate the changes and continuities in ordinary gardens from 1430-1900.

are also two interesting monuments to two successive Earls of Arundel who died within two years of each other in the mid 16th century.

Singleton is also the home of the famous **Weald and Downland Open Air Museum**, which has over 40 reconstructed historic rural buildings from all over southeast England. Founded in 1971 by J.R. Armstrong, the museum's buildings were all at one time under threat of demolition, before being transported here.

The buildings vividly demonstrate the homes and workplaces of the past and include Titchfield's former Tudor market hall, farmhouses and agricultural buildings from the 15th and 16th centuries,

This enchanting and unusual collection is situated in a delightful 50 acre park on the southern edge of the village. The museum also arranges demonstrations of rural skills and children's activities' days where traditional games, trades and crafts of the past, such as basket making and bricklaying, can be enjoyed.

WOODSTOCK HOUSE HOTEL

Charlton, Near Chichester, West Sussex, PO18 0HU
Tel: 01243 811666

Aiden and Lesley Nugent, the friendly owners of this licensed bed and breakfast hotel, do everything to ensure guests have an enjoyable stay. Set in the rolling countryside of the South Downs, **Woodstock House Hotel** has lovely gardens, a residents' lounge and all rooms are en suite with television and refreshment trays. It is within easy reach of Goodwood racecourse and motor racing circuit, West Dean Gardens, the Weald and Downland Museum and a host of golf courses, restaurants and country inns.

WEST DEAN

6 miles S of Midhurst on the A286

Just to the south of this pretty community of flint cottages, the land rises towards the ancient hilltop site known as **The Trundle**. One of the four main Neolithic settlements in Sussex, the large site was fortified during the Iron Age, when massive circular earth ramparts and a dry ditch were constructed. Named after the Old English for wheel, the site now enjoys fine views over Chichester, Singleton and Goodwood Racecourse.

Amidst the rolling South Downs, **West Dean Gardens** (see panel on page 245) reproduces a classic 19th century designed landscape with its highly acclaimed restoration of the walled kitchen garden, the 16 original glasshouses and frames dating from the 1890s, the 35 acres of ornamental grounds, the 40 acres St Roche's arboretum and the extensive landscaped park. All the areas of this inspiring and diverse garden are linked by a scenic parkland walk. A particular feature of the grounds is the lavishly planted 300 foot Edwardian pergola, designed by Harold Peto, which acts as a host for a variety of climbers including roses, clematis and honeysuckle. The beautifully restored Victorian glasshouses nurture vines, figs and soft fruits as well as an outstanding collection of chilli peppers, aubergines, tomatoes and extensive floral displays.

CHILGROVE

6 miles SW of Midhurst on the B2141

To the north of this village, which is situated in a wooded valley, lies **Treyford Hill** where a line of five bell shaped barrows, known as the **Devil's Jump**, can be found. Dating back to the Bronze Age, these burial mounds - where the

FORGE HOTEL

Chilgrove, Near Chichester, West Sussex
Tel: 01243 535333 Fax: 01243 535363
e-mail: reservations@forgehotel.com
website: www.forgehotel.com

Since the reign of Charles I, a flint and brick house has existed on this spot in the lovely Chilgrove valley. Originally a blacksmith's cottage, it has since been extended and now carefully restored by the owner Neil Rusbridger.

A classically trained chef, he is in his element when preparing food. Using only the finest quality ingredients, usually sourced from local suppliers, he creates mouth-watering dishes delightfully complemented with wine from the small, but interesting and well-selected, list. What appears on the menu is dependent on what Neil can source on a daily basis and will vary depending on season,

weather and local availability. Dishes may include local Selsey Crab and wild mushroom torte, champagne and fresh herb risotto topped with home-smoked fillets of lamb or pork fillet and duck rillettes served with a kumquat relish. Wicked desserts include the brandy snap mille-feuille layered with honeyed compote of local rhubarb. Irrespective of what he's planning to cook Neil, given a little advance notice, will make every effort to take account of his guests dietary requirements or individual tastes.

Dining at the Forge is a wonderful social occasion. Sitting round the oval oak table in the company of the other guests is a rewarding experience that has resulted in many lasting friendships.

THE WHITE HORSE AT CHILGROVE

Chilgrove, Chichester, West Sussex, PQ18 9HX
Tel: 01243 535219 Fax: 01243 535301
e-mail: info@whitehorsechilgrove.co.uk
website: www.whitehorsechilgrove.co.uk

The White Horse at Chilgrove is a perfect blend of traditional pub, high class restaurant and luxury hotel. It has been established as a coaching inn since 1765 and is situated in a beautiful downland setting just six miles north-west of Chichester. It is ideally placed for exploring West Sussex and visiting the many local attractions such as the Chichester Festival Theatre, motor racing at Goodwood, the renowned National Trust property of Uppark, the magnificent 18th century Stansted House and gardens, the Victorian West Dean Gardens and the Weald and Downland Museum, as well as the many Neolithic remains nearby. For those interested in country walking or sports such as golf, fishing, shooting or sailing, this is the perfect centre with all these facilities within easy reach. There is ample parking off the road and easy access to Chichester. The open fires and low exposed beams provide a restful rural sanctuary at the end of a day's sport or sight-seeing, while on warm summer evenings visitors can dally over meals and drinks in the gathering dusk at tables in front of this traditional wisteria covered inn.

Charles Burton bought the White Horse two years ago, having worked for the previous owner. With his team of French chefs, he has built up an enviable reputation for superb food here. In the recently extended bar customers can enjoy bar meals with a difference. The bar menu features Italian style open sandwiches, fresh scallops, renowned Selsey crab, crispy roast duck or calves liver. In the refurbished restaurant, the discerning gourmet can dine out in style with an à la carte menu, which is fast becoming a local legend. There is crab salad, or warm goats cheese salad, fresh rock oysters, freshly caught whole sea bass, grilled smoked steak and a selection of game, which includes partridge, grouse, and braised local hare and rabbit. This choice can be accompanied by a selection from the amazing 500 wines on the award winning wine list. This comprehensive collection covers all major wine producing areas of the world and many are available in half bottles, magnums or even larger sizes. For diners who take the choice of wine seriously, they will e-mail the wine list in advance to give plenty of time for thought. From high quality food to fine wines to knowledgeable and experienced staff, it is easy to see how this fine establishment merits its rosette for food.

The accommodation is equally fine and richly deserves the 4 diamonds that it has been awarded by the English Tourist Board. There are eight twin bedded or double bedrooms all en-suite and with telephone, TV, trouser press, hair dryer and all the facilities that visitors expect to find in a top quality hotel. A very special feature at the White Horse is the option of having a sumptuous breakfast hamper delivered to the room in the morning.

cremated remains of tribal leaders were interred in pottery urns - received their descriptive name as a result of the local superstitious habit of attributing unusual, natural features of the landscape to the work of the Devil.

WEST MARDEN

9 miles SW of Midhurst off the B2146

This picturesque place, much loved by artists, is the largest of the four Marden hamlets, which are all linked by quiet country lanes. It is, however, the only one of the four settlements without a church. **North Marden**, itself only a tiny place, is home to the Norman Church of St Mary which is one of the smallest in the county whilst, **Up Marden**'s minute 13th century church, which stands on the ancient Pilgrims' Way between Winchester and Chichester, is only a little bigger. Of the four Mardens, **East Marden**, is the most village-like and, on the village green, there is a thatched well house with a notice reading, 'Rest and be Thankful but do not Wreck me'. As the well is still very much in existence, the advice has been heeded down the centuries.

COMPTON

8 miles SW of Midhurst on the B2146

A tranquil settlement of brick and flint buildings, Compton lies under the steep slope of **Telegraph Hill**. Close to the hill is a grassy mound, which is, in fact, a Neolithic long barrow, known locally as **Bevis's Thumb**. This mysterious burial site was named after a local giant, Bevis

WEST DEAN GARDENS

West Dean, Chichester, West Sussex PO18 0QZ
Tel: 01243 818210 Fax: 01243 811342
e-mail: gardens@westdean.org.uk website: www.westdean.org.uk

With its sweeping lawns, punctuated by venerable trees, **West Dean** is a garden on an expansive scale. Peto's 300' foot pergola dominates the North Lawn, while in the Spring Garden, a laburnum tunnel

has been reinstated and two charming summer-houses restored.

Over 20,000 bulbs have been planted in the grounds giving a spectacular display in Spring through to early summer. The Victorian Walled Kitchen Garden, one of the finest in Britain, is a must for all visitors. A 2¼ miles parkland walk offers unspoilt views of the Gardens and the surrounding countryside.

The Visitor Centre (free entry) houses a licensed restaurant and an imaginative garden shop.

(the same Bevis who threw his sword from the battlements of Arundel Castle), who had a weekly diet of an ox washed down with two hogsheads of beer.

SOUTH HARTING

6 miles W of Midhurst on the B2146

One of the most attractive villages of the South Downs, South Harting has ancient thatched cottages and elegant red brick Georgian houses. The spire of the local church is, famously, covered in copper shingles, the bright verdigris hue of which can be seen from several miles away, acting as a signpost to this handsome place. Outside the church stand the ancient village stocks, along with a whipping post, and inside, there are several monuments including one commemorating the life of Sir Harry Fetherstonhaugh of Uppark.

South Harting can boast of being the home of the novelist Anthony Trollope for the last two years of his life. Though here only a short time before his death in 1882, Trollope wrote four novels whilst in South Harting and his pen and paper knife can be seen in the church.

The village stands at the foot of **Harting Down**, beneath the steep scarp slope of the South Downs ridge, which is traversed by the South Downs Way. This spectacular long distance footpath and bridleway stretches for nearly 100 miles, from Winchester to Beachy Head and, here, the path skirts around **Beacon Hill**. At 793 feet above sea level, the hill is one of the highest points on the Downs.

Just south of the village lies the magnificent house, **Uppark**, a National Trust property that is superbly situated on the crest of a hill. However, the climb up to the house was so steep that, when the house was offered to the Duke of Wellington after his victories in the Napoleonic Wars, he declined as he considered the drive to the mansion would require replacing his exhausted horses too many times. The house was built in the late 1680s for Lord Grey of Werke, one of the chief instigators of the Duke of Monmouth's rebellion of 1685. Lord Grey was let off with a fine and he retired from his none too illustrious military career and concentrated on building his house to the latest Dutch designs. As well as being a splendid house architecturally, the building of the house on this site was only made possible with the help of a water pump invented by Lord Grey's grandfather which brought water up to the hill top from a low lying spring.

It was a mid 18th century owner, Sir Matthew Fetherstonhaugh, who created the lavish interiors by decorating and furnishing the rooms with rare carpets, elegant furniture and intriguing objets d'art. At his death in 1774, Sir Matthew left his estate to his 20 year-old son, Sir Harry, who, with his great friend the Prince Regent, brought an altogether different atmosphere to the house. He installed his London mistress, Emma Hart (who later married Sir William Hamilton and became Lord Nelson's mistress), and carried on a life of gambling, racing and partying. However, in 1810, Sir Harry gave up his social life and, at the age of 70, he married his dairymaid, Mary Ann to the amazement and outrage of West Sussex society. He died, at the age of 92, in 1846 and both Mary Ann and then her sister, Frances, kept the house just as it had been during Sir Harry's

Uppark House

life for a further 50 years.

This latter era of life at Uppark would have been remembered by the young H.G. Wells who spent a great deal of time here as his mother worked at the house. As well as exploring the grounds and gardens laid out by the early 19th century designer Humphry Repton, Wells had a self-taught education from Uppark's vast stock of books.

After the upper floors of the house were destroyed by fire in 1989, the National Trust undertook an extensive restoration programme and reopened the house to the public in 1995. Luckily, most of the house's 18th century treasures were rescued from the fire and the fine pictures, furniture and ceramics are now on view again in their original splendid settings.

Also close to South Harting lies the site of the now demolished **Durford Abbey** - an isolated monastery founded in the 12th century by a community of Premonstratensian monks, a strict vegetarian order founded in 1120 by St Norbert at Premontre, France. Unlike other orders of their time, which grew wealthy on the income from their monastic estates, life at Durford seems to have been very much a struggle for survival. In fact, so harsh was the monks' existence here that, on the monasteries dissolution in the 16th century, is was described by a

commissioner as "The poorest abbey I have seen, far in debt and in decay." Although little of the abbey remains today, the monks of Durford succeeded in leaving an important legacy in the form of two 15th century bridges over the River Rother and its tributaries. (During the medieval period it was a duty of religious houses to provide and maintain such bridges.) Both Maidenmarsh Bridge, near the abbey site, and Habin Bridge, to the south of Rogate, are worth a visit and the latter, which consists of four semicircular arches, still carries the road to South Harting.

TROTTON
3 miles W of Midhurst on the A272

This pleasant village lies in the broad valley of the River Rother, once a densely wooded area known for its timber and charcoal. The impressive medieval bridge in the village dates back to the 14th century and is still carrying modern day traffic. The money for the bridge was given by Lord Camoys, who accompanied Henry V to Agincourt. Inside the parish church is a memorial to Lord Camoys, who died in 1419, and his second wife, Elizabeth Mortimer, who was the widow of Sir Henry 'Harry Hotspur' Percy. Here, too, can be found the oldest known memorial to a woman, a floor brass of Margaret de Camoys, who died here in around 1310.

BALLARDS BREWERY LTD

Unit C, The Old Sawmill, Nyewood, Near Petersfield,
West Sussex, GU31 5HA
Tel: 01730 821301 Fax: 01730 821742
e-mail: info@ballardsbrewery.org.uk
website: www.ballardsbrewery.org.uk

The first pint of **Ballards** was brewed in July 1980 in the
old cow house of the farm owned by Carola Brown's family.
It all started when Carola's husband got bored being a
lawyer and decided to join, what was then, the pioneers of
the micro-brewing industry. Now he has returned to his
law practice and Carola runs the brewery along with her
trusty trio of staff. Head brewer, Francis Weston who has
been with Ballards since 1981 and holds the certificate of
brewing competence, now produces some 1,500 gallons of
the stuff each week using traditional brewing methods and
top quality ingredients. The malted barley for the beers is
milled on the premises and made into a mash in a huge
wooden tub with whole flower English hops, water and
added yeast. Ballards don't use sugar, colourings or additives
in their brewing process. The liquor is strained off into large
stainless steel fermentation vessels to finish. When the
completed beer is put into the cask isinglass finings are then added to settle the yeast sediment.

Ballards produces real ales including 11 draught beers and four bottled. Five of the draught brews
are produced all the year round to cater for their core customer base of around 60 pubs. The rest of the
beers are seasonal. The bottled conditioned beers have been
added to the range to cater for the expanding demand from
people, who are becoming more quality aware and moving
away from pubs towards home drinking. Each beer is brewed
using an exclusive recipe and over the 20 odd years of its
existence Ballards has won several regional and national
awards including a Gold Medal for Nyewood Gold at the
Champion Beer of Britain Competition in 1999. This beer
had been specially produced for the Hop Growers
Association English Ale Awards using a single hop variety,
Phoenix, and lifted the gold medal there as well.

Visitors are welcome at the brewery during working
hours to purchase any of the cask or bottled beers available
as well as a large range of merchandise which includes T
shirts, sweatshirts, tankards, pump clips, key rings, lapel pins
and label designs. Brewery tours can be arranged for groups
of 12 to 30 people. They take place on weekday evenings
and include a complete introduction to the brewing process
as it is carried out in a small craft brewery. Naturally the
tour involves consuming generous quantities of what's
currently available. On the first Sunday of December, each
year, Ballards holds a Beer Walk to launch their latest 'Beer
of the Year'. The brewery is open from 10am until midday
with all products and merchandise on sale. The walk itself
can be anything from two to seven miles, through picturesque Sussex lanes and footpaths and visiting
up to four local pubs, serving Ballards for necessary refuelling. This is a great event but wellies are an
essential item of equipment.

PULBOROUGH

This ancient settlement has grown up close to the confluence of the Rivers Arun and Rother and it lies on the old Roman thoroughfare, Stane Street. Although it was a staging post along the old route between London and Chichester and was strategically located near the rivers, it was never developed like its rivals over the centuries. It remains today a pleasant and sizeable village, well known for its freshwater fishing. The centre of Pulborough, on the old Roman route, is now a conservation area with several fine Georgian cottages clustered around the parish church, which occupies a commanding hilltop position.

Just southeast of the village lies the **RSPB Pulborough Brooks Nature Reserve** where there is a nature trail through tree-lined lanes, leading to views overlooking the restored wet meadows of the Arun Valley.

AROUND PULBOROUGH

WISBOROUGH GREEN
5½ miles N of Pulborough on the A272

This pretty Sussex village has a large rectangular green, surrounded by horse chestnut trees, around which stand half-timbered and tile-hung cottages and houses. Nearby, the village **Church of St Peter ad Vincula** is particularly interesting as the original Norman building, to which the 13th century chancel was added, has walls almost five feet thick and a doorway 13 feet high! The suggestion is that this was an Anglo Saxon keep that was later enlarged into a church as the doorway is tall enough to admit a man on horseback. During the Middle Ages, this curious church was a

DYKE FARM

West Chiltington Road, Pulborough, West Sussex, RH20 2EE
Tel: 01798 872447

Sandra and Ken Martin started to farm 15 acres here in 1987. Two years later they opened **Dyke Farm** shop, initially to sell their own produce but soon added a comprehensive range of other foodstuffs. In the farm area are chickens, guinea pigs and rabbits and, yes, they do sell the guinea pigs as pets. The large, light and airy wooden shop was converted from a former farm building. Inside, the walls are lined with chilled display cabinets and shelves full of good quality fresh produce much of it organic. The fresh fruit and vegetables are mostly local as are the locally sourced cheeses made by small independent producers. The dairy section includes freshly churned butter, milk and cream. This friendly couple also sell free-range chickens from their own farm as well as ducks' and hens' eggs. Quails' eggs may be a speciality item but they are readily available in this shop. There's also a tasty selection of home-made pies, quiches, cakes and freshly baked bread plus a range of locally made jams, marmalades and chutneys.

For the gardener there is a superb choice of pot and bedding plants and a few garden accessories including bags of compost and bird tables. Fresh cut flowers can also be purchased.

The specialist selection of fresh fish on sale is sent daily from Grimsby. The choice is superb and includes cod, plaice, haddock, bream, Dover sole, lemon sole and salmon. Delicious fresh kippers are usually available as well. Orders can be taken for any fresh fish or shellfish and given notice there is very little that Ken and Sandra can't get.

MURRELLS NURSERY AND GARDEN CENTRE

Broomers Hill Lane, Pulborough, Sussex, RH20 2DU
Tel: 01798 875508 Fax: 01798 872695

This nursery and garden centre was established over 30 years ago by the Murrell family on a six acre site that was previously a farm. Although the original family is no longer involved, the business still retains the friendly and attentive ethos on which its reputation was built. The quality of the produce is first class with much of it being grown on site. The large greenhouses and surrounding grounds are bursting with a colourful display of plants, trees and shrubs. **Murrell's** stocks an extensive range of alpines, bamboos, conifers and ferns. There are ivies, bedding plants, fuchsias and geraniums. Hanging baskets are a speciality and can be purchased ready made or made to order.

Heathers and ornamental grasses of every hue abound, and the varieties of roses range from the

favourites of yesteryear to varieties newly propagated. For those gardeners interested in food the centre has an excellent choice of fruit trees and bushes to choose from and a full complement of vegetables ready to transplant into their own plots. All members of staff are unobtrusive and put no pressure on visitors to buy but are happy to assist customers with their selection and offer advice on the particular soil and climatic conditions needed for successful growing of the various plants. Open seven days a week, Murrell's is situated on the outskirts of Pulborough just off the A29 or the A283.

SUSSEX FARM FOODS

The Old Forge, Bury Gate, Pulborough, West Sussex, RH20 1NL
Tel: 01798 831985 Fax: 01798 831001

This conversion from a former village forge is a far cry from number 10 Downing Street yet Gilly Stuart-Smith one of the proprietors is the interior designer who was responsible for the design of England's most famous address when Mrs Thatcher was in residence.

Both she and her partner, Barbara Kirk, are farmers, and they opened the shop in 1996 so they could diversify from farming. The grade II listed building sits opposite what used to be a toll house and had been an antique shop for 30 years before Barbara and Gilly converted it. The interior of **Sussex Farm Foods** has the original black-beamed apex ceiling and a traditional wooden floor. Most of the display areas are in a style sympathetic with the age and atmosphere of the room in addition to the white and glass chill cabinets required by modern food hygiene laws. There is an excellent display of

unusual food products. Lots of items that are very hard to find elsewhere like whole, organic, Cornish brie, baby stiltons and free range goose. Much of the produce stocked is local and home cooked to exacting standards. There's freshly baked crusty bread, local honey, fresh cakes, biscuits and decidedly wicked champagne truffles. In season they stock damsons and quinces, sourced from the gardens of their friends, fresh vegetables including asparagus. This is a very high-class delicatessen, which could be described as being like Harrod's Food Hall, in miniature of course. It is situated on the A29 Bury to Pulborough Road near its junction with the B2138 to Fittleworth.

THE ACORN

Todhurst Site, Brinsbury College, North Heath, Pulborough,
West Sussex, RH20 1DL   Tel: 01798 873533   Fax: 01798 873533
e-mail: lindathompson@aldingbournetrust.co.uk
website: www.aldingbournetrust.co.uk

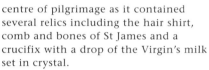

The coffee shop at the **Acorn**, with its delicious home baked cakes
and wonderfully friendly service is a good enough reason to visit but
there is much more. In the Acorn shop are some of the finest organic fruit and vegetables available in
the county, grown on site and Soil Association registered. There is also a large selection of unusual
herbaceous perennials. In this commercial setting students with learning difficulties receive work skills
training in preparation for employment. The Acorn is a registered charity.

centre of pilgrimage as it contained several relics including the hair shirt, comb and bones of St James and a crucifix with a drop of the Virgin's milk set in crystal.

The village is set in the undulating country of the Weald and, to the west of Wisborough Green, there are two areas of preserved woodland which give an indication to today's visitors of how most of the land north of the Downs would have looked many thousands of years ago. Looking at the countryside now it is hard to imagine that, in the 16th and 17th centuries, this area was an important industrial centre. Thanks to the seemingly limitless supply of trees for fuel, iron foundries and forges prospered here right up until the time of the Industrial Revolution. A plentiful supply of high quality sand from the coast supported a number of early glassworks. During the 16th century, Huguenot settlers from France and the Low Countries introduced new and improved methods of glass manufacture and the industry flourished until the early 17th century when lobbying by shipbuilders and iron smelters led to legislation banning the glassmakers from using timber to fire their furnaces.

Fishers Farm Park brings together the delights of the rural farmyard with the excitement of an adventure playground. As well as the combine harvester and pony rides, there is a whole assortment of animals, ranging from giant shire horses to goats, lambs and rabbits. For those who seek more mechanical diversions there is a merry-go-round from the 1950s and up-to-the-minute go-karts.

KIRDFORD

5½ miles N of Pulborough off the A272

This village, with its square green surrounded by stone cottages and tree-

WILLIAM HOCKLEY

The Malthouse, Fittleworth Road, Wisborough Green,
West Sussex, RH14 0ES
Tel: 01403 201917

Set in glorious countryside amidst its own extensive grounds,
the Malthouse is testimony to Derek and Valerie Thrower's
multi-faceted talents. Converted from a barn it now houses a
unique collection of antiques for the country house and
garden and serves as a base for Valerie's interior design and upholstery business. The stock includes a
large range of English, French and American wallpapers and fabrics and a superb collection of up-
market furniture ranging from Georgian chests of drawers to Victorian wardrobes

lined main street, has more the feel of a small town. Like its neighbour, Wisborough Green, Kirdford was a centre for glassmaking between 1300 and 1600 and the village sign incorporates diamonds of locally made glass. Iron smelting also prospered here for 100 years from the mid 16th century and this accounts for the rather lavish extensions to the village's original Norman church.

LOXWOOD

8 miles N of Pulborough on the B2133

This pleasant village, which lies off the beaten track and close to the county border with Surrey, is on the **Wey and Arun Junction Canal**, which opened in 1816 and linked London with the south coast. The coming of the railways saw an end to the commercial usefulness of this inland waterway and, in 1871, it was closed. However, certain stretches have been restored and it is now possible to

cruise along one of the country's most attractive canals or stroll along the peaceful towpath.

The village is also associated with the Christian Dependants, a religious sect founded by preacher, John Sirgood, in the 1850s. The group were nicknamed the 'Cokelers' because of their preference for cocoa over alcohol and their chapel and burial ground can still be seen in Spy Lane.

WEST CHILTINGTON

3 miles E of Pulborough off the A283

Built around a crossroads in the twisting lanes of the Wealdan countryside, this neat and compact village centres on the village green which is dominated by the delightful and relatively unrestored **Church of St Mary**. Famous for its medieval wall paintings discovered in 1882, this charming Norman church has an oak shingled spire and a roof of

THE OLD SCHOOL HOUSE

Church Street, West Chiltington, West Sussex, RH20 2JW
Tel:01798 812574

This was West Chiltington's Victorian village school, stone-built in 1876. **The Old School House** now offers charming self-catering accommodation in a totally self-contained wing. The original enormous high school windows, exposed beams and thick stone walls have been skilfully blended with the new high-quality fittings and furnishings to create luxurious accommodation on two levels. A king size bed, double - width power shower and fully- fitted kitchen all contribute to the comfort of the property. Facilities include a fridge-freezer, washer-dryer, microwave oven, dishwasher, electric oven and hob, colour television and gas central heating. There is ample off-street parking and guests can arrange to use the garden.

Ten minutes' drive from Pulborough Station, with a village shop and post office nearby, the village has a picturesque country church and three pubs, all serving food. Chichester, with its cathedral, Festival Theatre and harbour; Arundel, with its castle, and the coastal towns of Worthing and Brighton are all within easy reach, making this a superb base for a touring holiday. This part of Sussex is also ideal for country walking or bird- watching. Various other activities including ballooning, flying, boat trips, sailing and antique - collecting can all be indulged in from West Chiltington. The property is non-smoking throughout, no pets are allowed and it is not suitable for babies and children. From the cross-roads at the Queen's Head, the Old School House is along Church Street, on the right just before the church.

Horsham stone. Beside the churchyard gate are the old village stocks and whipping post.

COOTHAM

3 miles SE of Pulborough on the A283

The village is synonymous with **Parham** (see panel below), the most western and the grandest of the Elizabethan mansions that were built below the northern slopes of the Downs. Just west of the village and surrounded by a great deer park, the estate, in medieval times, belonged to the Abbey of Westminster and, at the Dissolution of the Monasteries, passed into the hands of the Palmer family. As was customary, the foundation stone of the great mansion was laid by a child, Thomas Palmer, in 1577. The grandson and heir to the estate, Thomas did not fare as well as the house and he died of smallpox in 1605 after having served with both Drake and Hawkins. In the meantime, the splendid though rather dour grey stone building was constructed and, although it appears E shaped from the front, this Elizabethan mansion is actually in the form of an H as the wings project both north and south.

In 1601, Thomas Bysshop, a London lawyer, bought the estate and, for the next 300 years, it remained with that family. In 1922, the house and park was purchased by a son of Viscount Cowdray, Clive Pearson and, in 1948 Mr and Mrs Pearson opened the property to the public. The splendid Elizabethan interiors have been restored to their former glory, including the magnificent 160 foot Long Gallery, Great Hall and Great Parlour, and an exceptional collection of period furniture, oriental carpets, rare needlework and fine paintings are on show.

The gardens too have been restored and the seven acres of wooded parkland contain a walled garden with herb beds and a Wendy House, greenhouses where plants and flowers are grown for the house, a lake and a statue garden. The house, now owned by a charitable trust, is home to Lady Emma Barnard, the Pearsons' great grand-daughter, and her family. The house and gardens are open to the public on certain days of the week between April and October.

PARHAM HOUSE & GARDENS

near Pulborough, West Sussex RH20 4HS
Tel: 01903 744888 Fax: 01903 746557
website: www.parhaminsussex.co.uk
e-mail: enquiries@parhaminsussex.co.uk

Idyllically situated in the heart of a medieval deer park, on the slopes of the South Downs, is **Parham** an Elizabethan manor house with a four acre walled garden and seven acres of 18th century Pleasure Grounds.

There is an important collection of paintings, furniture and needlework contained within the light, panelled rooms, including a Great Hall and Long Gallery. Each room is graced with beautiful fresh flower arrangements, the flowers home-grown and cut fresh from the walled garden.

Open on Wednesday, Thursday, Sunday and bank holiday afternoons from April to September, and Sunday afternoons in October. Licensed lunches and cream teas, picnic area, shop and plant sales area.

STORRINGTON

3½ miles SE of Pulborough on the A283

This old market town has a jumble of architectural styles from its small heavily restored Saxon church through to 20th century concrete buildings. However, from Storrington there is good access to the **South Downs Way** long distance footpath via Kithurst Hill. It was this beautiful surrounding countryside that inspired Francis Thompson to write his poem *Daisy* whilst he was staying in a local monastery and the composer, Arnold Bax, also lived in the area between 1940-51.

The heavily restored **Church of St Mary** has, inside, a Saxon stone coffin on which is the marble effigy of a knight who is thought to have been a crusader. When the author Dr A.J. Cronin moved to the old rectory in the 1930s he used this legend as the basis for his famous novel *The Crusaders*.

SULLINGTON

4½ miles SE of Pulborough off the A283

This hamlet is home to a 115 foot **Long Barn** which rivals many tithe barns that were such a feature of the medieval monastic estate. An exceptional building with a braced tie beam roof, the barn, which is privately owned, can be viewed by appointment. Just outside Sullington is **Sullington Warren** - owned by the National Trust this expanse of open

heathland was once used for farming rabbits and it now offers superb views across the South Downs. The Warren has nine prehistoric round barrows, all listed as Ancient Monuments.

AMBERLEY

4 miles S of Pulborough on the B2139

An attractive village of thatched cottages situated above the River Arun, Amberley is an ancient place whose name means 'fields yellow with buttercups'. Lands in this area were granted to St Wilfrid by King Cedwalla in around AD 680 and the village church of today is thought to stand on the foundations of a Saxon building constructed by St Wilfrid, the missionary who converted the South Saxons to Christianity. Later, in the 12th century, Bishop Luffa of Chichester rebuilt the church and it still has a strong Norman appearance.

At around the same time as the church was being rebuilt, a fortified summer palace for the Bishops of Chichester was also constructed. During the late 14th century, when there was a large threat of a French sea invasion, Bishop Rede of Chichester enlarged the summer palace and added a great curtain wall. Still more a manor house than a true castle, **Amberley Castle** is said to have offered protection to Charles II during his flight to France in 1651. Today, it is a privately owned luxury hotel.

During the 18th and 19th centuries, chalk was quarried from Amberley and taken to the many lime kilns in the area. Later, large quantities of chalk were needed to supply a new industrial process, which involved the high temperature firing of chalk with small amounts of clay to produce Portland cement. Situated just to the south of Amberley and on the site of an old chalk pit and limeworks is **Amberley Museum**, which concentrates on the industry of this area. Very much a working museum, which occupies a site of 36 acres, visitors can ride the length of the museum on a workman's train and view the comprehensive collection of narrow gauge engines, from steam to electric. The history of roads and road making is also explored and, in the Electricity Hall, there is an amazing assortment of electrical items from domestic appliances to generating and supply equipment. In the workshop section, there are various tradesmen's shops including a blacksmith's, pottery, boatbuilder's and a printing works.

To the north of Amberley there is a series of water meadows known as the **Amberley Wild Brooks**. Often flooded and inaccessible by car, this 30 acre conservation area and nature reserve is a haven for bird, animal and plant life. The trains on the Arun Valley line cross the meadows on specially constructed embankments, which were considered wonders of modern engineering when the line was first opened in 1863.

HARDHAM

1 mile SW of Pulborough on the A29

This tiny hamlet, on the banks of the River Arun, is home to the Saxon **Church of St Botolph**, which is famous for its medieval wall paintings. Considered some of the finest in England, the oldest of the paintings dates from around 1100 and among the scenes on view are images of St George slaying the dragon and the Serpent tempting Adam and Eve. The murals are thought to have been worked by artists based at St Pancras Priory in Lewes, who were also responsible for the paintings at Coombes and Clayton.

At one time Hardham had a small Augustinian monastic house and the site of **Hardham Priory** can be found just south of the hamlet. Now a farmhouse, the priory's cloisters have been incorporated into a flower garden. From here a footpath leads to the disused **Hardham Tunnel**, a channel, which was built to provide a short cut for river barges wishing to avoid an eastern loop of the River Arun.

BIGNOR

5 miles SW of Pulborough off the A29

The main thoroughfares of this pretty village are arranged in an uneven square and, as well as a photogenic 15th century shop, there are some

Amberley Museum

THE WHITE HART

Stopham Road, Stopham Bridge, Pulborough,
West Sussex, RH20 1DS
Tel: 01798 873321

This quintessential English country inn sits on the River
Arun by the ancient monument of Stopham Bridge. The
White Hart's owners, Dave and Sarah Darling, offer a
friendly and informal atmosphere coupled with superb
food. Resident chef, Nick Tribute, regularly produces a
delicious selection of starters and main courses, all
prepared from fresh ingredients and served piping hot.
The food choice encompasses traditional and modern. Old favourites such as Roast Beef and Yorkshire
pudding, Pork and apple sauce are joined by tasty newcomers. The venison and redcurrent sausages
are particularly succulent and the goats cheese asparagus tart is to die for.

On a cold day there are few dishes that can equal the comforting qualities of beef in beer with
miniature herb dumplings although the crispy duck and hoi sin sauce comes very close. Other dishes
include king prawns in filo pastry parcels served with a sweet and sour sauce and chicken and sweetcorn
soup. Vegetarians are very well catered for here with choices such
as delicious mushroom stroganoff and rice or roasted vegetable
salad with feta cheese. Puddings include the delightfully wicked
favourites Jam Roly Poly and Spotted Dick or the slightly less
calorific Crème brullee or glazed lemon tart. All this can be washed
down with fine wines from the old and new worlds or classic
beers like Fullers London Pride and Sussex bitter. During the warm
weather the food and drink can be enjoyed alfresco in the
delightful pub garden with its riverside setting.

PERSIAN CARPET GALLERY

Church Street, Petworth, West Sussex, GU28 0AD
Tel: 01798 343344 Fax: 01798 342673
e-mail: pcg1973@yahoo.co.uk

Ali Mandegaran has a Ph D in engineering and Zora his wife is a
scientist, but their love and knowledge of carpets is in the blood. Ali's
father was a carpet dealer in Iran and this family connection led them

to take over the well-established **Persian Carpet Gallery** in 1998. They specialise in old and new
oriental rugs and carpets including retailing, exchange, restoration, cleaning and valuation. They
have one of the largest collections of oriental rugs in the UK, offering a choice of 10,000 beautiful and
varied Persian rugs as well as some from Afghanistan, Pakistan, India, China and Turkey. Customers
can choose from a hard wearing Hamadan ideal in the hall way, an Isfahan fire side rug, a delicate silk
Qum for the bedroom or a pictorial Afshar Soumac to hang on the wall. Persian weavers work with
beautiful soft colours and simple designs, which will enhance any style of furnishing and interior
design. They also offer an interior design service from an experienced and qualified interior designer.

An important part of the business is the purchase and
exchange of old carpets, to increase the range available to
customers. The Persian Carpet Gallery is interested in
purchasing any size or style of oriental carpet from kilim to
needlework or tapestry and will happily sell pieces for customers
on a commission basis. Their repair and restoration service will
expertly restore the small tears and areas of wear, which are
often evident on old oriental rugs, while their hand cleaning
service will maintain the appearance and lengthen the life of
these valuable pieces.

charming ancient domestic buildings to be seen. In 1811, a ploughman working on the east side of the village unearthed a **Roman Mosaic Floor**, which proved to be part of a villa built at the end of the 2nd century AD. This is one of the largest sites in Britain with some 70 Roman buildings surrounding a central courtyard. It is thought that the find was the administration centre of a large agricultural estate. The villa, being the home of a wealthy agricultural master, was extended throughout the time of the Roman occupation and the mosaic decoration of the house is some of the finest to be seen in this country.

Unlike the Roman excavations at Fishbourne, this remains relatively undiscovered by tourists and, charmingly, the exposed remains are covered, not by modern day structures, but by the thatched huts that were first built to protect them in 1814. The 80 foot long mosaic along the north corridor is the longest on display in Britain and among the characters depicted on the mosaics are Venus, Medusa and an array of gladiators. The **Bignor Roman Villa Museum** houses a collection of artefacts revealed during the excavation work and a display on the history of the Roman settlement and its underfloor heating system or hypocaust.

Fittleworth
2½ miles W of Pulborough on the A283

An acknowledged Sussex beauty spot, this village has retained much of its charm despite its position on the main Pulborough to Petworth road. Its narrow roads wind through woods passing an old mill and bridge, lovely old cottages and lanes leading to the surrounding woods and heath. This rural idyll has been popular with artists over the years, particularly around the turn of the century. In the Swan Inn, the local hostelry, there is a number of paintings

of local views, supposedly left by artists in return for their lodgings.

Well known too amongst fishers, the village has excellent fishing on the River Rother and further downstream, where it joins the River Arun.

In the middle of woodlands is **Brinkwells**, a thatched cottage, once home to the village's most famous visitor, the composer Edward Elgar. He first came here in 1917, when he wrote his famous cello concerto, and returned for the last time in 1921. Appropriately, the Jubilee clock in the village church has a very musical chime.

Stopham
1 mile NW of Pulborough off the A283

This charming place, where a handful of cottages cluster around the early Norman church, lies on the banks of the River Rother. The family home of the Barttelot family, who can trace their ancestry back to the Norman invasion, **Stopham House** is still here as is the splendid early 15th century bridge, which the family were instrumental in constructing. The impressive **Stopham Bridge** is widely regarded as the finest of its kind in Sussex and, though the tall central arch was rebuilt in 1822 to allow masted vessels to pass upstream towards the Wey and Arun Canal, the medieval structure is coping well with today's traffic without a great deal of modern intervention.

Petworth
5 miles NW of Pulborough on the A283

This historic town, though now a major road junction, still has many elements of an ancient feudal settlement - the old centre, a great house and a wall dividing the two. Mentioned in the Domesday Book, where it appeared as *Peteorde*, this was a market town and the square is thought to have originated in the 13th century and its street fair dates back to

THE HALF MOON INN

Kirdford, Near Petworth, West Sussex, RH14 0LT
Tel: 01403 820223 e-mail: halfmooninn.kirdford@virgin.net
Fax: 01403 820224 website: www.the-halfmoon-inn.co.uk

Patrick and Francesca Burfield found their dream pub in the sleepy village of Kirdford, just off the A272 between Billingshurst and Petworth. Then they set about restoring the 16th century **Half Moon Inn** while retaining the inviting atmosphere of an ancient hostelry. Now the Half Moon boasts three dining areas, two of them non-smoking, and can accommodate a total of 62 diners. All areas are spotless, with sparkling glassware, linen tablecloths and fresh flowers. The Library, with its book collection available to customers, can also be used by private parties of up to 16. The Clock Room with its magnificent wood block floor is the choice of diners who want to smoke during or after their meal. Bright and well-lit, this room can seat 25 and takes its name from the collection of clocks which line the walls. The main restaurant retains the original quarry tile floor and 16th century beams. For those guests who stay in the Half Moon there are two tastefully furnished and decorated double bedrooms with full facilities.

But it is the Half Moon's reputation for fine food that is the major attraction. Sunday lunch is a speciality with splendid three-course meals available. In the dining rooms the menu changes regularly. Starters may include delicious crispy duck salad or mouth-watering tomato basil and courgette soup. Main course choices may be venison with crushed garlic or fillets of sea bass. Vegetarians will delight in roasted vegetable tart topped with cambazola, or tortellini with a pesto cream. Desserts are the last word in decadence, particularly the dreamy banana crumble and the ginger crème brûlée.

RIBBONS AND BOWS

Lowheath Cottage, Lowheath, Petworth, West Sussex, GU28 0HG
Tel: 01798 344088 Fax: 01798 344088

Sonia Pascoe is well known for her imaginative flair in the competitive world of Victorian art and crafts. She is an innovative designer who has developed her own unique range of hand decorated Toleware and can reproduce the design from any fabric or wallpaper onto a decorative item with stunning effect. She established her business here at Lowheath some 15 years ago in a workshop adjoining her lovely home. Her slogan 'Our reputation is our recommendation' speaks for itself.

Most of her toleware is produced to commission only and she is happy to discuss requirements with clients. In addition she has a limited range of 'off the shelf' toleware with a botanical theme. Planters and waste paper baskets come in several styles, mostly with a natural cream background. Other bolder designs have a dragged or stippled paint effect in a complementary colour finished with gold edging and set on a felt covered base.

Sonia has recently added occasional tripod tables and three section hand-decorated screens to her range of products. The tables come complete with a glass top recessed into the wooden frame and the wooden screens are hand decorated and made to the customer's specification. She also runs a series of instructional classes in the art of decorative techniques from her home. The courses are arranged by appointment only and include a delicious lunch, home cooked by Sonia. Students are limited to between four and six on each course, are very informal and held in a warm and friendly atmosphere.

1189. Between the 14th and the 16th centuries this was an important cloth weaving centre and a number of fine merchants' and landowners' houses remain from those days. **Daintrey House**, which has a Georgian front façade and Elizabethan features to the rear, has magnificent iron railings around the front garden. Another house, **Leconfield Hall**, dating from 1794, was the courthouse and council meeting place before becoming a public hall. The garden of **Lancaster House**, close by, is said to have been used as a hiding place for the church silver during the time of Cromwell.

As well as taking time to wander the streets here and see the many interesting houses, cottages and other buildings, visitors should make time to take in the town's two museums. The **Petworth Cottage Museum** is housed in a 17th century cottage of the Leconfield estate, restored to the days of 1910 when it was the home of Maria Cummings. She was a seamstress at nearby Petworth House and a widow with four grown up children. The

PETWORTH HOUSE

Petworth, West Sussex GU28 OAE
Tel: 01798 342207 Fax: 01798 342963
e-mail: spesht@smtp.ntrust.org.uk
website: www.nationaltrust.org.uk

Discover the National Trust's forest collection of paintings and sculpture, as well as fore furniture and ceramics displayed in a magnificent 17'~ Century mansion with a beautiful 700 acre deer park landscaped by 'Capability' Brown. Petworth House contains works by artists such as Van Dyck, Reynolds, Titian and Turner.

Highlights of the house include the newly restored Carved Room containing Griming Gibbons' limewood carvings and landscaped by Turner and the North Gallery with over 100 paintings on display. Fascinating Servants' Quarters show the domestic side of life at Petworth. The shop, licensed restaurant and events throughout the year make Petworth a great day out.

cottage recreates her domestic setting including her sewing room.

The unusual **Doll House Museum** has an interesting collection of over 100 doll's houses, inhabited by 2,000 miniature people, put together to capture the incidents of everyday life. Among the one twelfth size houses there are replicas of the Royal Albert Hall, a prison and a museum full of tourists.

However, what brings most visitors to Petworth is the grand estate of **Petworth House** (see panel on page 258), now in the hands of the National Trust. Built between 1688 and 1696, on the site of a medieval manor house belonging to the Percy family by Charles Seymour, the 6th Duke of Somerset, Petworth House is a simple and elegant building that has more the look of a French château than an English country house. Both French and English architects have been suggested. The construction of the house was completed by the Duke's descendant, the 2nd Earl of Egremont, who had the grounds and deer park landscaped by Capability Brown in 1752.

Today, the house is home to one of the finest art collections outside London and the layout of the house, with one room leading directly into another, lends itself perfectly to life as an art gallery. Amongst the works on view are paintings by Rembrandt, Van Dyck, Holbein, Reynolds, Gainsborough and Turner, who was a frequent visitor to Petworth House. On a less grand scale, in decoration terms, the servants' block is also open to the public and provides an interesting insight into life below stairs.

Just south of the estate is the **Coultershaw Water Wheel and Beam Pump**, one of the earliest pumped water systems, installed in 1790 to pipe water two miles to Petworth House. Restored to full working order by the Sussex Industrial Archaeology Society, it is now open to the public on a limited basis.

THE WEST SUSSEX WEALD

This area, to the north of the South Downs, is called a Weald, a word that is derived from the German word Wald, meaning forest. This would suggest an area covered in woodland and, though some areas of the great forest remain, the landscape now is one of pastures enclosed by hedgerows. From the Middle Ages onwards, until the time of the Industrial Revolution, the area was very much associated with iron working and, less so, glassmaking. The trees were felled for fuel to drive the furnaces and streams were dammed to create hammer ponds. The legacy of this once prosperous industry can be seen in the wealth of elaborate buildings and, particularly, the splendid churches, that were built on the profits of the industry.

Those interested in visiting grand houses will find that this region of West Sussex has several to offer. Close to East Grinstead Standen, a remarkable Victorian country house now restored to its original glory, is a wonderful example of the Arts and Crafts Movement. The low half-timber 15th century house, the Priest House, at West Hoathly, was built as an estate office for the monks from St Pancras Priory, Lewes. Now restored it is open to the public as a museum filled with 18th and 19th century furniture. The magnificent Elizabeth mansion, Danny, at Hurstpierpoint, has a very special place in history as this is where Lloyd George and his war cabinet drew up the terms of the armistice to end World War I. In private hands today, the house is occasionally open to the public.

Near Ardingly lies Wakehurst Place, a striking Elizabethan mansion built by the Culpeper family in 1590. Now leased to the Royal Botanical Gardens at Kew, the magnificent collection of trees and shrubs in the grounds are well worth seeing. Other great gardens can also be found in this region of West Sussex, including Leonardslee at Lower Beeding which was laid out in the late 19th century by Sir Edmund Loder and Hymans, which was created with the help of the 19th century gardening revivalists William Robinson and Gertrude Jekyll.

HORSHAM

This ancient town, which takes its name from a Saxon term meaning 'horse pasture', was founded in the mid 10th century. Some 300 years later, Horsham had grown into a prosperous borough and market town, which was considered important enough to send two members to the new Parliament established in 1295. Between 1306 and 1830, Horsham, along with Lewes and Chichester, took it in turns to hold the county assizes. During the weeks the court was held in Horsham, large numbers of visitors descended on the town giving it a carnival atmosphere. Public executions were also held here, either on the common or on the Carfax, including one, in 1735, of a man who refused to speak at his trial. Sentenced to death by compression, three hundredweight of stones were placed on his chest for three days. When the man still refused to speak, the gaoler added his own weight to the man's chest and killed him outright. **The Carfax** today is a thriving pedestrianised shopping centre and nothing is left of the horrors of its past.

Horsham's architectural gem is **The Causeway**, a quiet tree-lined street of old buildings that runs from the Georgian fronted town hall to the 12th century Church of St Mary, where can be found a simple tablet commemorating the life of Percy Bysshe Shelley, a celebrated local inhabitant. Here, too, can be found the gabled 16th century **Causeway House** - a rambling building that is now home to the **Horsham Museum**, a purpose for which its layout is ideal. This excellent museum has recreations of a Sussex farmhouse kitchen, a wheelwright's and saddler's shop, and a blacksmith's forge and, among the old prints and photographs, is an extraordinary

HORSHAM CHEESE SHOP & DELICATESSEN

20 Carfax, Horsham West Sussex, RH12 1EB
Tel: 01403 254272 Fax: 01403 254272
website: www.horshamcheeseshop.co.uk

With two decades of experience this is one of the best known delicatessens in the United Kingdom and sells the finest speciality cheeses obtainable anywhere. Voted the 11th best Deli in the UK in 2000 and twice winners of the Dairy Crest Cheese Retail award, the **Horsam Cheese Shop** is a member of the Good Food Guide of Great Britain, Taste of South East England Good Food and Drink Association and the Association of Cullinaire Francaise. The shop was founded in 1981 by Lesley Ward who used her knowledge of good food and drink to establish a reputation for excellent quality. She retired in 2001 and the shop was taken over by Walter Ostereicher, an Austrian chef who has worked in the UK and abroad.

Continuing the shops excellent relationship with the many small farmers and independent producers enables Walter to maintain the superb range of exciting foods on offer. Wines and chutneys are joined on the shelves by a wonderful selection of old-fashioned jars of sweets. They even stock McSween of Edinburgh's legendary haggis. Many items are produced exclusively for the Horsham

shop from special recipes and sold under their own Carfax brand, but is is undoubtedly the cheeses that are star of the show. Whole cheeses, cut cheeses and packaged cheeses are in the chill cabinet, in the counter and on shelves in front of the counter with Walter and his attentive staff peeking out over the top. There are over 183 different varieties from throughout Europe and Scandinavia including English, regional and local, and Scottish. Walter also supplies goods by mail order including a complete selection for wine and cheese parties.

ARCHITECTURAL PLANTS

Horsham: Cooks Farm, Nuthurst, Horsham, West Sussex RH13 6LH
            Tel: 01403 891772 Fax: 01403 891056 e-mail: horsham@architecturalplants.com

Chichester: Lidsey Road Nursery, Woodgate, Chichester, Sussex, PO20 6SU
            Tel: 01243 545008 Fax: 01243 545009
            e-mail: chichester@architecturalplants.com website:www.architecturalplants.com

Architectural Plants, set in four acres of wonderful Sussex countryside, is a Mecca for garden designers, stocking some of the most amazing botanical specimens available to buy in Britain. Angus White was a furniture maker with a passion for gardening but he could not buy any of the plants he wanted for his garden anywhere. He figured that if he wanted to buy these plants, other gardeners would too. So in 1990 he established Architectural Plants and in the intervening years continued to learn about the plants, who buys them and how they can be used. They supply plants to suit all climates and purposes. The Chichester Nursery on the south coast grows the plants propagated at Horsham on to specimen size.

Anybody wanting a year round garden, a jungle effect or to create a series of hidden corners should come here. Visitors are sure to find the plants they are looking for, as well as helpful advice from the knowledgeable and friendly staff. And there's no need to worry about fitting that massive palm in the boot of the car because nationwide delivery is available. The pagoda style building that serves as headquarters for the business looks more like some last outpost of the Empire than a typical Sussex building. The lavatory, which looks out over the valley garden has been described as the ' most beautiful in Europe'. And there's a playhouse to keep the children amused.

POTS AND PITHOI

The Barns, East Street (B2110), Turners Hill,
West Sussex, RH10 4QQ
Tel: 01342 714793 e-mail: info@pots-and-pithoi.co.uk
Fax: 01342 717090 website: www.potsandpithoi.com

Pots and Pithoi introduced Cretan terracotta to the United Kingdom in the late 1980s and since then has continued to search every region of Crete for further shapes. These beautiful examples of the potter's art are so versatile that there is always somewhere in the garden that would benefit from the addition of one or two of them. Small pots with herbs look great at the back door while beehive pots make captivating water features. Buying only from the best potters, they have built up the largest selection of these magnificent hand-made pots anywhere in the world. To ensure the pots will withstand the worst of British winters Pots and Pithoi insist on the highest quality in manufacture accepting only top grade clay, fired to 1150°C. The pots at their West Sussex HQ come in 240 different sizes from a few inches high to over four feet. The stock is massive, with over 14,000 pieces and 96 different styles, bought from just four potteries.

As well as the new pots, they have built up quite a collection of old and antique pots from Turkey, Greece, Portugal and Spain. These relics of a by-gone age were the storage jars of their time and were gradually replaced by tin and plastic containers. They are still undoubtedly things of beauty, the patina of years giving them an added attraction in the corner of a garden or inside the house or conservatory. Everything is on display and inside the stone barn they sell other things including hand-blown glass, Mediterranean blue glazed earthenware and Italian frescoes.

drawing of a hard labour machine that was installed in Horsham Goal. It consisted of a long row of hand operated cranks, linked to a vast wind vane, which beat the air for no apparent purpose other than to exhaust the convicts. Concentrating on local history in particular, the collection is varied and includes toys, costumes, 19th century literature and aspects of town life.

Just two miles southwest of Horsham lies the famous **Christ's Hospital School**, a Bluecoat school that was founded in London in 1552 by Edward VI. The school moved to Horsham in 1902 and the present buildings incorporate some of the original London edifices. Bluecoat refers to the traditional long dark blue cloak that is still worn by the pupils.

AROUND HORSHAM

RUSPER

3 miles N of Horsham off the A264

This secluded village of tile-hung and timbered cottages grew up around a 13th century priory. Rusper Priory is long gone and the only reminders of it are the medieval tower of the church and the graves in the churchyard of a prioress and four sisters. The church was rebuilt in the mid 19th century by the Broadwater family, whose wealth came from their piano manufacturing business. Lucy Broadwater, who died in 1929 and to whom there is a memorial tablet in the church, was a leading figure in the revival of English folk music.

GATWICK AIRPORT

7½ miles NE of Horsham off the A23

The airport opened to commercial air traffic in 1936 when the first passengers took off for Paris. The return fare was £4 5 shillings (£4.25) and this included the return first class rail fare from Victoria Station, London to the airport. A month later the airport was officially opened by the Secretary of State for Air. He also opened the world's first circular air terminal here which was immediately christened the Beehive. During World War II, Gatwick airport, like all other British airports, was put under military control and was one of the bases for the D-Day operations.

After the war, the terminal buildings were extended and, in 1958, the new airport was reopened. Amongst Gatwick Airport's notable firsts was the pier leading from the terminal to the aircraft stands giving passengers direct access to the planes, and Gatwick was the first airport in the world to combine air, rail and road travel under one roof. Further extensions have increased the airport's capacity to a point where it handles over 30 million passengers a year flying to destinations right around the world.

Gatwick Airport Skyview gives visitors the chance to see behind the scenes of this busy airport through its multimedia theatre and there is also a real aircraft and cockpit to explore.

CRAWLEY

6½ miles NE of Horsham on the A23

A modern town, one of the original new towns created after the New Towns Act of 1946, Crawley is really an amalgamation of the villages of Three Bridges and Ifield with the small market town of Crawley. Though much has been lost under the new developments, Crawley probably dates back to Saxon times though it remained a quiet and unassuming place until the late 18th century. A convenient distance from both London and Brighton, it was used by the Prince Regent and his friends as a stopping over point as they commuted between the south coast resort of Brighton and the

(Continued page 266)

WALK 7

St Leonard's Forest

Start	Forestry Commission's Roosthole car park, on minor road about 2 miles (3.2km) east of Horsham and 1 mile (1.6km) north of Mannings Heath
Distance	4 miles (6.4km)
Approximate time	2 hours
Parking	Roosthole car park
Refreshments	None
Ordnance Survey maps	Landranger 187 (Dorking, Reigate & Crawley), Explorer 134 (Crawley & Horsham)

St Leonard's Forest lies between Horsham and Crawley and in the Middle Ages was one of a series of adjacent, thickly wooded areas that occupied the 'Forest Ridge' of the Sussex Weald. Nowadays it is a pleasant mixture of conifer and broad-leaved woodland, farmland and heathland, which are all included in this easy walk, as is one of the ubiquitous hammer ponds, a reflection of the past importance of the iron industry in this area.

In the early 19th century William Cobbett described St Leonard's Forest as a 'miserable tract of heath and fern and bushes and sand'. It was the demand for charcoal from the local ironmasters that led to the felling of much of the forest, especially during the 16th and 17th centuries at the height of the Wealden iron industry, but some traditional woodland survives, considerably augmented by the more recent conifer plantations of the Forestry Commission. The forest is thought to get its name from a former chapel within it, dedicated to St Leonard.

From the car park turn left along the road for ¼ mile (400m) and turn down the first lane on the right Ⓐ, signposted to Mannings Heath. The lane heads gently downhill. At a left-hand bend turn

right over a stile Ⓑ, at a public footpath sign, to follow a path across a field, soon curving left to keep alongside a wire fence on the right to another stile. Climb it, entering the woodlands of Alder Copse, and keep along the inside left-hand edge of the wood to Roosthole Pond. This is one of the numerous hammer ponds in the forest; the overflow from them provided the power for the hammers used in the iron industry.

Cross the end of the pond, continue gently uphill, now along the inside right-hand edge of Coolhurst Wood, and climb a stile to rejoin the road Ⓒ. Cross over and walk along the broad, straight, tree-lined track opposite. After ½ mile (800m) you reach a metal gate; just in front of it turn right Ⓓ, at a footpath sign, onto a narrow path that squeezes between trees and bushes on the left and a hedge and wire fence bordering a field on the right. This path may be overgrown and awkward in places. When you have passed the end of the field bear left along an obvious and easier path across an area of rough grass and scrub, cross a track, then climb a stile at a public footpath sign and continue across an open landscape of grassland fringed by trees.

Where the path peters out bear slightly right, making for a wire fence at the field edge and keep alongside it to descend into woodland. Keep ahead at a public footpath sign and path junction – in front is a Forestry Commission sign for Lily Beds. Pass to the right of a shallow pond and continue gently uphill along a grassy track through mixed woodland. Keep a sharp look-out for a public footpath sign by a slight right-hand bend which directs you to bear left along a narrow path, still heading gently uphill. At a public footpath sign pass beside a wooden barrier to cross a track and

continue across an area of heathland, past another public footpath sign and continuing to the next one at a crossing of tracks and paths **E** .

Turn right here to walk along a wide, geometrically straight track and after ½ mile (800m) you reach a public footpath sign at another crossing of tracks and paths. Keep ahead for a few yards and then turn right **F** along an attractive forest track which leads directly back to the car park. ●

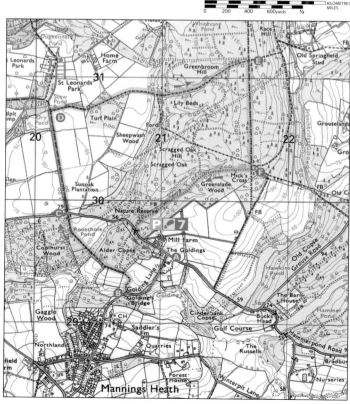

TULLEYS FARM

Turners Hill, Near Crawley, West Sussex, RH10 4PE
Tel: 01342 718472 Fax: 01342 718473
e-mail: shop@tulleysfarm.com website: www.tulleysfarm.com

Set amidst many acres of outstanding natural beauty **Tulleys Farm and Courtyard** is halfway between Turners Hill and Worth. They started in the early 1970s with the establishment of Pick Your Own and since then the farm has been in the forefront of marketing innovation. In 1999 they won the Marks and Spencer Grower Retailer of the Year Award.

During the spring and summer the Farm Shop Courtyard is transformed into a colourful array of bedding and herbaceous plants complemented by a wide range of containers from oak barrels and hanging baskets to glazed and terracotta pots. The shop, converted from a disused milking parlour, is the hub of the farm's activities. It stocks a selection of fresh produce, freshly baked bread, farmhouse cakes, cheeses, ice cream, cooked meats and preserves. Nearby in the old Victorian stable block is the Farmhouse Kitchen serving teas and coffees and a wide range of home-made country food. French doors lead to the Tea Garden where visitors can relax, while the children amuse themselves in the play

area or visiting the animal patch. Here they can see chipmunks, rabbits and guinea pigs or find Curly the pig and the goats. There's a giant maze open from July to September where the whole family can have hours of fun. In October the theme turns to Hallowe'en and pumpkins, when Tulleys is transformed with unpredictable special effects into the superb Creepy Cottage. It is such a fun place that it is easy to forget that people also come here to buy food and pick their own fruit and vegetables, starting with strawberries in June and ending with potatoes in October.

LODER PLANTS

Market Garden, Cyder Farm, Lower Beeding, Horsham,
West Sussex, RH13 6PP Tel: 01403 891412 Fax: 01403 891336
e-mail: cl@hortic.com website: www.rhododendrons.com

In 1992 Chris Loder founded his nursery on the site of an early kitchen garden dating back to 1852. Rhododendrons are 'in his blood' having been brought up with them since early childhood. He's horticulturally trained as well. Rhododendrons have been grown here for over a century and Chris can now supply some 1,200 different varieties. He also has a large stock of evergreen and deciduous azaleas and a variety of companion plants including alpines, bamboos, ferns, grasses, palms, shrubs and trees.

THE CAMELLIA GROVE

Market Garden, Cyder Farm, Lower Beeding, Horsham, West Sussex, RH13 6PP
Tel: 01403 891143 Fax: 01403 891336 e-mail: cl@hortic.com website: www.camellia-grove.com

In September 1957 Sir Giles and Lady Loder decided to thin out some oaks in Leonardslee Garden. A zigzag of paths was created and planted with several hundred varieties of camellia and a few oaks were left to provide shade. This has produced an area that allows the varying shades of the hybrids to grow together naturally. The plants available at the nursery are from cuttings of plants in the Leonardslee garden. The plant sales here are supplied by Camellia Grove nursery, which occupies the same site as Loder plants. It is, however, only open by appointment so that they can provide customers with undivided attention and advice. They will also endeavour to supply any of those from Leonardslee not included on the list.

Leonardslee Gardens

metropolis. However, the coming of the railways took away the need of a resting place and so Crawley returned to its quiet life.

MANNINGS HEATH

2 miles SE of Horsham on the A281

Just north of the village lies **St Leonard's Forest**, one of the few wooded heathland areas to survive the long term ravages of the timber fuelled iron industry of the Weald. Rising in places to around 500 feet, the forest lies on the undulating sandstone ridge that is bounded by Horsham, Crawley and Handcross. According to local folklore, St Leonard's Forest is the home of the legendary nine foot long dragon which roamed the heath and terrorised the surrounding villagers. Coincidentally, some dinosaur bones were discovered nearby in 1822 by Mary Mantell.

LOWER BEEDING

3 miles SE of Horsham on the B2110

The name of the village, along with that of its near namesake, Upper Beeding to the south, is somewhat confusing. Lower Beeding is actually situated on the summit of a hill whilst Upper Beeding lies in one of the lowest parts of West Sussex. However, this can be explained by looking at the derivation of the shared name. Beeding is derived from the Old English 'Beadingas' which means 'Beada's people' and the Upper and Lower refer to the importance of, rather than the geographical positions of, the two settlements.

Just to the south of the village lies the beautiful **Leonardslee Gardens**, in a natural valley created by a tributary of the River Adur. Laid out by Sir Edmund Loder who began his task in 1889, the gardens are still maintained by the family and are world famous for the spring displays of azaleas, magnolias and rhododendrons around the seven landscaped lakes. Deer and wallabies live in the semi-wild habitat around the small lakes. There are several miles of walks around this large area as well as small gardens, including a bonsai

Leonardslee Gardens

THE OLD TOLLGATE RESTAURANT AND HOTEL

The Street, Bramber, Steyning, West Sussex, BN44 3NE
Tel: 01903 879494 Fax: 01903 813399
e-mail: otr@fastnet.co.uk website: www.oldtollgatehotel.com

Travellers passing through Bamber were at one time obliged to interrupt their journey to pay a few pence at the toll-gate for the right to continue on their way. Today, many people still make a stop at this point, though now it is to enjoy the comfort and superb food offered by the **Old Tollgate Restaurant and Hotel**. This beautifully appointed hostelry is built on the site of the old Toll-House and during building works over the years the older, main part of the restaurant was still found to contain sections of the timber frame walls of the original building. Thirty one beautifully designed bedrooms have been decorated in four different styles, all are en-suite, contain a selection of toiletries, have colour television and are fitted with mini bars, trouser presses and direct dial telephone.

The famous carvery-style restaurant is acclaimed by many as unrivalled in the

variety and excellence of its food. A selection of hors d'oeuvre is followed by a choice of roasts, pies and casseroles, all cooked to perfection by the team of chefs. The final touch to a superb meal is the tempting display of deliciously wicked sweets and the superb cheese selection. This friendly countryside establishment carries both an AA and RAC three star rating and has lounges, bars and facilities in keeping with the high Best Western standards.

Tollgate Times is the title on the masthead of the Hotel's own newsletter. A recent issue carried profiles of two long-serving staff members, Head Chef Andrew Coburn who has been with them for ten years and Head Receptionist Suzie Christie, newly promoted from the Deputy position she held for two years. But the main story is devoted to the first run of Tollgate Melody, a three year-old racehorse and the latest in a line of horses, sponsored by the hotel. Owned by Peter and Nancy Crocker and trained by Richard Rowe at Storrington the hotel is not expecting a lot of her at

the moment as she is still young. But they do have high hopes for their other sponsored horse, Half the Pot. Coming from the same stable, this chaser is highly recommended and director, Reina Alston and all the staff are delighted with the four wins he has claimed so far. With racecourses at Goodwood, Brighton, Lingfield and Fontwell, the Old Tollgate is an ideal place for anyone interested in the sport of kings with the added advantage of having its own horse. The countryside round the hotel is ideal for those who enjoy riding and also for walking, golf and fishing. The village itself is both historically interesting and picturesque with the best known of local sights being the Norman castle standing on top of the hill just behind the hotel.

garden to enjoy. The Loder family collection of motor vehicles dating from 1889 to 1900 is an interesting and informative display of the various different designs adopted by the earliest car constructors.

COWFOLD

4 miles SE of Horsham on the A272

This picturesque village of cottages clusters around the parish **Church of St Peter**, which holds one of the most famous brasses in Sussex. Dating back to the 15th century, the life-size brass is of Thomas Nelond, Prior of Lewes in the 1420s, and the brass, along with its elaborate canopy, is over 10 feet long.

Looking at Cowfold today it is hard to believe that is was once an important centre of the iron industry. The abundance of timber for fuel and reliable streams to drive the bellows and heavy hammers made this an active iron smelting area from medieval times through to the end of the 18th century. In order to secure a steady supply of water to these early foundries, small rivers were dammed to form mill or hammer ponds and a number of disused examples can still be found in the surrounding area.

Just to the south of Cowfold and rising above the trees is the spire of **St Hugh's Charterhouse**, the only Carthusian monastery in Britain. Founded in the 1870s, after the order had been driven out of France, the 30 or so monks of this contemplative order live cut off from the rest of the world behind the high stone walls. Each monk has his own cell, or hermitage, complete with its own garden and workshop, and the monks only emerge from their solitude for services and dinner on Sunday.

UPPER BEEDING

13 miles S of Horsham off the A2037

A sprawling village of cottages along the banks of the River Adur, during the Middle Ages, Upper Beeding was the home of **Sele Priory**, a Benedictine religious house founded in the late 11th century by William de Braose. Long since destroyed, the site of the priory is now occupied by a private house.

Though a quiet place today, in the early 19th century an important turnpike road passed through Upper Beeding and the old village toll house, one of the last in the county to remain in service, is now an exhibit at the Weald and Downland Museum, Singleton.

BRAMBER

13 miles S of Horsham on the A283

Visitors seeing Bramber for the first time will find it hard to imagine that this small, compact village was once a busy port on the River Adur estuary during Norman times but its demise came as the river silted up. The name Bramber is derived from the Saxon 'Brymmburh' meaning fortified hill, and when William de Braose built his castle on the steep hill above the village it was probably on the foundations of a previous Saxon stronghold. Completed in 1090, the castle comprised a gatehouse and a number of domestic buildings surrounded by a curtain wall. An important stronghold whilst the port was active, the castle was visited by both King John and Edward I. However the castle did not survive the Civil War. It was all but demolished by the Parliamentarians. Today, the stark remains of **Bramber Castle** can be seen on the hilltop and the site is owned by English Heritage.

During the 15th century, the lands of the de Braose family were transferred to William Waynflete, the then Bishop of Winchester and founder of Magdalen College, Oxford. It was Waynflete who was responsible for constructing **St Mary's House**, in 1470, a striking

POSIES OF STEYNING

1 Cobblestone Walk, High Street, Steyning, West Sussex, BN44 3RD
Tel: 01903 816812

This is one of several small shops situated in Cobblestone Walk, an ancient and busy arcade. Behind the 16th century frontage of this quaint half timbered building is a fascinating pot pourri of crafts and cards, gifts and decorations. Shops like this act as a powerful magnet to browsers and at Posies they are made very welcome. Wendy Jones the owner of **Posies**

established her business here when the previous craft shop left. Prior to this she had been busy raising her family and in her spare time she worked on her exquisite artificial flower arrangements. These she sold at craft fairs and on shelf space she rented from the previous owner of the shop.

Now she continues to sell her own creations and has a wide variety of silk, dried and parchment floral arrangements. She will also take orders and produce arrangements to individual customer specifications and is happy to match these to samples of fabrics and wallpaper from her customers homes. She will either provide the containers for the arrangements or use those brought by her customers. Also on display in the shop is an eclectic collection of hand-crafted gifts and cards made by local artists and designers. Particular favourites with visitors are the locally handmade collectable Ramshackle Bears. Then there are the famous Yankee Candles, candle holders, pot pourri, swags, garlands and bunches, and a selection of fresh flowers.

ANCIENT & MODERN

No 3 Cobblestone Walk, off High Street, Steyning,
West Sussex BN44 3RD
Tel: 01903 815135 Fax: 01903 815123
e-mail: sivell@madasafish.com

Ancient & Modern is an absolute gem of a shop and an essential visit for anyone interested in fine furniture. Here are combined the twin passions of Kate Sivell and her husband Robert. Kate has always loved antiques and gained an excellent grounding in the business by working with Lady Jan Verney, one of Suffolk's most knowledgeable dealers, at the Clare Collector. A fluent French speaker with an extensive network of contacts in France, she is able to travel extensively there, selecting and purchasing the right pieces for the shop. Her speciality is French furniture from the 18th and 19th centuries, French faïence pottery and porcelain from the 19th century and early 20th century French linen.

Because she can source her own pieces Kate is able to buy them at a reasonable price and sell them at much lower prices than London dealers. Robert is a qualified and very experienced furniture maker

and his pieces account for the modern part of the shop's title. Some fine examples of his work will always be found here. Ranging from a magnificent serpentine mahogany chest to hand-crafted radiator covers. However what he offers customers is a complete, bespoke, furniture making service and he will make anything in any style to their specifications in his workshop in the nearby commercial centre. He's been providing this service for many years and has built a large customer base throughout Europe and in America.

St Mary's House, Bramber

medieval residence that was first built as a home for four monks who were bridge wardens of the important crossing here over the River Adur. Now a Grade I listed building, this is a classic half-timbered dwelling with fine wood panelled rooms, Elizabethan trompe l'œil paintings and medieval shuttered windows. However what remains today is only half of the original construction, which also acted as a resting place for pilgrims travelling to Chichester or Canterbury.

Following the Dissolution of the Monasteries, the house came into private ownership and was refurbished as a comfortable residence for a well-to-do family. The Painted Room was decorated for a visit by Queen Elizabeth I in 1585 and the room in which Charles II rested before fleeing to Shoreham and then France is known as the King's Room. Lovingly restored and with charming topiary gardens, the house was the setting for the Sherlock Holmes story *The Musgrave Ritual* and it has also featured in the *Dr Who* television series.

Finally, before the Reform Act of 1832

swept away the rotten boroughs, this tiny constituency returned two members to Parliament. This was despite the fact that, at one time, Bramber only had 32 eligible voters! One member of Parliament who benefited from the unreformed system was William Wilberforce who was more or less awarded one of the Bramber seats in recognition of his campaigning work against slavery.

STEYNING

13 miles S of Horsham off the A283

This ancient market town, whose High Street follows closely the line of the South Downs, was founded in the 8th century by St Cuthman. An early Celtic Christian, Cuthman travelled from Wessex eastwards pushing his invalid mother in a handcart. On reaching Saxon Steyning, the wheel on the handcart broke as they passed Penfolds Field and the nearby haymakers laughed and jeered as the old lady was thrown to the ground. St Cuthman cursed the field and the unhelpful haymakers, and the heavens are said to have opened and torrential rain poured and spoilt their labours. To this day, it is said to rain whenever Penfolds Field is being mown. St Cuthman took his calamity as a sign that he should settle here and he built a timber church.

By the late Saxon period Steyning had grown to become an important port on the then navigable River Adur and, as well as being a royal manor owned by Alfred the Great, it also had a Royal Mint. By 1100, the silting of the river had caused the harbour to close but, fortunately, the town was well-established and could continue as a market place. Designated a conservation area, there are many buildings of architectural and historical interest in the town's ancient centre. There are several 14th and 15th century hall type

Steyning Church

South Downs, this village's name is derived from the Saxon for 'settlement of the family of Wassa'. A pretty place, with a varied assortment of buildings, Washington stands between the chalk downland and the sandstone Weald and it was at the early 19th century inn, The Frankland Arms, that Hilaire Belloc found a "nectar brewed in the waxing of the moon and of that barley which Brutus brought hither in the first founding of this land".

Just southeast of the village, and not far from the South Downs Way, lies one of Sussex's most striking landmarks - **Chanctonbury Ring**. An Iron Age hillfort, the site is marked by a clump of beech trees, planted in 1760 by Charles Goring who inherited the hill along with Wiston Park. Unfortunately, many of the trees suffered during the October hurricane of 1987 but enough remain to make this an eye catching sight on the horizon. Meanwhile, the part-16th and part-19th century mansion of **Wiston House** is now leased by the Foreign Office and, though it is not open to the public, views of the house and the park can be seen from the road leading to village church.

The countryside around Chanctonbury Ring inspired the composer John Ireland who, towards the end of his life in the 1950s, bought **Rock Mill** which lies below the hill. A converted tower mill, a plaque on the wall records that Ireland lived the happiest years of his life here before his death in 1962.

houses as well as Wealden cottages but the most impressive building, built in the 15th century as the home of a religious order, is the famous **Old Grammar School**, now a successful comprehensive. An excellent place to discover Steyning's past is at **Steyning Museum** in Church Street where there are exhibitions showing both the town's history and local prehistoric finds.

Steyning's close proximity to the **South Downs Way** and the **Downs Link** (a long distance bridleway which follows the course of the old railway line to Christ's Hospital near Horsham and on in to Surrey), makes this a lovely base for both walking and riding holidays.

WASHINGTON

12 miles S of Horsham off the A24

Standing at the northern end of the Findon Gap, an ancient pass through the

SHIPLEY

6 miles S of Horsham off the A272

As well as its pretty 12th century village church, this pleasant village also features a small disused toll house and a distinctive hammer pond that, in the 16th century, would have supplied water to drive the bellows and mechanical hammers in the adjacent iron foundry. However, Shipley is perhaps best known for being the former home of the celebrated Sussex writer Hilaire Belloc. He lived at **King's Land**, a low rambling house on the outskirts of the village, from 1906 until his death in 1953 and, appropriately enough, as a lover of windmills, he had one at the bottom of his garden. Built in 1879, **Shipley Mill** is the only remaining working smock mill in Sussex and, whilst being the county's last, it is also the biggest. Open to the public on a limited basis, the mill was completely restored and returned to working order after the writer's death.

Belloc is not the only connection that Shipley has with the arts, for the composer John Ireland is buried in the churchyard of the village's interesting church, built by the Knights Templar in 1125. The poet and traveller, Wilfrid Scawen Blunt, also lived at Shipley where he entertained celebrities of the day including Oscar Wilde, William Morris and Winston Churchill.

DIAL POST

7 miles S of Horsham on the A24

Just to the east of the village lie the stark ruins of medieval **Knepp Castle**, a fortification built by William de Braose of Bramber to defend the upper reaches of the River Adur. All that remains of the once impressive Norman keep is a solitary wall standing on top of a low mound which is surrounded by a now dry moat.

BILLINGSHURST

6½ miles SW of Horsham on the A272

This attractive small town, strung out along Roman Stane Street, was, in the days before the railways, an important coaching town and several good former coaching inns, including the 16th century

---

RUMBOLDS FARM

Plaistow, Nr Billingshurst, West Sussex, RH14 0PZ
Tel: 01403 871404

The husband and wife partnership of Andrew and Alison Gibbs run this charming and picturesque family holiday property. Andrew's family have farmed here for over three generations and he was born in the 17th century grade II listed **Rumbolds Farm** and has farmed the land here all of his life. The couple run a farm shop specialising in organic dairy products, including milk, cheese and cream. The milk is pasteurised and available fresh, daily. Everything in the shop comes from the Guernsey herd of cows. They have five different varieties of cheese including hard, pressed and soft (soft cheese available summer only) and some very thick and exceedingly tasty double Guernsey cream.

They also sell organic lamb and beef from their own stock, all sold ready packed, frozen or fresh

and free-range eggs are from the farm of a neighbour. Alison's jams and marmalades are very popular with visitors as is the stock of local honey. The farmhouse has recently been undergoing conversion to make it available as a self-catering holiday let for a family or a group of friends. It has six bedrooms, one acre of garden and, being secluded and quiet, is an ideal base for a large family or group. There's a large Sussex barn available for functions where catering facilities can be arranged if required. Seating 80 round large circular tables it has a delightful rustic ambience created by the soft light falling on the ancient beams and timbers.

THE COACH AND HORSES

School lane, Danehill, Near Haywards Hill, Sussex, RH17 7JF
Tel: 01825 740369

Set in attractive countryside, this 19th century rural pub has a
relaxed and friendly atmosphere and a mix of chatty customers.
It is also home to Harvey, a five year-old blonde retriever who
is well-loved and a great favourite with visitors. There's a cosy
little bar with half-panelled walls, polished wooden floorboards
and a wood-burning stove in the fireplace. It has an intimate
atmosphere and is just the place for concentrating on a game of darts, with drinks available through
the big hatch into the bar. That is where the locals gather, crowding round the wooden counter or
sitting on the high bar stools enjoying the well kept Harvey's Best or guest beers like Adnams Best or
Badger Best from the handpump. This is as good as the traditional English country pub gets and
where the visitor can enjoy a realistic slice of village life from a bygone age.

In the summer it's a delight to sit outdoors in the large, attractive garden and enjoy the views over

the South Downs. Food is an important part of what the **Coach
and Horses** has to offer. Ian and Catherine Philpots, the owners,
pride themselves on their bar lunches and the constantly changing
evening menu. Standards like mouth-watering grilled ciabatta
with roasted pepper, goats cheese and pine kernels, appear beside
fresh herb risotto and spiced salmon fish cakes with a lime
mayonnaise. Old favourites appear on the main menu, like pork
and leek sausages and mash, alongside daily specials such as whole
lemon sole with capers and lime butter. There's a grand selection
of wines available to wash it all down.

LINDFIELD GALLERIES

62 High Street, Lindfield, West Sussex, RH16 2HL
Tel: 01444 483817 Fax: 01444 484682
e-mail: david@orientalandantiquerugs.com
website: www.orientalandantiquerugs.com

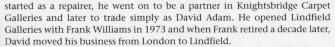

Lindfield Galleries sells an eye dazzling selection of carpets and
rugs from Persia, Turkey, Afghanistan and Turkmenistan as well as
fine antique tapestries and Aubusson carpets from Europe; indeed,
a wealth of hand-woven treasures to rival many of the oriental carpet
shops of London and other European capitals. The shop is owned and run by David Adam, who has
been in the oriental carpet business for nearly 50 years, and whose knowledge, enthusiasm and
experience is acknowledged and appreciated by customers and colleagues within the trade. Having

started as a repairer, he went on to be a partner in Knightsbridge Carpet
Galleries and later to trade simply as David Adam. He opened Lindfield
Galleries with Frank Williams in 1973 and when Frank retired a decade later,
David moved his business from London to Lindfield.

Specialising in old and antique carpets, rugs and kilims, Lindfield Galleries
is a member of the British Antique Dealers Association. Each area within the
carpet weaving world has it's own characteristics, weaves and designs and
David is happy to share his expertise with interested clients. He also selects
modern pieces that are well woven, often using natural dyes, that he feels are
of equal quality to older pieces. Such carpets make quality weaving accessible
to people who may not be looking to buy the older, and sometimes rarer,
pieces. Lindfield Galleries provide a cleaning and restoration service and will
give expert advice on keeping your carpet or rug in good order.

Olde Six Bells, can still be found in the old part of the town. The Norman parish **Church of St Mary**, has a 13th century tower but most of the rest of the building dates from the 15th to 16th centuries apart from some unfortunate Victorian restoration to the east end.

ITCHINGFIELD

3 miles SW of Horsham off A264

The parish church, in this tiny village, has an amazing 600 year-old belfry tower, the beams of which are entirely held together with oak pegs. During a restoration programme in the 1860s, workmen found a skull, said to have been that of Sir Hector Maclean, on one of the belfry beams. A friend of the vicar of the time, Sir Hector was executed for his part in the Jacobite Rising of 1715 and, presumably, his old friend thought to keep his gruesome souvenir in a safe place. In the churchyard of this early 12th century building is a little priest's house, built in the 15th century as a resting place for the priest who rode from Sele Priory at Upper Beeding to pick up the parish collection.

RUDGWICK

5½ miles NW of Horsham on the B2128

A typical Wealden village of charming tile-fronted cottages, the 13th century village church has a fine Sussex marble font in which the shells of sea creatures have been fossilised into the stone.

WARNHAM

2 mile NW of Horsham off the A24

This small and well-kept village is famous as being the birthplace of the poet Percy Bysshe Shelley. He was born, in 1792, at **Field Place**, a large country house just outside the village, and this is where he spent a happy childhood exploring the local countryside and playing with paper boats on the lake at the house.

Famously, the young poet was cast out of the family home by his father who did not approve of his profession, and while there are many Shelley memorials in the parish church Percy has no memorial. His ashes are buried in Rome, where he died in 1822, and his heart lies in his son's tomb in Bournemouth.

HAYWARDS HEATH

On first appearances, Haywards Heath appears to be a modern town, situated on high heathland. However, the conservation area around **Muster Green** indicates where the old settlement was originally based. A pleasant open space surrounded by trees, which is believed to takes its name from the obligatory annual 17th century custom of mustering the militia, the green was the site of a battle during the Civil War. Here, too, can be found Haywards Heath's oldest building, the 16th century **Sergison Arms** which takes its name from the landed family who once owned nearby Cuckfield Park.

The modern town has grown up around the station to which Haywards Heath owes its prosperity as the two nearby villages of Lindfield and Cuckfield both refused to allow the railway to run through them when the line from London to the south coast was laid in the 19th century.

AROUND HAYWARDS HEATH

LINDFIELD

1 mile NE of Haywards Heath on the B2028

This famous beauty spot is everyone's idea of the perfect English village: the wide common was once used for fairs and markets, the High Street leads up hill to the church and there are some

THE BIRMAN GALLERY

68 The High Street, Lindfield, West Sussex, RH16 2HL
Tel: 01444 482393

June and John Woodside are the friendly knowledgeable owners of the
excellent **Birman Gallery** which was originally June's idea. It's a small shop
on the High Street of a delightful Sussex village. The interior, though small, is
expertly lit and very well stocked. There are original paintings in all mediums
by local artists and others including Hilary Scoffield, Don Kinrade and Hagop
Kasparian. Original and limited edition prints are available as well as locally
made silver jewellery and handmade glassware.

splendid domestic buildings from tile-
hung cottages to elegant Georgian
houses. The village is also home to **Old
Place**, a small timber framed Elizabethan
manor house that is said to have been
Queen Elizabeth's country cottage and
the cottage next door is said to have
been Henry VII's hunting lodge. Sited on
a hill top, the 13th century village church
with its large spire was a useful landmark
in the days when the surrounding area
was wooded. Beside the churchyard is
Church House, which was originally The
Tiger Inn. During the celebrations after
the defeat of the Spanish Armada in
1588, the inn supplied so much strong
ale to the villagers that the bell ringers
broke their ropes and cracked one of the
church bells. The inn was one of the
village's busy coaching inns in the 18th
and 19th centuries when Lindfield was an
important staging post between London
and Brighton.

ARDINGLY

3½ miles N of Haywards Heath on the B2028

Ardingly is chiefly famous for being the
home of the showground for the South
of England Agricultural Society.
Although there is some modern building,
the old part of the village has remained
fairly unspoilt. **Ardingly College**, a
public school, founded by the pioneering
churchman Nathaniel Woodard in 1858
is a large red brick building with its own

squat towered chapel. The village
church, around which the old part of
Ardingly is clustered, dates from
medieval times though there is much
Victorian restoration work. Inside can be
found various brasses to the Tudor
Culpeper family whilst, outside, the
churchyard wall was used, in 1643, as a
defensive position by the men of
Ardingly against Cromwell's troops who
came to take the Royalist rector.

To the west of the village, a tributary of
the River Ouse has been dammed to form
Ardingly Reservoir, a 200 acre lake
which offers some excellent fishing as
well as waterside walks and a nature trail.

Just north of Ardingly, at the top end
of the reservoir, lies **Wakehurst Place**,
the Tudor home of the Culpeper family,
who arrived here in the 15th century. The
present house, a striking Elizabethan
mansion, was built in 1590 by Edward
Culpeper and the house and estate were
eventually left to the National Trust in
1963 by Sir Henry Price. Over the years,
but particularly during the 20th century,
the owners of Wakehurst Place have built
up a splendid collection of trees and
shrubs in the natural dramatic
landscapes of woodlands, valleys and
lakes. Now leased to the Royal Botanic
Gardens at Kew, the 500 acre gardens are
open to the public throughout the year.
As well as the varied and magnificent
display of plants, trees and shrubs,

Wakehurst Place

in 1894. Using Paddockhurst as his weekend retreat, Lord Cowdray, who had amassed a fortune through civil engineering works, spend thousands of pounds on improving the house, including adding painted ceilings and stained glass. After the lord's death, in 1932, the house was purchased by the monks as a dependent priory of Downside Abbey, Somerset and it became an independent house in 1957.

visitors can take in the exhibitions in the house on local geology, habitats and woodlands of the area. Wakehurst Place is also home to the **Millennium Seed Bank**, a project which aims to ensure the continued survival of over 24,000 plant species world-wide.

WORTH

8 miles N of Haywards Heath off the B2036

For those with a particular interest in historic churches, the ancient settlement of Worth, which is now all but a suburb of Crawley, is well worth a visit. Considered by many to be one of England's best churches, the Saxon **Church of St Nicholas** was built between 950 and 1050 though, for some reason, it does not feature in the Domesday Book. Still in use today, the church is massive and solid but the addition of a Victorian tower and broach spire is unfortunate.

The Benedictine monastery and Roman Catholic boys' public school, **Worth Abbey**, to the east of Worth, was originally built as the country house of a wealthy tycoon. Paddockhurst, as it was known, was built by Robert Whitehead, a 19th century marine engineer, who invented the torpedo. It was greatly added to by the 1st Lord Cowdray who purchased the property from Whitehead

EAST GRINSTEAD

10 miles N of Haywards Heath on the A22

Situated 400 feet above sea level on a sandstone hill, this rather suburban sounding town has a rich history that dates back to the early 13th century. East Grinstead was granted its market charter in 1221. Throughout the Middle Ages, it was an important market town as well as being a centre of the Wealden iron industry. The name, Grinstead, means 'green steading' or 'clearing in woodland' and, though Ashdown Forest is a few miles away today, it was once a much more extensive woodland which provided much of the fuel for the town's prosperity.

Although there is much modern building here, the High Street consists largely of 16th century half-timbered buildings and this is where the splendid **Sackville College** can be seen, set back from the road. However, this is not an educational establishment as the name might suggest, but a set of almshouses, founded in 1609 by the Earl of Dorset. A Grade I listed building, the dwellings built for the retired workers of the Sackville estates, are constructed around an attractive quadrangle. It still provides

ORCHARD NURSERY

Holyte Road, East Grinstead, West Sussex, RH19 3PP
Tel: 01342 311657 Fax: 01342 410272

Lynda Bradford's grandfather created his market garden on the site of a Victorian kitchen garden in 1960. In the 1980s Lynda and her late father established **Orchard Nursery**, still using the old walled garden and original green houses. Since then it has built a solid reputation as a supplier of high quality plants, offering one of the best selections of herbaceous plants in the area, most of them produced by the nursery on site. Container gardening is a speciality and in season the selection of pot grown trees, shrubs and plants is unbelievable. Plants include hardy geraniums and several varieties of anthemis, and encompass everything from old cottage garden favourites to the new and unusual.

The staff are knowledgeable and friendly and always willing to answer questions or offer help and advice on all aspects of gardening. Browsers are particularly welcome and nobody is put under any pressure to buy. Lynda is a former teacher and still keeps her hand in teaching swimming at the local swimming club. She also uses her educational skills to run a series of two hour long summer classes at the nursery, teaching the art of hanging basket and container gardening. In winter, Christmas workshops on wreath making and festive decorations for the home are run indoors. Even the Christmas trees sold here are home grown and can be dug or cut as required, selected from the stock of traditional, nordman and blue spruce trees.

SELF HEALTH ENTERPRISES

Bulrushes Farm, Coombe Hill Road,
East Grinstead, Sussex, RH19 4LZ
Tel: 0870 2202258 Fax: 01342 336909
e-mail: usherbs@aol.co
website: www.selfhealth.co.uk

Ulrich and Mary Sommer founded their business after the chance discovery of a book 'Cure for All Cancers' by Hulda Regehr Clark PhD, ND. An interest in the book led Ulrich to translate it into German and from then requests for the products written about spread like wildfire. Ulrich is originally from Schleswig Holstein and is a professional pharmacist. Mary, his wife, is a fitness trainer working with sports people and celebrities. The business they started to provide Dr Clark's products blossomed and within four years their customer base had grown from 300 people to over 20,000. They supply their products throughout the world to private customers, health food stores and wholesale.

Self Health provides products, books and programs according to Dr Clark's 'Cure for all Diseases' and other books. They also supply herbs and vitamins, for wellness, as well as minerals, super food and many more items. They provide cleanse advice and programs as well as nutritional and health consulting. In October 2000 they started providing GH1, an all natural product that aims to reverse and prevent the effects of ageing. Taken as drops or sprayed under the tongue the minute doses are also intended to strengthen the immune system, improve sexual performance, help remove wrinkles and cellulite, remove fat and improve muscle.

accommodation for elderly people but guided tours of the building are provided for visitors. The parish **Church of St Swithin** stands on an ancient site but it only dates from the late 18th century as the previous church was declared unsafe after the tower collapsed in 1785. Beside the porch are three graveslabs in memory of Anne Tree, John Forman and Thomas Dunngate, Protestant martyrs who were burnt at the stake in East Grinstead in 1665.

Before the Reform Act of 1832, only the occupants of East Grinstead's 48 original burgage plots (long, narrow housing allotments) were eligible to vote - making this one of the county's most rotten boroughs. As was common practice elsewhere, the local landed family, the Sackvilles, would ensure that they acquired enough votes to guarantee a comfortable majority.

The arrival of the railways in 1855 ended a period of relative decline in the town and, today, East Grinstead is a flourishing place. Perhaps, however, the town will always be remembered for the pioneering work carried out at the Queen Victoria Hospital during World War II. Inspired by the surgeon, Sir Archibald McIndoe, great advances in plastic and reconstructive surgery were made here to help airmen who had suffered severe burns or facial injuries. Following McIndoe's death in 1960, the **McIndoe Burns Centre** was built to further the research and the hospital remains the centre of the Guinea Pig Club, set up for and by the early patients of the pioneering surgeon.

The **Town Museum**, housed in East Court, is a fine building that was originally constructed as a private residence in 1769. An interesting place, which tells the story of the town and surrounding area, as well as the life of its inhabitants, the Greenwich Meridian passes through the town at this point.

To the south of East Grinstead lies **Standen**, a remarkable late Victorian country mansion that is a showpiece of the Arts and Crafts Movement. Completed in 1894 by Philip Webb, an associate of William Morris, for a prosperous London solicitor, the house was constructed using a variety of traditional local building materials. Morris designed the internal furnishings such as the carpets, wallpapers and textiles. Now fully restored, the house, owned by the National Trust, can be seen in all its 1920s splendour, including details such as original electric light fittings. Open to the public, the house is set in a beautiful hillside garden with views over the Ashdown Forest and the valley of the Upper Medway. From near Standen runs the **Bluebell Railway**, which offers a pleasant journey by steam train through the Sussex Weald to Sheffield Park, the railway's headquarters, via the 1930s station at Horsted Keynes.

Nearby **Saint Hill Manor**, one of the finest sandstone buildings in the county, was built in 1792 by Gibbs Crawfurd, the grandfather of the man, who brought the railway to East Grinstead in the mid 19th century. Other owners of the house include the Maharajah of Jaipur and Mrs Neville Laskey, a generous lady who accommodated the RAF patients of Sir Archibald McIndoe. L. Ron Hubbard, the author and founder of the Church of Scientology, was the house's last owner and it was he who oversaw the work to restore the manor to its former glory including the Monkey Mural that was painted in 1945 by Sir Winston Churchill's nephew, John Spencer Churchill. The house and gardens are open to the public.

WEST HOATHLY

5½ miles N of Haywards Heath off the B2028

Situated high on a ridge overlooking the Weir Wood Reservoir to the northeast, this historic old settlement grew up around an ancient crossing point of two routes across the Weald. The squat towered village church was begun before the Norman Conquest and, inside, there are a number of iron grave slabs of the Infield family from nearby Gravetye Manor. In the churchyard, on the south wall, is a small brass in memory of Anne Tree, one of the 16th century East Grinstead martyrs. Lying in woodland just north of the village is **Gravetye Manor**, a splendid stone Elizabethan house, built, in 1598, for the Infield family, who were wealthy, local iron masters. Much later, in 1884, William Robinson, the gardening correspondent of *The Times*, bought the house and, over the next 50 years, he created the splendid gardens, following the natural contours of this narrow valley. Today, the manor is a first class country house hotel.

However, the village's most impressive building is undoubtedly the **Priest House**, a low half-timbered 15th century house probably built as the estate office for the monks of Lewes Priory who owned the manor here. This would originally have been one vast room but, in Elizabethan times, it was altered to a substantial yeoman's house. It is now a museum belonging to the Sussex Archaeological Society, filled with 18th and 19th century furniture and a fascinating collection of kitchen equipment, needlework and household paraphernalia. The museum is set in a classic English country garden with a formal herb garden containing over 150 culinary, medicinal and folklore herbs.

BURGESS HILL

3 miles SW of Haywards Heath on the B2113

This small town, which has recently undergone much central redevelopment, owes its existence to the arrival of the railway in the mid 19th century. Compared to many of the settlements in the surrounding area, Burgess Hill is a relatively new addition to the landscape. It does, however, have a particularly spacious cricket pitch and some older buildings remaining from what was once a small settlement.

KEYMER

5½ miles SW of Haywards Heath on the B2116

Situated between two tributaries of the River Adur, this old village was once a centre of smuggling. In 1777 over £5,000 worth of goods were seized by customs. Keymer is, however, better known for its famous works that are still producing handmade bricks and tiles. Surprisingly, though, the double spire of Keymer's Church of St Cosmas and St Damian (patron saints of physician and surgeons) is covered not with tiles but with wooden shingles.

HURSTPIERPOINT

5½ miles SW of Haywards Heath on the B2116

Surrounded by unspoilt countryside, this pretty village, which takes its name from the Saxon for wood - *hurst* - and Pierpoint after the local landowning family, was mentioned in the Domesday Book. The narrow High Street here is particularly attractive with some fine Georgian buildings and a tall Victorian church, designed by Sir Charles Barry, the architect of the Houses of Parliament. Another imposing building, dominating the countryside to the north of the village, is **Hurstpierpoint College** chapel. Like nearby Lancing and Ardingly, the school was founded in the 19th century by Nathaniel Woodard.

To the south of the village lies the ancestral home of the Norman Pierpoint family. They settled here in the 11th

THE ROYAL OAK

Wineham Lane, Wineham, West Sussex, BN5 9AY
Tel: 01444 881252 Fax: 01444 881530

The Royal Oak is one of the oldest pubs in Sussex and is
mentioned in the Domesday Book. The present black and
white half-timbered building dates from the 13th century.
Inside, it has the low beams, inglenook and well worn brick
floor so characteristic of fine old country inns. It has been run
by the Peacock family for over 200 years and by the present member, Tim, for over 30 years.
CAMRA listed, it stocks real ales and fine wines and offers a good selection of freshly cut and
toasted sandwiches, home made soups and ploughmans lunches.

century close to their powerful relative
William de Warenne and **Danny** was, in
those days, a modest hunting lodge
situated below the grassy mound of
Woolstonbury Hill. In the mid 15th
century, the family had to flee after the
then owner, Simon de Pierpoint,
deliberately murdered some of his serfs,
and the house was burnt to the ground
in retaliation. The site stood empty
until, in the late 16th century, Elizabeth I
granted the estate to George Goring who
built the impressive classic Elizabethan E
shaped mansion seen today.

However, the history of Danny remains
a somewhat turbulent story as Goring, a
staunch Royalist, was forced to give up
his splendid mansion at the end of the
Civil War. It was the Campion family,
coming here in the early 18th century,
who added the Queen Anne south facing
façade as well as remodelling the interior
by lowering the ceiling in the Great Hall
and adding a grand, sweeping staircase.

Danny's finest hour came, in 1918,
when the Prime Minister, Lloyd George
rented the house, and it was here that
the terms of the armistice with Germany
were drawn up to end World War I. A
plaque in the Great Hall commemorates
the meetings held here by Lloyd George's
war cabinet and, during the time that the
cabinet was here, Lloyd George was
known to have walked up Woolstonbury
Hill to seek peace and solitude. The

house also saw service during World War
II when it was occupied by British and
Commonwealth troops. Today, Danny is
owned by the Country Houses
Association and let out in 28 serviced
apartments. The house is open to the
public on a limited basis.

CLAYTON

6 miles SW of Haywards Heath on the A273

This small hamlet, which lay on a Roman
road between Droydon and Portslade, is
home to a rather ordinary Saxon church
with some early medieval wall paintings,
which are undoubtedly the work of the
renowned group of artists from St
Pancras Priory, Lewes.

The settlement lies at one end of a mile
long railway tunnel, which was
constructed in the 1840s to take the still
busy London to Brighton track. An
engineering wonder of its day, the
northern end of **Clayton Tunnel** is
dominated by a large Victorian folly,
Tunnel House, built in a grand Tudor
style to house the tunnel keeper.

On a hill overlooking Clayton stand
two windmills, known rather
unimaginatively as **Jack and Jill**. The
larger of the pair, Jack, is a tower mill
dating from 1896. It fell into disuse in
the 1920s and, now without its sails, has
been converted into an unusual private
residence. Jill, a post mill that originally
stood in Brighton, was brought here by

oxen in 1852, has been fully restored and is still capable of grinding corn.

PYECOMBE
7 miles SW of Haywards Heath on the A23

This ancient village stands on a prehistoric track that runs along the South Downs from Stonehenge to Canterbury. Home to one of the smallest downland churches, this simple, Norman building has a 12th century lead font that survived the Civil War by being disguised by the crafty parishioners in a layer of whitewash.

Pyecombe is renowned amongst farmers, and particularly shepherds, as being the home of the best possible shepherd's crook, the **Pyecombe Hook**. It was the crook's curled end, known as the guide, that made the Pyecombe Hook so special as it was a very efficient mechanism for catching sheep though it was hard to fashion. Throughout the 19th and early 20th centuries, the village forge turned out these world famous crooks and, though they are no longer made today, several rare examples can be seen in Worthing Museum.

POYNINGS
8 miles SW of Haywards Heath off the A281

Once an iron working village, Poynings lies in a hollow below the steep slopes of **Dyke Hill** on top of which is situated an Iron Age hillfort. Just south of Poynings, and close to the hill, is one of the South Downs greatest natural features - the **Devil's Dyke**. Local legend has it that this great steep-sided ravine was dug by the Devil to drown the religious people of Sussex. Working in darkness, intent on digging all the way to the coast, he was half way to the sea when an old woman climbed to the top of a hill with a candle and a sieve. The light of the candle woke a nearby cockerel, whose crowing alerted the Devil. Looking up,

the devil saw the candle light through the sieve and fled thinking that the sun was rising.

During Victorian times, the Devil's Dyke became a popular place from which to view the surrounding downlands. A railway was built to connect the village with Brighton and a cable car was installed over the ravine. The cable car has now gone but the site is still a popular place with motorists, walkers and hang gliding enthusiasts.

FULKING
9 miles SW of Haywards Heath off the A281

The layout of this pretty village, situated under the steep downland slopes, has changed little since the 16th century when the sheep in the area far outnumbered the people. Beside the aptly named ancient village inn, The Shepherd and Dog, there is a spring and stream, which is now channelled through a Victorian well house. For centuries, the spring and the stream, which then flowed along the road side, was used for washing the sheep before the annual spring sheep shearing and shepherds would bring their flocks to Fulking in droves. After washing the sheep, the shepherds would retire to the inn with their dogs for a well earned drink. The spring provided the villagers with all their water until the 1950s when a mains water supply arrived.

SMALL DOLE
10 miles SW of Haywards Heath on the A2037

Just to the north of this small downland village, is **Woods Mill**, the headquarters of the Sussex Trust for Nature Conservation. As well as a nature reserve and the nature trail around the woodland, marshes and streams, the site is also home to an 18th century watermill which houses a countryside exhibition.

EDBURTON

10 miles SW of Haywards Heath off the A2037

This tiny hamlet is named after Edburga, the grand daughter of King Alfred, who is said to have built a church here in the 10th century. However, the present **Church of St Andrew** dates from the 13th century and, inside, can be seen one of only three lead fonts remaining in the county. Though battered and dented from the days of the Civil War, when it was used as a horse trough, the font escaped being melted down for ammunition. On top of the steep downland escarpment, which rises to its highest point here, stands **Castle Ring**, a mound and ditch which are the remains of an 11th century fort.

HENFIELD

8½ miles SW of Haywards Heath on the A281

Once an important staging post, the village not only has a couple of excellent old coaching inns but also some other fine buildings of architectural note. The church is Saxon and dates back to a charter of AD 770 though it was heavily restored in the Victorian age and only a few medieval features remain. However, the 16th century cottage, known as the **Cat House**, is a pretty if rather eccentric building, situated near the church. Fixed around the eaves is a series of stencils of cats with their paws outstretched as if chasing birds. This peculiar decoration

was supposedly put up by a previous owner of the house, Bob Ward who believed that the vicar's cat had eaten his canary.

CUCKFIELD

1 mile W of Haywards Heath on the A272

Pronounced *Cookfield*, this small country town dates back to Saxon times and though it would be particularly charming if the name were to have been derived from the Saxon Cucufleda meaning 'a clearing full of cuckoos', it is more likely that it means 'land surrounded by a quickset hedge'. Situated on the side of a hill, during the 11th century, Cuckfield belonged to the Norman, William de Warenne, who had a hunting lodge and chapel here.

Before the new turnpike road was built in 1807, Cuckfield stood on the main route from London to the south coast and, because of this, it became a busy staging post. George IV used to stop here on his way to Brighton. A horse-drawn coach service was maintained from here by an American right up until the beginning of World War I when the horses were needed for the war effort.

To the north lie **Borde Hill Gardens** (see panel on page 268), a splendid typically English garden of special botanical interest in some 200 acres of spectacular Sussex parkland and woods. Colonel Stephenson Clarke, by funding

OCKENDEN MANOR

Ockenden lane, Cuckfield, West Sussex, RH17 5LD
Tel: 01444 416111 e-mail: ockenden@hshotels.co.uk
Fax: 01444 415549 website: www.hshotels.co.uk

This magnificent Elizabethan Manor House sits at the end of a country lane in one of England's most picturesque villages. With fabulous views across the South Downs and nine acres of beautiful grounds it is the perfect place to relax. Enjoy the comfortable sitting room with its fine antiques, freshly cut flowers and log fire. Dine in elegance in the award winning restaurant or curl up with a book in one of the individually decorated guest bedrooms.

Borde Hill Garden

Balcombe Road, Haywards Heath, West Sussex, RH16 1XP
Tel: 01444 450326 Fax: 01444 440427
e-mail: info@bordehill.co.uk website: www.bordehill.co.uk

Borde Hill has been home to the Stephenson-Clarke family since 1893. Colonel Stephenson-Clark sponsored 'the great plant collectors' of the 19th century, who brought back trees and shrubs from all corners of the world. Through his foresight and hard work, Borde Hill now has a world-renowned botanical collection. Set in 200 acres of stunning Sussex parkland and woods, it is rated Grade II* by English Heritage. Borde Hill's many distinctive and themed 'rooms' make it unique among England's great gardens. Following an award from the Heritage Lottery Fund, work started has been completed on phase one of a garden renaissance.

Visitors will discover a touch of romance in the Italian Garden, marvel at the roses or retreat into the sub-tropical paradise of the Round Dell or the splendour of magnificent trees and shrubs from the Himalayas and the Andes. From the formal gardens it is possible to wander into the nearby woodland gardens where nearly every copse has its colony of exotic trees and shrubs. Warren Wood, Little Bentley and Stone Pits Wood offer a wonderful variety of enchanting and enticing woodland walks and nature trails. Afterwards, tired and satisfied there is nothing better to end the visit than a light lunch or cream tea in the Lavender Tea Rooms. Jeremy's Restaurant is also available for the discerning customer.

plant hunting expeditions to China, Burma, Tasmania and the Andes, established the collection of plants and trees, which is still maintained by the Colonel's descendants. With displays carefully planted to offer a blaze of colour for most of the year, this garden is well worth exploring.

Handcross

7 miles NW of Haywards Heath on the B2114

Close to this little village, which stood on the old London to Brighton road, are two glorious gardens. To the southeast lie the superb National Trust owned gardens of **Nymans**. Though much of the house that stood on this estate was destroyed by fire in 1947, the empty shell provides a dramatic backdrop to one of the county's greatest gardens. At the heart of Nymans is the round walled garden, created with the help of the late 19th century gardening revivalists William Robinson and

Gertrude Jekyll. Elsewhere, the gardens are laid out in a series of 'rooms', where visitors can walk from garden to garden taking in the old roses, the topiary, the laurel walk and the sunken garden.

Just northeast of Handcross is another smaller, though not less glorious garden, **High Beeches Gardens**. Here, in the enchanting woodlands and water gardens, is a collection of rare and exotic plants as well as native wild flowers in a natural meadow setting.

Nymans

Surrey's closeness to the capital and its transport links have defined much of its history. The Thames winds through Surrey and many of the present-day villages and towns developed as riverside trading centres in the medieval period or earlier. As the Thames led to the development of medieval and earlier villages, the arrival of the railway in the mid-19th century saw new villages spring up, while others expanded out of all recognition. Rail lines and major roads fan through the whole area from London with the latest contribution to the transport theme being the M25.

Royal Horticultural Society Wisley Gardens

However Surrey is full of historical traces. Great houses, as well as royal and episcopal palaces, were built here from medieval times, and many villages have evidence of Saxon, Celtic, Roman and even late Stone Age settlements. The site of one of England's defining moments, the signing of the Magna Carta in 1215 is at the riverside meadow of Runnymede. The most impressive of all buildings along the Thames is Hampton Court, where Henry VIII expanded Cardinal Wolsey's already magnificent palace.

Farnham, with its lovely Georgian architecture and 12th century castle, is the largest town in southwestern Surrey, while Guildford, the ancient county town of Surrey, is an obvious base for travellers interested in exploring Surrey.

Farnham Castle

Guildford has been the capital of the region since pre-Norman times and the remains of Henry II's castle and keep provide commanding views over the surrounding area. The old Georgian cobbled High Street, incorporates the Tudor Guildhall, with its distinctive gilded clock. Woking like many Surrey towns was transformed by the arrival of the railway in the 19th century. The Victorian influence is evident in many of the larger houses built by Norman Shaw and other proponents of the Arts and Crafts style. The more ornate style of Victorian architecture, designed to reflect the prosperity of a confident imperial power, is also represented in the two massive buildings funded by Thomas Holloway, the Royal Holloway College and the Holloway Sanatorium, which are near Egham in the north. The best of Edwardian architecture is well represented throughout Surrey by the work of Sir Edwin Lutyens, often working in partnership with the eminent gardener Gertrude Jekyll.

Canal Barges, nr Godalming

This varied architectural heritage belies the notion that Surrey is nothing more than a collection of anonymous suburbs of London. Much of Surrey is indeed the capital's commuter belt and conurbations like Kingston and Croydon spread out into a vast hinterland of suburbia. However around Guildford and Dorking and near the Sussex border there are small towns and wayside villages amid rough Down and Weald uplands or thickly wooded hillsides. The countryside is varied, from the well-maintained plantation of Kew Gardens, possibly the most famous gardens in the world, to numerous parks, greens, heaths, commons and open land. Rich farming areas give way to expanses of heath and woodlands with networks of paths for walkers and cyclists. The famous Hog's Back section of the A31 is one of the most scenic drives in the Southeast, with excellent views north and south as it follows the ridge between Farnham and Guildford through some of Surrey's most unspoilt countryside.

Outwood Post Mill

LOCATOR MAP

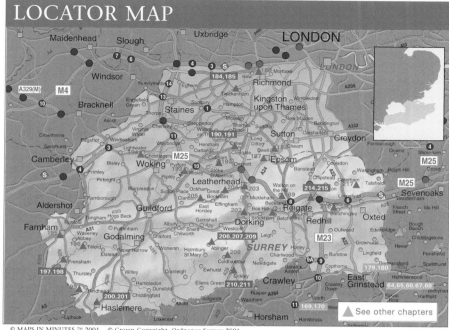

Maidenhead Slough Uxbridge **LONDON**

Windsor Richmond Kew Mortlake LONDON A205

A329(M) M4 Bracknell Englefield Green Egham Twickenham 184,185 Kingston upon Thames Wimbledon A232

Crowthorne Sandhurst Ascot Virginia Water Chertsey Staines Sunbury Hampton Moseley New Malden Sutton Beddington Croydon

Camberley Bisley Woking Byfleet M25 Weybridge Hersham Esher Ditton Cheam Epsom Banstead Coulsdon Warlingham Biggin Hill M25

Aldershot Farnborough Worplesdon Guildford Effingham Box Hill Reigate Redhill Oxted M25 Sevenoaks Westerham Ide Hill

Farnham Godalming Shalford Albury Shere Gomshall Westcott Dorking 206,207,209 Leigh **SURREY** M23 Oxted

Haslemere Thursley Witley Cranleigh Ewhurst Ockley 210,211 Crawley East Grinstead 64,65,66,67,68

Horsham Handcross See other chapters

© MAPS IN MINUTES ™ 2001   © Crown Copyright, Ordnance Survey 2001

ADVERTISERS AND PLACES OF INTEREST

NORTHEAST SURREY

Surrey's proximity to London often leads people to assume that it is nothing more than a collection of anonymous suburbs extending south and west from the capital. Indeed much of what had originally been - and which steadfastly continues to consider itself - Surrey was absorbed by London in the boundary changes of 1965. Growing conurbations such as Kingston and Croydon house and employ thousands. Rail lines and major roads fan through the area from London.

However this northeast corner of Surrey is full of historical traces, some well known and others truly hidden gems. Great houses, as well as royal and episcopal palaces, were built here from medieval times, and many villages have evidence of Saxon, Celtic, Roman and even late Stone Age settlements. The countryside is varied, from the well-maintained plantation of Kew Gardens to the rough Down and Weald uplands to the south and numerous parks, greens, heaths, commons and open land in between. The sound of birdsong ringing through the woods or the click of a cricket bat on a village green are as much a part of this stretch of Surrey as the whirring suburban lawnmower.

KINGSTON

The first impression most people have of Kingston is of high-rise office blocks and its famous by-pass, giving it the sense of being totally urbanised and something of a modern creation. However Kingston has been a thriving market town since the Middle Ages, the first of only four Royal Boroughs in England and Wales. In 838 AD it was referred to as 'that famous place called Cyningestun in the region of Surrey'. **The Guildhall**, built in 1935, is solid and functional, but nearby beside the 12th century Clattern Bridge over the River Hogsmill stands the Coronation Stone, said to have been used in the crowning of up to seven Saxon kings. Records show that Kingston was a prosperous town in Anglo-Saxon times. In the Domesday survey of 1086 it is recorded as having a church, five mills and three salmon fisheries.

Kingston has been a river crossing place since medieval times, the present stone bridge replacing the old wooden bridges in 1828. Regular street markets have been held on a site by the bridge since the 17th century, and around the market a well-preserved medieval street plan can be explored. Kingston parish church was completely rebuilt in neo-Gothic style in the 19th century, but its interior still contains many medieval monuments. On the London Road, however, is a real medieval relic - the chapel of **St Mary Magdalene**, dating from the 14th century.

Guided walks of Kingston's historical heritage start from the Market Place every Sunday in summer.

The district of **Coombe**, to the east of Kingston, was rebuilt by prosperous Victorians. Large houses, built in a variety of architectural styles, came to symbolise the solid financial standing of their owners. Unfortunately, few of these houses survive apart from their impressive gate lodges, but there are a few exceptions such as Coombe Pines in Warren Cutting.

John Galsworthy began the development of Coombe Hill, and two of his own houses survive - Coombe Leigh, which is now a convent, and Coombe Ridge, today a school. Galsworthy's son was the famous novelist and set Soames Forsyte's house in Coombe.

AROUND KINGSTON

Twickenham
4 miles N of Kingston on the A310

Lying on the west side of the Thames just a few miles north of Hampton Court Palace, Twickenham is a thriving community that makes the most of its riverside setting. Perhaps more than anything else Twickenham is renowned as the headquarters of Rugby Union Football in Britain, a role it has played since 1907. The recently rebuilt stadium plays host to England home internationals as well as the annual Varsity match between Oxford and Cambridge. The **Museum of Rugby** allows visitors to savour the history and atmosphere of the sport (see panel below). Running through the players tunnel is enough to get many people's blood rushing, and the museum provides a full account of Twickenham right up to its latest renovations.

Montpelier Row and Sion Row, wonderfully preserved 18th century terraces, are some of the fine old houses in the heart of Twickenham. At **Strawberry Hill**, just to the south of Twickenham, is the villa bought by the author Horace Walpole in 1749 and remodelled into a 'gothic fantasy', which has been described as "part church, castle, monastery or mansion". It is internationally recognised as the first substantial building of the gothic revival. Strawberry Hill is now St Mary's University College, a teachers' training college, but it is open for pre-booked tours on Sundays in summer. Those eager to pursue other historical associations from that era can find the tomb of the poet Alexander Pope in the Twickenham churchyard.

Orleans House and Gallery, which houses one of the finest art collections outside of London's national collections, enjoys an enviable location in a woodland garden on the Riverside between Twickenham and Richmond (see panel on page 290).

On the opposite riverbank, accessible by passenger ferry for most of the year, is **Ham House**, built in 1610, and then enlarged in the 1670s. Now in the hands of the National Trust, Ham's lavish Restoration interiors and magnificent collection of Baroque furniture provide a

THE MUSEUM OF RUGBY

Twickenham Stadium, Rugby Road,
Twickenham, TW1 1DZ
Tel: 0181 892 8877
Fax: 0181 892 2817
website: www.rfu.com

Few would dispute that sport has an appeal that crosses gender, age and racial barriers. But few people would connect the thrills and spills of top level competition with the standard museum environment.

How can a museum compete with drama, excitement and appeal of live sport? The answer is simple: today's sports museums with their hands on exhibits and interactive screens and sounds are more than just testaments to facts and figures, but living breathing ways of connecting with the unrivalled excitement that only sport can provide

You can find out all about rugby, its history and its star players by visiting **The Museum of Rugby**, Twickenham. The word's finest collection of rugby memorabilia is housed at the Museum of Rugby, which takes visitors through the history of the sport from 1823 to the present day. The Museum also offers fans a tour of Britain 's most famous Rugby Stadium.

ORLEANS HOUSE GALLERY

Riverside, Twickenham, Middlesex, TW1 3DJ
Tel: 020 8892 0221 Fax: 020 8744 0501
e-mail: galleryinfo@richmond.gov.uk
website: www.richmond.gov.uk/depts/opps/eal/leisure/arts/orleanshouse

Sheltered within six acres of natural woodland overlooking the Thames stands **Orleans House Gallery**, the principal public art gallery for the Borough of Richmond.

This choice setting, beside one of the loveliest curves of the River Thames, inspired James Johnston, Joint Secretary of State for Scotland under King William III, to have a stately home built here. The architect was John James, who later rebuilt Twickenham Parish Church. The Octagon, originally designed as a garden pavilion, was added to the house in 1720 in honour of a visit by Queen Caroline.

The House acquired its present name from its most famous resident, Louis Philippe, Duc d'Orleans, later French King, who lived here from 1815 until 1817 during his exile from France. Most of Orleans House was demolished in 1926 and 1927 but the Octagon and two wings were saved by the Hon. Mrs Levy, later the Hon. Mrs Ionides. The property, along with the Ionides' collection of paintings and prints of the locality, were bequeathed to the local Borough on her death in 1962 to become a public gallery.

The gallery hosts an innovative range of contemporary and historical temporary exhibitions in the main and Stables Gallery, and cares for the prestigious Richmond Borough Art Collection of over 2,000 works, which are displayed on a regular basis. Education is central to work at the gallery, and the gallery frequently runs activities during term time and holidays for a range of ages.

Admission: Free. Open Tuesday - Saturday; 1.00 - 5.30pm, Sunday; 2.00 - 5.30pm (April November), closes at 4.30pm (December March)

suitable setting for the popular summer ghost walks. It has extensive grounds including lovely 17th century formal gardens. Next door is **Marble Hill House** a Palladian villa, designed by Roger Morris and completed in 1728 or 1729 for George II's mistress, Henrietta Howard. Visitors can walk in the 66 acres of riverside grounds, take a look at the furniture and paintings displayed in the house, or enjoy a cream tea in the café.

RICHMOND

5 miles N of Kingston on the A307

Richmond is an attractive shopping centre with the usual chain stores and a number of small specialist and antique shops. However the lovely riverside setting along a sweeping curve of the Thames and the extensive Richmond Park help to retain a strong sense of its rich and varied history.

A good place to get acquainted with old Richmond is **Richmond Green**, a genuine village green, flanked on the southwest and southeast edges by handsome 17th and 18th century houses. The southwest side has an older, and more royal, history. It was the site of Richmond Palace, built in the 12th century and passing into royal possession in 1125, when it was known as Shene Palace. The palace was destroyed by Richard II in 1394 but subsequent kings had it rebuilt in stages. The site, right by the green, made it an ideal spot for organising jousting tournaments. The rebuilding and extensions reached their peak under Henry VII, who renamed the palace after his Yorkshire earldom. Elizabeth I died in the palace in 1603. Sadly the only surviving element of the palace is the brick gatehouse beside the village green.

Just off the northeast flank of the green is the **Richmond Theatre**, an imposing Victorian building with an elaborate frontage facing the street. It is a showcase for excellent theatrical productions. The combination of the repertoire and the lovely setting attracts a number of renowned actors.

Richmond Riverside, a redevelopment scheme dating from the late 1980s, stretches along the Thames. It comprises pastiche Georgian buildings complete with columns, cupolas and facades and includes houses, offices and commercial premises. Among the modern buildings, however, there remain a few of the original Georgian and Victorian houses, including the narrow, three-storey Heron House, where Lady Hamilton and her daughter Horatia came to live soon after the Battle of Trafalgar. The riverside walk ends at Richmond Bridge, a handsome five-arched structure built of Portland stone in 1777 and widened in the 1930s. It is the oldest extant bridge spanning the Thames in London.

Richmond's Old Town Hall, set somewhat back from the new developments at Richmond Bridge, is the home of the **Museum of Richmond**, a fascinating privately run museum which provides a unique perspective on

Flambeau

111 Kew Road, Richmond, Surrey, TW9 2PN
Tel: 020 8948 4571 Fax: 020 8948 4614

Chris Harding opened his Richmond showroom in December 2000 after 16 years of trading in Hove. Its impressive large glass exterior has a distinctive black frontage on Richmond Circus at the beginning of Key Road. Inside **Flambeau** there's a light airy, well-lit showroom with soft classical music playing in the background.

The business reflects Chris's long-term interest in marble and granite fireplaces. He can supply and fit all manner of high quality fireplaces. In the showroom are examples of traditional, antique and contemporary fireplaces. Mostly they are constructed from natural stone, marble and granite. Chris can also supply gas fires, with a coal, log or pebble effect, the latter being very popular amongst discerning younger clients. As a specialist in restoration of fireplaces Chris can also assist with applications for a Heritage Restoration Grant, which can make up to £500,000 available for selected listed properties.

Visitors to Flambeau are likely to find Chris sitting amidst a collection of antiques as he sells some fabulous objets d'art. The selection is constantly changing but could include exquisitely decorated inlaid trunks, urns and vases. He usually has a number of large mirrors, including wall mounted and overmantle. There's Venetian lighting, overhead and table lamps and a variety of occasional furniture, which could include pine Victorian blanket chests, hallstands and tables and maybe even a massive four poster bed. He's even had an ancient brass telescope mounted on a sturdy wooden tripod.

Richmond's history and special significance in English life. The Museum's permanent displays chronicle the story of Richmond, Ham, Petersham and Kew - communities that grew and prospered along the Thames downstream from Hampton Court. The collections of the Museum of Richmond concentrate on different aspects of this history, detailing the rich heritage from prehistoric times through to the present.

Special features and detailed models focus on some of the most noteworthy buildings, such as the Charterhouse of Shene, which was the largest Carthusian Monastery in England. The information about Richmond Palace is a bit of English history in microcosm. Built by Henry VII - and like the town named after his Yorkshire Earldom in 1501 - the Palace was later a favourite home of Elizabeth I.

A number of displays concentrate on the luminaries who have made Richmond their home over the years. Among the roll call of the great and the good are Sir Robert Walpole, Sir Joshua Reynolds, Lady Emma Hamilton, George Eliot, Virginia Woolf, Gustav Holst and Bertrand Russell.

The steep climb of Richmond Hill leads southwards and upwards from the centre of Richmond. The view from Richmond Terrace has been protected by an Act of Parliament since 1902. The Thames lies below, sweeping in majestic curves to the west through wooded countryside. Turner and Reynolds are among the many artists who have tried to capture the essence of this scene, which takes in six counties. A little further up the hill is the entrance to Richmond Park. This 2,400 acres of open land, with deer roaming free, was first enclosed by Charles I as a hunting ground. Set amidst this coppiced woodland are several landscaped plantations noted for their azaleas and rhododendrons.

KEW AND KEW GARDENS
7 miles N of Kingston off the A310

Kew, lying just a couple of miles North of Richmond, on a pleasant stretch of the Thames, is a charming 18th century village, favoured by the early Hanoverian kings. They built a new palace here and the handsome 18th century houses, which still surround Kew Green, were built to accommodate the great and the good around of the royal circle. The **Public Record Office** in Kew holds the national archive, 900 years of historical records, including the Domesday Book. The painter Thomas Gainsborough is buried in **Kew Church**.

However, Kew is best known for the **Royal Botanic Gardens**, arguably the most famous gardens in the world. Princess Augusta, mother of George III, laid out an eight acre botanical garden on the grounds of Kew Palace in 1759. Tranquil and spacious, this garden, now extending over 300 acres, has become an important botanical research centre. Over a million visitors a year are attracted to view the 40,000 species of plants and 9,000 trees which grow here in plantations and glasshouses. The most famous and oldest glasshouse, built in 1848, is the Palm House, which houses most of the known palm species. Nearby is the Water Lily House, full of tropical vines and creepers overhanging its lily pond. The Prince of Wales Conservatory, which opened in 1987, houses plants from ten different climatic zones, from arid desert to tropical rainforest.

Kew houses Britain's smallest royal residence. The three-storey Kew Palace built in 1631, sometimes nicknamed the Dutch House because of its Flemish-bond brickwork, measures only 50 feet by 70 feet. Queen Caroline acquired it for her daughters in 1730. The only king to have lived in this tiny royal residence was George III, confined here from 1802 during his infamous madness. Behind the palace is a restored 17ᵗʰ century garden, with labels identifying the herbs and their uses.

Another Kew landmark is the octagonal, 10 storey **Chinese Pagoda** standing 163 feet high. Originally, the building was flanked by the Turkish Mosque and the Alhambra, all designed by Sir William Chambers, Princess Augusta's official architect. The ground floor is 50 feet across, with each storey reducing in size until the tenth storey is 20 feet by 10 feet. Built as an exotic folly in the fashion of the times, it now serves a more practical purpose as a landmark for visitors.

MORTLAKE
7 miles N of Kingston on the A205

Mortlake is best known as the finishing point of the Oxford and Cambridge Boat Race. Although it was once an attractive riverside village, it is now dominated by the large brewery building. However a series of handsome 18ᵗʰ century houses stand along Thames Bank, towards Chiswick Bridge and the famous Victorian explorer Richard Burton is buried in an unusual tent-shaped tomb in the cemetery.

WIMBLEDON
3 miles E of Kingston on the A219

To most people Wimbledon is synonymous with the **All-England Lawn Tennis Championships** held each year at the end of June and in early July. However, the grounds of the All England Lawn Tennis and Croquet Club are open throughout the year and the Wimbledon Lawn Tennis Museum has a range of exhibits from the languid era of long flannel trousers to sweaty tie-breaks and disputed line calls. However there is more to Wimbledon than tennis. In fact, the Championship fortnight is a time to

avoid Wimbledon, since tennis fans throng the streets and every route in and out is clogged with traffic.

The centre of Wimbledon is a thriving commercial area, with stores lining the High Street. Here, cheek by jowl with anonymous 1960s buildings, are a few gems. Eagle House, just west of the National Westminster bank building, was built in 1613. Its Jacobean appearance, with three large bay windows by its central entrance, still conveys a harmonious grandeur, which in its day would have dominated its neighbours. From Wimbledon itself, Wimbledon High Street climbs steeply to the west towards Wimbledon Village, which has more of a boutique and bistro feel to it. Handsome residential streets lead off the High Street on its climb, and there are expansive views looking east across South London.

Further above Wimbledon Village is **Wimbledon Common**, covering more than 1,000 acres, criss-crossed by walking and riding trails and providing one of the capital's largest areas of public access. At the southwest corner is an Iron Age mound, called **Caesar's Camp**, although it is not Roman, but dates from around 250 BC. Archaeological evidence indicates that people have occupied this area since the paleolithic era, some 3,000 years ago. However it did not become common land with legal public right of access until the Wimbledon and Putney Commons Act of 1871, after local residents opposed Earl Spencer's intention to enclose it.

NEW MALDEN
2 miles S of Kingston on the A2043

Just a few miles east of Hampton Court and just south of both Richmond Park and Wimbledon Common is New Malden. Excellent road and rail connections link this neat suburb with Central London as well as points south.

New Malden makes a good base for exploring the nearby sights, particularly easy by public transport, avoiding traffic and parking problems.

There are a few surprises lurking in this corner of suburbia. Just by the church on Church Road is the red-brick Manor House, dating from the late 17th century. Further along, to the northeast, is a duck pond, flanked by the Plough Inn. This pub seems modern but its core was built more than 500 years ago.

SURBITON

1 mile S of Kingston on the A307

Surbiton is a well-heeled suburb adjoining Kingston, which escapes much of the traffic and commercial build-up that bedevils its northern neighbour. Handsome properties and good transport connections to London and the south coast make Surbiton one of the most desirable locations in the London commuter belt. Surbiton was called Kingston New Town and Kingston-on-Railway as it developed in the early 19th century. Most of the public buildings date from this period and the architecture of churches such as St Andrew and St Matthew are good examples of the Gothic Revival that was so dominant at the time.

The A307 follows the course of the Thames through Surbiton, with lovely views of Hampton Court Park on the opposite bank of the river. Hampton Court Palace is just over a mile away from Surbiton.

KINGSTON TO CROYDON

CHEAM

5 miles E of Kingston on the A217

Roughly equidistant between Kingston and Croydon, Cheam is one of the prettier suburbs of this area, retaining a green and leafy feel, largely due to the number of substantial houses with large gardens. Several houses in Cheam open their gardens as part of the National Gardens Scheme Charitable Trust.

As with so many other parts of Surrey where London has encroached, Cheam has lost much of its overtly medieval elements, but careful detective work can lead to some pleasant surprises. St Dunstan Church, built in the 1860s, is a large and uninspiring Victorian building but its courtyard contains the surviving portion of the medieval parish church - the **Lumley Chapel**, which was the chancel of the old church. The roof inside was remodelled in 1582 by Lord Lumley, who also commissioned the three finely carved marble and alabaster tombs. A series of delightful and well-preserved brasses commemorates Cheam notables from the 15th and 16th centuries.

Whitehall is a timber framed building built around 1500. The history of the house and of those who lived in it over its 500 years is chronicled within.

CARSHALTON

6 miles E of Kingston on the A232

The heart of old Carshalton is clustered around two ornamental ponds, which were created in the 18th century from the old mill pond and an adjoining area of wet land. The Portland Stone bridge was probably designed by the Italian architect Giacomo Leoni for Thomas Scawen, who owned nearby Stone Court. Part of his estate, remains as Grove Park, bought by the council in the 1920s 'to preserve it as an open space ... and to obtain control of the beautiful ornamental waters which form such an attractive centre to the area'. Around this area are several fine old houses with grounds that are open to the public.

One of them, **Carshalton House**, now

Saint Philomena's School, was finished in 1713 for Sir John Fellowes, a governor of the South Sea Company. The house is imposing, especially when first seen on the road from Sutton. It is a solid affair of red and yellow brick standing two storeys high, with an attic storey above the cornice. The harmonious, yet restrained look of the house is exactly the effect that so appealed to architects at the time of Queen Anne. The porch, built about 50 years later, with its Corinthian columns reflects a renewed love of classical embellishment. Outside is an impressive early 18th century water tower, which blends in with the architecture of the main house. It housed a water-powered pump, which lifted water from the river into a cistern, which fed the house.

Honeywood, now the **Honeywood Heritage Centre**, stands beside the upper pond. The original building is 17th century but was considerably extended at the turn of the century. Inside it is furnished in Edwardian style including the paint colours and has displays on local history including stucco and pottery from Nonsuch Palace.

Two miles south of Carshalton, on the downs, is a public park with some majestic trees. These formed part of the grounds of a stately home, The Mansion, which was destroyed in an air raid in 1944. It was the home of the 12th Earl of Derby, founder of the famous horse race that bears his name.

BEDDINGTON
7 miles E of Kingston off the A235

Croydon Airport, which was located east of Beddington village, closed down in 1959, leaving room for the development of several housing estates, which tend to dominate the village. However, traces of Beddington's past are visible in its church, St Mary, a large building, which

was probably begun in the 11th century. The local landowner, Sir Nicholas Carew, left money for rebuilding the church in the late 14th century, and the **Carew Chapel** bears his name. He, along with many of his descendants, is commemorated in brasses in this chapel and in the chancel of the church. One of the most attractive later additions is the organ gallery, built in 1869. The player's space is screened like a minstrel's gallery.

CROYDON
9 miles E of Kingston on the A23

Looking at the high-rise flats and offices, one-way systems and traffic lights, it is hard to imagine that Croydon was not much more than a large village less than two centuries ago. That historic past seems to have been obliterated in a headlong rush to development.

Yet, as with so many other large British towns, first impressions can be deceiving. Nestling beneath some of the most modern high-rises are some much older buildings, including some brick almshouses built in 1599 and now overshadowed by their modern neighbours. More intriguingly, and certainly worth seeking out, are the remains of the palace that was the summer residence of the Archbishops of Canterbury. The palace was built in the 11th century by Archbishop Lanfranc. It was considerably altered and expanded in subsequent centuries but remained an official residence until 1757. **The Palace** is now part of the Old Palace School for girls but the public can see some of the oldest surviving elements, including the Norman undercroft and the 15th century banqueting hall.

St John the Baptist Church is the largest parish church in Surrey, with a two-storey porch and fine tower. Its enormous size puts it in a league with St Mary Redcliffe in Bristol and St Martin in

HORTON COUNTRY PARK

The Ranger Service, Epsom & Ewell Borough Council, Town Hall, The Parade, Epsom KT18 5BY
Ranger Service   01372 741191   Horton Children's Farm   01372 743984
Equus Equestrian Centre   01372 743084   Horton Country Club   020 8393 8400

Horton Country Park is a rural landscape of fields, hedgerows, woods and ponds of great wildlife and historical interest. This range of habitats supports wildlife which is numerous and varied including many trees and flowers, a plethora of insects, many birds including the Park's emblem, the green woodpecker, and also mammals such as deer, foxes, and water voles.

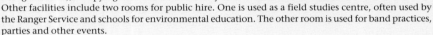

Good tracks and horse rides, most with gentle or no gradient, allow you to explore the Country Park, and many of the hard surfaced rides follow the route of the old Horton Light Railway.

There is also a children's farm, Equus Equestrian Centre, and the Horton Park Country Club (with an 18 hole golf course), occupying sites within the Country Park. Other facilities include two rooms for public hire. One is used as a field studies centre, often used by the Ranger Service and schools for environmental education. The other room is used for band practices, parties and other events.

Salisbury. The 15th century church burnt down in 1867 but was rebuilt by 1870 on the old foundations in a style that largely matches the earlier church. Some original elements of the medieval church remain in the restored tower and the south porch.

Croydon also has a handsome arts complex, the **Fairfield Halls**, which flank one edge of a modern flower-filled square in the heart of Croydon. It comprises a main concert hall, the Peggy Ashcroft Theatre, the Arnhem Art gallery and a general-purpose lounge which doubles as a banqueting hall. **Waddon Caves**, along Alton Road, were the site of late Stone Age and Iron Age settlements, which were inhabited until the 3rd or 4th century AD.

EPSOM

The old market and spa town of Epsom is a prosperous residential centre which lies on the edge of London's southwestern suburbs. In the early 17th century, it was observed that cattle were refusing to drink from a spring on the common above the town and subsequent tests revealed the water to be high in magnesium sulphate, a mineral believed to have highly beneficial medicinal properties. As the fashion for "taking the waters" grew towards the end of the century, wealthy people from London came in increasing numbers to sample the benefits of Epsom salts and the settlement grew from a small village to a town with its own street market, a charter for which was granted in 1685.

By the end of the 18th century, the popularity of Epsom's spa was on the decline, but by this time, the town's pleasant rural location within easy reach of the City of London was already starting to attract well-to-do business people; a number of substantial residential homes were built in and around the town during this period, several of which survive to this day. A lively street market continues to be held every Saturday in **Epsom High Street**, a wide and impressive thoroughfare, which contains some noteworthy old buildings, including a **Victorian clock tower**.

Epsom's other main claim to fame is as a horse racing centre. Each year in early June, the Downs to the southeast of the town take on a carnival atmosphere as tens of thousands of racing enthusiasts come to experience the annual Classic race meeting and the colourful fun fair, which accompanies it. Informal horse racing took place on **Epsom Downs** as long ago as 1683 when Charles II is said to have been in attendance. Racing was formalised in 1779 when a party of aristocratic sportsmen led by Lord Derby established a race for three year old fillies which was named after the Derbys' family home at Banstead, the Oaks; this was followed a year later by a race for all three year olds, the **Derby**, which was named after the founder himself, although only after he won a toss of a coin with the race's co-founder, Sir Charles Bunbury. (Had Lord Derby lost, the race would have become known as the Bunbury.) The Oaks and the Derby were a great success and soon achieved classic status along with the St Leger at Doncaster, the earliest to be established in 1776, and the 1,000 Guineas and 2,000 Guineas at Newmarket, established in 1814 and 1809 respectively.

AROUND EPSOM

EWELL
2 miles N of Epsom on the A240

It comes as something of a surprise to find shades of Xanadu in this leafy town lying just north of Epsom. **Nonsuch Park** is a reminder of a grand plan that Henry VIII had to build the finest palace in Christendom. The magnificent Nonsuch Palace was almost finished at Henry's death. Unfortunately it was demolished in 1682 and all that remains is the fine park, which surrounded it, noble in stature and perspective but singularly lacking its intended focal point.

A few other historical attractions make Ewell worth visiting. There is an ancient spring, which was discovered in the 17th century. The 18th century **Watch House**, on Church Street, was once the village lock-up. It is shaped like a small cube, with two narrow doorways under an arch. Its mean and spartan appearance alone must have deterred would-be felons.

Ewell Castle, now a school, is not a medieval fortification. It was completed in 1814 in what was known as the Gothic style. Crenellated and stuccoed, it gives the appearance of a real castle, but the effect is somewhat lessened by its location so close to the road. In addition **Bourne Hall Museum** is well worth a visit (see panel opposite).

BOURNE HALL MUSEUM

Spring Street, Ewell, Surrey KT17 1UF.

If you visit Ewell village, you will soon find **Bourne Hall**. Overshadowed by the trees of a Victorian park, it is a low lying, circular modern building. For the 1960s, when it was built, this was a revolutionary design. Entering Bourne Hall, you look up to the brightly lit mezzanine floor to see a museum. The galleries, which are open plan, have displays drawing on a collection of over 5,000 items acquired over the years through the generosity of local people. After your visit, you can enjoy lunch or a coffee in the newly refurbished restaurant next to the museum.

BANSTEAD

3 miles E of Epsom on the A217

Banstead is one of the many small towns of Surrey that alert travellers from London that they are entering the real countryside. With the expansion of the Southeast, particularly since the last war, new suburbs have emerged and even towns that were themselves once suburbs have now created their own ring of smaller satellites.

Banstead is one of the exceptions to this creeping urbanisation, and the Green Belt Act of 1938 has helped it retain much of its original country feel. It stands at the edge of the rolling green downs that provide ideal riding country. The high street has its fair share of nationally known outlets, but there is still a sense of local flavour and pride in its locally run firms.

All Saints Church is a small, flint and stone parish church, which was built in the late 12th century and early 13th century. It has a squat appearance, with a low, broad tower and a shingled spire. Like many Surrey churches it was renovated in the 19th century. In this case the Victorian intervention was restrained, and the church now looks much as it must have in the late Middle Ages. Just north of the church is the circular Well, with its large roof. The Well had formed something of a focal point in medieval times.

The Downs near Banstead are ideal for rambling. Traces of late Stone Age huts were found on the Downs, and the **Galley Hills** are formed by four bowl barrows from that same period.

CHIPSTEAD

7 miles E of Epsom on the A23

A mixture of architectural styles give Chipstead an unusual appearance, as it constitutes a mixture of Victorian model village combined with a few older houses

DIANE FRANCE ANTIQUES

43 Walton Street, Walton on the Hill, KT20 7RR
Tel: 01737 813147

Diane France and her husband Glenn were born in Surrey. They both have a long standing interest in collectables and antiques and are widely travelled. They decided to put all their knowledge and experience to good use and opened their shop, **Diane France Antiques**, in September 2001. Parts of this main street shop are very old indeed, dating back as far as the 16th century. It's a small shop and although full of

interesting and unusual things, they are well displayed and the clever lighting gives a spacious and uncluttered feel.

Diane and Glenn specialise in furniture and ceramics and are constantly changing the items on display. Beautiful dark wood bookcases with glass fronts, Georgian chests of drawers and exquisite, marble topped, Victorian wash stands are just a selection of items that regularly appear. Visitors may also find pine cabinets, mahogany and early English oak furniture. The ceramics include some collectable Doulton ware. There is a good collection of pictures and mirrors also on display.

and a good measure of suburban development. Some handsome cottages border a crossroads and there is a pretty ornamental pond in the centre. For a taste of real Victoriana though, it is worth making a short detour about half a mile south to view **Shabden**, a mansion built in the French Renaissance style but with a large timber porch added. The overall effect is a jarring mixture of styles that contrives to make an unattractive house out of potentially attractive ideas.

COULSDON
7 miles E of Epsom on the A23

Coulsdon is a pretty village that has managed to keep recent housing developments - notably Coulsdon Woods - discreetly removed from the traditional centre. There are pretty cottages in the heart of the village and some of the more substantial farmhouses nearby can be traced to the 15th century. **St John the Evangelist Church**, on the corner of the village green, was built in the late 13th century. The tower and spire were built more than 200 years later but the interior has some well-preserved elements from the original church. Most notable of these is the sedilla, with its circular piers and pointed arches. A sedilla was a seat for (usually three) priests and always located on the south side of the chancel.

The countryside around Coulsdon has more than its share of history. Traces of a 2nd century AD Romano-British settlement have been found on the ridge along **Farthing Down**, and 14 barrows on the ridge are the evidence of a 6th century Saxon burial ground. A number of iron knives, swords and other weapons have been dug from the site. Coulsdon Common, on the way to Caterham, is a tranquil and largely undeveloped spot. Since Saxon times it has been common land given over to grazing, its soil deemed too poor for cultivation.

The **Downlands Circular Walk** conveniently begins and ends at The Fox, an attractive pub which faces Coulsdon Common.

CHALDON
8 miles E of Epsom off the A23

It is well worth making the detour to Chaldon, two and a half miles to the west of Caterham, to have a look at the 11th century church of St Peter and St Paul which stands within striking distance of the old Pilgrim's Way. An unassuming flint-built structure with little to commend it (other than, perhaps, its south tower and shingled spire), the interior contains one of the most outstanding medieval wall paintings still in existence in Britain. Executed in creamy white on a deep red-ochre background, the mural covers the entire west wall of the church. It is believed to have been painted around 1200, but was covered over during the Reformation and remained undiscovered until 1870. The "Chaldon Doom", as it has become known, depicts gory scenes from the Last Judgement; a "Ladder of Salvation" can be seen reaching up to the Kingdom of Heaven from purgatory, a place where horrific punishments are meted out by fork-wielding devils to those guilty of having committed the Seven Deadly Sins. Realistic looking cauldrons, manned by infernal kitchen staff, await the wicked.

CATERHAM
8 miles E of Epsom on the B2031

The route into Caterham town centre from the south passes close to Foster Down, a section of the North Downs Way, which incorporates the impressive **Tupwood Viewpoint**; good views can also be enjoyed from the nearby 778 feet Gravelly Hill.

Caterham itself is a modern and prosperous residential town, which at first glance seems to have little to offer the casual visitor. On the other hand, the town is something of a time capsule. Until 1856 Caterham was a remote Downs village. The arrival of the railway in that year changed everything and the town developed around it and the barracks, which were built in the 1870s. The railway was never extended, so Caterham is a terminus rather than a through station. As such, the 19th century town plan remains unchanged. Near Caterham Railway Station is the **East Surrey Museum** in Stafford Road, which offers an interesting insight into the natural history and archaeology of the surrounding area as well as a collection of objects, which recall the area's rural past.

WARLINGHAM

8 miles E of Epsom on the B269

Successful enforcement of Green Belt policy since the Second World War has helped Warlingham retain much of its green and leafy look, and it is hard to imagine that it lies just a few miles south of bustling Croydon and its built-up suburbs. Warlingham's real fame stems from its church, All Saints, or more specifically two historic events that took place in it. The new English prayer book, authorised by Edward VI, was first used in the parish church. Its compiler, Archbishop Cranmer, attended the service. Four centuries later Warlingham parish church was chosen to host Britain's first televised church service. The church itself was restored and enlarged in Victorian times but dates from the 13th century. It still contains many old elements, including a 15th century wall painting of Saint Christopher and a 15th century octagonal font.

Modern housing has replaced most of the traditional cottages in the heart of Warlingham but there are a few survivors from past centuries. The **Atwood Almshouses**, a two-storey cottage flanked by single-storey cottages, were built in 1663. The vicarage, nearby, was built in the same year.

TATSFIELD

10 miles E of Epsom off the B269

Tatsfield, high up on the Downs, is something of a curiosity as well as a testament to the enduring power of hyperbole in advertising. In the 1920s a group of small, unassuming cottages sprang up in the wooded landscape just north of the old village green. The verdant setting, combined with the hilly location, led to a promotional campaign urging prospective house buyer to "Come to London Alps".

South of the green is St Mary, the parish church which dates from about 1300. It stands on its own, commanding panoramic views south over the Weald.

WALTON ON THE HILL

5 miles S of Epsom off the A217

The "Hill" referred to in the name of this village is one of the many rolling hills that comprise the North Downs. Travellers heading south from London have a real sense of space by the time they reach Walton, and the upland farms strengthen this impression. Buildings - both residential and commercial - have the harmonious red brick look so typical of this part of Surrey. They were built mainly in the Victorian era, but some of the earlier buildings were constructed from flint, hanging tile and weather-boarding.

Walton Manor is a good example of the tile-hung style and it was built in the 1890s. Its appearance shows the influence of the decorative Arts and Crafts movement, typified by architects such as Norman Shaw. Embedded in one end, however, are the walls of a stone-built manor house of the 14th century; a two storey hall and chapel protrude from the east of the house.

The view south from the centre takes in the extent of the Downs, with the North Downs Way - the traditional **Pilgrim's Way** to Canterbury - running along the ridge on the other side of the broad valley. In the foreground are the rolling grounds of the championship golf course.

NORTH SURREY

The Thames winds through Surrey to the north of Weybridge and many of the present-day villages and towns developed as riverside trading centres in the medieval period or earlier. Romans marched through this part of Surrey during their conquest of Britain, possibly following the trail of the Celts who were already ensconced there. Saxons left their mark later, bequeathing a number of place names, which duly entered the Domesday Book in the 11th century. The most impressive of all buildings along this - and perhaps any - stretch of the Thames is Hampton Court. Here England's most larger than life monarch acquired and substantially expanded Cardinal Wolsey's palace until it was fit to match his own personality.

The human mark is much in evidence on this landscape, and for every area of suburban sprawl there also seems to be a corresponding architectural gem. It might be a sensitively preserved church, as in Thorpe, or even an unlikely high street survivor such as the Salvation Army Youth Centre in Sunbury-on-Thames, the newest incarnation of an impressive mansion.

Just as the Thames led to the development of medieval and earlier villages, so too did the arrival of the railway in the mid-19th century. New villages sprang up, while others expanded out of all recognition. The 20th century's contribution to the regional transport theme is the M25, which provides the western and southern border for the area covered in this chapter.

Relatively compact, yet full of interesting detail and constant surprises, this north-central section of the county is a microcosm of Surrey itself.

WEYBRIDGE

Although in many people's minds the epitome of a comfortable and modern commuter belt settlement, Weybridge is a surprisingly long-established settlement. The town takes its name from the bridge over the River Wey on the highway to Chertsey, and there is evidence of such a bridge existing as early as 1235. Tradition also links Weybridge with Julius Caesar, and many historians believe he crossed the Thames near here in 55 BC.

The town once possessed a palace, **Oatlands Park**, in which Henry VIII married his fifth wife, Catherine Howard, in 1540; 110 years later, the building was demolished and the stone used in the construction of the Wey Navigation. Weybridge stands at the northern end of this historic inland waterway, which was one of the first examples of its kind when it was completed in 1670. It extends for almost 20 miles southwards to Godalming and incorporates large sections of the main river.

The middle of the 17th century, during the interregnum, also saw a remarkable development in Weybridge. **The Diggers**, a radical left-wing group, attempted to build a commune on St George's Hill, although they were thwarted by angry commoners.

Elmbridge Museum, situated in the library in Church Street, is an excellent source of information about the history - and prehistory - of Weybridge. A wide range of exhibits takes in archaeological artefacts, old maps, photographs and paintings of the district. The costume collection is particularly interesting, as it consists of clothes worn by local residents from the late 18th century to the present day.

In 1907, the worlds first purpose-built motor racing track was constructed on the **Brooklands** estate near Weybridge, and in the years which followed, this legendary banked circuit hosted competitions between some of the most formidable racing cars ever made. The Campbell Circuit was designed by record breaking driver Malcolm Campbell in the 1930s. With the outbreak of World War II however, racing came to an end; the track fell into disrepair and Brooklands never again regained its once-pre-eminent position in British motor racing.

In recent years, the circuit has undergone something of a revival with the opening of the **Brooklands Museum**, a fascinating establishment centred on the old Edwardian clubhouse, now restored to its pre-war elegance. There is a collection of the famous cars which raced here, and archive film and memorabilia of the circuit's hey day. Bicycles also raced on this circuit and a display of Raleigh bicycles and accessories charts the company's story from its inception in 1886 to the present day. The Wellington Hangar, built across the finishing straight of the track, houses a collection of Brooklands built aircraft including a World War II Vickers Wellington, salvaged from Loch Ness and carefully restored.

AROUND WEYBRIDGE

WALTON-ON-THAMES
2 miles NE of Weybridge on the A244

Standing almost directly opposite Shepperton on the other side of the Thames is Walton-on-Thames. This unassuming London suburb has a surprisingly long and varied pedigree. As with many of the riverside communities along this stretch of the Thames, Walton has a claim to be the site where Julius Caesar forded the Thames during his second invasion of Britain. Hard archaeological evidence for this claim is scant, but there is ample proof that there was a settlement here during the Saxon period. Walton appears as "Waletona" in the Domesday Book when the town was recorded as having a church, a fishery and two mills.

In 1516 Henry VIII granted the residents two fairs a year, and these continued until 1878. Walton's relations with Henry were ambivalent. However, in 1538, Walton along with surrounding communities, became incorporated with Henry VIII's Chase of Hampton Court, into what amounted to a private royal hunting preserve. Walton was outside the perimeter fence but it was forced to comply with forest law, which had a detrimental effect on cultivation. Luckily for the residents of Walton, this arrangement was discontinued when Henry died.

Until 1750 the Thames could only be crossed by ferry or ford, but in that year the first bridge was built. This original structure, a wooden toll bridge built by Samuel Dicker, was replaced by several other bridges until the present iron bridge one was built in 1864.

The part-Norman **Church of St Mary** stands on the highest point of the town. It contains a remarkable memorial to

Richard Boyle, the Viscount Shannon, which was sculpted by Louis Roubiliac in the mid 18th century.

In Manor Road is the handsome and imposing **Manor House** of Walton Leigh, a timber-framed brick building that dates from the medieval period. Old records indicate that John Bradshaw, President of the Court that sentenced Charles I to death, lodged here.

EAST & WEST MOLESEY

3 miles NE of Weybridge on the B369

Molesey can trace its history to the 7th century, when grants of land were made to Chertsey Abbey. Among the abbey's estates was "Muleseg", which meant Mul's field or meadow. The identity of Mul is lost in the mists of time, but his name is commemorated in two riverside communities.

The prefixes east and west, relating to Molesey, were not used until the beginning of the 13th century. In the Domesday Survey Molesey was recorded as comprising three manors tenanted by knights who had arrived with William the Conqueror. East Molesey was originally part of the parish of Kingston upon Thames but its growing independence led to its separation from Kingston under a Special Act in 1769.

East Molesey's location just opposite Hampton Court Palace provided a valuable source of income for residents, and ferries did good business until the first bridge spanned the Thames in 1753. The Bell Inn, one of the loveliest inns in Surrey, dates from the 16th century, right at the beginning of Molesey's links with Hampton Court. Matham Manor, about four centuries old, is another link with the past. The Old Manor House, although handsome and impressive, is something of a misnomer. It originally served as the parish workhouse and was never a manor.

West Molesey is a continuation of East Molesey. It is much larger than its parent, but it occupies an even prettier stretch of the Thames. The parish church stands on a site where there has been a church since the 12th century. The present church is largely a legacy of the Victorian era, although the 15th century tower remains. Inside are some other artefacts from the medieval era, including the piscina. The piscina is a small basin in a wall niche by the altar and was used for cleaning sacramental vessels.

Molesey Hurst, a low, open stretch of land, lies along the Thames in the north of the parish. The land was once used for sporting activities such as archery, cricket, golf and even illicit duelling. It can also claim a cricketing "first". It was here, in 1795, that a player was first given out leg-before-wicket.

HAMPTON COURT

4 miles NE of Weybridge on the A309

Hampton Court Palace occupies a stretch of the Thames some 13 miles southwest of London. In 1514 Thomas Wolsey, the Archbishop of York took a 99-year lease on the buildings at Hampton Court. Wolsey created a magnificent residence with new kitchens, courtyards, lodgings, galleries and gardens. Until 1528 Wolsey maintained Hampton Court as his home as well as for affairs of state. However at that point he had fallen from favour with Henry VIII, and found himself forced to appease the monarch by giving him his house. Henry comprehensively rebuilt and extended the palace over the following ten years to accommodate his wives, children and court attendants. Although much of Henry VIII's building work has been demolished over the years, the Great Hall and the Chapel Royal survive, the latter still in use as a place of worship. The Great Hall, which Henry had completed in 1534, having forced the builders to work night and day, has mounted stag heads and fine tapestries lining the walls beneath the intricate hammerbeam roof. It was the scene of theatrical productions during the reigns of Elizabeth I and James I, and among the performing troupes was that of William Shakespeare. Also intact are the the enormous Tudor Kitchens, with the huge fireplaces and assortment of ancient cooking utensils that would have been used in the 16th century to prepare a feast fit for a king. During the 17th century the Stuart kings lived there both as monarchs and prisoners. James I enjoyed the hunting in the park, while Charles I, was imprisoned here after the Civil War. Charles II built accommodation for his mistress at the south-east corner of the palace.

Approached through Trophy Gate, Hampton Court gives a first impression of grandeur and scale. The courtyards and buildings to the left still contain a number of "grace and favour" apartments, where Crown officials and dependants of the Royal family live. Two side turrets contain terracotta roundels with the images of Roman emperors, which date from Wolsey's time. Anne Boleyn's gateway, opposite Base Court, is carved with the initials H and A, for Henry and Anne. The many courtyards and cloisters cover six acres in a mixture of Tudor and Baroque styles, with fascinating curiosities such as Henry VIII's Astronomical Clock.

William III and Mary II made the first major alterations to the palace since Tudor times. They commissioned Sir Christopher Wren to rebuild the king's and queen's apartments on the south and east sides of the palace, although the queen's apartments were left unfinished at the queen's death. King William III's Apartments remain one of the most magnificent examples of Baroque state

apartments in the world. Almost destroyed in a terrible fire in 1986, there followed an ambitious restoration project which returned the apartments to the way they were when they were completed for William III in 1700. They can now be seen in their original glory, still furnished with the fine furniture and tapestries of 1700. An exhibition under the colonnade in Clock Court near the entrance to the King's Apartments details the history of the state rooms including the restoration.

The grand Queen's Staircase leads to the Queen's Guard Chamber. The Queen's state rooms run along the east wing of Fountain Court, and include the Queen's Drawing Room and the Queen's Bedroom. The Queen's Gallery contains ornate marble fireplaces with mantelpieces decorated with images of doves and Venus. Gobelins tapestries, on the theme of Alexander the Great, hang from the walls. Life-sized marble guardsmen flank the main chimneypiece. Hampton Court Palace contains a large part of the Royal Collection of art works, including many 16th 17th and early 18th century pieces.

There are over 60 acres of gardens to explore at Hampton Court including the Great Vine and the newly restored Privy Garden. Shrubberies that were allowed to grow in the Privy Garden in the 19th century have been removed to reveal the ancient formal beds and pathways. An exhibition on the East Front tells the story of the gardens and explains the restoration of the Privy Garden, opened in 1995. From the Privy Garden you can visit William III's magnificent Banqueting House and the Lower Orangery where Andrea Mantegna's *Triumphs of Caesar* are displayed. The Broad Walk runs from the Thames for half a mile past the east front and is lined with herbaceous borders. Just off the walk to the left and inside is the

Tudor Tennis Court, a Real Tennis court built by Henry VIII, who was a keen player. To the north of the Palace is the famous Maze, planted in 1714 within William III's "Wilderness" of evergreen trees. **The Maze** is extremely popular and can be surprisingly difficult to negotiate. Be warned.

THAMES DITTON

4 miles E of Weybridge on the A309

Thames Ditton is one of the two Dittons that lie along the Thames south of Hampton Court. The name probably derives from the "dictun", or farm by the dyke, and there were already a Saxon church and five manors in the area at the time of the Domesday Book. The heart of Thames Ditton dates mainly from the 19th century, but the harmonious blend of red brick and occasional black-timbered buildings along the High Street helps put visitors in mind of the town's earlier history.

A flower-decked path leads to **St Nicholas' Church**, which was first mentioned in the 12th century - roughly the time when Ditton was divided into two parishes. The building is of flint and stone and the interior contains a font decorated with mysterious motifs that still puzzle historians.

Thames Ditton benefited from its proximity to Hampton Court Palace and the church contains the grave of Cuthnert Blakeden, "Serjeant of the confectionary to King Henry the Eighth".

LONG DITTON

5 miles E of Weybridge on the A309

There is a peculiar lack of logic in the naming of the two Dittons; Thames Ditton is actually longer than Long Ditton but this more easterly village has a longer history than its neighbour. St Mary's Church, in the heart of Long Ditton, is a relative newcomer, having

been built in 1880 but it stands close to the site of a Saxon church built long before the Dittons separated into two parishes.

Long Ditton is a scattered parish, with only a few vestiges left of its extensive history. Much of its history, however, can be gleaned from a close look inside St Mary's. The interior of the church features monuments to the Evelyn family, who put Long Ditton on the map in the 16th and 17th centuries. George Evelyn, grandfather of the famous diarist John Evelyn, acquired the local manor in the late 16th century and then set about establishing gunpowder mills in the area. Business for gunpowder was booming, so to speak, in this turbulent period and the Evelyns amassed a huge fortune, eventually spreading their business further afield within Surrey.

OATLANDS

1 mile E of Weybridge on the B374

"The land where oats were grown" gave its name to the Tudor palace in Oatlands Park. This was already an established residence when Henry VIII forced its owner to cede him the title in 1538. Henry was in a rush to build a palace for his new queen, Anne of Cleves, although Ann never lived at Oatlands. However, the palace did become the home of subsequent monarchs, including Elizabeth I, James I and Charles I. In fact it was Charles who is said to have planted the proud cedar tree that stands beside the drive of what is now the Oatlands Park Hotel; he was celebrating the birth of his son, Prince Henry of Oatlands.

HERSHAM

2 miles E of Weybridge on the A307

Anglo-Saxons were the likeliest first settlers of Hersham, although prehistoric flint tools have been found on what is now Southwood Farm. In the 12th century the village was spelt Haverichesham and probably pronounced "Haverick's Ham". Two major events have shaped Hersham's history. The first occurred in 1529 when Henry VIII acquired Hampton Court from Cardinal Wolsey. Henry decided that his new estate lacked one of its necessities - a deer park - so he set about buying adjacent land and encircling the area with a perimeter fence. Other villages, such as Weybridge and Esher, were on the edge of the park and escaped being enclosed, but Hersham was not so lucky. Not surprisingly, Hersham had a well-developed anti-royalist streak by the time of the Civil War and one of Cromwell's prominent aides, Captain John Inwood, lived there.

Politics and warfare apart, Hersham continued largely untouched by the outside world until the 19th century. Until 1804, when it was enclosed by Act of Parliament, much of the land around Hersham Green was open heathland. The arrival of the railway in 1838 led to a huge rise in Hersham's population. Development accompanied this boom and much of Hersham's original appearance was altered completely. Local residents, however, would not let the process rip the heart out of their village and Hersham Green was actually enlarged in 1878. Despite extensive redevelopment of the centre in 1985, the charm of the village has been maintained in many of the older buildings around the village green. The village green is still used for a variety of local functions including a popular **Summer Fayre** with traditional entertainment.

CLAYGATE
4 miles E of Weybridge off the A3

Standing on a rich geological seam where dense London clay meets Bagshot sand, Claygate is well named. For many years this rich earth provided a living for many

local men, who would have to bear the brunt of jibes from neighbouring villagers about working in the Claygate "treacle mines". Taunts notwithstanding, Claygate did supply the raw material for countless bricks and fireplaces.

Claygate can trace its origins to the Saxon times when it was a manor within the parish of Thames Ditton. In the early Medieval period the estate passed into the ownership of Westminster Abbey, which retained possession until Henry VIII dissolved the monasteries. Henry simply added it to his estates in Hampton Court.

Constrained for centuries by monastic, then royal control, Claygate remained largely unchanged as a tiny community until the 19th century. In 1838, however, **Claygate Common** was enclosed, enabling residents to enlarge the village considerably. One of the first orders of business was to erect their own church, Holy Trinity, to save the two-mile walk to Thames Ditton.

Ruxley Towers is an interesting building that dates from around the same period. It has a Gothic tower, built in 1830 and is decorated with a frightening display of gargoyles.

ESHER
4 miles E of Weybridge off the A3

Esher's recorded history goes back to Anglo-Saxon times. During the reign of Henry VIII, Hampton Court dominated all the surrounding manors including Esher. The railway arrived in Esher during the 19th century, after which it quickly became a popular residential area for wealthy city businessmen.

Esher is well known as the home of **Sandown Park**, the world class race course, where horse racing is staged all year round. Created in 1875 by Sir Wilfred Brett, it soon attracted all the great and good of the racing world including the royal family.

The part 16th century St George's church has an unusual three-tier pulpit and a marble monument to Princess Charlotte of Wales who died at nearby Claremont House in 1817. The part of Surrey nearest to London is well supplied with racecourses: as well as at Kempton Park, near Sunbury, and at the classic course at Epsom, regular meetings are also held at Sandown Park on Esher's northern edge.

Near here, and well worth a visit is the beautiful National Trust-owned **Claremont Landscape Garden**, which lies on the southern side of the A307 Portsmouth road within a mile of the town centre. Begun in the 1715, this is believed to be one of the earliest surviving examples of an English landscape garden. Later in the century, it was remodelled by William Kent whose work was continued by Capability Brown. Over the years some of the

greatest names in garden history including Sir John Vanbrugh and Charles Bridgeman have been involved in its creation. The grounds have been designed to include a number of striking vistas and contain a grassed amphitheatre, grotto, lake and an island with a pavilion. Nearby Claremont House operates as a school and is only occasionally open to visitors. It was designed in the 1700s by Vanbrugh and substantially remodelled in 1772 for Clive of India.

COBHAM

4 miles SE of Weybridge off the A3

Cobham, now a busy residential town, with densely settled residential streets, is found in the Domesday book as 'Coveham'. However, it does possess some fine period buildings, which dominate a bend of the River Mole on the southeastern side of Cobham. An

GARSONS

Thomson Bros. (Esher) Ltd, Garson Farm, Winterdown Rd, West End, Esher, Surrey KT10 8LS
Tel: 01372 462261 Fax: 01372 460960
e-mail: peter@garson-farm.co.uk website: www.garsons.co.uk

Peter Thomson is the fifth generation in charge of this long established family business a few minutes drive from the centre of Esher. One of the largest garden centres in this part of Surrey, **Garsons** stocks quality and traditional foods, original gifts and garden supplies. Most of the fruit and vegetable produce is harvested by pick-your-own visitors. After their exertions they can then relax and enjoy home-style cooking in the Conservatory Restaurant.

ATIKA

87 High Street, Esher, Surrey KT10 9QA
Tel: 01372 470074 Fax: 01372 470074

Katia Smith, Carol Isle and Monica Doublet are three women who stock an incredible range of old and antique furniture in **Atika**, an interesting and unusual High Street shop. Wardrobes, drawers, tables and chairs from Holland, Belgium, England and Eastern Europe are complemented by a range of hand-made candles, cushions, hand-made lights as well as picture frames, vases and mirrors. Atika also has an interesting selection of gifts including aluminium boxes, silk flowers and trinket boxes

PAINSHILL LANDSCAPE GARDEN

Portsmouth Road, Cobham, Surrey KT11 1JE
Tel: 01932 868113 Fax: 01932 868001
Enquiries: 01932 864674
e-mail: info@painshill.co.uk website: www.painshill.co.uk

This once barren heathland was transformed by the celebrated plantsman and designer, the Hon Charles Hamilton, into one of Europe's finest 18th Century landscape gardens. **Painshill** was one of the earliest ' Naturalistic' gardens ever created, Hamilton conjured up a mysterious and magical place in which to wander- the equivalent of a 20th century theme park where fashionable society could wander through a landscape theatre, moving from scene to scene. Staged around a huge serpentine lake with surprises at every turn. A Gothic Temple, Chinese Bridge, Ruined Abbey, a Grotto, Turkish Tent, Gothic Tower and the most magnificent waterwheel all disappear and reappear as the walk proceeds.

But Hamilton eventually ran out of money and to discharge his debts sold the estate in 1773. Since then it has been in the possession of many owners but was eventually fragmented and sold off in

lots in 1948 and the gardens, which had been well maintained for nigh on two centuries, were allowed to deteriorate. By 1981 they lay derelict and overgrown and it seemed that what had been a national treasure would be lost for all time. However Elmbridge Borough Council, conscious of the importance of Painshill, purchased 158 acres and formed the Painshill Park Trust with a view to restoring the gardens and opening them to the public. The subsequent ongoing restoration has been one of the great success stories of garden conservation. Most of the principal features of the garden are open for viewing and the restored planting

schemes are steadily maturing. The restoration has been a slow process. It's not simply a matter of clearing undergrowth and repairing features. Lots of detailed and painstaking research is required. Archaeological excavation, documentary research and the identification and dating of trees, tree stumps and historic paths. From this, detailed plans and maps are created to show what the estate would have looked like in the 18th century and all the later stages to the present day.

Now there are a variety of walks which allow visitors to explore Hamilton's idyll. The historic circuit is a signposted two-mile long route that an 18th century visitor would have followed to view all the attractions of the garden. A shorter path round the lake passes delights such as the ruined abbey, boat house and crosses the Chinese bridge. A vineyard flourished at Painshill from 1740 to 1812. This has

been replanted with Pinot noir, Chardonnay and Seyval blanc grapes and once again wine is being produced at Painshill. Painshill is not allowed to call their sparkling white wine champagne but when Charles Hamilton was making wine here in the 18th century the French ambassador of the day, mistook Hamilton's product for the champagne of his native land. In a tribute to the man who made it all possible, the Painshill trust have named the new visitor centre restaurant Hamilton's. It's open from early morning serving breakfasts, coffee, light lunches and splendid afternoon teas. The shop is a cornucopia for present and souvenir buyers containing everything from trugs and dibbers to umbrellas, food, china, books, honey and beeswax candles and, of course, Painshill wine. Open April - October: Tuesday to Sunday and Bank Holidays 10.30am - 6.00pm (lasy entry 4.30pm); November - March: Tuesday to Thursday, Saturday, Sunday and Bank Holidays 11.00am - 4.00pm (last entry 3.00pm). Closed Christmas Day and Boxing Day.

impressive 19th century water mill stands on the site of earlier mills dating back to the middle ages. The red brick building has now been restored to full working order. Cobham is also home to the **Cobham Bus Museum**, which houses the largest collection of London buses in the world.

Cedar House, built in the mid-18th century, is a solid and well-proportioned brick building, which actually

Painshill Park

changes height halfway along its front. To the rear is a medieval section, which includes a large tracery window. Built somewhat earlier in the18th century is Ham Manor, with a mansard roof and an impressive Italianite decrease. About a mile north of Cobham is **Foxwarren Park**, a bizarre house with eerie gables and multi-coloured bricks. It was built in 1860, and contemporary Victorian architects were known to introduce a bit of macabre humour into some of their designs. In this case it is hard to decide whether the intended effect was self-mocking or whether the gloomy appearance conformed to the owner's tastes.

One mile west of Cobham is **Painshill Park**, a white 18th century house with a fine setting on a hill. The house is impressive but Painshill is more noted for its grounds (see panel opposite), which were laid out by the Hon. Charles Hamilton, son of the Earl of Abercorn, in the 1740s. These grounds were a talking point in the mid-18th century and were praised by luminaries such as Horace Walpole. Hamilton had let his imagination conjure up a series of landscapes and ornaments that created a profoundly Romantic atmosphere. An ornamental lake lay in front of a Gothic

brick abbey, while on an island in the lake were various tufa sculptures and perpendicular cliffs leading down to the water. Hamilton even built a hermitage, and then went one stage further by installing a hermit in it. The mounting catalogue of expenses took its toll on Hamilton, however, and he eventually went bankrupt. Although many of the features in the grounds are gone it remains an amazing spectacle. The walk around the lake, takes in a Gothic temple, Chinese bridge, a ruined abbey, a Turkish tent, and a waterwheel. The planting at Painshill makes it a gardener's delight as it changes with the seasons. The landscape is enhanced by cedars and original 18th century plantings, including tiers of shrubs, flowerbeds and a vineyard.

OXSHOTT

4 miles SE of Weybridge off the A3

Taking its name from the Old English for "Occa's Wood", Oxshott's history as a settlement stretches back thousands of years. A flint found on **Oxshott Heath** is believed to date back to 8000 B.C., making it the oldest tool ever discovered in the area. Another fascinating find in **Oxshott Woods**, now displayed in the British Museum is an intricately carved

Anglo-Saxon bronze brooch of the early tenth century. Oxshott remained a small hamlet set in woods and heather until the 1880s, when the completion of the Surbiton to Guildford Railway ushered in an era of growth and development. Some stretches of woodland have withstood the tide of new roads and houses, notably Oxshott Heath and Princes Coverts, which is a woodland owned by the Crown Estate. In the middle of Princes Coverts is a square red-brick building which was erected in the 18th century over a medicinal spring known as **"Jessop's Well"**. The mineral content of the spring water was said to compare with that of Cheltenham, but despite the Royal connection and the salubrious waters, Oxshott somehow never achieved true spa status.

Perhaps Oxshott was considered a bit too dissipated because for many years it was mildly notorious for having two public houses but no church. This imbalance between sacred and profane was partly offset in 1912, when St Andrew's Church was erected.

STOKE D'ABERNON
5 miles SE of Weybridge off the A3

Like Cobham, the northern part of Stoke d'Abernon is undistinguished; however, the older southern part, which reaches down to the River Mole, contains a fine mid 18th century part-Palladian, part-baroque manor house and an exceptional parish church, which is believed to be among the oldest in the country.

The south wall of **St Mary's Church** is believed to date back to the days of St Augustine in the 7th century, and indeed it has been found to contain brickwork and cornices belonging to a Roman structure, which once stood on the site. There are also traces of an early Saxon lord's gallery and one of the oldest monumental brasses in Britain, that of

Sir John d'Abernon who was buried in 1277. The church, with its wonderful mixture of styles is part-medieval with the magnificent walnut pulpit dating back to the early 17th century.

About half a mile south of Stoke d'Abernon is **Slyfield Manor**, which was built in the 17th century but incorporated a late medieval timber-frame building. Garden walls, with original archways, blend with the painstaking brickwork of the house to create an effect that reminds many visitors of the work of Inigo Jones, particularly in Covent Garden.

WHITELEY VILLAGE
2 miles SE of Weybridge on the B365

A mile and a half to the southwest of Weybridge, and close to the St George's Hill residential area much-favoured by famous media personalities, lies the remarkable Whiteley Village. This unique 230 acre model village was founded on the instructions of the proprietor of a famous Bayswater department store, William Whiteley, who was shot in 1907. He left one million pounds in his will to house the elderly poor. The charitable community was designed to be entirely self-contained with its own churches, hospital and shops, and was laid out in an octagonal pattern around a green containing a memorial to the project's benefactor. The buildings are Grade II listed and of great architectural interest. The site has been planted with a great many trees and flowering shrubs, and is at its best in late-spring and summer. It is a private estate and not open to the public.

CHERTSEY
3 miles NW of Weybridge on the A320

Chertsey is an ancient riverside town, which has altered almost beyond recognition over the centuries. The town once boasted a formidable abbey, whose influence stretched over a wide area of southern England. When it was demolished following the Dissolution of the Monasteries, its stone was used to build Hampton Court Palace and later, the River Wey Canal.

One of the abbey bells now hangs in the parish church, St Peter; at one time it was used to sound the evening curfew and it is associated with a local romantic legend concerning Blanche Heriot, a young Chertsey woman who, on hearing that her lover was to be executed at the sound of the curfew bell, climbed into the tower and clung onto the tongue until his pardon arrived. This heroic action was commemorated in the ballad *"The Curfew Must Not Ring Tonight"* by the American poet Rose Hartwick Thorpe.

Chertsey Museum, housed in a fine Regency building, near the Thames, has a large collection of items of both local and national interest including a 10th century Viking sword and a fascinating costume display exploring 300 years of high fashion. (This museum is likely to be closed for a year for extension and renovation from April 2002 to April 2003.)

Despite the upheavals that Chertsey has undergone, it still manages to preserve some lovely woodland scenery, with a number of green fields and commons including Chertsey Mead. A well-proportioned, seven arched bridge spans the River Thames in the centre of the town.

THORPE

6 miles NW of Weybridge off the M25

Many of the streets in Thorpe are walled, screening residential buildings and small parks, and planning authorities succeeded in preserving this feature - unique in Surrey - despite a postwar building boom. There are some ancient

elements in St Mary Church, including a plain 12th century chancel arch. An 18th century monument to Elizabeth Townsend features a praying cherub. On closer inspection this cherub has an unusual, almost Mongol appearance - an effect that was something of a trademark of its designer, Sir Robert Taylor. Old brick cottages line Church Approach. Some of the larger buildings in Thorpe betray its farming background. Spelthorne St Mary, on Coldharbour Lane, is a solid 18th century residence with a half-timbered barn dating from a century earlier. The Village Hall, to the east of Church Approach, was converted from a 17th century brick barn.

SHEPPERTON

3 miles N of Weybridge on the B376

Over the centuries Shepperton has capitalised on its strategic riverside location, and today's thriving market town is testimony to the entrepreneurial spirit of previous generations. It grew from its origins as a straggling collection of homesteads to become a bustling way station for west-bound traffic from London. This status was firmly established by the 15th century, and many of the lovely houses around the Church Square Conservation Area date from that period, or shortly afterwards.

This century brought a new wave of development, as the famous **Shepperton Film Studios** were built in the 1930s. Handy for London's Airport, first at Croydon then at Heathrow, Shepperton presented itself as an ideal site for a film venture. International stars were collected from their transatlantic flights or from their Mayfair flats. Moreover, Shepperton's position at the edge of the Green Belt meant that "rural" location shots could be managed just a few miles from the studios themselves. Recent films to made here include *Shakespeare in Love* and *Hilary and Jackie*.

STAINES

6 miles N of Weybridge on the A30

The ancient town of Staines stands at the point where the old Roman road from London to the South West crossed the Rivers Thames and Colne, and in the 17th and 18th centuries, it became an important staging point on the old coaching routes to the West Country. When walking beside the Thames, look out for the London Stone which was erected in 1285 to mark the boundary of the city's authority over the river. The old part of Staines contains some noteworthy buildings, including the part 17th century church of St Mary and the town hall built in Flemish-style on the Market Place.

The Spelthorne Museum, located in the old fire station of Staines, tells the story of Staines and its extensive history. Archaeological excavations in the 1970s confirmed that Staines stood on the site of the Roman settlement of Pontes.

The museum contains Iron Age and Roman artefacts and archaeological evidence as well as re-creations of life in Roman times, and provides a useful chronology for the successive riverside settlements on this site. There is a re-creation of a Victorian kitchen, a collection of brewing and bottling equipment and the Staines Linoleum display devoted to the company which first made linoleum.

The M25 to the south of Staines passes close to **Great Thorpe Park**, a 500 acre leisure park which has been built on an area of reclaimed gravel pits. The park incorporates a shire-horse centre, a series of historic reconstructions of life in ancient Britain, and a permanent theme park containing some of the latest roller coaster rides and fairground attractions.

LALEHAM

5 miles N of Weybridge on the B376

Located only a few miles from bustling Staines and only minutes north of the M3, Laleham sits on the banks of the Thames, with one of London's larger reservoirs backing onto it. A triangular green lies near the river, reached by Ferry Lane. It is a pretty village with many 18th and 19th century houses. Facing the green are a pair of early 18th century houses, **Muncaster House** and **The Coverts**.

Parts of All Saints Church at Laleham are 16th century but it is said to stand on the site of a Roman temple. **Laleham Riverside Park** was formerly the grounds of Laleham Abbey, which belonged to the Lucan family. Water understandably plays a large part in activities here, with boat hire available just a few hundred yards west of the trim Victorian centre.

LITTLETON

5 miles N of Weybridge on the B376

Littleton has undergone a number of dramatic changes in the last four decades and today it is hard to find much of the original village lying south of the huge reservoir serving the capital. New houses, car parks and a school have replaced what had been a harmonious medieval ensemble of church, rectory, manor farm and manor house.

Luckily, of this group the church remains intact. St Mary Magdalene is built of brick and dates back to the 13th century. The brick is a 16th century addition, the original nave and chancel had been made of ragstone and flint rubble. This modification constituted a decided visual improvement. The west tower was built at a later date; like the earlier modifications it is of brick, giving the church a cohesive appearance. Inside there are a number of curiosities, including a late medieval locker and a complete restored set of pews from that same period. The ornate choir stalls are said to have come from Winchester.

SUNBURY-ON-THAMES

3 miles N of Weybridge off the M3

With its high-rise office blocks and modern shopping precincts, today's Sunbury-on-Thames seems a far cry from its origins as a 10th century 'burgh' built by the Saxon Lord Sunna. However it developed as a medieval market town for a riverside district stretching from Chertsey all the way to Kingston and these bastions of commerce have simply kept in step with the passing of time. The local inhabitants seem happy enough to have retained the town's trading essence, even if it does mean that many of Sunbury's period buildings have long since been replaced.

A few of the town's period buildings remain, including the **Salvation Army Youth Centre**, which had been Sunbury Court, an 18th century mansion with Ionic decoration. A yew tree in the churchyard of the 18th century St Mary Church featured in 'Oliver Twist' by Charles Dickens. Between Sunbury Court and the church are some handsome Georgian residences.

NORTHWEST SURREY

The northwest corner of Surrey, lying to the west of the M25 and stretching westwards to the Berkshire and Hampshire borders and given a southern limit by the A3, shows the county's countryside coming into its own. Rich farming areas give way to expanses of heath and dotted woodlands, once the haunt of highwaymen but now safe for ramblers - as long as they steer clear of the well-marked military areas.

Woking is the principal town in this area, like many Surrey towns an established centre that was transformed by the arrival of the railway in the 19th century. The Victorian influence is strong throughout this part of Surrey, evident in many of the larger houses built by or under the auspices of Norman Shaw and other proponents of the Arts and Crafts style, which blossomed as a reaction against poor-quality, mass-produced building materials.

The more ornate style of Victorian architecture, which seemed to be the embodiment of a prosperous nation flexing its imperial muscle, is also represented in the two massive buildings funded by Thomas Holloway, the Royal Holloway College and the Holloway Sanatorium, which are near Egham in the north. That same northern extremity contains the site of one of England's defining moments, the signing of the Magna Carta in 1215 at the riverside meadow of Runnymede.

WOKING

Woking is a commuter town which lies on the main railway line to Waterloo. In fact it was the railway that defined the present appearance - and location - of Woking. The original village was what is now called Old Woking, and when the railway arrived in 1838 the station was built two miles away in what was then open heathland. The first residents drawn to Woking as a result of the railway were the dead. Brookwood Cemetery was opened to cope with London's problem of finding space to bury the dead. However, gradually the living were attracted and the town began to grow around the railway station and the original village centre dwindled. As a result, most of the heart of Woking dates from the middle of the 19th century.

Among these Victorian-era buildings, however, is an unexpected "first". The first purpose-built mosque to be founded in Britain - **Shah Jehan Mosque** - can be found in Woking's Oriental Street. The construction of this unusual onion-domed structure was largely financed by the ruler of the Indian state of Bhopal who visited the town in 1889. Woking was involved in another first, the beginnings of science fiction. H.G. Wells' Martians, in his 1898 novel *War of the Worlds*, landed on Horsell Common in Woking. The impressive Martian sculpture in the town centre was raised to commemorate the centenary of the book. Standing seven metres tall, the alien sculpture dominates its location. Even the paving around it is patterned to represent shock waves from the impact of the alien pod landing.

Old Woking is a former market town, which is now incorporated into the southeastern suburbs of its more modern neighbour. This is an old settlement, dating from the Saxon period and mentioned in the Domesday Book. Old Woking had the good fortune to be listed as a personal possession of the king and therefore it did not need to pay taxes. Its streets contain some noteworthy old buildings, including the 17th century old Manor House, and the part-Norman parish church of St Peter which has a late-medieval west tower.

AROUND WOKING

PYRFORD
1 mile E of Woking on the B382

Located roughly midway between Woking and Byfleet is Pyrford, which manages to retain many aspects of its village character despite being no more

---

RHS GARDEN WISLEY

Woking, Surrey, GU23 6QB
Tel: 01483 224234 Fax: 01483 211750
website: www.rhs.org.uk

The Royal Horticultural Society's garden at Wisley has 240 acres of beautiful and practical garden ideas. A gardener's paradise, the richly planted borders, luscious rose gardens and exotic glasshouses are a joy to wander through. But the garden also provides a test bed for countless cultivation methods and in a series of model gardens various growing conditions are applied. When the RHS was given Wisley in 1903, only a small part of the estate was cultivated as a garden, the remainder being woods and farmland. George Ferguson Wilson designed the original garden in 1878 as the 'Oakwood experimental garden' to try to grow difficult plants. Over the years as the garden expanded it has still remained true to the original concept.

Recent developments include the Walled Garden (West) planted with tender perennials, shrubs and climbers. The rich selection of plants from around the world has been chosen for their foliage. Cascades of water, streams and pools, terracotta pots and wrought iron work set against mellow York

paving add to the architectural planting. Wooden seating designed by Julian Chicester allows visitors to enjoy the sights and scents of this unusual garden. The Temperate Glass House has been recently re-organised with a section of dry bright conditions, a central section for temporary displays and the remaining part designed around a waterfall and pools with damp, shady conditions. A new feature for Wisley is a bonsai collection in a minimalist Japanese style garden. It is on the site of the former Garden for the Disabled and is easily accessible for wheelchairs.

Mill House, nr Newark Priory

were broken down for use in local buildings, although some of its features - including the east window - are said to have been taken to Ockham. Today only the walls of the south transept and those of the presbytery still stand, and visitors must use their imagination to work out where in the surrounding corn fields there might once have been the remainder of the monastic buildings.

than a couple of miles from its larger neighbours. It is set in meadows along the River Wey, with most of its original red-brick cottages still forming a core near the church. This parish church, the largely Norman **Church of St Nicholas**, has been preserved over the centuries without being the victim of intrusive restoration work. The south wall of the nave contains some unusual wall paintings of the Flagellation and Christ's Passion, which were painted around 1200. Research work carried out in the 1960s uncovered some even earlier murals beneath these paintings. The murals depict horsemen as well as a mysterious procession of men carrying staves.

About half a mile along the B367, to the south of Pyrford, is **Newark Priory**, an evocative ruin set in fields along the banks of the Wey. The priory was a house of Austin Canons who founded it in the 12th century. Like other monastic settlements it was a victim of the Dissolution under Henry VIII. Unlike others, however, it was never converted into a private residence. Instead its walls

WISLEY
3 miles E of Woking off the A3

The Royal Horticultural Society's internationally renowned **Wisley Garden** lies on the north side of the A3, one mile to the northwest of Ockham (see panel opposite). As well as containing a wide variety of trees, flowering shrubs and ornamental plants, this magnificent 250 acre garden incorporates the Society's experimental beds where scientific trials are conducted into new and existing plant varieties. Wisley also acts as a centre for training horticultural students, and offers a wide range of plants, books, gifts and gardening advice at its first-class plant centre and shop.

Wisley Gardens

RIPLEY

2 miles E of Woking off the A3

Just a mile or so to the southwest of Wisley is the attractive village of Ripley, a former staging post on the old coaching route between London and Portsmouth. The main street contains a number of exceptional brick and half-timbered buildings, including the charming Vintage Cottage with its unusual crown post roof.

Most of the attractive houses lie on the gracefully curving High Street. Unusually, the long and wedge-shaped village green lies beside the street on the west side. The village seems to have grown away from the green rather than around as in most English villages.

SUTTON PLACE

2 miles SE of Woking off the A3

Sutton Place was the creation of Sir Richard Weston, a protégé of Henry VIII who was a Knight of the Bath, a Gentleman of the Privy Chamber and eventually Under-Treasurer of England. He had accompanied Henry to France for the famous meeting at the Field of the Cloth of Gold in 1520, so in every respect he had the right to expect to live in sumptuous surroundings that reflected his high standing.

The house he had built, after receiving the grant of the Sutton estate in 1521, is seen by many critics as one of the most important English houses to be built in the years after Hampton Court was completed. It was built to describe almost a perfect square, with sides measuring about 130-140 feet surrounding a central courtyard. The north side was demolished in the 18th century, so today's house appears to comprise a two storey, red brick central building with two long projections.

Symmetry is important in **Sutton Place**, as English architects were busy putting to use the elements of the Italian Renaissance in their buildings. Doorways and windows are balanced in each wing.

The Italian influence is particularly evident in the terracotta ornamentation of the windows and even more dramatically in a series of terracotta panels depicting cherubs over the entrance. Terracotta had been first used as an architectural feature, mainly as faience, in Hampton Court in 1521. Sutton Court was built probably no more than a decade later - records show that Henry VIII was a guest in 1533 - so it was obviously at the forefront of this style of ornamentation. It is the exterior, with its strict adherence to Renaissance tenets, that makes Sutton Place so fascinating. Inside there have been alterations and additions that make the effect less wholly linked to one period.

Sir Geoffrey Jellicoe, the most renowned British landscape gardener of the century, partially completed visionary garden for Sutton Place's then owner, oil tycoon Stanley Seeger. Inspired by the philosophy of Carl Jung, Jellicoe created a series of symbolic gardens round the grand Elizabethan house. The most notable survival is the yew-enclosed garden which contains a vastly enlarged marble abstract 'wall' sculpture based on a small maquette by Ben Nicholson. The yew walk is breathtaking. The garden has been under the ownership of the Sutton Place Foundation for the last 13 years, during which several new gardens have been added by landscaper Paddy Bowe.

WORPLESDON

3 miles SW of Woking on the A322

Worplesdon retains a sense of its rural past in its setting on the edge of heaths, despite the threat posed by the expansion of Guildford which is just a couple of miles to the south. A number of brick houses dating from the early 18th century surround the triangular green, which is up on a hill. One of these houses displays a brick front, of around 1700, tacked on to a timber frame, creating an unusual effect.

St Mary's Church, standing above the village, was mentioned in the Domesday book. Although clumsily restored in the Victorian era, the oldest part is 11th century and it retains a number of interesting features from the medieval period. Chief among these is the late 15th century tower, which is compact and well-proportioned. At its base is a tower arch over an intricately carved door. The inner face has an inscription which reads "Richard Exfold made XIV fote of yis touor".

PIRBRIGHT

3 miles W of Woking on the A324

Pirbright is a village that is first recorded in 1166 as Perifrith, a compound of the two words "pyrige" (pear tree) and "fryth" (wooded country). It remained a hamlet of scattered homesteads until the 19th century when the railway's arrival in 1840 led to a boom in the population and a corresponding burgeoning of new construction.

Despite the rapid increase in the village population, and thanks also to the enlightened Green belt policies of this century, Pirbright has managed to keep most of its rural aspect. The huge village green, which forms its core is in fact a wedge of the surrounding heathland. Pirbright contains many listed buildings, including several medieval farmsteads. Information about these, as well as a selection of excellent walks, is contained in a lovingly produced booklet available from the vicarage.

Extensive colourful gardens, frequent winners of the Guildford in Bloom festival, surround The Royal Oak, an 18th century pub set by a stream in the heart of Pirbright. Altogether, the setting and relaxed atmosphere strengthen the feeling of being in a rural hideaway, although the village of Pirbright lies handily between Woking and Aldershot.

FARNBOROUGH

7 miles W of Woking off A331

Farnborough lies just over the border in Hampshire and although it is largely a commercial and shopping - rather than historical - centre, it is worth visiting for its links with Royal Aircraft Establishment. These ties are explained fully at the **RAMC** and **Royal Logistic Corps Museums**, which can also provide information about Farnborough's other claim to international fame, the annual Air Show.

FRIMLEY

7 miles W of Woking off the M3

Frimley is an extremely old village on the Hampshire border and a site of several important prehistoric and Roman finds which are displayed at the **Surrey Heath Museum** in Camberley. Much of the more recent history, unfortunately, has been less well preserved and the old sense of the village's coaching significance has been erased with a series of housing developments over the last four decades. The area around **Frimley Green**, however, gives some indication of what Frimley looked like in the late medieval period. Cross Farmhouse is one of the oldest surviving houses, its timber-frame and brick structure containing elements dating from the 15th century. The parish church of St Peter dates only from 1825 but its churchyard contains the graves of many famous people. Among them is Francis Bret Harte, the American novelist whose wanderings around the world led him to settle eventually in England.

Just south of Frimley, and also hugging the Hampshire border, is the village of **Mytchett**, which has also suffered from some unthinking urban planning.

The **Basingstoke Canal Visitors Centre**, which lies just east of Farnborough and only five minutes from the M3, offers a tranquil and relaxing way in which to discover the charming countryside. Visitors can take a leisurely trip on a narrowboat, gaining a fascinating insight into the points of interest from the informative guide. The Canal Exhibition provides an in-depth account of how barge skippers lived a century ago and how the Basingstoke Canal, and its wildlife habitats, have been conserved more recently.

CAMBERLEY

7 miles W of Woking off the M3

Prior to 1807, when the famous **Sandhurst Royal Military Academy** was relocated nearby, the substantial town of Camberley did not exist, and indeed its oldest part, the grid-patterned York Town, was constructed to house the academy's first instructors. (Lying just across the Berkshire border, Sandhurst Academy is set around a group of buildings designed in neoclassical style by James Wyatt.)

Although now resembling many other large towns with its High Street chains and modernised pubs, Camberley still displays much of the care and attention that marked its development in the mid-Victorian era. Unlike other towns, which sprang up willy-nilly, usually with the advent of the railway, Camberley had a measured growth and the town expanded along the lines of the grid shape of York Town. Shops and workers' houses predominated north of the

railway line while to the south were the larger houses of prosperous merchants set among stands of mature trees. These latter houses, many of which are good examples of the Arts and Crafts style of architect Norman Shaw and his followers, still stand although recent housing developments have encroached on much of the wooded areas.

The story of the development of Camberley and the surrounding area is well told at the **Surrey Heath Museum** on Knoll Road. Most of the exhibits have been designed to tell this story from a child's point of view, but adults will also enjoy seeing some of the curiosities and original documents from the 19th century. There are also displays on heathland crafts, the archaeology of the area and the notorious highwaymen who preyed on unwary travellers.

BISLEY

3 miles W of Woking on the A322

Surrounded by farmland and heaths, Bisley remains resolutely small-scale and unassuming. It is within easy reach of Camberley to the west and Woking to the east, but luckily much of the traffic comes in the form of ramblers who are equipped with the well-marked books of pub walks in the vicinity. Bisley's contribution to the pub supply is the Fox Inn, which stands opposite Snowdrop Farm, where a well-marked trail crosses the A322. Having crossed the A322, the trail cuts southwestwards across **Bisley Common**, where annual marksmanship competitions are held on the rifle ranges, past the pretty little Stafford Lake and into Sheet's Heath. Even making this short walk, which in fact is part of one of the longer "pub" trails, gives a good indication of the native landscape. Here the land is more or less in its natural state, with scrubby low bushes and bracken indicating why it was the more fertile soil east of the A322 that was more sought after for cultivation.

The attractive church of **St John the Baptist** likewise stands to the west of most houses in Bisley, giving it an almost lonely appearance. It is built of local sandstone with a short tiled spire topping its wooden tower.

LIGHTWATER

7 miles W of Woking off the M3

For many Londoners, Lightwater represents the first taste of countryside outside the metropolis. It has the advantage - from the visitor's point of view - of lying within easy reach of the M3. By turning south off the motorway, instead of north to Bagshot, drivers soon enter a countryside defined by heaths and scattered woodlands. Bagshot Heath, once a rough area peopled by highwaymen and duellists, begins at the western edge of Lightwater, and the village of **Donkey Town** lies just to the south, its name providing some confirmation of the area's rural nature.

Lightwater Country Park is over 57 hectares of countryside with two colour-coded trails guiding walkers across open areas of natural heath, and through pine and birch woodlands. There is also a Trim Trail fitness circuit set among pine woods. The steep climb to the summit of High Curley is rewarded by panoramic views of the surrounding countryside. Heathland Visitor Centre has a fascinating collection of exhibits about the history and natural history of this stretch of West Surrey countryside.

BAGSHOT

7 miles W of Woking on the A30

On the western edge of Surrey, on the Berkshire border lies the ancient village of Bagshot, which Daniel Defoe described

as "not only good for little but good for nothing". Bagshot today bears out Defoe's description, being built up with unimaginative suburban sprawl. However Bagshot village center and the Church Road area are now Conservation Areas. The village was on the main coaching route from London to the west and was a bustling post stop, catering for thousands of travellers every year. In 1997 two wall paintings, dating from the turn of the 17th century, were discovered in an old 14th century building. The paintings, which had been concealed behind wall panels, cover two walls and are now protected behind glass

WINDLESHAM

7 miles NW of Woking on the A30

Windlesham, lying in a setting of heath and meadow, is far prettier than its larger southern neighbour Bagshot. Victorian brick buildings - including some larger examples of the "prosperous merchant" variety - line the heath while the more fertile meadows obviously attracted earlier settlers. One of the most attractive houses in Windlesham is **Pound Cottage** on Pound Lane. This timber-framed, 17th century cottage has a lovely thatched roof, which comes down in hips to the ground floor ceiling. Like much of Surrey Heath, Windlesham was once part of Windsor Great Forest and developed as a traditional farming community centred around several manors and the church. Like Bagshot, Windlesham contains two conservation areas.

CHOBHAM

3 miles NW of Woking on the A3046

Enjoying a peaceful location just five minutes drive from Woking town centre is the attractive community of Chobham. The village is a Conservation Area and the High Street has developed

TENAKERS FARM SHOP

Scotts Grove road, Chobham, Woking, GU24 8DT
Tel: 01276 858637

This is a well-established business dating back to 1971. Present owner David Mould took over **Tenakers Farm Shop** in 1999. A Surrey man, born and bred, he has a long experience in horticulture. When he manages to get away from Tenakers he likes to unwind with a round or two of golf.

This is a typical farm shop with an excellent range of fresh fruit and vegetables and most important of all, a very friendly staff. Around the large and well-lit central aisle display, basket upon basket is piled high with fresh produce. This abundance of potatoes, onions, turnips, oranges, apples and lemons is locally grown, wherever possible.

Gardeners are well catered for with a wide variety of bedding plants, herbaceous plants and shrubs. They will also find all the usual gardening sundries in the nursery section. For those just looking for something to brighten up their homes or buy a gift there are always cut flowers, house plants, pots,

and vases to choose from and a selection of greetings cards to go along with them. Various seasonal items are on sale throughout the year like decorations at Christmas time and chocolate eggs at Easter. A chilled cabinet contains an excellent range of chilled foods and drinks, handy for those contemplating a picnic. If that's not enough there is the confectionary section, potato crisps and even bread. And just to ensure the family dog does not feel left out there is even food for dogs and other pets.

over the centuries into an attractive and generally harmonious stretch of buildings, the oldest dating back to the 16th century. The street itself curves up a hill, with the parish church of St Lawrence punctuating the row about halfway along. The original church was built in the 11th century but a restructuring in 1170 was the first of many alterations, including the tower, added around 1400, and the Victorian extension of the side aisle, that have left the church of St Lawrence more of an assembly of disparate elements than a harmonious whole.

VIRGINIA WATER

7 miles N of Woking on the A30

From Camberley, the A30 runs along the northeastern border of the county to Virginia Water, a surprising diversion, which lies in the heart of the Surrey stockbroker belt. The "water" referred to

is a mile and a half long artificial lake which is set within mature woodland at the southern end of **Windsor Great Park**; it was created by Paul and Thomas Sandby, two accomplished Georgian landscapers who were also known for their painting. The picturesque ruins standing at the lakeside are genuine remains of a Roman temple which once stood at Leptis Magna in Libya. **The Valley Gardens** also contain an unusual 100 foot totem pole which was erected here in 1958 to mark the centenary of British Columbia. A little further to the north, the Savill Garden is renowned as one of the finest woodland gardens in the country covering around 18 hectares. Begun by Eric Savill in 1932, it has continued to develop with various additions over the years, including herbaceous borders, a bog garden and a temperate glasshouse.

Holloway Sanatorium, now renamed

Crossland House, was designed by the Victorian architect W.H. Crossland for the eminent businessman and philanthropist Thomas Holloway. It was built to house middle-class people, afflicted with mental disease. Holloway Sanatorium looked to the continent for inspiration, to the architecture of Bruges and Ypres. The result was a brick and stone Gothic structure that stood as the epitome of high Victorian fashion, ironically constructed after the popularity of that overblown style had begun to ebb. This Grade I listed building had fallen into dereliction until 1998, when it was sensitively restored as part of a prize winning housing development at Virginia Park.

ENGLEFIELD GREEN

8 miles N of Woking on the A30

The green that gives Englefield Green its name is large and attractive, flanked by a number of interesting houses, including some several centuries old. The aptly named Old House dates from 1689, and most of it is a tribute to the red brick symmetry so beloved of that period. Next to it is **Englefield House**, built in the late 18th century. This is more of a curiosity, since it seems that the architect was unclear whether his brief called for something classical, neo-Gothic or Venetian. Castle Hill is the largest building around Englefield Green. Extended in the 19th century, the original 18th century building was a 'Gothic' structure, built for Sir John Elwell. When the common lands were enclosed in 1814, the green survived as open land on account of the wealth and influence of its surrounding residents.

EGHAM

8 miles N of Woking on the A30

Skirted by the River Thames and the historic fields of Runnymede, Egham is near a number of points of real interest. The centre of Egham is not particularly noteworthy, although the area by the Swan Hotel at the Staines Bridge, is attractive with a pretty row of old riverside cottages.

The Swan Sanctuary at Egham took over an area of disused land at Pooley Green in 1989 and consists of nursing ponds, rehabilitation lakes, and various facilities for cleaning and caring for injured swans. All birds are returned to the wild as soon as they are fit.

Between Egham and Englefield Green is one of Surrey's more memorable buildings, the **Royal Holloway College**. It is a huge Victorian building, modelled on the Chateau du Chambord in the Loire Valley in France. Opened by Queen Victoria in 1886, it was one of the first colleges for women in the country. Like the Holloway Sanatorium at Virginia Water, it was designed by W.H. Crossland for Thomas Holloway. Holloway's generous ideas on lodging - each student was allocated two rooms - dictated the enormous size of the building. In the form of a double quadrangle, it measures 550 feet in length and 376 feet across. Inside, the formal rooms include a remarkable library and a picture gallery, housing a collection of Victorian paintings by artists such as Millais, Landseer and Frith. Now part of the University of London, the college has a student population of over 4000 and male students have been admitted since 1965.

RUNNYMEDE

10 miles N of Woking on the A30

A meadow beside the River Thames to the north of Egham is where King John sealed the **Magna Carta** in 1215. The historic Runnymede Site and nearby Cooper's Hill are contained within a 300 acre tract of land which is now under the ownership of the National Trust.

Runnymede was an open space between the King's castle at Windsor and the camp of the rebel barons at Staines. The king was forced to agree to protect the barons from certain injustices but the important principle was established that the king, as well as his subjects, could be governed by the law.

The area contains three separate memorials: a domed neoclassical temple which was erected by the American Bar Association to commemorate the sealing of the world's first bill of democratic rights, a memorial to John F. Kennedy, and the **Air Forces Memorial**. Many come to see the memorial commemorating the men and women of the Commonwealth Air Forces killed in World War II, who have no known grave. From its position on Coopers Hill, above the river, it commands splendid views over the Thames Valley and Windsor Great Park. The river below is populated by slow-moving motor cruisers and pleasure craft, and river trips to Windsor, Staines and Hampton Court can be taken from Runnymede, daily between May and October, and at weekends during winter. The nearby **Runnymede Pleasure Ground** offers a range of children's leisure activities in a pleasant riverside setting.

FARNHAM AND THE WEST

Farnham, with its lovely Georgian architecture and battle-worn castle, is the largest town in southwestern Surrey, where the heel of the county extends westwards into Hampshire. Apart from Farnham, however, there are no large towns in this corner of the county, and its charms lie more in the array of attractive villages, scattered farmhouses, woodlands and open heaths in some of the hilliest parts of the southeast.

History plays an important role in this area, with Civil War battle cries still almost audible from the walls of Farnham Castle and the hint of plainsong hanging in the still air around the ruins of Waverley Abbey. "Stand and deliver" would seem to be a more appropriate sound to hear in the wilder sections of the southern extremity, and the Gibbet Memorial on Hindhead Common is a tangible reminder of the fate that awaited those highwaymen who had the misfortune to meet the long arm of the law.

The famous Hog's Back section of the A31 forms the northern edge of the area covered in this chapter. This lovely stretch of road is one of the most scenic drives in the Southeast, affording excellent views north and south as it traverses the ridge between Farnham and Guildford. Indeed, looking south from the Hog's Back provides an aerial perspective of many of the sites covered in the following pages, or at least the countryside surrounding them. The panorama is best viewed from the grassy verge by the side of the A31 at one of the many lay-bys.

FARNHAM

The most westerly town in Surrey is Farnham, a market town of particular architectural charm with its 12th century castle overlooking Georgian houses in the river valley below. This fine old settlement stands at the point where the old Pilgrims' Way from Winchester to Canterbury crosses the River Wey, and it has long been an important staging post on the busy trading route between Southampton and London. Remains of Roman, Saxon and Stone Age dwellings have been found within its boundaries. The town first became a residence of the Bishops of Winchester during Saxon times, and following the Norman conquest, the new Norman bishop built himself a castle on a pleasant tree-covered rise above the centre of the town. The castle is a blend of the fortified and residential. It underwent a number of alterations, most notably in the 15th century when the decorated brick-built tower was added, and it remained in the hands of the Bishops of Winchester from the 12th century until 1927.

Farnham Castle has been visited on a number of occasions by the reigning English monarch and was besieged during the English Civil War. Today, it is approached along Castle Street, a delightful wide thoroughfare of Georgian and neo-Georgian buildings which was laid out to accommodate a traditional street market. The old Norman keep, now owned by English Heritage, is open to the public throughout the summer. The residential part of the castle is now occupied by Farnham Castle International Briefing and Conference Centre. Fully residential, it is available for conferences as well as corporate and local events and there are guided tours on Wednesday afternoons.

Farnham contains a number of other

FARNHAM MALTINGS

Bridge Square, Farnham, Surrey GU9 7QR
Tel: 01252 726234
website: www.farnhammaltings.com

Over 300,000 people visit **The Maltings** every year. They come to Performing and Visual Arts events, courses and workshops; visit the Monthly Markets, trade fairs; or belong to one of the 40 or so societies which meet regularly there. But, whilst the Maltings has built up its reputation as an arts and community centre only since 1975, its history stretches back to the 18th century.

The earliest surviving document relating to the Maltings is dated 1729, but there is evidence of two previous owners. In those days it was a tanyard. In 1830 Robert Sampson set up as a maltster in the then separate East Wing. He was succeeded in business by his son, Sampson Sampson, whose sign can still be seen on the end of his cottage at 18 Bridge Square. Meanwhile, the tanyard was sold to John Barrett, who converted it into a brewery.

The building stood empty for 12 years before it was turned ino an arts and community centre. The conversion so far comprises the Great Hall, the Barley Room, Malt Room, Tannery, Main Bar, Forum, Maltings Gallery & Studio, Long Kiln Room, Dance Studio, South West Kiln, the East Wing Studios, Dressing Rooms, and Playgroup Studio. In1991 fully retractable theatre style raked seating in the Great Hall was installed.

interesting historic buildings, including a row of 17th century gabled almshouses. The informative **Farnham Museum** is housed in an attractive Grade I Georgian town house dating from 1718, known as Willmer House in West Street. The house has many original features including a pleasant walled garden at the rear. As well as some fine wood panelling, carvings and period furniture, the museum contains some interesting archaeological exhibits and a unique collection of 19th century glass paperweights.

Farnham Maltings (see panel above) in Bridge Square is a thriving arts and community centre which is housed in a listed early 18th century building, thought to have been a tanyard. As well as an excellent cafe and bar, the centre offers a regular programme of live music, films and exhibitions.

AROUND FARNHAM

WAVERLEY ABBEY

2 miles E of Farnham on the B3001

Lying within easy striking distance of
Farnham are the atmospheric ruins of
Waverley Abbey. Dating from the 12th
century, this was the first Cistercian
abbey to be built in England. The first
church was completed in 1160 and
destroyed during the dissolution of the
monasteries. Its monumental floor plan
was only revealed after excavations this
century. There is little in the way of
architectural detail remaining at the site
apart from some frater arches. However
architectural historians have suggested
that this early church might well have
inspired the famous Gothic churches of
Tintern, Fountains and Riveaulx abbeys.

The Abbey remains are open during
daylight hours and are said to have
provided the inspiration for Sir Walter
Scott's romantic novel, *Waverley*,
published in 1814 during his stay at the
nearby Waverley Abbey House whose
imposing structure was built with stone
taken from the abbey in 1723.

TILFORD

3 miles E of Farnham off the B3001

A lovely two mile riverside walk from
Waverley Abbey leads to Tilford, an
attractive village which stands at the
confluence of the two branches of the
River Wey. The monks of Waverley are
believed to have been responsible for
rebuilding Tilford's two medieval bridges
following the devastating floods of 1233
during which the abbey itself had to be
evacuated. At the heart of Tilford stands
a triangular village green which features
a 900 year-old oak tree with a 25 foot
girth which is known as the King's or
Novel's Oak; a pleasant early 18th century

inn can be found nearby. Tilford's parish
church of All Saints hosts a regular
spring festival of early church music. In
Reeds Road to the southwest of Tilford is
the **Rural Life Centre and Old Kiln
Museum** (see panel opposite)

RUNFOLD

2 miles E of Farnham on the A31

Runfold marks the beginning of the large
tracts of woodland that dominate much
of the landscape between Farnham and
Guildford. A well-marked turning off the
A31 indicates the small road that winds
south into the village. Runfold, like its
immediate - and even smaller -
neighbour Seale, was essentially a mixed
farming community in the medieval
period, and this way of life is displayed
in Manor Farm, which lies between the
two villages.

TONGHAM

2 miles E of Farnham on the A31

Tongham lies at an important junction,
where Surrey meets Hampshire.
Aldershot lies just west across the border
which is marked by the A331. With the
busy A31, linking Farnham and
Guildford lying just to the south,
Tongham is hard pressed to retain any
sense of the country. That it manages to
is to the credit of the planners, who have
ensured that many of its timber-framed
cottages are still seen to good effect. Look
out for the distinctive curved braces (the
timbers linking walls and roof) on some
of these cottages. Tongham boasts its
own brewery called the **Hogs Back
Brewery** which can be seen after the hill
to the east of the town and the stretch of
the A30 that continues to Guildford. It is
famous for its TEA (or Traditional
English Ale) and is based in an 18th
century barn, where they brew the beer
in the traditional way.

Rural Life Centre

Old Kiln Museum Trust, Reeds Road,
Tilford, Farnham, Surrey GU10 2DL
Tel: 01252 795571 Fax: 01252 795571
e-mail rural.life@lineone.net
website: www.surreyweb.org.uk/rural-life/

The Rural Life Centre is a museum of past village life covering the years from 1750 to 1960. It is set in over 10 acres of garden and woodland and housed in purpose-built and reconstructed buildings, including a chapel, village hall and cricket pavilion. Displays show village crafts and trade, such as wheelwrighting, of which the centre's collection is probably the finest in the country. An historic village playground provides enter-tainment

for children, as does a preserved narrow gauge light railway that operates on Sundays. There is also an arboretum with over 100 species of trees from around the world.

The centre is open Wednesday to Sunday and Bank Holidays from April until October.

Hog's Back

4 miles E of Farnham on the A31

The Hog's Back is the name given to the ridge which dominates the landscape between the level ground surrounding Guildford (looking north) and the wooded, more undulating terrain looking south towards Hindhead. Motorists refer to this stretch of the A31 as the Hog's Back, and the 4 mile stretch between Tongham and Compton is well served with picnic stops and the occasional lay-by to stop and admire the views.

The hamlet of Wanborough on the northern side of the A31 contains one of the smallest churches in Surrey. Built by the monks of Waverley Abbey, it stands in the shadow of a massive monastic tithe barn.

The old manor house was constructed between the 15th and 17th centuries on the site of pre-Norman manor and was used during World War II to train secret agents.

Puttenham

5 miles E of Farnham off the A31

The Hog's Back village of Puttenham lies stretched out along the route of the old Pilgrims' Way. An attractive mixture of building styles, the village contains a restored part-Norman church, several fine 15th and 16th century cottages, an 18th century farm with a number of period outbuildings and oast houses, and an impressive Palladian mansion, Puttenham Priory, which was completed in 1762.

The mixture of building styles arose because of Puttenham's location, where chalk gives way to sandstone. Cottages use one or the other - or both - of these materials, and the effect is enlivened with brickwork usually dating from the 18th century.

Elstead

5 miles E of Farnham on the B3001

The attractive village of Elstead lies surrounded by farmland and crossed by the River Wey. In fact it is this crossing that makes Elstead noteworthy. Its rough stonework bridge dates from the medieval period, crossing the river in a series of five graceful arches. It has a brick parapet, making the overall effect one of solidity and strength.

THE MARINERS HOTEL,

Millbridge, Frensham, Surrey GU10 3DJ
Tel: 01252 792050 Fax: 01252 792649
website: www.themarinershotel.co.uk

Carlo Genziana and his sister Melita have been running the **Mariners Hotel** in Millbridge for the last 18 years. The comfortable lounge bar is inviting on a chilly evening, a warm red brick chimney breast, a blazing fire reflected in the horse brasses and copper. While warm summer days can drift away at the outdoor tables enjoying the pleasant scenery. In either place visitors can enjoy a selection of real ales and fine wines with traditional pub grub. For something a little different, the bistro style restaurant, specialises in Italian and fresh fish dishes and serves an extensive daily buffet. It has gleaming wooden booths, a colourful harbour scene painted around the walls while nets, shells and other paraphernalia of the sea complete the marine ambience.

The hotel has 21 comfortable en-suite rooms with all the usual facilities. The rooms include a sumptuous and romantic bridal suite, family rooms for guests with small children and ground floor rooms for those who require easy access. Laundry and ironing services are also available. The hotel specialises in functions, whether it be wedding receptions, dinner dances or club week-ends. Equally suitable for business conferences the hotel has facilities for faxing and photocopying. This family-run hotel is dedicated to providing a friendly and professional service in the peaceful location of the Surrey countryside. Whether guests are on business, on holiday or simply dining out, Carlo and Melita will ensure they enjoy a warm welcome and wonderful food and drink.

FRENSHAM GARDEN CENTRE

The Reeds, Frensham, Surrey GU10 3BP
Tel: 01252 792545; Fax: 01252 792566
e-mail: info@frensham-gardencentre.co.uk
website: www.frensham.co.uk

Robert Tyler opened **Frensham Garden Centre** in 1993 and it has gone from strength to strength ever since. Trained in horticulture at Writtle College, Robert is well able to ensure that his friendly staff are trained and knowledgeable about gardening and the wide range of products stocked. Customers will find everything they could possibly need for their garden here, whether they are experienced or professional gardeners or novices. Many of the plants are grown in the centre's own nursery and other products are sourced from a wide variety of suppliers to ensure the best possible prices. As a result, customers will find here the lowest prices for high quality products.

In a beautiful woodland setting, Frensham Garden Centre invites customers to browse around its displays of plants, terracotta pots, wooden barrels and ornaments. Visitors can try out the garden furniture, investigate barbecues and weigh up a spade or fork. All the well-known quality names will be found here including Spear and Jackson, Wolf and Sandwik for tools and Swan Hattersley, Denewood and Alexander Rose for garden furniture. The garden centre has several other interesting and more unusual sections. At Camping World there is a wide selection of camping equipment including hiking gear and ski wear as well as the largest display of tents in the south. The Gift Box has a collection of craft items to browse through for that special present and finally the Frensham Coffe Shop offers a relaxing and pleasant environment to lunch or snack. Opening hours: Monday to Saturday 09.00am – 5.30pm, Sunday 10.30am – 4.30pm

Elstead Mill

centre of the village. Of particular interest is the large granary, built around 1600. It stands - resting on its 25 wooden pillars - at the centre of a quadrangle at the heart of the farm.

The **Church of St Nicholas**, in the centre of the village, was built in Norman times but was massively restored in the 19th century. The restoration, however, was conducted by A.W.N. Pugin, and there is great care evident throughout. St Nicholas represents something of a find for students of architecture since it appears to be one of the few churches where Pugin sought to create a Neo-Norman effect. Most of his work strove for the higher-flown Gothic styles. The ancient yew tree in the churchyard is probably more than 600 years old.

The other big attraction in the village is **Peper Harow House**, a Grade one listed building, built in 1768 and now converted into flats. It is a cube-shaped manor house, the bottom two storeys soberly classical. An extra floor was added in 1913 along with some Baroque ornamentation that clashes with the style of the original building. The outbuildings are almost as impressive as the house itself, in particular the three-sided stables. The park surrounding the house was designed by Capability Brown in 1763.

Unfortunately, the medieval effect is lessened somewhat by the modern bridge that runs parallel to it on the north side. Nevertheless, the bridge marks a delightful entrance to the village itself.

On the lane leading from the old bridge to the village green is the **Old Farm House**, a large timber-framed building that was completed in the 16th century. The green itself is compact and triangular and a small cul-de-sac leads from it to the 14th century **Church of St James**, which was overly restored in the 19th century.

Just west of the centre is **Elstead Mill**, an 18th century water mill. It stands four storeys high, its brick structure topped with a Palladian cupola. Six classical columns support a small lead dome at the very top. Now a restaurant, much of the machinery, including a working water wheel is displayed within.

PEPER HAROW
6 miles E of Farnham off the A3

Peper Harow is a small village lying just west of the A3 in completely rural surroundings. It has a number of interesting cottages reinforcing its rustic charm as well as one of the best collections of Surrey farm buildings at **Peper Harow Farm** just outside the

FRENSHAM
3 miles SE of Farnham off the A28

St Mary's Church was moved in the 13th century from its previous site on low ground beside the River Wey. The chancel walls were part of the original building. The tower is 14th century, with massive diagonal buttresses, but the whole church was subject to a major restoration in 1868.

The village of **Millbridge** lies just to the north of Frensham, and like Frensham it is set in heaths with occasional farmland dotted around it. The A287 to the south of the village runs between Frensham's Great and Little Ponds, two sizeable National Trust-owned lakes which provide good bird-watching and recreational facilities. These are now contained within a 1,000 acre country park which incorporates four prehistoric bowl barrows and the Devil's Jumps, three irregularly shaped hills whose origin, like many other unusual natural features, is attributed to Satan.

THURSLEY
6 miles SE of Farnham off the A3

Thursley is an exceptional village, which takes its name from the Viking god Thor and the Saxon word for field, or lea. The settlement was once an important centre of the Wealden iron industry and a number of disused hammer ponds can still be seen to the east. These artificial lakes provided power to drive the mechanical hammers and bellows in the once-bustling iron forges. Today, the village is a tranquil place arranged around a green containing an acacia tree which was planted as a memorial to William Cobbett, the Georgian traveller and writer who is best remembered for his book describing riding tours of England, "Rural Rides", which was published in 1830. Thursley is also the birthplace of the celebrated architect, Sir Edwin Lutyens, who at the age of only 19 converted a row of local cottages into a single dwelling now known locally as the Corner.

Thursley's two principal thoroughfares, the Lane and the Street, contain a wide variety of noteworthy domestic buildings. The latter leads to St Michael's Church, a part-Saxon structure which was heavily restored by the Victorians.

The spire and belfry are 15th century and are supported by massive timber posts with tie-beams and arched braces, a good example of late-medieval engineering.

The churchyard contains the grave of a sailor, who was murdered on Hindhead Heath in 1786 by three men he had gone to help. Although the villagers never discovered the victim's name, they gave him a full burial and erected an inscribed stone over his grave.

Two interesting old buildings stand near the church, the half-timbered and tile-hung Old Parsonage and the part timber framed Hill Farm, both of which date from the 16th century.

THE DEVIL'S PUNCH BOWL
7 miles S of Farnham off the A3

The Devil's Punch Bowl is a steep-sided natural sandstone amphitheatre through which the busy A3 Guildford to Petersfield road passes four miles to the southeast of Frensham Great Pond. As usual, Lucifer's name is invoked in the place name but the origins might have more to do with real events than with superstition. The deep valley provided excellent cover for thieves and highwaymen, and even in coaching days passengers would look on the natural wonder with a mixture of awe and apprehension.

HINDHEAD
7 miles S of Farnham on the A28

Hindhead stands near the top of a ridge and at 850 feet above sea level, is the highest village in Surrey. Perhaps surprisingly, it has only been in existence since the late 19th century. Before that the site was known primarily as a site for highwaymen planning their next heist while taking cover in the steep wooded countryside. Good stands of fir trees still surround Hindhead.

HEALTHWISE FOODS

Grayshott Health Food Stores, Headley Road, Grayshott,
Surrey GU26 6LE
Tel: 01428 604046 Fax: 01428 681776
e-mail: ken@healthwisefoods.demon.co.uk
website: www.healthwisefoods.demon.co.uk

Healthwise Foods has been established for over 30 years. Ken Dance
bought the company three years ago. Ken has worked for many years
in the food industry with Sainsbury's and has always had a keen interest in quality whole-food.
Grayshott Health Foods is situated in a parade of shops in the main street. Providing a wide range of
products, the shop caters for people with all sorts of special diets. There are sugar-free jams for diabetics,
wheat and gluten-free products for coeliacs and dairy free foods for vegans or those with allergic
reactions, and a variety of frozen vegetarian dishes. There is even ice cream suitable for coeliacs,
diabetics or vegans. For health conscious parents there are organic baby foods to give youngsters the
best possible diet from the start. The emphasis of the shop is on quality.

For those who would rather restrict their caffeine intake or eliminate it from their diet entirely,

there are numerous decaffeinated teas as well as fruit and flower
teas including such delightful concoctions as elderdown and lemon,
apple and ginger, wild fennel, blackcurrant and gurana. The shop
also carries a full range of cereals, pulses and dried fruit. In the
herbal section there is a selection of natural remedies and vitamin
and mineral supplements. Advice can be sought from the Therapy
Centre, where specialists in homeopathy, nutrition, reiki, chiropody,
counselling and reflexology provide alternative therapies for
maintaining a healthy mind in a healthy body.

The town grew up along the
Portsmouth Road (now the A3) and the
buildings date mainly from a
concentrated period in the 1890s. Shops
were built along the Portsmouth Road
and a number of comfortable residences
were dotted through the surrounding
woodlands. Most of these houses still
enjoy leafy settings even if today the
appearance is somewhat tamer. The late
1890s construction date means that these
residences betray the influence of the
Arts and Crafts movement. Most of them
derive from the designs of Norman Shaw,
the movement's great proponent. One of
the best examples of this style is
Thirlestane on the Farnham Road.
Making the most of the south-facing
situation, as well as the height, this V-
shaped house faces southwest so that
most of it acts as a suntrap. A deliberately
rough exterior, combined with the
hanging tiles, typify the attention to

quality materials while the deliberately
asymmetrical nature of the two wings
suggests the freedom of spirit that is
associated with that period.

HINDHEAD COMMON

7 miles SE of Farnham off the A3

Lying just to the east of Hindhead itself is
Hindhead Common, comprising a largely
untamed collection of wild heathlands,
pinewoods and steep valleys. The
National Trust owns 1,400 acres of
Hindhead Common, and maintains a
series of trails and paths that takes
visitors through evocatively named sites
such as Polecat Copse, Golden Valley,
Hurt Hill and Stoatley Green. On the
summit of Gibbet Hill is a granite
monument marking the spot where the
gibbet stood. The glorious views across
both the North and South Downs was
the last earthly memory of the thieves
and murderers who were executed here.

(Continued page 332)

WALK 8

The Devil's Punchbowl

Start	Hindhead
Distance	5½ miles (8.9km)
Approximate time	3 hours
Parking	National Trust car park on eastern edge of Hindhead
Refreshments	Pubs and cafés in Hindhead
Ordnance Survey maps	Landranger 186 (Aldershot & Guildford), Explorer 133 (Haslemere & Petersfield)

The Devil's Punchbowl is probably Surrey's most celebrated natural feature. This route follows its western rim before dropping down to cross to its eastern side. After climbing to the Portsmouth road, two little-used footpaths lead to Gibbet Hill – a superb viewpoint. From here it is a straightforward route back to Hindhead. There are some steep and lengthy climbs on this walk.

A track leads northwards from the western end of the National Trust car park, passing the toilets. After about 1¼ mile (400m) bear left to take the path along the western rim of the Punchbowl. Breaks in the trees start to occur more frequently, allowing spectacular views to the bottom of the natural amphitheatre. There is also a thoughtfully placed seat where you can sit and enjoy the scene.

Bear right on reaching a junction of two tracks by an electricity substation **A**, heading for Highcombe on the waymarked bridleway which continues along the top of the Punchbowl. A helpful aid to navigation is the power line that accompanies the sandy track, which first crosses to the right of the path, and then crosses back to the left side where it remains, usually within sight. At the point where the line returns to the left side of the track, you should bear right **B** on a path which is a detour to an excellent viewpoint. A memorial to the brothers of W.A. Robertson stands here. Both were killed in the First World War, and the Devil's Punchbowl was given to the

National Trust by the Robertson family to commemorate the men's sacrifice.

Continue past the monument to return to the main path which descends gently to reach a point where a bridleway leaves to the left. Keep straight on here and a little further on when another bridleway joins from the right. Make sure that you still have the power line in sight on the left, as the path will now begin to descend more steeply through Vanhurst Copse and in doing so becomes narrow and enclosed. A National Trust boundary-marker shows where you leave Trust land.

The steep path can be heavy-going after wet weather, but eventually it reaches Hyde Lane. Turn right here **C** to pass Ridgeway Farm. Now there is another steep section down a path with high banks to a footbridge over a small stream **D**.

Bear right after this up a track, forking left to reach a lane. Turn left again and then right **E** after 100 yds (91m), following the red arrow waymark of the Greensand Way. A long climb up a shady track with a good surface brings you to a National Trust signboard where the track divides. Bear right here, continuing to follow the Greensand Way, and then left a little further on. Go straight over the footpath junction which follows almost immediately. The climb continues, but at last the scenery changes to heathland and the sandy path reaches the top of the ridge, where there are views and a seat which overlooks the Punchbowl.

The sound of traffic on the Portsmouth road is now impossible to ignore – before reaching it there is a diversionary path to the left which avoids the churned bridleway and allows better views of the Punchbowl.

Cross the road **F** to a footpath just to the left of where you emerge onto the busy highway. This is not the Greensand Way (which continues from a point a little further down the Portsmouth road) but a more obscure footpath, marked FP94. Turn sharply to the left where the path divides, away from both alternative ways, which look better used. The path descends very steeply to a forest track that continues downhill. Cross a second gravelled forestry road to take a similar one heading west, which leads to Begley Farm.

Turn right here onto the road **G** and walk along it until just before Boundless Farm it swings left. Turn right at this corner **H** onto a footpath into Boundless Copse. Keep straight ahead when the path meets a forestry track and where this divides fork left. A steep climb follows through new plantings to a clearance at the top. The path is now on the crest of a ridge and it continues to gain height as the ridge grows broader. At a footpath junction

go straight across to reach Gibbet Hill **J**, with its monument and triangulation pillar. It is justly famous as a viewpoint.

With your back to the monument, walk westwards (with a small planting of trees on the right) to a car park, then continue down the road which leads from it. The Sailor's Grave is on the right, overlooking the Punchbowl. The unknown seafarer was murdered nearby in 1786. The culprits were caught and after execution their bodies were left to the mercy of the elements on the hilltop gibbet. The road from the car park leads to the main road opposite the car park where the walk started.

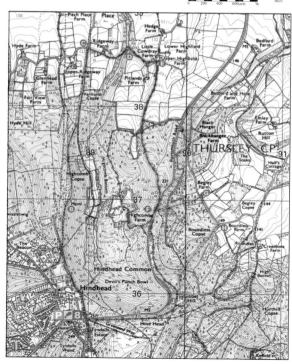

GUILDFORD AND THE SOUTH

Guildford, with its prominent setting on a hill visible from the A3, is an obvious base for travellers interested in exploring the southwestern section of Surrey that extends down t,o and then, traces the West Sussex border. Like the area around Farnham, this area contains some of Surrey's most unspoilt countryside. Rough, hilly, thickly wooded in places, the landscape comes as close as anywhere in the county to fitting the descriptive term "wild".

The interaction between landscape and human society provides the background for some of the most interesting sights covered in the following pages. From time-worn remnants of prehistoric hill forts to medieval bridges along the Wey Valley and even including some of the modern architecture to be found among Guildford's hilly streets, the imprint of necessity-driven design is everywhere. Is it any wonder that Sir Edwin Lutyens cut his teeth, architecturally speaking, with his designs for houses occupying hilly sites or tucked in narrow valleys?

The settlements become decidedly smaller and more scattered as the Sussex border is neared. It is in these villages, many no more than hamlets, that visitors can appreciate just how even the earliest settlers scraped a living, and how later inhabitants developed crafts that exploited the rich natural surroundings.

GUILDFORD

The route into Guildford from the northwest passes close to **Guildford Cathedral**, one of only two new Anglican cathedrals to have been built in this country since the Reformation (the other is

Liverpool). This impressive redbrick building stands on top of Stag Hill, a prominent local landmark which enjoys panoramic views over the surrounding landscape. The building was designed by Sir Edward Maufe with a superb high-arched interior and was begun in 1936. However, work was halted during World War II and members of the local diocese had to wait until 1961 for the new cathedral to be finally consecrated. Guided tours and restaurant facilities are available all year round. In 1968, the **University of Surrey** relocated from London to a site on a hillside to the northwest of the cathedral. Pleasant and leafy, the campus contains a number of striking buildings including the university library and art gallery.

From the university, it is only a mile to the heart of Guildford, the ancient county town of Surrey. Guildford has been the capital of the region since pre-Norman times and in the 10th century, it even had its own mint. Henry II built a **Castle** here on high ground in the 12th century which later became the county gaol. Today, the castle remains and the ruined keep provide a fascinating place from which to view the surrounding area.

Those visiting the town for the first time should make straight for the old High Street, a wonderful cobbled

Guildford Castle

thoroughfare of Georgian and older buildings which rises steeply from the River Wey.

Perhaps the most noteworthy of these is the **Guildhall**, a Tudor structure with an elaborately decorated 17ᵗʰ century frontage which incorporates a belltower, balcony and distinctive gilded clock.

Abbot's Hospital, a little further along, is an imposing turreted almshouse which was built in 1619 by the Guildford-born Archbishop of Canterbury, George Abbot; at the top of the High Street, the Royal Grammar School dates from the early 1500s and was subsequently endowed by Edward VI.

A number of interesting streets and alleyways run off Guildford High Street, including Quarry Street with its medieval St Mary's Church and old Castle Arch. The latter houses the Guildford Museum,

Guildford Guildhall

an informative centre for local history and archaeology which also contains an exhibition devoted to Lewis Carroll, the creator of *"Alice In Wonderland"* who died in the town in 1898.

A charming bronze memorial to Lewis Carroll (real name Charles Lutwidge Dodgson), which is composed of a life-sized Alice chasing the White Rabbit into his hole can be found on the far bank of the River Wey, midway between the two footbridges. The famous Yvonne Arnaud Theatre stands in a delightful riverside setting at the foot of the castle mound on the town side of the river. As well as offering top quality productions, the theatre has an excellent bar, coffee lounge and restaurant which remains open throughout the day. In summer, rowing boats and guided pleasure boat trips are available at the nearby Guildford Boat House.

AROUND GUILDFORD

CLANDON PARK
5 miles E of Guildford on the A247

Set in the farming countryside east of Guildford and south of Woking is the National Trust-owned property, Clandon

Mary Abbots Hospital, Guildford

Clandon Park

Park. This magnificent country mansion was designed in the 1730s by Giacomo Leoni, a Venetian architect, who combined Palladian, Baroque and European styles to create one of the grandest 18th century houses in England. The interior is renowned for its magnificent two-storey marble hall, sumptuous decoration and fine Italian plasterwork depicting scenes from mythology. The Gubbay collection of furniture and porcelain is also housed here, along with the Ivo Forde collection of humorous Meissen figures. The surrounding parkland was landscaped by Capability Brown in characteristic style and includes a parterre, grotto and brightly painted New Zealand Maori house.

GOMSHALL

5 miles E of Guildford on the A25

This once industrialised community has a Victorian heart and was once an important centre of the tanning and leather-working industries. The old packhorse bridge over the River Tillingbourne dates from the 1500s and the manor house at the southern

end of the village from the early 1700s. Gomshall is now known for its fine craft and antique shops, several of which are concentrated in an ancient and beautifully converted water mill, the **Gomshall Mill and Gallery**. This working water mill dates back to 1086 and now houses a variety of attractive and unusual shops, a tea room and a licensed restaurant.

SHERE

6 miles E of Guildford off the A25

Shere is one of the loveliest, and consequently most visited, villages in Surrey. Thankfully now bypassed by the A25, it lies at the foot of the North Downs in the river valley which is particularly known for the growing of watercress, a plant that requires a constantly flowing supply of fresh water. The village **Church of St James** dates from the 12th century and was tastefully restored in the 1950s. Among its many noteworthy features are the 13th century Purbeck marble font, the St Nicholas Chapel, and an unusual hermit's cell built in the 14th century for a local

Shere Village

woman who asked to be confined there for life.

The churchyard is entered through an impressive lych gate designed by Lutyens and close by stands the White Horse Inn, one of the many fine 16th and 17th century buildings to be found in the village. The **Shere Museum** in the Malt House contains an interesting collection of local artefacts, and the Old Farm behind the church is an open farm, which, at weekends, offers hands-on demonstrations of traditional farming techniques.

Albury

4 miles E of Guildford on the A28

Albury dates largely from the last century and was constructed in fanciful neo-Gothic style as an estate village for nearby **Albury Park**. This large country mansion was built on the site of a Tudor manor house in the early 18th century and was much altered by Pugin in the 1840s. The most eccentric feature of the house is its collection of chimneys, 63 of them built for only 60 rooms in an amazing variety of shapes and sizes. Although the mansion has now been

converted into flats, the estate gardens are open to visitors and are well worth a look. They were laid out by the diarist John Evelyn at the turn of the 18th century and feature a series of terraced orchards which rise above the house to the north. A number of smaller communities nestle around Albury.

Chilworth

3 miles E of Guildford on the A28

Chilworth is a former munitions and paper-making centre whose church, **St Martha on the Hill**, had to be rebuilt in 1850 following an explosion in the nearby gunpowder works. The result is a genuine success and shows great flair and sensitivity. There was no attempt made to copy the original exactly but the resulting reconstruction remains true to the Norman spirit of the destroyed church. On the hill to the south of the church are five circular banks, each about 100 feet in diameter, which have been identified as early Bronze Age henge monuments.

Chilworth Manor was built in the 1600s on the site of a pre-Norman monastic house. The exterior is a medley of styles but its 17th century gardens are complete, running up the side of the hill in terraces.

Shalford

3 miles S of Guildford on the A281

The residential community of Shalford contains a fascinating **Water Mill** which operated from the early 1700s right up to the World War I. Once powered by the waters of the Tillingbourne, this exceptional tile-hung structure retains most of its original machinery. During

Albury Village

the 1930s, it was bought and restored by Ferguson's Gang, a secretive group of conservationists who hid their identities behind eccentric noms de plume and who eventually donated the water mill to the National Trust.

Shalford stands near the northern entrance to the **Wey and Arun Junction Canal**, an ambitious inland waterway, which was constructed in 1816 to connect the Thames with the English Channel. Conceived during the Napoleonic wars as a way of avoiding attacks on coastal shipping, unfortunately it opened too late to fulfil its function and was soon superseded by the railways. A towpath providing some delightful walks runs along almost two-thirds of the canal's 36 mile length, a significant proportion of which has now been fully restored by enthusiastic teams of volunteers.

About a mile south of Shalford is **Great Tangley**, one of the finest 16th century half-timbered houses in Surrey. The exterior is made up of roughly square panels each with four curved diagonal braces. This combination creates a star shape for each panel, which is repeated across the sides of the house.

BLACKHEATH

4 miles SE of Guildford off the A248

Set in the hills above Albury, this tidy Victorian hamlet gives the visitor a sense of remoteness despite being within easy striking distance of Guildford. Blackheath has some fine late-Victorian buildings. One of the most interesting is Greyfriars, a Franciscan monastery built in neo-Gothic style in 1895. The church and dormitories of this stone-built structure are contained under one roof. Another Victorian curiosity is the somewhat austere timbered residence, the Hallams.

WONERSH

4 miles SE of Guildford off the A248

Wonersh is a former weaving centre with a fine 16th century half-timbered inn, the Grantley Arms, located along the high street, which presents a cheerful and harmonious appearance with its medley of brick, stone, tile-hanging and half-timbered buildings. An imposing Lutyens house, **Chinthurst Hill**, is just a few minutes' walk northwest of the heart of the village. Lutyens used the local Bargate stone to create a Tudor effect, this being between 1893 and 1895, before he had developed his own distinctive style. The house occupies a lovely hillside site and the terraced garden was planted by Gertrude Jekyll.

BRAMLEY

3 miles SE of Guildford off the A248

Despite being largely Victorian, Bramley has some attractive Georgian and Regency residential buildings. These appear somewhat haphazardly through the long winding street that forms the nearest thing to a core of the village. There are two Lutyens houses in Bramley. The small, L-shaped **Millmead**, a National Trust property, is located south of Gosden Green. It was built for the gardener Gertrude Jekyll between 1904 and 1907 and traces of her original garden survive. About half a mile north is **Little Tangley**, a late 19th century house to which Lutyens added a porch and staircase hall in 1899. The Stables, which is now a private house called Edgton, was one of the architect's first works.

GODALMING

5 miles S of Guildford on the A3100

The old market town of Godalming was once an important staging post between London and Portsmouth and a number of elegant 17th and 18th century shops and coaching inns can still be found in the High Street. A market was established here in 1300 and the town later became a centre for the local wool and textile industries. Perhaps the most interesting building in the old centre is the former town hall, affectionately known as **The Pepperpot**, which was built at the western end of the High Street in 1814. Now surrounded on all sides by

Winkworth Arboretum

heavy traffic, this unusual arcaded building once contained an interesting museum of local history. **The Museum** is now opposite the Pepperpot at the fascinating Wealden House, parts of which date from the 15ᵗʰ and 16ᵗʰ Centuries but which also has Victorian and Georgian additions. The museum has displays on geology and archaelogy as well as local history, including a display detailing Godalming's claim to fame as the first town to have a public electricity supply. Two of Godalming's most renowned former residents – Gertrude Jekyll, the gardener and Sir Edward Lutyens, the architect – are celebrated in a gallery exhibition and there is a Jekyll style garden. The timber-framed house once belonging to Gertrude Jekyll can be found in dense woodland on the opposite side of town. It was designed for her by Edwin Lutyens in characteristic rural vernacular style and partially constructed of Bargate stone, a locally quarried hard brown sandstone that was much-loved by the Victorians.

Godalming's part-Norman parish church of St Peter and St Paul is also built of Bargate stone. As is **Charterhouse School**, the famous public school, which moved from London to a

hillside site on the northern side of Godalming in 1872. Among its most striking features are the 150 foot Founder's Tower and the chapel designed by Giles Gilbert Scott as a memorial to those killed in the First World War. Three miles along the B2130 to the southeast of Godalming lies the renowned **Winkworth Arboretum**, a 95 acre area of wooded hillside which was presented to the National Trust in 1952. The grounds contain two lakes and a magnificent collection of rare trees and shrubs, many of them native to other continents. Hascombe, one mile further on, is another characteristic Surrey village with great charm.

Loseley Park

3 miles N of Godalming off the B3000

Loseley Park, a handsome Elizabethan country estate, was built in 1562 of Bargate stone, some of which was taken from the ruins of Waverley Abbey. **Loseley House** is the former home of the Elizabethan statesman, Sir William More. Both Elizabeth I and James I are known to have stayed here, and the interior is decorated with a series of outstanding period features, including hand-painted panelling, woodcarving, delicate

Loseley House

plasterwork ceilings, and a unique chimney-piece carved from a massive piece of chalk. The walled garden is a beautiful place to take a stroll, the surrounding gardens contain a terrace and a moat walk, and the nearby fields are home to Loseley's famous herd of pedigree Jersey cattle. Visitors can take a trailer ride to the traditional working dairy farm, where you can see the Jersey herd being milked every afternoon and discover the history of the estate.

COMPTON

4 miles N of Godalming off the B3000

The historic community of Compton was once an important stopping place on the old Pilgrims' Way. The village possesses an exceptional part-Saxon church, St Nicholas, with some remarkable internal features, including a series of 12th century murals, which were only rediscovered in 1966, an ancient hermit's, or anchorite's, cell, and a unique two-storey Romanesque sanctuary which is thought to have once contained an early Christian relic.

Compton is also renowned for being the home of the 19th century artist G.F. Watts, a chiefly self-taught painter and sculptor whose most famous work, Physical Energy, stands in London's Kensington Gardens. At the age of 47,

Watts married the actress Ellen Terry, but the couple separated a year later. Then at the age of 69, he remarried, this time to Mary Fraser-Tytler, a painter and potter 33 years his junior who went on to design Watts' Memorial Gallery, which today contains over 200 pieces of the artist's work, along with the Watts Mortuary Chapel, an extraordinary building which was completed in 1904 and is decorated in exuberant Art Nouveau style. The Watts Gallery is a fascinating place to visit, housing a unique collection of his paintings, drawings and sculptures. The nearby memorial chapel is also worth visiting.

EASHING

1 mile W of Godalming off the A3100

The tiny hamlet of Eashing is noted for the lovely medieval Eashing Bridge, which has segmented arches and uses cutwaters - pointed upstream and rounded downstream to stem the flow of the river. It is one of several surviving Wey Valley bridges of that period, the others being at Elstead and Tilford. Just to the east of the bridge is **The Meads**, an ancient house of two distinct parts. Half of it is 16th century, with timber framing and an original Tudor doorcase. The other is 18th century and brick and stone, with small dark chips of stone set in the mortar.

WITLEY

4 miles S of Godalming on the A283

The historic village of Witley comprises an attractive collection of fine tile-hung and half-timbered buildings loosely arranged around the part-Saxon church of All Saints, a much-altered structure which contains some rare 12th century frescoes and a delicately carved 13th century font, and incorporates a 17th century tower. The present village inn, the White Hart, was constructed in Elizabethan times to replace an even earlier hostelry. It is believed to be one of the oldest inns in the country and at one time stood adjacent to a market place which hosted a busy Friday market.

Witley's Old Manor was visited by a number of English monarchs, including Edward I and Richard II, and the village centre contains some delightful 15th and 16th century timber-framed houses, many of which are hung with characteristic fishtail tiles. These include the Old Cottage, Red Rose Cottage (so-called because the lease granted on Christmas Day 1580 called for an annual rent of one red rose), and Step Cottage, a former rectory, which was once the home of Reverend Lawrence Stoughton who died aged 88 after serving the parish for 53 years and outliving five wives.

At one time, Witley was a summer haven for artists and writers, the best known of which is perhaps George Eliot who wrote her last novel, *"Daniel Deronda"*, here between 1874 and 1876. Her home, the Heights, was designed by Sir Henry Cole, the architect of the Royal Albert Hall, and was visited by a series of eminent guests, including the novelist Henry James. Today, the building has been converted into a nursing home and is now known as Roslyn Court.

A large proportion of the common to the north of Thursley is a designated nature reserve which is known for its unusually large and varied population of dragonflies. The **Witley Common Information Centre** lies a few minutes drive from Thursley Common on the eastern side of the A3. This purpose-built nature centre is managed by the National Trust and is set in woodlands at the edge of a substantial area of Trust-owned heathland. Inside, there is an audio-visual display and an exhibition outlining the history, geology and natural history of the area.

Tigburne Court, which is regarded by many as Lutyens's finest work, is just over a mile south of Witley, standing right on the main Milford to Petworth road. It was built between 1899-1901 for Sir Edgar Horne. Lutyens was 30 years old when he designed Tigburne Court, and the house shows him at the height of his powers yet still full of youthful exuberance. He playfully mixed Tudor styles with 18th century classicism and used horizontal bands of tiles with the Bargate stone to create a powerful geometric effect. The gardens, like those of so many of the best Lutyens houses, are by Gertrude Jekyll.

HAMBLEDON
5 miles S of Godalming on the A283

This scattered settlement contains a number of interesting buildings, including the tile-hung **Court Farm**, which stands near the part 14th century church, the Old Granary, School Cottage, and Malthouse Farm and Cottage. The National Trust owns a small timber-framed dwelling in Hambledon known as Oakhurst Cottage which has been restored as an old artisan's home. Open by appointment only.

A memorial to one of the Trust's founders, the social reformer Octavia Hill, stands at the top of nearby **Hydon's Ball**, an unusual conical hill which at 593 feet above sea level, offers some fine views over the surrounding landscape.

HASLEMERE
9 miles S of Godalming on the A286

The genteel town of Haslemere lies in the southwestern corner of the county. Now a quiet and comfortable home for well-to-do commuters, it has central streets filled with handsome Georgian

SERENDIPITY ANTIQUES AND CRAFTS CENTRE

7 Petworth Road, Haslemere, Surrey GU27 2JB
Tel: 01428 642622

A history graduate of Rhodes, Elizabeth Moore has always been interested in antiques, in particular china and porcelain. Elizabeth exhibited at **Serendipidity** before she bought it in 1999. Various people exhibit their wares at this Aladdin's Cave of a shop situated just off the High Street in the delightful town of Haslemere. The themes are constantly changing and the window is expertly dressed every month to reflect the changes within. Recent themes have included textiles, costumes, militaria, far horizons, retro, English porcelain, pottery, desks, Art Deco, Victoriana, picnics and childhood. There are 14 different exhibitors at the centre, guaranteeing that a wide variety of tastes and interests will be reflected in the stock.

Housed in a former pub, the half-tiled frontage and small paned windows invite customers to put their noses to the glass and peer in at the enchanting displays. In the deceptively large interior, glass fronted cases and shelves hold collectable china and glass, jewellery, books, pictures, maps and more.

Furniture, pottery, brass or baskets may be found in the huge recesses of the ancient brick ingle nook fireplace while period furniture and crafts of all kind jostle for space in every nook and cranny. Visitors can browse to their heart's content in this treasure trove but they will be reluctant to leave without buying so wide is the appeal of this serendipidous collection. Anyone looking for something just a little bit different or searching for a particular item to add to a specialist collection is likely to find it here and at an affordable price. Opening hours: Monday to Saturday 10.00am - 5.00pm

COLDHARBOUR TRADING

The Ark, Town Car park, Haslemere, Surrey GU27 2HG
Tel: 01428 641817 Fax: 01730 893915
e-mail: turkishcarpets@coldharbourtrading.fsnet.co.uk
website: www.coldharbourtrading.fsnet.co.uk

Colin Fletcher and Anne Fabbri specialise in Turkish carpets. Each year they travel extensively throughout the carpet weaving regions of Turkey to find interesting and unusual pieces. The result is an exclusive collection of hand chosen rugs and carpets of diverse types and styles. The exclusivity is by no means reflected in the price. Colin and Anne manage to keep their prices down by avoiding wholesalers and arranging their own freight and customs.

The interior of Coldharbour Tradings premises in the centre of Haslemere are like any typical carpet shop found in the Bazaars of Istanbul or Konya. The carpets are displayed Turkish fashion, in rolls spread on the floor or hanging from the walls and their friendly welcome encourages customers to browse. They are able to tell potential customers the source and background of any of their pieces be it a newly woven Kilim or one of the antique or unusual carpets they have on display.

and Victorian buildings, most of which were constructed following the arrival of the railway in 1859. The building styles, including stucco, redbrick and tile-hung, combine to form an attractive and harmonious architectural mix. Some of Haslemere's finest pre-Victorian structures include the Town Hall, rebuilt in 1814, the **Tolle House Almshouses** in Petworth Road, Church Hill House, the Town House, and two noteworthy hotels, the Georgian and the White Horse.

Towards the end of the last century, Haslemere became something of a centre for the arts. Alfred Lord Tennyson settled nearby, and a group known as the Haslemere Society of Artists was formed whose number included Birket Foster and the landscape painter, Helen Allingham. At the end of the World War I, the French-born musician and enthusiastic exponent of early music, Arnold Dolmetsch, founded what has become a world-famous musical instrument workshop here. Dolmetsch's family went on to establish the Haslemere Festival of Early Music in 1925 which is still held each year in July.

Another of Haslemere's attractions is the **Educational Museum** in the High Street, an establishment which was founded in 1888 by local surgeon and Quaker, Sir James Hutchinson, and which now contains an imaginative series of displays on local birds, botany, zoology, geology and history.

CHIDDINGFOLD

6 miles S of Godalming on the A283

With its three-sided green, waterlily-filled pond, part 13th century church, medieval pub and handsome collection of Georgian cottages, this attractive settlement contains all the features of a quintessential English village. During the 13th and 14th centuries, it was an important centre of the glass-making industry, a once flourishing trade which used local sand as its main ingredient and employed skilled craftspeople from across northern Europe. Some fragments of medieval Chiddingfold glass can be seen in the small lancet window in St Mary's Church, below which a brass plaque can be seen which is inscribed with the names of several early glass-makers. The church itself was much altered during the 1860s. However, its west tower is 17th century and contains a peal of eight bells, one of which is believed to be around 500 years old. The churchyard is entered through an exceptionally fine lych-gate, a covered gateway with a wide timber slab which was used to shelter coffins awaiting burial.

Of the many handsome buildings standing around Chiddingfold's village green, the Crown Inn is perhaps the most impressive. This is another hostelry which claims to be the oldest in England, its existence having

Chiddingfold Village

first been recorded in 1383. The structure is half-timbered and incorporates a medieval great hall; Edward VI is reported to have stayed here in the 15th century. Other buildings in the village worthy of note are Chantry House, Manor House, and Glebe House, the last two of which have elegant Georgian facades.

DUNSFOLD

6 miles S of Godalming on the B2130

From Chiddingfold, a pleasant journey eastwards through the country lanes leads to another settlement with fold, (a Saxon term meaning "forest clearing"), in its name. Dunsfold is a narrow ribbon of a village, which lies on either side of a long unmanicured green. It contains a number of fine old brick and tile-hung cottages and houses, several of which date from the late 17th century, and an excellent pub, the Sun Inn which stands beside a towering oak tree which is said to have a girth of over 20 feet.

Dunsfold's finest feature, however, is situated half a mile from the village on top of a raised mound which may once have been the site of a pre-Christian place of worship. The **Church of St Mary and All Saints** dates from around 1280 and apart from the addition of a 15th century belfry, has remained virtually unchanged since. The structure was much admired by William Morris, the Victorian founder of the Arts and Crafts Movement, who particularly approved of the simple, rough-hewn pews, which were made around 1300 by the inhabitants of the surrounding farms. A leafy glade at the foot of the mound is the location of a holy well, whose water is reputed to be a cure for eye complaints and blindness. The site of the holy well is marked by a timber shelter erected in the 1930s.

ALFOLD

9 miles S of Godalming on the B2133

A former clearing in the Wealden forest, Alfold, is an exceptionally attractive village which was once an important glass-making centre. It reputedly supplied material for the windows of Westminster Abbey. Evidence of the medieval glassworks can still be made out in the woods on the edge of the village. The area around the church contains a number of interesting historic features, including an ancient yew tree in the churchyard, a charming Tudor cottage, and an old village whipping post and set of stocks.

Just at the edge of the village is the **Countryways Experience**, a series of interactive exhibits that covers the history and natural history of this area, giving visitors some perspective on how living conditions adapted to new styles of farming over the centuries. Visitors can feed a range of animals, including lambs, goats, piglets, calves, and chickens with food from the farm shop.

ELLEN'S GREEN

9 miles SE of Godalming on the B2128

This tiny hamlet on the Sussex border is one of the best preserved Surrey villages. It is set in unspoilt Weald country, with thick woodlands giving way to small fields. Cottages line the green but in a way that has no suggestion of excessive self-consciousness. Although singularly lacking in dramatic sights, Ellen's Green offers the visitor the chance to see the sort of small villages that were once typical of the area but are now in short supply.

CRANLEIGH

7 miles SE of Godalming on the B2128

The parish church, St Nicholas, in the quiet residential town of Cranleigh contains a carving of a grinning feline which allegedly provided the inspiration for Lewis Carroll's Cheshire Cat. The town also contains the country's first cottage hospital, opened in the 1850s, and a public school founded by local farmers in 1865, which still incorporates a working farm.

EWHURST

8 miles SE of Godalming on the B2127

Ewhurst is a long village containing a sandstone church, St Peter and St Paul, whose nave and south door are considered to be amongst the finest examples of Norman church architecture in the county. The rest of the structure would have been of a similar age had it not been for an unfortunate attempt to underpin the tower in the 1830s, which resulted in the collapse, not only of the tower, but of the chancel and north transept as well. The structure was eventually rebuilt in "Norman style"

with an unusual shingled broach spire. Inside, there is a carved 14th century font and a Jacobean pulpit, and outside, the churchyard contains a number of mature trees native to North America.

The remainder of the village, part of which is set around a small square, contains some fine 18th and 19th century residential buildings, including the Woolpit, built for the Doulton family in the 1880s. The 843 foot Pitch Hill is situated a mile to the north and can be easily reached along a pleasant footpath from the village.

DORKING

Dorking is a long-established settlement, which stands at the intersection of Stane Street, the Roman road which once connected London with Chichester, and the ancient **Pilgrims' Way**, the east-west ridge way route, which is roughly

THE RUG CENTRE

68 South Street, Dorking, Surrey R44 2HD
Tel: 01306 882202; Fax: 01306 882131

Near the centre of Dorking behind the classic bow-fronted Georgian windows of the **Rug Centre**, visitors will find rugs of all sorts stacked from floor to ceiling. Michael Woodman and John Hicks established the Rug Centre in Reigate some ten years ago. Their expertise in Oriental rugs, gained over 25 years in the business, extends to all the major producing areas. Five years ago they moved to Dorking and have now opened a branch in Exeter. The continuing expansion of the business indicates that more and more people are appreciating the look, feel and warmth of hand-made Oriental rugs.

Small Afghan, Gabbeh or Belouch items are available for around £22 while fine old Persian Isafahans and Kashans will cost many thousands. All the rugs are woven by hand, whether in city workshops, village craft centres or by nomadic peoples whose men guard the sheep while women weave with age-

old skill passed on from mother to daughter over many generations. The variation in colour and design is infinite from the glowing rich reds of old Turkoman to the delicate tracery of Chinese Silks. Thick Persian Bidjars will last for generations while Russian Soumaks make dramatic wall hangings. If customers choose a carpet in the shop, which doesn't quite work in their home, Michael will search for the perfect rug for their setting. People come from every corner of the UK and from the United States and Canada to browse and buy at the Rug Centre. The friendly staff are happy for customers to browse through the rugs or to help them find something to suit.

followed by the course of the modern **North Downs Way**. Despite evidence of Saxon and Viking occupation, present-day Dorking is a congested commuter town, which owes most of its character to the Victorians.

There are a small number of older buildings, most notably the part 15th century former coaching inn, the White Horse, and the shops and houses in North Street, West Street, and at the western end of the High Street. However, the town's two most distinctive architectural features are characteristically 19th century: the unexpectedly grand parish church of St Martin with its soaring spire, and the Rose Hill housing development, an assortment of Victorian villas arranged around a green and entered from South Street through an unusual neo-Gothic arch. **St Paul's Church** in Dorking is a fine piece of architecture, designed by Benjamin Ferray and constructed in 1857.

Perhaps Dorking's most attractive feature is its close proximity to unspoilt countryside, a testimony to the success of the southeast's Green Belt policy. As well as the open spaces in the downs to the north, **Holmwood Common**, two miles along the A24 to the south, is another tract of National Trust-owned land which offers some pleasant way-marked walks through mature oak and birch woodlands and disabled access to the pleasant picnic area around **Fourwents Pond**.

Boxhill
2 miles N of Dorking off the A25

The 563 foot Box Hill lies a couple of miles from **Polesden Lacey** on the eastern side of the River Mole. This popular local landmark rises sharply from the valley floor to an impressive tree-covered summit, 400 feet above. The hill takes its name from the mature box trees which once grew here in profusion but which

were seriously depleted in the 18th century to supply the needs of London wood-engravers. By then, the site had already been known for over a century as a beauty spot and had been visited by, among others, the diarist John Evelyn.

Today, the National Trust owns over 800 acres of land around Box Hill which has now been designated a country park. The area around the summit incorporates an exhibition centre, a late 19th century fort and a take-away cafe, and can be reached either by footpath or by a narrow winding road, which leads up from Burford Bridge. The hillside is traversed by a series of nature walks, and there are also several picnic sites, which enjoy breathtaking views across the Weald to the South Downs.

The Burford Bridge Hotel stands on the banks of the River Mole at the foot of Box Hill and is connected to it by stepping stones across the river. In the early 19th century, the establishment was known as the Hare and Hounds and it was here that in 1805, Admiral Nelson said his farewells to Lady Hamilton prior to the Battle of Trafalgar. Keats is also believed to have completed his second volume of poems *"Endymion"* here in 1818. **Chapel Farm** at nearby West Humble is an open farm, which offers visitors the chance to see a working livestock farm at close quarters.

Mickleham
3 miles N of Dorking on the A24

Mickleham is a highly picturesque village with a good pub, the Running Horses, and a restored Norman church, St Michael, containing a rare Flemish stained-glass window. It is worth examining the churchyard because this is one of the few parish churches to preserve the Surrey tradition of grave-boards. These are wooden tombstone planks, which are carried between two posts. Most of the grave-boards in St Michael's are 19th century although they have been carefully preserved and renovated where necessary.

LEATHERHEAD

5 miles N of Dorking on the A24

Leatherhead is a pretty Mole Valley town, which manages to retain some measure of tranquillity despite being crossed by a number of major trunk routes. Several buildings in the narrow streets of the old town are worthy of note, including the 16th century Running Horse Inn and the attractive part 12th century parish church of St Mary and St Nicholas. The grave of Anthony Hope (real name Sir Anthony Hawkins), the author of *"The Prisoner Of Zenda"*, can be found in the churchyard, and a short distance away in Church Street, the informative **Leatherhead Museum of Local History** is housed in a

charming 17th century timber-framed cottage with its own small garden.

GREAT BOOKHAM

4 miles N of Dorking on the A246

Although heavily built up since the Second World War, the residential area to the west of Leatherhead manages to retain something of its historic past. The earliest mention of a settlement in the area dates back to the 660s AD when a manor at Bocheham is recorded as belonging to Chertsey Abbey.

Present day Great Bookham contains an exceptional parish church, **St Nicholas**, which has an unusual flint tower with a shingled spire dating back to the Norman era in the 12th century. A substantial part of the building, including the chancel, is known to have been rebuilt in the 1340s by the Abbot of Chertsey, and the church was again remodelled by the Victorians. Inside,

FIRE AND IRON GALLERY

Rowhurst Forge, Oxshott Road, Leatherhead, Surrey KT22 0EN
Tel: 01372 386453
e-mail:lucyquinnell@aol.com website:www.fireandiron.co.uk

Described by Miranda Innes in Country Living Magazine as *"a mecca for metal maniacs"*, Lucy Quinnell's **Fire And Iron** is a lively, eccentric collection of metalwork and jewellery by some of the leading local, national and international makers. Delightfully situated in a 15th century Surrey farmhouse set in several acres of countryside, the gallery hosts one of the finest display of the art of the metalworker – anywhere. Metalwork may be the name of the game but there are no coal-black smiths or bellows-blown forges here. Throughout the year a series of special exhibitions by individual artists complements a slowly changing permanent display of work from the world's leading artist-blacksmiths.

Although there's always a wide variety of designs on display, ranging from unusual wedding rings to life size steel animals, Lucy is delighted to arrange for a specially commissioned piece from any of the artists, be it a simple ring or a weathervane. The gates of the Globe Theatre in London was one of the Gallery's largest projects, taking ten years to organise and involving the work of 120 blacksmiths from around the world. Other clients include former Beatle, the late George Harrison, The Duke of Westminster and Elton John. Visitors who would like to try their hand at producing artwork like that seen in the gallery can sign up for one of the popular weekend blacksmithing courses which Lucy runs.

LINCOLN JOYCE FINE ART

40 Church Road, Great Bookham, Surrey KT 23 3PW
Tel: 01372 458481; Fax: 01372 458481
e-mail: rosemarylincolnjoyce@hotmail.com
website: www.artgalleries.uk.com

The Lincoln Joyce Fine Art Gallery in the centre of
Bookham offers a changing range of pictures and some
sculptures by contemporary and 20th century artists.
Long committed to providing a showcase for talented
artists, it was established in 1987 by the late John Storey
and taken over in 2000 by Rosemary Pearson. Rosemary
is well qualified to enhance the reputation for quality that the gallery has already gained. She has
studied painting and the art world for many years, gaining depth and breadth of knowledge in her
time at Sotheby's. She is a specialist in 19th and early 20th century art and her unerring eye for quality
ensures that only the finest paintings and sculptures are displayed here. Edwin Pollard, who managed

the gallery for the previous owner, continues to
work closely with Rosemary, to build on and
maintain the gallery's well-deserved reputation
among art lovers.

Visitors are sure to enjoy viewing the wide
selection of works by well known artists such as
Rowland Hilder, Edward Stamp, David Bellamy,
Sir Frank Brangwyn, Charles Edward Dixon, Sir
Claude Francis Barry as well as others by up and
coming artists. This provides customers with an
opportunity to invest in the future of the art
world and enjoy works of art, which will sustain
a lasting appreciation. The subjects are varied,
including landscape, marine, figurative, still-life
and semi-abstract but the watch word is quality.

Situated near the centre of the village of
Bookham, the charming half-timbered building,
which houses the gallery, was built in the 1920s and was originally a dairy. Behind the fascia walls, the
original tiles depicting cows, chickens and sheep vividly recall its rural past. However its historic use is
in little evidence within, where the under-stated elegance of the décor and an excellent lighting system
exhibit the works of art to perfection. An amazing range and number of pictures and sculptures are
displayed in this fairly small area yet there is a wonderful feeling of light and spaciousness. Visitors are
made to feel welcome to linger and enjoy the experience. All works of art on display here are personally

chosen by Edwin and Rosemary and they love
sharing their wide knowledge and expertise with
anyone seeking additional background and
information on pictures and artists. Art lovers will
return again and again to this friendly and
discerning gallery for the standard of art on view,
for their commitment to the future and for the sheer
pleasure of browsing in delightful surroundings
with expert advice and information readily to hand.
No matter how many times visitors return they will
find that the constantly changing exhibitions will
always present something new and fresh to
appreciate. Gallery hours: Tuesday to Saturday;
10.00am - 5.00pm.

there is some fine 15th century stained glass and a number of noteworthy monumental brasses and memorials to the local lords of the manor. An early 18th century owner of the Bookham estate, Dr Hugh Shortrudge, left an endowment in his will to four local churches on condition that an annual sermon was preached on the subject of the martyrdom of Charles I. St Nicholas continues to uphold the tradition of the "Shortrudge Sermon" which is preached each year on the final Sunday in January.

Polesden Lacey

Nearby **Little Bookham** has a small single-roomed church with a wooden belfry which is believed to date from the 12th century. The adjacent 18th century manor house now operates as a school. Bookham Common and Banks Common to the northwest of Little Bookham provide some welcome relief from the commuter estates and offer some pleasant walking through relatively unspoilt open heathland. The commons are recorded in the Domesday Book as providing pannage, the right to graze pigs on acorns, for Chertsey Abbey. Now under the ownership of the National Trust, they are particularly known for their rich and varied birdlife.

Another National Trust-owned property, **Polesden Lacey**, stands on high ground two miles to the south of Great Bookham. The estate was once owned by the writer R B Sheridan who purchased it in 1797 with the intention of restoring its decaying 17th century manor house. However, a lack of funds prevented him from realising his ambitions, and following his death in 1816, the building was demolished and the estate sold. During the 1820s, the architect Thomas Cubitt built a substantial Regency villa in its place which was subsequently remodelled and enlarged by successive owners throughout the 19th century.

In 1906, the estate was acquired by Captain Ronald Greville and his wife Margaret, the daughter of a Scottish brewing magnate and a celebrated high society hostess. Over the following three decades, they invited a succession of rich and influential guests to Polesden Lacey whose number included Edward VII, and George VI and Queen Elizabeth (the Queen Mother), who spent part of their honeymoon here in 1923. The Grevilles carried out a number of alterations of their own during this period and the extravagant "Edwardian-Louis XVI" internal decoration remains as a testimony to Margaret Greville's taste or lack of it.

Whatever the perspective, the house contains an undeniably fine collection of furniture, paintings, tapestries, porcelain and silver, which the Grevilles accumulated over 40 years, and Margaret's personal collection of photographs provides a fascinating record of British high society at play during the early part of the century. The surrounding grounds amount to over

1,000 acres and incorporate a walled rose garden, open lawns, a YHA youth hostel and a large area of natural woodland. An annual festival in late June and early July is held in the charming open-air theatre. This has expanded over the years and now presents a variety of theatre and entertainment including Gilbert and Sullivan, light operetta, grand opera, ballet, classical concerts, jazz, big bands, music hall, folk dancing and spectacular fireworks. There is always a Shakespearean production.

The Polesden Lacey estate is bordered to the south by Ranmore Common, another area of National Trust-owned upland, which is criss-crossed by scenic footpaths and bridleways.

RANMORE COMMON
1 mile NW of Dorking off the A2003

Ranmore Common's location on the top of the Downs provides some excellent views, especially looking south. This unspoilt setting, which can feel remote in bad weather despite its proximity to Dorking, is a testament to enlightened Green Belt policy. The common is in reality a long green, with only a few houses dotted around it, thereby preserving its exposed nature. Part-owned by the Forestry Commission, it is a Site of Special Scientific Interest and provides an excellent habitat for many birds and mammals.

EFFINGHAM
5 miles NW of Dorking on the A246

Efffingham is an old village that was famous as the home of the Howards of Effingham, one of whom was the Commander-in-Chief of the English fleet, which defeated the Spanish Armada in 1588. His home was **Effingham Court Palace**, which survives only as remnants at Lower Place Farm.

F. CONISBEE AND SON

Park Corner, Ockham Road South, East Horsley, Surrey KT24 6RZ
Tel: 01483 282 073 Fax: 01483 284859

F. Conisbee and Son is a long established family butchers, poulterers, graziers and caterers, who have been mastering the trade for over two centuries. The current Conisbee is Neil who runs the business with his sons Stephen and James. Unlike supermarkets and many modern butchers, they still buy their cattle 'on the hoof' every week from the local fat stock market. Generations of experience enable them to select the very best cattle being raised by local Surrey farmers. All the meat is hung as carcasses and quarters, allowing the meat to mature naturally. This ensures tenderness and improved flavour without the tainting or discolouration often found in vacuum packed meat. Further ensuring quality from start to finish, the family rear their own beef cattle on their farm in Fetcham.

The farm produces 5,000 prize winning turkeys each year, mostly for Christmas. In 2000 one lifted the Champion Turkey award at the South of England Fat Stock Show. The business has expanded considerably since the early years and they now have a resident chef in the kitchen at their Park Corner premises. Robert turns out a wide variety of excellent frozen home cooked ready meals and caters for anything from an intimate supper to a birthday celebration, wedding, conference or dinner dance. But Conisbee's speciality has to be its barbeques. Whole pigs and lambs or spit roasts are cooked over a bed of hot coals with all staff and equipment supplied. That and of course, their sausages, including Mexican chilli, apple and cider, garlic, chive and tomato or even your own recipe.

There were two other important manors in Effingham. One is the moated grange in Great Lee Wood, once the manor of Effingham la Leigh. The other was the medieval property of the Earls of Gloucester, East Court, which is now incorporated in a boarding school, St Theresa's Convent.

EAST HORSLEY

6 miles NW of Dorking on the A246

Suburban building has caught up with East Horsley, leaving the town centre bereft of the sort of charm associated with Ranmore Common or some of the other villages that are nearer Dorking. It does, however, possess one of the more dramatic country houses in Surrey, at least as it is viewed from the road. **East Horsley Towers**, built in the 1820s, seems to capture the spirit of the 19th century imagination as it moved from Romantic to the nostalgic re-creations so beloved of the Victorians. A long entrance leads to the house, which presents itself with a huge round tower by the entrance. Another tower, to the west, is built in the Gothic style. The house itself displays Tudor influences but has multi-coloured vaulting ribs throughout for support. Another tower, this time Germanic looking with a pointed roof, dominates the east wing of the house. It now operates as a luxurious management training centre.

OCKHAM

10 miles NW of Dorking on the B2039

Ockham once possessed a fine Jacobean mansion, **Ockham Park**. A serious fire in 1948 destroyed everything except for the orangery, stables, kitchen wing, and a solitary Italianate tower. The village church of All Saints still stands within the grounds of the estate; this largely 13th century building was constructed on the site of a pre-Norman structure and is

known for its remarkable east window, a surprising combination of seven tall pointed lancets finished in marble with distinctive carved capitals. The window dates from around 1260 and is thought to have been brought here from nearby Newark Abbey following its dissolution in the 16th century. The church incorporates a brick chapel, which contains a robed marble effigy of the first Lord King, a former owner of Ockham Park who died in 1734.

On **Chatley Heath**, 1 mile to the north of Ockham, there is a unique **Semaphore Tower** which was once part of the Royal Navy's signalling system for relaying messages between Portsmouth and the Admiralty in London. Although the semaphore mechanism soon fell into disuse, the structure has remained in good order and is open to the public at weekends. As well as offering outstanding views over the surrounding landscape, the **Chatley Heath Semaphore Tower** houses an interesting exhibition and model collection. It can be reached along a pleasant woodland pathway and is open throughout the summer at weekends and Bank Holidays.

EAST CLANDON

7 miles W of Dorking on the A246

This attractive small village straddles the A246 Leatherhead to Guildford route. The road zig-zags between brick and half-timber cottages, several of which are clustered around the Norman church of St Thomas. This small church was extensively restored at the end of the 19th century but the architects ensured that one of is most distinctive features - the bulky shingled bell tower - retained its original appearance.

The village also contains an interesting old forge and a lovely old manor farmhouse dating from the late 17th century. A striking National Trust

PARK HOUSE FARM

Abinger Common, Dorking, Surrey RH5 6LW
Tel: 01306 730101 Fax: 01306 730643
e-mail: Peterwallis@msn.com
website: www.smoothhound.co.uk/hotels/parkhous

A warm welcome awaits visitors to **Park House Farm** from Ann and Peter Wallis. They love to make guests feel relaxed in their large spacious home set in 25 acres of Surrey's beautiful countryside. Tastefully furnished with fine antiques, the house is warm and luxuriously comfortable throughout. The four sumptuous bedrooms are beautifully furnished and decorated with rich colour co-ordinated drapes, headboards and bed covers in quality matching patterns. All rooms are en-suite with excellent facilities and wonderful views. Full English breakfast is included but they will try to provide anything that guests require. This kind of care and attention to detail ensures that they retain their well-deserved ETC 4 diamonds.

This is an ideal base from which to explore the countryside on foot – nearby Leith Hill one of the highest points in Surrey has panoramic views for miles. The excellent rail link to London takes only 40 minutes to whisk visitors to the art galleries, museums, monuments, cathedrals, palaces, theatres and shopping of the capital. Park House is just off the A25 between Guilford, the historic County town of Surrey and Dorking, which is famous for its antique shops. The transport hub of road, rail and air links is complete with easy access from here to both Gatwick and Heathrow. Ann and Peter's policy of no smoking anywhere in the house ensures a pleasant environment for all guests. They regret that they cannot accommodate pets - simply because they have some of their own.

THE STEPHAN LANGTON INN

Friday Street, Abinger Common, Near Dorking, Surrey RH5 6JR
Tel: 01306 730775

Jonathan and Cynthia took over the Stephan Langton Inn in November 2000 following experience in various prestigious venues in London. Jonathan was previously head chef at Snow's on the Green, as well as the Mirabelle and the Chiswick. Cynthia was General Manager at the Chiswick. Set in a picturesque location in a densely wooded area, the inn has the appearance of an ancient traditional inn. In fact, it was built in 1930 on the site of an older inn. Its namesake was a 13th century Archbishop of Canterbury who was involved in drawing up the Magna Carta.

With ample parking outside, the interior has a cosy bar with wooden floors and an open fire. The bar serves Adnams and Sussex Best Bitter. The non-smoking dining room, with black beams, polished wooden tables and comfortable seating is separate from the bar. In summer, patio areas to the front and back allow customers to enjoy the surroundings and the sound of the running stream nearby.

However, delightful as the setting is, it is Jonathan's flair with the food, which draws increasing numbers of customers here. Specialising in modern British Cooking, he makes sure that all food is freshly prepared on the premises. Fresh sea food and meats, a fine selection of piquant cheeses and imaginatively cooked vegetables are accompanied by an excellent selection of wines. The bread, pasta and ice cream are all home-made by Jonathan. Puddings include a light and refreshing lemon sorbet, chocolate brownies or a delicate baked custard. Opening hours: Bar Monday to Friday 11.00 – 15.00 and 18.00 – 23.00, Saturday 11.00 – 23.00, Sunday 12.00 – 21.00.

property is located one mile to the northeast; **Hatchlands Park** is a distinctive brick-built house, which was designed in the mid 18th century for Admiral Boscawen after his famous victory in the Battle of Louisburg. Inside, there are some splendid examples of the early work of Robert Adams, some fine period furniture and paintings, and a wonderful assortment of historic keyboard instruments, the Cobbe collection, which was moved here in 1988. The grounds, originally laid out by Repton, were remodelled by Gertrude Jekyll. In recent years, parts of the garden have been restored to original designs and planting plans of Jekyll and Repton.

WESTCOTT

2 miles W of Dorking on the A25

Westcott is a tidy village that lies on the main road linking Dorking with Shere. Although most of the houses are from the same Victorian period, they display a variety of building styles. This diversity stems from the fact that Westcott lies almost exactly at the junction of the chalk North Downs and the sandstone Surrey Hills. Both of these stone types figure in the design of the cottages, and sometimes both are used in the same house. **Churtgate House**, built in the 16th century, pre-dates nearly all the other buildings in Westcott; it is located on the main road at the corner of Balchin's Lane.

ABINGER

4 miles SW of Dorking off the A25

The parish of Abinger contains two villages, Abinger itself (or **Abinger Common**) which lies one mile west of Friday Street at the southern end of the parish, and **Abinger Hammer** which lies on the A25 Dorking

to Guildford road to the north. Abinger claims to be one of the oldest settlements in the country, having been settled by Middle Stone Age people around 5000 BC. The remains of a Mesolithic pit-dwelling were discovered in a field near Abinger's old Manor House, which, when excavated in 1950, revealed over 1,000 tools and artefacts which are now on display in an interesting little museum.

Abinger's parish church of St James is an unlucky building. This part 12th century structure was largely destroyed by an enemy flying bomb during World War II. It was rebuilt, with great sensitivity, but was severely damaged in 1964 after being struck by lightning. In the churchyard there is a war memorial designed by Lutyens, and in the corner of the three-side village green, a set of old wooden stocks and a whipping post.

Abinger Common is a delightful hamlet that lies one and a half miles north of Leith Hill, the birthplace of the first Archbishop of Canterbury whose name lives on in the title of an enchanting pub, The Stephen Langton Inn.

Abinger Hammer, just over a mile to the northwest, lies in the valley of the River Tillingbourne, a fast-flowing stream which in the 15th and 16th centuries was used to power the mechanical metal-

Abinger Hammer Clock

THE PLOUGH INN

Coldharbour Lane, Coldharbour, Dorking, Surrey RH5 6HD
Tel: 01306 711793 Fax: 01306 710055
e-mail: theploughinn@btinternet.com

Surrounded by beautiful National Trust land in the picturesque village of Coldharbour, the **Plough Inn** dates back to the 17th century, when it was a coaching inn, supplying the needs of travellers for good food, comfortable lodgings and transport. Anna and Rick Abrehart, who took over in 1989 have continued the centuries old tradition of warmth, hospitality and friendly service, catering to the needs of modern travellers as well as local people. The mark of quality of an establishment is the opinion of the locals and they would testify that The Plough Inn well deserved its award of Surrey pub of the year in 1997.

Those who appreciate good ale will find it here, brewed on the premises in the Leith Hill Brewery, set up by Rick in 1996. The two ales are brewed in the traditional way using only natural ingredients. Available in the bar, they are unique to the Plough Inn. The flagship brew, Crooked Furrow, is a well-rounded and fruity best bitter. Tallywhacker, on the other hand, is a strong, dark ale with subtle overtones of roasted barley.

It's worth a detour to sample the beer alone but the food is of an equally high standard. Food is served in the restaurant, bar or garden, and Rick and Anna are meticulous about fresh ingredients and quality. From gourmet to traditional English the food is exciting and varied. The daily menus include meat, pasta, vegetarian dishes and game. The pudding selection is to die for, the main problem is choosing.

For those wanting to throw a party, where could be better than The Barn. In the grounds of the Plough, this 17th century barn offers a warm, friendly rustic atmosphere for any gathering. There is room to seat about 60 people and it is ideal for parties, dinners and discos.

For those wishing to investigate the outdoors, nearby Leith Hill is the highest spot in South East England. From the National Trust Tower here it is possible to see 13 counties with the naked eye. The Plough is in an ideal centre from which to explore the lovely surrounding countryside, to stop overnight on a longer journey or to spend some time in nearby Dorking or Guildford. What may not be so readily noticed is that the Plough is only 30 minutes from Gatwick and one hour from Heathrow. It is ideal for travellers

and if guests need to catch an early flight, a taxi can easily be arranged to get to the airport with plenty of time to spare. The inn has six rooms, all en-suite, five double and one single. Decorated in an individual country house style, simple but tasteful, with polished antique furniture and iron bed heads, the rooms have all the facilities you would expect in a top quality hotel yet they avoid the anonymous feel of hotel room décor. For a special occasion such as an anniversary or birthday, nothing could be more romantic than champagne and flowers awaiting guests' arrival in the lovely Bay Room.

KINGFISHER FARM SHOP

Abinger Hammer, Dorking, Surrey RH5 6QX
Tel: 01306 730703 Fax: 01306 731654

Kingfisher Farm Shop run by Barrie Arminson with his wife Margaret and daughter Marion is part of a long family tradition of providing high quality food for the discerning consumer. Barrie's great grandfather started growing watercress in 1850 and Barrie continues to produce watercress for the local market. It is grown in spring water, which provides all the nutrients required, without the aid of fertilisers or insecticides.

However the farm shop has been a growing part of the business since the family started selling fruit and vegetables in 1971. The watercress packing shed at Abinger Hammer became the present shop in 1999. As well as their own fresh watercress, the Arminsons sell as much regional and local food as they can. Tables outside are piled with a wide range of fresh fruit and vegetables in season as well as plants and herbs. In the brightly lit interior an abundance of fresh fruit and vegetables meets the eye. Nearby shelves are groaning with bread, cakes, pies and biscuits alongside locally produced jams and chutneys. In chill cabinets and freezers there are fresh and frozen meats, while dairy products include milk, cream, ice cream and a great selection of cheeses. Vegetarian and a range of whole food products are also available. The latest innovation for the Arminsons is the Off Licence, which stocks English wines and beers from Surrey and Sussex as well as cider from Devon. As members of Taste of the South East, the Kingfisher Farm Shop specialises in providing high quality local and home made food, of a kind unavailable in supermarkets. Opening Hours: Monday to Saturday; 09.00am - 6.00pm except Sunday and Bank Holidays: Summer; 10.00am - 5.00pm. Winter; 10.00am - 4.00pm.

working hammers from which the settlement takes its name. At one time, the village was known for the manufacture of cannon balls and a busy blacksmith's workshop can still be found here. Abinger Hammer's industrial past is reflected in the famous "Jack the Smith" hammer clock, which was erected in 1909. This unique clock overhangs the road on the site of an old iron forge and is characterised by the figure of a blacksmith who strikes a bell with his hammer every half hour.

HOLMBURY ST MARY

6 miles SW of Dorking on the B2126

Until 1879 the village was called Felday and was a hide away for smugglers and sheep stealers. Holmbury St Mary was the invention of well-to-do Victorians, one of whom, George Edmund Street, designed and paid for the church in 1879. Much of the village was developed in the 19th century. It is ideally situated for access to the 857 foot Holmbury Hill, an upland with an altogether wilder feel than Leith Hill, its taller neighbour across the valley. A pleasant walk leads to the remains of an eight acre Iron Age hill fort whose fading earthwork fortifications lie hidden amongst the undergrowth on the hillside.

COLDHARBOUR

5 miles SW of Dorking off the A29

A remote hamlet set 700 feet up in the Surrey Hills, Coldharbour has an atmosphere that is light-years away from most people's preconception of surrey as a county of cosy suburbs and smiling farmland. Sturdy, stone-built houses cling to the hilltop, from which there are magnificent views sweeping south over the Weald.

Just to the north of Coldharbour is **Anstiebury Camp**, an Iron Age fort

THE HANNAH PESCHAR SCULPTURE GARDEN

Black and White Cottage, Standon Lane, Ockley, Surrey RH5 5QR
Tel: 01306 627269 fax: 01306 627662
e-mail: hpeschar@easynet.co.uk
website: www.hannahpescharsculpture.com

Situated in a wooded valley with natural running water this sculpture garden has been developed over the last 18 years by **Hanna Peschar** and her husband Anthony Paul. The water was previously channelled into millponds and an earlier 20th century garden had added paths and exotic plantings. Now the remains of the old water garden have been combined with an ever-changing display of sculpture and ceramics in a specially designed and unique setting.

Anthony Paul is a freelance landscape designer, whose work on the landscape of this lively, unorthodox, garden has been so subtle as to be easily mistaken for nature itself. Streams, ponds, waterfalls and bridges provide the artwork with a setting that is dramatic and theatrical and at the same time sensuous and tactile. Existing trees have been trimmed to improve their form and new plants chosen for both form and colour to provide dense planting and contrasting open areas. Tall grasses and massive leafed plants frame and enhance the art collection.

It's a place where surprises abound. *Fragment* a stoneware and lead face by Graham Clayton lies on the ground beside a tree and may evoke memories of Shelley's poem *Ozymandius of Egypt*. Neil Wilkin's *Umbrella Tree* is a study in crystal and stainless steel, which appears to be in a perfectly natural setting on the banks of a stream, surrounded by wild flowers and grasses while the bronze mesh forms of David Beggbie's *Three Truncs* create an almost ghostly, ethereal atmosphere as they hang suspended between two tree trunks against a backdrop of lush vegetation.

Hannah Peschar has built up an international reputation for promoting young and exciting talent. All the art works in the garden have been chosen by her and most are by British artists. The range is wide with styles covering everything from the figurative to the abstract. Materials can be metals, glass, wire, ceramic, marble, wood and even plastic or fibreglass. It is not a static exhibition and the installations are changed regularly. Most of the sculptures are for sale and with a possibility of paying in instalments. Sculptures can also be shipped and placed worldwide and individual commissions arranged with any of the artists exhibiting.

The garden is easy to find. Exit the M25 at Junction 9 and take the A24 south towards Dorking. Bypass that town and at the Beare Green roundabout take the A29, signposted Bognor Regis, to the village of Ockley. Look out for the Old School House pub on the right and just after it, turn right into Cat Hill Lane. Turn left at the T junction into Standon Lane and the garden entrance will be on the right some 500 yards past the left turning to Oakwood Church.

probably dating from the 1st or 2nd century BC. The fort is oval in plan, covering more than 11 acres and is defended by triple banks with double ditches to the north and northeast.

LEITH HILL

5 miles SW of Dorking on the B2126

The 965 foot National Trust-owned, Leith Hill is the highest point in the southeast of England. In 1766, a 64 foot tower was built on the tree-covered summit by Richard Hull, a local squire who lived at nearby Leith Hill Place. He now lies buried beneath his splendid creation. Present-day visitors climbing to the top on a clear day can enjoy a panorama, which takes in several counties and reaches as far as the English Channel.

The part 17th part 18th century Leith Hill Place stands within beautiful rhododendron filled grounds, which are open to the public throughout the year. In its time, the house has been owned by the Wedgwood and Vaughan Williams families, and inside, there is a fine collection of Wedgwood pottery and paintings by such artists as Reynolds and Stubbs. An Edwardian country house designed by Sir Edwin Lutyens can be found on the northern slopes of Leith Hill. Goddards on Abinger Common, now the centre of activities of the Lutyens Trust, stands within attractive grounds laid out by Gertrude Jekyll. The

garden is open on a limited basis throughout the summer and the house itself can be rented by the week or for a few days from the Landmark Trust.

OCKLEY

8 miles S of Dorking on the A29

At Ockley there is a village green which, at over 500 feet in diameter, is one of the largest in Surrey. In summer, village cricket is played in this classic English setting which is enhanced by a number of handsome period houses and cottages. Ockley has had a long and eventful history: the village once stood on Stane Street, the old Roman road between Chichester and London which is now partially followed by the route of the A29, and in the mid 9th century, a momentous battle between the forces of King Ethelwulf of the West Saxons and the marauding Vikings reputedly took place near here. Following the Norman invasion, the surrounding woodlands were designated a royal hunting forest and in the 12th century, the Normans built a fortification half a mile to the north of the present village green which has long since disappeared. However, the nearby part 14th century church of St Margaret remains, although this was extensively remodelled by the Victorians during the 1870s.

Among the many other noteworthy buildings in Ockley are the 18th century

(Continued page 358)

THE INN ON THE GREEN

Stane Street, Ockley, Surrey
Tel: 01306 711032

Martin Earp is the genial host, of this fine establishment. **The Inn on the Green** is a 16th century coaching inn situated opposite the village green. Warm and comfortable, with beamed ceilings and a roaring log fire, it attracts lovers of comfort, good food and drink. It is a free house with a changing selection of real ales including regulars like Old Speckled Hen and Green King Abbot. It excels in fish and meat dishes such as whole seabass, beef Wellington or that old favourite, steak and ale pie.

WALK 9

Leith Hill and Friday Street

Start	National Trust's Landslip car park below Leith Hill, near Coldharbour village
Distance	6½ miles (10.5km)
Approximate time	3½ hours
Parking	Landslip car park
Refreshments	Pub at Friday Street, kiosk at Leith Hill Tower (weekends)
Ordnance Survey maps	Landranger 187 (Dorking, Reigate & Crawley), Explorer 146 (Dorking, Box Hill & Reigate)

At 965ft (294m) Leith Hill is not only the highest point in Surrey but also the highest in south-east England. It is a magnificent viewpoint, one of a series that crown the well-wooded greensand ridge a few miles south of the North Downs. This walk is mostly through the lovely pine and beech woods and over areas of sandy heathland that is characteristic of greensand country, and although fairly hilly in places it is relatively undemanding. However, do follow the route instructions carefully; the large number of tracks and paths in this area, much of which is owned by the National Trust, can be confusing at times.

Begin by taking a path that leads up from the car park, following the first of a series of signs with a tower symbol on them, towards Leith Hill Tower. At a track turn right to head quite steeply uphill. Bear left in front of a gate marked 'Bridleway' at a junction and climb again to reach Leith Hill Tower **B** . This was built in 1766 by Richard Hull of nearby Leith Hill Place to compensate for the hill just failing to top the 1000ft (305m) mark; the extra height pushes it to 1029ft (313m). There is a small admission charge to the tower, from where there is one of the finest and most extensive panoramas in the south-east: northwards across to the North Downs and beyond that to London and the Chilterns, and southwards over the Weald to the South Downs and the English Channel.

Just past the tower the path forks. Take the right-hand path here, at a second fork take the left-hand one and at a third fork take the left-hand one again. Shortly after,

a well-defined path joins from the left. Continue ahead for about ½ mile (800m), following the straight main path across Wotton Common to reach a crosstrack **C** . Turn right here along a fairly straight path and after ½ mile (800m) bear left at a T-junction to a lane **D** . Turn left and almost immediately turn right, at a public footpath sign, along a path that keeps along the inside edge of woodland, with a fence on the right.

On the edge of the woodland go through a fence gap and follow a path across a field to climb a stile at the far end. Continue along an enclosed path to the right of houses, soon re-entering woodland, and descend, by a wire fence on the left, to a crossroads **E** . Turn right along a track that winds through the beautiful woodlands of Abinger Bottom, briefly emerging from the trees to reach a lane. Keep ahead along the lane and opposite the drive to a house called St Johns bear right to continue along a wooded track. After passing a barrier the track becomes a tarmac lane, which you follow through the charming and secluded hamlet of Friday Street to a T-junction.

Turn right to pass across the end of the millpond, a former hammer pond and one of many in the area that were created to power the hammers of the local ironworks up to the time of the Industrial Revolution. The view across it nowadays could hardly be more tranquil. On the far side, turn half-right **F** , at a public footpath sign, along a path that heads uphill away from the pond, passing to the left of a National Trust sign for Severells Copse, and continue steadily uphill to a lane. Cross over, keeping ahead to cross another lane and continue along the path in front. Take the right-hand path at a fork – not easy to spot – and head downhill along a sunken path, bearing slightly right on meeting another path to continue downhill, curving left to a lane.

Turn left through Broadmoor, another attractive and secluded hamlet, and opposite a riding centre turn sharp right **G** , at Greensand Way and public bridleway waymarks, onto a track. Keep on this straight and broad track through Broadmoor Bottom for 1 mile (1.6km) and, just over ¼ mile (400m) after passing to the right of Warren Farm, look out for a crossing of paths and tracks by a bench **H** . Turn half-left here onto a path; after a few yards cross a stream, by a National Trust sign for Duke's Warren, and a few yards further on at a fork take the right-hand path. This is a most delightful part of the walk, initially between woodland on the right and more open sloping heathland

dotted with trees on the left, later the path re-enters woodland and heads steadily uphill, finally curving left to a junction.

Bear left for a few yards to a fork and take the right-hand track, following the direction of a blue waymark, to emerge alongside the right-hand edge of the cricket pitch on Coldharbour Common. Just after the end of the cricket pitch, turn sharp right to continue along a path that has a wooden footpath post **J** , ignoring all side turns and following the main path all the while. To the left there are grand views over the Weald to the South Downs on the horizon. Opposite a barrier on the right **A** , turn left to rejoin the outward route and head downhill back to Landslip car park, following footpath signs that have a car symbol with the letter 'L' on them. ●

Ockley Court, which stands opposite the church, and the groups of cottages surrounding the green which are built in a variety of styles and materials, including brick, tiling and weather-boarding. An interesting private sculpture and ceramics gallery, the **Hannah Peschar Gallery-Garden**, which incorporates a delightful water garden can be found in Standon Lane (see panel on page 354).

A short distance to the southwest of Ockley, a chapel was built in the 13th century to serve the population of this once-isolated part of the Weald. Known as the Okewood Chapel, it was later endowed by a local nobleman after his son narrowly avoided being savaged by a wild boar when a mystery arrow struck and killed the charging animal.

NEWDIGATE
5 miles S of Dorking off the A24

A turning east off the A24 at Beare Green leads to the village of Newdigate. This historic settlement contains an interesting parish church, St Peter's, which is believed to have been founded in the 12th century by the Earl de Warenne as a "hunters' chapel", a place of worship built to be used by Norman hunting parties during their expeditions in the Wealden forest. The tower, with its shingled spire, was constructed around a massive cross-braced timber frame in the 15th century, a time when Newdigate was relatively prosperous thanks to its flourishing iron-founding industry. The oak shingles on the spire had to be replaced in the late 1970s after their Victorian predecessors had warped in the hot summer of 1976.

Present-day Newdigate contains a number of exceptional old timber-framed buildings, several of which date back to the 16th century and before.

CHARLWOOD
8 miles SE of Dorking off the A24

A charming period village on the Sussex border, Charlwood is all the more admirable in that it is so near Crawley and Gatwick Airport and yet preserves so much of its own rural identity. Although it lacks the sense of remoteness which it must once have possessed, Charlwood still has many 18th century cottages and a sprinkling of earlier, slightly larger yeomen's houses such as the 15th century Charlwood House to the southeast of the village centre.

The parish Church of St Nicholas was built in the 11th century and underwent a series of alterations, extensions and renovations beginning in the 13th century. The impression, surprisingly, is one of an organic building that has evolved with the centuries. One of its prized possessions is the late medieval screen, one of the most intricately carved pieces of ecclesiastical woodwork in Surrey.

BROCKHAM
1 mile E of Dorking on the A25

Brockham is a picture-postcard village set around a quintessential three-sided village green on which cricket is played in summer, a Guy Fawkes' bonfire is lit in autumn, and Christmas carols are sung in winter. The legendary cricketer W.G. Grace is even said to have played here. This delightful tree-lined setting is enhanced by a splendid view of Box Hill, some fine old cottages, and an elegantly proportioned parish church with a tall spire which was built in the 1840s in uncomplicated Early English style. Other noteworthy buildings in the village include the late 18th century **Brockham Court**, which can be seen on the eastern edge of the green, and the part 17th century Feltons Farm, which lies a short distance away to the southwest. The

Brockham Village

a well-marked trail along much of its route, look down on its modern, secular, counterpart, the M25.

The countryside in this southeastern corner is far less wooded than south-central or southwestern Surrey. Instead it is a land of open fields and church spires spotted on the horizon. Only at the southern edge, where it nears the Weald of Kent, does the landscape begin to become defined by its dense woodlands.

remains of some 19th century industrial kilns can be seen on the Downs above the village in the disused Brockham Quarries.

SOUTHEAST SURREY

The southeast corner of Surrey abuts both Kent to the east and Sussex to the south. Not surprisingly there are elements of both counties in some of the Surrey border villages, noticeable in particular in the way that Kent weather-boarding features in the villages and hamlets near Lingfield.

The M25 marks the northern extremity of the area covered in this chapter. As with so many other parts of the county, the towns and villages lying just south of the motorway have fought - and largely won - a battle to preserve their sense of identity. Perhaps it is simply because they have had many centuries to grow accustomed to east-west traffic. The valleys and ridges here comprised the route followed by religious devotees on their way from London and further afield to Canterbury. Indeed many stretches of the original Pilgrims' Way, which is now

REIGATE

Reigate is a prosperous residential town whose expansion at the hands of postwar developers has done much to conceal its long and distinguished history. The settlement was once an important outpost of the de Warenne family, the assertive Norman rulers whose sphere of influence stretched from the Channel coast to the North Downs. As at Lewes, they built a castle on a rise above the village streets of which nothing remains today except for an arch, which was reconstructed in the 1770s from material recovered from the original castle walls. Today, this striking neo-Gothic reproduction stands at the heart of a pleasant public park.

A steep path leads down from the castle mound to the attractive mixture of Victorian, Georgian and older buildings, which line Reigate's High Street. The **Old Town Hall**, a handsome redbrick building constructed in 1729, stands at its eastern end, and a short distance away to the north, the entrance to a disused road tunnel can be seen. This was built beneath the castle mound in 1824 to ease

MIMI'S DELICATESSEN AND ESPRESSO BAR

65A/B High Street, Reigate, Surrey RH2 9AE
TEL: 01737 216121

Mouth-watering food, freshly prepared from quality ingredients coupled with a friendly and personal service combine to make **Mimi's Delicatessen and Espresso Bar and Take Away** one of the most popular eateries in Surrey. Situated in a former antique shop on the High Street, its location and stool seating in the two large front windows add to its appeal. Although seating is limited, Mimi's never feels cramped. Spacious tables with bright covers and a motley collection of chairs combine with the blue and yellow décor to create a cheerful and restful ambience.

Two counter refrigerators hold a bewildering array of food - continental cheeses from France, Spain, Italy and England, together with a selection of hams, salamis, freshly baked pastries, crostini, fresh bread and real ice cream. Each day sees a different selection of pasta, pizza and vegetarian dishes as

well as salads, artichoke hearts, olives, sun-dried tomatoes, roasted vegetables and mushrooms and fish including sardines, tuna and anchovies. A thriving take away service produces a constant stream of freshly baked ciabatta, focaccia, baguettes and panini all stuffed to the brim with a variety of fillings and offer excellent value for money. The fillings can also be served in a toastie with olive oil gently drizzled on it. Even if you're not hungry, call in just for a coffee or hot chocolate as it comes highly recommended and will make your day.

the through-flow of traffic on the busy London to Brighton coaching route.

Other noteworthy buildings in this part of town include the timber-framed and tile-fronted La Trobes in the High Street, and the 400 year-old **Old Sweep's House** in the charmingly named Slipshoe Street.

As well as being effective administrators, the de Warennes were known for their devout religious beliefs, and again as at Lewes, they founded a priory in the town some distance from the centre. After the Dissolution, this became the home of Lord Howard of Effingham, the commander-in-chief of the English navy at the time of the Spanish Armada. **Reigate Priory**, now a Grade 1 listed building set in 65 acres of parkland, has been remodelled on a number of occasions, in particular during the Georgian era. It now operates as a school and museum. The interior contains some fine period features

including a Holbein fireplace and a fine 17th century oak staircase. Also set away from the town centre, and probably standing on the site of pre-Norman Reigate, is the pale stone-built church of St Mary Magdalene. This contains a number of striking memorials, including one carved by Joseph Rose the Elder around 1730.

AROUND REIGATE

BETCHWORTH
3 miles W of Reigate off the A25

Betchworth was once a much more important settlement than it is today. In the 14th century, it had its own fortress, Betchworth Castle, which stood beside the River Mole on a site now occupied by the local golf course. This has now virtually disappeared and the only reminder of Betchworth's past glory is

SENIOR AND CARMICHAEL

Whitehouse Workshop, Church Street,
Betchworth, Surrey RH3 7DN
Tel: 01737 844316 Fax: 01737 844464
e-mail: rupert@seniorandcarmichael.co.uk
website: www.seniorandcarmichael.co.uk

Furniture makers **Senior and Carmichael** are
situated in picturesque Church Street leading to
St. Michael's Church, which was made famous
by the film *Four Weddings and a Funeral*.

The partners Rupert Senior and Charles
Wheeler-Carmichael both trained at Parnham
College of Furniture. They are personally
involved in the making of every piece of furniture
in the workshop. Working with a talented team of craftsmen, they carry out every part of the furniture
making process in-house. Working to commission, the partnership produces some of the very best
hand-made one-off contemporary furniture in the country. Senior and Carmichael have now been
awarded 12 coveted Guild Marks from the Worshipful Company of Furniture Makers, Britain's hallmark
of excellence in design and craftsmanship. Their work is featured in numerous specialist books and
they exhibit all over the world. All their exceptional pieces of contemporary furniture have been tailored
to individual requirements, using predominately wood but also incorporating metal, glass and stone.
They have a wealth of experience of working alongside other trades specialising in traditional crafts
such as leatherwork, inlay or woodcarving.

Some of their more extraordinary commissions have included an expanding mechanical dining
table, the largest bookcase in the world, a 60 foot conference table for the Royal Saudi Arabian Embassy
in London and a Folio Table for a major stately home, which last commissioned furniture in 1780.
They are regularly commissioned to design and make dining tables, chairs, coffee tables, cabinets,
revolving bookcases and desks for homes and offices all over the country. Each piece of work is
individually signed, numbered and dated which assures its authenticity. As these pieces are treasured
and passed on as unique heirlooms, the place of Senior and Carmichael in history is guaranteed.

Recently Senior and Carmichael have started producing some limited editions of their more popular
pieces such as the Hurricane Chair. These hand-made wooden chairs are constructed in a combination
of local timbers, salvaged from those blown down in the Great Storm of 1987. The woodlands of this
area were devastated, affecting many of the finest specimen trees, some as much as 250 years old. Oak,
ash, yew, sycamore, acacia, London plane and walnut are among the woods used to make these historical
chairs. Each has a unique story to tell and for those with a romantic turn of mind, the two furniture

makers can identify where almost
every log came from

The Whitehouse Workshop was
built in the late 19th century and is a
rare example of a weather-boarded
joiners shop, once very common in
the towns and villages of Southern
England. Senior and Carmichael
have been established here for the
last 20 years continuing the long
tradition of furniture making on this
site. As the workshop is fully
operational, visitors should make an
appointment to discuss a commission so that the partners can give
them their undivided attention.

the parish **Church of St Michael**, a surprisingly imposing structure which incorporates some ancient Saxon masonry, a Norman arch and a succession of more recent architectural modifications. Inside, there is a fascinating map of the local manor dated 1634 showing the vestiges of the feudal field system and a wooden chest which is reputed to have been made before the Norman invasion from a single piece of timber taken from a 1,000 year old oak tree. There is also an unusual font dating from the 1950s. The church is situated at the end of a wide cul-de-sac, which also contains an early 18th century vicarage, an old long barn, and a collection of attractive 17th and 18th century cottages.

A number of interesting buildings can be seen in other parts of Betchworth, including the 16th century Old Mill Cottage, the slender **Queen Anne Old House**, and **Betchworth House**, an impressive part-Georgian manor house which is surrounded by pretty parkland.

BUCKLAND

3 miles W of Reigate on the A25

Buckland is a pretty settlement which suffers from being sited on the busy main road. The road divides Buckland's tidy rectangular green from the parish church of St Mary, a part 13th century structure, whose interior is worth a look for its 15th century stained-glass east window and 17th century pews and oak panelling. The A25 to the east of Buckland passes along the northern edge of Reigate Heath. This narrow area of open heathland is the home of the unique **Windmill Church**, the only church in the world to be situated in a windmill.

Buckland Village and Pond

LEIGH

4 miles SW of Reigate of the A217

Leigh (pronounced lye) is a well-kept village, which, like at least a dozen others in Britain, takes its name from the Saxon term for forest clearing. Like Newdigate and Charlwood to the south, Leigh was an important centre of the Wealden iron-founding industry which prospered from the 14th century until it was superseded by Northern-based coal-fired smelting in the 18th century. Indeed, this now-tranquil area was once known as Thunderfield-in-the-Forest because of the number of iron furnaces it contained.

HORLEY

5 miles S of Reigate on the A23

The pleasant town of Horley lies on the Sussex border and not far from Gatwick Airport to the south. The proximity to the airport, surprisingly, has done little to alter the character of Horley although the town did undergo a transformation in the Victorian era after the arrival of the main railway line. The present arrangement of streets, set mostly in a gridiron pattern, branched out from the rail line to provide housing for railway workers and shops to cater to their needs. This neighbourhood, which constitutes most of the core of Horley, is trim and neat, and the overall effect is pleasant. Dotted among the 19th century buildings are a few survivors of earlier eras, including a lovely tile-hung cottage by the church.

OUTWOOD

5 miles SE of Reigate off the M23

Although Outwood is accessible from the M23, a more pleasant approach leads southwards from Bletchingley along a country road across the Weald. **Outwood Common**, the area of high ground to the east of village, is best known for being the location of one of the most interesting windmills in the country.

The Post Mill is acknowledged as the oldest working windmill in England. It was built in 1665 and it is said that from the top of the mill, some 39 feet up, the Great Fire of London was visible 27 miles away. Unlike other ancient buildings in England, the Post Mill's early history is not shrouded in mystery and conjecture. It was built by Thomas Budgen, a miller of Nutfield, and the original deeds are still in existence.

The term "post mill" describes the structure and mechanism of this remarkable building. The whole body of the mill, including its sails and machinery, balances on a huge central post. This post is made from oak, which, it is said, was drawn seven miles by oxcart from Crabbet Park, near Crawley, where it was felled. It is supported by four diagonal quarter bars and two crosstrees. These in turn rest on four brick piers. The purpose of this post system is to allow the mill to be turned to face the breeze. It is so finely balanced that a single person can turn the sails into the wind. Another special design

Outwood Post Mill

feature incorporated around 100 years later allows the angle of the sails to be adjusted to suit different wind conditions using a system of elliptical springs.

For over a century, a second "smock" windmill stood nearby, and the pair were known locally as the Cat and Fiddle; sadly, the Fiddle blew down in a storm in the early 1960s.

BURSTOW

8 miles SE of Reigate off the B2037

The lanes to the south of Outwood lead through Smallfield to Burstow, a well-kept village whose church, St Bartholomew's, has a surprisingly well preserved late medieval timber-framed tower. This hefty 15th century structure supports a peal of six bells, the largest of which weighs over half a ton. The church itself is an attractive mixture of Norman, Perpendicular, and Victorian influences;

the chancel contains the remains of John Flamsteed, a former rector and the first Astronomer Royal, who is best remembered for his maps of the night skies which were compiled in the late 17th century as an aid to marine navigation.

About one mile north of Burstow is **Smallfield Place**, regarded by many as the best example of a stone-built country home in Surrey. Its almost forbidding appearance is at odds with the mellow brick or aged timber exteriors of so many Surrey manor houses. The house was built at the beginning of the 17th century and presents a long, largely unadorned two-storey Wealden stone face to the curious public.

LINGFIELD

12 miles SE of Reigate off the A22

Lingfield is a large village, which is set within delightful wooded countryside in the southeastern corner of the county. Almost large enough to be called a town, "leafy Lingfield" is perhaps best known to the world at large for its racecourse. However, the settlement has long been an important agricultural centre, whose largely Perpendicular church of St Peter and St Paul has been enlarged over the centuries to create what has become known as the "Westminster Abbey of Surrey". As well as having a rare double nave and an exceptional collection of monumental brasses, the church also contains a surprising number of memorials to members of the Cobham family, the medieval lords of the manor who lived at the now demolished **Starborough Castle**, a mile and a half to the east. Each of the first four barons has a sizeable tomb showing an effigy of its occupant. These date from between 1361 and 1471 and are particularly fascinating to those with an interest in the development of late-medieval armour over this period.

The broad thoroughfare leading down from the church is lined with characteristic weather-boarded and tile-fronted buildings, including Pollard Cottage, with its unusual 15th century shop front, the 16th century Old Town Stores, and the Star Inn Cottages, built around 1700. The country library on the opposite side of the church is a former farmhouse, which was built in the 17th century on the site of a Carthusian college founded in the 1400s by Sir Reginald Cobham. Elsewhere in Lingfield, a couple of interesting features can be found near the pond in Plaistow Street: the 15th century village cross and the old lock-up, a small local gaol which was built in 1772 and in use until 1882.

Greathed Manor, to the southeast of Lingfield, is a substantial Victorian manor house built in 1868 for the Spender Clay family.

CROWHURST

11 mile SE of Reigate off the A22

Crowhurst contains a yew tree estimated to be around 4,000 years old, thought to be one of the oldest yew trees in the country. Its branches are said to enclose an area over 30 feet in diameter. During the 1820s, a covered cafe was formed by removing some of the central branches and installing tables and chairs.

Crowhurst Place, to the southwest, was rebuilt after the First World War on the site of a 15th century moated manor house.

DORMANSLAND

12 miles SE of Reigate off the B2029

Dormansland presents itself as evidence for a bit of social history detective work. The cottages in this hamlet near the Sussex and Kent borders date from the Victorian era, with some 17th and 18th century examples mixed in. However, they share a common limitation - their size. Other Surrey hamlets have workmen's cottages but there is usually much more diversity in scale. Several social historians have proposed that these tiny cottages were built by people who were squatting in common land.

Just outside the village is an altogether grander structure, **Old Surrey Hall**, built in 1450 on the remote border with Sussex. Much of the 15th century section, with its close timbering exterior, survives, but the overall moated quadrangle of today's house dates from 1922 and represents a renovation work of near genius by the architect George Crawley.

REDHILL

2 miles E of Reigate on the A23

Redhill developed around the railway station after the London to Brighton line opened in the 1840s. The new rail line ran parallel to the corresponding road (now the A23) and cut through previously open landscape. Most of Redhill's buildings consequently date from that period or the decades shortly afterwards. The parish church of St John has an exceptionally tall and elegant spire, and the Harlequin Theatre in the Warwick Quadrant shopping precinct offers a full programme of drama, film and musical entertainment in addition to having a pleasant bar, restaurant, and coffee shop.

BLETCHINGLEY

4 miles E of Reigate on the A25

Bletchingley is a highly picturesque village and former "rotten borough" which once had its own castle and street market. Traces of the Norman fortification thought to have been built by Richard de Tonbridge in the 12th century can be seen in the grounds of

FANNY'S FARM SHOP

Lodge Farm, Markedge Lane, Merstham, Nr Redhill,
Surrey RH1 3AW
Tel: 01737 554444 website: www.fannysfarm.com

Fanny Maiklem started **Fanny's Farm Shop** in 1979 to sell her own excess garden produce. It slowly evolved over the years to become the eclectic collection of shops, which are all run as a family business. The Lodge, which is Fanny's home was once gate house to Upper Gatton House, built by Sir Jeremiah Coleman, the Mustard Baron. Beside it in three former poultry sheds are housed: The Blooming Flower Shop, The Quaint Tearoom and The Bric-a-Brac. Visitors can and regularly do spend hours browsing through the memorabilia, cards, pictures and baskets. They can then finish off with a delicious cream tea with home made scones and jam before departing with bags full of fresh vegetables, home-made marmalade, honey and home baked produce. They probably only popped in for a bag of apples. Outside, the sheds are decorated with plants and flowers with fruit and vegetables displayed on a couple of brightly painted traditional market barrows. Inside the main shop are shelves of jams,

preserves and honey from Fanny's own hives as well as boxes of fruit and vegetables, fresh bread, free range eggs and home baking from local villagers.

Fanny's daughter Nell, a trained florist, runs the flower shop while son Angus and his girlfriend Lisa handle all the maintenance and look after the 'pick your own' kitchen garden. Fanny is a well-known local celebrity and is often heard broadcasting on BBC Southern Counties Radio with her series, 'Behind the Scenes at Fanny's Farm Shop'.

BOORS GREEN FARMHOUSE

Harps Oak Lane, Merstham, Surrey RH1 3AN
Tel: 01737 643903 Mobile: 07968 239234
e-mail: enquiries@boorsgreenfarmhouse.co.uk
website: www.boorsgreenfarmhouse.co.uk

Set within an area of outstanding natural beauty
and standing in just under two acres of informal
gardens surrounded by fields, **Boors Green
Farmhouse** is one of rural Surrey's true gems.
Exceedingly comfortable, and with a reputation
for providing a legendary breakfast, it's ideally
situated for exploring or for simply getting away
from it all and relaxing. Public footpaths run close to the house allowing guests to enjoy the beauty of
the countryside at a leisurely pace. The small lake in the garden is regularly visited by wildlife and
ducks while in the nearby woods pheasant and deer can often be seen. Richard and Rosemary Williams,
the owners, are a very friendly and hospitable couple.

They personally welcome all their guests in a large hall with vaulted ceiling and a traditional
wood-burning stove and do everything they can to ensure their visit is an enjoyable experience. Guests
are free to enjoy the grounds or curl up in front of a blazing log fire with a book selected from the
galleried library. Or they can take a short walk across the fields to the local farm shop for a ploughman's
lunch or a cream tea or browse the home produce and livestock which includes several ' free range'
Vietnamese pot-bellied pigs. Both Richard and Rosemary are keen sports people. She is a former
Marathon runner who still runs many miles each week but for enjoyment rather than training for
competitions. Richard is a competent golfer with a superb knowledge of all the local courses.

THE CIDER HOUSE GALLERY

Norfolk House, 80, High Street, Bletchingley, Surrey RH1 4PA
Tel: 01883 742198 e-mail: info@ciderhousegalleries.com
Fax: 01883 744014 website: www.ciderhousegalleries.com

Established in 1970 by Tony Roberts's father, **The Cider House
Gallery** is now run by Tony and his wife Helen. Both extremely
knowledgeable about art, Helen specialises in portraits while
Tony has particular expertise in marine paintings. In their
Victorian warehouse in the centre of Bletchingley they have a
vast stock of paintings, dating from the 17th to the mid 20th century. The emphasis of the collection is
on 18th and 19th century British paintings and country house pictures. At any time they normally have
around 900 pictures in stock as well as a range of sculptures.

Formerly a grain and cheese store, the warehouse's opening in the 1840s as an emporium known as
Bristow's was reported in The Times. There is a small display window to the front, giving little hint of
the spacious two floors of display space to the rear, where a constantly changing range of exciting and
interesting paintings can be viewed in comfortable and relaxed surroundings. Visitors can browse

through the pictures at their leisure or take advantage of Tony
and Helen's expertise to find precisely what they want.

The gallery is a member of the London and Provincial
Antique Dealers Association. Over the quarter century of its
existence it has gained an international reputation among the
art dealers, collectors and decorators it supplies, frequently
lending works to other galleries, particularly in London. The
gallery also provides a valuation and restoration service.

Castle Hill, a private house lying to the south of the A25. Closer to the centre, the old market in Middle Row is an exceptionally lovely thoroughfare, which, like the nearby High Street, contains some wonderful old timber-framed and tile-hung houses and cottages.

Some fine early buildings can also be found in **Church Walk**, the lane leading to Bletchingley's Perpendicular church of St Mary. The oldest part of this sizeable sandstone structure, the Norman west tower, dates from the end of the 11th century; it had a spire until a bolt of lightning destroyed it in 1606. Inside, there is a 13th century hermit's cell, a wonderful assortment of medieval gargoyles, a 16th century monumental brass of a local tanner and his wife, and an extravagant sculpted monument to Sir Robert Clayton, a City money lender and former Lord Mayor of London who died in 1707. The church also contains the sizeable tomb of Sir Thomas Cawarden, the former owner of Bletchingley Place, who acquired the manor house from Anne of Cleves after she had won it from Henry VIII in her divorce settlement.

A couple of interesting settlements lie within easy reach of Bletchingley. **Pendell**, a two-minute drive to the northwest, contains the striking Jacobean-style Pendell Court, which was built in 1624, and the neo-classical Pendell House, which was built 12years later on an adjacent site. Brewer Street, one mile to the north, contains the remains of Anne of Cleves's manor house. This was remodelled in the 18th century and is now known as Place Farm.

GODSTONE

6 miles E of Reigate off the A22

Although Godstone is now thankfully bypassed by the A22, the A25 east-west route still passes through its heart, making a sharp change in direction as it does so. Fortunately, the village's Tudor and Elizabethan character has survived relatively intact. Godstone's most distinguished building, the White Hart Inn in the High Street, claims to have been visited by Richard II, Elizabeth I, Queen Victoria, and even the Tsar of Russia who broke his journey here in 1815. A series of attractive lanes and alleyways connects the High Street to the village green, a broad open space with a cricket pitch, which is surrounded by a wonderful collection of 16th and 17th century buildings, including the Tudor-built Hare and Hounds Inn.

Godstone's parish church of St Nicholas is situated half a mile east of the centre and can be reached from the White Hart along an old thoroughfare known as Bay Path. Although Norman in origin, the building was virtually rebuilt in the 1870s by Sir George Gilbert Scott, a local resident at the time. Inside, there is a marble memorial to a cousin of John Evelyn, the famous 17th century diarist. The area around the church contains some fine old buildings, including a row of 19th century almshouses and the 16th century timber-framed Old Pack House, which lies a short distance away to the south. Bay Path also leads to a former hammer pond, **Bay Pond**, which is now a designated nature reserve. At one time, its water would have been used to power the mechanical hammers in a nearby iron foundry, an indication of Godstone's lost industrial past, which also included the manufacture of gunpowder and leatherware. **Godstone Farm**, in Tilburstow Hill Road to the south of the village, is an open farm where children experience life on the farm at first hand.

OXTED

8 miles E of Reigate off the A25

Oxted is an old town that prospered because of its position just below the Downs and consequently a good trading link with the rest of Surrey. Today, however, Oxted constitutes two distinct parts. New Oxted lies between the original town and Limpsfield. It grew up around the railway station, which was built in the 19th century. Old Oxted is also largely Victorian to the eye, but occasionally the visitor notices some survivors of earlier centuries such as the Forge House and Beam Cottages, with their medieval core and 17th century exteriors. Streeters Cottage, built in the 17th century, presents a large timber-framed gable to the road.

LIMPSFIELD

9 miles E of Reigate on the B269

The churchyard at Limpsfield, three miles to the east of Godstone, contains the grave of the composer, Frederick Delius, who despite having died in France, left instructions that he should be buried in an English country graveyard. Detillens, a rare 15th century "hall" house, is also located in Limpsfield. This striking building has an unusual "king-post" roof, and despite having been given a new facade in the 18th century, is a good example of a house belonging to a Surrey yeoman, a member of the class of small freeholders who cultivated their own land. Inside, there is an interesting collection of period furniture, china and militaria.

Limpsfield Chart, or simply The Chart, constitutes a hilltop common with some lovely views eastwards across Kent. Next to the common is a 17th century Mill House. The windmill itself was removed in 1925. Elsewhere in The Chart there are handsome groupings of stone-built houses, cottages, and farm buildings, best exemplified by the ensemble at Moorhouse Farm.

BEECHWOOD RIDING SCHOOL

Hillboxes Farm, Marden Park, Woldingham, Surrey CR3 7JD
Tel: 01883 342266 Fax: 01883 330849
e-mail: horses@beechwoodridingschool.co.uk
website: www.beechwoodridingschool.co.uk

Beechwood Riding School is run by Jakki Garnham and Colin Trice and is one of only a handful of riding establishments, which hold the coveted Association of British Riding Schools, Riding School Principals Diploma. Jakki is also a British Horse Society Approved Instructor who has been teaching children and adults to ride since 1969. Having trained at a busy London Equestrian Centre she graduated to a large Devonshire stud and riding school where she developed her talent for teaching younger riders, while expanding her knowledge of the horse from birth to maturity. She has considerable experience of teaching at home and abroad, often teaching at rallies of the Pony Club with whom she maintains a close association.

At Beechwood the philosophy of teaching aims to achieve a happy and harmonious relationship between horse and rider and offers tuition to those interested in classical equitation. All of the horses and ponies have been carefully chosen for their temperaments to ensure that they are suitable mounts for both novice and advanced children and adults. The selection includes warmbloods, thoroughbreds, cobs and ponies. The format of lessons is flexible and varied, including half hour lessons for young riders, pony parties, "own a pony" weeks, private assessment and tuition for adults, group lessons, day rides and hugely enjoyable pub rides. Beechwood is easy to reach, a mere handful of miles from the M25.

TOURIST INFORMATION CENTRES

KENT

ASHFORD

18 The Churchyard
Ashford
Kent
TN23 1QG

Tel: 01233 629165
e-mail: tourism@ashford.gov.uk

BROADSTAIRS

68 High Street
Broadstairs
Kent
CT10 1LH

Tel: 01843 862242

CANTERBURY

34 St Margret's Street
Canterbury
Kent
CT1 2TG

Tel: 01227 766567
e-mail: canterburyinformation
@canterbury.gov.uk

CLACKET LANE

(Motorway Service Area)

Clacket Lane
Junction 5/6 M25
Westerham
Kent
TN16 2ER

Eastbound Tel: 01959 565063
Westbound Tel: 01959 565615

CRANBROOK

(summer only)

Vestry Hall
Stone Street
Cranbrook
Kent
TN17 3ED

Tel: 01580 712538

DEAL

Town Hall
High Street
Deal
Kent
CT14 6BB

Tel: 01304 369576

DOVER

Townwall Street
Dover
Kent
CT16 1JR

Tel: 01304 369576
e-mail: tic@doveruk.com

EDENBRIDGE

Stangrove Park
Edenbridge
Kent
TN8 5LU

Tel: 01732 868110

FAVERSHAM

Fleur de Lis Heritage Centre
13 Preston Street
Faversham
Kent
ME13 8NS

Tel: 01795 534542

FOLKESTONE

Harbour Street
Folkestone
Kent
CT20 1QN

Tel: 01303 258594
e-mail: tourism@folkestone.org.uk

GRAVESEND

10 Parrock Street
Gravesend
Kent
DA12 1ET

Tel: 01474 337600

HERNE BAY

12 William Street
Herne Bay
Kent
CT6 5EJ

Tel: 01227 361911
e-mail: hernebayinformation
@canterbury.gov.uk

HYTHE

(summer only)

En-route Travel
Red Lion Square
Hythe
Kent
CT21 5AU

Tel: 01303 267799

MAIDSTONE

The Gatehouse
Palace Gardens
Mill Street
Maidstone
Kent
ME15 6YE

Tel: 01622 602169

MAIDSTONE

M20 - Roadchef Service Area
Juction 8
Hollingbourne
Kent
ME17 1SS

Tel: 01622 602169

MARGATE

12-13 The Parade
Margate
Kent
CT9 1EY

Tel: 01843 583333/583334

NEW ROMNEY

(summer only)
Magpie
Church Approach
New Romney
Kent

Tel: 01797 364044

RAMSGATE

17 Albert Court
York Street
Ramsgate
Kent
CT11 9DN

Tel: 01843 583333/583334

ROCHESTER

95 High Street
Rochester
Kent
ME1 1LX

Tel: 01634 843666

SANDWICH

The Guild Hall
Cattle Market
Sandwich
Kent
CT13 9AH

Tel: 01304 613565

SEVENOAKS

Buckhurst Lane
Sevenoaks
Kent
TN13 1LQ

Tel: 01732 450305

TENTERDEN

(summer only)
Town Hall
High Street
Tenterden
Kent
TN30 6AN

Tel: 01580 763572

TONBRIDGE

Tonbridge Castle
Castle Street
Tonbridge
Kent
TN9 1BG

Tel: 01732 770929

TUNBRIDGE WELLS

The Old Fish Market
The Pantiles
Tunbridge Wells
Kent
TN2 5TN

Tel: 01892 515675

WHITSTABLE

7 Oxford Street
Whitstable
Kent
CT5 1DB

Tel: 01227 275482
e-mail: whitstableinformation
          @canterbury.gov.uk

EAST SUSSEX

BATTLE

88 High Street
Battle
East Sussex
TN33 0AQ

Tel: 01424 773721
Fax: 01424 773436

BEXHILL-ON-SEA

51 Marina
Bexhill-on-Sea
East Sussex
TN40 1BQ

Tel: 01424 732208
Fax: 01424 212500

BOSHIP

Boship Roundabout A22
Lower Dicker
Hailsham
East Sussex
BN27 4DP

Tel/Fax: 01323 442667

BRIGHTON

10 Bartholomew Square
Brighton
East Sussex
BN1 1JS

Tel: 01273 292599

EASTBOURNE

3 Cornfield Road
Eastbourne
East Sussex
BN21 4QL

Tel: 01323 411400
Fax: 01323 649574

HASTINGS

Queens Road
Hastings
East Sussex
TN34 1TL

Tel: 01424 781111
Fax: 01424 781186

HASTINGS

Old Town
Hastings
East Sussex
TN34 1EZ

Tel: 01424 781111
Fax: 01424 781186

HOVE

Church Road
Hove
East Sussex
BN3 3BQ

Tel: 01273 292589

LEWES

187 High Street
Lewes
East Sussex
BN7 2DE

Tel: 01273 483448
Fax: 01273 484003

RYE

The Heritage Centre
Strand Quay
Rye
East Sussex
TN31 7AY

Tel: 01797 226696
Fax: 01797 223460

SEAFORD

25 Clinton Place
Seaford
East Sussex
BN25 1NP

Tel/Fax: 01323 897426

WEST SUSSEX

ARUNDEL

61 High Street
Arundel
West Sussex
BN18 9AJ

Tel: 01903 882268
Fax: 01903 882419
e-mail: tourism@arun.gov.uk
website: ww.sussexbythesea.com/

BOGNOR REGIS

Belmont Street
Bognor Regis
West Sussex
PO21 1BJ

Tel: 01243 823140
Fax: 01243 820435
e-mail: tourism@arun.gov.uk
website: ww.sussexbythesea.com/

BURGESS HILL

96 Church Walk
Burgess Hill
West Sussex
RH15 9AS

Tel: 01444 247726
Fax: 01444 233707
e-mail: touristinformation
@burgesshill.gov.uk

CHICHESTER

29a South Street
Chichester
West Sussex
PO19 1AH

Tel: 01243 775888
Fax: 01243 539449
e-mail: Chitic@chichester.gov.uk

CRAWLEY

County Mall
Crawley
West Sussex
RH10 1FP

Tel: 01293 545322
Fax: 01293 545319
e-mail: VIP@countymall.co.uk

EAST GRINSTEAD

Library Buildings
West Street
East Grinstead
West Sussex
RH19 4SR

Tel: 01342 410121
Fax: 01342 410262
e-mail: sa81@dial.tipex.com

HORSHAM

9 The Causeway
Horsham
West Sussex
RH12 1HE

Tel: 01403 211661

LITTLEHAMPTON

Windmill Complex
Littlehampton
West Sussex
BN17 5LH

Tel: 01903 713480
e-mail: tourism@arun.gov.uk
website: ww.sussexbythesea.com/

MIDHURST

North Street
Midhurst
West Sussex
GU29 9DW

Tel: 01730 817322
Fax: 01730 817120

PETWORTH

Market Square
Petworth
West Sussex
GU28 0AF

Tel: 01798 343523
Fax: 01798 343942

SHOREHAM

Adur DC
Commerce Way
Lancing
Shoreham
West Sussex
BN15 8TA

Tel: 01273 263147
Fax: 01273 263131

WORTHING

Chapel Road
Worthing
West Sussex
BN11 1HL

Tel: 01903 210022
Fax: 01903 236277
e-mail: wbctourism
@pavilion.co.uk

SURREY

CROYDON

Croydon Clocktower
Katharine Street
Croydon
Surrey
CR9 1ET

Tel: 020 8253 1009
Fax: 020 8253 1008
e-mail: tic@croydononline.org

FARNHAM

Council Offices
South Street
Farnham
Surrey
GU9 7RN

Tel: 01252 715109
Fax: 01252 725083
e-mail: itourist@waverley.gov.uk

GUILDFORD

14 Tunsgate
Guildford
Surrey
GU1 3QT

Tel: 01483 444333
Fax: 01483 302046

RICHMOND

Old Town Hall
Whittaker Avenue
Richmond
Surrey
TW9 1TP

Tel: 020 8940 9125
Fax: 020 8940 6899
e-mail: information.services
          @richmond.gov.uk

INDEX OF ADVERTISERS

JARROLD PATHFINDER WALKS

Definitive UK walks

- Ordnance Survey mapping - the most accurate mapping
- 28 walk routes – best value for money available
- Graded: easy, moderate and challenging walks
- Information on parking and refreshments
- Useful advice for walkers
- Durable 'sewn' format
- 48 titles – complete UK mainland coverage

www.jarrold-publishing.com

Travel Publishing

The Hidden Places

Regional and National guides to the less well-known places of interest and places to eat, stay and drink

Hidden INNS

Regional guides to traditional pubs and inns throughout the United Kingdom

GOLFERS GUIDES

Regional and National guides to 18 hole golf courses and local places to stay, eat and drink

COUNTRY LIVING MAGAZINE

RURAL GUIDES

Regional and National guides to the traditional countryside of Britain and Ireland with easy to read facts on places to visit, stay, eat, drink and shop

For more information:

Phone: 0118 981 7777
e-mail: travel_publishing@msn.com

Fax: 0118 982 0077
website: www.travelpublishing.co.uk

Easy-to-use, Informative
Travel Guides on the British Isles

Travel Publishing Limited

7a Apollo House • Calleva Park • Aldermaston • Berkshire RG7 8TN

ORDER FORM

To order any of our publications just fill in the payment details below and complete the order form. For orders of less than 4 copies please add £1 per book for postage and packing. Orders over 4 copies are P & P free.

Please Complete Either:

I enclose a cheque for £ [   ] made payable to Travel Publishing Ltd

Or:

Card No: [   ]   Expiry Date: [   ]

Signature: [   ]

NAME: [   ]

ADDRESS: [   ]

TEL NO: [   ]

Please either send, telephone, fax or e-mail your order to:

Travel Publishing Ltd, 7a Apollo House, Calleva Park, Aldermaston, Berkshire RG7 8TN
Tel: 0118 981 7777   Fax: 0118 982 0077   e-mail: karen@travelpublishing.co.uk

	Price	Quantity		Price	Quantity
Hidden Places Regional Titles			**Hidden Places National Titles**		
Cambs & Lincolnshire	£7.99	....	England	£11.99	....
Chilterns	£8.99	....	Ireland	£11.99	....
Cornwall	£8.99	....	Scotland	£11.99	....
Derbyshire	£7.99	....	Wales	£11.99	....
Devon	£8.99	....			
Dorset, Hants & Isle of Wight	£8.99		**Hidden Inns Titles**		
East Anglia	£8.99	....	Heart of England	£5.99	....
Gloucestershire & Wiltshire	£7.99	....	Lancashire & Cheshire	£5.99	....
Heart of England	£7.99	....	South	£5.99	....
Hereford, Worcs & Shropshire	£7.99	....	South East	£5.99	....
Highlands & Islands	£7.99	....	South and Central Scotland	£5.99	....
Kent	£8.99	....	Wales	£5.99	....
Lake District & Cumbria	£8.99	....	Welsh Borders	£5.99	....
Lancashire & Cheshire	£8.99	....	West Country	£5.99	....
Lincolnshire & Nottinghamshire	£8.99	....			
Northumberland & Durham	£8.99	....	**Country Living Guides to Rural England**		
Somerset	£7.99	....	East Anglia	£9.99	....
Sussex	£7.99	....	South of England	£9.99	....
Thames Valley	£7.99	....	South East of England	£9.99	....
Yorkshire	£7.99	....	West Country	£9.99	....

Total Quantity [   ]   **Total Value** [   ]

READER REACTION FORM

The *Travel Publishing* research team would like to receive reader's comments on any visitor attractions or places reviewed in the book and also recommendations for suitable entries to be included in the next edition. This will help ensure that the *Country Living series of Rural Guides* continues to provide its readers with useful information on the more interesting, unusual or unique features of each attraction or place ensuring that their visit to the local area is an enjoyable and stimulating experience. To provide your comments or recommendations would you please complete the forms below and overleaf as indicated and send to:

The Research Department, Travel Publishing Ltd,

7a Apollo House, Calleva Park, Aldermaston, Reading, RG7 8TN.

Your Name:

Your Address:

Your Telephone Number:

Please tick as appropriate: Comments ☐ Recommendation ☐

Name of Establishment:

Address:

Telephone Number:

Name of Contact:

READER REACTION FORM

Comment or Reason for Recommendation:

....

....

....

....

....

....

....

....

....

....

READER REACTION FORM

The *Travel Publishing* research team would like to receive reader's comments on any visitor attractions or places reviewed in the book and also recommendations for suitable entries to be included in the next edition. This will help ensure that the *Country Living series of Rural Guides* continues to provide its readers with useful information on the more interesting, unusual or unique features of each attraction or place ensuring that their visit to the local area is an enjoyable and stimulating experience. To provide your comments or recommendations would you please complete the forms below and overleaf as indicated and send to:

The Research Department, Travel Publishing Ltd,

7a Apollo House, Calleva Park, Aldermaston, Reading, RG7 8TN.

Your Name:

Your Address:

Your Telephone Number:

Please tick as appropriate: Comments ☐   Recommendation ☐

Name of Establishment:

Address:

Telephone Number:

Name of Contact:

READER REACTION FORM

Comment or Reason for Recommendation:

....

....

....

....

....

....

....

....

....

....

INDEX TO TOWNS & PLACES OF INTEREST